Dreamweaver® CS5
ALL-IN-ONE
FOR
DUMMIES®

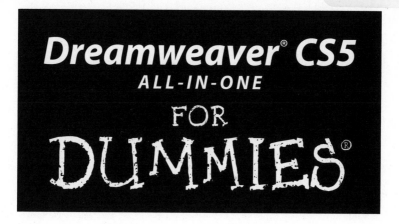

Dreamweaver® CS5
ALL-IN-ONE
FOR
DUMMIES®

by Sue Jenkins and Richard Wagner

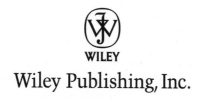

WILEY

Wiley Publishing, Inc.

Dreamweaver® CS5 All-in-One For Dummies®

Published by
Wiley Publishing, Inc.
111 River Street
Hoboken, NJ 07030-5774

www.wiley.com

For general information on our other products and services, please contact our Customer Care Department within the U.S. at 877-762-2974, outside the U.S. at 317-572-3993, or fax 317-572-4002.

For technical support, please visit www.wiley.com/techsupport.

Wiley also publishes its books in a variety of electronic formats. Some content that appears in print may not be available in electronic books.

Library of Congress Control Number: 2010926841

ISBN: 978-0-470-61077-0

Manufactured in the United States of America

10 9 8 7 6 5 4 3 2 1

WILEY

About the Authors

Sue Jenkins is a Web designer, graphic designer, illustrator, photographer, teacher, writer, and the owner of Luckychair (www.luckychair.com), a professional design studio serving companies across the United States since 1997. Sue is the author of several books on design, including *Web Design All-in-One For Dummies, Web Design: The L-Line, The Express Line to Learning, How To Do Everything Illustrator CS4*, and the upcoming *Smashing Photoshop: 100 Professional Techniques*. She can also be seen as the software instructor in four of ClassOnDemand's (www.classondemand.com) Adobe Training DVDs: *Dreamweaver for Designers* (winner of a 2007 Bronze Telly Award), *Designer's Guide to Photoshop, Designer's Guide to Illustrator* (winner of a 2009 Annual Communicator Award of Distinction), and *Fundamentals of Photoshop Elements* (winner of a 2009 DV Magazine Award of Excellence). In addition, Sue is an Adobe Certified Expert and Adobe Certified Instructor and teaches three-day courses in Dreamweaver, Illustrator, and Photoshop at Noble Desktop in New York City. Sue lives with her husband and son in Pennsylvania.

Richard Wagner is a Senior Developer at Maark, LLC as well as author of several Web-related books, including *Building Facebook Applications For Dummies, Professional iPhone and iPod touch Programming, XSLT For Dummies, Creating Web Pages All-in-One For Dummies, XML All-in-One For Dummies, Web Design Before & After Makeovers*, and *JavaScript Unleashed* (1st and 2nd editions). Previously, Richard was vice president of product development at NetObjects. He was also the inventor and chief architect of the award-winning NetObjects ScriptBuilder. A versatile author with a wide range of interests, he is also the author of *The Expeditionary Man* and *The Myth of Happiness*.

Dedication

To Phil and Kyle for their cooperation, time, love, and humor.

— Sue Jenkins

Authors' Acknowledgments

A hearty round of thanks go out to several people, including my coauthor, Rich Wagner, my agent, Matt Wagner, senior acquisitions editor Bob Woerner, project editor Susan Pink, technical editor Jon McFarland, and everyone in composition services at Wiley who helped with the production of this edition.

— Sue Jenkins

I would like to thank Susan Pink for her excellent job of managing this project. Thanks also to Jon McFarland for his technical insights to ensure the accuracy of the book.

— Richard Wagner

Publisher's Acknowledgments

We're proud of this book; please send us your comments at http://dummies.custhelp.com. For other comments, please contact our Customer Care Department within the U.S. at 877-762-2974, outside the U.S. at 317-572-3993, or fax 317-572-4002.

Some of the people who helped bring this book to market include the following:

Acquisitions and Editorial

Project Editor: Susan Pink

Acquisitions Editor: Bob Woerner

Copy Editor: Susan Pink

Technical Editor: Jon McFarland

Editorial Manager: Jodi Jensen

Editorial Assistant: Amanda Graham

Sr. Editorial Assistant: Cherie Case

Cartoons: Rich Tennant
  (www.the5thwave.com)

Composition Services

Project Coordinator: Sheree Montgomery

Layout and Graphics: Ana Carrillo,
  Joyce Haughey

Proofreaders: Melissa Cossell,
  The Well-Chosen Word

Indexer: Broccoli Information Mgt.

Publishing and Editorial for Technology Dummies

  Richard Swadley, Vice President and Executive Group Publisher

  Andy Cummings, Vice President and Publisher

  Mary Bednarek, Executive Acquisitions Director

  Mary C. Corder, Editorial Director

Publishing for Consumer Dummies

  Diane Graves Steele, Vice President and Publisher

Composition Services

  Debbie Stailey, Director of Composition Services

Contents at a Glance

Table of Contents

Book VII: Building Web Applications 601

Introduction

*W*hen professional Web designers want to build a Web site, they nearly always choose Dreamweaver. With more than 80 percent of all designers using Dreamweaver, it is definitely the top dual-platform (PC and Mac) Web design software application on the market today.

What makes Dreamweaver so great is the combo WYSIWYG *(What You See Is What You Get)* and coding interface that allows you to build HTML files containing text, graphics, and other media, all the while seeing the page layout and its code as you create pages in Dreamweaver's Design and Code views.

Dreamweaver accurately generates all the HTML, CSS, and JavaScript source code needed for Web developers to create HTML- and XHTML-compliant Web pages. This means no more sweating intricate coding issues such as merging table cells, creating rollover effects, and applying CSS to text. In addition, Dreamweaver integrates well with Fireworks, for roundtrip graphic editing, with Photoshop, for quick image optimization, with InContext Editing, for browser-based Web editing, and with Contribute CS5, for Web site maintenance and the publishing of content changes by a nondesigner.

Dreamweaver CS5 enhancements include access to Adobe BrowserLab; enhanced CSS tools such as CSS enable and disable, incremental pagination, and CSS Inspect; access to dynamically related files; Live Changes and Live View navigation; improved PHP code hinting; and several workspace updates. You'll also find a better coding environment; integrated support for JavaScript, CSS, and server-side scripting; accessibility standards–compliant code; and improved dynamic content creation tools for connecting to databases such as MySQL and for working with a variety of scripting technologies including PHP, ASP, JSP, ASP.NET, and ColdFusion. In addition, you can easily integrate XML content with both XSL and the Spry framework for Ajax. The program contains all the tools you need to streamline page development, and many of the tools are customizable through the Preferences dialog box.

Use *Dreamweaver CS5 All-in-One For Dummies* as your complete guide to the exciting world of Web design.

About This Book

This is a Dreamweaver reference book rather than a how-to book, which means that, rather than reading the book from cover to cover, you have the freedom to jump around from topic to topic and chapter to chapter, reading whatever section you want as the need arises. In fact, think of each minibook as its own little reference zone, with each zone split into chapters about performing specific tasks in Dreamweaver CS5.

Everything you find in this book is written so that you don't have to wade through complicated technical help files or commit anything to memory. To keep things simple, you'll find detailed, step-by-step, easy-to-follow instructions. When more technical information is needed to clarify a particular process, it's often set apart from the main text in sidebars or noted in the margins with a Technical Stuff icon.

The bottom line is that we want to make you comfortable with Dreamweaver CS5 and hope that you'll continue to use this book frequently and consider it the main resource of your Web design library.

Conventions Used in This Book

To help with new terms and concepts, the following typographical rules, or *conventions,* are used in this book:

✦ **New terms:** New terms are set apart with italics. For example: Dreamweaver CS5 comes with the commonly used JavaScripts, which it refers to as *behaviors,* ready to insert into your pages from the Behaviors panel.

✦ **Placeholder text:** Text that is a placeholder is set in italic. For example, in the phrase Type *username* here, *username* is a placeholder for your actual username, so it is set in italic.

✦ **Code samples:** We include short code samples in monospaced text in the paragraph, like this: `<img src="logo.gif">`. We set longer code samples apart from the text, like this:

```
<frameset rows="80,*" cols="*" frameborder="NO"
    border="0" framespacing="0">
<frame src="top.html" name="topFrame" scrolling="NO"
    noresize title="topFrame">
```

When we want to draw your attention to particular parts of code samples, we indicate the important parts in bold, as in this example:

```
<div id="sidebar"></div>
```

✦ **Reader entry:** Anything you need to type is in **boldface**.

✦ **Cross-platform:** Whenever PCs and Macs have different shortcuts, we include both the Windows equivalent (for example, right-click) and the Mac equivalent (for example, Control+click).

✦ **Web addresses:** Web addresses are set apart in monofont, such as `www.adobe.com`.

What You Don't Have to Read

You don't have to read any part of this book that doesn't interest you. For example, if you never intend to use Fireworks, skip that chapter! And if you see a sidebar that covers more technical information than you care to know, pass it by. The main thing is that you know what is available and read only what is useful to you.

Assumptions About You

With only a general idea of the kinds of people who will buy this book, we must make certain broad assumptions about all our readers to write this book with enough specificity for each of you. Therefore, we assume that you're a human being living on planet Earth who knows how to operate a computer and visit Web sites on the Internet, and has a desire to find out how to use Dreamweaver to build Web sites. Beyond that, some prior knowledge of Web design, HTML, JavaScript, CSS, or Dreamweaver would be helpful but is not required to use this book.

How This Book Is Organized

This book is divided into nine minibooks, each of which is further divided into relevant chapters organized by topic. Each minibook relates to the most important concepts in Dreamweaver.

Book I: Getting Started

Begin your trip into the world of Web design with a look around the Dreamweaver workspace and a review of site design. Then find out how to create and manage sites in Dreamweaver — an important step that enables you to take full advantage of Dreamweaver's automated features.

Book II: Mastering the Basics

Book II shows you everything you need to know to create and save new documents; add and format text on a page; insert graphics and create rollover buttons; convert text and graphics into clickable links to other Web pages; add movies, sound, and other media files to your pages; add tables for organizing content; and build fantastic forms for collecting data from visitors.

Book III: Working Like the Pros

Book III walks you through the process of styling your pages with Cascading Style Sheets (CSS), building sites using Dreamweaver templates, and using Library items. You also find out about working with server-side includes, creating and using code snippets, recording and saving custom commands with the History panel, and using Dreamweaver with Fireworks for roundtrip image optimization. The final chapter in this minibook contains information on using Dreamweaver with other software applications, such as Flash, Photoshop, Bridge, Device Central, AIR, ConnectNow, and InContext Editing.

Book IV: Energizing Your Site

When you're ready to add more zing and pizzazz to your pages, turn to Book IV. Here you find out how to work with layers instead of tables, create opportunities for visitor interactivity by adding JavaScript behaviors to objects on your pages, work with Spry effects and Spry widgets, and design pages built with frames. The final chapter in this minibook shows you the benefits of XHTML and how to configure Dreamweaver to write XHTML-compliant code.

Book V: Publishing Your Site

Book V shows you how to run Dreamweaver's reports and use other tools to test and fix any coding errors before you publish your site. You also find out how to publish your Web site, which involves learning to select and set up a remote connection to your host server and transfer files to the remote site.

Book VI: Working Collaboratively

Dreamweaver has several tools to assist you with multiuser page management. In Book VI, you find out how to enable collaborative tools such as Design Notes and Check In/Check Out as well as create sites that are editable by nondesigners through two integrated page editing tools. If you'll be using Adobe's Contribute CS5 software, read Chapters 2 and 3 for information on setting up, connecting to, and managing a Contribute site. Alternatively, if you'll be working with InContext Editing, be sure to read Chapter 4 for help with creating and managing InContext Editable Web sites.

Book VII: Building Web Applications

Book VII discusses how to select and add Web and application servers along with how to configure, edit, and delete database connections. When working with databases, troubleshooting problems is important, so we also discuss resolving permission problems, database connection issues, and error messages.

Book VIII: Making Pages Dynamic

In Book VIII, you find out how to define data sources and make them available for use in your dynamic pages. We also show you how to add simple dynamic data to your Web pages, as well as create HTML tables for your recordsets, navigate through your recordsets, and dynamically control them. In addition, you discover how to test the functionality of your dynamic site by using Dreamweaver's Live Data view. This minibook also includes a chapter on working with ColdFusion components, adding Web services to your site, and putting custom server behaviors to work.

Book IX: Developing Applications Rapidly

Book IX shows you how to build several types of pages, such as master and detail pages; search and results pages; and record insert, update, and delete pages. We also get into more complicated territory, such as calling ASP command objects, working with JSP prepared statements, and using stored procedures. Finally, you find out how to restrict site access.

Icons Used in This Book

To make your experience with the book easier, you'll find a handful of icons in the margins of the book to indicate particular points of interest.

Tip icons alert you to interesting techniques or hints that can save you time and effort.

The New icon highlights important features and enhancements that are new in Dreamweaver CS5.

The Remember icon is a friendly cue about things to keep in mind when performing certain tasks or important information that can benefit you in understanding how Dreamweaver works.

When you see the Warning icon, watch out! Paragraphs marked with this icon include important information that will help you avoid common design or coding mistakes and steer clear of trouble.

Occasionally, we include some technical information that, while interesting to some, is not essential reading for everyone. Nevertheless, consider at least glancing at the text marked with the Technical Stuff icon just in case it applies to your situation.

Where to Go from Here

Read through the Table of Contents to find what interests you. In addition, consider the following jumping-off topics:

✦ For an overview of Dreamweaver in general and the new features in Dreamweaver CS5 in particular, go to Book I.

✦ For information about working with text, graphics, and links, read Book II.

✦ For information on using Cascading Style Sheets, templates, and server-side includes, see Book III.

✦ To discover how to work with layers, use JavaScript behaviors, and work with Spry framework widgets, see Book IV.

✦ For information on publishing your site, see Book V.

✦ For details about working collaboratively with a team, using Contribute, and InContext Editing, see Book VI.

✦ For instructions on building Web applications, go to Book VII.

✦ To build dynamic Web pages, read Book VIII.

✦ For information on rapid application development, see Book IX.

Beyond this book, loads of valuable Dreamweaver resources to help you build Web sites are available on the Internet. The following is a sample of some useful sites you'll find out there.

Adobe Resources

Dreamweaver Support Center: www.adobe.com/support/dreamweaver/

Dreamweaver Exchange: www.adobe.com/cfusion/exchange/index.cfm?event=productHome&exc=3&loc=en_us

Author Resources

Luckychair: www.luckychair.com

Standards, Guidelines, and Initiatives

World Wide Web Consortium (W3C): www.w3.org

Web Accessibility Initiative: www.w3.org/WAI/

Dreamweaver Extensions

Project Seven: www.projectseven.com

Hot Dreamweaver Fever: www.hotdreamweaver.com

Kaosweaver: www.kaosweaver.com

Web Developer Resources

Web Monkey: www.webmonkey.com

W3 Schools: www.w3schools.com

JavaScript Resources

Dynamic Drive DHTML Scripts: www.dynamicdrive.com

EarthWeb JavaScripts: http://webdeveloper.earthweb.com/webjs/

JavaScript Source: http://javascript.internet.com

CSS Resources

W3C's CSS: www.w3.org/Style/CSS/

CSS Zen Garden: www.csszengarden.com

Sitepoint CSS Reference: http://reference.sitepoint.com/css

W3Schools CSS Tutorial: http://w3schools.com/css/default.asp

CSS Beauty: www.cssbeauty.com

Free CSS Templates: www.freecsstemplates.org

Book I

Getting Started

The 5th Wave   By Rich Tennant

Contents at a Glance

Chapter 1: Cruising Around the Dreamweaver CS5 Workspace

In This Chapter

✔ **Getting to know the Dreamweaver workspace**

✔ **Understanding the panels and Properties inspector**

✔ **Setting Dreamweaver preferences**

✔ **Finding help in the Help files, tutorials, and Reference panel**

A general understanding of the Dreamweaver workspace can greatly assist you with using the program. If you're familiar with earlier versions of Dreamweaver but new to Dreamweaver CS5, use this chapter as a review of the workspace basics.

This chapter provides an overview of the workspace and Document window, a review of the panels and Properties inspector, a quick look at setting preferences, and tips on how and where to find Dreamweaver help.

Choosing a Workspace Layout

When you launch Dreamweaver for the very first time, the program automatically opens a dialog box asking you to choose which file extensions should be associated with the project, and then displays the newly updated default Designer layout. After the program is open, you can switch to another available layout option by choosing Window➪Workspace Layout, or by clicking the Workspace Switcher menu on the Application bar.

With the release of CS5 (which uses the darker and more angular OS Widget Library (OWL) interface introduced in Dreamweaver CS4), the workspace options are now nearly identical for both Windows and Macintosh platforms. So now, regardless of platform, all Dreamweaver CS5 users have equal access to the same workspace layouts. Here is a closer look at the available layout options:

✦ **App Developer:** Select this layout to have the CSS Styles, AP Elements, Databases, Bindings, Server Behaviors, Files, Assets, and Snippets panels docked on the left with the Document window displayed in the center and no Properties inspector.

✦ **App Developer Plus:** Select this layout to have most of the App Developer panels mentioned in the preceding bullet docked on the left; the Document window set to Split Code view (code on top) in the center; the Properties inspector below the Design view; and the iconic view of the Insert, Databases, Bindings, and Server Behaviors panels docked along the right. Click the double-arrows at the top of either panel dock to expand and collapse the panels as needed.

✦ **Classic:** This layout most closely mirrors the default Designer layout setup from previous CS versions of Dreamweaver. The right edge of the screen displays the most used docked panels, while the rest of the workspace is composed of the old tabbed Insert panel across the top, the Document window in Split Code view below that, and the Properties inspector along the bottom. In all other CS5 layouts, the Insert panel appears at the top of the dock area. Remember, you can dock and undock (make free-floating) all panels, which gives you the flexibility of customizing your workspace.

✦ **Coder:** Select this layout to have the CSS Styles, AP Elements, Files, Assets, and Snippets panel groups on the left—similar to several popular programming software applications—with the Document window in Code view in the center of the screen.

✦ **Coder Plus:** This layout shows the Files, Assets, and Snippets panel group on the left; the Document window in Code view in the center of the screen; and the iconic view of the Insert, CSS Styles, and AP Elements panels docked along the right.

✦ **Designer:** Select this layout to have the Insert, CSS Styles, AP Elements, Business Catalyst, Files, and Assets panels docked on the right, with the Document window in Split Code view in the center, and the Properties inspector along the bottom.

✦ **Designer Compact:** Select this layout to have the iconic Insert, CSS Styles, AP Elements, Business Catalyst, Files, and Assets panels docked along the right, with the Document window in Split code view in the center, and the Properties inspector along the bottom.

✦ **Dual Screen:** Select this layout if you have a secondary monitor to the left or right of your primary monitor. Initially, the panel dock is displayed on the left monitor and the Document window and code view are displayed on the right; however, you can customize this setup if you prefer working with a different configuration.

Each workspace layout is designed to assist you with a particular task. Choose an Application Developer layout if you'll be developing applications, select a Coder option if you'll be working only with code, select a Designer layout if you'll be working with the WYSIWYG editor (Design view) and Code editor, pick the Classic option if you're not quite ready to start using one of the other layouts, and choose the Dual Screen layout when working with two monitors. If you are unsure of which layout to use, we recommend that you select the Designer option. Alternatively, feel free to open and arrange any of the panels to your liking and save your customized workspace by clicking the Workspace Switcher menu and choosing New Workspace.

Getting to Know the Dreamweaver Workspace

Because most Dreamweaver users are designers, we'll explore the workspace using the Designer layout, which consists of the Application bar at the top of the screen, the Document window in the center, the panel dock and panels on the right, and the Properties inspector along the bottom, shown in Figure 1-1 for Windows and Figure 1-2 for Macintosh. All of these layout elements work in harmony to assist you with adding and editing the content in any open document.

Figure 1-1:
The Dreamweaver CS5 workspace for Windows.

Document toolbar

Menu bar

Application bar   Document tab bar   Workspace Switcher

Document tab   Code view

Coding toolbar   Panel dock   Insert panel

Tag selector   Document window   Status bar   Files panel

Design view   Properties inspector   Panel group

Figure 1-2:
The Dream-weaver CS5 workspace for Macintosh.

Document tab

Coding toolbar

Application bar

Workspace Switcher

Document close bar

Menu bar

Document tab bar

Document toolbar

Code view

Insert panel

Tag selector   Design view   Status bar   Panel dock   Panel group

Document window

Properties inspector

Files panel

You find these elements in the Dreamweaver workspace:

- ✦ **Welcome Screen:** When you launch Dreamweaver, the Welcome Screen, which is automatically enabled, appears in the open workspace area any time no files are open. The Welcome Screen (shown in Figure 1-3) contains quick links to open recent files, create new documents, and access Web links to Dreamweaver Exchange and a library of top-featured Adobe training videos. In addition, you'll find links to "Getting Started," "New Features," and "Resources," all of which are helpful for users seeking quick details about what's new in CS5.

TIP

Hide and show the Welcome Screen by selecting or deselecting the Show Welcome Screen check box in the General category of the Preferences dialog box. (See "Setting Dreamweaver Preferences," later in the chapter, for more on the Preferences dialog box.)

Figure 1-3:
Use the
Welcome
Screen to
quickly open
recent files,
create new
documents,
and launch
a browser to
view online
videos.

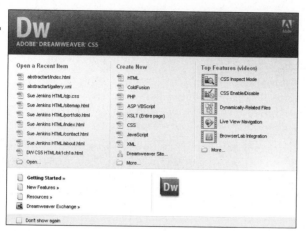

 ✦ **Application bar:** The Application bar includes the Dreamweaver logo
("DW"), menus, a Layout menu for choosing different code and design
views, an Extend Dreamweaver menu for accessing Dreamweaver
Exchange, a Site menu for quickly managing new Dreamweaver sites
and editing existing ones (see Book I, Chapter 3), a Workspace Switcher
menu for toggling between the workspace layout options, a search field
for finding help in Dreamweaver, and a CS Live Services button that
offers quick links to services such as BrowserLab, Acrobat.com, and CS
News and Resources.

 ✦ **Insert panel:** The Insert panel, when visible, appears as its own panel
at the top of the panel dock. The Insert panel displays a variety of icons
for quickly adding objects such as images and tables into an open file.
A more in-depth description of this panel appears in the "Using the
Insert panel" section, later in the chapter.

 ✦ **Document window:** This window shows the active document as you
design and edit it. View the document in Code, Split (half code and half
design), or Design view. When more than one document is open, you
can toggle between them by clicking their document title tabs.

 ✦ **Document toolbar:** This toolbar is located at the top of every open
document just below the document's title tab. The toolbar includes the
Code, Split, and Design view buttons as well as quick links for other
features such as the Live Code and Live View settings. For more details
about the different buttons and icons located here, see the "Document
toolbar" section, later in this chapter.

 ✦ **Coding toolbar:** This toolbar, which adds special quick-coding icons to
the left edge of the Code view area, is particularly useful to programmers and users who like quick access to frequently used code shortcuts.

Shortcut icons include options to collapse and expand lines of code, add or remove line numbers and comment tags, and highlight invalid code. Toggle this toolbar on and off by choosing View➪Toolbars➪Coding. Remember, the Coding toolbar is visible only in Code or Split view.

✦ **Standard toolbar:** This toolbar, which is off by default, has shortcut links to common tasks on the File and Edit menus, such as New, Open, Browse in Bridge, Save, Save All, Print, Cut, Copy, Paste, Undo, and Redo. To toggle this toolbar on and off, choose View➪Toolbars➪Standard.

✦ **Style Rendering toolbar:** This toolbar has shortcut icons to show how a page would look using different media types, presuming the page uses CSS (Cascading Style Sheets) specific to those media types. For instance, the <body> tag may have different CSS attributes for handheld devices, such as a BlackBerry, versus screen media, such as a browser. Other icons include options for toggling CSS on and off in Design view; toggling on and off Design-time Style Sheets; increasing, decreasing, and resetting text size; viewing hyperlink states (link, visited, hover, active, and focus) when those CSS link attributes are styled in the CSS. To view this toolbar, which appears in the open Document window below the Document toolbar or Browser Navigation toolbar, choose View➪Toolbars➪ Style Rendering.

To find out more about CSS in general, see Book III, Chapter 1. To find out more about CSS for specific media types, visit the World Wide Web Consortium at www.w3.org/TR/CSS21/media.html.

✦ **Properties inspector:** The Properties inspector is docked under the Document window at the bottom of the screen. The contents of this inspector change according to the contents selected in your document. Select an object or text in Design or Code view, and then add or change properties of that selection in the Properties inspector. See "Using the Properties inspector," later in this chapter, for a more detailed description of its capabilities.

✦ **Files panel:** Use the Files panel, located at the bottom of the panel dock, to access and manage all your site files, assets, and folders. For a more in-depth description of this panel, page ahead to "Working with the Files panel," later in this chapter.

✦ **Tag selector:** This status bar area is at the bottom of the open Document window. Here you see the hierarchy of tags around a selection or wherever you have placed the insertion point on the page. Click any tag in the Tag selector to quickly select that tag and its contents. This tool is extremely handy when adding CSS to objects in a document.

✦ **Panel groups:** Within the panel dock, related panels are combined into a single panel group with individual tabs. A more in-depth description follows in the section "Accessing panels and panel groups."

Exploring the Document Window

The Document window is made up of several parts, some of which are always visible and others that you can toggle on and off. The following section describes the following features of the Document window: the Document tab bar; the Document toolbar; the rulers, grids, and guides; and the status bar.

Document tab bar

The Document tab bar is located directly below the Application bar and displays the document filename tab of an open file. When multiple files are open, the tabs of every open file are displayed from left to right inside the tab bar. If you would prefer to see the documents in a particular order, you can drag-and-drop them by their tabs into the desired position. The path (location) of the open file, which used to also be displayed on the tab, has been moved in CS5 to the Browser Navigation bar's Address field. However, you may still view the local path to any open file by moving your mouse over the document's filename tab.

When an open page is linked to other documents, such as an external CSS style sheet, a server script, or an include file, the names of these *dynamically related* files will appear in an extended area of the document tab directly below the tab of each open document. For example, if your index.html file is linked to an external style sheet named mystyles.css, the tab of your open document will look like the example shown in Figure 1-4. To toggle between the Code view of the open document and any related file, click the related filename and that file's contents will appear in the Code view of the open Document window. To return to your document, click Source Code.

Figure 1-4:
Dynamically
related files
appear
below
the open
document
tab.

As part of CS5's enhancements to improve workflow and maximize the workspace, instead of showing a read-only document's status by adding the words *[Read Only]* at the end of the document's path, Dreamweaver now displays a Read Only lock icon to the left of the filename in the document tab.

Document and Browser Navigation toolbars

The Document toolbar (shown in Figure 1-5) is located at the top of every open document (just below the Application and Document tab bars) and displays options and details associated with the active document. Directly below the Document toolbar is the new Browser Navigation toolbar, which allows you to navigate through your linked documents when Live View is activated.

Figure 1-5:
The
Document
toolbar.

Code view | Live Code | Refresh Design view | File Management

Code and Design | Check Browser | Inspect | Visual Aids | Title

Design view | Live View | Preview/Debug in Browser

The Document toolbar has buttons and icons that display different views of your page, as well as quick links for other features such as adding a page title and previewing the page in a browser. When you hover your cursor over each button or menu icon, a handy tool tip appears, giving you that feature's name and function. Click the menu icons to select options from their submenus:

✦ **Code view:** Use this setting to hand-code and edit HTML, CSS, JavaScript, server-side programming code (for example, PHP, ASP, or CFML), and other code in the open Document window. The different parts of the code in your document are precolored for easier development, but you can change that if you are visually impaired or just prefer a certain color palette. The default display font for text in Code view is 9-point Courier New. You can change the font in the Fonts category of Dreamweaver's Preferences.

✦ **Design view:** This *WYSIWYG* (What You See Is What You Get) editor displays a visual rendering of all the code between the <body> tags of the open document. Manipulate text and other objects in this view by selecting, editing, and applying properties to the content. Although similar to what you see in a browser window, this view cannot display many interactive code elements, such as links or JavaScript, so be sure to test the page in a browser or use the Live View button.

✦ **Split view:** The best of both worlds, use Split view to see simultaneously both Design and Code views in the open Document window. Resize the two panes by clicking and dragging the divider bar between them.

Note: If the contents of an open document exceed the visible area of the workspace in the Code, Design, or Split view, scroll bars appear to help you scroll to the hidden areas of the page.

Four additional layout options are available, but these are accessible only through the Layout Menu icon on the Application bar:

- **Split Code view:** Use Split Code view to see simultaneously two different Code views of the same open document. Both panes can be resized by clicking and dragging the divider bar between them.

- **Design View on Top:** Code view can sit on the top or bottom of the screen as opposed to the default left or right. To change the Code view position, you must first deselect Split Vertically. Then choose Design View on Top from the Application bar Layout menu or click the View Options icon on the Document toolbar and choose Design View on Top.

- **Split Vertically:** The Split Code, Code, and Design views can have their horizontally split panels converted to vertically split panels by choosing the Split Vertically option from the Application bar Layout menu.

- **Design View on Left:** After you choose Split, the code in Code and Design views appears on the left of the Document window. To flip the Code view to the right side of the Document window, choose Design View on Left from the Application bar Layout menu.

✦ **Live Code:** When Live View is enabled, click the Live Code button to select objects in Design view and quickly identify the corresponding code in Code view.

For more information about working with live data in Live View and Live Code, as well as planning dynamic pages, see Book VIII.

✦ **Live Changes:** As an enhancement to the Live Code feature, CS5 now includes a service called Live Changes. When Live Code is enabled, the source code for the open page is updated to show the new state of any interactive page elements such as menus and Spry tabbed panels. In other words, Live Changes highlights the background of any code that changes between the normal and active states of any interactive element as you move your mouse over those elements. If you find this feature distracting, you can turn it off by choosing View➪Live View Options➪Highlight Changes in Live Code. You may also customize the highlight color through the Code Coloring category in Dreamweaver's Preferences.

For more information about working with live data in Live View and Live Code as well as planning dynamic pages, see Book VIII.

✦ **Check Browser Compatibility:** This tool checks the open file for cross-browser compatibility issues. The Results panel displays any errors. You can use this menu also to check spelling, cross-reference the CSS Advisor Web site for issues, report a browser rendering issue, or adjust the target browser's version compatibility settings.

✦ **Live View:** This option, which was introduced in CS4, allows you to see your code, along with any dynamic content, *live* in Design view by clicking the Live View button or choosing View➪Live View.

✦ **Inspect:** This button works with Live View to help you identify CSS markup in your HTML. When enabled, the Inspect mode allows you to hover your mouse over various page elements to view the CSS box model attributes for any block-level element. Any selections in Live View are highlighted in Code view. Furthermore, highlighted CSS styles can be quickly viewed through the CSS panel in Current Selection mode.

✦ **Preview/Debug in Browser:** Preview or debug the open file in Device Central, Adobe BrowserLab, or any browser listed in the drop-down list. Add browsers through the Preferences dialog box.

✦ **Server Debug (ColdFusion only):** Click here to see a report of the page to help with debugging in ColdFusion. This icon appears only when a managed site uses a ColdFusion test server.

✦ **Visual Aids:** The Visual Aids menu lets you toggle on and off various tools to assist you with page layout, including CSS Layout Box Model, CSS Layout Outlines, AP Element Outlines, Table Borders, and Invisible Elements.

✦ **Refresh Design View:** Refresh the document's Design view after making changes in Code view. Code view changes do not automatically appear in Design view unless you save the file, press F5, or click this icon.

✦ **Title:** Enter a title for your page here, which is displayed in the browser's title bar. You may also type a title directly in the code between the `<title>` tags.

For open documents that have been edited but not saved, Dreamweaver adds an asterisk next to the filename in the Document filename tab as a visual reminder of the document's unsaved status. Save the document, and the asterisk goes away.

✦ **File Management:** Select a function from the File Management drop-down list.

✦ **Live View Navigation:** The Browser Navigation toolbar (shown in Figure 1-6) is a new feature in Dreamweaver CS5 that works with the Live View option. The toolbar is off by default, but you can turn it on and off by choosing View➪Toolbars. Once enabled, the toolbar works much like a regular browser navigation bar, with navigational buttons to move forward and backward, to stop loading the page, to refresh CSS styles, to edit the Live View page, and to return to the original document.

The Browser Navigation toolbar works in two modes:

• **Normal Mode:** Use this toolbar in normal working mode to view the local path to the open document window.

- **Live View Mode:** When Live View is activated, the address bar shows the path to the specific file displayed in the Live View window. Use the toolbar's navigation buttons (forward, back, stop, and home) to navigate through your linked pages as you would in a regular browser. You can also type a URL in the address field and edit any nondynamic pages you have browsed to as long as they are part of one of your managed sites.

Use the Live View Options menu to the right edge of the Browser Navigation toolbar hen troubleshooting display issues in Live View, The Live View menu has options that allow you to freeze or disable JavaScript, disable plug-ins, highlight changes in Live Code, follow links in the page, switch between a staging server for document source or local files for document links, and access and modify the HTTP Request settings.

By default, the Follow Links option is deselected for each document and document session, but you can easily turn on this feature by choosing the Follow Links option from the Live View menu or by choosing View⇨Live View Options⇨Follow Links. After the option is selected, you can use the Live View feature to follow links in your open document. If you also select Live Code, the code of the followed link is displayed (but can't be edited) in Code view.

Figure 1-6: Use the Live View Options menu on the Browser Navigation toolbar to assist with trouble-shooting display issues in Live View.

Rulers

Rulers, when enabled, appear along the top and left edges of the Document window and assist you with the measurement and placement of objects in your document. Rulers can be displayed in pixels, inches, or centimeters. The ruler's X/Y coordinates, which represent the 0/0 measurement mark for the horizontal and vertical axes and are located by default at the top-left edge of the file, can be moved to any location in the open Document window by clicking and dragging the origin square at the top-left edge of the rulers, and then releasing the origin point anywhere inside the visible Document window. The X/Y coordinates then jump to 0/0 at that new position. To reset the X/Y coordinates to the default location at the top-left edge of the Document window, choose View⇔Rulers⇔Reset Origin. Toggle rulers on and off by choosing View⇔Rulers⇔Show.

Grids

Use the grid to assist with laying out content in Design view. Because the grid lines extend in regular intervals through the entire document, from left to right and from top to bottom, you can use them as guides for exact positioning of objects in your document, as shown in Figure 1-7. For precise alignment, turn on the Snap to Grid option by choosing View⇔Grid⇔Snap to Grid. Control the grid settings, such as grid coloring and spacing, with the Grid Settings dialog box by choosing View⇔Grid⇔Grid Settings. Hide and show grids by choosing View⇔Grid⇔Show Grid.

Figure 1-7: Use the rulers, guides, and grids in Design view to assist you with the placement of objects.

Guides

Guides are horizontal and vertical guide lines that you can drag into the open Document window to assist you with the measurement and placement of objects. For example, you may want to place the top-left edge of an AP Element (layer) exactly 150 pixels in from the left edge of the Document window. A guide placed at the 150-pixel vertical mark with the Snap to Guide option enabled would allow you to snap the layer to the guide at that position. Dreamweaver's guides work much like the guides in Adobe Photoshop and Illustrator; they are visible on-screen in the work environment but aren't visible in print or on a Web page.

To create guides, choose View⇨Rulers⇨Show to turn on the Rulers, and then click and drag guides out from the top and left ruler bars. When the guide is in the desired position, release the guide onto the document. Lock or unlock guides as needed for easy repositioning or quick removal by dragging the guide back onto the ruler bar. Choose View⇨Guides⇨Snap to Guides to have elements snap to guides when positioning objects, such as layers, in the Document window. Quickly hide and show guides by choosing View⇨Guides⇨Show Guides.

Status bar

Dreamweaver's Status bar (shown in Figure 1-8) includes many handy features to improve your productivity. The Tag selector is on the bottom-left edge of the Document window and allows for easy tag and tag content selection. On the bottom-right edge, the Status bar shows the current size (in pixels) of the Document window, as well as a file size and estimated file opening time reflecting the file preferences for projected site visitors. For example, an open document may display 1100 x 435 and 35K/5 sec, meaning that the current page has a 35K file size and would take 5 seconds to load in a browser on a computer using a 56K modem. Keep in mind that the size of the Document window is not the same as the fixed width of your Web site layout; the numbers presented here merely represent the pixel dimensions of the Design view portion of the open Document window.

Figure 1-8:
The Status
bar.

Set magnification menu
Zoom tool   Window size menu
Hand tool   Download size/Download time
Tag selector   Select tool   Document encoding

You can manually resize the Document window to a predetermined size to approximate the inside of a browser window for testing by dragging the dividers between the panel dock and the Document window. To view a set of standard window sizes based on monitor resolution, click the Window Size/Download Size/Download Time pop-up menu.

In addition, the Status bar includes magnification tools to assist you with editing page content:

✦ **Select tool:** Use the Select tool to select content in the Document window. This is the default tool for selecting objects and text in your file in Design view. For example, single-click an image to select it with the Select tool.

✦ **Hand tool:** Use the Hand tool with a Zoom view to move the section of the page you're viewing in the Document window. For example, at 1600% view, the Hand tool allows you to reposition what you see in the Document window at that magnification.

✦ **Zoom tool:** The Zoom tool allows you to zoom in and out of the Design view window. Select the tool and click in the Document window to zoom into the page. Press and hold Alt (Windows) or Option (Mac) and click again to zoom out. Double-click the Zoom tool icon to return to 100% view.

✦ **Set Magnification menu:** The Magnification menu displays Zoom settings in percentages from 6% to 6400%. Select a preset magnification view from the drop-down list or type a number in the percentage field and click Enter (Windows) or Return (Mac) to view the page with a custom magnification.

Understanding the Panels and the Properties Inspector

Dreamweaver uses panels to help you organize, select from, and modify content, as well as to provide access to common features and functions. The main panels you will use most frequently are the Insert panel, the Files panel, and the Properties inspector. With the exception of the Properties inspector, all panels are located in the panel dock area, either individually or inside a panel group. You can, however, open, resize, reposition, undock, redock, and close any panel and panel groups to customize your workspace.

Understanding the panel dock

The panel dock is a fixed rectangular area at the left edge, the right edge, or both edges of the workspace (depending on your selected layout) that contains the currently open panels and panel groups. Each dock can be shown in *expanded* or *collapsed* mode by clicking the tiny double-arrows in the dark gray bar at the top of the dock:

✦ **Expanded mode:** When the dock is expanded, the individual panels can be individually expanded (showing the panel's contents) or collapsed (showing just the panel's tab).

✦ **Collapsed mode:** When the dock is collapsed, the panels appear in iconic mode with just an icon and a panel name. You can then access panels as temporary flyout menus by clicking the desired panel icon.

All panels have common features that make them easy to understand and use:

✦ **Options menu:** Each panel has an Options menu at the top-right corner of the panel. Use the Options menus to access panel-specific tasks.

✦ **Expanding/Collapsing:** Double-click the panel tab or panel tab bar to expand and collapse the panel or panel group window.

✦ **Repositioning:** Reposition panels by clicking and dragging the panel tab. Panels can be reordered within a panel group, repositioned inside and outside panel groups within the dock, and moved outside the dock to become free-floating panels.

✦ **Resizing:** To resize the height of docked panels, place your cursor on top of the divider line between two panels. When the cursor turns into a double-sided arrow, click and drag to resize the panels. To resize undocked panels, place your cursor at any edge of the panel window. When the cursor turns into a double-sided arrow, click and drag to resize the panel.

Accessing panels and panel groups

Dreamweaver has many panels to help you do your work. You can open and close most panels using the Window menu.

Panel groups are sets of related panels combined as separate tabbed layers in a single panel, either inside or outside the dock. Access each panel by clicking the tab at the top of the panel group. For example, the CSS panel group displays both the CSS Styles and the AP Elements panels; to see the AP Elements panel in that panel group's window, click the AP Elements tab.

Create new and modify existing panel groups by dragging and dropping panels to their new locations. Expand and collapse panel groups by double-clicking any of the tabs in the group. If docked to the right or left side of the Dreamweaver workspace, you can undock panels or entire panel groups by clicking the tab of a panel or the gray unused area next to the panel tabs within a panel group, and dragging the panel or panel group to the new location, either inside or outside the dock.

Using the Insert panel

The Insert panel (shown in Figure 1-9) has several sets of gray buttons for adding common *objects,* such as tables, images, and media, to an open document. By default, the Common set of buttons is displayed; you can access other sets through the drop-down menu at the top of the panel.

Figure 1-9:
The Insert
panel.

As you hover your cursor over the icons, a tool tip reveals the icon name and the colors on them become visible. If you'd prefer to see color icons instead of gray icons, select the Color Icons option from the Insert panel's Options menu at the top-right edge of the panel. Each icon, when clicked, adds the correct code to your page for the object or action selected. For instance, to insert an image, click the Images icon (and select the desired graphic); the appropriate HTML code is added to your page, such as `<img src="logo.gif">`. Although adding objects this way is fast and easy, you can also add the same objects to your page by using the Insert menu.

By default, the Insert panel displays the icons and labels for the options in the different available categories, such as Common, Layout, or Data. When you first open the panel, you should see the icons for the Common category. If you change the category, Dreamweaver remembers your last used setting. In addition to viewing the icons with labels, you can also choose to display the icons without the labels by choosing Hide Labels from the panel's category drop-down menu. Expand and collapse the Insert panel by double-clicking the panel's tab. Hide and show labels and access Help files by using the panel's Option's menu.

To add any of the objects or assets in the Insert panel to an open document, select one of the categories (such as Common, Layout, or Forms) and then do one of the following:

✦ Click an icon to insert the object.

✦ Click the icon and select an option from the icon's drop-down menu to insert the object.

Some icons insert an object (or perform an action) automatically, whereas others open object- or action-specific dialog boxes prompting you to select a file or add attributes or parameters to the object or action. When inserting objects from the Insert panel into Code view instead of Design view, you may also encounter the Tag editor. In that case, enter the appropriate information and click OK to add the object to your page.

Using the Properties inspector

The Properties inspector is the panel to use for adding HTML and CSS formatting and other attributes or properties to selected objects in your document.

The most versatile of all the panels, the contents of the Properties inspector change according to the object or text selected in Code or Design view. For instance, when you select text in your document, the Properties inspector displays options for adding properties to text; when you select a graphic, the inspector displays options for adding properties to images, as shown in Figure 1-10. This works for most object selections. The main thing to remember is that you must select the desired object or content *before* adding properties.

Figure 1-10:
When an image is selected, the Properties inspector displays options for adding image properties.

Working with the Files panel

Use the Files panel to manage (organize, select, and open) all your site files and folders, view both remote server and local file listings, access other files on your hard drive, and manage sites within Dreamweaver.

Rather than relying on your Explorer window (Windows) or Finder (Mac) to find and open files, create a "managed site" (see Book I, Chapter 3) for each project you work on in Dreamweaver and use the Files panel to locate and open all your site files. Your life will be much easier when you centralize this task to the Files panel.

The Files panel is displayed in its collapsed mode in the Designer workspace, and when displaying a "managed" site, it lists all the files and folders of the specified directory. You can also expand the panel into two panes to show both local and remote server views in one window; see the following list for details.

At the top of the Files panel, two drop-down menus assist you with site-management tasks. These two menus, Site Management and Site View, are shown in Figure 1-11. Here is a brief description about these menus:

Site Management

Site View

Figure 1-11:
The Files
panel.

+ **Site Management:** This menu lists all the managed sites you've created in Dreamweaver. A site becomes *managed* when you define a folder on your local computer for the HTML files of a specific project, and tell Dreamweaver where to find that folder. To get the most out of Dreamweaver's features, you need to create a managed site for each project you work on. . To view a list of managed sites, scroll to the bottom of this menu and choose Manage Sites to open the Manage Sites dialog box. For more information on creating a managed site, see Book I, Chapter 3.

+ **Site View:** When the Files panel is collapsed, use the Site View menu to toggle among four views:

  • **Local view:** Select this view to see the file structure of the local managed site. You may also use this view to see both local and remote server sites with the Files panel split into two panes. Use the Expand/Collapse icon to toggle between viewing one and two panes. By default, the local site appears in the right pane and the remote server appears in the left, but you can modify this in the Site category of Dreamweaver's Preferences if you'd prefer having the local pane appear on the left, as in many older FTP programs.

  • **Remote server:** Select this view to see the file structure of the remote server site. A remote server site is a version of your local site sitting on a remote hosting server accessible from the Internet. You must set up a remote server site in advance to see the remote site files.

  • **Testing server:** This view shows a directory listing of both the testing (staging) server and local site files. You must set up a testing server in advance to see the testing server site.

- **Repository view:** This feature is used when Dreamweaver is set up to use Subversion, a version control application. Choosing this option invokes the Version Control context menu, inside which files can be compared, viewed, and reverted.

Below the drop-down lists are a series of helpful icons to aid with transferring files to and from a remote server. Book V, Chapter 4 outlines how to use these icons, which are Connect/Disconnect, Refresh, Get Files, Put Files, Check Out Files, Check In Files, and Expand/Collapse.

Use the Files panel Options menu to create new files and folders by choosing File⇨New File or File⇨New Folder. New files and folders are added automatically to the bottom of the Files panel with the name *untitled* for easy renaming. To quickly open a file using the Files panel, double-click the filename or drag-and-drop the file to the workspace.

In addition to the features-rich Options menu at the top of the panel, the bottom of the Files panel has a Log button, to open the background file activity log, and a status bar, which displays important file data for individual selected files, such as title, creation date and time, and file size.

Customizing the Workspace

The Dreamweaver workspace is highly customizable, so you can create a work environment that best meets your needs and then save the layout for future use. The panels, for instance, are docked to their respective locations, but you can reposition and resize them by clicking and dragging them by their tabs. When you create and save a custom layout, all the panel locations, groupings, sizes, and expanded or collapsed states are saved along with the Document window and application window sizes and positions.

Here's how to work with a custom layout:

✦ To save a custom layout, choose Window⇨Workspace Layout⇨New Workspace. Give your layout a name and click OK.

✦ To open and use a saved layout, choose Window⇨Workspace Layout and then select the layout name.

✦ To rename a saved layout, choose Window⇨Workspace Layout⇨Manage Workspaces, select the layout from the listing in the Manage Workspaces dialog box, and click the Rename button.

✦ To delete a selected layout, choose Window⇨Workspace Layout⇨Manage Workspaces, select the layout from the listing in the Manage Workspaces dialog box, and click the Delete button.

✦ To revert a layout to its default settings and arrangement, choose Window⇨Workspace Layout⇨Reset *Layout Name*.

Setting Dreamweaver Preferences

You can modify many settings in Dreamweaver's Preferences dialog box to further customize your workspace and workflow. To access the Preferences dialog box, choose Edit⇨Preferences (Windows) or Dreamweaver⇨Preferences (Mac).

The Preferences dialog box offers several categories for customization. Select a category from the list on the left to reveal that category's preference settings on the right side of the dialog box. Figure 1-12 shows the Preferences dialog box with the General category selected.

Figure 1-12:
Use the Preferences dialog box to customize Dreamweaver.

Many of the category settings can stay as they are. In some instances, however, you may choose to modify the settings to improve your work experience. You can find entries throughout this book that reference the Preferences settings and suggest ways to customize specific categories.

Finding Help

We all need help from time to time, and the best place to find it (for Dreamweaver, at least) is through the options inside the Help menu. There you find links that open special dialog boxes or browser windows revealing a variety of help topics. Read about these topics in more detail in the following sections.

To find help for a specific Dreamweaver feature, choose Help from the panel menu or click the Help button or icon found in most dialog boxes. The Adobe Community Help dialog box appears to display information for the most closely related topic. For instance, to find out more about setting properties for graphic files, select an image inserted in a document and then click the Help icon in the Properties inspector. The Help Viewer window opens to a Setting Image Properties page.

Using Dreamweaver Help (F1)

The most resourceful link on the Help menu by far is Dreamweaver Help, which launches the Adobe Community Help CS5 dialog box full of local help files and remote help resources, from which you can search for help by topic or any keyword. In addition to being thorough and helpful, most results also contain quick links to related topics as well as related online resources such as tutorials and videos.

You must have a live Internet connection to access these online help files, which can be launched by choosing Help➪Dreamweaver Help or by pressing F1.

Search the Help files by selecting a category and drilling down into the topic area you want to learn more about. When you select a topic, its details appear on the right side of the window. You can also search for specific topics by typing keywords into the Search field and restrict search results to Local Help, Adobe.com Help, or Community Help by choosing an option from the Search Location menu. Results are listed by order of relevance. Select the topic that most matches your query to view the results of your search. In addition, when viewing a topic, use the navigation icons to go forward and backward within the topic area.

Working with the Reference panel

The Reference panel displays reference information for all the markup languages, programming languages, accessibility standards, and CSS you can use when building your Web site.

Open this panel by choosing Help➪Reference. The Results panel appears below the Properties inspector, and displays the Reference area as one of several tabs in the panel, alongside other helpful tools such as Search and Validation (covered in later chapters). Select a book from the panel's Book drop-down list to display information from that reference book, as shown in Figure 1-13. Each entry contains descriptions and examples of the styles, tags, and objects in your code.

Figure 1-13:
Select a reference book from the Book menu.

To reference a specific tag, keyword, or attribute selected in the Code view of an open document, do one of the following:

✦ Right-click (Windows) or Control+click (Mac) the item and choose Reference from the context menu.

✦ Place the insertion point in a tag, keyword, or attribute and press Shift+F1.

If the reference contains an example you want to copy and paste into another document, select it from the Reference panel and copy it using the panel's context or Options menu.

Visiting Adobe's Dreamweaver support portal

Several Help menu links launch browser windows for online Adobe Help and Support for Dreamweaver. The entire Adobe Web site is updated regularly and includes tips, updates, examples, and detailed information on advanced topics, so check the site often.

To help you find specific destinations in Adobe's online Help and Support Resource Center, Dreamweaver provides quick access to the following locations through the Help menu:

✦ **Spry Framework Help:** Launch the Spry Framework for Ajax online developers guide.

✦ **Business Catalyst InContext Editing Help:** Launch the Adobe InContext Editing page, where you will find documentation about this new online Web editing service.

✦ **Omniture Help:** Launch the Adobe Omniture.com Web site, where you can learn about products and services, explore resources, participate in the Omniture online community, access Web-based training, become a partner, and more.

✦ **ColdFusion Help:** Launch the Adobe ColdFusion online documentation.

✦ **Reference:** Launch the Reference panel in the Dreamweaver workspace.

✦ **Dreamweaver Support Center:** Launch the Adobe Community Help CS5 dialog box to search for help by topic or keyword.

✦ **Dreamweaver Exchange:** Go to the Dreamweaver Exchange page to search for, purchase, and download free Dreamweaver extensions.

✦ **Manage Extensions:** Launch Dreamweaver Extension Manager for help installing, removing, and submitting extensions to and from the Adobe Exchange.

✦ **CSS Advisor:** Launch the CSS Advisor section of the Adobe Developer Connection Web site to find detailed information on all things CSS, including browser compatibility, solutions and workarounds to common display issues, and comments from the Adobe community.

✦ **Adobe Online Forums:** Open a page providing access to several Adobe Web-based and newsreader-based online forums, where you can talk with other Dreamweaver users about Dreamweaver topics and technical issues.

✦ **Complete/Update AdobeID Profile:** Open a browser window to sign up or sign in to Adobe.com to complete your product installation, create an AdobeID profile, or update your existing profile.

✦ **Product Registration:** Connect to the Internet to register your product online.

✦ **Deactivate:** Deactivate your serial number and prevent the application from running. It is highly recommended that you deactivate before uninstalling the software.

✦ **Updates:** Connect to www.adobe.com to check for software updates.

✦ **Adobe Product Improvement Program:** Sign up for Adobe's Product Improvement program. With your permission, Adobe automatically receives information about your usage to help with improving future versions of the software.

Chapter 2: Planning and Designing Your Site

In This Chapter

✔ Figuring out who your audience is

✔ Taking a look at the site design

✔ Adding graphics to your design

Putting a Web site on the Internet involves more than figuring out how to build Web pages. Creating a site that people enjoy using requires careful planning and design, based on site visitors' expectations and your (or your client's) Web site goals.

Planning a good Web site involves conducting market research, defining business needs, making decisions about Web-based technology, discussing search engine optimization and accessibility strategies, gathering and organizing content, setting a budget and signing contracts, purchasing a hosting plan, designing and optimizing graphics, constructing the site in HTML, CSS, JavaScript, or some combination thereof, and adding the required dynamic features and functionality. Discussing all these topics in detail is beyond the scope of this book; instead, this chapter focuses on a few key aspects of Web design that you need to think about. If you want more in-depth information on Web design, check out *Web Design All-in-One For Dummies* (Wiley) by Sue Jenkins.

Whether designing a site for yourself, your company, or a freelance client, the overall planning and design process is relatively the same. This chapter discusses knowing your audience, reviewing design considerations, and tips for designing a successful site.

Understanding the Web Design Workflow

Building a Web site has a logical workflow. The different stages of the Web design workflow are as follows:

Define > Design > Build > Test > Launch

Each stage requires cooperation from all parties involved — including the client, designers, and programmers — because each is responsible for different parts of the process. Table 2-1 shows who should be involved with each step of the workflow process.

Table 2-1	**Web Design Workflow**			
Define	*Design*	*Build*	*Test*	*Launch*
Client and designer	Designer	Designer and programmer	Client, designer, and programmer	Designer and programmer

Typically, the client provides content, the designer (you) creates the design and builds the site, the programmer adds dynamic functionality, everyone gets involved in testing, and finally, the designer or programmer or both launch (publish) the site on the Internet.

Knowing Your Audience

The aim of a Web site is to meet the audience's needs while achieving the client's mission. Both the client and you (the designer) need to have knowledge of the target market, an understanding of the demographics of that target audience, and a good overview of the existing online competition.

Defining the client's expectations

Use the client's mission statement as a starting point to define the client's goals for the Web site. If the client doesn't have a mission statement, you need to ask some questions to help define the goals. For example, what does the client hope to achieve with the Web site? Here are some goals the client may have for the site:

+ Provide information to existing customers

+ Generate leads to find new customers

+ Sell products and services

+ Provide information to the general public

When defining Web site goals, consider and focus on the three most important aspects about the business that make it unique and beneficial to customers. The look of the site should be largely determined by the industry and Web site needs, and the organization of the site should be defined by the content being delivered.

Exploring the audience's expectations

Market research is one of the best ways to determine site visitors' expectations. Here's the information you need to assemble:

✦ The target demographic. Be specific. Who are they?

✦ The target visitors' Web browsing habits. Determine whether they are seeking products, information, or a consultation, or have information to share with others.

✦ The target visitor's bandwidth capabilities. Not all Internet users have access to high-speed Internet, especially visitors from across the globe. If this is a consideration, a fast-loading Web page will be one of your main priorities.

✦ The target visitor's Internet browsing equipment. Some of your visitors may want to view your site on mobile devices in addition to using an Internet browser, which means you may need to develop separate mobile content or mobile-ready Web pages.

✦ The money that target visitors have available to spend on the client's products or services.

✦ Whether the target audience prefers to purchase online or shop in a brick-and-mortar store.

Collecting this information can help you determine the site's design direction, layout, and structure. For instance, if the site is aimed at a worldwide audience, you may need to consider language and cultural issues.

You can find Web sites for every conceivable industry in the world, so a good place to start the design process when creating a new Web site is to review what's already on the Internet. Do a general online search for companies in the same industry worldwide or countrywide. Then do additional searches for competition in the same general geographic region, such as statewide, countywide, and citywide. Think about design, usability, budget, time frame, and technical issues. Look at the competitors' sites and take notes about what works and what doesn't with regard to content and layout.

After gathering data about competitors' sites, draw diagrams and sketch design ideas, write copy, and make a list of key points that the site should address. You may even want to generate a preliminary site map, or wireframe, of all sections of your new site based on your research of competitor's sites, client feedback, and so on. A clear understanding of the target audience helps define the site's organization and structure.

Examining Issues that Affect the Site Design

Several issues affect the design of your site, such as cost, timeframe, marketing, target audience, accessibility issues, content, and browser optimization. The following sections introduce you to these concepts and provide ideas for making the most of your site.

Balancing time, cost, and scope

When you're designing a Web site, whether for yourself or for a client, keep in mind these three main components to any Web project:

✦ **Time:** Decide when you can deliver the job.

✦ **Cost:** Determine how much the project is going to cost.

✦ **Scope:** Determine what you hope to achieve.

Most projects begin with specific limitations with regard to these project components. One frequent limitation has to do with budget; a client may specify that he or she hopes to keep their cost within a specific budget for a new Web site that achieves the defined scope and is delivered by a specific time. Although that may be an ideal goal, achieving all three components of the Web project may not be feasible. For example, if a project needs to be delivered in a short time frame, the project cost may need to increase, or if the client only has X dollars to pay for the project, only parts of the scope may be met. Obviously, the three Web project components have a strong dependency between them; if the project cost, time frame, and scope are in sync, all three can be achieved. However, if limits are placed on any one of the components, a compromise may need to be reached.

Conveying your message

When you're considering the best way to transmit a message on a Web site, you need to take into account several site design considerations, including design, usability, accessibility, copyright, budget, and technical issues. For instance, is the new site selling a product or service, is it a nonprofit organization, or is it a personal Web site? Decide whether the new site will be a *brochureware* site (a print brochure in Web format) or will have any dynamic functionality for gathering information, selling products, or providing password-protected content.

Web site design concepts

Before beginning any Web project, spend some time reflecting on the following site concepts:

✦ **Design:** The visual design of the page is the most important aspect of the site. Not only does the look help communicate the information contained on the page, but it also says a lot about the client, the product or service being sold, the professionalism of the person (or team) who designed it, and the site owner's level of professionalism and competence.

The design itself should be simple with a clear navigation plan. The navigation scheme and company logo or other identifying icon should appear on every page in the same general location, allowing easy access to the home page at all times. You want visitors to move through the site easily and find what they're looking for as quickly as possible.

Programs such as Adobe Photoshop and Adobe Fireworks have a ton of neat features for designing graphics and optimizing them for use in a Web site. However, sometimes beginner designers get carried away and lose focus on the overall design in favor of showing off the fancy effects they have learned. For instance, there is no need for text with a drop shadow, inner bevel, inner glow, outer glow, and a gradient overlay. The same applies to Adobe Flash; it's great that you can create animations and buttons that fade on mouse up and mouse down, but the design will suffer if a visitor can't figure out how to navigate the Web site.

✦ **Usability:** Consider in advance how users will interact with the pages and the Web site as a whole. Is the site easy to understand and navigate? Can users access information quickly, and is it formatted logically in an easy-to-read way? You need to clearly define the main idea of each page. Keep text short and to the point and include links and graphics relevant to the rest of the site. Above all, proofread the site for spelling errors and double-check links. If you have the time, consider asking another designer, friends, or family members for quick feedback about usability issues. Often times they may be able to point out something obvious you have missed or attempt to use a feature differently than you had imagined.

✦ **Accessibility:** Making a site accessible to people with visual, auditory, motor, and other disabilities has implications for a site's design. Consider adding text navigation links instead of (or in addition to) graphical links for visitors with browsers that don't support graphics or visitors using disability software such as speech readers and text viewers. Dreamweaver has tools that let you author accessible content. See the "Designing Web sites with accessibility" sidebar in this chapter for more information about accessibility issues.

Perhaps Ed Tittel, author of *HTML, XHTML, & CSS For Dummies* (Wiley), said it best on his book's companion Web site (`www.edtittel.com/html4d6e/index.php?option=com_content&view=article&id=73:web-site-accessibility&catid=31:general&Itemid=41`): "If you have a small vanity site and simply don't care about making its content accessible to those with reading or vision impairments, then perhaps site accessibility doesn't matter . . . to you. But for any kind of site that may eventually wish to reach a broader audience, or whose sponsor wants to attract government business at any level (most cities, counties, states, and the feds all require their vendors to offer accessible sites to users of their products or services), accessibility isn't an option — it's a mandate."

✦ **Copyright:** Make sure that any graphics, text, music, video, and other media you add to the site is original or legally licensed to avoid copyright infringement. In other words, assume everything online is copyrighted and legally belongs to someone else unless otherwise stated.

✦ **Budget:** You need to know the budget defined for the project so that you can appropriately allocate time to designing and building, and possibly even maintaining, the site. Extra costs may also be incurred for hosting, training, and other Web site needs. Plan, too, for the cost of the project changing scope due to the client's requests for revisions. Changes can also affect the timeline, so be sure to build in extra time as a cushion for the unexpected. Scope creep (unforeseen or whimsical client requests for project changes) happens all too often so be prepared for hourly cost increases or contract addendums or both.

✦ **Technical:** When designing and building a Web site, you have many technical considerations that affect how visitors experience the site, including the browsers and operating systems the site supports, whether the site will use any dynamic functionality, and whether the site requires a secure server for data protection. For instance, information collected from visitors needs to be kept secure and protected.

Also, the coding and database for dynamic functionality, if any, depends on the Web server type (Linux and UNIX servers use PHP and MySQL and Microsoft servers use .NET and SQL databases), so designers and developers need to plan accordingly.

Designing Web sites with accessibility

When designing Web sites, you need to consider whether the audience will include people with visual and other disabilities. If so, you should add accessibility features, such as image labels and keyboard shortcuts, to your site. Dreamweaver has the tools that let you author accessible content that complies with government guidelines. In addition, Dreamweaver supports designers who need accessibility features themselves to create accessible sites. Although adding site accessibility is not a requirement for every Web site, doing so is considered a *best practice*. When in doubt, make your sites accessible.

Accessibility features in Dreamweaver prompt you to add Accessibility tags and attributes to objects as they are inserted in a page. To turn on these features, follow these steps:

1. Choose Edit➪Preferences (Windows) or Dreamweaver➪Preferences (Mac).

   The Preferences dialog box appears.

2. Choose the Accessibility category on the left to reveal the accessibility options on the right.

3. Next to the Show Attributes When Inserting options, select the content that you want to be prompted for.

For example, to always be prompted to add accessibility tags or attributes to images inserted on a page, select the Images option.

4. For Web designers with disabilities who are using Dreamweaver to create accessible Web pages, consider the following options:

The Keep Focus In the Panel When Opening option accesses an accessibility panel after you open it. This is a good option for Web designers using screen readers who need accessibility settings to create Web pages in Dreamweaver.

Consider disabling the Off-Screen Rendering option if using a screen reader. This option is turned on by default but may cause conflicts for designers using screen readers.

5. Click OK to accept the new preferences.

In addition to these accessibility features, Dreamweaver comes with several sample Web page designs that comply to accessibility standards. To access these sample designs, choose File➪New to open the New Document dialog box, and then select a layout from the Blank Page or Blank Template categories.

If you do use accessibility settings on your Web pages, be sure to run an accessibility report to test your page or site against the government's Section 508 guidelines as part of the testing process before publishing your site. See Book V, Chapter 1 for more about testing.

To find out more about accessibility initiatives, visit the Web sites for both the World Wide Web Consortium Web Accessibility Initiative (www.w3.org/WAI) and Section 508 of the Federal Rehabilitation Act (www.section508.gov).

Considering resolution, optimization, and content

Before building the site, you need to decide on other issues that affect the overall design of the site, including monitor resolution, browser optimization, and breadth of content. We discuss these issues in detail in the sections that follow.

Monitor resolution

When visitors come to your Web site, how much of the Web site design they see in their browsers is somewhat determined by the elements, or chrome, in their browser, such as the address bar, navigation buttons, status bar, and scroll bars, but mostly determined by their monitor resolution setting. Monitor resolutions can be set anywhere from 600 x 400 to 2560 x 2048. The smaller the numbers, the larger the site appears in the monitor display.

Currently, most monitors come with a factory preset resolution of 1024 x 768 or higher. Nevertheless, because you have no control over what monitor resolutions visitors will have, consider doing some market research to find out who your audience will be and what monitor resolution they're likely to have. This information helps you determine the ultimate width of your Web site design. For a few years, the standard was to design a Web site for a monitor resolution set to 800 x 600. However because less than 4 percent of all Internet traffic uses that resolution anymore, the new standard is to design for monitors optimized for 1024 x 768 and higher resolution settings. That said, because a design at 1024 x 768 pixels is too wide to fit in a browser window with the aforementioned browser chrome, the design would need to be a little smaller — about 955 x 600 pixels — to fit without invoking horizontal scrollbars.

For a great discussion about designing for multiple screen sizes, check out the still relevant 2005 whitepaper titled "Screen Size Matters" by Catalyst Group Design at `www.catalystgroupdesign.com/cofactors/upload/catalyst_resolution_whitepaper.pdf`.

Browser optimization

Another issue to consider is browser optimization. Taking a look at browser trends can give you insight into important design considerations, such as layout size and CSS (Cascading Style Sheets) support. For example, according to W3 Schools.com (one of the best Web tutorial sites), the most popular browser is Firefox, the most used operating system is Windows XP, and the most common monitor display resolution is 1024 x 768 or higher.

The W3 Schools Web site lists browser and operating system usage statistics on a monthly basis dating back to 2003. Examples are shown in Tables 2-2 and 2-3. For the most current browser optimization statistics, visit `www.w3schools.com/browsers/browsers_stats.asp`.

Table 2-2				Browser Usage Statistics			
2010	*IE 8*	*IE 7*	*IE 6*	*Firefox*	*Chrome*	*Safari*	*Opera*
January	14.3%	11.7%	10.2%	46.3%	10.8%	3.7%	2.2%

Table 2-3				Operating System Usage Statistics			
2010	*Windows 7*	*Windows Vista*	*Windows 2003*	*Windows XP*	*Windows 2000*	*Linux*	*Mac*
January	11.3%	15.4%	1.4%	59.4%	0.6%	4.6%	6.8%

In a perfect world, all Web sites would function flawlessly on all browsers, but in the real world this rarely happens without significant effort. There most definitely are subtle differences to how a Web site is interpreted by different browsers from the things like the actual layout and placement of images and text, font sizes, or even the functionality of forms. This fact is extremely frustrating for beginners and seasoned designers, but underlines the importance of proper testing, validation, checking compatibility and accessibility. Remember to design and test for the majority of your audience;

although it would be nice if the Web site works on all browsers, spending three months past your deadline fixing bugs on a Web site for some random non-name browsers with .05% of the browser market isn't an effective use or your time.

Content

Before building a Web site, you (or your client) need to create and gather content and other site assets. Content gathering includes writing copy for every page and creating or licensing image, sound, and video files. It's important to gather these assets in advance so that you don't have to stop site development repeatedly to create or find any missing content.

Gathering content is a big undertaking, even for the smallest sites, so unless you're also being compensated by your client as the project or content manager, this process should be the *client's* sole responsibility *before the project begins;* otherwise, you may be blamed for significant delays, even though you're not the one holding up the project. Before you sign contracts, make sure you reinforce the idea that it's the client's responsibility to gather the content before you start the project time clock. Trust us: You'll be glad you did.

After you've gathered the content, organize everything electronically in a place that's easily accessible when it comes time to build the site. For example, you may decide to create a folder on your computer called Websites, and in that folder create a subfolder for the client. Inside the client's folder, you may create several additional subfolders for all the different assets, as shown in Figure 2-1.

Figure 2-1:
Organize file assets into folders.

Planning the Site Layout

You can save time by planning and designing the site layout before working in Dreamweaver. A consistent layout and design helps create a good user experience. Site layout applies to the look of all the pages on the site, as well as how the pages are logically arranged and how they interact with each other. This phase is where you're creating the site's *architecture,* or structure.

With regard to the layout of the pages themselves, consider designing a mock-up that has fixed as well as editable areas. Dreamweaver allows you to create templates and library items for page layouts and elements to make them consistent on every page. For instance, the navigation element may be at the top of every page, with an area for subnavigation on the left margin and page-specific content in the center of the page below the navigation.

As you create the design, think about the site visitors' experience:

✦ Visitors should be able to move from page to page with ease. Therefore, navigation should be consistent throughout the site.

✦ Visitors should know where they are inside the site and how to return to the home page. Use indexes and subnavigation to assist visitors with finding information. Also provide a method for contacting the company in case a visitor wants to communicate by telephone, fax, mail, or e-mail.

After you gather and organize your data, you may want to create some HTML sitemap or wireframe pages to help organize the site's structure. A *wireframe* is a tree diagram or flowchart of a Web site that includes all its pages. Each wireframe indicates links between pages but doesn't typically include any reference to the design of the site or the content on any specific pages. You can create additional wireframes for the individual pages to assist with the organization of content on the page, before you have real content.

To create a wireframe for your Web site, consider using a graphics program, such as Adobe Illustrator or Adobe Photoshop, or a diagramming program, such as Microsoft Visio, Dia, or Gliffy. In addition to labeling each page on the wireframe, these programs have the tools you need to customize the diagram with graphic elements, color, text, specific fonts, and other information.

To find out more about wireframes, check out the SitePoint article by Matt Beach at www.sitepoint.com/article/wire-frame-your-site.

After creating a wireframe and before building the site in Dreamweaver, you may also want to create a mock-up, or *comp,* of the site design on paper or in a graphics program such as Adobe Photoshop, Adobe Illustrator, or Adobe Fireworks. A key benefit to designing a mock-up in a graphics program is that after the client approves the mock-up, you can use it to generate many if not all of the graphics.

A mock-up differs from a wireframe in that the mock-up is a design of the site that contains all the graphical information for the Web site layout including company identity, navigation, headers, text, and other graphics. In other words, the mock-up should have all the elements that the client has requested for the site. For instance, clients may tell you that they "want the logo on the top of the page, the navigation below that, an area for links to frequently accessed pages, and a section for a photo gallery." In response to these needs, you plan the layout of the page and the site. Then you show the mock-up to the clients to make sure the design meets their needs.

> Both the creation of the mockup and the wireframe are critical elements to planning a successful Web site. Giving the client the opportunity to see the site structure (wireframe) and the design (mockup) *before* the site gets built provides you and the client with the opportunity to hash out ideas and agree to the final design. The designer then has a good understanding of the Web site project and the exact design that the client is expecting so there are no misunderstandings later.

Designing and Optimizing Graphics

After the design is finalized, the next step is to slice and optimize the graphics. *Slicing* and *optimizing* describe the process of dividing a large flat mockup into individual pieces, or *graphics,* that are then compressed into GIF, JPEG, or PNG files and reassembled on the Web page with HTML and CSS, much like the pieces of a puzzle.

The number of graphics overall should be limited to ensure that the page loads quickly in a browser. If you're considering rollover button functionality and other interactive features on the site, create the graphics for these elements at this stage of the process, in advance of optimization.

Before adding graphics to Web pages, you need to compress them, because in their native format (PSD, PDF, AI, EPS, TIFF, and so on), the file sizes are much too large to download quickly over the Internet.

When compressing images for the Web, you can choose from three graphics formats: GIF, JPEG, and PNG, as shown in Table 2-4. Web browsers have widely supported GIF (Graphics Interchange Format) and JPEG (Joint Photographic Experts Group) for years; however, the PNG (Portable Network Graphic) format has more recently gained in popularity and is now also widely supported. Nonetheless, due to some older browser incapability issues, you may still want to be mindful when using PNG files. For example, IE6 interprets transparent PNG files into a wonderful shade of baby blue!

Table 2-4	Graphics File Formats	
Format	*Is Best For*	*What It Supports*
GIF	Images with large flat areas of color	Maximum of 256 colors (8-bit); both animation and background transparency
JPEG	Photographs and graphics with lots of color and gradient blends	Millions of colors (24-bit) but not animation or transparency
PNG	GIF replacement (as recommended by the W3C); supports images with large flat areas of color	PNG-8, maximum of 256 colors (8-bit); PNG-24, millions of colors (48-bit); background transparency but not animation

Each compressed image type uses a different compression format to crunch data and create smaller file sizes. With all formats, the compression goal is to achieve the best image quality possible while reducing the file size. Fortunately, because the Web displays images at low resolution (72 ppi, or *pixels per inch*), most of the loss in image quality from the compression is hard to see on screen.

To optimize the images, use an image-compression program such as Adobe Fireworks, Corel Paint Shop Pro, an old copy of Adobe ImageReady (CS2 and earlier), or the built-in compression engine in Adobe Photoshop or Adobe Illustrator. Most applications allow you to slice, optimize, and export graphic files and HTML. Other non-Adobe compression programs and plug-ins are also available, such as NetMechanic's GIFBot (www.netmechanic.com) and ReaSoft's ReaCompressor (www.reasoft.com).

Whichever program you choose, be sure to consult the program's Help files for further instruction on image sizing and optimization.

Chapter 3: Creating and Managing Sites

In This Chapter

✔ Understanding how Web sites are made

✔ Setting up a managed site

✔ Keeping track of multiple sites

A *Web site* is a group of pages that are linked and share common features such as design, navigation, content, and purpose. Dreamweaver enables you to organize all the pages and assets of your site in one convenient location. To take advantage of Dreamweaver's great site-management features, such as uploading files and managing links, first you need to create a *managed site* in Dreamweaver, which is really just a way to tell Dreamweaver where to create and save files locally for each Web site project. When managing your site, you'll likely adopt a general Web site structure and opt for either a root-level or document-level organization for your files.

In this chapter, you find out how to create a managed Web site, gain an understanding of root-level and document-level site organization, review the settings in the Site Definition dialog box, and discover how easy it is to manage multiple sites in Dreamweaver.

Understanding General Web Site Structure

Before you manage your first Dreamweaver Web site, you need to be familiar with the general structure of a Web site and have a basic understanding of the different types of root-level organization, as discussed in the sections that follow.

Web site construction folders

When building a Web site, you need to work in two or three locations:

+ **The local folder:** This folder, also called the *local root folder*, holds all the files, images, and other assets of a managed site. The root level, simply put, is the top level or starting point a browser uses for finding objects in a Web site. The local folder typically sits somewhere on your computer's hard drive, though it may also be on a mapped drive or a network server. Wherever it resides, you must specify the location of the local root folder in the Site Setup dialog box when defining a managed site. See the "Setting Up a Managed Site" section, later in this chapter, for instructions.

✦ **The live server folder:** This folder is where you publish your site, typically on a remote live Web server. For example, when you purchase a Web hosting plan, you're essentially renting a parking space for your Web site in the virtual parking lot of the Internet. That space is on the host's remote live Web server. You'll be transferring files to the remote live server folder from the local folder to ensure that the published Web site is functional and up to date. You can choose from several types of live servers. See Book V, Chapter 3 for more info on setting up a live server folder.

✦ **The testing server folder:** This folder is where Dreamweaver processes dynamic data to create dynamic content and connect with a database while you create and test your site. Your testing server can be on the local computer, a development or testing server, or a production server. We don't recommend that you use the live server folder for the testing server folder because that can cause confusion and create other problems. See Book VII, Chapter 1 to set up your testing server.

For most simple, nondynamic sites, you will build your site in the local folder and publish your site to the remote live server folder. For dynamic sites, you will build in the local folder, test in the testing server folder, and publish to the live server folder.

Root-level organization

After deciding on the general Web site construction folder locations for your site, the next step is to determine how to organize and link the files in your site relative to the *root* (top-level) folder.

Each page on a Web site has a unique address, or URL (Uniform Resource Locator), such as `http://www.monkeybarsdesign.com/about.html`. When you make a *local link* (a link from one file to another on the same site), you don't generally need to specify the entire URL of the file you're linking to, as in `<a href="http://www.monkeybarsdesign.com/contact.html">Contact Us</a>`. Instead, you just need to set the *relative path*, which is the path from the current file or the site's root folder to the linked file. For instance, to link from an about.html page to a contact.html page, both of which sit at the root level of a URL, the local link code would look like this: `<a href="contact.html">Contact Us</a>`.

When building your Web pages, use one of these three types of link paths: document-relative paths, site root–relative paths, or absolute paths. All three are described in this section.

Document-relative path

A link using a document-relative path specifies the path and name of the document being linked to, such as about.html or photogallery/MollySurfing. html. The general idea behind document-relative paths is that you don't need to add the *absolute* (full) URL including `http://` because all the linked files are located at the root level or inside a subfolder of the local root folder.

Using the Pacific Surf site structure shown in Figure 3-1 to create a document-relative path to a page inside a subfolder at the root level, add a forward slash after the folder name containing the file you want to link to, as in the path

```
photogallery/MollySurfing.html
```

Figure 3-1:
This site
uses
document
relative
paths.

This path tells the browser to move down a level in the folder hierarchy, from the root level into the photogallery folder, to find a file called MollySurfing.html. To move from inside a subfolder back up to the root level, such as adding a text link from the MollySurfing.html page to the about.html page, you add two periods and a slash (`../`) before the filename in the link code, as in `../about.html`. The `..` tells the browser to move up a level in the folder hierarchy. Table 3-1 shows different folder scenarios that might help you understand the path structure a little better.

Table 3-1	Linking Explained
Link from A to B	*Link Example*
From index.html to about.html	`about.html`
From about.html to MollySurfing.html	`photogallery/` `MollySurfing.html`
From MollySurfing.html to KimAndJeff.html	`KimAndJeff.html`
From MollySurfing.html to contact.html	`../contact.html`

Be sure to save new files to your Dreamweaver managed site before creating document-relative paths to ensure that the path is saved correctly. Otherwise, you may see a temporary path starting with `file://` in the code until the file gets saved and Dreamweaver can update all the temporary paths to relative paths.

Site root–relative path

Links using site root–relative paths display the path and name of the document being linked to, but they direct the browser to always begin searching for the path by starting at the root level of the site. To indicate this starting point, you include a forward slash before the first folder or filename in the link code, as in the following two examples:

```
/contact.html
/services/marketing.html
```

The forward slash stands for the site's root folder. Use site root-relative paths for large sites sitting on several servers, a site that has multiple hosts, or sites that use server-side includes (SSIs), as described in Book III, Chapter 3.

Absolute path

An absolute path is the full URL to the linked document, as in

```
http://www.example.com/services/marketing.html
```

You must use absolute paths (sometimes called *hard-coded* paths) for pages that sit outside your Web site on other servers, such as when adding a link on your site to purchase a specific *For Dummies* book from Amazon.com or a link that takes you to a particular page on someone else's blog site. Using absolute paths is somewhat discouraged for local site pages because links can easily be broken when you move files from one domain name or folder location to another. So unless you have a particular reason for using absolute paths (such as hard-coding links to other files and images in a customized header in a WordPress blog), try to use document-relative paths for local links whenever possible.

Setting Up a Managed Site

Setting up a managed site simply means defining a local site on your computer so that Dreamweaver knows where to save documents and find files related to that site. You'll want to create a managed site for each project that you work on so that you can open and edit site-specific files from the Files panel. Always try to define or manage a site before you start development to ensure that the site takes advantage of Dreamweaver's great site-management features, such as sitewide filename change support and the sitewide link checker.

In earlier versions of Dreamweaver, the Site Definition dialog box offered two ways to manage new sites, depending on your comfort level:

✦ **Basic:** This tab included a wizard with step-by-step prompts to guide you through the site setup process.

✦ **Advanced:** This tab allowed you to manually set all local, remote server, and testing folder settings as well as other category options.

In Dreamweaver CS5, the entire site-management process has been dramatically simplified and improved. All settings are now contained in a single unified location called the Site Setup dialog box. Even better, if you occasionally forget to manage a site before you begin working on a new project, certain tasks, such as saving a template or adding dynamic content, now trigger Dreamweaver to automatically open Site Setup for your convenience.

In addition, site management now includes a User Guidance feature, in which icons and highlighting in the dialog box visually assist you when you create a site within a given workflow, such as trying to preview a page with dynamic content in a browser before you have set up a testing server. For example, a green check mark appears next to menu items that have been successfully completed, an orange asterisk appears next to items with an unfinished status, and a red x mark appears next to times that were filled out incorrectly,

To get your site up and running locally, follow these steps:

1. **Choose Site⇨New Site.**

The Site Setup dialog box appears to the Site category, which displays fields for the Site Name and Local Site Folder, as shown in Figure 3-2.

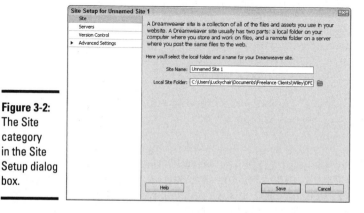

Figure 3-2:
The Site category in the Site Setup dialog box.

2. **In the Site Name field, enter the name of your site.**

   Choosing a name that matches the name of the client or indicates your site's purpose is best, such as ABC Company or My Blog.

3. **In the Local Site Folder field, verify that the path points to the folder on your computer that you want to use for this site.**

   For example, if you have a folder on your computer dedicated to local Web sites (local_sites), and you want to create a folder inside that to house the files for a new ABC Company Web site, your Local Site Folder path might be something like

   ```
   Users\YOURUSERNAME\Documents\local_sites\ABC Web
   ```

4. **Click Save to close the dialog box.**

   Your new managed site opens, displaying all the existing files and folders (if any) in the root folder in the Files panel.

   In the Server section that follows, you find out how to configure the Server category of the Site Setup dialog box to transfer files to a remote server. You can easily adjust these site settings at any time by choosing Site➪Manage Sites.

If your server or work computer is not backed up regularly, seriously consider making a local backup copy of your site before you modify it each time. Having backups is a great practice, one that can serve you well when mistakes are made, data is lost, or you need to revert your site to a previous backup version.

To begin building a site, you only really need to fill out the Site category. However, if you also want to use Dreamweaver to upload your site to a remote live server, you also need to complete the Server section. We discuss how to set up a live server in Book V, Chapter 3.

The following sections describe the other categories in the Site Setup dialog box, which you can configure as needed.

Servers

The Server category is where you set up the remote connection to a live server. The live server is the place that will host your pages on the Internet. It can also be a location you use for collaboration, testing, staging, production, and deployment of your Web files. The live server has several connection options, depending on your needs and setup. See Book V, Chapter 3 for more info on setting up a remote live server.

In addition to using the Server category for setting up your remote server connection, you can use this category to set up a testing server. A testing server area is the place where your dynamic pages will be processed. In other words, the folder specified here is an alternative location to your local site, where you can test your files on a server with an identical database setup — without having to deploy the files to the live site while they're still under development. The testing server can be on your local computer, or on a staging, development, or production server. Check out Book VII, Chapter 1 if you need to set up a testing server.

Version Control

The Version Control category is where you can set up remote access to a server running Subversion software. On this remote server, the site's files can be viewed, compared, and reverted to previous versions of the site. If you're not using Subversion software for version control, ignore this setting. Otherwise, see Book VI, Chapter 1 for details on Version Control setup.

Advanced Settings

Use the options in the Advanced Settings category to customize your workspace, take advantage of some of Dreamweaver's special features such as cloaking and Design Notes, and configure your software for administering a site in Adobe Contribute.

Local Info

The Local Info section contains settings that allow you to specify a path to the current site's default images folder, choose whether to use document-relative or site root-relative links, set the Web URL of the live server, enable case-sensitive link checking, and enable the cache feature.

✦ **Default Images folder:** Most image folders are located at the root of the local site folder and named images or img. For instance, if you are creating an images folder for a customer called ABC, the path to this folder might be something like:

```
Users\YOURUSERNAME\Documents\local_sites\ABC\images
```

✦ **Links Relative To:** By default, the Links Relative To option is set to Document. This option creates link paths that reference other files by their positions relative to the active file. One major benefit of this link type is that you can easily move your site to a different directory without destroying or having to rebuild your links. The Site Root-Relative option creates link paths that are always relative to the site root.

✦ **Web URL:** If desired, in the Web URL field, type the path to the site's Web address, as in http://www.MYWEBADDRESS.com.

✦ **Case-sensitive links checking:** Leave the Use Case-Sensitive Link Checking check box deselected so that Dreamweaver ignores the case of names in links.

✦ **Enable Cache:** When enabled, this option speeds up working with files in Dreamweaver.

Changing the link path

By default, Dreamweaver uses the document-relative path for links. If you would rather use site root–relative paths for links, you need to change a setting in the Site Setup dialog box.

To change from the default document-relative path setting to site root–relative paths, follow these steps:

1. Create a new site or open an existing site by choosing Site➪New Site or Site➪Manage Sites.

2. For a new site, enter a site name and local site folder path in the Site category. Otherwise, when the Manage Sites dialog box appears, select the site you want to edit from the list and click the Edit button.

3. Click the Advanced Settings category, on the left side of the dialog box.

The category expands to reveal several subcategory options.

4. In the Local Info category, change the Links Relative To setting from Document to Site Root.

This step doesn't change the paths of existing links but does apply to any new links you create in Dreamweaver.

When using site root–relative paths, remember that the pages don't appear when you preview the files in a browser. This is because browsers don't recognize site roots — servers do. To preview the paths in a browser while working in Dreamweaver, choose Edit➪Preferences (Windows) or Dreamweaver➪Preferences (Mac) to display the Preferences dialog box. Then select the Preview Using Temporary File option in the Preview in Browser category.

Cloaking

Cloaking prevents specified files and folders from being included in a variety of site operations, such as site file synchronization between local and remote servers. For example, you may want to cloak large movie files or Design Notes folders from being uploaded each time you update site files to the remote server. For more details on how to enable site cloaking, see Book V, Chapter 3.

Design Notes

Dreamweaver lets you create and share Design Notes about site files, which are then stored in a separate location. Enable the Design Notes feature when communicating within a design team or workgroup about a shared managed site. You can attach Design Notes to documents, templates, images, Flash movies, ActiveX controls, and applets. Refer to Book VI, Chapter 1 for details on Design Notes.

File View Columns

In the expanded Files panel, Dreamweaver displays file and folder details in columns next to the filenames. You can customize which file and folder details show up there by making changes to the File View Columns category.

For instance, you can hide and show, add and delete, reorder, share, and rename column settings. Find out more about defining File View Columns in Book VI, Chapter 1.

Contribute

When creating a site for use with Adobe Contribute software, you must enable Contribute compatibility before administering the site in Dreamweaver. The Contribute category allows you to enter Administration settings. See Book VI, Chapters 2 and 3 for the lowdown on using Dreamweaver with Adobe Contribute.

Templates

By default, the Template Updating option is set to *not* rewrite document-relative paths. To turn this feature off, deselect the check box here. To learn more about the joys of working with templates, turn to Book III, Chapter 2.

Spry

If desired, you could specify the folder location for Spry assets. However, by default a folder named SpryAssets is preset to drop into the local root folder if and when any Spry assets are used on the site. Don't change this unless you really know what you're doing. You can learn more about working with Spry in Book IV, Chapter 2.

Managing Multiple Sites

Because you create a new managed site for each project you work on in Dreamweaver, keeping track of all your sites is relatively easy. You can view a list of all your managed sites as follows:

✦ **Files panel:** The Files panel lists the files from the selected managed site. To change from viewing one site's files to another site's files within the panel, choose the desired site from the list of managed sites appearing in the Site Management menu.

✦ **Manage Sites dialog box:** Choose Site⇨Manage Sites to display the Manage Sites dialog box, shown in Figure 3-3. Select your desired site from the list and click the Done button to switch to the selected site and see that site's files listed in the Files panel. You may briefly see the Opening Site and Uploading Site Cache dialog boxes as Dreamweaver opens the selected site. You can also open the Manage Sites dialog box by selecting the Manage Sites option from the Files panel's Site Management menu.

Figure 3-3:
The Manage
Sites dialog
box.

Duplicating sites

Create duplicate copies of any existing defined site by clicking the Duplicate button in the Manage Sites dialog box. Dreamweaver copies all the settings and creates the new site with the same filename appended with the word *copy*. For example, if duplicating a site called *Coffka Café*, the name of the new duplicate managed site would be *Coffka Café copy* until you rename it.

This doesn't copy the actual files. It just creates a duplicate managed site pointing to the same Local folder with the same settings, which you can then modify as needed. If you intend to work on a duplicate copy of the same site, you'll also want to duplicate the local folder and all its files and adjust the local site folder path, to ensure that both copies of the site are totally separate.

Exporting and importing sites

Dreamweaver allows you to save and reopen sites as XML files using the Import and Export buttons in the Manage Sites dialog box. In other words, you'll export a site with all its settings as an XML file and then import the site with the same settings later, either on the same machine or on another machine. This method is handy when you want to get a new computer up and running with all the sites you're currently managing.

Exporting sites

To save a site as an XML file, follow these steps:

1. **Choose Site⇨Manage Sites to open the Manage Sites dialog box.**

2. **Select one or more sites and click the Export button.**

Use Control+click (Windows) or ⌘+click (Mac) to select multiple files.

3. **Browse to, select, and save the location for the export of each site.**

The exported file gets saved as an XML file with the .ste file extension.

Importing sites

To import previously exported XML files back into Dreamweaver, follow these steps:

1. **Choose Site⇨Manage Sites to open the Manage Sites dialog box.**

2. **Click the Import button.**

3. **Browse to and select one or more sites with the .ste file extension for importing.**

   Use Control+click (Windows) or ⌘+click (Mac) to select multiple files.

4. **Click Open to begin the importing process.**

   The Manage Sites dialog box lists the site name when the import process is complete.

Removing sites from the Manage Sites list

When removing sites, keep in mind that sites listed in the Manage Sites dialog box are merely pointers to the location of files on the specified computer and not the actual files and folders themselves. Therefore, removing a site from the Manage Sites list removes *only* the location information Dreamweaver needs to work on the files in the specified site; it does *not* delete any files from your local computer.

As a backup, before you remove a managed site from the listing, you may want to export the site using the export steps mentioned previously, in the "Exporting and importing sites" section. That way, you'll have a copy handy should you ever need to import it back into Dreamweaver.

To remove a site from Dreamweaver, select the site by name from the Manage Sites dialog box and click the Remove button. Dreamweaver gives you the *You cannot undo this action* message. Don't be unnerved; if you accidentally delete a managed site from the list, you can just re-create it.

Book II

Mastering the Basics

The 5th Wave   By Rich Tennant

SCREEEEEK

"Is this really the best use of Flash animation on our e-commerce Web site? A bad wheel on the shopping cart icon that squeaks, wobbles, and pulls to the left?"

Contents at a Glance

Chapter 1: Creating Documents

In This Chapter

✔ Creating a new document

✔ Saving files

✔ Setting page properties

✔ Importing data

Creating documents is the basis for everything you'll do for the Web. Dreamweaver provides several ways to create them, several types of new documents to choose from, and even several premade design files to use as starting points for your own designs.

This chapter explores document types, document creation, document saving, and document opening. You also discover how to set page properties, work with invisible page elements, and import Word and Excel files (Windows only).

Creating a New Document

When you first launch Dreamweaver, the default Welcome Screen appears in the workspace. The Welcome Screen allows you to open existing files from a list of the nine most recent documents, create new files by file type (such as HTML, CSS, or PHP), jump directly to the Site Setup dialog box to manage a new site, and launch a browser to watch the top-featured videos from Adobe.com. If you don't see the Welcome Screen when you launch the program, you can enable it by following the steps in the "Enabling the Welcome Screen" sidebar in this chapter.

When the Welcome Screen is visible (shown in Figure 1-1), the quickest way to create a new blank document is to click one of the file types in the Create New column. Click the HTML link, for instance, and a new untitled Document window appears, complete with basic HTML structural code, ready for adding content and saving with a filename and an extension.

Enabling the Welcome Screen

You can enable and disable the Welcome Screen through Dreamweaver's Preferences. To turn on the Welcome Screen (after disabling it by selecting the Don't Show Again box at the bottom of the Welcome Screen), follow these steps:

1. Choose Edit⇨Preferences (Windows) or Dreamweaver⇨Preferences (Mac).

   The Preferences dialog box appears.

2. Select the General Category to reveal general category options.

3. Add a check mark to the Show Welcome Screen check box in the Document Options area on the right. Then click OK.

Dreamweaver displays the Welcome Screen in the center of the workspace.

Figure 1-1:
Use the
Welcome
Screen
to quickly
create new
documents.

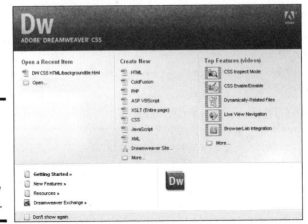

In addition to creating new documents through the Welcome screen, you can create new documents through the File menu by following these steps:

1. Choose File⇨New to launch the New Document window, shown in Figure 1-2.

   This dialog box is divided into various columns to assist you with selecting the desired file type, such as a Blank Page or Page from Template. In this chapter, we discuss the Blank Page, Page from Sample, and Other Page options; Book III, Chapter 2 shows you how to work with templates.

Figure 1-2:
Select a
category,
page type,
layout,
document
type, and
Layout CSS
location,
and enable
InContext
editing.

2. **In the column on the left, select the type of document you want to create.**

   The default document type is set to Blank Page. If you are unsure which type to select, select Blank Page.

3. **In the Page Type column, select the desired document type, such as HTML or CSS.**

4. **In the Layout column, choose <none> to build your own custom layout or select one of the preset layout options from the list.**

   Take some time to explore the layout options in the Layout column, when applicable, in each category. Dreamweaver supplies you with a nice group of blank documents and sample design files to use as a starting point for your own projects. For example, the Blank Page category for the HTML page type has several prewritten code layout options for you to choose from. You'll also find several CSS color schemes in the CSS Style Sheet folder of the Page from Sample category, each filled with preset colors, fonts, and sizes for you to use as a starting point for further development or with another style sheet.

   Beginners may want to select one of the preset layout options that include prewritten HTML and CSS layouts — such as the HTML 2 Column Fixed, Right Sidebar style layout — as a starting point to customizing the code. Later, as you become more familiar with Dreamweaver, it will be easier to create blank HTML pages and write your own CSS.

5. **(Optional) To set default document preferences for all new documents (such as document type, file extension, and encoding), click the Preferences button at the bottom of the New Document window.**

When finished, click OK to close the Preferences dialog box and continue setting options for your new document.

The Get More Content link at the bottom of the New Document dialog box takes you to Adobe's Exchange Web site where, after you register, you can download even more design files and plug-ins to enhance your copy of Dreamweaver. (See Book IV, Chapter 2 for more on the Dreamweaver Exchange.)

6. **Select an option from the DocType drop-down list.**

The default document type is currently XHTML 1.0 Transitional, but you can choose from any of the other options available in the drop-down list including the HTML 4.01 Transitional.

When a DocType (Document Type Definition) is specified here, Dreamweaver automatically writes the selected DTD code at the top of your new document above the opening <html> tag, and at times may append the <html> tag itself, like this:

```
<!DOCTYPE html PUBLIC "-//W3C//DTD XHTML 1.0 Transitional//EN"
    "http://www.w3.org/TR/xhtml1/DTD/xhtml1-transitional.dtd">
<html xmlns="http://www.w3.org/1999/xhtml">
```

If you're unsure of which option to choose, either leave the setting at XHTML 1.0 Transitional for XHTML or select the HTML 4.01 Transitional option for HTML. For a more detailed discussion of XHTML, turn to Book IV, Chapter 4.

7. **(Optional) If you selected a CSS layout from the one of the Page Types with a Layout column, choose a location for the page's CSS files from the Layout CSS drop-down menu.**

Select Add to Head to have the CSS embedded in the <head> of the current page; select Create New File to have Dreamweaver place the CSS in a new external CSS file and link the new file to your page; or select Link to Existing File to specify an existing CSS that already has the required CSS rules for this page.

If you have a different external CSS file — unrelated to the CSS layout — that you'd like to link to the new document, click the Attach Style Sheet link icon next to the Attach CSS File field.

8. **(Optional) If you plan on creating a site that is editable using InContext Editing, select the Enable InContext Editing check box.**

To learn more about Business Catalyst InContext Editing, click the Learn More link directly below the check box.

9. **When you have finished making your selections in the New Document window, click the Create button.**

The new file appears in the Document window.

By default, the window appears in a vertical split instead of a horizontal split. To switch to the Horizontal Split option, deselect the Split Vertically option from the Layout menu on the Application bar.

Saving Documents

When saving a document, give the file a unique name with the appropriate file extension and save it to the root level of the managed site folder.

To save a new file, follow these steps:

1. **Choose File➪Save.**

The Save As dialog box appears. Be sure you choose File➪Save and not File➪Save As. The Save command automatically prefills the file name with the proper extension (untitled.html) whereas the Save As command leaves off the extension (untitled), forcing you to remember to add it. Fortunately, if you do forget, Dreamweaver should add the extension to your filename for you. Nonetheless, you'd be wise to get in the habit of making sure your new files include the .html file extension.

2. **In the Save As dialog box, navigate to the folder where you want to save the new file.**

Remember to save your file in a managed Dreamweaver site. If you haven't managed your site yet, turn to Book I, Chapter 3.

3. **In the File Name text box, type the name of your file.**

When naming the file, consider using all lowercase letters and avoid using special characters such as ñ or ö, spaces, or punctuation, such as periods or slashes. Although filenames can be any length in Windows, keep filenames under 29 characters to avoid Mac OS issues if your computer is running an older OS. (The published Mac character-length recommendation is 31 characters, but OS X has no limits.)

By default, Dreamweaver assigns a default file extension to your untitled document, which for HTML files can be either .html or .htm (see the "Changing the default file extensions" sidebar for instructions on setting the default file extension). Regardless of which extension you choose to work with, be consistent and use the same extension throughout your entire Web site. The extension on the filename ensures that the files are displayed correctly in a browser window. If needed, choose a different file type from the Save as Type drop-down list.

4. **Click Save.**

After the file has been named and saved, you can continue saving new changes to the file by choosing File➪Save. This overwrites the previously saved version with the same file name.

Changing the default file extensions

In versions of Dreamweaver earlier than Dreamweaver 8, the default extensions for all document types were listed in an external XML file. To change the default extension, you had to manually open the XML file and edit the code by hand. Thankfully, since Dreamweaver 8, you may now change the default HTML file extension in the Preferences dialog box. (To change any other document-type file extensions — though you'll probably never need to do so — you still open the XML file.)

To edit the default document type and preferences, follow these steps:

1. Choose Edit⇨Preferences (Windows) or Dreamweaver⇨Preferences (Mac) to launch the Preferences dialog box.

2. Click the New Document category on the left.

3. On the right, change the preferences as needed for Default Document, Default Extension, Default Document Type (DTD), and Default Encoding.

4. Click OK when you're finished.

The new default file extensions work immediately for all newly created documents.

After you initially save your document, you have some additional options when saving it in the future. For instance, you can save a copy of the file, save several files at once, or revert to a previous version of the file, as described in the following sections.

Saving a copy of a file

You can save changes to a document after the initial save with the document's existing name and location, thereby overwriting the previous version of that file. You can also save a file as a copy using the Save As command.

To save a copy of the file using Save As, follow these steps:

1. **Choose File⇨Save As.**

The Save As dialog box appears.

2. **In the Save As dialog box, navigate to the folder where you want to save a copy of the file.**

You can save a copy of the file with the same or different filename in a new folder, or save a copy of the file with a different filename in the same folder.

3. **In the File Name text box, enter a different filename.**

4. **Click Save.**

Saving multiple documents at once

Another save command that can often come in handy is Save All. This command saves all open documents in the workspace, no matter their type, with one command.

To save all open files at once, choose File⇨Save All. If any open documents are unsaved, the Save As dialog box appears for each unsaved file. For each unsaved file, enter filenames with file extensions, navigate to the folder where you want to save the file, and then click the Save button.

If Save All is a function you intend to perform often, create a custom keyboard shortcut for the Save All command! See Book III, Chapter 4 for details.

Reverting to a previous version of a file

Inevitably, a time comes when you need to revert to the last saved version of a file. During each work session, Dreamweaver allows you to revert to the previously saved version, whether that's the state the file was in when you opened it or the state the file was in three minutes or three hours ago when you last saved your updates.

Follow these steps to refer to the previous version of an open file:

1. **Choose File⇨Revert.**

A dialog box appears and asks if you want to discard any changes you've made to the current file and revert to the previous version.

If your Revert command appears dimmed, you may have already saved the file with any updates, so there is nothing to revert to. If you haven't saved yet, however, the Revert option is selectable.

2. **Click Yes to revert; click No to cancel.**

This function works only during the current Dreamweaver session. When you close Dreamweaver and restart it, you can no longer revert to a previous version of a file.

Opening Existing Files

After creating, saving, and closing a file, you can reopen it at any time for editing in Dreamweaver. Furthermore, you can open any existing Web page or text-based file in Dreamweaver, even if it was created in another program. Other file types you can open in Dreamweaver include JavaScript (.js), CSS (.css), XML (.xml), and text files (.txt). However, you can't open Word (.doc) files directly in Dreamweaver.

Here's how to open an existing file:

1. **Choose File⇨Open or press Ctrl+O (Windows) or ⌘+O (Mac).**

The Open dialog box appears.

2. **Navigate to and click the file you want to open.**

3. **Click Open.**

The file opens in the Document window. With HTML files, you can choose Code, Split, or Design view for editing purposes. JavaScript, CSS, and text files open by default in Code view. (See Book I, Chapter 1 for more on these views.) You can also open files directly by double-clicking the file in the Files panel.

If the file you open in Dreamweaver is a Microsoft Word file that's been saved as a Microsoft Word HTML file, you need to clean up the Microsoft markup so that it doesn't conflict with your HTML and CSS. Choose Commands⇨Clean Up Word HTML to have Dreamweaver remove all unnecessary Microsoft markup. Although this command doesn't remove everything related to CSS styling, it does a good job of removing most of it. For more information, check out Book V, Chapter 2.

Setting Page Properties

Dreamweaver lets you set a page's default formatting properties for a single page in the Page Properties dialog box (see Figure 1-3). This is helpful if you're creating a single file and want to centralize CSS and other formatting options within that file. However, if you plan on using the same styles for an entire Web site, we strongly recommend that you use a single linked external CSS file instead.

Figure 1-3:
Set the appearance and other properties of a page.

Page Properties formatting options include setting the page's default appearance (font family, size, color, background color, background image, and so on) and margin spacing; define CSS link styles and headings; enter the page title, DTD, and other encoding options; and specify a tracing image. Any page can have its own property settings, and you can modify these settings at any time.

In Dreamweaver CS5, page properties settings are added to the page as inline HTML formatting tags or as CSS (Cascading Style Sheet) markup in the <head> area of the page. To find out more about CSS, turn to Book III, Chapter 1.

To access the Page Properties dialog box from any open document, use one of the following methods:

✦ Click the Page Properties button in the Properties inspector.

✦ Press Ctrl+J (Windows) or ⌘+J (Mac).

✦ Choose Modify⇨Page Properties.

After you open the Page Properties dialog box, select the layout and formatting properties that you need from the Appearance (CSS), Appearance (HTML), Links (CSS), Headings (CSS), Title/Encoding, and Tracing Image categories.

**Book II
Chapter 1**

Creating Documents

Understanding Invisible Page Elements

When you are building your Web pages, sometimes you'll need to add code, such as JavaScript or comment tags, to the body of your page, but you don't want that code to appear in a browser or on your page in Design view. For these instances, Dreamweaver uses special little yellow icons called *invisible elements*. For example, when invisible elements are enabled, Dreamweaver displays an invisible element icon to show you where that code sits in Code view, rather than displaying an entire swatch of JavaScript code in Design view. Any invisible element icon can be easily moved around the page, edited in Code view, or deleted.

By default, about half the available invisible elements are enabled and appear in Design view when you choose View⇨Visual Aids⇨Invisible Elements. A check mark next to Invisible Elements means the option is turned on.

You may notice that content in Design view shifts slightly when invisible elements appear. Therefore, for precision with layout, you may need to toggle the invisible elements on and off from time to time; if you prefer to leave them on, preview your page in a browser or in Live View often to test the accuracy of the layout.

Use the settings in the Invisible Elements category of the Preferences dialog box to further control which invisible elements appear in Design view. For instance, you may want to show an invisible icon for named anchors but not for line breaks. Table 1-1 provides a brief description of all the invisible elements.

Table 1-1	Invisible Elements
Invisible Element	*What Its Yellow Icon Hides in the Code*
Named Anchors	Marks the spot where each named anchor (`a name=" "`) sits in the code.
Scripts	Marks the spot where JavaScript or VBScript sits in the body part of the file. The invisible element spans from the opening to closing `<script>` tags and includes the entire contents of the script. Edit the content of the script in Code view and change the language, source, and type in the Properties inspector by selecting the invisible element icon in Design view. *Note:* Script invisibles don't appear for inline JavaScript or JavaScript URLs.
Comments	Marks where you find HTML comments. Edit the comments in the Properties inspector by selecting the invisible element icon in Design view.
Line Breaks	Displays icons for every line break (` ` or ` `) in the code. Select the invisible element icon to move or delete the break.
Client-Side Image Maps	Marks the spot of each client-side image map in the code.
Embedded Styles	Marks the spot where CSS is embedded in the body of the file rather than in the head of the file or in an external CSS. Technically, `<style>` tags should be only in the head, although Dreamweaver lets you manually put them in the body.
Hidden Form Fields	Displays an icon for every instance of a hidden form field with the type `"hidden"` attribute.
Form Delimiter	Appears as part of the `<form>` tag and appears in Design view as a red dotted border to show where you can insert form elements. This feature is a good one to leave on, because you must insert form fields inside the dotted line for the form to work properly.
Anchor Points for AP Elements	Displays an icon to visually represent each AP element (layer) in the file. You can position the AP element itself anywhere on the page, but the icon typically sits at the top-left corner. Click the AP element icon to see the AP element's contents.
Anchor Points for Aligned Elements	Marks the spot where code can have the `align` attribute, including tables, images, plug-ins, and applets.

Invisible Element	What Its Yellow Icon Hides in the Code
Visual Server Markup Tags and Nonvisual Server Markup Tags	Marks the spot where server markup tags, such as ASP and ColdFusion, sit in the code even though they don't appear in the Document window.
CSS Display: none	Displays the location of page content that has been hidden with the CSS "Display: none" property in any linked or embedded CSS file. The "Display: none" property effectively hides content from view on the page.
Show Dynamic Text As	Displays dynamic text in the format of {Recordset:Field}. To prevent long values from distorting page formatting, change the display setting here to {}.
Server-Side Includes	Displays the contents of any SSI include files.

To turn invisible elements on or off, follow these steps:

***1.* Choose Edit⇨Preferences (Windows) or Dreamweaver⇨Preferences (Mac).**

The Preferences dialog box appears.

***2.* Click the Invisible Elements category.**

On the right side of the dialog box, shown in Figure 1-4, you see a list of invisible elements that can be enabled to display as icons in Design view.

Figure 1-4: The Preferences dialog box with the Invisible Elements options.

3. **Place a check mark next to the name of each invisible element that you want to show on your pages in Design view.**

   For example, to see an icon when JavaScript is added to the body of your page, put a check mark next to Scripts. Note that about half the invisible elements are preselected. We recommend that you leave these checked.

4. **Click OK.**

Your changes take effect immediately. Modify these settings at any time by reopening the Preferences dialog box.

You can easily add some invisible elements, such as comments or named anchors, to your document by using the icons in the Common area of the Insert panel. Plus, with an invisible element selected in Design view, you can quickly edit its contents in the Properties inspector.

Importing Tabular Data Files

Tabular data files are delimited text files containing records that are separated, or *delimited,* by a specified character, such as a tab or comma, that doesn't appear in the data. You can create delimited text files in most spreadsheet and database programs, such as Microsoft Excel and Access.

After you convert an Excel or database file into a delimited text file, you can import it into a Web page with Dreamweaver. During the import process, you select the delimiter type that you originally used to separate the data. The delimiter is then used to separate data into individual table cells. This gives you a new level of control over your imported data that wasn't available before!

To import a tabular data file, follow these steps:

1. **Choose File➪Import➪Tabular Data.**

   The Import Tabular Data dialog box appears, shown in Figure 1-5.

Figure 1-5: The Import Tabular Data dialog box.

Import Tabular Data		
Data file:	Browse...	OK
Delimiter: Tab		Cancel
		Help
Table width: Fit to data		
Set to: Percent		
Cell padding: Format top row: [No Formatting]		
Cell spacing: Border: 1		

2. **Browse to and select the data file to import.**

3. **From the Delimiter drop-down list, select the delimiter type used when the file was saved.**

   Select Tab, Comma, Semicolon, Colon, or Other. If Other, enter the character that was used as the delimiter.

4. **(Optional) Enter other settings as desired to format the table that will hold the imported data.**

5. **Click OK.**

After importing, save your page and edit the imported data as you need.

Importing Word and Excel Files (Windows Only)

Windows users can import Word and Excel files right into any new or existing Dreamweaver page. During the import process, Dreamweaver automatically strips the Microsoft files of unnecessary code, including style formatting, and converts the content into HTML code. You can even choose what level of formatting to retain during the import. The only cautionary restriction is that the file must be smaller than 300K after importing.

Follow these steps to import the entire contents of your Word or Excel file:

1. **Choose File⇨Import and then choose either Word Document or Excel Document.**

2. **In the Import Word Document or Import Excel Document dialog box, browse for and select the file to open, choose the desired formatting setting from the Formatting menu, and click Open to begin the import.**

   Figure 1-6 shows the Import Word Document dialog box. If your computer alerts you that the server is busy and that the action cannot be completed because another program is busy, click the Switch To or Retry button to correct the problem and import the file.

3. **Edit the imported data as necessary.**

   You're making changes in the new document, not altering the original Microsoft file.

4. **Choose File⇨Save.**

To include only part of a Microsoft file and preserve formatting, copy the data directly from the open Microsoft file and paste the portion of the file directly in the Web document.

Figure 1-6:
Import a
Word file
with the
Import Word
Document
dialog box.

Chapter 2: Working with Text

In This Chapter

✔ Adding, editing, and removing text

✔ Inserting text with the Paste and Paste Special commands

✔ Using the Properties inspector

✔ Creating inline style sheets

✔ Creating bulleted and numbered lists

✔ Searching with Find and Replace

*A*dding text to your pages in HTML is as easy as typing in a word processing document or text editor. You can insert, change, or delete text, as well as style, order, and structure it. You can even paste text from another file into an open Dreamweaver Document window.

Text is the keystone of all Web pages. In fact, a Web page is simply a text file (it may also contain other objects, such as images and tables) that uses a set of HTML tags and Cascading Style Sheet (CSS) markup to describe to a browser how to format and display the text. Use text to describe a company's products or services, provide contact information, make important facts and figures available to visitors, tell stories, and more. In addition, text on a Web page is searchable by search engines, which means what you add to a page should be easy to read and understand.

This chapter covers everything you need to know about working with text including adding, editing, and removing copy; using the Properties inspector to create inline CSS; making lists; and using the Find and Replace tool for robust text and code editing.

Adding Text

You can type text directly in the Document window in Design view or Code view. To begin adding text in Design view, open a new or existing document and begin typing. In Code view, you can add text straight to the code anywhere inside the opening and closing `<body>` tags, including inside table cells, `<div>` tags, and `<span>` tags.

In Split view, when you select a word, sentence, or paragraph in the Design pane, the corresponding code also gets selected in the Code pane. Likewise, when you select content in the Code pane, that content also gets selected in Design pane. You can switch freely between typing text in Design, Split, and Code views.

As you add text to your page and leave your cursor hovering over the workspace in Design or Code view, you may notice a small square gray icon with a ship's steering wheel appear. This is the icon for the Code Navigator tool, which pops up to provide you with quick access to CSS rules and other code sources that affect your selection (or the content near your cursor when no selection is active). To find out more about the Code Navigator tool, see Book III, Chapter 1.

Editing Text

To edit text, select the text you want to edit and start typing. By selecting the text first, you automatically overwrite the text in the selection when you type. Make a selection by double-clicking a word to select the whole word, or triple-clicking a word to select an entire block of text.

When selecting with a triple-click in Design view, only the copy is selected. When triple-clicking in Code view, both the content and the content's HTML container tags are selected.

If the content between any two tags includes any unnecessary breaks in the text (not including `<br>` or `<p>` breaks), however, the triple-click in Code view selects only a single line rather than the entire content block between the two tags. If that happens, clean up the code by removing unnecessary spacing between characters and try the triple-click again.

Text containers include `<body>`, `<p>`, `<h1>` through `<h6>`, `<div>`, `<span>`, `<td>`, and `<li>`. If a paragraph of text is contained in a paragraph tag, the opening and closing `<p>` tags aren't selected along with the text in Design view but are selected in Code view, as shown in the following examples.

When triple-clicking a word inside a paragraph in Design view, only the text is selected, as in this example:

```
"Philosophy, rightly defined, is simply the love of wisdom." --Cicero
```

When triple-clicking a word inside a paragraph in Code view with no unnecessary breaks in the content, the following text and code appears instead:

```
<p>"Philosophy, rightly defined, is simply the love of wisdom." --Cicero</p>
```

When triple-clicking a word inside a paragraph in Code view with an unnecessary break in the content — in this example the break is after the word *simply* — you see this selected:

```
<p>"Philosophy, rightly defined, is simply
```

Removing Text

To remove text from your page, select it and then delete it by pressing Delete or Backspace on the keyboard or by choosing Edit⇨Clear or Edit⇨Cut from the main menu. The Delete key, the Backspace key, or the Clear command removes the selection; the Cut command places the deleted selection onto the Clipboard. The keyboard shortcut for the Cut command is Ctrl+X (Windows) or ⌘+X (Mac).

**Book II
Chapter 2**

Working with Text

Pasting Text from Another File

When pasting data into Dreamweaver from a Word document, Web site, or other word processing file, Dreamweaver often preserves that document's formatting when you use the regular Paste command. (Formatting includes the font face, size, formatting, and alignment.) If you want to preserve formatting, choose Edit⇨Paste.

On the other hand, if you want to have some control over which parts of the formatting are retained when pasted into Dreamweaver, follow these steps:

1. **Copy the text you want to paste and then choose Edit⇨Paste Special.**

   The Paste Special dialog box appears, as shown in Figure 2-1.

Figure 2-1:
Set
formatting
preferences
for pasted
text.

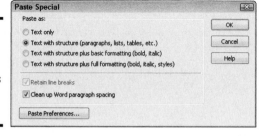

2. **Select one of the following paste options:**

   - **Text only:** Paste the copied text as unformatted text. Any formatting attributes copied from the original source file — including line and paragraph breaks, bold or italics, font size, and font color — are stripped.

   - **Text with structure:** Paste the copied text with its existing paragraph structure, including line and paragraph breaks, lists, and tables. Its formatting attributes, such as bold or italic, are not included.

   - **Text with structure plus basic formatting:** Paste the copied text with preexisting structure and formatting, including paragraphs, line breaks, and tables, and basic text markup using tags such as `<h1>`, `<strong>`, `<em>`, and `<hr>`.

   - **Text with structure plus full formatting:** Paste the copied text into Dreamweaver with its original structure, HTML formatting, and pre-existing internal CSS data. This option does not include the copying of styles that come from sources external to the copied file, such as an external CSS file, or from any programs that don't allow style information to be copied to the Clipboard.

3. **Select the Retain Line Breaks option.**

   Enable this option to keep line breaks, or disable this option to remove the unwanted line breaks that some applications add at the ends of each line of text. This option is not available for the Text Only option. *Note:* If this option is dimmed, click the Paste Preferences button to edit the default settings in the Copy/Paste category of the Preferences dialog box.

4. **Select the Clean Up Word Paragraph Spacing option.**

   Enable this option when using the Text with Structure or Text with Structure plus Basic Formatting option to remove extra spaces between paragraphs in the pasted text.

5. **Click OK.**

   The copied text is pasted into your document with the selected settings.

The paste preferences you select in the Paste Special dialog box remain in effect until you change them, so feel free to change them as often as needed.

Setting Text Properties in the Properties Inspector

The Properties inspector is context specific, so when you're adding text to the page, it displays options for formatting and linking text. The Properties inspector has two tabs, or views: one for HTML and one for CSS. To toggle between these views, click the HTML or CSS button at the left edge of the panel.

In the HTML view, shown in Figure 2-2, you can specify a font format such as Paragraph or Heading 1, add bold or italics tags, set a CSS class or ID, create ordered or unordered lists, indent or outdent text, and enter hyperlink information. All these settings, or *styles*, are applied immediately to selected content, and you can change them at any time.

Figure 2-2:
The Properties inspector displays HTML formatting options for selected text.

In the CSS view, shown in Figure 2-3, settings include specifying a targeted rule, selecting the font family, size, and color, adding bold or italic, and setting font alignment. You can also quickly access a CSS rule in the CSS Styles panel for any selected content by clicking the CSS Panel button, and edit that rule, if desired, by clicking the Edit Rule button.

Figure 2-3:
The Properties inspector also displays CSS formatting options when text is selected.

When your text or other content is located in a table, the bottom half of the Properties inspector displays table formatting fields for horizontal and vertical alignment, width and height dimensions, no wrap and header check boxes, and a background color selector. See Book II, Chapter 6 to learn more about working with tables.

When you add bold or italic formatting by clicking the B or I icon in the Properties inspector, Dreamweaver writes the standards-compliant `<strong>` and `<em>` (for emphasis) tags in the code instead of the deprecated `<b>` and `<i>` tags. This is because `<b>` and `<i>` are formatting tags, whereas `<strong>` and `<em>` are structural tags. Both tags format text, but *structural tags* can also provide clues about the text's importance that can help improve search engine rankings by emphasizing important keywords or phrases as well as complying with Web accessibility guidelines to improve the way screen readers interpret text on a page with speech inflections. Although browsers still support the old `<b>` and `<i>` tags, we recommend that you use only the standards-compliant `<strong>` and `<em>` tags.

HTML Properties Inspector

Here's an overview of the text options in the Properties inspector when you select the HTML view:

+ **Format:** Choose the paragraph style that's applied to the selected text. Style options are None, Paragraph `<p>`, Preformatted `<pre>`, or Headings `<h1>` through `<h6>`.

+ **ID:** Select an ID in any linked or internal CSS style sheet. An ID identifies the contents of a tag pair with a unique name, which you can then format and position with CSS, as in `<span id="onsale">Now On Sale!</span>`

+ **Class:** Display a list of custom styles in the internal CSS, or attached external CSS, if any, or both. Select and apply a style by name, remove an already applied style attribute by selecting None, or launch dialog boxes to rename a style or attach an external style sheet to the open document. When no style is applied, the drop-down list appears blank or says None, and when multiple styles are applied, the drop-down list is blank.

+ **Bold:** Add the `<strong>` tags around selected text to emphasize the selection with boldness.

+ **Italic:** Add the `<em>` tags around selected text to emphasize the selection with italics.

+ **Link:** Add hypertext links to selected text or graphics. To add a link to a particular file, select the text or graphic in Design or Code view and do one of the following:

- In the Link text field, type the URL or filename of the link.

- Click the Browse for File icon to browse for and select a file by name.

- Click and drag the Point to File icon onto the name of the file in the Files panel. Release the icon, and Dreamweaver writes the filename in the Link text field for you. This is a great feature that saves time and helps you avoid typos!

To create a text link or an image link before you know what the final URL or filename will be, enter # or javascript:; in the Link text box. You can replace this dummy link with the correct filename or URL later.

✦ **Unordered List:** Convert the selected text to a bulleted list.

✦ **Ordered List:** Convert the selected text to a numbered list.

✦ **Text Outdent** and **Indent:** Uniformly apply indenting and outdenting to lists and blocks of text in container tags, such as <p>. Click the Indent and Outdent icons in the Properties inspector to add and remove margin spacing evenly around the selected text. You can apply indents and outdents also from the main menu or the context menu. Indenting regular text adds the <blockquote> tag around a selection, and outdenting removes the tag. By contrast, clicking the Indent and Outdent icons with list text creates sublists using nested <ol> or <ul> and <li> list tags. You can then format your multitiered lists with CSS to apply font styles and control margin spacing.

Indenting with the <blockquote> tag typically adds about 40 pixels of uniform padding on the left and right margins and a little extra white space above and below. For better control over your content, consider using CSS to create a custom style that indents your content without the need for <blockquote> tags.

✦ **Title:** Add a title attribute to a selected hyperlink for enhanced accessibility for visitors using assistive devices. Titles are often used to improve search engine listings and rankings, so be sure to include a title for every hyperlink you create.

✦ **Target:** Specify where the linked page appears, whether in the same browser window, another browser window, or a frame inside a frameset. Without adding a target, the default setting is to open the linked page in the same browser window. Choose _blank to display the linked page in a new browser window, _new to display the linked page in a new window or reload the content into that new window, _self to open it in the same browser window, _parent to open the file in the parent frameset or the same frame as the link, or _top to open the file in the full browser, breaking any existing frames. (Although frames are no longer recommended in Web design, you can learn more about using frames in Book IV, Chapter 3). The Target option is dimmed until you activate it by entering a link in the Link field.

Book II
Chapter 2

Working with Text

✦ **List Item:** Specify a list type from a dialog box when formatting lists. For unordered lists, choose a list style of Bullet or Square. For ordered lists, choose from Numbers (1, 2, 3), Roman Large (I, II, III) or Roman Small (i, ii, iii), and Alphabet Large (A, B, C) or Alphabet Small (a, b, c). The list item button remains dimmed until you create a list on your page and place your cursor anywhere inside, but not selecting, part of the list. Two additional options, Directory List and Menu List, appear in the list type menu, but we recommend that you avoid using these because both styles are deprecated.

✦ **Page Properties:** Display the Page Properties dialog box, from which you can modify the properties of the currently open page, including the default font set, size, and color, background color, and margin spacing. See Book II, Chapter 1 for details on the Page Properties dialog box.

CSS Properties Inspector

When you select the CSS view in the Properties inspector, the following text formatting options are available:

✦ **Targeted Rule:** Apply rules from an existing CSS file, create new CSS rules, add new inline styles, and apply or remove existing classes to selected text.

  • **Cascade:** List id, tag, or compound styles in a linked external CSS file. Use this feature to modify the selected style's attributes appearing in the Properties inspector. To modify additional attributes of the selected style, click the Edit Rule button.

  • **New Rule:** This section offers two options for creating new CSS styles. **New CSS Rule:** Choose any of the font, size, color, or other formatting options in the Properties inspector to launch the New CSS Rule dialog box, which then adds your new style to an external CSS file. **New Inline Style:** Add inline CSS style formatting to selected text using the options in the Properties inspector.

  • **Apply Class:** Remove a custom class style from or apply a custom class style to a selection. **Remove Class:** Strip external custom class CSS styles applied to selected text. This feature does not, however, strip any inline, id, tag, or compound styles. **Custom Style:** Select a custom style by its name from the list to apply the desired custom class style to selected text.

✦ **Edit Rule button:** Launch the New CSS Rule dialog box for the CSS style applied to selected text (or the CSS style applied to text surrounding the current location of your cursor). In the dialog box, make adjustments to that CSS style.

✦ **CSS Panel:** Open the CSS Styles panel when it is unopened or inactive in the panel dock area, or expand the panel when it is collapsed.

Hexadecimal numbers and the Web-safe palette

Colors on a Web page, whether used to format page properties, text, table cells, or other objects, are displayed in a browser by using special color codes called *hexadecimal numbers*. These color codes are actually a set of three hexadecimal number pairs, where each digit in a pair represents a value for red, green, and blue, as in #RRGGBB. A number symbol (#) always precedes the six digits when they appear in the HTML or CSS code, and each digit can have a value from 0–F (0–9 and A–F), as in #CC33FF. On the 0–F scale, 0 has a null value and F has the highest value of 15. The biggest value for any of the RGB pairs is FF, which is equal to 255 in the normal decimal system. This means, for example, that a value of #00FF00 yields the highest amount of green possible.

Web-safe colors refer to the 216 colors that can be accurately displayed in Web browsers on both Mac and PC computers with 8-bit monitors. These browser-safe colors use only the following hexadecimal values: 00, 33, 66, 99,

CC, and FF. In addition to using the hexadecimal values, you can specify Web-safe colors using a color name, such as cornflowerblue, crimson, or plum.

To make specifying a color in Dreamweaver easy, click in the Text Color box in the Properties inspector to choose a color from the Web-safe palette or the System Color Picker. Or if you happen to know the hex value or name of the color, type it in the Text Color box.

You can find a listing of all acceptable color names along with a swatch with their color and hexadecimal equivalents at www.w3schools.com/html/html_color names.asp.

These days — with monitors capable of rendering millions of colors — using a Web-safe color is no longer the critical issue it was in the early days of the Internet. Nonetheless, knowing about the Web-safe palette and understanding how to use it can help you to use color successfully on the Web.

✦ **Font:** Show a list of font sets to choose from to apply to the selected text. In a font set, if the first font is unavailable on the visitor's computer, the second font is used for onscreen display. If the second font is unavailable, the third font is used, and so on. When you select a font set, the New CSS Rule dialog box appears so you can create your own custom class, tag, or ID style with the `font-family` style attribute to your style sheet, as in `font-family: "Arial Black", Gadget, sans-serif;`.

✦ **Bold:** Launch the New CSS Rule dialog box so you can create your own custom class, tag, or ID style with the `font-weight: bold;` style to your style sheet.

✦ **Italic:** Launch the New CSS Rule dialog box so you can create your own custom class, tag, or ID style with the `font-style: italic;` style to your style sheet.

✦ **Align Left, Align Center, Align Right,** and **Justify:** Launch the New CSS Rule dialog box so you can create your own custom class, tag, or ID style with the `text-align: left;`, `text-align: right;`, `text-align: center;`, or `text-align: justify;` style to your style sheet. The selected custom style is then automatically applied to your selection.

✦ **Size:** Launch the New CSS Rule dialog box so you can create your own custom class, tag, or ID style with the "font-size: n unit;" style to your style sheet, as in `font-size: 36px;` which will automatically be applied to your selection. The size can be set in pixels (px), points (pt), inches (in), centimeters (cm), millimeters (mm), picas (pc), ems (em), exs (ex), or percentages (%). Because fonts render uniformly on both platforms when specified in pixels, pixels are currently the preferred measure for specifying precise font sizes. Percentages and ems are also popular proportional sizing units.

Table 2-1 lists descriptions for all the acceptable units of measure. Enter an exact number and unit, select from preset sizes ranging from xx-small to xx-large.

✦ **Text Color:** Turn the selected text to the specified RGB color by launching the New CSS Rule dialog box so you can create your own custom class, tag, or ID style with the `color: #hexvalue;` style to your style sheet. The custom style is then automatically applied to your selection. To select a hexadecimal color representing an RGB value, type a color name, such as aqua, in the text field next to the Text Color box, or enter a hexadecimal number, such as #000000 for black. Click the Text Color box to choose a color from the Web-safe color palette or the System Color Picker (it's the rainbow colored circle icon at the top of the Web-safe color palette).

✦ **Page Properties:** Open the Page Properties dialog box, from which you can modify the CSS properties of the currently open page, including the default font set, size, and color, background color, and margin spacing in the Appearance (CSS), Appearance (HTML), Links (CSS), and Headings (CSS) categories. See Book II, Chapter 1 for details on the Page Properties dialog box.

Table 2-1	Units of Measure
Unit of Measure	*Description*
px	Pixels
pt	Points; 1 point equals 1/72 inch
pc	Picas; 1 pica equals 12 points
%	Percentage
in	Inches
cm	Centimeters

Unit of Measure	Description
mm	Millimeters
em	A proportional unit of measure equal to the point size of the current font; for example, if the current font is 10 point, 1.2 em is equal to 12 points
ex	A proportional unit of measure equal to half the point size of the current font; for example, if the current font is 10 point, 1.2 ex is equal to 6 points

Creating Inline Styles

By default, Dreamweaver writes internal or external CSS instead of HTML to add text formatting to your pages. (See Book III, Chapter 1 for a full discussion of Cascading Style Sheets.) However, you can add inline CSS styles using the New Inline Style Targeted Rule in the CSS area of the Properties inspector, which writes code similar to this:

```
<p style="font-family: Arial, Helvetica, sans-serif; font-size: 18px; color:
    #900;">This is how a sentence gets marked up with an inline style.</p>
```

For inline CSS style markup, set the Targeted Rule to New Inline Style, and use the Properties inspector's font, size, color, bold, italic, list, and align fields to add inline formatting to the page (as described in the preceding section). Then, if you need to add list formatting, indenting, outdenting, or a link, you can toggle to the HTML side of the Properties inspector to that information. For example, bold, linked text looks like this:

```
<a href="http://www.google.com"><strong>Google</strong></a>
```

When choosing a Web font, select one that is likely to be available for any site visitor (whether using Mac OS or Windows). Here's an acceptable list of fonts to choose from when specifying the font face for your HTML text: Arial, Verdana, Helvetica, Times, Times New Roman, Courier, Courier New, Georgia, Geneva, Impact, Palatino, Palatino Linotype, Tahoma, Trebuchet, Serif, and Sans-serif.

For additional information about browser-safe fonts in general and a complete list of fonts that come preinstalled in Windows and Macintosh computers, check out www.websitenotes.com/websitenotes-37-20041220BrowserSafeFonts.html or www.ampsoft.net/webdesign-1/WindowsMacFonts.html.

To help further with font selection, Dreamweaver allows you to select font sets to style your text. *Font sets* are lists of fonts that browsers read and use to display text. The browser looks for the first font listed in the set and renders the page using that font face. If the first font listed is unavailable, the browser searches for the next font in the list, and so on. Most font sets end with serif or sans-serif, which are standard to all computers. A typical font set is Arial, Helvetica, Sans-serif. The benefit of using font sets instead of a single font is that a font set gives you more control over which fonts the browser attempts to use to display the text on the page. By contrast, if a single font is not found on the computer viewing the page, the text on that page is displayed with the browser's default font face.

To set the default font set, size, and color for an entire Web site, you create an external Cascading Style Sheet, as described in Book III, Chapter 1.

Inserting Special Characters

From time to time, you may need to add special characters such as © or ® or ñ to your pages when typing text in the Document window. Rather than looking up the HTML code for the appropriate character on the Internet and typing it in Code view, use Dreamweaver to add these special characters to your file. All special characters and symbols are represented in HTML with a name or number. Dreamweaver calls each of these an *entity*. For instance, you can code the copyright symbol with the © or © entity.

If you need to use the greater- and less-than brackets in your text and don't want HTML to interpret them as tags, use the > entity symbol for greater than (>) and < for less than (<).

To add a special character to an open file, follow these steps:

1. **Place your cursor where you want to add the special character.**

   Single-click in Design view or Code view to place the insertion point in the correct position.

2. **Choose Insert➪HTML➪Special Characters. On the flyout menu, choose from the list of commonly used special characters.**

   For instance, you can insert a copyright, a yen, or an em-dash symbol.

3. **If you don't see the character you want to use, choose Other at the bottom of the flyout menu.**

   The Insert Other Character dialog box appears, as shown in Figure 2-4.

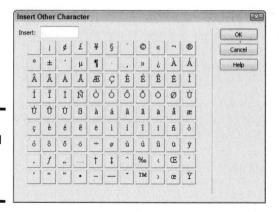

Figure 2-4:
Add special characters to your page.

Book II
Chapter 2

Working with Text

4. **Select the character you want, and then click OK to insert that character.**

   You can also copy and paste the HTML code from the Insert field at the top of the Insert Special Character dialog box. For instance, the HTML code entity for the copyright symbol is `&copy;`.

   For a complete list of commonly used ISO-8859-1 symbols for the Web (the default character set used by most browsers), see `www.w3schools.com/tags/ref_entities.asp`.

Creating Lists

As mentioned earlier in the chapter, the List Type menu in the List Properties dialog box displays four list types: Bulleted List, Numbered List, Directory List, and Menu List. This book omits the Directory and Menu options because those styles are deprecated and we recommend that you avoid using them.

The Bulleted and Numbered lists are classified as either unordered or ordered:

✦ **Unordered:** A bullet precedes all the list items. The style of the bullet can be a bullet (a solid circle), a circle (a hollow disc), or a small square. Dreamweaver lets you choose only a bullet or a square, however. To use the circle style, you need to modify the code by hand, as in:

```
<ul type="disc">
```

✦ **Ordered:** The list type can be Number (1, 2, 3), Roman Large (I, II, III), Roman Small (i, ii, iii), Alphabet Large (A, B, C), or Alphabet Small (a, b, c) To specify the desired list type, use A, a, I, i, or 1 as the type, as in:

```
<ol type="i">
```

In addition to the number type, ordered lists can have a starting value different than 1. For example, to start an ordered list using Alphabet uppercase at the letter J, add the start value of 10 (J is the 10th letter) to the <ol> tag:

```
<ol type="A" start="10">
```

To add a start value to a list item <li> tag instead of the ordered list <ol> tag, use the value attribute instead of the start attribute:

```
<li value="10">
```

If you don't specify a list type, the default unordered list is bulleted with a solid circle, and the default ordered list is numbered (1, 2, 3). To learn how to customize the look of your bulleted lists with custom graphics and CSS formatting, turn to Book III, Chapter 1.

To convert selected text into list format, follow these steps:

1. **Select the text you want to convert to a list.**

You can also type your first entry, convert it to a list format, and then continue adding items. Dreamweaver automatically continues to format your list.

2. **Click the Unordered or Ordered List icon in the HTML area of the Properties inspector.**

The Unordered List icon looks like a bulleted list, and the Ordered List icon looks like a numbered list (refer to Figure 2-2).

3. **Deselect the text by clicking the cursor inside any list item.**

When the list is deselected, the List Item button becomes active in the Properties inspector.

4. **Click the List Item button in the Properties inspector.**

The List Properties dialog box appears.

5. **Select a list type and list style. If desired, enter a start count, or apply a CSS style through the New style menu, or both.**

If you need to adjust a list item so that it is displayed with a different style or count than the rest of the items in the list, use the New Style menu to set a style for the selected list item or use the Reset Count option to set a different starting number for the selected list item. In a numbered list, for example, you could specify that the third item use the *a* type with a start value of 4, thereby forcing that list item to appear with a lowercase letter *d*.

6. **Click OK to close the List Properties dialog box.**

To change the list type of an existing list, place your cursor anywhere in the list and select another list type from the List Properties dialog box. You can also convert unordered lists into ordered lists, and vice versa. The list icons in the Properties inspector are toggle buttons allowing you to add and remove list formatting to selected text as needed.

Editing with the Find and Replace Tool

The Find and Replace dialog box is a powerful editing tool that can save you valuable time and effort. For example, you could use the Find and Replace tool to search for all instances of a copyright date of 2009 and replace them with 2010. Use this feature to find and replace text or source code in a selection, in an open document, for a specified folder, or for the currently managed site. This is a great tool for replacing filenames, stripping unnecessary tags, adding or removing site root-relative path formatting, and replacing entire blocks of code with other content.

**Book II
Chapter 2**

Working with Text

The following sections explain how to search for specific tags and attributes, search for text in specific tags, save and reuse search strings, and search using regular expressions.

Searching for tags and attributes

The most common use of the Find and Replace tool is to search for and modify specific tags and attributes. For example, you may need to find all instances of the old <b> tag and strip them from the code, or you may need to find all occurrences of the word *Principle* and replace them with the word *Principal.* Whatever your need, the general find-and-replace method is the same. The differences are where you're searching, what you're searching for, and what you want to do with the results when you find them.

Follow these steps to search for specific tags or attributes:

1. **Open the file you want to search in, or select the document or folder you want to search in the Files panel.**

2. **Choose Edit⇨Find and Replace.**

   The Find and Replace dialog box appears, as shown in Figure 2-5.

Figure 2-5:
Find and
Replace
content
such as
text, source,
code, and
specific
tags.

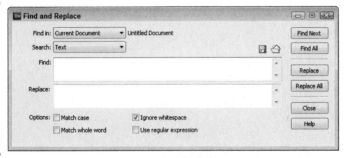

3. **Select the files to be searched in the Find In drop-down list.** These are your options:

   - **Selected Text:** Search only in text selected in the open document.
   - **Current Document:** Search the open file.
   - **Open Documents:** Search any file that's open in the workspace.
   - **Folder:** Search only in the specified folder.
   - **Selected Files in Site:** Search only the files and folders selected in the Files panel.
   - **Entire Current Local Site:** Search an entire local or remote managed site.

4. **Select a search type in the Search drop-down list:**

   - **Source Code:** Search for specific HTML code or tags.
   - **Text:** Search for specific words or word combinations and ignore HTML. For example, searching for `the perfect car` would match both `the perfect car` and `the <strong>perfect </strong>car`.
   - **Text (Advanced):** Search for specific text inside or outside tags. For instance, searching for `chocolate cake` and specifying Inside Tag and the `<b>` tag would find only the first instance of the words `chocolate cake` in the following text: *I wanted to eat `<b>chocolate cake</b>` for breakfast but my mother told me I had to wait until after dinner. I had a piece of chocolate cake anyway, right after she left the kitchen.*
   - **Specific Tag:** Search for specific tags, their attributes, and those attribute values, such as all `<td>` tags with align set to bottom: `<td align="bottom">`.

 To search for a Return character, add line breaks in the search query by pressing Shift+Enter (Windows) or Shift+Return (Mac). Just be sure to turn off the Ignore Whitespace option if regular expressions are not part of the search (You discover more about regular expressions later in the chapter). Doing so ensures that the search finds a Return and not a `<br>` or `<p>` tag.

5. **Enter additional options as needed to further define the search:**

   - **Match Case:** Match uppercase and lowercase letters as defined by your input. For example, if you search for `Chocolate Pudding`, you won't find `chocolate pudding`.
   - **Ignore Whitespace:** Read any white space except `<p>` and `<br>` tags as a single space for the purposes of matching items in your search. With the option turned on, `me and you` would match `me and you` and `me and   you`, but not `meandyou`. This option is not available when using regular expressions, so if you use them, you need to write the expression to ignore white space.

- **Match Whole Word:** Search for text matching a whole word or phrase, similar to the regular expression search for strings starting and ending with \b.

- **Use Regular Expression:** Force specific characters and strings such as \b or ? to be interpreted as regular expression *operators*. See the upcoming section "Using regular expressions in your searches" for more information on regular expressions.

When starting a search from in Code view, Dreamweaver may let you know that it's synchronizing views before beginning the search. If that happens, click OK to continue.

6. **Search for your text by clicking the appropriate button:**

Book II
Chapter 2

Working with Text

- **Find Next:** Jump from each found instance to the next, and if searching in multiple documents, jumps from one document to the next.

- **Find All:** Open the Search panel and displays search results.

- **Replace:** Replace your search criteria with your replacement text in the Replace or To field. Click Find Next to move to the next instance.

- **Replace All:** Find all instances of your search criteria and replaces them with your replacement text in the Replace or To field.

You can't undo these commands, so be sure to perform a backup of your files before clicking the Replace All button. Or be really careful that you're replacing exactly what you want to be replacing.

7. **Click the Close button when you are finished.**

Note: The dialog box automatically closes and results are displayed in the Results panel after you click Find All or Replace All.

Press F3 (Windows) or ⌘+G (Mac) to search for the same criteria again without relaunching the Find and Replace dialog box.

You can also click the Save Report icon (it looks like a disk) in the search results panel and save the results as an XML file, which you can drag into Microsoft Excel and view as a nice chart. This is handy for showing bosses and clients how many text items were replaced.

Searching for text in specific tags

When searching in code for specific tags, you may find that including attributes is helpful as a way to narrow the search. Dreamweaver lets you search not only for specific tags but also for the attributes of those tags and the attribute values, as shown in Figure 2-6.

Figure 2-6:
Search for
attributes
in specific
tags.

For instance, to ensure that all your images have `alt` attributes for W3 accessibility compliance, you may need to search for all the `<img>` tags without `alt` attributes. You can set parameters to add the attribute with an empty value (`alt=" "`) by leaving the To field blank.

To search for text in specific tags, follow Steps 1 through 3 in the preceding section and then continue with these steps:

1. **In the Search drop-down list, select Specific Tag.**

2. **(Optional) Click the plus (+) icon to add a tag modifier:**

- **With Attribute:** Specify the attribute type and attribute value of the tag to be a match.

- **Without Attribute:** Specify that, to be considered a match, a particular attribute is not in the search, such as searching for all `<span>` tags without the `class` attribute

- **Containing:** Specify text or a tag that must be present in the specific tag to be a match.

- **Not Containing:** Specify that certain text or a tag must not be in the first tag to be a match.

- **Inside Tag:** Specify that a tag must be found in the first tag to be a match.

- **Not Inside Tag:** Specify that a tag must not be found in the first tag to be a match.

Note: When the search does not need any tag modifiers, click the minus (–) icon to remove any tag modifiers.

3. **(Optional) To further limit the search, repeat Step 2.**

4. **If replacing content, choose an action on the Action menu and then input additional information as prompted:**

- **Replace Tag & Contents:** Enter Replace With information for the new tag and contents.

- **Replace Contents Only:** Enter Replace With information for the contents of the specified tag.

- **Remove Tag & Contents:** Remove the selected tag and everything in between.

- **Strip Tag:** Remove specified tags but not their content.

- **Change Tag:** Select another tag type in a drop-down list.

- **Set Attribute:** Select a tag and specify its attribute, if any.

- **Remove Attribute:** Select an attribute to be removed from the specified tag.

- **Add Before Start Tag:** Enter data to add before the specified start tag.

- **Add After End Tag:** Enter data to add after the specified end tag.

- **Add After Start Tag:** Enter data to add after the specified start tag.

- **Add Before End Tag:** Enter data to add before the specified end tag.

5. **Search for your text by clicking the appropriate button:**

- **Find All:** Open the Results panel and display search results.

- **Find Next:** Jump from each found instance to the next, and if searching in multiple documents, jump from one document to the next.

- **Replace:** Replace your search criteria with your replacement text in the To field. Click Find Next to move to the next instance.

- **Replace All:** Find all instances of your search criteria and replace them with your replacement text in the To field.

6. **Click the Close button to exit the Find and Replace dialog box.**

**Book II
Chapter 2**

Working with Text

Saving and reusing searches

When creating complex search parameters in the Find and Replace dialog box, you may need to reuse a search in the future. To save a search to reuse later, enter the desired search options and click the Save Query icon, which looks like an old floppy disk and is located near the Find All button. When prompted, name the search with the .dwr file extension (older versions of Dreamweaver used the .dwq extension), browse to the location where you want to save the search, and click Save.

To use a previously saved search, launch the Find and Replace dialog box and click the Load Query icon, which looks like an open folder with a page being filed inside it. In the Load Query dialog box, navigate to the folder where you saved the search, select it, and click Open. After the search is loaded, click any of the Find or Replace buttons.

Using regular expressions in your searches

Regular expressions are patterns made up of letter, symbol, and number combinations used in searches to help narrow search terms. Dreamweaver allows you to use regular expressions in your searches. Common regular expression characters include the following:

✦ \d: Matches a single digit between 0 and 9

✦ ^: Matches at the start of the line

✦ \b: Matches at a word boundary

For example, to compile a search for a specific e-mail address (`info@company name.com`) in the entire Web site, your search criteria is the following:

✦ Look for the specific tag, in this case, `<a>`, which needs to be written as only *a* in the field.

✦ The tag must contain text including the regular expression, in this case, `^info`.

✦ Replace the text with the e-mail address.

Take a look at Figure 2-7 to see this search.

Figure 2-7:
Search
using
regular
expressions.

To find out more about regular expressions, visit `www.regular-expressions.info/` or see the "Introduction to Regular Expressions in Dreamweaver" article on the Dreamweaver Developer Center Web site at `www.adobe.com/devnet/dreamweaver/articles/regular_expressions.html`.

Chapter 3: Inserting Graphics

In This Chapter

✔ **Inserting, editing, repositioning, and deleting images**

✔ **Setting image attributes with the Properties inspector**

✔ **Adding interactive page elements, such as rollover images and image maps**

*G*raphics give a Web page personality. They help create the look and feel that represents the product, service, company, or person the Web site is about. Graphic images are great for navigation buttons, logos, photographs, icons, buttons, background images, design elements, illustrations, and more.

You're limited to using only certain types of graphics on Web sites. The three main types of graphics supported by most browsers are GIF (pronounced "JIF," like the peanut butter, though some people say "GIF" with a hard G as in *gate*), PNG (pronounced "ping"), and JPEG or JPG (pronounced "J-peg"). Each format takes high-resolution images and compresses the data to keep file sizes smaller than their high-resolution counterparts. Because most browsers can support only 72 pixels per inch for on-screen display, you need to reduce your Web graphics to 72 pixels per inch. Fortunately, what is lost in resolution is made up for in reduced file sizes, which helps to make the Web images load faster in a browser window.

When optimizing your images for the Web, GIF and PNG-8 files are best used for graphics with large, flat areas of color with a maximum of 256 colors, and JPEGs and PNG-24s support millions of colors and are best used for photographs and images with gradients. Although the PNG-24 file format is far superior to the PNG-8 format, especially because it supports transparency much like a GIF file, PNG-24 files are not quite yet the norm. This is primarily because so many people are still using older browsers that don't support this format. Now, if everyone switched tomorrow to using the latest versions of Firefox, Safari, Opera, or Internet Explorer, we'd be set. Until then, if you use PNG-24, understand that older browsers can't display that format correctly. As such, this chapter limits discussion of PNG files to the PNG-8 format.

This chapter presumes your graphics are optimized in the GIF, PNG-8, or JPG format and are ready to insert in your Web page. Besides learning how to insert images, you find out how to edit, delete, and move graphics, set image attributes such as borders, create rollover buttons and image maps, build an image-based navigation bar, and work with graphics and HTML generated in Adobe Fireworks.

Inserting Images in Your Web Page

As with many features of Dreamweaver, you have several ways to add images to a Web page. Often, the insertion method you choose is simply determined by where the cursor happens to be on-screen. For instance, if your cursor is closest to the Files panel, you'll probably insert the image from there. Of course, you can use keyboard shortcuts any time you like, which is also a nice timesaver.

Before you begin adding images to your Web page, be sure you save all your graphics in an images folder at the root level of your managed Web site. (If the folder doesn't exist yet, create one.) Organizing your graphics in a common folder can help you keep track of files as the site grows.

When inserting your images, whatever method you choose, Dreamweaver automatically writes the code for you, including the path where the image is. If the image is outside the managed site folder, Dreamweaver may prompt you to copy the graphic file to the current managed site. Furthermore, whenever the Select Image Source dialog box appears, you can select File System to choose a graphic from a specific folder on your computer, or choose Data Sources to specify a Spry Data Set (dynamic image source) in the Bindings panel.

Using the Insert panel

The easiest way to insert images is by using the Images pull-down menu in the Common category of the Insert panel. To insert an image, follow these steps:

1. **Place your cursor where you'd like to add the image, click the Images menu icon in the Common category of the Insert panel, and then click the Image icon.**

   The Image icon looks like a little tree in a grassy field.

   The pull-down menu displays the icon of the last icon selected. Therefore, when the icon on the menu displays the image type you need, you can simply click it to insert that type of graphic. Otherwise, use the pull-down menu to select the type of image you want to insert.

   The Select Image Source dialog box appears (see Figure 3-1), where you can navigate to and select the graphic you want to insert. The dialog box has a panel to display the files by name and a preview area including an image preview, image dimensions, format, size, and probable loading time.

Figure 3-1:
Use the
Select
Image
Source
dialog box
to select an
image to
insert.

2. **Select the image you want to insert, and then click OK.**

   For unsaved files, you will see a dialog box alerting you that your document must be saved to create a document-relative path for your image.

By default, Dreamweaver enables the Image Accessibility Attributes feature, which can be toggled on and off through Dreamweaver's Preferences. When this feature is enabled and you are inserting an image on the page, the Image Tag Accessibility Attributes dialog box automatically appears so you can add accessibility attributes for Alternate Text as well as a Long Description to your image. Enter one or both accessibility attributes.

At the minimum, we highly recommended that you add Alternate Text to describe the image in 50 characters or less. The Alternate Text attribute (for example, `alt="apples"`), you enter is read by Browser screen-reader software used by the visually impaired. For the Long Description, enter a filename or URL to a page that has a longer description of that image, as in `longdesc="apples.html"`. Then click OK.

To bypass Accessibility options and insert the image without the Alternate Text or Long Description attribute, click Cancel. To discover more about designing Web sites with accessibility, see Book I, Chapter 2.

You can also drag-and-drop the Image icon from the Insert panel into the open file in Design or Code view. Believe it or not, you can even drag-and-drop an image from the desktop into an open Dreamweaver document.

When working in an unsaved file, Dreamweaver writes a `file:///` reference to the image but converts that reference to the document-relative path upon saving the file. For instance, before saving your file, the image path may look like this:

```
<img src="file:///C|/Documents and Settings/Administrator/My Documents/ Clients/
    ClientX_HTML/images/logo.gif" width="200" height="200" alt="logo" />
```

But after saving the file, the path may look like this:

```
<img src="images/logo.gif" width="200" height="200" alt="logo" />
```

Using the Insert menu

Use the Insert menu as an alternate method of inserting images. Choose Insert⇨Image to insert an image. As with the Insert panel method described in the preceding section, navigate to and select the image to insert in the Select Image Source dialog box.

Using the Assets panel

To use the Assets panel to insert images, you must define your site first (see Book 1, Chapter 3 for details) and make sure you've placed all optimized graphics for the site into an images folder at the root level of the managed site. After defining the site, click the Images icon located at the top-left corner of the Assets panel (see Figure 3-2) to see a list of images. The Assets panel has a preview window that shows a thumbnail of any selected graphic file in the managed site. Below the preview window, graphics are listed alphabetically by name and also show the file dimensions in pixels, the file size in KB, the file type (GIF, PNG, JPG, and so on), and the full path and filename of the image. If you don't see your image listed here after adding it to the page or site, click the Refresh Site List icon at the bottom of the panel.

Figure 3-2:
The Assets panel displays images.

To insert an image from the Assets panel, select the image and do one of the following:

✦ Click the Insert button at the bottom of the panel.

✦ Drag-and-drop the image into the page at the desired location.

Using the Files panel

To add images to an open document from the Files panel, simply select, drag, and drop the chosen image into the desired location on the page. If you have enabled Accessibility preferences, the Image Tag Accessibility Attribute dialog box prompts you to enter accessibility attributes for the image. Enter those values and click OK, or click Cancel to bypass accessibility options and insert the image without the Alt and Long Description attributes.

Book II
Chapter 3

Inserting Graphics

Editing, Deleting, and Moving Inserted Images

After you insert the image, you can do many things with it:

✦ **Edit:** Select the image to modify any of the image attributes or replace the image with another image in the Properties inspector. For the low-down on modifying image attributes, see the section "Setting Image Attributes with the Properties Inspector," later in the chapter.

✦ **Delete:** Select the image and press Delete or Backspace, or choose Edit⇨Clear or Edit⇨Cut.

✦ **Move:** In Design view, drag the image to its new location and release the mouse button. You can also cut and paste the image in both Design and Code views. Keep in mind, however, that you can't place an image in a particular spot on the page without first creating a container, such as a layer or table, to position it. To find out more about layers, see book IV, Chapter 1. To discover more about tables, go to Book II, Chapter 6.

Using an Image Placeholder When a Graphic Isn't Ready

Placeholder images are great to use if you know you need graphics in parts of your layout but the graphics aren't ready yet. Placeholder images can be any size in pixels, and the width and height attributes are displayed in the center of the placeholder image itself.

Image placeholders don't appear in browser windows and are intended for use only in the Dreamweaver environment. Therefore, before publishing a Web page or site, be sure to replace any image placeholders with the desired GIF, PNG, or JPEG files.

To insert a placeholder image, follow these steps:

1. **Select the Image Placeholder option on the Images drop-down menu in the Common category of the Insert panel.**

   The icon has an image of two tiny squares overlapping; one has a picture of a tree on it and the other has a big dimmed X. You can also choose Insert⇨Image Objects⇨Image Placeholder. The Image Placeholder dialog box appears, as shown in Figure 3-3.

Figure 3-3: Set Image Placeholder attributes.

2. **Enter the placeholder image attributes: Name, Width, and Height (in pixels), Color, and Alternate Text.**

   The Name field is used to create both `name` and `id` attributes, which will be used later for identifying the graphic with CSS and JavaScript.

   The Color attribute (which is technically the `background-color` attribute for your placeholder image) should match the surrounding layout or the predominant color of the graphic, because code for this attribute will be added to your placeholder image and will not be removed when you replace the placeholder with the real image. In other words, if the background color of your placeholder is a contrasting color and you don't remove the style code manually after inserting the real image, site visitors may see that contrasting color momentarily as the image loads in their browser.

   To choose a color, click the icon to the right of Color and choose your color in the pop-up palette. The hexadecimal number then appears in the text box to the right. You can also type a color name, such as green, or a hexadecimal number, such as #FF9933, in the text box. (See Book II, Chapter 2 for more about using hexadecimal numbers.)

   In Figure 3-3, the placeholder name is submit, the width is 150, the height is 30, the color is #286987, and the Alternate text is Sign me up!

3. **Click OK.**

   The placeholder image is inserted on the page. In Code view, you see the following HTML for the example:

   ```
   <img src="" alt="Sign me up!" name="submit" width="150" height="30"
        id="submit" style="background-color: #266984" />
   ```

Figure 3-4 shows how this image looks in Design view. The image placeholder displays the name, dimensions, and color you input in the dialog box.

Figure 3-4:
A place-
holder
image.

When you're ready to replace the placeholder image with the real image, double-click the placeholder image in Design view to open the Select Image Source dialog box, select the replacement image, and click the OK button. The name, id, background color, and alt attributes from the place-holder image remain, and the source of the image and its width and height are updated with the new filename.

Setting Image Attributes with the Properties Inspector

After you insert an image into your document, you'll want to add other HTML markup and possibly style attributes to the image. Most of the attributes can be added to the image by using the Properties inspector, including applying any custom CSS styles you may have already created. (See Book III, Chapter 1 for the lowdown on creating style sheets.)

Suppose, for example, that you insert an image called logo.gif into a Web page. After the image is inserted, select it to apply attributes. As shown in Figure 3-5, a thumbnail of the selected image is displayed in the top left of the Properties inspector, along with the file size in K, width and height sizes, the image source, the ID, and Alternate text. If your Properties inspector also displays a Photoshop or Fireworks icon in the Edit area, you can click that icon to open the selected graphic in that program for editing.

If you can't see all the image properties shown in Figure 3-5, click the expander arrow in the bottom-right corner of the Properties inspector.

Naming your images

It's a good idea to give an ID to all your images so you can quickly apply Dreamweaver behaviors, JavaScript, CSS, or VBScript to them later. To give an ID to your images, select the graphic and enter a name in the ID field of the Properties inspector (refer to Figure 3-5).

Specifying the width and height of images

By default, when images are inserted in a page, Dreamweaver reads image dimensions, writes them into the code in pixels, and displays them in the W and H fields of the Properties inspector. Although Dreamweaver inserts dimensions in pixels, you can adjust the dimensions to percentages. In the example image in Figure 3-5, the logo graphic is 192 x 201 pixels. If the image is resized, the new image dimensions would appear in the W and H fields.

Although you are allowed to specify sizes in the W and H fields in percentages (by adding the % symbol after the number, as in 80%), we don't recommend that you do so because the image can easily become skewed and look terrible.

Figure 3-5:
The Properties inspector displays fields to add image attributes.

File size

Edit Image Settings

Thumbnail Image   ID   Edit in Photoshop   Update from Original

Pointer Hotspot | Polygon Hotspot   Crop   Expand/Collapse Panel

Rectangle Hotspot   Resample | Sharpen

Circle Hotspot   Brightness and Contrast

Resizing and resetting images

Resize images by either dragging the resize handles located on the right, bottom, and bottom-right corners of the selected image or by entering new image dimensions in the W and H fields in the Properties inspector. After you stretch or scrunch an image beyond its normal size, the Reset Size icon appears between the W and H fields in the Properties inspector and the W and H values appear in bold. To revert an image to its normal size, click the Reset Size icon.

It's a good idea — especially if you're scaling up — to create new graphics with an external image editing program rather than resize them in Dreamweaver. Inserting correctly sized images reduces browser download time as well as helps to maintain the integrity of the image as it appears elsewhere on the site.

Adding vertical or horizontal padding

To push the edges of a graphic away from surrounding text, you may want to add padding to your images. Today CSS is the norm, but in the past designers would often use the V Space and H Space HTML markup fields to add uniform vertical or horizontal padding. For vertical padding above and below the image, enter a measurement in pixels in the V Space field. For horizontal padding on the left and right sides of the image, enter a measurement in pixels in the H Space field.

A better method of adding padding to images is to use CSS, especially because it allows you to apply nonuniform padding around an image, such as padding on just the top and left sides. See Book III, Chapter 1 to learn more about CSS.

Adding image links

The Properties inspector has a Link field, where you can enter the filename or full path of a page or document that the graphic can link to. To add a link to an image, select the image and enter the filename (including the file extension), the path, or both in the Link field. For alternate link options and detailed instructions on linking, see Book II, Chapter 4.

Adjusting targets

When an image contains a link, the Target field becomes active so you can set the browser frame or browser window into which the linked file should load. When unspecified, the default target for all links is _self. In other words, when you click a link in a browser window, the linked document appears in the same browser window. If that's what you want to happen when clicking the link, leave the Target field blank. Otherwise, to specify that the link opens a new window for displaying the linked page, select _blank in the Target drop-down list. (You can read more on setting link targets in Book II, Chapter 4.)

Specifying the original file

The Original field allows you to specify the location and filename of the original file used to create the optimized Web graphic. Then you can quickly edit that file in the image editor you specify in External Editors preferences by clicking the Edit application icon next to the Link field. See the "Using the image editing icons" section, later in the chapter, to find out more about editing Web graphics in Dreamweaver.

Adding image borders

By default, images with no links have no borders, but you can add black borders of any pixel width using HTML markup. Images with links have a border that takes on the properties of text links. For example, if the default text link color is blue, a linked image has a blue border.

Although adding an HTML border by entering a number for the width of the border in the Border field in the Properties inspector may seem like a great advantage, the major drawback to it is that you can't choose a different border color through the Properties inspector. (Similar to Henry Ford and his Model-T: "People can have the Model T in any color — as long as it's black.") Technically, the border color can be the same color as the surrounding text color, so you could control the border color with the old `<font>` tag if for some reason you don't want to use CSS, as in the following example:

```
<p><font color="#CC0066">This text is pink, which means the image will have
    the same border color. <img src="images/logo.gif" width="192" height="201"
    border="1"></font></p>
```

Today most major browsers don't consistently support this *deprecated* (old, outdated, and no longer recommended) method, so be sure to test it if you intend to use it. A better method is to create a custom CSS style. CSS borders can be any color or thickness, one of a handful of different styles, and applied to any or all of the image's four sides. Turn to Book III, Chapter 1 to redefine tags and create custom styles in Cascading Style Sheets.

Providing Alternate text

As mentioned previously in the chapter, when accessibility features are enabled in Dreamweaver's Preferences, you can add accessibility attributes to your images as you insert them onto your pages. However, when the accessibility features are disabled, be sure to add these attributes manually to your images through the Properties inspector before publishing the Web site. The two most important accessibility attributes for images are Alternate Text and Long Description. Alternate Text, or *Alt text,* is useful for site visitors who use text-only browsers, have their browsers set to manually download images, or use speech synthesizer software to read the descriptions of the image. In some browsers, Alt text appears in place of the images when images are downloading and when the mouse pointer hovers over an image. Furthermore, some search engines use Alt text to help determine site ranking by presuming that the words used in Alt text are more relevant and important than text found in `<meta>` tags.

You can make Alt text as brief as one word or as long as a 50-character paragraph, though you should enter a complete, meaningful sentence rather than a list of keywords. If you want to provide a longer description for your image, you can also include a Long Description attribute that links to a separate Web page containing the longer description. The code for an image with both Alternate Text and a Long Description looks something like this:

```
<img src="images/brooklynbridge.jpg" alt="The Brooklyn Bridge" width="400"
    height="300" border="10" longdesc="bridge.html" />
```

Aligning images

You can align selected images on your page in two ways, one using HTML markup and the other using CSS, which is the more modern, standards-compliant, W3C (World Wide Web Consortium) recommended practice. Here's a description of each alignment method:

✦ **HTML: Wrap elements — such as text — around the image** by selecting an option in the Properties inspector Align drop-down list (shown in Figure 3-6). When no alignment is specified, the default alignment is Left. This alignment method adds the `align` attribute to the `<img>` tag.

✦ **CSS: Make images float to the left or right of text or other objects** by applying a custom style to an image. To do so, select the style by name in the Class drop-down list (shown in Figure 3-5).

**Book II
Chapter 3**

Inserting Graphics

Figure 3-6:
Image
alignment
options.

With CSS, each style can have multiple properties, or *rules*. For example, you can create a style that adds a 1-pixel-wide, four-sided navy blue border; 5 pixels of uniform padding; and right alignment to an image:

```
<style type="text/css">
<!--
.alignright {
padding: 5px;
border: 1px solid #000033;
clear: right;
float: right;
}
-->
</style>
```

Using the image editing icons

Dreamweaver has several tools for editing images without the need to launch an external image editor, though you can also launch the default editor from here. You can use these editing tools with any GIF, PNG, or JPEG file inserted on a page. The following seven image editing tools are located under the Alt field in the Properties inspector when you select an image on a page in Design or Code view (refer to Figure 3-5):

✦ **Edit:** Launch the default image editing program, which in most cases is Fireworks. You can specify an alternate image editor in the File Types/Editors category of the Preferences dialog box. Choose Edit⇨Preferences (Windows) or Dreamweaver⇨Preferences (Mac).

✦ **Edit Image Settings:** Launch the Image Preview dialog box, where you can make simple adjustments to the selected image. The dialog box has two tabs, Options and File. In the Options tab, you can adjust the image format and quality; add image smoothing, progressive browser display, and sharpening color edges; set a matte color; remove unused colors, crop the image, and view RGB values for the image showing in the preview window. Essentially, the dialog box works like a mini Web graphics optimization program. In the File tab, you can adjust the image scale and export area.

✦ **Update from Original:** Adjust the selected image using the original source file instead of the optimized graphic. You must specify in the Original field of the Properties inspector the original file that was used to create the optimized graphic.

✦ **Crop:** Crop the graphic. Clicking this icon displays an alert dialog box that warns you about the permanence of any changes you make. Click OK in the alert dialog box to continue. Cropping handles then appear around the image so that you can crop the image. Press Enter (Windows) or Return (Mac) to accept the cropping.

✦ **Resample:** Resample a resized image to improve the quality of the image at the new size. This feature appears only after you resize an image. Try to keep resampling to a minimum (especially resampling up) because this process can degrade the image quality. If you really need a graphic at a different size, create a new graphic in an image editing program.

✦ **Brightness and Contrast:** Adjust the brightness and contrast of the image. Like the Crop tool, the Brightness and Contrast icon displays an alert dialog box that warns you about the permanence of any changes you make to the image. Click OK in the dialog box to continue and a Brightness/Contrast dialog box appears. Move the sliders in the dialog box to the right or the left to increase or decrease, respectively, the brightness and contrast. Click OK to accept the new settings or Cancel to close the Brightness/Contrast dialog box without changes.

✦ **Sharpen:** Adjust the overall image contrast and edge pixel clarity. The Sharpen dialog box uses a sliding scale of 0–10 to adjust the image sharpness; the higher the number, the more intense the image's definition or sharpness.

Creating Interactive Images

Besides inserting the occasional static graphic here and there on a Web page, Dreamweaver greatly simplifies the process of adding interactive image options on a Web page, including creating rollover images, image maps, and adding Fireworks HTML to a Web page.

The following sections discuss these interactive techniques. All interactive image icons are accessible in the Common category of the Insert panel, as shown in Figure 3-7.

Book II
Chapter 3

Inserting Graphics

Image button

Figure 3-7: Choose an interactive image option.

Adding rollover images

Rollover images are graphics that change to a different image in a browser window when a visitor moves the cursor over the image. To make a rollover button, you need two graphics — one for the normal state and one for the over state — that are the same pixel width and height but look different enough that a visitor will notice the rollover effect.

Dreamweaver lets you quickly create rollover images by inserting JavaScript into the code that tells a browser to display one image for the normal state and another image for the mouseover state.

Before creating your rollover images in Dreamweaver, optimize the identically sized graphics for both normal and rollover states, give them similar names, such as nav01.gif and nav01-over.gif, and save them in an images folder at the root level of your managed site.

To create rollover images, follow these steps:

1. **Place the insertion point in the Document window where you want the rollover image to go.**

   The spot you click in the Document window is where the rollover image will appear on the page.

2. **Click the Images icon in the Common category of the Insert panel and choose Rollover Image in its drop-down list (refer to Figure 3-7).**

   Or choose Insert⇨Image Objects⇨Rollover Image. The Insert Rollover Image dialog box appears, as shown in Figure 3-8.

Figure 3-8:
Specify a
rollover
image.

3. **Enter an image name, browse to and select the graphics to use for both the original and rollover images, add Alternate text, and type a filename or URL for a link to another file.**

   By default, the Preload Rollover Image option is enabled. This option adds JavaScript to the page that tells the browser to preload this graphic into the browser's cache as the page is loading. Leave this option selected so that the over state graphic is ready to appear by the time a visitor places the cursor on the rollover graphic's normal state.

4. **Click OK.**

   Dreamweaver inserts the original image and writes all the JavaScript necessary to perform the rollover function. JavaScript is attached to the <img>, <head>, and <body> tags.

To preview or test JavaScript behaviors in Design view, click the Live View button on the Document toolbar. To test the effect in a browser, choose File⇨Preview in Browser. You can tell the rollover effect is working properly by positioning the cursor over the rollover button. *Note:* Internet Explorer blocks ActiveX content such as JavaScript when previewing the page. If you see the security alert bar at the top of the browser, select the Allow Blocked Content option to view the page.

Creating image maps

An *image map* is an image that has shaped regions, or *hotspots,* defined by pixel coordinates in the code and that can be assigned a behavior (such as a hyperlink). When a visitor clicks the hotspot, an action occurs (for example, another page is displayed). Hotspots can be rectangular, oval, or polygonal in shape. The following example shows how image maps are defined in the code for a hotspot in the shape of a circle:

```
<img src="images/logo.gif" width="192" height="201" border="1"
    usemap="#Map1"><map name="Map1" id="Map1"><area shape="circle"
    coords="97,98,75" href="#">
```

Images can have multiple hotspots as well as multiple behaviors assigned to a hotspot. For instance, you may have a photograph of a map of the United States and want to turn each state's shape into a unique hotspot linking to information elsewhere on the site specific to that state. (See Book IV, Chapter 2 for more on behaviors.)

You can draw hotspots on a selected image using the Rectangle Hotspot, Circle Hotspot, and Polygon Hotspot tools, which are below the image thumbnail in the Properties inspector (refer to Figure 3-5). You can adjust the hotspot border with another tool, the Pointer Hotspot.

Here's how to create a hotspot on a graphic:

1. **Select the image in Design view.**

By selecting the image in Design view, you activate the image hotspot options in the Properties inspector.

2. **In the Properties inspector, enter an ID for the image in the ID field and a name for the image map in the Map field.**

If unspecified, image maps will be assigned a default name such as Map1, Map2, Map3, and so on. If you specify an ID but not a name, the image map will be named after the ID, as in logoMap when the ID is logo. If creating multiple image maps in the same document, definitely use separate ID and map names for each.

3. **Select a hotspot tool and draw a hotspot shape on the image:**

- **Rectangular:** Drag and release the mouse to create an enclosed rectangular shape. To create a square, hold down the Shift key while dragging.

- **Circle:** Drag and release the mouse to create a circle shape.

- **Polygon:** Create a nonuniform polygonal shape by selecting this tool and clicking the image multiple times to insert anchor points for the hotspot shape. Click the Pointer Hotspot tool to finish the shape.

To select these hotspot tools, click one of the icons in the bottom-left corner of the Properties inspector (see Figure 3-9) or select one from the Images pull-down menu in the Common area of the Insert panel. If prompted to add accessibility attributes, enter them.

4. **Use the Pointer Hotspot tool to select the hotspot and assign `link`, `target`, and `alt` attributes to it in the Properties inspector.**

   When the hotspot is selected, the Properties inspector displays fields for assigning a link, a link target, and Alternate text to the hotspot. You can also reposition the hotspot and adjust the anchor points of the hotspot shape with the Pointer Hotspot tool.

5. **Deselect the hotspot or image or both by clicking away from the image with the Pointer Hotspot tool in Design view.**

   Figure 3-9 shows an image with a hotspot.

6. **To continue adding hotspots to the same image, select another hotspot tool and repeat Steps 1 through 5.**

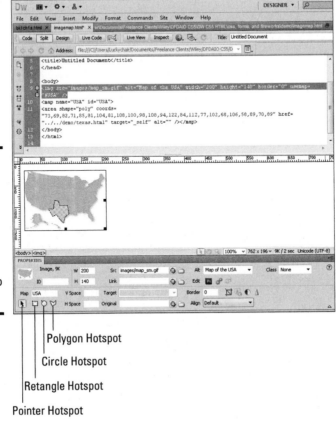

Figure 3-9: Create image map hotspots with the hotspot tools and assign behaviors to hotspots.

Polygon Hotspot

Circle Hotspot

Retangle Hotspot

Pointer Hotspot

Inserting Fireworks HTML

Fireworks lets you create, slice, and optimize images for the Web, and because it's an Adobe program, it integrates beautifully with Dreamweaver. One of the main things you can do with Fireworks is create a page layout and then export the file as an HTML page including images and rollover effects. After you export the file, you can import it into Dreamweaver. Dreamweaver lets you quickly add design elements generated by Fireworks, such as animated rollovers, pop-up menus, and other images, into an open document. Fireworks has an export command that lets you specify which Dreamweaver managed site folder to place the code into so you can easily import the code into Dreamweaver when you're ready.

To import Fireworks content into an open Dreamweaver document, follow these steps:

1. **Click in the page to place the insertion point where you want to add the Fireworks HTML.**

2. **Click the Images icon in the Common category of the Insert panel and choose Fireworks HTML in its drop-down list (refer to Figure 3-7).**

   You can also choose Insert➪Image Objects➪Fireworks HTML. The Insert Fireworks HTML dialog box appears, as shown in Figure 3-10.

Figure 3-10:
Insert
Fireworks
HTML.

3. **Browse to and select the Fireworks HTML file that you want to import.**

   To have Dreamweaver delete the Fireworks HTML after inserting it on your page, select the Delete File After Insertion check box.

4. **Click OK.**

   Dreamweaver imports the HTML, graphics, and any associated JavaScript to support rollover effects and other interactivity.

For more on using Dreamweaver with Fireworks, see Book III, Chapter 5.

Chapter 4: Making Links with Text and Images

In This Chapter

- ✔ Making links with text
- ✔ Making links with images
- ✔ Creating e-mail links
- ✔ Editing and deleting links
- ✔ Coding with the Tag Chooser
- ✔ Coding by hand

*W*eb pages become a Web site when they are joined by hyperlinks. *Hyperlinks* (often called just *links*) convert nearly any content — including text or graphics — into clickable pointers that lead the site visitor through other pages on a site, winding through text and graphics along the way.

Links can point to another Web page on the same site; to another page on a different Web site; to a section of the same or another page, PDF, Word or PowerPoint document, graphic, sound file, movie, Zip or SIT file; or to downloadable software. They can open a blank e-mail message with the recipient's address already in place, or they can be temporary placeholders for behaviors and scripts to attach to.

You can add, edit, or remove links from a page at any stage of the site building process. Although they look like working links inside the Dreamweaver Document window in Design view, they don't work when you click them there, so be sure to launch a browser window by pressing F12 (Windows) or Option+F12 (Mac) or click the Live View button to test the functionality and accuracy of your links.

This chapter takes an in-depth look at the different kinds of links that you can create in Dreamweaver.

Understanding Hyperlinks

You can create four types of hyperlinks in Dreamweaver:

+ **Regular:** Link pages together by converting content, including text, graphics, and other objects, into hyperlinks.

+ **E-mail:** Launch a computer's default e-mail program and prompt the site visitor to send e-mail to the e-mail address in the link.

+ **Named anchor:** Take the site visitor to a link location embedded on the same page as the link or to an anchor link location embedded on another page.

+ **Temporary:** Convert selected content into undefined links for adding detailed link information or behaviors at a later time. The two kinds of temporary links are called *null* and *script* links.

Before adding links, be sure you understand the difference between document-relative, absolute, and site root–relative paths because the link syntax varies slightly depending on the path type. Turn to Book I, Chapter 3 for a general discussion about paths.

One of the fastest ways to add links to your page is to select some text, graphic, or object on the page and type the link information in the Link field in the Properties inspector. Type the link by entering the filename or full URL, including `http://` and the file extension. After you enter the link, the Target field becomes activated. Then, you can select a target window or destination for the link (see the "Setting Link Targets" section in this chapter).

In the HTML view of the Properties inspector, two icons (shown in Figure 4-1) are to the right of the Link text field so that you can add links to any selected text, graphic, or object on the page. Both methods are faster and more accurate ways of linking files (because no typing is involved):

Link field   Browse to File

Point to File   Target field

Figure 4-1:
The
Properties
inspector
helps you
add links.

+ **Browse to File:** Click the folder icon to display the Select File dialog box. Browse to and select the file you want to link to, and then click OK; Dreamweaver writes the link of the filename in the Link field on the

Properties inspector for you. After you specify the link, enter any target information in the Target field.

✦ **Point to File:** Click this icon and drag the pointer icon to a file listed in the Files panel. Release the mouse button when the cursor is on top of the desired file and Dreamweaver writes the link of the filename in the Link field of the Properties inspector. Enter your target information in the Target field. The Point to File icon works also for selecting named anchors on a page (See the "Creating Named Anchor Links" section, later in the chapter, to find out more).

To test a link, you must launch a browser window (or preview your page in Live View). Here's how to open a browser to test your link:

Book II
Chapter 4

✦ To preview an open page, save your page and then press F12 (Windows) or Option+F12 (Mac) to launch your primary browser or press Control+F12 (Windows) or ⌘+F12 (Mac) to launch your secondary browser (see Book V, Chapter 1 to specify a primary and secondary browser). The currently open document appears in a browser window.

✦ To preview a file listed in the Files panel, right-click (Windows) or Control+click (Mac) the file, choose Preview in Browser, and choose the browser type from the list.

✦ To preview a page in a variety of different browsers using Adobe's new BrowserLab, click the Preview/Debug in Browser icon next to the Inspect button on the Document toolbar and then choose Preview in Adobe BrowserLab.

To open a locally linked file inside Dreamweaver, select the link in the Dreamweaver Document window and choose Modify➪Open Linked Page. Alternatively, press Ctrl (Windows) or ⌘ (Mac) and double-click the link to open the linked document in Dreamweaver's Document window.

All links use the <a> tag plus one or two different attributes to convert selected text or graphics into links. The next few sections give separate descriptions and examples of the four link types.

Creating Text Links

You can create *text links* from a word, a phrase, a sentence, a paragraph, or even an entire page of text. The link HTML code surrounds a selection of text and converts it to a clickable hyperlink. Text links use the <a> tag with the href attribute. The href attribute stands for *Hypertext REFerence,* and the attribute points either to a file at the root level of the defined site or to an external Web page by including the http:// and full path to that page. The target attribute, which tells the browser whether to open the link in the same or another browser window, also goes inside the opening <a> tag.

Making Links with
Text and Images

This example link displays the Google home page in a new window:

```
<a href="http://www.google.com" target="_blank">Search on Google</a>
```

This example displays an About page in the same browser window:

```
<a href="about.html" target="_self">About Us</a>
```

To create a text link, follow these steps:

1. **Select the word, phrase, sentence, or paragraph that you want to convert into a text link.**

The selected text must be a single word or a unified block of text. If you are creating a new link from an as-yet unwritten word or phrase, skip ahead to Step 2.

2. **Choose Insert➪Hyperlink or click the Hyperlink icon in the Common category of the Insert panel.**

The Hyperlink icon looks like a chain link. The Hyperlink dialog box appears, as shown in Figure 4-2. Any preselected text appears in the Text field.

Figure 4-2: Complete these fields to create a text hyperlink.

3. **Enter the following information in the dialog box:**

- **Text:** Enter (or edit) the text you want to make into a link, such as Learn More or Contact Us.

- **Link:** Type the path or filename or both of the linked page. If the linked page is on the same site, enter only the filename, such as contact.html, or the filename and directory, as in about/ourmission.html. However, if the linked page is external to the current site, enter the full URL including the `http://`, as in http://www.dummies.com.

- **Target:** By default, linked pages automatically appear in the same browser window. To override this setting, select _blank to have the link appear in a different browser window. See the "Setting Link Targets" section for more about other target settings.

- **Title:** Add a simple text description for the link. The title appears as a tool tip in some browsers when a visitor mouses over the link. In addition, well-written titles can both improve visitor accessibility and assist in better search engine indexing and ranking.

- **Access Key:** Add a one-letter keyboard equivalent that visitors can use with the Tab key to select the link in the browser. After they select the link, they can press Enter (Windows) or Return (Mac) to visit that linked page.

- **Tab Index:** Add a number for the tab order of this link, relative to other links on the page. The tab order, which defines the order of accessible elements on a page using the Tab key, begins at the top of the browser window and moves downward from left to right, as when reading a book.

4. **Click OK.**

   Dreamweaver adds the link to the page.

Making Image Links

Image links work the same way text links do, but the link code surrounds an image instead of text. Here's an example of a link to visit Google using a GIF file:

```
<a href="http://www.google.com" target="_blank"><img src="images/googlelogo.
    gif"></a>
```

Here's an example of a link to a page at the root level of a defined site using an About Us button graphic:

```
<a href="about.html"><img src="images/aboutus.gif"></a>
```

To create an image link from an optimized graphic inserted on your page, select the image on the page in Design view and type the filename or path of the linked page in the Link field in the Properties inspector. Add a `title` attribute, and if desired, add a link target to define where the linked page will appear.

When you add a link to an image, the border around the image becomes a hyperlink. To remove the link border from your linked image, set the Border property on the Properties inspector to 0.

You can also create an image link the same way you create a text link. See the preceding section to find out how to do so.

Inserting E-Mail Links

E-mail links, when clicked in a browser window, tell the site visitor's computer to launch the computer's default e-mail program, open a blank e-mail message window, and populate the Send To field with the e-mail address in the link. E-mail links use the `<a>` tag with the `href` attribute just like text links do. But instead of listing `http://` before the filename, an e-mail link uses the `mailto:` attribute before the e-mail address (`mailto:` is a URL just like `http://` is), like this:

```
<a href="mailto:me@example.com">me@example.com</a>
```

Adding an e-mail address to a Web page using this type of standard HTML e-mail link makes the e-mail address extremely vulnerable to spambots and spam spiders, which crawl the Web in search of anything that has the `me@example.com` format or for links containing the `mailto:` attribute. For e-mail encryption ideas, check out the nearby sidebar "Encrypting e-mail addresses" or search online.

Encrypting e-mail addresses

E-mail addresses listed on Web sites are extremely vulnerable to being harvested by spam gathering software and then sold to zillions of spam lists. To better protect your e-mail address, encrypt it or use some other form of hiding the e-mail address so that it can't be electronically harvested or easily obtained.

Try these suggestions for hiding or encrypting e-mail links on Web pages:

- Encrypt your e-mail address with a JavaScript encryption software application. Several freeware and shareware versions are available, including Email Riddler at `www.dynamicdrive.com/email riddler/` and the HiveLogic Enkoder Form at `http://hivelogic.com/enkoder/form`. Do a search for Email Address Encryptor to find others.

- Enter your e-mail address in Code view using URL code entities for all special characters. For example, `me@example.com` becomes `me%40example%2Ecom`. Visit the W3Schools Web site (`www.w3schools.com/tags/ref_urlencode.asp`) to convert your e-mail address into URL Unicode.

- Include your e-mail address on the page but don't turn it into a link. Your e-mail address is still vulnerable, but less so than as a standard e-mail link.

For a great article about e-mail harvesters and the countermeasures you can take to fight them, read Tim Williams's take on e-mail at `http://members.cox.net/timandbeth/spam/`.

To create a standard HTML e-mail link, follow these steps:

1. **Choose Insert⇨Email Link to launch the Email Link dialog box.**

   Or, in the Common category of the Insert panel, click the Email Link icon, which looks like an envelope.

2. **In the Text field, enter the text that will appear in the browser window as linked text, such as** Contact Us **or** contact@company.com.

3. **In the EMail field, enter the e-mail address for the link, such as** contact@company.com.

4. **Click OK.**

   Dreamweaver writes the e-mail link code in the page.

Creating Named Anchor Links

Named anchor links are great for creating links that jump to another location on the same page or to a specific part of another page in the same Web site. Use named anchor links for FAQ lists, Table of Contents, Indexes, Back to Top links, and other page elements in which internal linking would be useful.

Creating a named anchor link requires two steps:

1. **Place the anchor in the spot on your page where you want to link to and give it a name.**

2. **Make a link (from text, an image, or an object) that points to the named anchor you just placed.**

Suppose you have a page with two FAQs (frequently asked questions) and want to list the questions at the top of the page and the answers in sequence below the questions. The text on your page may look something like this:

1. Question?

2. Question?

First Question Answer
Answer to first question. Answer to first question. Answer to first question. Answer to first question. Answer to first question.

Second Question Answer
Answer to second question. Answer to second question. Answer to second question. Answer to second question. Answer to second question.

To link each question at the top of the page to its answer below, you create a named anchor right before each answer and then link the question to it. This type of link is called a named anchor because it uses the name attribute of the <a> tag. You'll notice, however, that the code for named anchors includes both name and id attributes:

```
<a name="Q1" id="Q1"></a>
```

The name and id attributes have the same values so that they share the same domain value space, which means you could use either one when specifying the link to the anchor. For example, you can create an anchor using the name attribute, as the following example shows:

```
<a name="Q1">1st Question Answer</a>
```

Or you can turn another element into an anchor using the id attribute, as this example shows:

```
<h1 id="Q1">1st Question Answer</h1>
```

After the anchor is placed, the link to the anchor uses the same name:

```
<a href="#Q1">Go to question 1 answer</a>
```

Dreamweaver tries to simplify the process by including both name and id attributes in the code when you create a named anchor.

The following sections cover the two-step process for creating a named anchor.

Step 1: Place the named anchor

Remember to create your page with all the text before creating the named anchors. Then place an anchor at each of the destination points. For example, in a FAQ list, you want to place an anchor right before the text for each answer in the list.

To place a named anchor, follow these steps:

1. **Place your cursor in the document where you'd like the anchor to be placed, and then click the Named Anchor icon in the Common category of the Insert panel or choose Insert⇨Named Anchor.**

   The Named Anchor icon looks like a golden anchor (when color icons are enabled; otherwise it is gray). The Named Anchor dialog box appears, as shown in Figure 4-3.

Figure 4-3:
The Named
Anchor
dialog box.

2. **Enter a name for your anchor and click OK.**

   Try not to use any spaces or funny characters in your anchor names nor start an anchor name with a number, and do not put any anchors inside a layer. In Design view, a little yellow invisible element marks where the named anchor sits in the code.

If you don't see the invisible element in Design view, be sure the Invisible Elements Visual Aids option is selected in the Document window and that the invisible elements in the Preferences dialog box are set to display named anchors. To see visual aids, choose View⇨Visual Aids⇨Invisible Elements.

Step 2: Link to the named anchor

Creating the link to the named anchor uses the `href` attribute just like standard text and image links, but it has one unique twist: Instead of linking to a filename or URL, the link name attribute is preceded by a number symbol (#) to tell the browser to look for the named anchor on the same page, like this:

```
<p><a href="#Q1">1. Question</a></p>
```

To create a link to a named anchor, do one of the following:

+ Select the text that will become the link, and in the Link field of the Properties inspector, type the number symbol (#) followed by the anchor name, as in #Q1. Alternately, you can use the Point to File feature in the Properties Inspector to point to the named anchor.

+ Select the text that will become the link, and choose Insert⇨Hyperlink, which displays the Hyperlink dialog box (refer to Figure 4-2), from which you can select the named anchor in the Link drop-down list. (See the earlier section, "Creating Text Links," for details.)

You can use named anchor links also when linking from one page to another by typing, after the name of the file being linked to, the number symbol (#) followed by the anchor name. For example, if you want a visitor to click a link in one page and go right to a particular section of another page, your link may look something like this:

```
<a href="contact.html#wholesale">Learn more about Wholesale Pricing</a>
```

In this example, the visitor is taken to a named anchor destination called `wholesale` in the page called `contact.html`.

Book II
Chapter 4

Making Links with Text and Images

Creating Temporary Links

The most common types of links are the links you create to other files and named anchors, but you can add other link types to a page:

+ **Script:** These links call JavaScript functions or run JavaScript code to provide information to the site visitor without the visitor having to leave the page, such as when a JavaScript alert box appears. JavaScript links can do other page processing duties, such as form validation, when the visitor interacts in some way with the page, such as clicking a particular button. For an excellent tutorial on JavaScript, go to `www.w3schools.com/js/default.asp`.

+ **Null:** These empty links don't go anywhere but still treat the text or object like a link. When you create null links, you can use them to attach behaviors or scripts to the text and objects on the page. (You can find more about behaviors in Book IV, Chapter 2.)

To create a script link, follow these steps:

1. **Select the text, graphic, or object in Design view.**

2. **Enter** javascript: **(the word** *javascript* **followed by a colon) in the Link field in the Properties inspector, followed by a JavaScript or function call.**

For instance, to create a JavaScript link that closes the currently open browser window, type the following text in the Link field:

```
javascript:parent.close();
```

The script for the link appears in the code like this:

```
This is a <a href="javascript:parent.close();">Close</a> link.
```

where the JavaScript code appears between double quotation marks as a value of the `href` attribute. If you need to include double quotation marks as part of your script, be sure to add escape marks before each double quotation mark, as `\"This link goes to the home page\"`.

To create a null link, do one of the following:

+ Select the text, graphic, or object in Design view and type javascript:; (the word *javascript* followed by a colon, followed by a semicolon) in the Link field in the Properties inspector.

+ Select the text or graphic and enter a number symbol (#) in the Link field in the Properties inspector.

Some browsers jump to the top of the page when you use a number sign as a null link; therefore, the JavaScript null link is preferred.

Whenever you're ready to convert the temporary link to a permanent link, replace the temporary link with the appropriate filename or URL.

Setting Link Targets

After adding a link to text or a graphic, you can assign a *target* in the Target field of the Properties inspector. The target defines where the linked file opens: whether in the same browser window, a new browser window, or a specific frame in a frameset. When unspecified, the linked page typically opens in the same browser window. For further details on setting text properties with the Properties inspector, see Book II, Chapter 2.

Editing and Deleting Links

Links aren't set in stone after you create them; you can edit and even delete them any time. You can even edit all instances of a single link used on several pages of your site at the same time.

Editing links

To edit a link after inserting it in your page, select the link — whether it's a text, graphic, or object link — and then do either of the following:

✦ Edit or replace the link by using the Properties inspector.

✦ Choose Modify⇨Change Link. The Select File dialog box appears, so you can search for and select another file for the link.

Dreamweaver has a great feature that allows you to change a link throughout an entire managed site (for instance, change the August newsletter link to a September newsletter link). To do this, follow these steps:

1. **Select a file in the Files panel that includes the link you want to change, and then choose Site⇨Change Link Sitewide.**

The Change Link Sitewide dialog box appears, as shown in Figure 4-4, with the filename you selected in the Change All Links To box.

**Book II
Chapter 4**

Making Links with Text and Images

Figure 4-4:
The Change
Link
Sitewide
dialog box.

2. **In the Into Links To box, enter the new filename (or click the Browse button) and then click OK.**

The Update Files dialog box appears with a list of files that will be changed.

3. **Click the Update button to convert all those links in the site, or click the Don't Update button if you change your mind.**

Deleting links

To delete an existing link, do one of the following:

✦ Select the link text, graphic, or object and remove the link attributes from the Link field in the Properties inspector.

✦ Select the link text, graphic, or object and choose Modify⇨Remove Link.

✦ Delete the opening and closing link tag code by hand in Code view.

Using the Tag Chooser

The Tag Chooser is a special place you can go to find and insert specific tags on your page. The Tag Chooser bills itself as "A collection of Markup Language Tags." That's because, in addition to all the HTML tags, the Tag Chooser contains tags for several other markup languages: CFML, ASP, JSP, ASP.NET, PHP, and WML. You'll learn more about how to use these correctly in Books VII, VIII, and IX.

What's more, each language is housed in its own tag library folder and has its tags categorized into logical subfolders to help you find the right tag. For example, if you're looking for a tag to add an iframe, or inline frame, to your page, you'd open the HTML Tags Language folder in the Markup Language Tags folder, and search for the tag in the Page Elements category, as shown in Figure 4-5. When you select a tag in the panel on the right side of the dialog box, the Tag Info panel at the bottom of the dialog box reveals tag reference information such as syntax and tag usage.

Figure 4-5: Find and insert specific markup language tags with the Tag Chooser dialog box.

To use the Tag Chooser, follow these steps:

1. **Choose Insert⇨Tag.**

The Tag Chooser dialog box appears (refer to Figure 4-5). This dialog box provides access to all the tags in a variety of markup languages.

2. **In the left pane, select the language folder you want to use and then navigate to that folder's subcategories to find the type of tag to insert.**

Expand folders as needed to narrow the tag search.

3. **Search the right pane for the specific tag you want to insert.**

Tags in each subcategory are listed in the right pane of the dialog box, and descriptions for each tag appear in the bottom panel of the dialog box, below the Tag Info button. If you don't see the description panel, click the Tag Info button so that its arrow points downward.

4. **To insert a tag on your page, select the tag and click the Insert button, or simply double-click the tag name.**

If the tag is listed in the right pane with angle brackets surrounding it (such as `<u></u>`), the complete tag pair will be inserted in your document at the insertion point or surrounding any selected content. All other tags, however, require additional information from you.

If the tag needs more information, the Tag Editor dialog box appears. Figure 4-6 shows an example of the Tag editor set to insert properties for the `<iframe>` tag.

Figure 4-6: Enter tag details in the Tag Editor.

5. **Enter the tag and attribute details.**

The Tag Editor is context-specific, which means it displays all the property fields available for the selected tag. If you're unsure of what to add in any field, leave it blank for now because you can always edit the tag using the Properties inspector at a later time.

Book II
Chapter 4

Making Links with Text and Images

If the Tag Editor displays multiple categories, such as General, Browser Specific, and Style Sheet/Accessibility, look at those category options and add any tag attributes as desired.

6. Click OK in the Tag Editor.

The selected tag is inserted onto your page.

7. To add more tags to your page, repeat Steps 2–6. Otherwise, click the Close button to close the Tag Chooser.

Coding Links by Hand

If you happen to know the HTML markup syntax, by all means feel free to hand-code your links. Simply go right to Code view and type away. Just be sure you remember to close your link tags with the closing </a> tag. Table 4-1 shows examples of the link types.

Table 4-1	Sample Links
Link Type	*Link Example*
Hyperlink with text, including target attribute, title attribute, and link to file on same site	`<a href="about.html" target="_self" title="About Us">About Us</a>`
Hyperlink with text, including target attribute, title attribute, and full path of link	`<a href="http://www.google.com" target="_blank" title="Google">Google</a>`
Hyperlink with graphic, including target attribute, title attribute, and link to file on same site	`<a href="about.html" target="_self"><img src="images/about.gif" title="About"></a>`
Hyperlink with graphic, including target attribute, title attribute, and full path of link	`<a href="http://www.google.com" target="_blank" title="Google"><img src= "images/google.jpg"></a>`
E-mail link	`<a href="mailto:me@example.com">me@example.com</a>`
Named anchor	`<a name="anchor1" id="anchor1"></a>` (Anchor laid down at destination point) `<a href="#anchor1">Go to Anchor 1</a>` (Link to anchor at destination point)

Chapter 5: Adding Flash, Movies, Sound, and More

In This Chapter

✔ Adding Flash SWFs

✔ Adding Flash Video (FLV/F4V)

✔ Inserting Shockwave movies, Java applets, and ActiveX controls

✔ Working with Netscape Navigator plug-ins

✔ Adding other video and sound

You've probably seen Web sites that include Flash intros, MPEG videos, MP3 songs, QuickTime movies, YouTube videos, and other kinds of sound and video. Dreamweaver makes it easy to insert these media clips, as well as adjust the attributes that determine how the media appears on a Web page, and, if applicable, change how the user can interact with the media files.

This chapter shows you how to add Flash, movies, sound, and other media objects to a Web page. You also find a brief discussion about acceptable sound file formats and the differences between linking and embedding video and sounds.

Flash Elements You Can Add to Your Web Site

Your basic Flash movie uses the most common SWF (referred to as Small Web Format or Shockwave Flash) file format, but you can add other Flash elements to your Web pages. Before you begin adding them, however, you need to understand the subtle differences between the different Flash file formats:

✦ **.fla** files, or *Flash files,* are Flash movies. These are the original, editable source files for creating SWF files.

✦ **.swf** files (pronounced "swiff") are compressed, portable versions of .fla files that you can preview in Dreamweaver and play in browsers.

✦ **.swt** files are Flash template files that allow you to change information in SWF files.

✦ **.swc** files are Flash element files or special SWF files that make customizable Rich Internet applications.

✦ **.flv** files, or *Flash video files,* play movies that have encoded audio and video data that allows the free Flash player to play them. For example, a Windows Media or QuickTime video could be encoded with special software into FLV files for viewing in a Flash player. Flash's Video Encoder, which is integrated with Flash (www.adobe.com), and Sorensen Squeeze (www.sorensonmedia.com) are two recommended encoders. To discover more about the process of encoding videos, visit www.adobe.com/devnet/video/.

✦ **.f4v** files are renamed Flash MP4 files and can also play movies that have encoded audio and video data in the MPEG-4 format, which allows the free Flash player to play them. For more information about this relatively new file format, visit www.adobe.com/devnet/flv/.

To add Flash movies and Flash video to your site, you must first create the SWF and FLV (or F4V) files in Flash. Inserting FlashPaper, unfortunately, has been deprecated for CS5. To learn more about this feature for earlier versions of Dreamweaver, visit www.adobe.com/products/flashpaper/.

Flash is a great tool, but beginners should be aware that it can be misused on the Web. Before you add Flash movies to your Web site, do a little research to become aware of the benefits (animation, sound, interactivity) and drawbacks (search engines ignore Flash movies so it's not good for Search Engine Optimization (SEO), many Web visitors dislike Flash, and beginners tend to overuse it) of Flash.

Inserting Flash Movies (SWFs)

Inserting Flash movies into your Web page in Dreamweaver is a simple two-step process. Before you can insert a Flash movie in Dreamweaver, however, you must first create the movie in the Flash program and save it as an SWF file. Check out *Flash Professional CS5 & Flash Catalyst CS5 For Dummies* by Finkelstein and Leete if you need help preparing your Flash movie.

Adding a Flash movie to your page

To add a Flash movie (SWF) to a Web page, follow these steps:

1. **Place your cursor where you want the Flash movie to appear on your Web page.**

2. **Choose Insert⇨Media⇨SWF.**

You can also choose the Media: SWF option from the Media menu in the Common area of the Insert panel. The Select SWF dialog box appears.

3. **Select the Flash SWF movie file you want to insert on the page, and then click OK.**

4. **If you have enabled Accessibility options in Dreamweaver's Preferences, do the following:**

   a. **Add a title, an access (shortcut) key, and a tab index number to the SWF file in the Object Tag Accessibility Attributes dialog box that appears.**

   b. **Click OK.**

Dreamweaver embeds the SWF movie with all the Flash HTML code needed for the movie to play in most major browsers by including the `<object>` tag for Microsoft ActiveX controls, hidden comments to identify the different parts of the code, and HTML that prompts visitors using browsers with older versions of the Flash player to download the current version. The following example code shows how you would embed an SWF file called sample.swf on a page:

Book II
Chapter 5

Adding Flash, Movies, Sound, and More

```
<object classid="clsid:D27CDB6E-AE6D-11cf-96B8-444553540000" width="210"
    height="180" id="FlashID" accesskey="1" tabindex="A" title="Flash SWF
    Sample">
<param name="movie" value="sample.swf" />
<param name="quality" value="high" />
<param name="wmode" value="opaque" />
<param name="swfversion" value="6.0.65.0" />
<!-- This param tag prompts users with Flash Player 6.0 r65 and higher to
    download the latest version of Flash Player. Delete it if you don't want
    users to see the prompt. -->
<param name="expressinstall" value=". ./Scripts/expressInstall.swf" />
<!-- Next object tag is for non-IE browsers. So hide it from IE using IECC. -->
<!--[if !IE]>-->
<object type="application/x-shockwave-flash" data="sample.swf" width="210"
    height="180">
<!--<![endif]-->
<param name="quality" value="high" />
<param name="wmode" value="opaque" />
<param name="swfversion" value="6.0.65.0" />
<param name="expressinstall" value=". ./Scripts/expressInstall.swf" />
<!-- The browser displays the following alternative content for users with Flash
    Player 6.0 and older. -->
<div>
<h4>Content on this page requires a newer version of Adobe Flash Player.</h4>
<p><a href="http://www.adobe.com/go/getflashplayer"><img src="http://www.adobe.
    com/images/shared/download_buttons/get_flash_player.gif" alt="Get Adobe
    Flash player" width="112" height="33" /></a></p>
</div>
<!--[if !IE]>-->
</object>
<!--<![endif]-->
</object>
```

Dreamweaver displays the embedded Flash SWF movie on the page in Design view as a gray placeholder box with a tabbed blue outline (see Figure 5-1). The tab displays the file format (SWF), the FlashID, and an eye icon that toggles visibility between the movie and the download information that visitors without Flash installed will see in the browser window. The Document window doesn't automatically preview the Flash SWF movie, but you can preview it both inside and outside Dreamweaver.

To preview the Flash SWF movie, save your file, select the movie in Design view, and do one of the following:

+ Click the Play icon in the Properties inspector. Click the Stop icon to stop the preview.

+ Click the Live View button on the Document bar to watch the movie as you would in a browser window. Click Live View again to stop the preview.

+ Press F12 to preview the movie in a browser window.

Figure 5-1: The Flash movie appears as a gray box in Design view.

Setting Flash movie attributes

After inserting the SWF movie onto the page, select the Flash placeholder in Design view and use the Properties inspector to set the desired movie attributes. If you don't see all the movie properties, click the expander arrow in the bottom-right corner of the Properties inspector:

✦ **Flash ID:** Input the movie ID. The default name is FlashID.

✦ **Loop:** Play your SWF movie continuously in the browser. If you do not select this option, your movie plays once and then stops. *Note:* If the movie contains a loop, it will play continuously regardless of whether the Loop option is selected or deselected.

✦ **Autoplay:** Start playing the movie automatically when the page loads in a browser window. This option is on by default.

✦ **W** and **H:** Change the size by entering different values here. However, the size should automatically match the size of the movie.

✦ **V Space** and **H Space:** Set white space in pixels above and below, and on both sides of the movie. Better yet, add padding to your SWF file using CSS.

✦ **File:** Specify the path of the Flash .swf file. If you ever need to change the file displayed here, browse for and select the alternate file using the Browse to File icon or the Point to File pointer, or type the filename and path.

✦ **Src:** Specify the location of the original Flash .fla file used to create the .swf file. Browse for and select the file using the Browse to File icon or the Point to File pointer, or type the path to the desired file.

✦ **Quality:** Adjust the *anti-aliasing,* or smoothing, of the movie during playback. High settings make the movie smoother but could slow the display of the movie. By contrast, low settings load faster but look less crisp. Auto Low and High options improve appearance or emphasize quality, respectively.

✦ **Scale:** Determine how the movie fits into the pixel sizes displayed in the W and H text boxes:

   • **Default (Show all):** Display the entire movie at 100 percent.

   • **No Border:** Maintain the original movie dimension aspect ratio but fit the movie, without borders, in the sizes set in the W and H text boxes, which means that any parts of the movie that extend beyond the W and H settings are cut off.

   • **Exact Fit:** Squishes the movie into the specified dimensions, regardless of the original size of the movie.

**Book II
Chapter 5**

**Adding Flash,
Movies, Sound,
and More**

✦ **Align:** Set the alignment of the movie relative to the page.

✦ **Wmode:** Prevent conflicts with DHTML elements such as Spry widgets by setting the Wmode for the SWF file in the browser window. . Choose from any of the following:

  • **Window:** Force the SWF on top of all page elements.

  • **Opaque:** Allow DHTML elements to flow on top of the SWF; this is the default setting.

  • **Transparent:** Force DHTML elements to appear behind the SWF. This is often a problem when combining Flash with DHTML menus. If your menu falls behind the Flash movie, switch the Wmode to Opaque or Window.

✦ **Bg:** Add a background color behind the movie. This color is displayed only if the movie is not playing.

✦ **Edit:** Provide access to the source FLA file for the SWF movie when Flash is loaded on the same computer. If no Flash application is detected, this icon is disabled.

✦ **Play/Stop:** Start and stop movie previews in Design view.

✦ **Parameters:** Display a dialog box so that you can enter more parameters for the movie if the movie has been created to accept these parameters. For a complete list of Flash object and embed tag attribute parameters, visit `http://kb2.adobe.com/cps/127/tn_12701.html`.

✦ **Class:** Apply a CSS-specific class style to a movie, such as a style with borders, positioning, or alignment attributes.

Inserting Flash Video

Flash video is different from a regular Flash movie in that a Flash video uses the FLV file format and allows you to add prerecorded video to a Web page in a format that most visitors can view with the free Adobe Flash player. A Flash movie, by comparison, is more of a limited animation clip delivered on the Web using the SWF file format.

Flash videos start as captured video, which itself can be in many formats, including those produced with Avid Xpress DV, Adobe After Effects, Apple QuickTimePro, and Apple Final Cut Pro. After you capture the video, it gets encoded into the Flash Video format (FLV). You can then decide on a delivery mechanism and add the video to your Web site.

You need to acquire the video and encode it into the FLV format, or at least obtain the FLV files before adding them to your site. You can add the Flash video to your page using the Dreamweaver Insert Media FLV command. This tool enables you to add Flash video to your pages without using the Flash program, and it enables browsers to play the inserted Flash video with playback controls.

Find out more about Flash video from the Flash Learning Guide, including tips on encoding video with Flash CS5 and other programs, at www.adobe. com/devnet/flash/articles/video_guide.html.

When inserting a Flash video, you have two options for the video type: Progressive Download and Streaming. The decisions you make for inserting Flash video vary slightly depending on which type you choose:

+ **Progressive Download Video:** Download the FLV file to the user's computer and play it there. The benefit of FLV is that the video starts to play during the download.

+ **Streaming Video:** Stream the Flash video and play it in the browser window. Streaming video typically buffers for a few seconds before playback, resulting in a smoother playback. Streaming requires that the file be served by your own Flash Media Server or by a hosted server running Flash Video Streaming Services.

These types of streaming servers aren't common to most basic servers, so be sure to check with your Web host for recommendations.

To insert Flash video using the Progressive Download Video type, follow these steps:

1. **Open a document and place the insertion point where you want the Flash video to appear.**

2. **Choose Insert⇨Media⇨FLV.**

You can also click the Media menu and click the FLV icon in the Common area of the Insert panel. The Insert FLV dialog box appears, as shown in Figure 5-2.

Figure 5-2:
The Insert FLV dialog box set to Progressive Download Video.

3. **Select Progressive Download Video as the video type.**

4. **Set the following options:**

   - **URL:** Enter the relative or absolute path of the FLV file. Or click the Browse button to choose a FLV file. For absolute paths, type the complete URL including `http://`, as in `http://www.mySample Site.com/video.flv`. If you're using a Mac, you must use an absolute path when FLV files sit more than two levels up from the HTML file into which the video is inserted.

     Note: The FLV files must contain metadata to work properly as a video player. Many encoders automatically add metadata to the FLV files, but some do not.

   - **Skin:** Select an appearance for the video player from the Skin drop-down list. A preview window displays an approximation of how each option looks.

   - **Width** and **Height:** Enter a dimension in pixels for both the width and height of the FLV file. Click the Detect Size button to have Dreamweaver attempt to automatically read the FLV file dimensions; if the dimensions are unreadable, manually enter Width and Height sizes. The Total with Skin dimensions displayed after the dimensions are detected represent the total Width and Height of the FLV file plus the Width and Height of the chosen skin.

   - **Constrain:** Maintain the aspect ratio between the width and height of the FLV movie. This option is selected by default.

   - **Auto Play:** Play the video as soon as the Web page loads in the browser window.

   - **Auto Rewind:** Return the video playback to the start position when the video reaches the end.

5. **Click OK to close the dialog box and insert the Flash video on your page.**

   Along with the appropriate code for inserting the FLV file, Dreamweaver includes version detection that prompts visitors to download a newer version of the free Adobe Flash Player, if their browser's version is out of date.

   To play the FLV video in a browser, Dreamweaver automatically creates a video SWF file and a SWF skin file. These files are added to the same directory as the HTML file into which the video has been inserted. In the example shown in Figure 5-3, these files are called `Clear_Skin_1.swf` and `FLVPlayer_Progressive.swf`.

Figure 5-3:
The
Properties
inspector for
Progressive
Download
Video.

You must also upload the FLVPlayer and Clear_Skin files to your server
for the video to play properly. Dreamweaver automatically uploads
these files as dependents during the File Transfer Protocol (FTP) session
as long as you opt to upload dependent files during the upload process.

After inserting the FLV on your page, you can modify in the Properties
inspector some Flash video settings, such as Auto Play, Auto Rewind, and
the Skin (refer to Figure 5-3).

To insert Flash video using the Streaming Video type, follow these steps:

1. **Open a document and place the insertion point where you want the
Flash video to appear.**

2. **Choose Insert⇨Media⇨FLV.**

You can also click the Media menu and click the FLV icon in the
Common area of the Insert panel. The Insert FLV dialog box appears, as
shown in Figure 5-4.

3. **Select Streaming Video as the video type.**

4. **Set the following options:**

• **Server URI:** Enter the server, application, and instance names provided by your host provider, as in `rtmp://www.mySite.com/`
`application_name/instance_name`.

Figure 5-4:
The Insert
FLV dialog
box for
streaming
video.

- **Stream Name:** Enter the name of the FLV file (either with or without the .flv extension), as in video3.flv or video3.

  Note: The FLV files must contain metadata to work properly as a video player. Many encoders automatically add metadata to the FLV files, but some do not.

- **Skin:** Select an appearance for the video player in the Skin drop-down list. A preview window displays an approximation of how each option looks.

- **Width** and **Height:** Enter a dimension in pixels for both the width and height of the FLV file. Click the Detect Size button to have Dreamweaver attempt to automatically read the FLV file dimensions; if the dimensions are unreadable, manually enter Width and Height sizes. The Total with Skin dimensions displayed after the dimensions are detected represent the total Width and Height of the FLV file plus the Width and Height of the chosen skin.

- **Constrain:** Maintain the aspect ratio between the width and height of the FLV movie. This option is enabled by default.

- **Live Video Feed:** Enable this option only when the video feed is live. When live, the player plays a live video streamed from the server. The name in the Stream Name text box is the name of the live video feed. Because a viewer can't manipulate live video, only the volume control appears on the skin. Furthermore, the Auto Play and Auto Rewind options are also inoperable with live video. If prompted, choose a halo skin for live video content support.

- **Auto Play:** Begin playing the video as soon as the Web page loads in the browser window.

- **Auto Rewind:** Return video playback to the start position when the video reaches the end.

- **Buffer Time:** Enter the time it takes, in seconds, before the video begins to play in a browser. By default, the buffer is set to 0, but you can increase the number of seconds to have the player pause before the video begins to play, which may be helpful for sites that have occasional bandwidth issues when visitor traffic is high. When Auto Play is enabled, however, the buffer time is ignored.

5. **Click OK to close the dialog box and insert the Flash video on your page.**

   Along with the appropriate code for inserting the FLV file, Dreamweaver includes version detection markup that prompts visitors to download a newer version of the free Adobe Flash Player, if their browser's version is out of date.

   A video SWF file and SWF skin are also created to play the video in a browser. You must upload the SWF files to your Web server and the ASC file to the Flash Communication Server for the video to play properly. Dreamweaver automatically uploads these files as dependents when transferring files with FTP as long as you opt when prompted to upload dependent files during the upload process.

Flash videos may require different players depending on which codec the video was created with. For more information about Flash video, visit the Flash Developer Center at `www.adobe.com/devnet/flash/` and read the Flash Video with Dreamweaver tutorial by Jen deHaan at `www.adobe.com/devnet/flash/articles/flv_tutorial.html`.

Adding Shockwave Movies, Java Applets, and ActiveX Controls

In Dreamweaver, you can add Shockwave movies, Java applets, ActiveX controls, and other sound and video files to any open, saved file. If the object you want to add is not one of these types, use a Netscape Navigator plug-in instead (as described in the section "Adding Netscape Navigator Plug-ins," later in the chapter). You need to prepare these objects before inserting them on your page. Table 5-1 describes the type of objects you can add to your Web page.

Table 5-1	Media Types
Media Type	*Description*
Shockwave movie	Adobe's standard for interactive multimedia files on the Web, typically created from compressed Adobe Director files. Shockwave movies download fast and can be displayed in browsers with the appropriate free Shockwave player installed.
Java applet	Lightweight Web page applications *(applets)* generated with the Java programming language.
ActiveX control	Reusable components that behave like Netscape Navigator browser plug-ins. (ActiveX controls were formerly called OLE controls.) They run only in Windows versions of Internet Explorer. You can assign these controls additional attributes and parameters in Dreamweaver.
QuickTime movie	A movie format created with Apple's QuickTime program that can include video, audio, and other bitstreams, such as images and animations.
Non-FLV video	Any non-FLV video, such as MPEG or AVI. These movies can be linked to or embedded in your Web page. To view a particular streaming video, visitors must also typically download a special plug-in file, such as RealMedia or Windows Media.
Netscape Navigator plug-in	A plug-in, or helper application, that allows a Netscape Navigator browser to display multimedia content (audio, video, animation, virtual reality, and 3D objects) in a range of file formats. Plug-ins include RealPlayer, QuickTime, and MP3 files, among many others.

Follow these steps to insert a media object on your Web page:

1. **Choose Insert⇨Media and select the desired media type (Shockwave, Applet, ActiveX, or Plug-in).**

Or click the Media icon in the Common category of the Insert panel to select the media type from its drop-down list. The Select File dialog box appears.

2. **Browse to and select a source file, and set any parameters for the media file.**

For information on adding parameters for media files, see the nearby sidebar "Controlling media objects with parameters."

To insert a media placeholder and bypass having to select a source file or set any preferences (though the Tag Accessibility dialog box may still pop up when Accessibility features are enabled), press and hold Control (Windows) or Option (Mac) while inserting the media object. For example, to insert a placeholder for a plug-in without selecting the plug-in file, press and hold Control or Option and choose Insert⇨Media⇨Plug-in, or click the Plug-in icon in the Media drop-down list in the Common category of the Insert panel.

3. **Click OK to insert the media.**

4. **If an Accessibility Attributes dialog box appears, do the following:**

   a. **Add a title, a shortcut** *(access)* **key, and tab index options to the media file in the object's Tag Accessibility Attributes dialog box that appears.**

   b. **Click OK.**

      Or click Cancel to add the media file or placeholder without the Accessibility attributes.

Setting Shockwave movie properties

Shockwave movies, which are compressed multimedia files created with Adobe Director, are embedded in a page in a similar fashion and have the same options as Flash files. Although often confused with Flash files, they are not Flash.

To specify the properties for Shockwave movies, select the movie placeholder in Design view and apply attributes to it from the Properties inspector. See the earlier section "Setting Flash movie attributes" for a description of each property.

Setting Java applet properties

You can also add Java applets to HTML files with Dreamweaver. Java (not to be confused with JavaScript, a scripting language) is a programming language that creates *applets,* or little applications.

After inserting the Java applet on the page, select the applet placeholder in Design view and set the applet attributes in the Properties inspector (see Figure 5-5):

Figure 5-5:
Set properties for a Java applet.

✦ **Applet Name:** Enter the applet name in the text box.

✦ **W** and **H:** Set the width and height of the applet in pixels.

✦ **V Space** and **H Space:** Set white space in pixels above, below, and on both sides of the applet.

✦ **Code:** When you select the applet, this field is filled in automatically. To change the Java applet source file, click the folder icon or type a different filename.

✦ **Base:** If you selected a file in the Code field, the location or path of the applet appears in this box.

✦ **Align:** Set the alignment on the applet relative to the page.

✦ **Alt:** Set alternative content and specify a graphic file that is displayed if the user's browser doesn't support Java applets or has Java disabled. You can also insert Alternate Text instead of a graphic. When you add an image, the `<img>` tag is inserted between the opening and closing `<applet>` tags. To specify both an image and Alternate Text, insert the image first, and then add the `alt` attribute to the `<img>` tag in Code view:

```
<applet code="myapplet.class" codebase="applet/" width="32" height="32">
<img src="applet/myapplet.gif" width="100" height="50" alt="Spinning
    Counter" />
</applet>
```

✦ **Class:** Apply CSS to an applet.

✦ **Parameters:** Click the Parameters button to enter more parameters for the applet. See the upcoming sidebar "Controlling media objects with parameters" for more info about setting parameters.

If you don't see all these properties, click the expander arrow in the bottom-right corner of the Properties inspector.

Setting ActiveX control properties

ActiveX controls, formerly known as OLE controls, are mini-applications that behave like browser plug-ins and can be reused as often as you need. The ActiveX object lets you add attributes and parameters for an ActiveX control in a user's browser.

ActiveX controls run on Windows with Internet Explorer but not in IE on a Mac or in any Netscape browser, so use them with consideration.

Select the ActiveX control placeholder in Design view, and set the attributes of the `<object>` tag and the parameters of the ActiveX control in the Properties inspector (see Figure 5-6).

Figure 5-6:
Set properties for the ActiveX control.

TECHNICAL STUFF

Controlling media objects with parameters

With most media objects, the Properties inspector includes a Parameters button when you're specifying properties for that media object. Parameters are special values for Shockwave movies, Java applets, ActiveX controls, Netscape Navigator plug-ins, and Flash SWF files. These values are attached to the `<object>`, `<embed>`, and `<applet>` tags in the code, and usually set specific attributes for the type of media object being added to the page. For instance, a Shockwave movie can have a URL parameter that is part of the `<embed>` tag as in the following line of code (where `swURL` is the name and `filename.html` is the value of the parameter):

```
<embed src="swmovie.dcr" height="100"
    width="100" swURL="filename.html">
```

To find out what attributes you can add to an object, see the documentation for the media object you're inserting. Whatever parameters you do add, the process for adding them is the same.

To add parameters to media objects, follow these steps:

1. Select the media file placeholder in Design view.

2. Click the Parameters button in the Properties inspector.

The Parameters dialog box appears, as shown in the figure.

3. Enter a value for the parameter. Click the plus (+) icon to add a parameter or the minus (–) icon to remove a parameter.

4. Enter the parameter name in the Parameter column and the value in the Value column.

5. Repeat Steps 3 and 4 to add or remove parameters as needed.

6. To reorder the parameters, click the up and down arrow icons.

7. Click OK when you've finished setting parameters.

You can also view the assigned attributes of any selected media object by viewing the Attributes tab of the Tag Inspector panel. There you can add, edit, and delete attributes such as `src`, `width`, and `height`.

✦ **ActiveX:** Enter the name of the ActiveX media file in the ActiveX text box in the top-left corner of the Properties inspector. The name assists with scripting the object.

✦ **W** and **H:** Set the width and height of the object in pixels.

✦ **V Space** and **H Space:** Set white space in pixels above, below, and on both sides of the object.

✦ **ClassID:** Select a value from the drop-down list or type a value, such as RealPlayer or Shockwave for Flash. This field identifies the control to the browser. If the browser can't find the ActiveX control specified, it tries to download it from the URL listed in the Base field.

✦ **Embed:** Activate the Netscape Navigator plug-in equivalent of the ActiveX control using the `<embed>` tag within the `<object>` tag. ActiveX property values assigned in Dreamweaver are applied to their Netscape Navigator plug-in equivalents.

✦ **Src:** If you enabled the Embed option, type or browse to and select the data file for a Netscape Navigator plug-in. If you don't specify a filename, Dreamweaver attempts to find the value using the other ActiveX properties.

✦ **Base:** Identify the URL with the ActiveX control. If the control is not already installed on the user's computer, IE prompts the user to download it. Without the proper ActiveX control installed, the browser can't display the object.

✦ **ID:** Set the ID for the ActiveX control to load. If you don't have information for this parameter, leave this field blank.

✦ **Data:** Set the data file for the object to load in the browser. Some ActiveX controls, such as RealPlayer, don't use this parameter. Leave the field blank if you don't have information for this parameter.

✦ **Alt Img:** Specify a graphic file to be displayed if the user's browser doesn't support the `<object>` tag. The Embed option must be deselected to use this feature.

✦ **Align:** Set the alignment of the object relative to the page.

✦ **Play/Stop:** Start and stop ActiveX control previews in Design view.

✦ **Class:** Apply CSS to an object.

✦ **Parameters:** Enter more parameters for the ActiveX control. See the sidebar "Controlling media objects with parameters" for more info about setting parameters.

Adding Netscape Navigator Plug-ins

Typical plug-ins for Netscape Navigator (the precursor to Firefox and other non-IE browsers) include QuickTime movies, RealPlayer content, and MP3s. If you want to insert an object that is *not* a Flash, Shockwave, applet, or ActiveX object, try inserting it on your page as a Netscape Navigator plug-in. You can create your own content or get it from another source, and then use Dreamweaver to insert the file into your HTML page. To insert a Netscape Navigator plug-in, follow the steps in the earlier section "Adding Shockwave Movies, Java Applets, and ActiveX Controls" and choose the Plug-in option in Step 1.

Setting Netscape Navigator plug-in properties

After adding the Netscape Navigator plug-in object, select the plug-in place-holder in Design view and set its properties in the Properties inspector (see Figure 5-7). Here are your options:

Figure 5-7:
Set
properties
for the
plug-in.

✦ **Plug-in ID/Name:** Enter the name in the Plug-in text box in the top-left corner of the Properties inspector.

✦ **W** and **H:** Set the width and height of the plug-in object in pixels.

✦ **V space** and **H space:** Set white space in pixels above, below, and on both sides of the plug-in object.

✦ **Src:** If you selected a source file for the plug-in when you inserted it, this field is already filled in. If not, identify the source data file of the plug-in by typing the filename or click the folder icon to browse to and select the file.

✦ **Plg URL:** Specify the URL where users can download this plug-in. If the user's computer doesn't have the plug-in, the browser downloads it from this URL.

✦ **Border:** Set the width of a black border, in pixels, around the entire plug-in. When left blank or set to 0, no border appears.

✦ **Align:** Set the alignment of the object relative to the page.

✦ **Play/Stop:** Start and stop plug-in control previews in Design view.

+ **Class:** Apply CSS to an object.

+ **Parameters:** Enter more parameters for the Netscape Navigator plug-in. See the sidebar "Controlling media objects with parameters" for more info about setting parameters.

Playing Netscape Navigator plug-ins

Dreamweaver lets you preview movies and animations that use Netscape Navigator plug-ins (but not ActiveX controls) in Design view. As long as you've installed the appropriate plug-ins, you can play previews of all the plug-ins at once or play them separately.

Be sure to also test the plug-ins in as many browsers as possible to ensure that your site visitors have the most consistent experience viewing them. Choose File➪Preview in Browser➪Adobe BrowserLab to test the page in BrowserLab (you must sign in to use this service), or use the online testing site at www.browsershots.org.

Here's how to preview movies and animations with Netscape Navigator plug-ins:

+ **To preview a single movie or animation:** Select a media file inserted on the page and click the Play icon in the Properties inspector. The media file plays in Design view. Or choose View➪Plugins➪Play.

+ **To preview all the media files on a single document:** Choose View➪Plugins➪Play All. All the media files on the same page play. Alternately, you can try to preview the plug-ins by clicking the Live View button on the Document toolbar.

+ **To stop playing the media files:** Click the Stop icon in the Properties inspector. For multiple media files, you can also choose View➪Plugins➪Stop All. For Live View previews, click the Live View button again to toggle out of Live View.

If for some reason the plug-in content does not play in the Document window, try the following troubleshooting tips:

+ Be sure the plug-in is installed on the test computer and that the plug-in content is compatible with the plug-in version installed. For instance, if a movie runs with QuickTime V7, but only the QuickTime V5 player is installed, the movie won't play.

+ Open the Configuration/Plug-ins/UnsupportedPlug-ins.txt file in a text editor to see if the plug-in is listed. This file automatically adds problematic plug-ins to the list.

✦ Check the computer to see if enough memory is allocated to run the file. Many plug-ins need an extra 2MB to 5MB of memory just to run! That said, most modern operating systems don't use memory allocation, so this issue may be more applicable for Mac OS9, Windows 95, and earlier operating systems.

Acceptable Sound File Formats

Several common sound file formats are available, each with their own set of benefits and drawbacks. Here are the most common file formats:

✦ **.mp3 (Motion Picture Experts Group Audio, or MPEG-Audio Layer-3):** This sound file compresses files so they are much smaller in size. The quality is very good — even close to CD quality if recorded and compressed in the right way. One of the great things about this format is the ability to stream data so the user doesn't have to wait for the entire file to download before listening to it. Most podcasts are MP3 or ACC.

One possible drawback is the overall file size, which can get pretty big, making download times on a dialup connection seem impossible. The user's computer must have helper applications, such as iTunes, QuickTime, RealPlayer, or Windows Media Player, to play MP3 files.

✦ **.qt, .qtm, .mov, or QuickTime:** This format is great because it can contain both sound and video. Developed by Apple, QuickTime is the default sound and video player for Macintosh computers. PCs can play QuickTime files too, but the user needs to download and install the free QuickTime player first. The encoding formats supported by QuickTime include JPEG, MPEG, and Cinepak.

✦ **.ra, .ram, .rpm, or RealAudio:** Like MP3s, this format allows for streaming audio data. It also compresses files, but into even smaller file sizes than MP3s. Visitors need to download and install the RealPlayer application to play these files. That said, RealAudio is on the decline so you might want to shy away from using it.

✦ **.wav (Waveform Extension):** These files have good sound, are widely supported by browsers, and don't need any special plug-ins to play. They tend to have very large file sizes, so sound clips need to be small enough to add to Web pages. Most computers allow you to record your own WAV files in some way with a microphone.

✦ **.midi or .mid (Musical Instrument Digital Interface):** These files are intended for instrumental music only. Small files can provide long sound clips, too. The sound quality, however, is dependent on the sound card on the user's computer. Like WAV files, MIDI files are supported by most browsers and don't require special plug-ins. The biggest drawback to MIDI files is that you can't easily record them; they must be synthesized using specific software and hardware.

✦ **.aif (Audio Interchange File Format, or AIFF):** Like the WAV format, these sound files have good sound, are supported by most browsers, and don't need plug-ins to play. AIFF files can be recorded to CDs and tapes using a microphone through your computer, but because of their large file sizes, sound clips need to be small enough to add to Web pages.

If you come across another file format that you want to use on your Web page, check with the format creator's technical help files to find out about browser support.

Adding Other Video and Sound to a Page

Dreamweaver supports adding sound to a Web page. You can choose from many types of sound files and formats, such as .wav, RealPlayer, and .mp3, as described in the preceding section.

Before you decide on a format and how to add the sound to your page, consider the audience, the file size, the sound quality, and the different ways browsers support these files because different browsers handle sound files very differently. If you're trying to create a consistent experience for your visitors — regardless of their browser type — consider adding the sound to a Flash SWF file rather than having it linked to or embedded in the page. Ultimately, testing the sound and video files in multiple browsers is the best way to decide what to add and how to add it.

Linking versus embedding video

You can link or embed your prepared video files (non-Flash) in a Web page, depending on the video format and preferred method of display. That means you can set up the video to download to the user's desktop, or embed it in the page so that it streams in the browser while downloading.

Follow these steps to link or embed a short video in your page:

1. **Add the video clip to your site folder.**

Video clips often use the MPEG or AVI file format.

2. **Link or embed the clip to your page by doing one of the following:**

• **Linking:** Type the text that you want to appear on your page (such as Download Video), select that text, and in the Link field in the Properties inspector, type the video filename with extension, use the Point to File tool to point to the file in the Files panel that you want to link to, or click the Browse to File icon to browse for and select the video file.

- **Embedding:** Follow the steps in the earlier section, "Adding Shockwave Movies, Java Applets, and ActiveX Controls." Streaming video requires that the user's computer has a helper application, such as RealMedia, Windows Media, or QuickTime, for the video to play.

Be sure to upload the video file to the server along with the file it's linked to so the site visitor can download or watch the video.

Linking versus embedding sound

Linking to a sound file is the best way to add sound to a Web page because it allows users to decide for themselves whether they want to listen to the file before hearing it.

Embedding sound, by contrast, adds the sound directly into a Web page so it plays automatically, as long as the user's computer has the right plug-in and the speakers are turned on. Embedded files can play background music, for instance. Sound plug-ins often embed volume control as well as On/ Mute control.

Although both methods are possible, the more widely used practice is to embed sound in a Flash file, which avoids the need for visitors to download a bunch of different plug-ins.

Linking to a sound file

To add a link to a sound file on a Web page, follow these steps:

1. **Select the image or text that you want to use as the link to the audio file.**

2. **In the Properties inspector, type the filename in the Link text box,** use the Point to File tool to point to the file in the Files panel that you want to link to, **or click the Browse to File icon to browse for and select the audio file you want to use.**

Be sure to upload the sound file to the server along with the file it's linked to so the site visitor can access the sound file. This method makes the sound file available to the widest audience.

Embedding a sound file

To embed a sound file on a Web page, follow these steps:

1. **In Design view, place the insertion point on the page where you want to embed the file.**

2. Choose Insert➪Media➪Plugin.

Or click the Media icon in the Common category of the Insert panel and choose Plugin from its drop-down list. The Select File dialog box appears.

3. Browse to and select the sound file you want to insert.

4. Click OK to insert the sound file.

After inserting the sound object, select the sound placeholder object in Design view and enter values in the attribute fields in the Properties inspector. The W and H values, for example, determine the size of the audio controls displayed in the browser window.

Be sure to upload the sound file to the server along with the file it is embedded in so the site visitor can hear and play the sound file.

Launching a Media External Editor

Dreamweaver allows you to launch many external editors for a variety of media types if you need to edit those media files while working in Dreamweaver. For example, you can launch Fireworks to modify GIF and PNG files, Photoshop to modify JPG files, and oXygen or Altova XMLSpy to modify XML files. Launching an external editor from within Dreamweaver to edit most media types is a simple process that requires only a few steps.

First, you need to associate the media file type with the editor on your computer. To so do, follow these steps:

1. Choose Edit➪Preferences (Windows) or Dreamweaver➪Preferences (Mac) and then select the File Types/Editors category in the Preferences dialog box, as shown in Figure 5-8.

Figure 5-8:
The File Types/ Editors Preferences.

2. **Select the file extension in the Extensions panel to see any associated editors in the Editors panel.**

   For example, in Figure 5-8, the .png extension is associated with the Fireworks editor, which is also the primary editor.

3. **If needed, add or change extension types by clicking the plus (+) or minus (–) icon. To make an editor the primary editor, click the Make Primary button.**

4. **When you finish, click OK to save your changes.**

After you establish the file types and editor preferences, double-click the media file in the Files panel to start the external media editor. The primary editor associated with that media type opens.

If you'd prefer to occasionally not use the primary editor to edit the media file, right-click (Windows) or Control+click (Mac) the media file from the Files panel or from Design view and choose Open With or Edit With from the context menu.

Book II
Chapter 5

Adding Flash,
Movies, Sound,
and More

Chapter 6: Organizing Data with Tables

In This Chapter

✓ Creating tables

✓ Using table visual aids

✓ Formatting tables and table cells

✓ Adding content to table cells

✓ Importing tabular data

With the increasing popularity of CSS layout and CSS best practices, table-based Web sites are becoming less and less common. Most Web designers have switched to a CSS layout model, which is widely recognized as being more flexible than a table-based layout.

That said, tables themselves are still a great way to organize tabular data and other content, such as a listing of store locations or detailed product information, in a visually pleasing way. HTML tables can have as many rows and columns as needed, and additional tables can be nested inside other table cells ad infinitum for more complex layouts. Tables are made up of one or more rows, and each row has one or more cells. The cells make up columns, and though the columns are not explicitly defined in HTML, Dreamweaver allows you to manipulate rows, columns, and cells.

As far as styling goes, tables can have borders, background colors, background images, and be aligned relative to the page. Their individual table cells can also have similar attributes. Furthermore, table content can include text, graphics, links, movies, sound, and other plug-ins, and each of these can have their own formatting or style attributes.

This chapter guides you through the process of inserting, editing, and deleting tables as well as formatting and adding content to them. Plus we provide some general tips for using tables to improve the overall look and feel of a Web page.

Creating Tables

Although creating Web page layouts with CSS and *AP Elements*, or *layers*, is the preferred method of design these days, you can still use tables for laying out and organizing other content. It's also important to understand how tables have been used in the past for layout, because you may someday inherit a Web site built with a tables-based layout and need to convert it to layers, or at the very least edit the content in the table's cells.

To add a table to your page, simply insert the table in an open file in the Dreamweaver Document window, add content to the table cells as needed, and format the table and content inside the cells according to a predetermined design or your own personal aesthetic. For instance, you can create a table that organizes UPS second-day air shipping rates by state and number of units sold, as shown in Figure 6-1.

UPS 2nd Day Air												
2ND BUSINESS DAY												
STATE	UNITS 1	2	3	4	5	6	7	8	9	10	11	CASE
CT, NY	$12	$15	$18	$22.50	$25.50	$28	$31	$33	$34	$36.50	$38.50	$40.50
DC, NH, VA	$13	$16	$20.50	$24.50	$28	$30	$34	$37.50	$38.50	$40.50	$43	$45
NC, OH, WV	$14	$18	$23.50	$28	$32	$35.50	$41.50	$44	$46	$50.50	$52.50	$55.50
AK, GA, IL, IN, MI SC	$16	$21.50	$28	$34	$40.50	$44	$51.50	$55.50	$58	$63	$66.50	$70.50
FL, IA, LA, MN, MO, ND, WI	$18	$25.50	$35.50	$43	$52.50	$58	$68.50	$74	$78	$84.50	$91	$97.50
NE, TX	$19	$27	$36.50	$45	$55.50	$61	$72	$78	$82	$90	$96.50	$104
CA, CO, ID, NM, NV, OR, WA, WY	$21.50	$28	$38.50	$47	$56.50	$63	$74	$80	$84.50	$93	$97.50	$100

Figure 6-1: Use tables to organize content within a page.

When your table contains a lot of text, it's best to fix the width of the table cell to a readable size, usually 500 pixels wide or less. To contain text inside a fixed area of the page, insert a fixed-width table with one row and one column and paste or insert the content inside the table cell. When opened in a browser window, the text then wraps inside the cell boundaries instead of expanding and collapsing with the edges of the browser window.

In the Layout category of the Insert panel, shown in Figure 6-2, you can choose from two layout modes when working with tables:

✦ **Standard:** By default, Dreamweaver uses Standard mode, which shows tables as a grid of rows and columns.

✦ **Expanded:** For even easier editing, try using the Expanded mode, which adds temporary cell padding and cell spacing for more precise selections.

Figure 6-2:
The Layout
category of
the Insert
panel.

To switch layout modes, click the desired Layout mode button in the Layout category of the Insert panel. You can also switch modes by choosing View➪ Table Mode and then selecting a layout mode option from the submenu.

In the following sections, you find out how to insert a basic table in your Web page.

Inserting a basic table in your page

To create a basic table in Dreamweaver, follow these steps:

1. **Place your cursor where you want the table to appear on the page.**

2. **Choose Insert➪Table.**

   You can also click the Table icon on the Layout category of the Insert panel. The Table dialog box appears, as shown in Figure 6-3.

3. **Specify the following attributes for the new table:**

   • **Rows** and **Columns:** Enter the number of rows and columns for your table.

   • **Table Width:** Enter a fixed width in pixels or a percentage width between 1 and 100 percent.

   • **Border Thickness:** Enter the size, in pixels, for the table border. If left blank, the border is displayed as if it were set to 1 pixel. To remove a border, set the thickness to 0.

   • **Cell Padding:** Enter a number in pixels to increase the space between the cell's walls and its contents. If left blank, the cell padding is displayed as if it were set to 1 pixel. To remove cell padding completely, set the size to 0.

- **Cell Spacing:** Enter a number in pixels to increase the thickness of the walls of the table between the cells. If left blank, the cell spacing is displayed as if it were set to 2 pixels. To remove cell spacing completely, set the size to 0.

Figure 6-3:
Set table
options
before
adding a
table to the
page.

4. **(Optional) Choose a Header for the table.**

   The content in header rows or columns formats differently (bold and centered) than content in other table cells (regular and left aligned). In addition, screen readers identify the content in header rows or columns differently to assist visually impaired visitors in understanding the content in the table.

5. **In the Accessibility area, fill in the following fields:**

   - **Caption:** Enter a title for the table, which appears outside the table cells, directly above the first table row.

   - **Summary:** Type a description for your table. This information is added to the opening Table tag and appears hidden from view in a browser but can be read by screen readers.

6. **When you finish, click OK to create your table.**

   Dreamweaver adds the table and all the appropriate HTML table code to your page with the specified settings.

7. **Add content to your table cells.**

   You can insert text, graphics, media, and other files in a table cell — anything that can exist on a page can be placed and formatted in a table cell. For details, see the "Inserting Text and Images in Table Cells" and "Formatting Individual Table Cells" sections.

TIP

After inserting the table, you can also nest tables inside the table's individual cells. To nest a table inside a table cell, place your cursor inside the table cell and repeat Steps 2 through 7.

Turning On Table Visual Aids

Creating tables can sometimes be a tricky business, so Dreamweaver created some interesting visual aids. They help you select table cells, columns, and rows, edit the tables themselves, and view table attributes such as cell widths in pixels or percentages.

By default, the visual aids for tables should already be on; however, you can toggle them on and off by choosing View⇔Visual Aids⇔Table Widths or View⇔Visual Aids⇔Table Borders. You can also turn Visual Aids on and off through the Visual Aids menu of any open document window. Figure 6-4 shows an example of a table with and without Table Visual Aids.

**Book II
Chapter 6**

**Organizing Data
with Tables**

When you turn on Table Visual Aids, Dreamweaver presents a table header menu, which displays table widths and column widths when the table is selected or the cursor is somewhere inside the table. Next to the widths you see tiny green arrows that, when clicked, quickly access a few of the table-related commands.

Figure 6-4:
A table with
and without
visual aids
enabled.

Visual Aids

If two numbers are specified for the width dimensions, check the HTML code to ensure that the column widths add up to the total table width. For instance, one column's width may be set to 100 pixels, but after adding a long sentence or large graphic, the cell stretches to 300 pixels. The first number (100) is the HTML-specified cell width, and the number in parentheses (300) is the visual width as displayed on-screen. Fix the table dimensions in the code by clicking the table header menu and selecting Make All Widths Consistent. Then preview the page in a browser window — F12 (Windows) or Option+F12 (Mac) — to test for visual accuracy.

Formatting Tables with the Properties Inspector

After creating a table, you can set formatting options for the entire table, or for specified rows, columns, or cells in the Properties inspector.

To select a table to format it, do one of the following:

✦ Click the table's outer edge.

✦ With your cursor anywhere inside the table, click the table tag on the Tag Selector bar at the bottom of the Document window.

When a table is selected, its outer edges turn bold, selection handles appear on the right-center, bottom-center, and bottom-right corners of the table, and the Properties inspector displays table formatting options, as shown in Figure 6-5.

Table formatting attributes are optional. Use them in any combination to format tables in harmony with the data contained in them and the overall look of the Web site design. When adding formatting to a table, keep in mind that cell formatting takes precedence over row formatting, which takes precedence over table formatting. In other words, a cell with a background color displays that color in the browser even if the row or entire table has a different background color attribute.

Also keep in mind that most of the decorative table styling should be applied with CSS rather than with HTML table formatting tags. You can apply your CSS styles along with other formatting using the ID and Class fields in the Properties inspector.

The Properties inspector includes these table formatting options:

✦ **Table ID:** Input the table name. IDs are now used instead of Name attributes for easier assignment of CSS, Dreamweaver behaviors, and JavaScript events. Adding Table IDs to each of your tables is a Web-standards compliant way of coding, and it also helps you keep better track of them.

✦ **Rows** and **Cols:** Change the numbers in the Rows and Cols fields to adjust the table rows and columns accordingly (see the "Adding Rows and Columns to a Table" section).

✦ **W:** Adjust the width of the table in pixels or percentages. Widths are generally specified for tables automatically, and the overall height is determined by the contents of the table. When specifying dimensions in percentages, the width is relative to the open browser window or containing cell. For instance, W=80% (or in the code view, width="80%") means the table expands to 80 percent of the open browser window, or 80 percent of a containing cell if the table is nested within another table. If you need to set the height of a table to a specific dimension, use CSS.

✦ **Border:** Add a border to the outer edges of a table. By default, the Border field is blank. Enter any number from 0 to 750. Borders without a border color attribute appear beveled.

For better borders, create a custom CSS style. See Book III, Chapter 1 to learn more about Cascading Style Sheets.

✦ **Class:** Apply a custom style, such as a background color, border, or background image, to a table or table cell from an internal or external CSS.

Figure 6-5:
The Properties inspector shows table formatting options when a table is selected.

Selection handles

To gain further control over the look of your tables, consider adding cell padding, cell spacing, and cell alignment attributes:

✦ **CellPad:** Add uniform spacing in pixels inside all the cells in a table, padding cell contents away from the cell walls.

✦ **CellSpace:** Add uniform spacing in pixels to the walls of the cells in the table.

✦ **Align:** Determine where the table sits relative to other content on the page. The browser determines the default alignment, but most browsers have the default set to Left. To ensure that the table aligns properly, select Left, Center, or Right from the drop-down list, or better yet, use CSS to position the table within the browser.

By default, the CellPad and CellSpace fields are blank, but both apply the equivalent of 2 pixels by default. To remove the default spacing attributes, enter 0 in both fields.

Merging and Splitting Rows and Columns

Editing rows and columns in Dreamweaver is a coder's dream come true! Adobe has made splitting and merging cells so easy that you might never want to go back to hand-coding your tables (although hand-editing tables after they're built can often be faster than editing through the Properties inspector and Design view).

It's important to understand what's happening to the code when you split or merge cells. For example, when merging two cells in a row into one cell, the two cells are combined by making the first cell span across two columns, using the colspan attribute in the <td> tag:

```
<table width="300" border="1">
<tr>
<td colspan="2">Merged Cells</td>
</tr>
<tr>
<td>Bottom Left</td>
<td>Bottom Right</td>
</tr>
</table>
```

By contrast, when merging two cells in a column, those cells actually span across two rows, this time using the rowspan attribute in the <td> tag:

```
<table width="300" border="1">
<tr>
<td rowspan="2">Merged Cells</td>
<td>Right Top</td>
</tr>
<tr>
```

```
<td>Right Bottom</td>
</tr>
</table>
```

Figure 6-6 shows examples of what a merged row and a merged column look like in Design view, compared to normal tables with no merged cells.

Seems simple enough, but this process can get confusing the more complex your tables get. Imagine having to figure it out and code it by hand! Thankfully, Dreamweaver handles all this merging and splitting with ease — in fact, Dreamweaver makes everything about designing Web sites a breeze by giving you the option of working in either Code or Design view. The following sections explore ways to split and merge cells as well as add rows and columns.

You can merge or split any number of cells using icons on the Properties inspector. For instance, you may want to select all the cells in a particular row and merge them into one wide cell, or take one cell somewhere in the table and split it into three cells.

If you forget which icon is which (merge or split) in the Properties inspector, hover your cursor over the icon to read the tool tip description. Merge says *Merges selected cells using spans* and Split says *Splits cell into rows or columns.* The merge icon has two boxes that look like they are being combined or pushed together, whereas the split icon has two boxes being pushed away or separated from one another.

Book II
Chapter 6

Organizing Data
with Tables

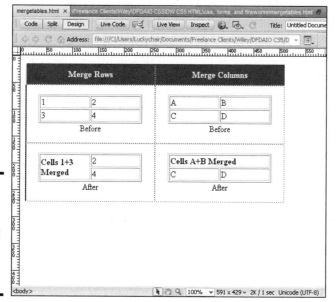

Figure 6-6:
Before and after views of a merged row and a merged column.

Merging cells

To perform a merge, follow these steps:

1. **Select the cells that you want to combine by clicking and dragging across several cells.**

   For the merge to work, selected cells must be *contiguous,* or touching, as well as evenly matched horizontally and vertically (in the shape of a rectangle). If the selection is unbalanced in some way, the Merge icon is dimmed. As long as the merge icon is active, the merge can take place with the selection.

2. **Click the Merges Selected Cells Using Spans icon in the lower-left corner of the Properties inspector.**

   Dreamweaver merges the selected cells into a single cell.

To remove a merge, place your cursor inside a single cell and do one of the following:

   ✦ Choose Modify➪Table➪Decrease Row Span to split the selected cell.

   ✦ Choose Modify➪Table➪Decrease Column Span to split the selected cell.

Splitting a cell

To split a cell, follow these steps:

1. **Place the cursor inside the cell you want to split.**

2. **Click the Splits Cell Into Rows or Columns icon in the Properties inspector.**

   You can also choose Modify➪Table➪Split Cell. The Split Cell dialog box appears, shown in Figure 6-7.

Figure 6-7: The Split Cell dialog box.

3. **Select Rows or Columns as the Split Cell Into type and enter a number for the split in the Number Of field.**

4. **When you're finished, click OK.**

   Dreamweaver splits the cell.

Setting Table Width and Heights

When first creating a table, the overall size of the table is determined by the pixels or percentages settings in the width (W) field. Both pixels and percentage settings split cells and rows evenly but without adding exact pixel dimensions into the W field for each row or column. The reason for this is that most table cells use their contents to determine their size. However, sometimes you need to fix a table, table row, table column, or table cell's dimensions. To do so, select an entire row or column, or place your cursor inside any cell to modify the dimensions of the cells, and then enter width attributes in pixels or percentages in the Properties inspector.

Alternately, you can specify the exact width and height of a table, table row, column, or cell using Cascading Style Sheets.

Take care when manually entering W cell sizes to your cells because if the math doesn't add up right, the table may not be displayed accurately in a browser window. Therefore, be sure each row or column adds up to 100 percent or the total amount of pixels specified for the table. For example, in a table with two columns that is 200 pixels wide, check to see that the total cell width equals 200 (100 pixels wide each). Unequal columns can be any size as long as they equal 200, as in the following code, where 85 is the width for the first column and 115 is the width for the second column:

```
<table width="200" border="1" cellpadding="5">
<tr>
<td width="85" rowspan="2">Coffee</td>
<td width="115">Regular</td>
</tr>
<tr>
<td>Decaffeinated</td>
</tr>
</table>
```

Adding Rows and Columns to a Table

There are several was to add rows and columns to an existing table in Dreamweaver, so feel free to use the method that works best for you.

Adding a row

To quickly add a row to a table, do the following:

✦ To **add a row above** a certain row, place your cursor inside a cell and choose Insert➪Table Objects➪Insert Row Above. You can insert a row above a selected cell also by clicking the Insert Row Above icon in the Layout category of the Insert panel.

✦ To **add a row below** a certain row, place your cursor inside a cell and choose Insert⇨Table Objects⇨Insert Row Below. You can insert a row below a selected cell also by clicking the Insert Row Below icon in the Layout category of the Insert panel.

Adding a column

To quickly add a column to a table, do the following:

✦ To **add a column to the left** of a certain column, place your cursor inside a cell and choose Insert⇨Table Objects⇨Insert Column to the Left. You can insert a column to the left of a selected cell also by clicking the Insert Column to the Left icon in the Layout category of the Insert panel.

✦ To **add a column to the right** of a certain column, place your cursor inside a cell and choose Insert⇨Table Objects⇨Insert Column to the Right. You can insert a column to the right of a selected cell also by clicking the Insert Column to the Right icon in the Layout category of the Insert panel.

Adding multiple rows or columns

When adding columns, the rightmost column is duplicated and added to the right edge of the table. When adding rows, the bottom row is duplicated and added to the bottom of the table. With this method, the arrangement of the cells is duplicated but the contents are not.

To add multiple rows or columns, place your cursor inside the cell next to where you want to add the rows or columns, and follow these steps:

1. **Choose Modify⇨Table⇨Insert Rows or Columns.**

The Insert Rows or Columns dialog box appears, shown in Figure 6-8.

Figure 6-8:
The Insert
Rows or
Columns
dialog box.

2. **Select either the Rows or Columns option icon, and then enter the number of rows or columns that you want to insert.**

3. **Select one of the following options: Above the Selection, Below the Selection, Before Current Column, or After Current Column.**

4. **Click OK.**

   Dreamweaver inserts the specified number of rows or columns into your table.

Deleting rows and columns

Delete rows and columns quickly with any of these methods:

+ Place your cursor inside a cell of the row or column to be deleted and choose Modify➪Table➪Delete Column or Delete Row.

+ Select an entire row or column and press Ctrl+X (Windows) or ⌘+X (Mac), or choose Edit➪Cut.

+ Select an entire row or column and click the Delete or Backspace key.

Inserting Text and Images in Table Cells

Add text and graphics to table cells just as you'd add them to a page. Click inside the cell and begin typing to add text, or use the Insert panel to add an image (see Book II, Chapter 3). Insert other media to table cells in the same way by browsing for and selecting the media that you want to insert.

You can also paste contents from other sources — such as a word processing document — into a cell. Apply text and graphics formatting attributes with the Properties inspector or with the help of CSS. (See Book III, Chapter 1 for more on CSS.)

Formatting Individual Table Cells

In addition to standard text formatting options, the cells themselves can have specific formatting attributes, which are slightly different from formatting options for an entire table. If you don't see cell formatting options in the Properties inspector, click the down expander arrow in the bottom-right corner to reveal the cell's formatting area.

As with table formatting, we recommend that you use CSS for styling rather than HTML formatting. Nonetheless, it's important that you know some HTML formatting options, in case you inherit an older site that uses them. Format several cells at once or one at a time depending on your needs using any of these formatting options in the Properties inspector (see Figure 6-9):

Figure 6-9:
Set cell
properties.

+ **Horz** and **Vert:** Set the Horizontal and Vertical alignment options for any cell, row, or column. The default horizontal alignment is Left for regular cells and Center for header cells. Horizontal alignment options include Left, Center, and Right. Vertical alignment options include Top, Middle, Bottom, and Baseline. Both dimensions also have a Default option, which aligns the contents of the cells left and center.

+ **W** and **H:** Set the width and height for an entire selection. Enter dimensions in pixels or percentages. Or, for more control, use CSS to set the dimensions of individual cells.

+ **No Wrap:** Force text or other content in a cell to not wrap, thereby pushing out the cell walls and adjusting the cell sizes if the content extends beyond the cell's specified size. Use this feature for addresses or other information that needs to be on one line.

+ **Header:** Turn any regular cell into a header cell; the <td> tag is converted into a <th> tag. Table headers have preset formatting attributes (bold and centered) to help set their content apart from the rest of the content in the table. Headers are typically used only on the top row or left column of a table.

+ **Bg:** Set the background color of a cell or set of selected cells. Background cell colors sit on top of, or *hide,* a table background color. To specify a background color, click the color picker icon and select a color or enter in the Bg Color field the hexadecimal number preceded with a **#** (number sign), such as #FF3300. If you forget to add the **#** before the hex value, the color may not appear in certain browsers. Alternately, you can use CSS to style your cells with background colors, borders, and images.

+ **Page Properties:** Open the Page Properties dialog box, where you can set HTML and CSS properties for this page only. If you'd prefer to set these attributes for an entire site, use the CSS panel. To find out more about working with CSS turn to Book III, Chapter 1.

Changing Table Measurements from Pixels to Percentages

Another great feature Dreamweaver provides when working with tables is the ability to convert a table's measurements from pixels to percentages, and vice versa. This is especially useful when you want the flexibility of adjusting a table with percentages but need to convert to fixed pixel widths before publishing.

To change table measurements from pixels to percentages (or vice versa), select the entire table and choose a conversion option from the submenu when you select Modify⇨Table. Or, for even faster conversions, use the table property conversion icons located in the Properties inspector, as shown in Figure 6-10.

Covert Table to Pixels

Clear Column Widths │ Convert Table Width to Percent

Figure 6-10:
The table
property
conversion
icons.

Clear Row Heights

A description of each is provided in the following list:

✦ **Clear Column Widths:** Remove any width attributes from column cells in the entire table.

✦ **Convert Table Widths to Pixels:** Convert all table widths from percentages to fixed pixels.

✦ **Convert Table Widths to Percent:** Convert all table widths from fixed pixels to percentages.

✦ **Clear Row Heights:** Remove any width attributes from row cells in the entire table.

✦ **Convert Table Heights to Pixels:** Convert all table heights from percentages to fixed pixels.

✦ **Convert Table Heights to Percent:** Convert all table heights from fixed pixels to percentages.

Importing Tabular Data

Dreamweaver can swiftly import tabular data saved as tab-delimited .txt files and convert it to HTML tables. This is great news to anyone who has ever tried to paste table data from Microsoft Excel or Access into an HTML page. Windows users can import Excel files directly into Dreamweaver (choose File⇨Import⇨Excel Document) or import tabular data as described next.

Mac users, however, can't import Excel files into Dreamweaver, and must therefore (for now) use the Import Tabular Data command.

To insert tabular data, choose File⇨Import⇨Tabular Data. The Import Tabular Data dialog box appears, and you can enter the filename of the tab-delimited data file, set the delimiter type, and perform other table formatting. Turn to Book II, Chapter 1 for more info about importing tables.

Sorting Information in a Table

Another great Dreamweaver table tool is the Sort Table command. Although normally you'd sort your data before inputting it in a table in Dreamweaver, you may want to improve the order of the information in your table after populating the table cells. Use this sort command to sort your alphabetical or numerical table data in an ascending or descending order, such as alphabetizing a list of client names or store addresses, or ordering a list of items by their unique ID numbers.

Because Dreamweaver can sort data only along a single column of data and the sorting command physically changes the order of the content in your tables, this feature does not work on tables with colspan or rowspan attributes. Therefore, you should perform this task before you merge or split any cells in your table.

With the table filled with your data selected, follow these steps to sort the information in the table:

***1.* Choose Commands⇨Sort Table.**

The Sort Table dialog box appears, as shown in Figure 6-11.

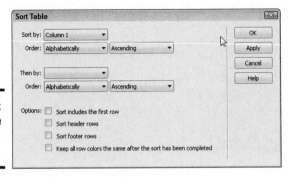

Figure 6-11:
Select table sorting options.

2. **In the Sort By drop-down list, select which column you want to sort by.**

For example, if your table has two columns, select either Column 1 or Column 2.

3. **In the two Order drop-down lists, choose whether you want to sort the column alphabetically or numerically and in ascending (A to Z or 1 to 100) or descending (Z to A or 100 to 1) order.**

To alphabetize a list from A to Z, select Alphabetically and Ascending.

4. **In the Then By list, choose another column number for a secondary sort, or leave the field blank.**

This option offers a second level of organization for your sort. For example, you may want to sort a list of names by last name and then by first name.

5. **In the Options area, further refine your results:**

   - **Sort Includes the First Row:** Select this option if your table doesn't include headings, so the first row of data gets included in the sort. If your table does include headings, leave this option deselected.

   - **Sort Header Rows:** This option sorts all the rows in the table's thead, separate from the sorting of the data in the rest of the table. To find out about the <thead> tag, open the Reference panel by choosing Help⇨Reference.

   - **Sort Footer Rows:** This option sorts all the rows in the table's tfoot, separate from the sorting of the data in the rest of the table. To find out about the <tfoot> tag, open the Reference panel by choosing Help⇨Reference.

   - **Keep All Row Colors the Same After the Sort Has Been Completed:** Select this option to have any row attributes stay with the data after the sort. This option doesn't work well with tables formatted with alternating row colors; rather, this feature is best for tables that have row attributes specific to the content in each row.

6. **To see the sorting results before committing to them, click the Apply button. If you're satisfied with the result, click OK. Or to exit without sorting, click Cancel.**

If you are happy with the new ordering, save the changes to the table.

If you want to immediately revert the table contents to the order the table was in before the sort command, choose Edit⇨Undo Sort Table.

Working with Tables Created by Other Programs

If you want to harness the power of another program to do much of the table organization for you — especially with regard to graphics — several Web optimization programs can help you convert your graphic layouts from flattened artwork or layered files to a tables-based or CSS-layers-based HTML file with sliced graphic images in each table cell or layer. Most notable are Adobe Fireworks and the built-in Save for Web & Devices dialog box in Photoshop and Illustrator, but other programs do essentially the same thing.

Several Web services, such as MarkUpNow.com and psd2html.com for a modest fee, gladly convert your flat artwork into standards-compliant, cross-browser-compatible, valid page layouts complete with optimized graphics, XHTML, CSS, and sometimes JavaScript!

When using an optimization program yourself, you'll probably cut the graphic into smaller pieces, or *slices,* which in turn are converted into individual GIF, PNG, or JPEG files upon optimization. Many of these programs also allow you to add to the slices JavaScript behaviors including rollover button behavior, animation, and graphical styles or effects. After all these extras have been applied to the slices in the optimization program, all the slices (or selected slices) can be optimized and converted to HTML and CSS-ready files. Typical options for exporting optimized graphics from an optimization program include HTML and Images, Images only, CSS Layers, and HTML only. After the optimization process is complete, you can bring the HTML files and graphics into Dreamweaver for further editing.

For HTML files generated in Fireworks, Photoshop, or Illustrator, which typically include an index.html page and an attending images folder, move or copy these files to a logical location on your local computer.

After the exported files are in the appropriate folder on your computer, define (manage) a new Dreamweaver site, as described in Book I, Chapter 3. Taking this step is essential to ensuring that you have access to all managed-site tools in Dreamweaver. From within the managed site, open the individual Fireworks-, Photoshop-, or Illustrator-generated HTML files and apply further formatting, links, and so on.

Using Fireworks-generated HTML is slightly different and more sophisticated than using other optimization programs. For more about Fireworks HTML and how to use it in Dreamweaver, see Book III, Chapter 5.

Chapter 7: Building Fabulous Forms

In This Chapter

✔ **Constructing a Web form**

✔ **Adding fields to your form**

✔ **Performing form validation with JavaScript**

✔ **Performing form validation with Spry Assets**

*F*orms are great tools for collecting information from site visitors. Forms allow users to request information, send comments and questions, sign up for services or newsletters, fill out an online application, or enter payment information for purchasing products or services.

Before building a form for your Web page, spend some time figuring out what specific data you need to collect and consider how to organize that data logically so your form is easy to understand and navigate. As a best practice, try to keep the form as brief as possible and only request information that you really need. Otherwise, you risk people leaving the page and searching elsewhere.

Forms, by default, are not secure documents. If you need your forms to be secure—a must if you're collecting confidential personal information such as a credit card or password—speak to your host provider about purchasing an SSL (Secure Sockets Layer) digital security certificate of some kind. SSL encrypts data and provides secure connections for e-commerce and communication so your site visitors can feel confident that their personal information is protected and safe. VeriSign (www.verisign.com), GeoTrust (www.geotrust.com), and Thawte (www.thawte.com) are the most popular SSL encryption certificates.

Other options are using a third-party online credit card processing service, such as PayPal, GoogleCheckout, or Authorize.net, or using an online shopping cart service such as Americart.com, which, for a minimal transaction fee, takes on the risks of liability that comes with credit card processing.

You can do many other things to make your forms secure, such as creating a secure login script, using cookies, and creating XForms with XML, but those topics falls beyond the scope of this book. To find out more about Web security in general, visit the VeriSign, GeoTrust, and Thawte Web sites. For more on XForms, visit the W3C (`www.w3.org/TR/xforms`) and W3Schools (`www.w3schools.com/xforms/default.asp`) Web sites.

In this chapter, you find out how to create fabulous HTML forms, validate them with JavaScript and Spry assets, and submit them to your server for processing.

Organizing Data in Your Form

Although you can't nest forms inside other forms, you can have multiple forms on a single page, if needed. To organize your form data, use tables, line breaks, paragraph breaks, and CSS formatting, just as you would anywhere else on the page.

One of the best ways to organize your form is to use a table. (See Book II, Chapter 6 for the lowdown on creating tables.) Although you can build your form in any order, it's often easier to add all your form labels first before adding form fields. For instance, in a two-column, multirow table, enter form labels for first and last name, address, city, state, ZIP, phone, e-mail, and so on down the left column of cells, and then add all the matching form fields down the right column. By labeling all the form fields, the users will know what information to provide. Figure 7-1 shows a simple form requesting billing information to make a purchase.

For more complex data collection needs, your form may need a more intricate layout, so feel free to nest tables within tables to further help with organization. For instance, you may have a section of the form that describes an event as well as listing the event's location and date. If the data needs to be broken up into categories, it may benefit from being organized inside a nested table.

Check box   Text fields

Book II
Chapter 7

Figure 7-1:
A sample
form
requesting
billing
information.

Building
Fabulous Forms

Radio buttons   Drop-down lists

Creating a Fabulous HTML Form

This section describes how to create an HTML form. If you want to use Dreamweaver to make dynamic Web forms, turn to Book VIII, Chapter 4 for more information.

When creating a form, you start by adding the <form> tag to an open document. If you forget the <form> tag, Dreamweaver prompts you to add it when you insert your first form field. Nevertheless, inserting the <form> tag yourself before you build your form is a good habit to get into.

When a visitor enters information in your form and clicks the Submit button, the data needs to go somewhere for processing. In most cases, that somewhere is a server-side script or program; check with your host provider about what their Web server can handle so you choose the correct scripting language. Forms are often processed with ASP, PHP, CGI, or ColdFusion scripts. The script or program then processes the data and responds by returning information to the user, performing an action based on the form's instruction (such as sending the user to a Thank You page), or sending an e-mail directly to a specified e-mail recipient. Host providers often have a form processing method available as part of your hosting package, so be sure to check with your host provider for details and instructions.

To create a form and link it to a script, follow these steps:

1. **Place the cursor where you want the form to appear on the page.**

2. **Choose Insert➪Form➪Form.**

You can also click the Form icon (it looks like a little square with a dotted red outline) in the Forms category of the Insert panel.

In Design view, the <form> tag appears on your page as a dotted red line in the shape of a large rectangle. In Code view, the inserted form tag looks like this:

```
<form id="form1" name="form1" method="post" action=""></form>
```

If you don't see the dotted red line, which Dreamweaver considers an *invisible element* that appears in Design view but doesn't show up in the browser, choose View➪Visual Aids and check that invisible elements are selected.

After you insert the <form> tag, the Properties inspector displays the form formatting options, as shown in Figure 7-2.

3. **Give your form a unique name by typing it in the Form ID text box in the Properties inspector.**

Names are important if you plan to add JavaScript or VBScript to control the form in some way. If you forget to name the form, or don't need to add scripting, Dreamweaver uses the form*n* syntax to name your forms, where *n* is equal to the number of each form that is added to a page, such as id=form2.

Book II
Chapter 7

Building
Fabulous Forms

Figure 7-2:
Add form
processing
details to
your form
tag with the
Properties
inspector.

4. **In the Action field, click the Browse to Folder icon to browse to and select the script, program, or file that will process the collected data in the form.**

   If the script is on the server, type the path to that script. For example, many forms use CGI or Perl scripts located in a CGI-BIN folder on the server, such as the following script, where the name email.pl should be replaced with your script filename:

   ```
   <form id="form1" name="form1" method="post" action="cgi-bin/email.pl">
       </form>
   ```

   The CGI script is something that your host provider or system administrator provides you.

5. **Select a method for transmitting collected form data to the server from the Method drop-down list:**

   • **Default:** Use the browser's default setting to send the data. Because the default is usually—but not always—the GET method, it's better to specify GET or POST rather than using the default.

   • **GET:** Add the value of the collected data to the URL requesting the page, making this URL bookmarkable, and therefore vulnerable to hackers. Also, because URLs can have a maximum of only 8192 characters, this method is not useful for long forms. GET is best for repeatable, stateless form applications.

- **POST:** Hide the form data inside the HTTP request, preventing the collected data page from being bookmarked. The data, however, is not encrypted (it's also vulnerable to hackers), so be sure to use a secure connection to a secure server, especially if you're collecting personal information such as credit cards, usernames, and passwords.

6. **(Optional) In the Enctype drop-down list, select the MIME encoding type of the data being sent to the server.**

   By default, this field is blank. Select `application/x-www-form-urlencode` as the default type for the `POST` method, or select the `multipart/form-data MIME` type when adding a file-upload field to a form. If you're unsure about what to select here, leave the field blank and check with your host provider or system administrator for assistance.

7. **Set the target browser location for any returned data or documents in the Target drop-down list:**

   - **_blank:** Display the returned document or data in a new browser window.

   - **_new:** Similar to _blank, display the returned data in a new browser window. However, because this is not really a valid target for the `<a href>` tag, we recommend that you use _blank instead.

   - **_parent:** Use the parent window of the current file.

   - **_self:** Display the returned data in the same window.

   - **_top:** Use the current open window even if other windows are open.

You have now completed the preliminary steps for adding a form to your page. The dotted red line marks the boundaries of your form. Within this border, you can add *form objects,* such as text fields, check boxes, radio buttons, lists, and menus, as described in the next section. If you plan to organize your form objects inside a table, now is the time to add the table to your page. (See Book II, Chapter 6 for details on creating tables.)

Adding and Labeling Form Fields

Dreamweaver calls all the form input fields *form objects*. These are what you use to collect data from the site visitor. The following sections describe adding each type of form object to your form and customizing it with its respective property setting options.

Text fields

Use text fields to collect text or numerical data, such as a name, an address, a telephone number, an e-mail address, or a password.

Inserting a text field

To insert a text field in your page, follow these steps:

1. **Place your cursor in the form area on your page where you want to insert a text field.**

For example, if you've already inserted form tags and created a table inside the form tags with labels to indicate the data you will be collecting in the form, place your cursor in the table cell (next to the cell containing the first form label) where you intend to insert the first text field. If you haven't yet inserted a form tag, see the earlier section, "Creating a Fabulous HTML Form."

2. **Choose Insert⇨Form⇨Text Field.**

You can also click the Text Field icon in the Forms category of the Insert panel. If form accessibility preferences are turned on in Dreamweaver's Preferences, the Input Tag Accessibility Attributes dialog box appears, prompting you to enter accessibility attributes to the form field. Complete the dialog box and click OK to insert the image or click Cancel to insert the field without accessibility attributes.

3. **In the TextField box in the Properties inspector, enter an ID for the text box you just inserted.**

All text fields need a unique name/ID for the form to work properly. Names can contain numbers and letters as well as the underscore character but can't include any spaces or special characters. Figure 7-3 shows an example of a form layout including the form tag (red dotted outline), form labels (Name, Address, Phone, and so on), and form fields to collect data. The Properties inspector displays the properties for the Address field, as shown in Figure 7-3.

This text field name is the variable that stores the value of the field (which is the data the user inputs) and is sent to the server for processing. For example, a text field with the name `Address` and corresponding input by a user of `123 Main St.` may be returned to you as `Address=123 Main St.`

4. **In the Type area, indicate whether you want the text field to be a single-line, multiline, or password field:**

- **Single Line:** This option uses the `<input>` tag with the `type=text` attribute.

- **Multi Line:** This option creates multiline text input fields. Multiline fields use the `<textarea>` tag with the `cols` attribute for character width and the `rows` attribute for number of lines.

- **Password:** This option, which uses the `<input>` tag with the `type=password` attribute, makes asterisks or bullets appear instead of the characters when typing in the form field in a browser. The data, however, is not encrypted. To provide encryption, talk to your host provider about buying an SSL certificate.

Figure 7-3:
Add properties to selected form fields with the Properties inspector.

Figure 7-4 shows examples of the three types of text fields.

Figure 7-4:
Types of text fields.

5. **In the Char Width box, enter the maximum number of characters that you want displayed in the text field.**

   This determines the width of the text input field. Additional characters may be accepted, but not displayed, depending on the value you enter in the Max Chars field. Controlling the width of an input field with CSS is better than inputting a number here in the HTML code because different browsers interpret this attribute in different ways.

6. **In the Max Chars field, enter the maximum number of characters that can be entered into the text field.**

   This is especially useful for limiting phone numbers to ten digits, ZIP codes to five digits, or other data that requires a limited number of characters. If a visitor enters more characters than defined by this field, the browser tells the visitor's computer to make an alert sound.

7. **In the Num Lines box (for multiline only), the height is determined by the number of lines entered here.**

   For example, enter 4 for a multiline text field that is four lines high.

8. **(Optional) In the Init Val box, enter text that should appear in the form object when the page loads.**

   This text can then be replaced with information from the user.

9. **(Optional) In the Class drop-down list, select a CSS style to apply to the form object.**

   For example, you may have created a custom CSS for all your text input fields. Choose the style from the menu to apply it.

10. **(Optional) Select the Disable option, or the Read-Only option, or both.**

    The Disabled option disables the text field. The Read-Only option makes the text field a read-only text area.

Inserting a text area

A text area object is exactly the same as a text field object set to multiline, only you don't need to set the Multi-line type in the Properties inspector yourself. Like the text field object, the text area object has fields for you to specify the character width and number of lines as well as entering any initial value text to appear in the field when the page loads and setting the wrap preferences, as described in the preceding section.

Hidden fields

For times when you need to hide information from the site visitor while providing information about the form to the server during form processing, or for when you want to store information entered by a user, add hidden fields to your form. For example, you can use a hidden field to specify an e-mail address or a subject with an input name and value, such as the following:

```
<input name="recipient" type="hidden" id="recipient" value="contact@example.com">
<input name="subject" type="hidden" id="subject" value="usercomments">
```

To insert a hidden field in your form, open your document and follow these steps:

1. **Place your cursor in the form area on your page where you want to insert a hidden field.**

   Hidden fields are typically placed right after the opening `<form>` tag. If you haven't yet created a form, see the earlier section, "Creating a Fabulous HTML Form."

2. **Choose Insert⇨Form⇨Hidden Field.**

   You can also click the Hidden Field icon in the Forms category of the Insert panel. The Properties inspector, shown in Figure 7-5, shows the properties for the hidden field.

3. **In the HiddenField box in the Properties inspector, enter an ID for the field.**

   The ID labels the hidden field, such as Redirect, Recipient, Subject, or Title.

4. **In the Value field, enter a sentence, an e-mail address, a URL, or other information.**

   The following are examples of hidden fields, including type, name, and value:

```
<input type="hidden" name="Redirect" id="Redirect" value="http://www.
    example.com/thankyou.html">
<input type="hidden" name="Recipient" id="Recipient" value="info@example.
    com">
<input type="hidden" name="Subject" id="Subject" value="Brochure
    Request">
```

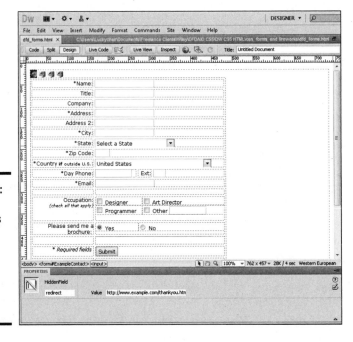

Figure 7-5: Use the Properties inspector to set the name and value of hidden fields.

Check boxes

Check box fields allow users to specify multiple responses when presented with a single question. You can add as many check boxes to the form as you want to support the question being asked. Figure 7-6 shows an example with four check boxes.

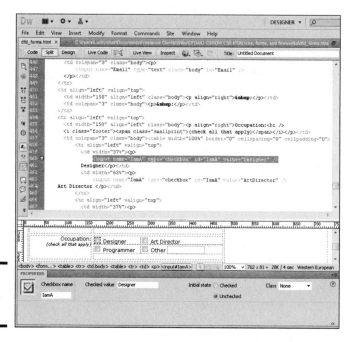

Figure 7-6:
Four check
boxes.

To insert a check box in your form, follow these steps:

1. **Place your cursor in the form area on your page where you want to insert a check box.**

   If you haven't yet created a form, see the earlier section, "Creating a Fabulous HTML Form."

2. **Choose Insert⇨Form⇨Checkbox.**

   You can also click the Checkbox icon in the Forms category of the Insert panel. The Input Tag Accessibility Attributes dialog box appears.

3. **Enter the appropriate accessibility attributes, and then click OK to proceed.**

4. **In the Properties inspector, enter a name for the check box in the Checkbox Name field and a value in the Checked Value field.**

When listing multiple questions with check boxes on a form, be sure to give each check box a unique ID to identify it within the form. The ID must not contain spaces or special characters, but the checked value can contain letters, numbers, and spaces, as in the following:

```
<input name="chkGrapes" type="checkbox" id="chkGrapes" value="Likes
    grapes" checked="checked"> Grapes
<input name="chkBanana" type="checkbox" id="chkBanana" value="Likes
    bananas" checked="checked"> Bananas
<input name="chkApple" type="checkbox" id="chkApple" value="Likes
    apples"> Apples
```

5. **Select the initial state of the check box to be either checked or unchecked, and if needed apply a CSS style from the Class menu to style the field.**

6. **Repeat Steps 2–5 to insert additional check boxes.**

Another way of adding check boxes to your forms is to use the Checkbox Group icon, which launches a dialog box to build an entire check box group rather than making buttons one at a time. All the same rules apply to check box groups as to check box buttons, with the benefit of having Dreamweaver write `<label>` tags for you to identify the text associated with each check box button. When you launch the Checkbox Group dialog box, simply enter labels and values for each button, name the group, and select a layout type.

To insert a check box group in your form, follow these steps:

1. **Place your cursor in the form area on your page where you want to insert a check box group.**

   If you haven't yet created a form, see the earlier section, "Creating a Fabulous HTML Form."

2. **Choose Insert➪Form➪Checkbox Group.**

   You can also click the Checkbox Group icon in the Forms category of the Insert panel. The Checkbox Group dialog box appears, as shown in Figure 7-7.

Figure 7-7:
The Checkbox Group dialog box lets you quickly build and insert check box groups.

3. **In the Checkbox Group dialog box, enter a name for the Checkbox button Group in the Name field.**

   The group name identifies all the buttons as belonging to the same group and adds the same name and id attribute (such as name="magazines" id="magazines") to each button.

4. **In the Label column, type a label for each check box button in the group.**

   Each item in the list represents a button in the check box group. To add new buttons, click the plus (+) icon. To remove any buttons, select the item to be removed from the list and click the minus (–) icon.

   To reorder the buttons listed in the group, select a button from the list and click the up or down arrows.

5. **In the Value column, type a checked value for each check box button in the group.**

   The checked value represents the value that is submitted as the selected choice for this radio group, such as a particular magazine.

6. **Choose Line Breaks or Table as the layout option for the check-box group.**

   The check box buttons that are inserted onto your page can be separated by line breaks or by table cells.

7. **Click OK to insert the check box group on the page.**

8. **Select one (or more) of the buttons in the group to be checked by default by entering the initial state as checked in the Properties inspector.**

   Use the Properties inspector to make further adjustments to the check box buttons in the group.

Radio buttons

Radio button fields allow users to specify either-or choices when presented with a question. You can have as many radio buttons as you want for any question, but the user can select only one answer.

Inserting radio buttons one at a time

To insert a radio button in your form, follow these steps:

1. **Place your cursor in the form area on your page where you want to insert a radio button.**

   If you haven't yet created a form, see the earlier section, "Creating a Fabulous HTML Form."

Book II
Chapter 7

Building
Fabulous Forms

2. **Choose Insert⇨Form⇨Radio Button.**

   You can also click the Radio Button icon in the Forms category of the Insert panel. The Input Tag Accessibility Attributes dialog box appears.

3. **Enter the appropriate accessibility attributes, and then click OK.**

4. **Select the radio button then, in the Properties inspector, enter a name for the radio button in the Radio Button field and enter a value in the Checked Value field.**

   A group of radio buttons must have the same name but different values to make the selection mutually exclusive. Therefore, provide the same ID to each radio button in your list and add a word in the Checked Value field to match the question being asked. You should also set one of the radio button's initial state value to checked. For instance, if asking people to choose their preference for chicken, beef, or vegetarian, the name for each radio button would be meal and the value for each is equal to the individual meal choice; if they fail to make a selection on their own, they'll get chicken. Here is the code:

   ```
   <input type="radio" name="meal" id="meal" value="chicken"
       checked="checked">
   <input type="radio" name="meal" id="meal" value="beef">
   <input type="radio" name="meal" id="meal" value="vegetarian">
   ```

   Figure 7-8 shows how to configure the radio buttons using the Properties inspector.

Figure 7-8:
Set radio button name and value attributes with the Properties inspector.

5. **Select an option to set the initial state of the radio button to checked or unchecked.**

   The radio button doesn't actually show a check mark; rather, it appears with a small dot in the center to indicate that it's been checked (selected).

6. **Repeat Steps 2–5 to insert additional radio buttons.**

   Make sure that radio buttons are always used in sets of two or more. Then be sure to only select one radio button as checked by default; if you specify more than one button with a checked value, it can create problems with data collection.

Inserting a group of radio buttons

The Radio Group icon launches a helpful dialog box to build an entire radio group all at once rather than creating a group of buttons one button at a time. In a group, only one option can be selected, whereas with individual buttons you could theoretically select them all. Selecting multiple buttons defeats the purpose because radio buttons are intended to be used as either-or selection fields. All the same rules apply to radio groups as to radio buttons with the benefit of having Dreamweaver write <label> tags for you to identify the text associated with the radio button. When you launch the Radio Group dialog box, simply enter labels and values for each button, name the group, and select a layout type.

To insert a radio group in your form, follow these steps:

1. **Place your cursor in the form area on your page where you want to insert a radio group.**

   If you haven't yet created a form, see the earlier section, "Creating a Fabulous HTML Form."

2. **Choose Insert⇨Form⇨Radio Group.**

   You can also click the panel. The Radio Group dialog box appears, as shown in Figure 7-9.

Book II
Chapter 7

Building
Fabulous Forms

Figure 7-9:
Create
a group
of radio
buttons all
at once.

3. **In the Radio Group dialog box, enter a name for the radio button Group.**

   The group name/ID identifies all the buttons as belonging to the same group and adds the same name and id attribute (such as id="dessert") to each radio button.

4. **In the Radio Buttons Label column, type a label for each radio button in the group.**

   Each item in the list represents a radio button in the radio group. To add new buttons, click the plus (+) icon. To remove any buttons, select the item to be removed from the list and click the minus (–) icon.

   To reorder the buttons listed in the group, select a button from the list and click the up or down arrow.

5. **In the Value column, type a checked value for each radio button in the group.**

   The checked value represents the value that is submitted as the selected choice for this radio group.

6. **Choose Line Breaks or Table as the layout option for the radio group.**

   The buttons can be separated by line breaks or by table cells.

7. **Click OK to insert the radio group on the page.**

8. **Select one of the buttons in the group to be selected by default by entering the initial state as checked in the Properties inspector.**

   Use the Properties inspector to make further adjustments to the radio buttons in the group.

Lists and menus

The list/menu form object creates both list- and menu-type form fields. Use this object to provide a list or menu in your form that allows users to make a selection from a specified category, such as a state or country.

To insert a list or menu in your form, follow these steps:

1. **Place your cursor in the form area on your page where you want to insert a list/menu object.**

   If you haven't yet created a form, see the earlier section, "Creating a Fabulous HTML Form."

2. **Choose Insert➪Form➪Select (List/Menu).**

   You can also click the Select (List/Menu) icon in the Forms category of the Insert panel.

3. **If you enabled form accessibility features:**

   a. **Complete the Input Tag Accessibility Attributes dialog box that appears.**

   b. **Click OK to insert the list/menu object or press Cancel to insert the field without accessibility attributes.**

4. **Click the List Values button in the Properties inspector.**

   The List Values dialog box appears. You use this dialog box to add labels and values to your list or menu (see Figure 7-10).

Book II
Chapter 7

Building
Fabulous Forms

Figure 7-10:
Add labels
and values
to lists and
menus.

- **Item Label:** This text appears as a selection in the list. To add new list items, click the plus (+) icon. To remove an item from the list, select the item to be removed and click the minus (–) icon. To sort items, select an item from the list and click the up or down arrow.

- **Value:** This value is returned with the collected data when the item is selected, as in CA for California.

5. **After you add all the items to your list, click OK to close the List Values dialog box.**

6. **With the list/menu object still selected, select a list Type in the Properties inspector.**

   Choose Menu to make a drop-down menu or List to make a scrollable box that displays a list of menu options. A list also allows users to select multiple items.

7. **If you selected List in Step 6:**

   a. **Enter a number in the Height box to represent the number of lines to be displayed in the list.**

   If the contents of the box exceed the box height, scroll bars appear.

   b. **(Optional) Click the Allow Multiple option next to Selections to allow users to Shift-click when making multiple selections from the list.**

8. **In the Initially Selected field, select an item in the list or menu to appear as the initial item.**

   For example, if you have a menu of U.S. states, the first item in the list, called Select a State, can be the initially selected item.

Jump menus

A jump menu consists of a list of items that a visitor can select from; after the visitor makes a selection, the browser jumps to another page or URL. Jump menus automatically add the necessary JavaScript behaviors required to instruct the browser to go to another page. This type of menu can be a useful tool for quick navigation on a Web site.

To find out how to set up a jump menu, see Book IV, Chapter 2.

Image fields

The Image Field option inserts an image into the form, for when you prefer to use your own graphic for a Submit button or other form input field.

Images in forms become clickable Submit buttons by default, unless you apply different JavaScript to the image.

To add an image field to your form, follow these steps:

1. **Place your cursor in the form area on your page where you want to insert an image field.**

   If you haven't yet created a form, see the earlier section, "Creating a Fabulous HTML Form."

2. **Choose Insert⇨Form⇨Image Field.**

   You can also click the Image Field icon in the Forms category of the Insert panel. The Select Image Source dialog box appears.

3. **Browse to and select the image you want to add to the form. If you enabled accessibility features:**

   a. **Complete the Input Tag Accessibility Attributes dialog box that appears.**

   b. **Click OK to insert the image or click Cancel to insert the field without accessibility attributes.**

   The image is inserted onto your page, as shown in Figure 7-11.

4. **In the Alt field in the Properties inspector, enter Alternate text for the image.**

   Typically, the text in the Alt field mirrors the text on the button graphic.

Figure 7-11:
With the
Image Field
form object,
you can use
your own
graphics.

5. **(Optional) In the Align drop-down list, select an alignment option for the graphic.**

Alignment options are Default, Top, Middle, Bottom, Left, and Right.

6. **(Optional) In the Class drop-down list, choose a CSS style to apply to the form object.**

For example, you may have created a custom CSS style for all your text input fields. Choose the style from the menu to apply it.

7. **In the ImageField field, enter Submit or Reset to use the image as a Submit or Reset button.**

Alternatively, you can give your button a unique ID to use the button with a JavaScript behavior. For example, you can create a button that, when clicked, runs a script to launch a pop-up window.

File upload fields

Add a File Field object to your form when you want to allow visitors to search for a file on their own computers and upload it to the server. When adding a file field, Dreamweaver inserts a text field with a Browse button next to it.

To use a file field on a Web page, you must make sure that your server has a server-side script that can accept this type of data submission. File fields require the POST method for transmitting files from the browser to the server. Select `enctype="multipart/form-data"` as the encryption type for the form. The data is posted to the address in the form's action field; you can use a regular HTTP URL as the value as long as your application has the right server permissions to be able to write files accepted this way.

Be sure to test this feature in your target browsers before publishing the page, because the file field is displayed differently in different browsers: Safari, Internet Explorer, Opera, and Firefox all have their own ideas about how to handle this field, including how much space they take up and what words are displayed.

To insert a file field in your form, follow these steps:

1. **Place your cursor in the form area on your page where you want to insert a file field.**

   If you haven't yet created a form, see the earlier section, "Creating a Fabulous HTML Form."

2. **Choose Insert⇨Form⇨File Field.**

   You can also click the File Field icon in the Forms category of the Insert panel.

3. **If you enabled Accessibility features:**

   a. **Complete the Input Tag Accessibility Attributes dialog box that appears.**

   b. **Click OK to insert the file field, or press Cancel to insert the field without accessibility attributes.**

4. **In the Properties inspector, enter the following attributes:**

   - **FileField Name:** Enter the ID for the file field.

   - **Char Width:** Enter the number of characters to set as the width of the file field.

   - **Max Chars:** Enter the maximum number of characters that a visitor can enter in the file field.

   - **Class:** If you've created a custom CSS style to format this field, select it by name from the Class drop-down list.

Buttons

Add a form button to your form for visitors to click when they're ready to submit data or trigger other form processing operations. Typical form buttons are labeled as Submit, Reset, or Send, but you can create buttons with other labels that perform tasks such as calculating shipping charges based on a user's geographical zone.

To create a button, follow these steps:

1. **Place your cursor in the form area on your page where you want to insert a form button.**

    If you haven't yet created a form, see the earlier section, "Creating a Fabulous HTML Form."

2. **Choose Insert⇨Form⇨Button, or click the Button icon in the Forms category of the Insert panel. If you enabled Accessibility features:**

    a. **Complete the Input Tag Accessibility Attributes dialog box that appears.**

    b. **Click OK to insert the button, or press Cancel to insert the button without accessibility attributes.**

    The Properties inspector displays the properties for the button, as shown in Figure 7-12.

3. **In the Button Name field in the Properties inspector, enter a name/ID for your button.**

4. **In the Value field, enter the text to appear on the button face.**

    For instance, if you want a button that says Join Mailing List, type **Join Mailing List**.

Figure 7-12:
Add a button to your form so visitors can submit data or trigger other operations.

5. **(Optional) In the Class drop-down list, select a custom CSS style to apply to the button.**

6. **Choose an action from the Action field:**

   - **Submit form:** This default form button type submits the collected data to a script or processing application on the server. Submit buttons can have any label as long as the Action type in the Properties inspector is set to Submit.

   - **Reset form:** A Reset form button clears the form fields by returning the form to its original state before the visitor submitted the form to the server. You can label reset buttons with any text, such as Reset or Clear All.

   - **None:** A third option creates a button with customized text that you can attach a behavior to, such as a Go button for a jump menu. Select None as the Action type in the Properties inspector and apply a JavaScript behavior using the Behaviors panel (see Book IV, Chapter 2 for more about behaviors).

Label tags

The `<label>` tag is used for enhancing accessibility attributes. When the `<label>` tag wraps around a form item, not only can screen-reader software read the label, but a *focus rectangle* surrounds both the label and form field in some browsers, which allows the user to click anywhere in the text and form field area to select it. This grouping is especially helpful when using radio buttons and check boxes!

If you label your form objects without using the `<label>` tags, the label isn't associated with the form object, as in the following sample code:

```
<input name="Dessert" id="Dessert" type="radio" value="Apple" checked="checked"
    />Apple Crumble
```

With the `<label>` tags, however, the label is associated with the form object, as in the following:

```
<label><input name="Dessert" id="Dessert" type="radio" value="Apple"
    checked="checked" />Apple Crumble</label>
```

If you've enabled accessibility preferences, the Input Tag Accessibility Attributes dialog box automatically appears any time you insert a form object on your page. There you can wrap your object with the `<label>` tag.

To insert a `<label>` tag in your form after you add objects to your form, follow these steps:

1. **Select the objects in your form that you want to wrap with the `<label>` tag.**

    If you would rather insert the `<label>` tag first and then edit the code by hand so that it wraps around a specific form field, place your cursor in the form area on your page where you want to insert the tag. If you haven't yet created a form, see the earlier section, "Creating a Fabulous HTML Form."

2. **Choose Insert➪Form➪Label.**

    You can also click the Label icon in the Forms category of the Insert panel. The `<label>` tag is inserted in your page code, as shown in Figure 7-13.

Figure 7-13: Use the `<label>` tag to group form objects and their labels.

If you're adding a `<label>` tag to an existing form object, such as a check box or radio button, check the code to ensure that the label for the form object sits between the opening and closing `<label>` tags.

Fieldset tags

A `<fieldset>` tag is used as a container for other form objects. Use fieldsets to define multiple fields into logical groups in the form. For instance, one fieldset may include text input fields for name and e-mail information, and another fieldset may include username and password information (see Figure 7-14).

Figure 7-14:
Use the
`<fieldset>`
tag to group
form objects
together.

You can use the `<legend>` tag with the `<fieldset>` tag to label each field
set, as in the following example:

```
<form method="post" action="">
<fieldset>
<h2>
<legend>Contact Information</legend>
</h2>
<label>
Name:
<input name="name" type="text" id="name" />
</label>
<br />
<label>Email:
<input name="email" type="text" id="email" />
</label>
</fieldset></form>
```

These tags create an interesting look in a browser. Figure 7-15 shows how
the example appears in Firefox on a PC.

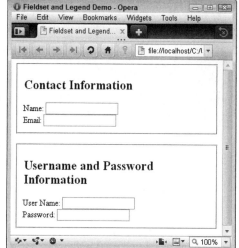

Figure 7-15:
The
`<fieldset>`
and
`<legend>`
tags format
form data
in a unique
way.

To insert `<fieldset>` and `<legend>` tags, follow these steps:

1. **Open a file containing a form in which you want to insert `<fieldset>` and `<legend>` tags.**

   If you haven't yet created a form, see the earlier section, "Creating a Fabulous HTML Form."

2. **Select all the form elements that you want to group inside the `<fieldset>` tags.**

3. **Choose Insert⇨Form⇨Fieldset.**

   You can also click the Fieldset icon in the Forms category of the Insert panel. The Fieldset dialog box appears.

4. **In the Fieldset dialog box, enter a name for the legend and then click OK.**

   The legend is like a heading for the objects grouped in the `<fieldset>` tags. If desired, apply a different format setting to the legend, such as H2, so that it stands out more than the rest of the surrounding paragraph text.

   Dreamweaver wraps the selected content with `<fieldset>` and `<legend>` tags. After the `<fieldset>` and `<legend>` tags have been added to your code, you can style the content with CSS.

As an alternative to the `<legend>` and `<fieldset>` tags, consider using `div` tags and CSS, which provide greater control for spacing, margins, background, colors, fonts, and so on.

Validating a Form with JavaScript

If you've ever filled out a form and received a pop-up message back from your browser that says you filled out the form incorrectly or that you didn't enter data in a particular field, you've witnessed form validation in action. Validation can be performed dynamically with PHP, ASP, JSP, or ColdFusion code. However, for most nondynamic sites, a simple client-side JavaScript Validate Form action does the trick.

The Validate Form behavior cross-checks all the fields against the validation rules you specify to ensure that the user entered the data correctly before submission. This way, you can check the form on the client side for completion and accuracy before the server collects the data.

You can attach validation events to as many fields in the form as you want. A couple of validation events follow:

+ **onBlur:** Validate individual fields as the form is being completed.

+ **onSubmit:** Review the entire form input data all at once when the visitor clicks the form's Submit button.

To validate a form with the Validate Form action, follow these steps:

1. **To validate the entire form, select the form's `<form>` tag. Or to validate an individual field, select that form object.**

2. **Open the Behaviors panel (which is technically a tab in the Tag Inspector panel) by choosing Window⇨Behaviors.**

3. **Click the plus (+) icon in the Behaviors panel and choose Validate Form from the Add Behavior pop-up menu.**

   The Validate Form dialog box appears, as shown in Figure 7-16, showing a list of all named fields in your form.

Figure 7-16:
The Validate
Form dialog
box.

4. **Select a form input field from the Fields listing, and then choose the desired validation settings for it:**

   - **Value Required:** The field must contain data of some kind, rather than stay blank.

   - **Accept Anything:** The user can input any type of data into the form field. If you select this option, you must also set the selected field to Required.

   - **Accept Email Address:** The validation script verifies that the field contains the @ symbol.

   - **Accept Number:** The validation script checks that this field contains only numbers.

   - **Accept Number From/To:** Specify a range for acceptable numbers.

   When validating the entire form, you must set a value and accept an option for each field in the form.

5. **Repeat Step 4 for every form input field listed in the Fields listing.**

6. **Click OK.**

Dreamweaver adds the Form Validation JavaScript code to the `<form>` and `<head>` tags. When validating an entire form, the `onSubmit` validation event automatically appears next to the Validate Form Events menu in the Behaviors panel. If validating only a single field, however, the default validation event is either `onBlur` or `onChange`.

Validating a Form with Spry Assets

Like JavaScript validation, Spry validation is another cool way to validate your forms, only this method uses the more advanced tools in the Spry framework. The Spry framework, which you find out more about in Book IV, Chapter 2, is a library of JavaScript that helps Web designers and developers with a basic understanding of HTML, CSS, and JavaScript build XLM-rich Web pages that provide more interactive experiences for site visitors.

Spry validation form fields, or *widgets*, include the Text field, Textarea, Checkbox, Select (List/Menu), Password, Confirm, and Radio Group. To use these widgets, you need to insert the Spry fields into your form instead of inserting the regular HTML form field tags. After you've inserted these Spry fields, you customize how each field validates data and, if desired, modify the look and feel of how the field appears in the browser. All Spry Validation widgets are styled with an external CSS file, such as SpryAssets/ SpryValidationTextField.css, that Dreamweaver automatically adds to the root level of your managed site when you insert the first Spry Validation form field. In addition to the CSS file, an adjoining JavaScript file (such as SpryAssets/SpryValidationTextField.js) is also added to your managed site.

To get the most use out of the Spry Validation form fields, you need a firm understanding of HTML, CSS, and JavaScript. Spry widgets are more advanced Dreamweaver tools intended for the experienced Dreamweaver user. As such, the following information includes general guidelines for using the Spry Validation tools. For detailed online help and information about working with Spry Validation, see `http://help.adobe.com/` `en_US/dreamweaver/cs/using/WS2442184F-3DF4-4240-96AF-` `CC6D792E2A62a.html`.

The Spry Validation widgets are at the bottom of the Forms category of the Insert panel, as shown in Figure 7-17, as well as in the Spry category of the Insert menu. You can insert these widgets in your form in the same way that you insert regular form fields What is different about each of them, however, is how they are styled and the kind of interactive opportunities they offer to site visitors. For example, with the Spry Validation Text field, visitors can be prompted to enter the correct date format and see an error message (*Invalid format* or *The value is required*) when the format entered does not match the formatting hint you provided or no input is made to the field.

Figure 7-17:
Insert Spry Validation form fields from the Forms category of the Insert panel.

Figure 7-18 shows examples of the four types of visual prompts: A. Hint activated, B. Correctly entered data, C. Incorrect data entered, and D. Missing data in required field.

Figure 7-18:
Visitors are
prompted to
enter data
correctly.

As you insert each Spry Validation field, Dreamweaver saves a linked Spry Assets CSS and JavaScript file to your managed site. These files must be uploaded to the server along with the page(s) using the Spry Validation fields for the Spry Validation form fields to function properly in a browser.

To insert any of the Spry Validation Fields into your page, follow these steps:

1. **Place your cursor in the area in your form where you want to insert a Spry Validation Field.**

2. **Click the desired Spry Validation field icon in the Forms category of the Insert panel. If the Input Tag Accessibility Attributes dialog box appears, complete the fields and click OK.**

   The selected Spry Validation Field is automatically added to the page in the specified location. The Spry Validation form fields look like their regular HTML form field counterparts, except the Spry versions are surrounded by a blue outline and tab that identifies the form field as a Spry Validation form field.

   You can also insert any of the Spry Validation form fields by choosing Insert⇨Spry and then choosing the desired option from the submenu.

3. **Select the new Spry Validation field in Design view to customize the field in the Properties inspector.**

   Like the normal form field, as described earlier in the chapter, you can set parameters for the Validation field with the Properties inspector.

4. **Select the Validation field's blue tab (not the field) and set the validation Type and Format in the Properties inspector.**

   When you click the Validation field's tab, a different set of information appears in the Properties inspector. You need to set the correct type and format to match the data you intend to collect from site visitors, such as a phone number, currency, dates, or credit card information.

For a complete listing of types and formats, see `http://help.adobe.com/en_US/dreamweaver/cs/using/WS267C8659-3AEF-4956-8268-E38CA4CAFAD3a.html`.

5. **Specify when the validation event will occur.**

   Select as many as you like, or deselect them all:

   - **Blur:** Validate the field when the user clicks outside the field.
   - **Change:** Validate the field while the user enters text inside the field.
   - **Submit:** Validate the field when the user submits the form.

6. **Set other options as required by the Validation field.**

   For example, when you select the Spry Validation Text Field tab, other options are setting the minimum and maximum number of characters, setting the min and max values, displaying the preview widget states, changing the required status of a field, creating a hint, and blocking invalid characters.

After the Spry Validation field is inserted and its properties are set in the Properties inspector, the field's style and error message (if any) can be customized in the CSS. Finding the right field's CSS style can be tricky on your own, so be sure to consult the online help files to ensure that you're editing the correct CSS style.

To find the correct CSS and learn more about advanced styling, go to `http://help.adobe.com/en_US/dreamweaver/cs/using/WSC12A0F2F-F242-4be0-868C-E8D539AFE5A6a.html`.

Book III

Working Like the Pros

Contents at a Glance

Chapter 1: Looking Good with Cascading Style Sheets (CSS)

In This Chapter

✔ **Understanding Cascading Style Sheets**

✔ **Creating internal and external style sheets**

✔ **Creating new CSS styles**

✔ **Enabling and disabling CSS Properties**

✔ **Editing, deleting, and renaming styles**

✔ **Attaching Design Time Style Sheets**

✔ **Using the Code Navigator**

✔ **Identifying styles with CSS Inspect**

C ascading Style Sheets (CSS) are a recommended standard from the
World Wide Web Consortium (W3C) to provide Web designers with
more control over the layout and appearance of HTML and XML files.
Cascading Style Sheets perform a similar function as formatted text in a
word processor. You can set default formatting for particular styles such as
paragraphs and headings. You can also create your own custom styles for
text, graphics, tables, and layers, plus create styles that control the format
and position of block-level assets like margins and borders.

With CSS, you can control page elements such as

- ✦ Fonts, font sizes, font styles, and font colors
- ✦ Line spacing and letter spacing
- ✦ Margins, padding, indenting, and outdenting
- ✦ Background images and colors
- ✦ Border style, width, and color
- ✦ List and link formatting
- ✦ Size, alignment, positioning, and visibility of elements on the page
- ✦ Page breaks, filters, and cursor visual effects

Dreamweaver CS5 formats text with CSS as the default text styling method (instead of HTML tags) because CSS has been implemented in all modern browsers including the top five: Firefox, Internet Explorer, Opera, Safari, and Google Chrome. For a side-by-side comparison of the top ten browsers, see `http://internet-browser-review.toptenreviews.com/`.

You'll enjoy these benefits with CSS:

✦ Style sheets separate content from the style and formatting information.

✦ Style sheets simplify HTML code and reduce file size (because all the styling information is in one location — either at the head of the file or in an external style sheet — rather than inline with the text) without compromising the structure of the content.

✦ Style sheets give you more control over the presentation of your pages.

✦ Using style sheets means your HTML files have faster download times across multiple browsers.

✦ With an external CSS, you have a centralized location for the Web site design, so you can change an entire site's look by changing just one file.

✦ Site visitors with disabilities have better access to pages using CSS.

✦ Older browsers can still view pages.

This chapter presents an overview of Cascading Style Sheets, including the difference between internal, external, and inline style sheets. You discover the three general types of styles and how to create, edit, rename, and delete your own CSS using the Dreamweaver CSS Styles panel. You also find a full explanation of the categories of the CSS Rule Definition dialog box, learn how to use the new CSS Inspect and Enable/Disable CSS Properties features, and discover when and how to use Design Time CSS.

Understanding Cascading Style Sheets (CSS)

In the early days of the Internet, how content looked on a Web page was largely the work of specialized formatting tags used inside the HTML code, such as `<font face="Arial" size="2">` . . . `</font>`, which instructs a browser to display the text in a specific font (Arial) and size (2). In late 1997, the advent of HTML 4—which began supporting Cascading Style Sheets and scripting, among other great enhancements—meant that most formatting was now written with style sheets, either inside the HTML document itself or outside the document in an external style sheet file.

Cascading Style Sheets (CSS) separate form from content by taking control over the appearance of the text through the specification of font style, font size, text color, and alignment, as well as positioning and additional formatting attributes for other elements such as images, tables, layers (called AP

Elements in Dreamweaver), and forms. HTML is now primarily used for organizing and identifying content, whereas the external CSS typically has all the formatting and positioning instructions.

One of the great benefits of separating form from content with CSS is that when you need to make formatting changes, you only need to edit the CSS file rather than modifying the style attributes inside the HTML code for every page. As you find out in the following sections, CSS code can be placed in any of three locations: *inline* with the HTML, *internal* in the head of your HTML file, or as an *external* file that is linked to all the pages on your site. External CSS is the preferred method of professional Web designers because it is the most organized and flexible way to format content.

For example, a sentence using the old <font> tag with face, size, and color attributes looks like this:

```
<p><font="Verdana, Arial, Helvetica" size="2" color="#990000">Search the Internet
    to find the best restaurants in your neighborhood.</font></p>
```

In comparison, using a style sheet that defines a custom style called .restaurants with attributes of Verdana, 12px, #990000 looks like this:

```
<style type="text/css">
<!--
.restaurants {
font-family: Verdana, Arial, Helvetica, sans-serif;
font-size: 12px;
color: #990000;
}
-->
</style>
```

and when applied to the same sentence, the sentence code simply looks like this:

```
<p class="restaurants">Search the Internet to find the best restaurants in your
    neighborhood.</p>
```

When you place the CSS in an external file, you can simply upload the revised CSS to the hosting server to change the look of your entire site. By contrast, when HTML styles are used and you want to make a sitewide change, all the pages on the site must be modified before uploading to the server.

Another great feature about CSS is that style sheets allow you to somewhat control what site visitors see when they visit your page regardless of the platform they're browsing in. Like the old HTML tags, CSS styles override default browser font face and font size settings, but in a much cleaner way.

Exploring Different Style Sheet Types

Dreamweaver CS5 uses CSS, rather than HTML tags, as the default method for editing text. If you like, you can still use HTML tags for styling your text by applying attributes to selected content through the HTML tab on the Properties inspector or by hand-editing the code with the old HTML tags. The trend, however, is to use CSS.

By using the Targeted Rule menu on the CSS tab of the Properties inspector, you can place your style sheet information in one of three locations, relative to the HTML code:

✦ **Internal, (inside the document):** You can create an internal style sheet through the CSS Styles panel and automatically add styles between the <head> tags of the document through the CSS tab of the Properties inspector.

✦ **External (outside the document in a separate CSS file):** You can create an external style sheet through the CSS Styles panel and then link it to your document.

✦ **Inline (putting the CSS markup right next to the HTML):** You need to know the proper syntax to add inline CSS so you can manually type the style code in the HTML.

You can use all three style sheet types (internal, external, and inline) in combination. For instance, you may have some internal styles and an external style sheet linked to the same document, plus an inline style or two throughout the code. You may even use multiple style sheets on a page or in an entire site. Just remember that whatever styles are closest to the content typically (though not always) take precedence over styles that are farther away.

Internal styles

After adding text to a Web document, you can apply certain styling attributes to your text with the formatting options on the HTML and CSS tabs of the Properties inspector, or by creating and applying styles through the CSS Styles panel.

The options on the HTML tab, shown in Figure 1-1, add HTML markup to your code. The HTML Properties inspector settings add the following inline formatting tags to the HTML code: Format, ID, Class, Link, Bold (Strong), Italic (Em), Unordered List, Ordered List, Indent, Outdent, List Item, Title, and Target.

Figure 1-1:
The HTML
formatting
options
in the
Properties
inspector.

The options on the CSS tab, shown in Figure 1-2, can be used to add CSS
markup to the <head> area of your open document, to an external style
sheet, or inline with the text. The CSS Properties inspector settings add the
following CSS markup internally to the <head> of the open page, inline with
the HTML, or to an external CSS file: Targeted Rule, Font, Size, Color, Bold
(Strong), Italic (Em), and Align (Left/Center/Right/Justified).

Figure 1-2:
The CSS
formatting
options
in the
Properties
inspector.

WARNING!

As you may have noticed, both tabs on the Properties inspector include a
Page Properties button, which applies only CSS formatting to the currently
active page. If you're new to CSS, ignore this button for now and concentrate
on learning how to apply CSS to your pages through the CSS Styles panel.

When adding a New CSS rule to your file, if you select the Arial font from
the Font drop-down menu in the CSS Properties inspector, the New CSS
Rule dialog box appears, prompting you to choose a selector type for your
CSS rule. For instance, you can create a custom class CSS style, such as
.saleprice to apply to any HTML element on your page, or specify the
HTML tag that will be redefined with the new font style attribute, such as the
<p> tag for all paragraphs. You learn more about CSS contextual selector
types in the "Understanding CSS Style Types" section, later in this chapter.

In the New CSS Rule dialog box, you can also choose whether this new style
will be defined in the current open document by selecting This Document
Only, or in a new or preexisting external CSS file by selecting New Style

Sheet File or an external CSS file by name. When you add the style to This Document Only, the following style sheet code is added to your HTML document between the `<head>` tags:

```
<style type="text/css">
<!--
.saleprice {font-family: Arial, Helvetica, sans-serif}
-->
</style>
```

By contrast, when you put the new style in an external CSS file, only the style attributes are added to the file:

```
.saleprice {font-family: Arial, Helvetica, sans-serif}
```

With internal CSS, the style sheet markup begins and ends with the `<style>` and `</style>` tags, respectively. Nested between those are opening and closing comment tags (`<!--` and `-->`), which comment out (hide) the style attributes so that older browsers don't display them as text in the body of the page. You use comment tags to insert text in your code that isn't displayed in a browser. The style attributes go between the comment tags.

Each time you style content on your page with the CSS Properties inspector, you are prompted to add a new custom style to the internal or external style sheet. After your new custom styles are added to the internal or external style sheet, the Targeted Rule menu in the Properties inspector (refer to Figure 1-2) displays those styles by name and previews them. You can also apply your custom CSS styles to selected content using the Class menu on the HTML Properties inspector.

When adding internal CSS styles to the open document, be aware that those internal CSS styles alter the contents on only that particular page. To use a single style sheet for multiple pages on a Web site, you must create an external style sheet, described next.

External styles

External styles refer to style descriptions saved in a single separate, external file with the .css file extension. External style sheets are often named after the company or project they're used with, or with some acronym or abbreviation relative to the Web site, such as monkey.css for a site about monkeys, although some designers simply refer to their CSS files as style.css so that every project uses the same naming convention.

The external style sheet links to the HTML pages using a special line of code. When the link is present and the page is displayed in a browser window, the browser interprets and displays the page's contents using the external style sheet information. You place the link to the external style sheet inside the `<head>` tag of the document with the `href` attribute referencing the location and filename of the CSS, as in this example:

```
<link href="monkey.css" rel="stylesheet" type="text/css" />
```

External style sheet styles use the same syntax and formatting as internal style sheets to define styles, with one tiny exception: The styles in an external style sheet do not need to be surrounded by the `<style>` and `<!--comment-->` tags that internal styles require. Furthermore — and this is what makes external style sheets so powerful — external style sheets are best when working with a multipage Web site because a single external style sheet can control the formatting for all the pages on the site. For example, if you need to change the style attributes of all the Heading 1s (`<h1>`) site-wide, you need to modify only the one external style sheet to make all the pages conform to the new style definitions!

Another major benefit of using external CSS, as opposed to HTML, inline CSS, or internal CSS, is that you can build your own master CSS file and use it again and again on each new Web project, customizing the fonts, colors, styles, and so on to match each project's design. See `www.crucialweb host.com/blog/master-stylesheet-the-most-useful-css-technique/` for a great example of this.

Inline styles

Occasionally, you may need to add an inline style to a document rather than using internal or external style sheets. For example, if you're creating an HTML e-mail, you might use tables instead of CSS layers, but still use inline styles for text formatting because many e-mail programs prefer to interpret HTML tags over CSS for layout and positioning. What's more, when the style data is inline with the content, a visitor can also read the mail offline and view it styled as you intended.

Inline style descriptions are written inside the code, surrounding the selected text or object, oftentimes appending whatever existing tag is closest to the content to be styled, or by adding a `<span>` tag with the style attribute, as in the following two examples:

```
<p style="font-size: 12px; color: #990000;">Inline styles are "in line" with the
    text.</p>
<p>This example uses the span tag to selectively apply a <span style="font-size:
    12px; color: #990000;">custom style</span> to selected text.</p>
```

To add an inline style to your page using the Properties inspector, follow these steps:

1. **Select the word or words to which you'd like to apply an inline style.**

For example, you may want to style the words *On Sale Now!*

2. **In the CSS Properties inspector, choose <New Inline Style> from the New Rule section of the Targeted Rule menu.**

Essentially, you'll be formatting the `style` tag attribute in a similar way to how the old `<font>` tag used to be coded.

3. **Apply the desired font, size, and color attributes to the selected text, as well as bold, italics, and alignment settings, if desired.**

When the inline style is applied to an entire paragraph, the style markup is added to the opening `<p>` tag, like this:

```
<p style="font-family: Georgia, 'Times New Roman', Times, serif; font-weight:
    bold; color: #F63; font-size: 16px;">On Sale Now!</p>
```

When the inline style is applied to a single word or selection of words inside a paragraph, the inline style markup surrounds the selected text using the `<span>` tag, like this:

```
<p>We have thousands of products <span style="font-family: Georgia,
    'Times New Roman', Times, serif; font-size: 16px; font-weight: bold;
    color: #F63;">On Sale Now!</span></p>
```

Working with the CSS Styles Panel

Use the CSS Styles panel to create and manage your internal and external style sheets. If the panel is not visible, open it by choosing Window➪CSS Styles. Although you can apply a handful of styles through the Properties inspector, we strongly recommend that you use the CSS Styles panel for creating and editing all your CSS because it provides access to the full range of CSS resources.

The Dreamweaver CSS Styles panel has many enhancements from versions prior to CS3, including multiple panes, incremental (faster!) pagination, and two new CS5 features, CSS Enable/Disable and CSS Inspect, which you learn about later in this chapter.

The panel is split into two parts. Two buttons appear at the top of the panel: All and Current, as shown in Figure 1-3, each of which display different views of the CSS Styles panel. The bottom half of the panel, called the Properties pane, displays the properties for selected styles. Resize panes within the panel at any time by clicking and dragging the divider line between the panes up or down.

The following sections discuss each of these views in detail.

Figure 1-3:
The CSS
Styles panel
in All mode
(left) and
Current
mode (right).

All mode

Click the All button and the CSS Styles panel splits into two panes:

✦ **All Rules:** The top pane displays a list of all the styles attached to, or contained inside, the currently selected open document.

✦ **Properties:** Select a style in the top pane, and the bottom pane displays its specific attributes. You can quickly make a change to an existing property or add more properties by clicking the Add Property link.

Current mode

Click the Current button and the CSS Styles panel divides into three panes:

✦ **Summary for Selection:** The top pane shows an attributes summary of the currently selected style. Properties display in order of specificity. Class styles have a higher specificity than Tag selectors.

✦ **Rules:** You can toggle this area to display data in two views by clicking the buttons on the top-right edge of the section's title bar. The left About icon displays information about a selected property (for example, Color is defined in an inline style attribute in index.html), whereas the right Rules icon shows the style name and the tag in the code that the selected style is applied to (such as `.onsale <span>` or `<inline style> <p>`).

✦ **Properties:** The bottom pane displays the attributes of the selected style in an editable format. Make a change to a property or add more properties by clicking the Add Property link.

CSS Styles panel viewing icons

The bottom edge of the CSS Styles panel, shown in Figure 1-4, displays icons that are shared by both All and Current views and allow you to select from different viewing and editing options.

Figure 1-4:
These icons display viewing and editing options.

The panel's bottom right edge displays five icons:

✦ **Attach Style Sheet:** Launch the Attach External Style Sheet dialog box to select an external style sheet to link to or import to the current file, as well as to specify the desired media type(s) that the attached CSS should be associated with.

✦ **New CSS Rule:** Open the New CSS Rule dialog box for naming, choosing a selector type, and specifying the location for the new style rule.

✦ **Edit Style Sheet:** Open the CSS Rule definition dialog box when a style is selected in the CSS Styles panel.

✦ **Disable/Enable CSS Property:** Toggle the visibility of selected style properties by clicking the gray space to the left of the property declaration in the Properties pane of the CSS Styles panel. You learn more about this feature in the "Enabling/Disabling CSS Properties" section, later in this chapter.

✦ **Delete CSS Property:** Permanently remove a selected rule or property from the CSS Styles panel, as well as any formatting from elements to which it was applied. This option doesn't, however, delete references in the HTML markup to that style. When you select the `<style>` tag of an internal CSS in the All Rules section of the CSS Styles panel, this icon deletes the embedded styles. Likewise, when you select an external CSS file, this icon unlinks the linked CSS style sheet.

The panel's bottom-left edge displays three icons that change the display of the listing in the Properties pane of the panel:

✦ **Show Category View:** Split CSS properties into nine categories: Font, Background, Block, Border, Box, List, Positioning, Extensions, and Tables, Content, Quotes. Each category's properties are displayed in an expandable list format. You can expand and collapse the list by clicking the plus (+) or minus (–) icon next to the category name. Properties in each category are listed alphabetically with set properties sorted on top in blue text.

✦ **Show List View:** Display CSS properties in descending alphabetical order with set properties in blue text at the top of the list.

✦ **Show Only Set Properties:** Display only set properties. This is the default view.

In all the CSS Styles panel views, any set properties are displayed in blue text. The other properties appear in black text unless they are irrelevant properties (when the rule is not inherited by the style or is overridden by another style), which are displayed with a red strikethrough line. In addition, irrelevant rules contain explanatory pop-up messages that you can see when you hover your mouse over the rule.

Understanding CSS Style Types

All Cascading Style Sheet rules are written in two-part syntax consisting of the selector and the declaration:

✦ The *selector* defines the style's name or location in the HTML that the style should be applied to. For example, a selector could be a tag such as <p> or <h1>, or a custom class name such as .tableheader. There are four selector types, as defined in the following section.

✦ The *declaration* specifies all the style's elements, such as font face, size, color, margin, and padding. Rules can contain multiple declarations as long as each is separated by a semicolon (;) as shown in the following example.

Here's an example of a CSS rule where p is the selector and everything inside the curly brackets ({}) is the declaration:

```
p {
font-family: Verdana, Arial, Helvetica, sans-serif;
font-size: 12px;
color: #993300;
}
```

Note that the declarations themselves have two parts separated by a colon (:): the property (such as color) and the value (such as #993300). In the rule for p in the preceding example, a style has been defined for all <p> tags, meaning that all content in the document between any pair of opening and closing <p> tags is displayed as Verdana, 12px, and #993300 (which is the hexadecimal code for a deep brick red color). (To find out more about *hex* colors, see Book II, Chapter 2.)

The *cascading* part of Cascading Style Sheets refers to the capability of adding multiple style declarations to the same rule as well as applying multiple rules to the same elements. For instance, one rule can define the style of text and another rule can define the margin and line spacing around it. In a greater sense, however, the term refers to the ability to use multiple style sheets and multiple style inheritances in a cascading way that determines which styles take precedence over the others. To find out more about CSS cascading rules, see the "About.com" article on CSS types at `webdesign.about.com/od/css/f/blcssfaqcascade.htm`.

In addition to the ability to hand-code, Dreamweaver provides you with two more ways to create CSS styles for your documents:

+ **Properties inspector:** As we mentioned previously, you can automatically create and add internal, externally linked, or inline styles to your page when styling selected content by using the CSS Properties inspector.

+ **CSS Styles panel:** Using the CSS Styles panel (as described in the section "Adding a Style to a New or Existing Style Sheet"), you can add internal or external styles to your files by accessing the full library of style properties in the CSS Rule Definition dialog box.

Before you begin creating your styles, you need to be familiar with the different style types. You can create four general types of styles using the CSS Styles panel: class styles, ID styles, tag redefines, and compound CSS selectors. Each type modifies different parts of the HTML, as described in the following sections.

Class styles

If you want to selectively style content, use custom class styles. For instance, in the sentence, *When collecting seashells, remember to bring a bucket or other container with you*, you could create a class style for the word *seashells*. That class style might look something like this:

```
.seashells {
font-family: Verdana, Arial, Helvetica, sans-serif;
font-size: 12px;
color: #3366CC;
font-style: italic;
}
```

Class style names, whether placed on internal or external style sheets, must have a period (.) before the style name to appear properly in a browser window. Dreamweaver lists, in preview form, all class styles in the Targeted Rule and Class drop-down lists in the Properties inspector.

To apply the class style to a document, select the content in Design view, and select the class style by name in the Targeted Rule or Class drop-down lists in the Properties inspector. Dreamweaver modifies the selection by surrounding it with the <span> tag with the designated class attribute, as the following example shows:

```
<p>When collecting <span class="seashells">seashells</span> remember to bring a
    bucket or other container with you.</p>
```

Figure 1-5 shows how this sentence looks in Design and Code views.

ID styles (ID)

Use the ID styles to create custom styles that are automatically applied to any object on the page with the ID matching the ID style name.

To illustrate, say you have an AP Element (layer) filled with a listing of different models of low-flow showerheads, like the one shown in Figure 1-6. If you then give the layer an ID attribute of "showerheads", using the syntax id="showerheads", and create a style using the syntax #showerheads, that ID style is automatically applied to the layer. As long as the ID style name is preceded with the number symbol (#), the style is automatically applied to the object with a matching ID. This is different from class CSS styles, which must be hand-applied to selections using the Targeted Rule or Class menu in the Properties inspector.

Figure 1-5:
Selectively apply custom styles to content on your page with the <span> tag.

Figure 1-6:
ID Styles are automatically applied to elements with the same ID.

Here's an example of how you write an ID style in the CSS:

```css
#showerheads {
    font-family: Georgia, "Times New Roman", Times, serif;
    background-color: #09C;
    border: 1px solid #039;
    color: #FFF;
    position: absolute;
    width: 330px;
    height: 180px;
    z-index: 1;
    left: 50px;
    top: 50px;
    padding-top: 0px;
    padding-right: 10px;
    padding-bottom: 0px;
    padding-left: 15px;
    }
```

And here is what the HTML markup looks like:

```html
<div id="showerheads">
    <h3>Jet-Stream Low-Flow Showerheads</h3>
    <ul>
     <li>Institutional - E-102</li>
     <li>Classic - E-202</li>
     <li>Freedom - E-302</li>
     <li>Liberty - E-422</li>
     <li>Luxury - E-622</li>
     </ul>
</div>
```

Tag redefine styles

You can use *tag redefine CSS styles*, created with the CSS Styles panel, to modify the preformatted look of existing HTML tags, such as the `<p>`, `<h1>`, and `<td>` tags. For example, the Heading 1 tag (`<h1>`) is preformatted to be large and bold, using whatever font styles the browser's default H1 setting are set to display it in. By redefining the tag in the CSS, you can force content styled with the `<h1>` tag to be displayed with your chosen style attributes, such as 36 pixels, Verdana, navy blue, and bold:

```
h1 {
font-family: Verdana, Arial, Helvetica, sans-serif;
font-size: 36px;
color: #000033;
font-weight: bold;
}
```

Whatever properties or tags you don't redefine in the CSS, however, remain set at the browser defaults, which can vary from browser to browser.

Compound styles

Compound styles are like the muscles of CSS, where you can create some amazing layout and formatting styles. The only drawback to these CSS workhorses is that compound styles can at first seem complicated for the beginner. The W3C (`www.w3.org/TR/REC-CSS1`) has technical definitions of all the things you can achieve with CSS and these *advanced selectors*, but if you're new to CSS, these instructions may be difficult to understand. For a more basic breakdown, read the "Advanced Selectors" article by Ross Shannon on the HTML Source Web site at `www.yourhtmlsource.com/stylesheets/advancedselectors.html`.

The most common use of the compound selector type is to modify the color of links. The default link color for browsers is royal blue, and the default visited link color is purple. If those colors don't blend well with the colors of your Web site, create custom link colors with the compound style type.

What's more, in addition to changing the link and visited link colors, style sheets allow you to add two additional link states to your links:

✦ The hover state, for when you mouse over the link

✦ The active state, for when you click the link

The order in which you create these link states is important. Create the normal link state first, and then the visited state, and then the hover and active states. A different order may cause the links to not work properly. If you have trouble remembering the order, try using the mnemonic "LoVe HAte" for Link, Visited, Hover, Active.

When added to a style sheet, the following code changes the link color for each of the states using a hexadecimal value for the color:

```
a:link {
color: #990000;
}
a:visited {
color: #FF0000;
}
a:hover {
color: #6600CC;
}
a:active {
color: #000000;
}
```

Use any hexadecimal color needed to match your design. In addition to the text color, you can also modify the text decoration (the type of underline attribute the link has), background color (behind the text), font weight (bold), and other style attributes in the CSS Styles panel.

The second most common usage for the compound selector type is for creating styles that are either combinations of tags or tags that are nested inside other tags. Tag combinations are for times when you need to create a style that you'll apply to multiple tags, such as the <body>, <th>, and <td> tags:

```
body,th,td {
margin: 0px;
padding: 0px;
font-family: Verdana, Arial, Helvetica, sans-serif;
font-size: 10px;
color: #99FFFF;
font-weight: bold;
}
```

Nested compound tag styles are used when you want to apply a style to a specific part of a page. For example, in the following code, the selector name applies to all <td> elements that are within any <tr> elements that are within any <html> elements with id "showerheads". In other words, this style is only applied to content inside cells inside a table with the id="showerheads":

```
#showerheads tr td {
font-family: Georgia, "Times New Roman", Times, serif;
font-weight: bold;
color: #393;
}
```

Other great resources for finding more about CSS and compound selectors include the following:

```
www.w3schools.com/css/
http://reference.sitepoint.com/css
www.csszengarden.com/
www.meyerweb.com/eric/css/
www.htmlhelp.com/reference/css/
```

Adding a Style to a New or Existing Style Sheet

To create an internal or external style sheet, you start by defining a style. You can create a class style, tag redefine, ID style, or compound style (all of which are described in the preceding section) using the CSS Styles panel.

Open your HTML document and follow these steps to add a style to a new or existing style sheet:

1. **Click the New CSS Rule icon at the bottom of the CSS Styles panel.**

You can also choose Format⇨CSS Styles⇨New. The New CSS Rule dialog box appears, as shown in Figure 1-7.

Figure 1-7: Create a new CSS rule (style).

2. **Choose a selector type from the following options:**

- **Class:** Create a custom style that you can apply to any content such as a word, phrase, sentence, graphic, or layer.

- **ID:** Create a style for tags with specific ID attributes.

- **Tag:** Redefine the look of an existing tag, such as <p> and <h1>.

- **Compound:** These selectors style links, combinations of tags, and nested tags. They can also be used to create styles using combinators, attribute selectors, pseudoclasses, and pseudoelements.

3. **For the Selector Name, depending on the selector type you chose in Step 2, do one of the following:**

- **Class (can apply to any HTML element):** Enter a name for your new style in the Selector Name text box with a period (.) before the style name, as in **.discount**.

Class names must begin with a period and can have any combination of numbers and letters, but no spaces or other special characters. Fortunately, if you forget to enter the period before the style name, Dreamweaver automatically enters it for you. This, however, is not foolproof; if your style doesn't appear in a browser, check the CSS to see if the period is missing before the class name.

- **ID (applies to only one HTML element):** Choose or enter the ID of the element you'd like to style in the Selector Name text box, as in #showerheads. After you enter an ID, any object with the same ID is automatically styled with this CSS rule.

- **Tag (redefines and HTML element):** Enter an HTML tag in the Tag text box or select the tag that your style redefines in the Tag drop-down list, such as <h1>, <table>, or <p>.

- **Compound (based on your selection):** Select a pseudoclass selector in the drop-down menu for redefining the different link styles in the Selector drop-down list, or type the HTML tag, the combination of tags separated by commas, or the nested tag sequence of the new style in the Selector Name text box.

  For example, typing **#showerheads tr td** creates a style that would automatically apply to any content inside a table cell inside an element with the ID "showerheads", typing **body,th,td** creates a style that automatically applies to multiple tags, and typing or selecting **a:link**, **a:visited**, **a:active**, or **a:hover** creates a style that redefines one of four link state styles. If you know how to create the more advanced compound selector styles, type the proper syntax for that compound selector style into the Style text box.

  After you choose or enter a name for your selector, a description appears in the description box below the Selector Name field.

To understand these compound style descriptions more readily, be sure to click the Less Specific or More Specific buttons (when applicable) below the description area.

4. **In the Rule Definition area, choose one of the following options to specify the location of the new style information:**

   - Choose **(New Style Sheet File)** to create a new external style sheet.

   - Choose **(This Document Only)** to create an internal style sheet.

   - Choose the filename of an existing external CSS file, if available, in the drop-down list.

5. **If you chose to add the new style to a new style sheet in Step 4, enter a name for your new CSS in the Save Style Sheet File As dialog box that appears when you click OK. Click Save to save it to the specified directory. Then skip ahead to Step 7.**

Be sure to name your new CSS with the .css file extension and save it to the root level of your currently managed site. Upon closing this dialog box, Dreamweaver automatically displays the CSS Rule Definition dialog box for defining the new style.

6. **Click OK to close the New CSS Rule dialog box.**

   The CSS Rule Definition dialog box appears, as shown in Figure 1-8. Depending on your selection in Step 3, the title bar in the CSS Rule Definition dialog box may display slightly different text. For instance, if adding a style to an existing CSS, the title bar reads CSS Rule Definition for *.example* in *example.css*.

Figure 1-8: Choose style attributes when creating a new style.

Book III Chapter 1

Looking Good with Cascading Style Sheets (CSS)

7. **Enter the style information for the new style, in any combination of categories.**

   Select a category from the listing on the left, and the right side of the panel changes to support that category's options. The upcoming section "Exploring the CSS Rule Definition Dialog Box" covers all category options in this dialog box.

   To preview before committing to the style settings, click the Apply button. Don't feel pressured to get the style to look exactly right during the creation process, because you can easily edit the style at any time (see the "Editing a CSS Style" section, later in this chapter).

8. **Click OK.**

   The new style is added to the style sheet and is displayed in the CSS Styles panel. To cancel out of the New CSS Rule dialog box without adding a style, click the Cancel button.

9. **Repeat Steps 1 through 8 to create additional styles in the same internal or external CSS.**

You can add as many styles as you want to the CSS, and you can create both internal and external styles at any time. For greatest ease of use, we recommend that you create a single external CSS file and place all your style rules there. That way, you can use a single style sheet for an entire Web site!

Attaching a Style Sheet to Your Document

You can attach an existing style sheet to your document at any stage of development. It can be a fully realized style sheet or a blank one that you build as you style your document. For the purposes of attaching the style sheet, its contents don't matter as long as the file is created and saved in advance with the .css file extension.

If you have an existing external style sheet (perhaps a copy of one used on another project or one provided by a member of your team) or want to use one of Dreamweaver's sample style sheets, save it to the local root folder of your currently managed site or in a folder at the root level of that site. Then follow these steps:

1. **Open the CSS Styles panel and click the Attach Style Sheet icon at the bottom of the panel (refer to Figure 1-4).**

The Attach External Style Sheet dialog box appears, as shown in Figure 1-9.

Figure 1-9:
Attach an external CSS to a page.

2. **In the File/URL field, enter the name of the existing style sheet or click the Browse button to navigate to and select the existing style sheet.**

Dreamweaver has several sample style sheets you can use either as-is or as a starting point for customizing your own style sheet. To use one of the existing style sheets, click the Sample Style Sheets link in the dialog box. The Sample Style Sheets dialog box appears so you can preview and select a style sheet from the listing. Click OK and Dreamweaver instantly attaches that selected style sheet to your page.

3. **In the Add As field, choose the Link or Import option:**

Link: Add the CSS as an external file, where a line of link code containing the CSS file you specified is inserted into the head of the page:

```
<link href="example.css" rel="stylesheet" type="text/css">
```

Import: Add a special `@import` link to the CSS internally in the head area of the page:

```
<style type="text/css">
<!--
@import url("example.css");
-->
</style>
```

Both options link to external CSS files. However, the second method is less reliable with older browsers than the first, so when linking, choose the Link option or simply include both methods in the code.

4. **In the Media field, select an option in the drop-down list or leave this field blank.**

Media types refer to the different types of devices or media a user can view your page with — such as a screen device (for example, a browser), a handheld device (for example, a BlackBerry), or a printer. Select a media type in the drop-down list to identify the linked CSS as being the one to use when that device is used to view the page.

To enter multiple media types at once, separate each type with a comma, for example, **screen, printer, handheld.**

To find out more about CSS for media, visit the World Wide Web Consortium at www.w3.org/TR/CSS21/media.html.

5. **Click the Preview button to see how the CSS will change the appearance of your document.**

6. **Click OK to attach the CSS to your document.**

The CSS Styles panel displays the newly attached external style sheet. To tell the difference between internal and external styles, look for the word `<style>` or the name of the external CSS; internal styles are displayed in a list below a `<style>` tag, whereas external style sheets are displayed below the CSS filename.

Applying a Class Style

You can apply class styles you've created in your internal or external style sheets to any selected asset in an open document. For example, you may want certain words in a sentence to stand out from the rest of the text or style graphics with uniform styling attributes. Before applying a class style, create the style with the CSS Styles panel (see the preceding section).

To apply a class style to your document, follow these steps:

1. **Select the content to be styled in Design or Code view.**

   To assist in selecting an exact tag, select the desired tag in the Tag selector bar at the bottom-left edge of the Document window.

2. **Using the Properties inspector, select the custom style in the Targeted Rule or Class drop-down list.**

   The Targeted Rule and Class menus both list the class styles by name, but the Class menu also shows a preview of class style names (as shown in Figure 1-10), making them easier to recognize.

Figure 1-10:
Apply custom styles with the Class menu.

Dreamweaver styles your selection by adding the <span> tag with your class style around your selection or by appending an existing tag with the new class style:

```
<p>Applying <span class="special">custom</span> styles is easy!</p>
<p class="special">Applying custom styles is easy!</p>
```

To remove a class style, select the text or object in Design view and choose None from the top of the Class drop-down list in the HTML tab of the Properties inspector. Or, in the CSS tab of the Properties inspector, remove a class style from a selection by selecting <Remove Class> from the Targeted Rule drop-down list (refer to Figure 1-2).

Editing a CSS Style

Editing styles in the CSS Styles panel is as easy as creating a new style. Essentially you're changing the style attributes in the same dialog box you used to initially create the style. You can use Current or All mode to enter the style changes.

Editing in All mode

To edit a CSS style with the CSS Styles panel in All mode, open your HTML document and follow these steps:

1. **Click the All button at the top of the panel.**

A list of style rules used on the entire document appears in the All Rules pane, whether internal or external.

2. **Select the style that needs editing.**

Now you have two options: You can edit that style's properties directly in the Properties pane at the bottom of the panel, or you can reopen the Rule Definition dialog box, inside which you can make adjustments to the selected style. .

3. **To edit the style directly in the Properties pane, click the property attribute to activate it and then type, select, or browse for the new property.**

For example, to change the source for a background image, you'd click a Browse button to open a dialog box, where you can select the replacement image.

You may also click the Add Properties link to add a new property to the selected style.

If editing your properties here, you do not have to complete the remaining steps. Otherwise, to find out how to edit styles using the Rule Definition dialog box, proceed to Step 4.

4. **To edit the style in the dialog box, click the Edit Rule icon at the bottom of the panel (refer to Figure 1-4).**

The CSS Rule Definition dialog box appears, identifying the style by name for internal styles, or the style by name and location for external styles, such as CSS Rule Definition for *.example* in *example.css*.

You can also reopen the CSS Rule Definition dialog box by

- Double-clicking the style name in the CSS Styles panel.

- Right-clicking (Windows) or Control+clicking (Mac) the style name and selecting Edit from the context menu.

- Clicking the Edit Rule icon in the CSS Properties inspector.

5. **Edit the style information as needed in any of the style categories in the CSS Rule Definition dialog box.**

The upcoming section "Exploring the CSS Rule Definition Dialog Box" covers the different options in this dialog box. To preview before committing to the edited style settings, click the Apply button.

6. **Click OK.**

The edited style with its new style attributes is displayed in the CSS Styles panel. To cancel out of the New CSS Rule Definition dialog box without modifying the style, click the Cancel button.

**Book III
Chapter 1**

**Looking Good with
Cascading Style
Sheets (CSS)**

Editing in Current mode

To edit a selected CSS style with the CSS Styles panel in Current mode, follow these steps:

1. **Click the Current button at the top of the panel.**

   A summary of style properties for any currently selected style appears.

2. **Select a text element or other asset in your open document to view its style properties.**

   The CSS Styles panel shows the summary for the current selection including detailed information about the style location and editable style properties.

3. **To edit any of the style's properties, select a rule in the Summary for Selection pane and edit those properties directly in the Properties pane at the bottom of the panel.**

   Or you can double-click the rule in the Summary for Selection pane to enter changes in the CSS Rule Definition dialog box. This option is available only if you've enabled the Edit Using CSS Dialog setting in the CSS Styles category of Dreamweaver's Preferences.

   The upcoming section "Exploring the CSS Rule Definition Dialog Box" covers the different options in this dialog box. To preview before committing to the settings, click the Apply button.

4. **Click OK.**

   The edited style with its new style attributes is displayed in the CSS Styles panel. To cancel out of the New CSS Rule Definition dialog box without modifying the style, click the Cancel button.

You can also edit your styles by hand in Code view.

Adding properties to a CSS style

Add properties to any existing CSS style at any time by following these steps:

1. **Choose a rule in the All Rules pane in All mode, or choose a property in the Summary for Selection section of Current mode.**

2. **Do one of the following:**

   - Click the Show Only Set Properties icon and then click the Add Properties link in the Properties pane.

   - Click either the Show Category View or Show List View icon, and fill in the new property value next to the property you want to add.

You can also add properties to an existing style at any time by hand-coding in Code view or by selecting the rule in All mode and reopening the CSS Rule Definition dialog box by clicking the Edit Rule icon at the bottom of the CSS Styles panel.

Deleting a CSS Style

Sometimes you create a style to see how it looks and by the end of a project discover that you've never used it. To help clear the CSS file of unnecessary style information — which also helps to keep the overall file size low — delete any unused styles from your style sheet before publishing your site.

To delete a style from a style sheet listed in the CSS Styles panel, follow these steps:

1. **Click the All button at the top of the panel.**

A list of style rules used in the entire document appears, whether those styles are internal on the page or external on a separate file.

2. **Select the style you want to delete.**

3. **Click the Delete CSS Rule icon at the bottom of the panel (refer to Figure 1-4).**

You can also right-click (Windows) or Control+click (Mac) the style name and choose Delete from the context menu.

If you feel comfortable doing so, you can also hand-delete internal styles from your document or external styles from an external CSS file in Code view.

Removing styles by either method removes the style only from the CSS, not from the HTML code of your pages. To remove the application of a removed style from HTML, use the Find and Replace dialog box to search the entire site for that style attribute. For details about using the Find and Replace dialog box to remove specified content, see Book II, Chapter 2.

Enabling/Disabling CSS Properties

When troubleshooting the way pages are appearing in different browsers, most Web designers look to their CSS code to see if they can find the source of the problem. Typically, designers will "comment out" different styles or properties in the CSS, one style at a time, until they can identify and isolate which CSS rule is disrupting the display of their page in a browser.

To make this troubleshooting process faster and more intuitive, use Dreamweaver's new and helpful Enable/Disable CSS Property feature. With this simple tool, you can quickly and efficiently turn style properties on and off manually, turn all disabled properties back on at once, and delete all disabled properties at once.

Turn style properties on and off in the Properties pane of the CSS Styles panel:

✦ **Disable a CSS property:** To toggle the visibility on and off for a particular style property, click the empty space to the left of the property declaration name on the left side of the panel. After the property is disabled, the gray space next to it displays the red universal *no* sign, as shown in Figure 1-11.

✦ **Enable a disabled CSS property:** To enable a disabled style, click the red universal *no* sign. The *no* sign disappears and the style is reinstated.

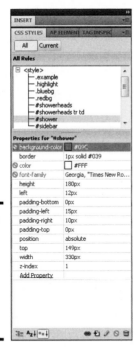

Figure 1-11: Disabled CSS properties display the red universal *no* sign.

When a property is disabled, three things happen:

✦ In Design view, disabled properties will not display on the page, even though the code may still indicate that the style is present.

✦ In the code, disabled properties are wrapped with comment tags preceded by [disabled]. For properties containing comment tags, Dreamweaver leaves those intact and disables only the property, as shown in Figure 1-12.

Figure 1-12: Disabled styles are "commented out" in the code.

```
35   #shower {
36       /* [disabled]font-family: Georgia, "Times New Roman", Times, serif; */
37       /* [disabled]background-color: #09C; |* Not sure if we'll keep this *| */
38       border: 1px solid #039;
39       position: absolute;
40       width: 330px;
41       height: 180px;
42       z-index: 1;
43       left: 12px;
44       top: 149px;
45       padding-top: 0px;
46       padding-right: 10px;
47       padding-bottom: 0px;
48       padding-left: 15px;
49       /* [disabled]color: #FFF; */
50   }
```

✦ In the Code Navigator (which you can invoke by Alt+clicking or Option-clicking on the Mac in Design or Code view), styles containing disabled properties display the red universal *no* sign when you hover your mouse over those styles (see Figure 1-13). To learn about the Code Navigator, see the "Using the Code Navigator" section later in this chapter.

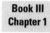

Figure 1-13: The Code Navigator can also identify disabled styles.

```
cssdem
#show    font-family: Georgia, "Times New Roman", Times, serif;
         background-color: #09C;
         border: 1px solid #039;
         position: absolute;
         width: 330px;
         height: 180px;
         z-index: 1;
         left: 12px;
         top: 149px;
         padding-top: 0px;
         padding-right: 10px;
         padding-bottom: 0px;
         padding-left: 15px;
         color: #FFF;
Alt+click to show              Disable  indicator
```

To clean up the CSS code when you are finished testing your styles, you have two options regarding disabled styles:

- **Remove Disabled Styles:** To remove all disabled properties in your style sheet, select Delete All Disabled in Selected Rule from the CSS Styles panel menu or context menu.

- **Re-enable Disabled Styles:** To re-enable all disabled properties in your style sheet, select Enable All Disabled in Selected Rule from the CSS Styles panel menu or context menu.

Note: This feature has some limitations in Live View.

Exploring the CSS Rule Definition Dialog Box

With the CSS Rule Definition dialog box, Adobe has created a simple user interface to create, test, edit, and apply styles. The dialog box includes eight distinct categories of style rules that you can use in any combination to create your styles. These categories are type, background, block, box, border, list, positioning, and extensions.

To use the dialog box, first select a category on the left side of the panel, and then select styling options on the right side of the panel. The right side of the panel's options are determined by the category you select on the left.

As a general rule, when entering individual values to rules with Top, Bottom, Left, and Right fields, enter 0 or None for sides that should not contain values. Doing so improves the chances of different browsers rendering your styles consistently.

Type properties

Use the Type category (shown in Figure 1-14) to create CSS styles with specific font attributes and type styles. In addition to the font face, you can customize the font size, line height, style, decoration, and weight, among other settings.

Figure 1-14: Create text styles with the Type category settings.

Not all browsers support all type properties, and some elements appear differently on a Mac than they do on a PC, so be sure to test the CSS styles in all your target browsers on both platforms before publishing your site. This gives you the opportunity to select different style attributes for your styles if needed. If you don't have access to both platforms or all target browsers, use Adobe's BrowserLab tool at `http://browserlab.adobe.com`.

The following rules are available in the Type category:

✦ **Font-family:** Select a Web-safe font-family in the drop-down list or type the name of the Web-safe font or font set you want to use. Default sets include cross-platform–compatible fonts such as "Verdana, Arial, Helvetica, Sans-serif."

To create your own custom font sets, select the Edit Font List option at the bottom of the drop-down list. The Edit Font List dialog box appears, wherein you create new lists from available system fonts. (For more of a discussion on font sets, see Book II, Chapter 2.)

✦ **Font-size:** Select a preset font size ranging from 9 to 36 in the drop-down list or type a number in the size field. Specify font size in px (pixels), pc (picas), pt (points), in (inches), mm (millimeters), cm (centimeters), em (ems), ex (exs), or % (percentage). Although using pixels is generally recommended over points (the primary unit for print design) to ensure a uniform display on both Macs and PCs, many CSS tutorials now suggest you use ems for font sizes instead due to a resizing issue in Internet Explorer. Additionally, when font sizes are set to ems, they resize correctly if the browser's default text size setting is changed. Resizing will not occur if the fonts are set to pixels.

✦ **Font-style:** Select normal (the default), italic, or oblique as the font style. The oblique style is similar to italic, only it typically refers to a sans-serif font that's tilted about 12 degrees before being adjusted to improve the font's appearance.

✦ **Line-height:** This setting, also called *leading,* sets the text line height from baseline to baseline. Choose Normal to use the automatically calculated standard ratio of font size to line height, or select (value) and enter a number value in pixels, points, in, cm, mm, picas, ems, exs, or %.

✦ **Text-decoration:** The following options are available for text decoration:

• **Underline:** Add an underline to the selected text. This setting is the default for links.

• **Overline:** Add an overline to the selected text. The overline looks just like an underline, only it's above the characters rather than below them. It's a strange-looking style, to be sure, so try not to use it for styling links unless you know your audience is sharp enough to figure it out.

• **Line-through:** Add a line-through, or *strikethrough,* effect to the selected text.

• **Blink:** Make the text blink, or *flash,* in the browser window. (This setting is not a recommended practice and is annoying to site visitors, so don't use it.)

• **None:** Remove all decorative formatting, including underlines on links. This setting is the default for normal text.

**Book III
Chapter 1**

**Looking Good with
Cascading Style
Sheets (CSS)**

+ **Font-weight:** The default font weight is normal, but you may specify the amount of boldness using other font weight options which are bold, bolder, lighter, and numerical bold settings in increments of 100 from 100 to 900, where normal is equal to 400 and bold is equal to 700.

+ **Font-variant:** Select normal or small caps. Normal refers to the default font variance of uppercase and lowercase figures. A small caps setting converts text to small caps.

+ **Text-transform:** Options are capitalize, uppercase, lowercase, and none. For example, selecting uppercase changes the display from normal upper and lowercase lettering to all uppercase letters.

+ **Color:** Select a color from the Web-safe palette or system color picker (the circle at the top-right edge of the pop-up palette). You can also type the hexadecimal code in this field; just remember to include the number symbol (#) before the hex number, as in #990033 or #903 (which is shorthand when the characters in each pair match: 99 becomes 9, 00 becomes 0, and 33 becomes 3), so the color renders properly in the browser.

Background properties

The Background category's rules (see Figure 1-15) define the background settings of various elements on a document. For example, you can add a background color to a page, a table cell, a layer, or selected text.

Figure 1-15:
Add custom background properties to your styles.

The following rules are available in the Background category:

+ **Background-color:** Apply a background color to the body of the page, text, tables, table cells, layers, and more. Select a background color from the Web-safe palette or system color picker, or type the hexadecimal code along with the number symbol (#) before the hex number (as in #990033), so the color renders properly in the browser.

+ **Background-image:** Type a filename or browse to and select the location and filename of an image. You can apply background images to the body of the page, text, a table, a table cell, or a layer.

+ **Background-repeat:** Instruct the browser how to display the background image. By default, background images automatically repeat, or *tile*, both vertically and horizontally unless otherwise specified:

  • **No-repeat:** Display the background image once, without any horizontal or vertical repeating.

  • **Repeat:** Mirror the default setting of continuous horizontal and vertical repeating of a normal background image.

  • **Repeat-x:** Force the specified background image to tile only horizontally. Images are cut off at the borders to fit the element's dimensions.

  • **Repeat-y:** Force the specified background image to tile only vertically. Images are cut off at the borders to fit the element's dimensions.

+ **Background-attachment:** Choose how the background image interacts with content above it:

  • **Fixed:** Treat the background image as if it were immovably fixed to the background of the browser, while text and other assets on the page scroll past or over it.

  • **Scroll:** Add the background image to the page so that text and other assets on the page scroll along with it.

  • **Inherit:** Inherit the fixed or scroll rule from a parent asset, such as a table cell inside a table. This option doesn't appear in the attachment field in Dreamweaver, but you can type it in the text box. (In fact, the Inherit option can be ascribed to every property, including the repeat and font-size properties.)

Browsers inconsistently support the preceding features, so use them with caution.

+ **Background-position (X):** Determine where in the browser window the background image begins its horizontal display or repeat. Enter positioning settings for Left, Center, or Right, or type your own value in pixels, points, in, cm, mm, picas, ems, exs, or %.

+ **Background-position (Y):** Determine where in the browser window the background image begins its vertical display or repeat. Add positioning settings for Top, Center, or Bottom, or type your own value in pixels, points, in, cm, mm, picas, ems, exs, or %.

To center a single image in the browser window, create a style for the `<body>` tag and set the Horizontal and Vertical alignment to Center with a fixed, nonrepeating, background attachment. In the following example, a file called logo.gif is used as the single centered background image:

Book III
Chapter 1

Looking Good with
Cascading Style
Sheets (CSS)

```
<style type="text/css">
<!--
body {
background-attachment: fixed;
background-image: url(images/logo.gif);
background-repeat: no-repeat;
background-position: center;
}
-->
</style>
```

Block properties

The Block rules (shown in Figure 1-16) control the space and alignment of styled tags and attributes. Elements that Dreamweaver treats as CSS layout blocks are

✦ `<div>` tags assigned with absolute or relative positions

✦ `<form>` and `<table>` tags

✦ Images assigned with absolute or relative positions

✦ Tags using the `display:block` style

✦ Paragraphs assigned with absolute or relative positions

Figure 1-16:
Add style properties to set spacing and alignment.

You can view CSS layout block properties such as layout outlines, backgrounds, and box models with Dreamweaver's Visual Aids. To toggle the visibility of these properties on and off, choose View➪Visual Aids and then select the visual aid you want from the submenu.

The following rules are available in the Block category:

+ **Word-spacing:** Select or enter a numerical value in pixels, points, in, cm, mm, picas, ems, exs, or % to evenly control the space between individual words. Positive and negative values are acceptable.

+ **Letter-spacing:** Evenly increase or decrease space between letters and characters by adding positive or negative numerical values in pixels, points, in, cm, mm, picas, ems, exs, or %. Be aware that these settings override text justification. Internet Explorer 4 and up supports this rule.

+ **Vertical-align:** Choose Baseline, Sub, Super, Top, Text-top, Middle, Bottom, Text-bottom, or (Value) to enter a value in pixels, points, in, cm, mm, picas, ems, exs, or %. Preview these alignments in a browser window (except for any in an <img> tag) to see their effect (press F12 in Windows or Shift-F12 on a Mac).

+ **Text-align:** Choose Left, Right, Center, or Justify to align text.

+ **Text-indent:** Enter a text indent numerical value in pixels, points, in, cm, mm, picas, ems, exs, or % to set the rule for indenting the first line of text. Indent sizes may be positive or negative values.

+ **White-space:** Determine how white space inside a block element is displayed:

  • **Normal:** Collapse any white space.

  • **Pre:** Leave the white space as it was coded.

  • **Nowrap:** Wrap text only when the code contains the line break <br> tags. Netscape Navigator and Internet Explorer 5.5 and later support this rule.

+ **Display:** Determine whether or not the element is displayed in the browser, and if so, how. You may, for instance, want to use one of these settings to turn off a style attribute in a CSS for print media:

  • **none:** Turn off, or hide, the display of the styled element.

  • **inline:** Display the element inline with other elements, typically inside the current block.

  • **block:** Display an element as a block.

  • **list-item:** Display elements as a list item with bullets, similar to the <ul> and <ol> tags.

  • **run-in:** Force a block box following a run-in box to become an inline box of the block box. Only Opera 5 and later currently supports this feature.

  • **inline-block:** Display an element as an inline block, which is placed inline but behaves like a regular block.

- **compact:** Style a box of content in such a way that subsequent block boxes are displayed to its left when room permits. Though a bit buggy, this feature is currently supported by Opera 5 and 7+. (For a visual illustration of this feature, see `www.quirksmode.org/css/display.html#compact`.)

- **marker:** Add a marker setting to format content inside a marker box, such as adding numbers or graphics to a list or special notations to styled content.

- **table:** Display elements as a table. Nested elements are displayed as table-row and table-cell; they appear if contained in typical `<tr>` and `<td>` tags. Other table display settings in this list are inline-table, table-row-group, table-header-group, table-footer-group, table-row, table-column-group, table-column, table-cell, and table-caption.

- **inherit:** Inherit the display rule from a parent asset, such as a table cell inside a table.

For more details regarding block display properties, visit the W3C Web site at

```
www.w3.org/TR/REC-CSS2/visuren.html#display-prop
www.w3.org/TR/REC-CSS2/generate.html#markers
www.w3.org/TR/REC-CSS2/tables.html#value-def-table-column
```

Box properties

The Box rules (shown in Figure 1-17) define tags and attributes that control the size and position of assets in the document. Box rules apply to individual sides of the styled asset when adding margin and padding values.

Figure 1-17: Create styles to set the position of page content.

Select the Same for All check box next to Padding and Margin to have uniform (four-sided) box settings.

Unless you have other rules for other sides of an asset, when entering individual values to rules with Top, Bottom, Left, and Right fields, enter 0 or None for sides that don't contain values.

The following rules are available in the Box category:

✦ **Width/Height:** Select Auto or enter a value in pixels, points, in, cm, mm, picas, ems, exs, or %. Auto adjusts the layer's size to fit the area of the layer's contents, whereas a fixed value expands the layer to a fixed size. Note that the width refers to the space inside the padding, except in Internet Explorer, which is buggy.

✦ **Float:** When you float an object (such as an image, paragraph, div, or list), it turns into a block-level element that can then be positioned left or right, relative to the current line. Choose Left, Right, or None to control the position of the element that in turn controls the direction in which other objects float or flow around an object.

✦ **Clear:** Choose Left, Right, Both, or None to control the side of an asset that does not allow AP Elements to sit next to them. When an AP Element appears on the side specified with a clear setting, the asset with the clear setting is bumped to the area below it.

✦ **Padding:** Add space between the content of an element and its border or inner margin, such as a word inside a table cell. Enter individual padding values in pixels, points, in, cm, mm, picas, ems, exs, or % to the Top, Right, Bottom, and Left sides of the styled element. Deselect the Same for All box to adjust sides individually.

✦ **Margin:** Add space between the border of an asset and other nearby assets, such as the area surrounding a sentence or the margin space on the outer edge of the browser window. Add individual margin values in pixels, points, in, cm, mm, picas, ems, exs, or % to the Top, Right, Bottom, and Left sides of the styled asset. Deselect the Same for All box to adjust sides individually.

Border properties

Use the Border rules (shown in Figure 1-18) to define the style, width, and color for border features around styled content.

Select the Same for All check box next to Style, Width, and Color to create uniform border settings, or deselect these options to adjust the sides individually.

**Book III
Chapter 1**

Looking Good with Cascading Style Sheets (CSS)

Figure 1-18:
Create
custom
border
styles with
the Border
category.

The following rules are available in the Border category:

✦ **Style:** Add border styles to your assets using the following settings: None, Dotted, Dashed, Solid, Double, Groove, Ridge, Inset, or Outset.

✦ **Width:** Enter border thickness as Thin, Medium, or Thick, or enter a value in pixels, points, in, cm, mm, picas, ems, exs, or % to the Top, Right, Bottom, and Left fields.

✦ **Color:** Select a border color from the Web-safe palette or system color picker, or type the hexadecimal code along with the number symbol (#) before the hex number, as in #990033, so the color renders properly in the browser.

List properties

Lists in HTML can be ordered (numbered) or unordered (bulleted), and when styling lists with CSS, both list types can have different style options than HTML alone provides for. With CSS, for instance, you can use a custom image in place of the default bullet types. Figure 1-19 shows the List category. You can also set the position of the bullet image relative to the list item text.

The following rules are available in the List category:

✦ **List-style-type:** If creating bulleted lists, select from Disc, Circle, or Square as the list type. If creating numbered lists, choose from Decimal, Lower-roman, Upper-roman, Lower-alpha, Upper-alpha, or None.

✦ **List-style-image:** Type the filename and path location of the graphic, or browse to and select the graphic to be used as the bullet image. When the image is located outside the remote site, be sure to enter the full URL to the image.

✦ **List-style-Position:** Determine how the list item text interacts with the list item's bullet or number. The two options are

  • **Outside:** Force the text to indent and wrap around the bullet/ number.

  • **Inside:** Wrap the text along the left margin.

Figure 1-19:
Create
custom list
styles with
the List
category.

Positioning properties

Use the Positioning rules (shown in Figure 1-20) to tell the browser how to position a selected element such as a layer or content block. For example, you can control an AP Element layer or an image's position in the browser window using positioning rules.

Figure 1-20:
Choose
options for
setting the
position
of an AP
Element or
image.

The following rules are available in the Positioning category:

✦ **Position:** Using the coordinates entered in the Placement boxes, determine the positioning of the layer or tag relative to the browser window:

- **Absolute:** Positioning is relative to the top-left corner of the browser.

- **Fixed:** Positioning is fixed to the top-left corner of the browser.

- **Relative:** Positioning is relative to the styled object's position in the text flow of the file. You must preview this effect in a browser (press F12 or Shift-F12).

- **Static:** Similar to Relative, Static positioning puts the styled object at its location in the text flow, causing elements to stack vertically. This option is the default position of elements when no type is selected.

✦ **Width:** Select Auto or enter a width value in pixels, points, in, cm, mm, picas, ems, exs, or %. Auto sets the layer's size to fit the width of the layer's contents, whereas a fixed value holds the width open to a fixed size.

✦ **Height:** Select Auto or enter a height value in pixels, points, in, cm, mm, picas, ems, exs, or %. Auto sets the layer's size to fit the height of the layer's contents, whereas a fixed value holds the height open to a fixed size.

✦ **Visibility:** Set the initial display settings of the layer. The choices are

- **Inherit:** Force the layer to inherit the visibility property of the layer's parent. If no parent exists, the layer is visible.

- **Visible:** Display the layer's contents, regardless of a parent's visibility value.

- **Hidden:** Hide the layer's contents, regardless of a parent's visibility value.

✦ **Z-Index:** Determine the styled layer's stacking order relative to the browser window. The choices are

- **Auto:** Get the next available z-index number.

- **Inherit:** Inherit a parent's z-index.

You can also manually enter a specific number. The lower the number, the closer to the background; the higher the number, the closer to the viewer. Layers can have both positive and negative values.

You can also change the z-index number of AP Elements quickly through the AP Elements panel.

✦ **Overflow:** Specify how the browser handles the content in a CSS layer or AP Element that exceed the boundaries of the box the layer sits in. The choices follow:

- **Visible:** Increase the layer's size (usually its `height` attribute first, then its `width`) so that all the layer's contents are visible.

- **Hidden:** Maintain the width and height settings of the layer's original size and cuts off, or clips from view, any content that exceeds this size.

- **Scroll:** Add scroll bars to the layer regardless of whether the content fits or exceeds the layer's size. You must preview this option in Live View or in a browser window (press F12 or Shift+F12), because it doesn't appear in the Dreamweaver workspace.

- **Auto:** Add scroll bars automatically if the contents of the layer exceed the layer's width and height. You must preview this option in Live View or in a browser window (press F12 or Shift+F12) because it doesn't appear in the Dreamweaver workspace.

✦ **Placement:** Set the exact size and position of the block element. Browsers then rely on the Type setting for interpreting the location. Be aware that sizes may be overridden if the content exceeds the block element's size. The default units for size and position are pixels, but for CSS layers, you can also use points, in, cm, mm, picas, ems, exs, or % to the Top, Right, Bottom, and Left sides of the layer.

✦ **Clip:** Set the visible area of the layer relative to the layer's top-left edge. Besides clipping content, the clipped area can be accessed with JavaScript to manipulate the values and thereby create special effects such as *wipes* that hide or reveal content on absolutely positioned layers. Enter clip region dimensions in pixels, points, in, cm, mm, picas, ems, exs, or % to the Top, Right, Bottom, and Left sides of the layer.

Extensions properties

Extensions apply forced page breaks and unusual visual effects including pointer styles to your documents. Most browsers don't support many of these extensions, but support may be forthcoming in the next few years, so be sure to test extensively before publishing them on your site. In fact, many more options are in this category than are displayed in the CSS Rule Definition dialog box. To view all the options in the Extensions category, click the Show Category View icon at the bottom of the CSS Styles panel and expand the Extensions category in the Properties pane. Figure 1-21 shows the Extensions category.

Book III
Chapter 1

Looking Good with
Cascading Style
Sheets (CSS)

Figure 1-21:
Add visual
effects and
page breaks
to your files.

The following style attributes are available in the Extensions category of the CSS Rule Definition dialog box:

✦ **Page-break-before/Page-break-after:** Force a page break during the printing process before or after an asset styled with this option. For instance, you may want to force a page break after every instance of a particular image on the Web page styled with this feature. Enter Auto, Always, Left, or Right in the Before and After fields.

✦ **Cursor:** Select a different cursor to be displayed when the visitor's pointer hovers over an object controlled by the style. Cool cursor effects are crosshair, text, wait, default, help, e-resize, ne-resize, n-resize, nw-resize, w-resize, sw-resize, s-resize, se-resize, and auto. For a complete explanation of each cursor style, visit www.w3schools.com/CSS/pr_class_cursor.asp.

✦ **Filter:** Apply several special-effect filters, such as drop shadow and glow, to the styled asset. Remember to test the selected setting in multiple browsers before publishing (press F12 or Shift+F12) because many of these settings are not fully supported.

Renaming CSS Styles

Dreamweaver CS5 streamlines the process of renaming custom styles. In the past, you'd have to change the name in the style sheet and update all the instances of the style name on all the pages of the site for the name change to be complete. Now, you can edit the name in one location and Dreamweaver handles all sitewide updates.

To rename a custom (class) CSS style, follow these steps:

1. **In the Properties inspector, select Rename from the Class drop-down list.**

Or, in the CSS Styles panel, select the style name and choose Rename Class from the panel menu. With this option, all dialog box options are labeled Class instead of Style.

The Rename Style dialog box appears, as shown in Figure 1-22.

2. **Select the style you want to rename in the list of available styles in the Rename Style drop-down list, and then enter the new name in the New Name field.**

Be sure not to use any spaces or special characters in the new filename.

3. **Click OK.**

When the style is in an internal CSS, the change takes place automatically and the Results panel appears showing you all instances of the edited style name. When the style is in an external CSS, however, Dreamweaver alerts you of this and offers to correct the name change in all documents sitewide using the Find and Replace dialog box.

4. **Click the Yes button to change the style name in all documents, the No button to change the name on the style sheet only without updating the site, or the Cancel button to stop the name change process.**

When you click Yes, the Find and Replace dialog box appears.

5. **If you clicked Yes in Step 4, the Find and Replace dialog box appears, ready to make the global update.**

Dreamweaver autopopulates the Find and Replace dialog box with the appropriate settings to correct the name change, but you must decide where the updates should occur. Select Current Document, Open Documents, Folder, Selected Files in Site, or Entire Current Local Site.

**Book III
Chapter 1**

**Looking Good with
Cascading Style
Sheets (CSS)**

6. **Click the Replace All button.**

   A warning dialog box opens to remind you that you cannot undo the operation.

7. **Click OK to proceed or Cancel to cancel the operation.**

   If you clicked OK, the search panel appears in the workspace and displays the results.

Exporting Internal Styles to an External Style Sheet

Placing all your CSS styles in one external file makes it easier to manage your styles sitewide. Fortunately, you can export internal styles to an external style sheet in Dreamweaver in a couple of ways. For example, you may have started a new project using one of the provided Dreamweaver HTML/CSS Layouts, which places CSS styling and positioning rules in the head of the page, and are ready to relocate the CSS to an external file. The first way is to cut the styles from the internal style sheet in Code view, and then paste them into an external style sheet. The second way uses the CSS Styles panel, requires no hand-coding, and is as fast as clicking a few buttons!

To export internal styles to an external style sheet, follow these steps:

1. **Click the All button at the top of the CSS Styles panel.**

   You see a list of all style rules used in the entire document, including internal and external styles.

2. **Below the All button, in the All Rules pane, select all the styles under the <style> tag.**

   To select them all, click the top style, and then Shift+click the bottom style. All the contents of the internal style sheet are selected.

3. **In the CSS Styles panel menu, select Move CSS Rules.**

   The Move to External Style Sheet dialog box appears.

   You can also select the Move CSS Rules option in the CSS Styles panel context menu by right-clicking or Control-clicking one of the selected styles.

4. **Move the selected styles to an existing or new style sheet:**

   • **Style Sheet:** Select an existing CSS file in the drop-down menu or by clicking the Browse button.

   • **A New Style Sheet:** Enter a filename for the new exported CSS file, or select an existing CSS file in the drop-down menu or by clicking the Browse button.

5. **If you elected to move the style to a new style sheet, click OK to save the exported file.**

   Name the file and save it into the existing managed site or navigate to and select another folder to save the new CSS file into.

6. **Remove the internal style tags from the page.**

   With the `<style>` tag still selected in the CSS Styles panel, click the Delete Embedded Style Sheet (trash) icon at the bottom of the panel (refer to Figure 1-4).

7. **If you moved the internal styles to a new external style sheet, you need to attach the new CSS to your HTML file if it's not already attached:**

   a. **Click the Attach Style Sheet icon at the bottom of the panel to add a link to the new external CSS.**

   b. **Enter the File/URL of the new CSS.**

   c. **Click the Add as Link or Import option, enter a media type, and then click OK.**

   Dreamweaver adds the link or `@import` code to attach the selected CSS to the open document.

The CSS Styles panel now lists the name of the newly linked external CSS. Continue using the new external CSS by adding new styles and editing existing styles as needed.

To move styles from within Code view, select the style(s) you'd like to move to an external CSS file and click the Move or Convert CSS icon on the Coding toolbar. This displays the Move to External Style Sheet dialog box as described previously.

Converting Inline Styles to CSS Rules

From time to time, you may want or need to convert an inline style to a normal CSS rule and place that new rule in an internal or external CSS file. For example, an inline style like this:

```
<p>Life is <span style="font-family: Georgia, 'Times New Roman', Times, serif;
    font-size: 16px; font-weight: bold; color: #F63;">sweet!</span></p>
```

can be converted into a regular CSS rule with the custom class name, .sweet, like this:

```
.sweet {
font-family: Georgia, 'Times New Roman', Times, serif;
font-size: 16px;
font-weight: bold;
color: #F63;
}
```

The sentence in the first block of code could then be simply written as

```
<p>Life is <span class="sweet">sweet!</span></p>
```

To convert an inline style to a CSS rule, follow these steps:

1. **Select or place your cursor inside the code of the object styled with an inline style, and choose Format⇨CSS Styles⇨Convert Inline Style to CSS Rule.**

The Convert Inline CSS dialog box appears, as shown in Figure 1-23. You can access this dialog box also by selecting the same option from the context menu when right-clicking (Windows) or Control-clicking (Mac) the object in Design view. Access the dialog box in Code view by clicking the Move or Convert CSS icon on the Coding toolbar.

Figure 1-23: Convert inline CSS to CSS rules.

2. **Select one of the following options from the Convert to drop-down menu:**

- **A new CSS class:** Create a new custom class style. Be sure to use the syntax `.stylename` with a period before the name of the style.

- **All <*n*> tags (where *n* is equal to the name of the selected tag):** Create a new style that redefines the selected tag.

- **A new CSS selector:** Create a style that is automatically applied to any object with a matching ID attribute. Be sure to use the syntax `#stylename` with a number symbol (#) before the name of the style.

3. **Enter a name for your converted CSS style in the field to the right of your Convert To selection.**

4. **In the Create Rule In area, select a new location for the converted style:**

Style sheet: Select an existing CSS file in the drop-down menu or by clicking the Browse button.

The head of this document: Move the converted inline style to the internal style sheet in the head of the document.

5. **Click OK to complete the conversion.**

The newly converted inline style is now applied to the same selection but as a CSS rule on an internal or external CSS file.

Using Design Time Style Sheets

Design Time Style Sheets allow you to view, edit, and hide multiple style sheets while working on a document in Design view. Although most sites use only one external CSS file, you may need multiple style sheets if you are developing two versions of the same Web site (one for Windows and one for Macintosh-only site visitors) or want to develop two different CSS files (one for the screen and one for the print).

This multiple style sheet option is enabled only in Dreamweaver's Design view to assist you with editing style sheets. In a browser window, only the style sheet that is attached inside the document appears to style the page.

Follow these steps to set up Design Time Style Sheets:

1. **Choose Format➪CSS Styles➪Design-Time** from the main menu.

The Design-Time Style Sheets dialog box appears, as shown in Figure 1-24.

Figure 1-24:
Add multiple CSS files to the workspace.

Design-Time Style Sheets	☒
⊞ ⊟	OK
Show only at design time: [ ]	Cancel
	Help
⊞ ⊟	
Hide at design time: [ ]	

2. **In the dialog box, add the settings to hide or show selected style sheets:**

- **Show a style sheet:** Click the plus (+) icon above the Show Only at Design Time field. Browse to and select the style sheet from the Select File dialog box. Repeat to add additional style sheets as needed.

- **Hide a style sheet:** Click the plus (+) icon above the Hide at Design Time field. Browse to and select the style sheet from the Select File dialog box. Repeat to add additional style sheets as needed.

- **Remove a style sheet:** Select the style sheet you want to remove in either category and click the minus (–) icon above that category.

3. **Click OK to close the dialog box.**

The CSS Styles panel is updated to reflect the new style sheet settings, with hidden or design indicators to show each style sheet's Design Time status.

Using the Code Navigator

The Code Navigator, which was introduced in Dreamweaver CS4, displays a pop-up window like the one shown in Figure 1-25, which lets you view and access the CSS code related to a selection or the area surrounding your cursor.

Code Navigator icon

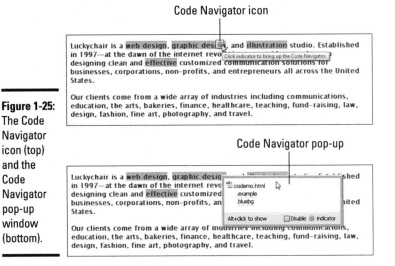

Figure 1-25:
The Code Navigator icon (top) and the Code Navigator pop-up window (bottom).

Code Navigator pop-up

You can access the Code Navigator in any of the following ways:

✦ **Alt-click (Windows) or Option-click (Mac) an element:** This method is the default method for opening the Code Navigator pop-up window.

✦ **Click the Code Navigator icon in Design View:** When you select an object, or let your cursor rest for a moment somewhere on the page, the Code Navigator icon appears. Click the icon to open the pop-up window.

✦ **Click the Show Code Navigator icon in Code View:** To access the Code Navigator icon in Code view, click the Show Code Navigator icon on the Coding toolbar.

✦ **Select View⇨Code Navigator:** This option (near the bottom of the View menu) displays the Code Navigator pop-up window.

Click the Disable icon in the pop-up window to turn the Code Navigator icon on and off.

After the pop-up window appears, you can hover your mouse over any listed CSS style to view the complete style, with all its selectors and declarations. This can be helpful if you're trying to find the hex value of a color or a font used for a particular word or sentence.

To edit a style listed in the pop-up window, click it and the corresponding CSS code appears both in Code view and in the CSS Styles panel, so you can quickly view and edit the code if desired. All changes to the CSS are live, so adjusting the style in Code view is the same as adjusting the style in the CSS Styles panel and (nearly) all changes appear immediately on your page in Design view.

To test any changes you make to the CSS, click the Live View button or launch a browser window by clicking the Preview/Debug in Browser icon on the Document toolbar.

Use the Code Navigator with Live View or Live Code view to quickly view and edit related relevant code and files.

In addition to displaying CSS code, the Code Navigator displays related documents when launching the Code Navigator on objects using JavaScript and server-side includes. Related files might include a Dreamweaver template (DWT file), a library file (LBI file), a CSS file, an external JavaScript file, an iframe source file, or an external SSI (SHTML, CFML, PHP, ASP, ASPX, and so on).

Identifying Elements with CSS Inspect

If you've ever used a Web inspection tool such as Web Inspect or Firebug, you know how helpful it can be to be able to edit, debug, and monitor the CSS, HTML, and JavaScript code in your (or someone else's!) Web pages. With that knowledge comes the understanding that those tools require the use of a browser and an element of patience while you search for information.

In CS5, you now have the option of searching for HTML elements and CSS styles within the Dreamweaver workspace. To use the new CSS Inspect feature (which works only when Live View is enabled), simply click the Inspect button on the Document toolbar.

To make the most out of each CSS Inspect session, we recommend that you work in Split Code, have Live View activated, have the CSS Styles panel open in Current mode, and have Live Code enabled. Because it's likely that you may forget to set up your workspace in this manner before you begin, Dreamweaver displays a simple warning message directly below the Document toolbar along with a Switch Now link that automatically reconfigures your workspace to maximize your CSS Inspect session.

With Live View and CSS Inspect turned on, the next step is to move your cursor around the workspace in Design view to see the highlighting of box model attributes for block-level elements in your code. When highlighted, each block-level element displays different colors for the border, margin, padding, and content, as shown in Figure 1-26.

Figure 1-26: CSS Inspect highlights block-level elements in your code.

Furthermore, block-level elements highlighted in Design view are simultaneously highlighted in Code view, making it even easier for you to identify the HTML tags and code of each block-level element. Fantastic!

But that's not all. You can also use the CSS Styles panel (in Current mode) with CSS Inspect to identify styles associated with the highlighted elements. As you move your cursor around the document, the CSS Styles panel is updated automatically. Then, if you need to edit a property, you can simply click that element in the CSS panel and make your changes.

When CSS Inspect is enabled, other panels—Code View, Live Code, the Tag Selector, the Code Inspector, and the Property Inspector—are updated with the selected element style information.

You can learn more about the box model on the W3C Web site at `www.w3.org/TR/CSS21/box.html`.

Chapter 2: Building Sites with Templates

In This Chapter

✔ Creating a template

✔ Creating editable template regions

✔ Nesting templates

✔ Creating a template-based document

✔ Editing templates and the pages that use them

Dreamweaver has created a quick and easy way to manage the look of your Web site with a master file process called templates. You can unify the overall design of your Web site into one file, called a *template,* and then use that file as the basis for creating all the other pages on your site.

This chapter gives you the lowdown on templates and why they're such a powerful tool, especially for small-to-medium–sized Web sites. You also find detailed instructions for creating, using, editing, and deleting templates.

If you are building a larger site or a site that uses dynamic functionality, other solutions may work better, such as server-side includes (see Book III, Chapter 3) or building a dynamic site using a database and a programming language such as ASP, JSP, PHP, or ColdFusion (see Books VII, VIII, and IX).

Introducing Templates

Templates enable you to control which parts of the template-based pages on your site can be edited and which parts remain fixed across all the pages on a site:

✦ The *editable regions* on a template are defined areas for specific parts of a Web document that have different content on each page of the site, such as the page header, the main text of the page, or a subnavigation element. You need to define and name each editable region in the template. This helps you keep track of the content that should be placed inside it when you create template-based documents.

For example, the main text editable region on the template-based Contact page would display detailed contact information, and the main text editable region on the template-based About page would display detailed information about the company.

✦ The *uneditable areas* of a template, by contrast, are the parts of the layout and design that are constant throughout the Web site. You don't need to define uneditable areas in the template as you do with editable regions.

For example, your navigation and company logo placement should be in the same location from page to page throughout the site; these areas would be uneditable on any template-based pages. Uneditable areas are a particularly useful tool when you work in a team with other designers, writers, and Web developers.

You discover the true beauty and power of Dreamweaver templates when you need to update part of your master layout or design (that means changing any of the uneditable areas of the template). Instead of having to individually modify those elements on each of the pages on your managed site, you only need to edit and save the template, and Dreamweaver automatically updates those elements on all the pages that utilize that template!

You can apply templates to blank or existing documents, and if you change your mind after applying a template to a page, you can simply detach it.

You can also remove template markup or export a page without template markup. After editing a template, Dreamweaver can selectively update pages that use the template or update code inside the entire managed site. Furthermore, from within a page created from a template, you can modify editable tag attributes such as image source or width. One of the most amazing functions of templates, however, is that you can completely modify the entire look of a Web site without having to redo the content, just by attaching a different template to the page!

When you publish your site, you don't need to upload templates to the remote server because they do not affect site functionality. Rather, Dreamweaver uses them as a local tool to help you control the code for common areas on all the pages that use the template file. What you do need to upload to the remote server are all the pages created from the template.

Creating a Template

You can create a template from an existing HTML, Adobe ColdFusion, or Microsoft ASP document, or you can build a template from scratch with a new, untitled, blank template file. After creating the file, you can add editable regions to the template, as described in the later section "Working with Editable Regions." You can also add Design Notes to the file (see Book VI, Chapter 1 for details), as well as modify the default highlighting and code colors in the Preferences dialog box (skip ahead to the "Creating editable regions" section).

Using server scripts in templates

Of necessity, some server scripts must be added to the document code above and below the opening and closing `<html>` tags. When server scripts are placed in templates, however, Dreamweaver may not always copy the script code — or subsequent changes made to it — to pages generated using a particular template, and that could cause significant server errors when scripts in the body of a template-based document depend on these "outside HTML" scripts.

Although Dreamweaver warns you about changing outside HTML scripts, the program doesn't actually do anything to prevent server errors. Fortunately, you can avoid this problem altogether by adding the following code to the `<head>` area of the template:

```
<!-- TemplateInfo
        codeOutsideHTMLIsLocked="true"
    -->
```

The addition of this line of code to the head of the template forces Dreamweaver to copy any changes to scripts outside the `<html>` tags to documents based on that template.

Keep in mind that adding this code removes the ability to edit these scripts in the template-based documents. You can either edit the scripts in the template or edit them individually in the template-based documents, but not both.

In the process of creating a template, Dreamweaver marks up the document code with special Dreamweaver template comment tags that identify the document as a template and define the various areas of the template. The first template comment tag is inserted right after the opening HTML tag, as in the following example:

```
<!-- InstanceBegin template="/Templates/mytemplate.dwt" -->
```

Additional template comment tags, such as the ones that mark the beginning and ending of editable regions, are inserted throughout the file to assist Dreamweaver with sitewide editing.

Dreamweaver templates use a series of comment tag markup code to define areas of the template as editable or uneditable. Although it's not necessary that you know what these tags mean or even how they work to use templates, you can learn more about them on Adobe's Web site at `http://help.adobe.com/en_US/dreamweaver/cs/using/WScbb6b82af55445 94822510a94ae8d65-7a79a.html`.

Converting an HTML page into a template

Although you can convert any existing HTML page into a template, we suggest that you take the time to create a master page with the design layout you want to use for the entire Web site. For greatest efficiency when designing your master HTML page, we recommend the following workflow: Add the text and graphics to the page, enter alternate text tags to images, create hyperlinks where needed, assign JavaScript rollover button behaviors, add text formatting with Cascading Style Sheets, check for spelling mistakes, and include any other media and dynamic settings necessary on the page.

Before you convert your master HTML page into a template for your site, test the page in multiple browsers for link accuracy, layout consistency, and dynamic functionality to ensure that the new template you create from this master page doesn't contain any errors.

When you're confident that the master HTML page is fully functional and is displayed correctly across several browsers, open the page in the Dreamweaver workspace window and follow these steps to convert the file into a Dreamweaver template:

1. **Choose File➪Save as Template.**

Be sure to choose Save as Template rather than Save from the File menu. You can also click the Templates icon in the Common category of the Insert panel and select Make Template from the Templates drop-down list to begin the conversion process.

The Save As Template dialog box appears (see Figure 2-1).

Figure 2-1:
Save your template file with a unique name.

Save As Template
Site: Dreamweaver CS5
Existing templates: (no templates)
Description:
Save as: mytemplate

Buttons: Save, Cancel, Help

2. **In the Site drop-down menu, select a site from the list of all your managed sites into which the new template will be saved.**

When creating a template in a managed site, that site's name should automatically be selected.

3. **In the Description field, enter a short description.**

The description appears in the Description field of the New from Template dialog box when creating a new template-based page.

4. **In the Save As field, enter a name for the template.**

For simplicity, name the template after the project, client, or specific function (such as shoppingcart), and use all lowercase letters (for XHTML compliance) with no spaces or special characters, as in xyzcompany.

5. **Click the Save button. If prompted to update links, click the Yes button.**

   Always say yes; if you click the No button, the links and paths in your page will no longer function properly.

   Dreamweaver creates a Templates folder in the Files panel and places the newly created template file with the .dwt file extension inside that folder, which means the template's location relative to the other files on the site has changed; it's now inside a Templates folder at the root level.

   Leave the template .dwt files inside the Templates folder and do not store any nontemplate files there. This helps you avoid causing errors to template paths.

6. **To create an editable region in your new Template file, select the object, content, or region on the template that you would like to be editable and choose Insert⇨Template Objects⇨Editable Region. Enter a name for the editable region and click OK.**

   Each editable region can contain any asset or combination of items such as a word or a block of text, a graphic, a layer, a table cell, a table row, or even an entire table. Dreamweaver prompts you to name each editable area. Name them using a descriptive term that defines their purpose, such as header, bodytext, or storephoto. When naming editable regions, use single or conjoined words written in all lowercase letters without spaces or any special characters.

   For a more in-depth discussion of editable regions, see "Working with Editable Regions," later in this chapter.

7. **Save and close the template.**

   Should you need to edit the template later, simply open the file in the Files panel. To learn more about editing templates, see the upcoming section "Editing Templates and Updating pages."

Creating a new template from scratch

To create a new, blank template into which you add all the necessary content, follow these steps:

1. **Choose File⇨New to open the New Document window, which is shown in Figure 2-2.**

2. **To create a new, untitled template page, select Blank Template from the Category list and select a template type, such as HTML Template, from the Template Type list.**

   If desired, select a DocType from the DocType menu and attach an existing external CSS file by clicking the Attach Style Sheet icon.

Figure 2-2:
Create
a new
template
using the
Blank
Template
category.

3. (Optional) Select the Enable InContext Editing option if you would like to create pages that can be editable using the InContext Editing system.

(The Enable InContext Editing option becomes active when you choose an HTML page type and a Dreamweaver preset layout.) To learn more about InContext, see Book III, Chapter 6.

4. Click the Create button.

The new template page is displayed as an untitled, unsaved template file in the Dreamweaver workspace.

5. Add content to the new template.

When adding content to the template, pay attention to the document-relative links and paths in the Properties inspector (see Book I, Chapter 3 for details). A correct path includes code that points from the Templates folder to the linked document and appends the link with the appropriate document-relative code, such as `../contact.html` instead of `contact.html`. For best results, use the Point to File or Browse to File icons in the Properties inspector to ensure that the links to other files, images, and objects are correct.

6. To create an editable region, select the desired content in the template and then choose Insert⇨Template Objects⇨Editable Region. Enter a name for the editable region and click OK.

Read the upcoming section "Working with Editable Regions" for instructions on all the editable template region types.

7. Choose File⇨Save As Template.

The Save As Template dialog box appears (see Figure 2-3).

Figure 2-3:
Enter
template
details in
this dialog
box.

8. **In the Site drop-down list, select a managed site to save the new file into.**

9. **(Optional) Add a description for the template.**

The description appears in the Preview area of the New Document window.

10. **In the Save As field, provide the template with an appropriate filename. Click Save.**

Although you can use a combo of uppercase and lowercase letters, for XHTML compliance we recommend the use of all lowercase letters with no spaces or special characters for the template name, as in abcwidgets. Template files automatically are saved in the Templates folder with the .dwt file extension. If the folder doesn't exist yet in your managed site, Dreamweaver will create it automatically.

Working with Editable Regions

The editable regions of a template are the parts that are unlocked, or editable, in a template-based page. These editable regions are perfect for areas that are specific to the page's purpose. For instance, each page may have its own header graphic, text, and subnavigation or sidebar areas.

Each editable region can contain any element or combination of elements such as a block of text, a graphic, a layer, and a table. Although you may create as many editable regions as you want, each template should have at least one editable region.

Editable regions are the most basic form of editable areas on a template. In addition to these, you can also create optional editable regions, repeating regions, repeating tables, and editable tag attributes, as described later in this chapter.

Creating editable regions

To create an editable region in a template, follow these steps:

1. **Select the content in the template file that you want to set as an editable region.**

For example, select a header graphic that displays the name of the page in a special font (as shown in Figure 2-4). Or, rather than selecting content, place the insertion point at the point on the page where you want to insert an editable area.

When creating editable regions that include tables and layers (AP Elements), pay attention to the source code of your selection. For example, when you select the `<td>` tag of a table and convert it into an editable region, that editable region includes both the table cell and its contents. By contrast, when you make the contents of a cell into an editable region, only the contents of the cell become editable and any formatting associated with the table cell itself remains uneditable. Likewise with creating editable areas in layers, when you select a `<div>` tag along with the layer's contents, the layer's positioning and contents are editable. But if you select and convert the contents of a layer into an editable region, only the contents are editable and the layer's position remains fixed.

2. **Choose Insert➪Template Objects➪Editable Region.**

You can also click the Templates icon in the Common category of the Insert panel and choose Editable Region from the drop-down list. The New Editable Region dialog box appears, as shown in Figure 2-5.

3. **Enter a name for the new editable region.**

Name editable areas using a descriptive term (such as header, phone, or headshot), using single or conjoined words written in all lowercase letters without any spaces or other special characters.

4. **Click OK.**

Dreamweaver converts your selection into an editable region by wrapping the content with template markup comment tags in Code view. These editable content regions begin and end with the following code:

```
<!-- TemplateBeginEditable name="EditRegion1" --> . . . <!-- TemplateEndEditable
    -->
```

The space between the two template markup tags indicates areas that remain editable in template-based documents. Take care, however, not to modify the template markup when working in Code view because Dreamweaver uses this markup to manage template updates.

Turn this header graphic into an editable region

Figure 2-4:
Select
template
content,
such as
a header
graphic,
to convert
it into an
editable
region.

Figure 2-5:
Name
editable
template
regions.

In Design view, editable regions in a template are surrounded by a greenish-blue rectangular outline, topped by a tab labeled with the name you just provided (see Figure 2-6). The greenish-blue color is Dreamweaver's preset editable region color, which you can change in the Highlighting category of the Preferences dialog box. Choose Edit➪Preferences (Windows) or Dreamweaver➪Preferences (Mac).

Editable regions in pages created from templates are also shown with the same greenish-blue label and outline, clearly marking where content can be edited.

Editable region

Figure 2-6:
Editable regions are defined by a blue outline and tab label.

Removing editable regions

From time to time, you may need to remove an editable region from your template. For example, because nested editable regions are not allowed in Dreamweaver, you may decide to enlarge or reduce the size of an existing editable region to better define the editable areas on the template, which requires you to delete an existing region before defining a new area.

To remove an editable region from a template, follow these steps:

1. **Open the template in the Dreamweaver workspace window.**

2. **Select the region by clicking the greenish-blue tab in the upper-left corner of the editable region.**

   Or place your cursor in the editable region you want to delete so that Dreamweaver knows which code you want to remove.

3. **Choose Modify⇨Templates⇨Remove Template Markup.**

   Dreamweaver instantly removes the template markup for that editable region, including the code in Code view and the greenish-blue outlines in Design view. The content in that region isn't deleted on the template. For template-based files, however, you need to resolve the issue of where to place any content that used to be in the removed region, which we talk about in the next section.

Renaming editable regions

If you accidentally misspell an editable region label, you could remove and then reapply the editable region with the correct spelling. But for simple name changes to an editable region, Dreamweaver has an even better solution:

1. **Open the template in the Dreamweaver workspace window.**

2. **Select the region you want to rename by clicking the greenish-blue tab in the upper-left corner of the editable region.**

For example, suppose you have an editable region called email that you want to rename as address.

3. **Choose Modify⇨Quick Tag Editor.**

The Quick Tag Editor appears, as shown in Figure 2-7. This is where you adjust the code.

Figure 2-7:
Use the Quick Tag Editor to edit code.

Book III
Chapter 2

Building Sites
with Templates

If you prefer, you can also modify the code directly in Code view. The code in the Quick Tag Editor looks something like this:

```
<!-- TemplateBeginEditable name="email" -->
```

4. **Type the new editable region name in the area in quotes.**

Using the same example, change email to address:

```
<!-- TemplateBeginEditable name="address" -->
```

An even quicker method for renaming the editable template region in a template is to select the editable region by clicking the editable region's greenish-blue tab and changing the name in the Properties inspector.

5. **Choose File⇨Save to save the template.**

If you've previously created template-based pages from this template, Dreamweaver displays the Update Template Files dialog box. Click the Update button to update all template-based files in the managed site.

We don't recommend clicking the Don't Update button because doing so updates only the template file, not any template-based files.

Dreamweaver then launches the Inconsistent Region Names dialog box, shown in Figure 2-8, to map any new region names to any old region locations. If you fail to map the regions, content in the old region name area may be discarded on pages using the template.

Figure 2-8:
Use the
Inconsistent
Regions
Names
dialog box
to map old
editable
region
names
to new
editable
regions.

6. **In the Name column under Editable Regions, select the old editable region name. Then choose the new region name in the Move Content to New Region drop-down list.**

   After selecting the new region name, you see the new region name listed in the Resolved column of the dialog box.

7. **If you adjusted the name of more than one editable region before saving, continue mapping the remaining regions.**

8. **Click OK.**

   Dreamweaver automatically closes the Inconsistent Region Names dialog box and finishes the region renaming process by updating all the pages on the site that use the template you just modified.

9. **Click the Close button on the Update Pages dialog box.**

   The process of changing the region name is complete. If you have any files open that use the template you just modified, save the files before closing them to accept the most recent changes.

Exporting a site without any template markup

In addition to removing or renaming editable regions, Dreamweaver can export an entire Web site full of template-based files—without any template markup—to another folder. The exported site file can even be in XML format if you like. One benefit of removing the markup is that the file sizes may be slightly smaller. Furthermore, when you export an XML version, the XML file is transportable as well as easily importable back into Dreamweaver and other applications.

To export a site without any template code, follow these steps:

1. **Select the managed site that you would like to export from the menu at the top of the Files panel, and open any file from that site, such as the homepage (index.html) or a template page. Then choose Modify⇨Templates⇨Export Without Markup.**

The Export Site Without Template Markup dialog box appears, as shown in Figure 2-9.

Figure 2-9: Export template-based Web files without template markup.

2. **In the Folder field, click the Browse button to choose a destination folder outside the current managed site.**

3. **To save an XML version of exported template-based documents, select the Keep Template Data Files check box. To update changes to files that have already been exported, select the Extract Only Changed Files check box.**

XML (eXtensible Markup Language) is a simple text format that is used to describe data for electronic publishing and for exchanging data on the Web. Visit the W3.org (www.w3.org/XML) and W3Schools (www.w3schools.com/xml/xml_whatis.asp) Web sites to discover more about XML.

4. **Click OK.**

Creating Optional and Optional Editable Regions

Use optional regions on a template for content such as graphics or text that may or may not be needed on every template-based page. For example, you can create an optional region for a Back to Top link that can be set to either visible or hidden in the template-based page, depending on the length of the text placed on the page above it. By using optional regions, you can decide on-the-fly whether you want to include the optional region in the pages you're adding content to.

Within optional regions, you can also set values for template parameters (such as true/false operations) and make conditional statements (such as if . . . else statements) that you can edit later in the template-based file. Dreamweaver adds template comment tags to the page code for the new optional region in two locations. In the head, you see something like this:

```
<!-- TemplateParam name="saleImage" type="boolean" value="true" -->
```

Then in the body code, where the optional region appears, you see additional comment tags like this:

```
<!-- TemplateBeginIf cond="saleImage" -->
<p><img src="/images/onsale.gif" width="100" height="23"> </p>
<!-- TemplateEndIf -->
```

Similar to regular optional regions, *optional editable regions* are also controlled by the template user from within the template-based page, but have the added feature of allowing the template user to edit the optional region's contents.

Creating optional regions

To create an optional region in your template, follow these steps:

1. **Open the template in the Dreamweaver workspace window.**

2. **Select the content that you want to set as the optional region.**

3. **Choose Insert⇨Template Objects⇨Optional Region.**

   You can also click the Templates icon in the Common category of the Insert panel and choose Optional Region from the drop-down list. The New Optional Region dialog box appears, as shown in Figure 2-10.

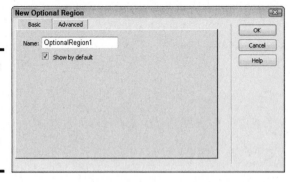

Figure 2-10:
Use this dialog box to specify optional regions in a template.

4. **On the Basic tab, enter a name for the new optional region and select or deselect the Show by Default option.**

   When Show by Default is selected, the new optional region appears on the template-based page; when deselected, the optional region is hidden from view on the template-based page.

5. **(Optional) On the Advanced tab, enter additional parameters or expressions for the new optional region:**

   • **Use Parameter:** Choose an existing parameter in the drop-down list that the selected content should be linked to.

   • **Enter Expression:** Write your own template expressions for controlling whether the region is visible or hidden by default, such as the expression COUNTRY=='United States'.

   Use parameters to control the display of the optional region or expressions to define conditional statements, such as if . . . else statements or true/false operations. Regions can have a default setting of either show or hide. If you do not specify a parameter or expression, you must select the Basic tab before clicking OK.

6. **Click OK.**

   The new optional region is inserted into the template. You can identify the optional regions from normal editable regions by the light blue color of the optional region's tab and outline.

Creating optional editable regions

To create an optional editable region in your template, follow these steps:

1. **Open the template in the Dreamweaver workspace window.**

2. **Click your cursor in the template file where you want to insert the optional editable region, and then choose Insert➪Template Objects➪Editable Optional Region.**

   Insert the optional editable region before inserting the content into the region: You can't wrap an editable region around a selection.

   You can also click the Templates icon in the Common category of the Insert panel and choose Editable Optional Region from the drop-down list. The New Optional Editable Region dialog box appears.

3. **On the Basic tab, enter a name for the new optional editable region.**

4. **(Optional) Click the Advanced tab (shown in Figure 2-11) to add other options such as parameters for conditional statements or expressions.**

   See Step 5 in the preceding section for details on setting parameters and entering expressions.

5. **Click OK.**

Book III
Chapter 2

Building Sites
with Templates

Figure 2-11:
Specify optional editable regions in a template.

Modifying optional regions

After you add an optional editable region to a template, you can modify its settings, including whether the default status for the region is hidden or displayed.

To modify an optional region, follow these steps:

1. **Open a template-based document in the workspace window.**

2. **In the Document window, do one of the following to open the Optional Region dialog box:**

   • **Design view:** Click the template tab of the optional region you want to edit.

   • **Code view:** Click the comment tag of the optional region you want to edit.

3. **Choose Modify⇨Template Properties.**

   The Template Properties dialog box appears.

4. **Make any desired changes to the selected optional region, such as changing the region's visibility or allowing nested templates to control the region.**

5. **Click OK.**

Creating Repeating Regions and Tables

Repeating regions in a template are wonderful to use when you have consistent content areas that repeat, such as rows in a table, but are unsure as to how many sections any particular page may need. With a repeating region, the number of sections can be controlled from within the template-based page, whereas the overall layout and design is still controlled by the template.

For example, Figure 2-12 shows a repeating table in a template-based page that lists all ABC Company's store locations by name, phone number, and address. From inside the template-based page, you can add, delete, and reorder table rows by clicking the repeating region icons.

Move row down

Delete row

Add row | Move row up

Figure 2-12:
Click these
icons to
manage
the content
inside the
repeating
region.

Repeat: contacts	Phone Number	Address
store	phone	address
Our Main Store	800-555-1212	123 Main Street
store	phone	address
Downtown Store	800-555-2121	456 Front Street
store	phone	address
Waterfront Store	800-555-3333	789 Water Street
store	phone	address
Warehouse Store	800-555-5555	15 Market Blvd.
store	phone	address
Corporate Headquarters	800-555-2323	1000 Capital Ave.

Adjust table rows with the repeating region icons:

✦ **Add a new row:** Click the plus (+) icon.

✦ **Delete a row:** Place your cursor inside an editable area in the row you want to remove and click the minus (–) icon at the top of the table.

✦ **Move an entry up or down:** Place your cursor inside an editable area on the row you want to adjust and click the Up or Down arrow icons at the top of the table.

You can also choose Modify➪Templates and then choose a repeating entry or move position option from the submenu.

In Dreamweaver, you can add two kinds of repeating regions to a template file: repeating regions and repeating tables.

Creating repeating regions

Although *repeating regions* are mostly used for tables, you can use them for other purposes, such as a product detail layout including text and graphics. If you need a region's contents to be editable, create a regular editable region from that content because the repeating regions themselves are not editable.

To create a repeating region, follow these steps:

1. **Open the template in the Dreamweaver workspace window.**

2. **Place the cursor where you want to insert the new repeating region, and then choose Insert⇨Template Objects⇨Repeating Region.**

   You can also click the Templates icon in the Common category of the Insert panel and select Repeating Region in the drop-down list. The New Repeating Region dialog box appears.

3. **Enter a name for the new repeating template region.**

   When naming repeating template regions, use single or conjoined words written in all lowercase letters without spaces or any special characters.

4. **Click OK.**

   Dreamweaver inserts the new repeating region in the template.

Creating repeating tables

Use a repeating table for making editable areas with repeating rows. You can also set table attributes and select which consecutive rows within the table repeat.

Follow these steps to create a repeating table:

1. **Open the template in the Dreamweaver workspace window.**

2. **Place your cursor inside the file where you want to insert the table, and then choose Insert⇨Template Objects⇨Repeating Table.**

   You can also click the Templates icon on the Common category of the Insert panel and choose Repeating Table in the drop-down list to open the dialog box. The Insert Repeating Table dialog box appears, as shown in Figure 2-13.

Figure 2-13: Add a repeating table to your template.

TIP

Add alternating row background colors

After (and only after) you insert a repeating table in your template, you can add some template markup to create background colors for alternate table rows in your template-based pages. The markup is added to the first repeating region <tr> tag in the template, in Code view:

```
<tr bgcolor="(_index & 1 ? '#FFFFFF' :
        '#FFFFCC')">
```

You can change the #FFFFFF (white) and #FFFFCC (pale yellow) hexadecimal values of the alternating rows in the sample code to any other colors to match your particular Web design color scheme. The main thing is that the syntax is correct and the code is placed in the right part of your template.

The following example shows the template's repeating table code with repeating regions and alternating background row colors (see the figure):

```
<table width="600" border="1"
        cellpadding="3" cellspacing="0"
        bordercolor="#666666">
<tr><th>First Name</th><th>Last Name</
        th><th>Telephone</th></tr>
<!-- TemplateBeginRepeat name="contacts"
        -->
```

```
<tr bgcolor="(_index & 1 ? '#FFFFFF' :
        '#FFFFCC')">
<td> <!-- TemplateBeginEditable
        name="firstname" --> firstname
        <!-- TemplateEndEditable -->
</td>
<td> <!-- TemplateBeginEditable
        name="lastname" --> lastname
        <!-- TemplateEndEditable -->
</td>
<td> <!-- TemplateBeginEditable
        name="telephone" --> telephone
        <!-- TemplateEndEditable -->
</td>
</tr>
<!-- TemplateEndRepeat -->
</table>
```

After you add this markup (shown in bold in the preceding example) to the first repeating region <tr> tag on your template, any new rows added to the repeating region of the table in the template-based page use the alternating row colors you specified in the code.

Repeat: contacts +|–|▼|▲	Phone Number	Address
store	phone	address
Our Main Store	800-555-1212	123 Main Street
store	phone	address
Downtown Store	800-555-2121	456 Front Street
store	phone	address
Waterfront Store	800-555-3333	789 Water Street
store	phone	address
Warehouse Store	800-555-5555	15 Market Blvd.
store	phone	address
Corporate Headquarters	800-555-2323	1000 Capital Ave.

Building Sites
with Templates

3. **Specify the following attributes for the new repeating table:**

   • **Rows** and **Columns:** Enter the number of rows and columns for the repeating table.

   • **Cell Padding:** Enter a number in pixels to increase the space between the cell's walls and its contents. If left blank, the cell padding is displayed as if it were set to 1 pixel. To remove cell padding, set the size to 0.

   • **Cell Spacing:** Enter a number in pixels to increase the walls of the repeating table between the cells. If left blank, the cell spacing is displayed as if it were set to 2 pixels. To remove cell spacing, set the size to 0.

- **Width:** Enter a number to set the fixed width of the repeating table in pixels, or enter a percentage width between 1 and 100 percent.

- **Border:** Enter the number in pixels for the table border. If left blank, the border is displayed as if it were set to 1 pixel. To remove a border, set the border size to 0.

- **Starting Row:** Enter the row number that begins the repeating region in the repeating table.

- **Ending Row:** Enter the row number that marks the end of the repeating region in the repeating table.

- **Region Name:** Specify a name for the repeating region in the repeating table.

4. **Click OK.**

The repeating table is inserted into your template.

Creating Editable Tag Attributes

Editable tag attributes let you create unlocked tag attributes in a template that can be modified from within the template-based page. For instance, a table may be locked into the page design, but with editable tag attributes, its width or border thickness may be adjusted in the template-based page. Set as many editable tag attributes in the template as you want. Attributes can include text, Boolean (true/false), URL, and color data types.

To create an editable tag attribute, follow these steps:

1. **Open the template in the Dreamweaver workspace window.**

2. **Select the tag of the object to which you want to add an editable tag attribute.**

   For example, if you want to make a particular image editable, select that graphic's <img> tag.

3. **Choose Modify⇨Templates⇨Make Attribute Editable.**

   The Editable Tag Attributes dialog box appears, as shown in Figure 2-14.

4. **Enter details for the attribute you want to make editable.**

   Attribute: If the attribute you want to make editable is listed in the drop-down list, select it. If the attribute is not listed, click the Add button to enter the name of the new attribute.

Figure 2-14:
Specify
editable tag
attributes
in your
templates.

Make Attribute Editable: Enable this feature to make the attribute editable. After you enable this field, the remaining fields in the dialog box become active.

Label: Type a unique name for the attribute to help identify its purpose, such as tableBorder or buttonSrc.

Type: Choose a value from the drop-down list that helps set the attribute's editability. Your options are

- **Text:** Type a text value to edit the tag attribute. For example, you can use text to define the value (left, right, or center) of the align attribute.

- **URL:** Add a link to an object, such as the path to the source file of a graphic.

- **Color:** Select a color from the color palette.

- **True/False:** Change the value of an attribute from true to false, or vice versa.

- **Number:** Type a number for the value of an attribute, such as when you want to change the border attribute of an image.

Default: This field shows the value of the selected object's current attribute, such as . ./images/birds.gif. If needed, type a new initial value for the parameter in the template-based file.

5. **If creating multiple editable tag attributes for the selected tag, repeat Steps 2 through 4 until you've set all the editable tag attributes.**

6. **Click OK to accept the settings.**

Each editable tag attribute adds template parameters to the code whereby the initial value of the attribute is set in the template and the parameter can be changed from within the template-based document, as described in the next section.

Changing editable tag attributes in template-based files

To modify an editable tag attribute from within a template-based document, open the file in the Dreamweaver workspace window and do the following:

1. **Choose Modify⇨Template Properties.**

   The Template Properties dialog box appears, as shown in Figure 2-15.

Figure 2-15: Editable tag attributes can be modified in template-based files.

2. **Select the editable tag attribute to modify in the Name column.**

   The bottom half of the dialog box updates to display the corresponding attribute editing options.

3. **Modify the selected editable tag attribute.**

   For instance, if one of the attributes allowed for changing the value of the page's background color, the bottom of the dialog box displays a Background Color Picker field for selecting a new background color.

4. **If modifying multiple editable tag attributes at once, repeat Steps 2 and 3.**

5. **Click OK.**

Resetting an editable tag attribute to uneditable

To change an editable tag attribute to an uneditable one, open the template and follow these steps:

1. **Select the editable tag in Code view.**

   Selecting the tag makes the editable attribute for this tag automatically appear in the Attribute field of the Editable Tag Attributes dialog box after it opens.

2. **Choose Modify⇨Templates⇨Make Attribute Editable.**

   The Editable Tag Attributes dialog box appears (refer to Figure 2-14).

3. **Deselect the Make Attribute Editable check box next to the attributes you want to disable, and then click OK.**

4. **Save the template and if you have created any template-based files, be sure to say Yes to update them.**

Building Nested Templates

Nested templates are templates whose design layouts and editable areas are based on another template file. A nested template is created when a template-based file is modified and then resaved as a new template file with additional new editable regions. For example, you can create a nested template that contains specific layout elements, such as a real-estate listing Web site where the detail information for each listing shares the same layout yet the overall page layout and design instructions come from the original template.

To make nested templates quickly, begin the creation process with a new template-based document that uses the base template you intend to modify.

Creating nested templates

To create a nested template, follow these steps:

1. **Create a template-based document from the base (original) template.**

   Choose File⇨New and click the Page from Template button in the New Document dialog box. Select the managed site from the Site listing, select the template that you want to use, and then click the Create button in the dialog box. A new template-based document opens in the workspace window.

   The nesting feature doesn't work if you attempt to create a new template from an existing template file. You must create the nested template from a template-based document.

2. **Choose File⇨Save as Template.**

   You can also click the Templates icon on the Common category of the Insert panel and choose Make Nested Template in the drop-down list.

   The Save As Template dialog box appears.

3. **Name the new nested template, and then click Save.**

4. **Add content and new editable regions to the nested template.**

For example, a new nested area can contain a table layout with an image, a header graphic, and a nested table for displaying content. For details on creating an editable region, see "Working with Editable Regions," earlier in the chapter.

5. **When you finish making changes, save the file before creating any template-based pages from the new nested template.**

Modifying nested templates

By default, the base template passes along any editable regions to the nested template. To convert an editable region passed through from a base template to a nested template into an uneditable region, you need to add some markup to the nested template.

To prevent an editable region from being passed to the nested template, follow these steps:

1. **Open the nested template in the Dreamweaver workspace.**

2. **In Code view, add the following code to the editable region code you want to block:**

```
@@(" ")@@
```

Add this code anywhere between the template markup tags: <!-- InstanceBeginEditable --> <!-- InstanceEndEditable -->

For example, code would change from

```
<td><!-- InstanceBeginEditable name="Address" -->
Address 1
<!-- InstanceEndEditable --></td>
```

to this:

```
<td><!-- InstanceBeginEditable name="Address" -->
@@(" ")@@ Address 1
<!-- InstanceEndEditable --></td>
```

Blocked editable regions inside nested templates are displayed with a little expression marker inside their boundaries, as shown in Figure 2-16. In Design view, they are also displayed with an orange highlighting color around the region, compared to the greenish-blue used to identify regular editable regions.

Figure 2-16:
In Design
view,
uneditable
regions
in nested
templates
display
a small
expression
icon.

Expression icon

Although nested templates look nearly identical to base templates, they do not necessarily share common areas when edits are made to the base template. For example, if you add a sentence to a noneditable region on the base template, that content doesn't pass through or appear on the nested template.

Creating a New Document from a Template

After you create a template and set all the editable regions needed inside it, you can begin building the Web site with pages generated from the template.

Create a new template-based page by following these steps:

1. **Choose File➪New to open the New Document dialog box.**

2. **Click the Page from Template button to select the template by site and template name.**

3. **Be sure that the Update Page When Template Changes check box is selected. Then click the Create button.**

The new template-based page appears in the Document window.

4. **Choose File⇨Save to save the new template-based file to the local root folder of the managed site with the name of your choice**

The template-based file is saved as a regular HTML file. As shown in Figure 2-17, template-based pages are quickly identifiable by the yellow highlighted rectangle displaying around the inside of the entire document, topped by a yellow Template: *filename* tab at the top-right edge of the page in Design view.

Figure 2-17:
The Template tab in Design view.

Template tab

5. **Add page-specific content to the editable areas of the page.**

Add text, graphics, tables, and other elements as you need. Locked uneditable regions are easily identifiable because the mouse pointer changes to the locked region pointer (see Figure 2-18).

Figure 2-18:
The locked symbol identifies uneditable regions in the template-based file.

Continue building all the pages for the Web site in a similar fashion until your site is complete, fully tested, and ready for publishing on the Web.

Editing Templates and Updating Pages

Whenever you modify and save a template, Dreamweaver not only recognizes that the template has changed but also gives you the option of automatically updating all the documents on the local managed site that were created with that template. If you'd rather selectively update template-based documents one at a time, Dreamweaver provides a method for that as well.

Modifying a template and updating all the pages that use it

You can update a template in Dreamweaver whenever you want and then apply the changes to all the files based on that template. For example, suppose that you want to change the name of one of the main navigation links (for example, changing Buy to Order) on all the template-based pages on your site. To make the change, open the template that you used to create the template-based pages and modify the link and any other content that may need changing. When you save the template with these changes, Dreamweaver gives you the option of updating all the pages created with that template.

To edit a template and update all the pages that use the template, follow these steps:

1. **Open an existing template by double-clicking the template file listed in the Templates folder of your managed site in the Files panel.**

You can also select the template from the Templates folder in the Files panel and then choose File➪Open from the Files panel menu.

2. **Make any changes to the template.**

As long as the template file is open in the Dreamweaver workspace, you can perform multiple undos from the History panel or choose Edit➪Undo.

3. **Choose File➪Save.**

Dreamweaver recognizes any changes made to a template and displays the Update Template Files dialog box (shown in Figure 2-19), which prompts you to let the program automatically update all pages that use the template.

4. **To update any pages that use this template, click the Update button to launch the Update Pages dialog box, which automatically runs the update.**

When the update is complete, the Update Template Files dialog box displays a status log to confirm how many files were examined and updated. Dreamweaver actually hard-codes the changes into all the files that use the template. You can now confidently upload all the changed documents to the live server.

Figure 2-19:
Dream-
weaver
automates
the
template-
based page
updating
process.

 Another automatic feature Dreamweaver performs when saving changes to templates is syntax checking to ensure that any expression or template parameter added in Code view is accurate. If the syntax is bad, Dreamweaver displays an error message with a reference to the line of code containing the error. You can manually check template syntax at any time by choosing Modify⇨Templates⇨Check Template Syntax.

 Although you can edit nontemplate and template-based pages in Adobe Contribute and InContext, you must edit templates in Dreamweaver. For more information about working with Contribute sites, turn to Book VI. To learn more about Business Catalyst InContext Editing, visit www.adobe. com/products/incontextediting/.

Selectively updating pages with the most recent version of the template

If you make edits to a template but don't want to apply them to all the pages based on it, such as when you add a template to your site from an external source or edit the template in another program, you can manually update the pages. This is also how you can make modifications to a template before committing to updating all the pages on the site, as long as you click No to the Dreamweaver prompt that asks if you want to update all the files that use that template. You can use two methods to selectively update template-based pages.

To update a single template-based document, follow these steps:

1. **Open the template-based document in the workspace window.**

2. **Choose Modify⇨Templates⇨Update Current Page.**

   The current page updates to reflect the most recent version of the template file upon which it is based.

3. **Choose File⇨Save to save the open page.**

   You must save the page to save the updates.

You can update multiple template-based documents — an entire site or just the files attached to the specified template — at once by following these steps:

1. **Choose Modify⇨Templates⇨Update Pages.**

The Update Pages dialog box appears.

2. **Choose one of the following options:**

- **Update the entire site:** Select Entire Site in the Look In drop-down list, and then select your site in the second drop-down list.

- **Update pages with a specific template:** Select Files That Use in the Look In drop-down list, and then select the Dreamweaver template .dwt file that you want to use to perform the update.

3. **Click the Start button to begin the update.**

The Update Pages dialog box performs the update. To see the status log, click the Show Log check box. Updates are immediate.

4. **When you finish your update, click Close to close the dialog box.**

Applying Templates to Pages

You can selectively apply templates to pages open in the Document window with the Assets panel, regardless of whether you previously applied the template.

To apply a template to a new, open document from the Assets panel:

- ✦ Click the Templates icon along the left margin of the Assets panel, select the template from the list, and click the Apply button at the bottom of the panel.

- ✦ Click the Templates icon along the left margin of the Assets panel, then drag and drop the template file into the open Document window.

If you want to apply a template to a document that currently uses a different template, follow these steps:

1. **Open the document in the Dreamweaver workspace.**

2. **Choose Modify⇨Templates⇨Apply Template to Page.**

The Select Template dialog box appears.

3. **Choose a site in the list of managed sites and a template in the list of available templates in that site.**

4. **Click the Select button in the dialog box.**

When regions in the old and new templates have the same names, content in those editable regions are automatically matched up. If all regions match up, the mapping process happens automatically.

However, if the new template contains editable regions with different names than the previously applied template, the Inconsistent Region Names dialog box appears.

5. **If the Inconsistent Region Names dialog box appears, map the editable regions from the old template to the new template. In the Name column under Editable Regions, select the old editable region name. Then choose the new region name in the Move Content to New Region drop-down list.**

    This tells Dreamweaver where the editable region in the old template should be placed in the new template. For instance, the old template may have two editable regions called leftcol and heading, whereas the new template has two regions called main and header. Select and match those regions from the old template to the regions in the new template so the content on the existing page moves to the specified region of the new template.

    If you do not properly map the regions from the old template to the new one when prompted, the information in those regions will be discarded when the new template is applied.

6. **Choose File⇨Save to save the updated page.**

For an alternate nonautomated method, create a new template-based page and then transfer content (by copying and pasting) from the editable regions in the original file to the editable regions in the new template-based page.

Detaching Templates from Pages

Why would you want to detach a template from a template-based page? You may need a page that looks like the rest of the site but is not controlled by the template, or perhaps a particular page needs to be significantly different from the rest of the site, and modifying a template-based page is easier than building the new page from scratch. Or maybe you want to quickly remove all the editable regions and other template markup on a page rather than having to selectively remove the restrictive code. Whatever your reason, the detachment process is simple.

To detach a template from a page, follow these steps:

1. **Open the template-based document in the Dreamweaver workspace.**

2. **Choose Modify⇨Templates⇨Detach from Template.**

    All template-specific markup is automatically removed from the file, making any formerly uneditable areas in the code fully editable again.

3. **Save the file.**

You can reattach the template by choosing Modify⇨Templates⇨Apply Template to Page. Additionally, you can reattach the template by undoing the detachment through the History panel as long as you keep the document open (see Book III, Chapter 4 for more on the History panel). However, after you save and close the file, you have to reattach the template manually.

Managing Templates

Use the Assets panel for renaming and deleting any of your existing templates. To display the list of templates in a managed site, click the Templates icon along the left margin of the Assets panel (see Figure 2-20).

Figure 2-20: Manage your site's templates in the Assets panel.

Templates

Refresh | Edit Template

New Template

Delete Template

Book III Chapter 2

Building Sites with Templates

Renaming a template

Should you ever need to rename a template, Dreamweaver can automate the name change across all the files in the managed site.

To rename a template in the Assets panel, follow these steps:

1. **In the Templates listing in the Assets panel, click to select (but not open) the template name that you want to change.**

Make sure that the template file you're renaming is not open. You can also rename the template in the Files panel.

2. **Click the filename again so the text becomes selectable; type a new filename.**

   If you accidentally double-click and open the template for editing, close the template and try the single-click, pause, single-click method again to activate the template filename.

3. **Press Enter (Windows) or Return (Mac) to complete the name change.**

   In the Update files dialog box that appears, Dreamweaver prompts you to update all template-based documents that use this file.

4. **Click the Update button to update all template-based files.**

Deleting a template file

At the end of a project, you may need to delete template files that weren't used on the site:

1. **From the templates listing in the Assets panel, click to select the template that you want to delete.**

2. **Click the Delete icon at the bottom of the Assets panel.**

   After clicking the icon, you're prompted to confirm the deletion.

When deleting files, remember that after they're gone, your files are gone for good. If you think you may need the file in the future, make a backup of the entire managed site before making the deletion.

Documents based on a deleted template are not automatically detached from it; rather, they keep their existing format, including editable regions. If you need to, you can convert template-based files into regular HTML files by choosing Modify⇨Templates⇨Detach from Template.

Chapter 3: Using Library Items and Server-Side Includes

In This Chapter

✔ **Creating library items**

✔ **Editing and managing library items**

✔ **Creating server-side includes (SSIs)**

✔ **Inserting and editing SSIs**

*D*reamweaver provides you with two ways to create reusable assets for your Web pages: library items and server-side includes. You can add both to documents, templates, and template-based pages, and both can contain any content that normally goes in the body of the page. Here's a closer look at the two options:

✦ **Library items:** These special files contain content of your choice that you can insert in multiple Web pages, yet manage the contents of in one location. After a library item is inserted on a page, its contents are hard-coded into the HTML surrounded by special Dreamweaver library item comment tags. Any time you edit the master library item's contents, all the pages that contain instances of the library files are automatically updated. Library items are great for subnavigation, data tables, copyright notices, and other common page elements that need frequent editing.

✦ **Server-side include (SSI) files:** Like library items, SSIs are special files containing specific content that you can add to multiple Web pages and update in one centralized location. The main difference from library items, however, is that SSI content isn't hard-coded into the HTML file that it's inserted into; instead, SSI files are saved as external HTML files and are then linked — similar to CSS — to a file. When the page is viewed in a browser, the browser finds the external SSI file and displays that file's contents as if it were coded into the page. Use SSIs for sections of Web pages that need frequent or constant editing on larger Web sites, such as a navigation item, daily menu, or class schedule.

This chapter shows you how to create, use, and edit library items and server-side includes.

Introducing Library Items

Library items work in a similar way as Dreamweaver's templates (discussed in Book III, Chapter 2). Whereas templates are the master documents from which you create new documents, *library items* are simply master page elements (such as navigation menus, tables, and images) containing whatever content you want that can be repeated multiple times throughout a site yet managed in a single location. You can use library items as many times as you want without the need for rewriting the code each time. Library items can be placed inside templates or used as standalone master elements in regular or template-based pages.

To understand more plainly how library items work, think of the original/ duplicate relationship of a rubber stamp. Your rubber stamp has the original design, and when you ink it, you can stamp it to make as many copies of that stamp's design as you like. Similarly, with library items, you create the original library item, save it, and then insert an instance, or copy, of it when and where you need it on your Web pages.

Creating Library Items

Create library items from any selected content in the body of your page, including text, graphics, forms, tables, layers, media, and JavaScript. If the selected content includes images or other linked items, those items must stay in their original locations for the library item to work properly.

When your library items include Dreamweaver JavaScript *behaviors* (which let visitors interact in some way with your Web page), Dreamweaver also copies the element and its *event handler* (an action that specifies when the event occurs, such as `onMouseOver`) to the library item file. Then, when you insert an instance of that library item in another document, Dreamweaver automatically adds the necessary JavaScript functions in the `<head>` area of the file so the copied library item containing the behavior works in the new file. By contrast, when hand-coding JavaScript behaviors, be sure to use the Call JavaScript behavior as part of the library item to execute the code; this behavior allows you to set a function or line of script to execute when a particular event happens in the browser. (See Book IV, Chapter 2 for more on behaviors.)

Here are some general guidelines of when to use library items:

✦ Your Web site is small (less than 30 pages).

✦ You manage the site yourself.

✦ You expect to make periodic changes to the library items or you anticipate the library item content may need altering in the future.

✦ You understand that making edits to the library items requires an automated updating of all the pages on your site that use those library items, which therefore means you must upload all the updated files to your server before site visitors can view those changes.

✦ Your Web site host provider doesn't support server-side includes.

✦ Every bit of processor speed is important to you (pages with SSIs take a little longer to load in a browser than pages containing library items).

Here are some good uses for library items:

✦ Footers

✦ Navigation elements

✦ Parts of your page or site that appear on multiple pages and may require periodic updating, such as product tag lines, sponsorship listings, and contact information

✦ Copyright notices

One great use for a library item is a copyright notice at the foot of a page, such as: *Copyright 2010. All rights reserved.* The library item uses the current year now, but come January 1st, you need to update the year. Fortunately, when you're ready to make a date change like this, you update only the original library item—Dreamweaver updates all the pages that use the library item with the new code.

Creating a selection-based library item

Follow these steps to create a library item based on content you've created:

1. **In the Files panel, click the Assets panel tab and then click the Library icon (which looks like an open book) at the bottom of the left margin of the Assets panel.**

If you don't see the Assets panel tab, choose Window➪Assets to open the panel. The Library options appear in the Assets panel, as shown in Figure 3-1. From here, you can create, edit, delete, preview, and otherwise manage the library items in your managed site.

2. **In Code or Design view of the open document, select the content you want to convert into a library item.**

Library items can contain text, graphics, links, tables, layers, JavaScript, Flash movies, and other HTML code elements. In the copyright example, select the copyright sentence in your document such as: *Copyright 2010. All rights reserved.*

Figure 3-1:
The Library
Items
view in
the Assets
panel.

Refresh | Delete Library Item

New Library Item

Edit Library Item

3. **Click the New Library Item icon at the bottom of the Assets panel.**

You can also choose Modify➪Library➪Add Object to Library to create
a new library item. Dreamweaver converts your selected code into a
library item with the .lbi file extension, and then creates a Library folder
and puts your newly created library item there. Visually, you can tell
that your code converted properly into a library item because it is displayed in your page as a block of code with pale yellow highlighting.

4. **Type a descriptive name for your new library item, such as copyright, and press Enter (Windows) or Return (Mac) to accept the
name change.**

By default, new library items are called untitled.lbi until you rename
them in the Assets panel. See the later section, "Renaming library items"
for more on this.

Creating an empty library item

For times when you know you need a library item on your site but don't
have the content for it yet — such as when a client still needs to send you
approved text — you can create and use an empty library item. You can then
edit the library item when the content becomes available.

Changing library highlighting preferences

You can change the yellow highlighting color and the visibility of the highlighting of library items in the Preferences dialog box.

To alter the highlight color, follow these steps:

1. **Choose Edit⇨Preferences (Windows) or Dreamweaver⇨Preferences (Mac) to open the Preferences dialog box.**

2. **Select the Highlighting category on the left side of the dialog box.**

3. **On the right side of the panel, click the Library Items color box and select a new** highlight color with the color picker or type the hexadecimal value in the text box.

4. **Click the Show check box to see the highlighted library color in your documents or deselect the Show option to hide the highlighting.**

5. **Click OK.**

To see the library item highlighting colors in your documents, choose View⇨Visual Aids⇨Invisible Elements. This setting toggles on and off the display of library item highlighting.

You can create an empty library item for later editing by following these steps:

1. **In the Files panel, click the Assets panel tab.**

   You do not need to have any documents open to perform this task.

2. **Click the Library icon at the bottom of the left margin of the Assets panel.**

3. **Click the New Library Item icon at the bottom of the Assets panel.**

   A new untitled library item is added to the Library folder. However, the new library item is not inserted in your page.

4. **Give your new library item a descriptive name and press Enter (Windows) or Return (Mac).**

   You can now edit the content of this library item and add it to your pages at any time.

Inserting a Library Item in Your Document

When you insert a library item in a document, the entire contents of that library item are coded into the page along with library item markup tags, as shown in the following example:

```
<!-- #BeginLibraryItem "/Library/copyright.lbi" -->&copy; Copyright 2010. All
    rights reserved.<!-- #EndLibraryItem -->
```

Follow these steps to insert a library item on a page:

1. **Place your cursor in the open document where you want to insert the library item.**

Setting the insertion point determines the location of the library item. For example, if you want to insert a library item that includes a copyright notice, place your cursor at the foot of a page.

2. **Open the Library area of the Assets panel by choosing Window➪ Assets and then clicking the Library icon at the left edge of the panel.**

The Library area of the Assets panel contains a list of all available library items for the currently managed site.

3. **Select the library item that you want to insert.**

If you have already created library items but do not see them in this listing, click the blue Refresh Site List icon at the bottom of the Assets panel.

4. **Click the Insert icon at the bottom of the Assets panel to add the library item to your page.**

You can add library items to your page also by dragging and dropping the library item from the Library area of the Assets panel to your open document.

Note that when you insert your library item, Dreamweaver writes opening and closing comment tags along with your library item contents, as shown in Figure 3-2.

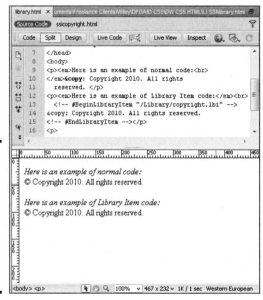

Figure 3-2: Highlighting and comment tags appear when inserting library items.

If you want to insert the contents of a library item in a page without the library item markup, press Ctrl (Windows) or Option (Mac) while dragging the item to the document from the Assets panel. When inserted this way, this instance of the library item is independent from the library source, so the library item no longer controls its contents.

Using library items sounds so easy that you may be wondering why you wouldn't use them. The main criticism about library items is this: Because the library items are hard-coded into your pages, when you edit them, any pages on your site that contain them must also be updated with the new code and subsequently uploaded to your live server before site visitors can see those changes. When your site has many pages, the time the uploading process takes to complete is a major consideration. This issue is especially valid when your site uses the Check In/Check Out system. Furthermore, updating library items alters the Last Modified time of each file, making it more difficult for you to track when a file's unique content was actually last changed.

Editing and Managing Library Items

After you successfully create a library item, you can edit it any time. You can then apply those changes to a single page, the entire site, or all the files that use the library item.

In addition to regular content updates, you may occasionally need to perform other management tasks such as renaming, deleting, detaching, duplicating, or re-creating a library item.

Editing library items

Follow these steps to edit a library item:

1. **In the Files panel group, click the Assets panel tab and then click the Library icon in the left margin of the Assets panel.**

2. **Select the library item that you want to edit.**

   If you're unsure of the name of the library item you want to edit, look in the preview pane of the Library area of the Assets panel to see a thumbnail of the selected library item.

3. **Click the Edit icon on the bottom of the Assets panel to open the library item in the Dreamweaver workspace window.**

   You can also open the library item into its own Document window by selecting the library item in Design or Code view and clicking the Open button in the Properties inspector.

4. **Edit the library item and save the changes by choosing File⇨Save.**

   Because library items are hard-coded into your pages, Dreamweaver automatically prompts you to update all the pages that contain that item.

5. **Click Update if you want Dreamweaver to launch the Update Pages dialog box to automatically find all instances of the original library item code on any pages on your site and update them to match the changes you just made.**

   If you happen to skip this updating prompt, manually perform updates by choosing an update option from the Modify⇨Library menu.

Updating documents and sites that use library items

After editing a library item, you may want to manually update the files that use it rather than having Dreamweaver automate that process for you. You can update a single page from within that document, your entire site, or just the files that use a particular library item.

Updating the current page

To update a library item within the open document, choose Modify⇨ Library⇨Update Current Page.

Updating specific files or an entire site

To update an entire site or all files using a specific library item, follow these steps after you edit the library item:

1. **Choose Modify⇨Library⇨Update Pages.**

   The Update Pages dialog box appears, as shown in Figure 3-3.

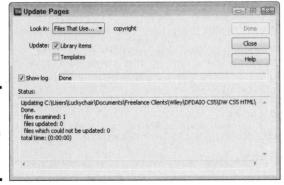

Figure 3-3:
Update
library items
on an entire
site.

2. **Select an option in the Look In drop-down list, depending on what you want to do:**

- **Update the library item sitewide:** Select Entire Site, and in the right drop-down list, select the name of the managed site.

- **Update the library item in all files:** Select Files That Use, and in the right drop-down list, select the library item name.

3. **Check to see that Library Items is selected as an Update option.**

4. **Click the Start button to begin the update process.**

   Select the Show Log check box to view a status log of the update process. The log displays a record of the number of files on the site that were successfully examined and updated, plus any files that Dreamweaver was unable to update.

5. **When the update is complete, click Close.**

Renaming library items

You can easily rename library items in the Library area of the Assets panel of a managed site. We highly recommend that you perform your library name changes from within Dreamweaver.

Renaming a library item outside Dreamweaver breaks the library links to the documents that use them.

To rename a library item, follow these steps:

**Book III
Chapter 3**

1. **In the Files panel group, click the Assets panel tab and then click the Library icon in the left margin of the Assets panel.**

2. **Select the library item you want to rename.**

   If you're unsure of the library item's current name, look in the preview pane of the Library area of the Assets panel to see a thumbnail of the selected library item.

3. **Click the library item name again, so that the text becomes editable, and type the new name.**

   If you accidentally double-click and open the library item for editing, close the library item and try the "single-click, pause, single-click method" to edit the library item filename.

4. **After entering the new name, press Enter (Windows) or Return (Mac) to complete the name change.**

   Dreamweaver displays the Update Files dialog box.

5. **Click the Update button.**

   Dreamweaver automatically updates all documents in the managed site that use this library item. To prevent Dreamweaver from performing the automatic update, click the Don't Update button. For example, you may want to delay updating documents in the managed site until after changing multiple library files on a site.

Deleting library items

To help keep your library items organized while developing your site, delete any unused or unnecessary library items in the Library area of the Assets panel by following these steps:

1. **In the Files panel group, click the Assets panel tab and then click the Library icon in the left margin of the Assets panel.**

2. **Select the library item that you want to delete.**

   If you're unsure of the name of the library item that you want to delete, select an item from the list and look in the preview pane to see a thumbnail of the selected item.

3. **To permanently delete the library item from the Library, press the Delete key on your keyboard and confirm the deletion.**

   You can also click the Delete button at the bottom of the Assets panel and confirm the deletion.

This deletion process permanently removes the library item from the Library, although it doesn't delete instances of that item from the contents of any documents that used it. Therefore, delete your library items with care.

Detaching library items

After you insert a library item into a document, you can't edit an individual instance of it unless you break the link between the library item and the document by detaching it, thereby converting the library item into editable text. Then, when you update the original library item after an instance is detached, the detached instance doesn't update along with the other instances of the library item.

You may want to detach an instance of a library item from its source for many reasons:

✦ You need to modify a significant portion of the library item on a single page.

✦ You've used the library item only on a single page.

✦ You want to insert a library item created for another site. You insert it on a page, detach it to break the links to that other site, and then re-create the link within the currently managed site.

To detach an instance of a library item from its source and convert it into editable content, follow these steps:

1. **Select the library item in the document that you want to convert into editable content.**

2. **Click the Detach from Original button in the Properties inspector.**

Dreamweaver alerts you that making the item instance editable prevents it from receiving updates from the original library item.

3. **Click OK.**

The selected library item instance then loses its library item highlighting and markup to become normal, editable content.

To modify instances of library items that contain Dreamweaver behaviors, you must detach the library item from its source to make the behavior editable. After editing the behavior, use the updated content to create a new library item or use it as a replacement for its previous version.

Copying a library item from one site to another

To use an existing library item on one Web site in another managed site, follow these steps:

1. **In the Files panel group, click the Assets panel tab and then click the Library icon.**

2. **In the list of Library items that appears, select the library item that you want to duplicate.**

3. **To make a copy inside another managed site, choose Copy to Site from the Assets panel menu and then choose the desired managed site by name from the submenu.**

Dreamweaver copies the duplicate library item into the selected managed site. If the new site does not already have a Library folder, Dreamweaver creates one and places the copied library item into it.

Re-creating library items

Occasionally, you delete a library item from the Library area of the Assets panel even though instances of it still remain throughout the site. If you want the library item back to control modifications made to all the instances, you must re-create it.

Here's how to re-create a library item:

1. **In an open document, select the instance of the library item that you need to re-create.**

2. **Click the Recreate button in the Properties inspector.**

A new library item is added to the Library area of the Assets panel. If a library item already exists there with the same name, Dreamweaver asks if you want to overwrite the existing file. Click OK to proceed or click Cancel. If you'd still like to save the library item, but with a different name, click the New Library Item icon at the bottom of the panel.

A master copy of the re-created library item is inserted into the Library folder.

Understanding Server-Side Includes

If you understand how to create and use library items (as described earlier in the chapter), you can quickly grasp the concept behind server-side includes (SSIs). Like library items, SSIs can comprise any combination of HTML, JavaScript, and graphics. But unlike library items, they have no opening and closing comment tags surrounding the code and the content of the SSI is not hard-coded into your Web page. Rather, a simple line of code is added to your page that points to the external SSI file on your live server, like this:

```
<!--#include file="serversideinclude.html" -->
```

Only the reference to, and not the contents of, the SSI file are part of the include instructions.

An SSI is an external HTML file that a live server automatically adds to the page it's inserted on when a browser requests that page from the server. The server then processes the include instructions and delivers a document that replaces the SSI statement code with the content of the SSI file.

When making the decision to use SSI, keep these points in mind:

✦ Servers process, or *parse,* pages with SSIs differently than regular HTML documents, and that may put more demand on a server's processor, which in turn could lead to slower page serving for all the pages on your entire site.

✦ When you preview the file with the include instructions in a browser locally (before testing it on a live server), your browser doesn't parse the SSI, in which case you may not see the include content on the page.

To solve this issue, Dreamweaver lets you preview documents in Design view exactly as they'll appear on a server. Furthermore, by selecting the Preview Using Temporary File option in the Preview in Browser category of Dreamweaver's Preferences dialog box, you can create a temporary copy of the file for preview and testing that displays the SSI in your local browser by mimicking how the file would behave on a server.

✦ The SSI markup syntax must match the type of Web server the files are being displayed on. Some servers are configured to examine all files to see if they have server-side includes, whereas other servers examine only files with the .shtml, .shtm, or .inc file extension.

Your particular server may require that you rename all files containing SSIs with the .shtml, .shtm, or .inc file extension. For example, you may need to rename a file with an SSI named menu.html to menu.shtml for the page to be displayed properly. Check with your system administrator or host provider to see whether you're required to change the file extension for documents with SSIs.

The bottom line is that you should test files containing SSIs on a live server before publishing them on the Internet, just in case the host server isn't configured to display them properly or you need to modify your code to support them.

Creating and Inserting Server-Side Includes

Like a regular HTML file, a server-side include file (an example of which is shown in Figure 3-4) comprises the content you want to include on another page and should be saved with the .html or .htm file extension. What it shouldn't contain in the code, however, are any <doctype>, <meta>, or opening or closing <html>, <head>, <title>, or <body> tags. This is because the SSI is *included* on another page that already has those HTML tags. Figure 3-5 demonstrates how an SSI file is included in the code of another document.

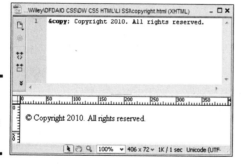

Figure 3-4: A server-side include file.

Book III Chapter 3

Using Library Items and Server-Side Includes

Figure 3-5: A server-side include inside another document.

If one or more of the following general guidelines apply, you may want to use server-side includes:

✦ Your Web site is large (more than 30 pages).

✦ Two or more people manage the site from different locations.

✦ Your site content needs frequent editing.

✦ You are confident that your host provider supports SSIs.

✦ Your clients want to update part of the site regularly, and they understand and can write the SSI content in HTML themselves.

✦ You love the fact that you have to upload only the SSI files to the server when their content changes, rather than uploading all the files that contain them, as you must do for library items.

✦ Your site is database driven (ASP, JSP, PHP, CFML). Although your site does not need to have a database to use SSIs, if it does, that alone is a big enough reason to consider using SSIs.

✦ You've tested your server and are confident that the SSIs work.

Here are some good uses for SSIs:

✦ Footers

✦ Copyright notices

✦ Navigation elements

✦ Jump menus

✦ Parts of your page or site that may require periodic updating, such as class schedules, course descriptions, or news items

✦ Parts of your site that require regular updates, such as a menu, a features list, technical data, or an event listing

If you're uncertain whether library items or server-side includes are best for your projects, consider this general rule: If the site is small, use library items. If the site is large and needs regular updates to certain parts of the content, your server supports SSIs, and you don't mind the ever-so-slightly slower page opening times, use SSIs.

Creating a server-side include

One fast way to create an SSI file is to build the content in a normal Dreamweaver HTML file, and then copy the content from that file and paste it into an empty document that doesn't contain any HTML markup.

Presuming that you've already created a document with the content for the SSI, follow these instructions to convert that content into a server-side include file:

1. **Open the document that has the content for the SSI file.**

2. **Select the content and choose Edit⇨Copy.**

The copied content is temporarily placed on your computer's Clipboard.

3. Close the open document.

4. Choose File➪New to open a new Blank Page HTML document in the Dreamweaver workspace window.

5. In Code view, choose Edit➪Select All to select all the HTML code in the file, and then press the Delete or Backspace key on your keyboard.

Be sure the entire document is empty of all code before proceeding.

6. With your cursor still in Code view of the empty file, choose Edit➪Paste to paste the copied content from the original file.

7. Save the new SSI file with an appropriate filename and the .html or .htm file extension.

If you plan to use several SSI files in the same Web site, consider saving all the SSI files into one folder at the site's root level for better organization of the SSI files.

You can now insert the SSI file into another file, as described in the next section.

Inserting a server-side include

Dreamweaver writes the appropriate syntax into your code when you use the built-in SSI command. Insert your server-side include files into regular documents, dynamic documents, templates, or template-based files.

To insert an SSI into a page, follow these steps:

1. Open the document that you want to add the SSI to.

2. Click the cursor where you want the SSI to appear.

Use Design view or Code view.

3. Choose Insert➪Server-Side Include.

The Select File dialog box appears.

4. Browse to and select the SSI .html file.

If you've saved your SSI files into a separate folder, navigate to that folder and select the appropriate SSI file.

5. Click OK.

Dreamweaver adds the appropriate SSI code to your document, as shown in the following example, where the SSI file, called copyright. html, is located in a folder called ssi:

```
<!--#include file="/ssi/copyright.html" -->
```

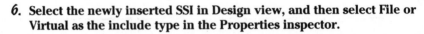

6. **Select the newly inserted SSI in Design view, and then select File or Virtual as the include type in the Properties inspector.**

You can choose from two SSI types: File or Virtual. Depending on the type of server you have, you may need to replace the word *file* with *virtual* in the include code instructions. Apache servers typically use the Virtual setting, whereas File is the standard for Microsoft Internet Information Server (IIS) (this is the Dreamweaver default). If you're not sure which one to choose, try the first one, and if that doesn't work, try the second, or better yet, ask your host provider or system administrator for guidance.

When the server runs IIS software, ask your host provider or system administrator about installing special software that will allow you to include a file in a folder above the current folder in the site root folder hierarchy.

If your server uses another kind of software besides Apache or IIS, check with your host provider or system administrator for which SSI type to use.

Dreamweaver immediately displays the include file's content in Design view, such as

```
© Copyright 2010. All rights reserved.
```

while showing include instruction markup in Code view, such as

```
<!--#include file="/ssi/copyright.html" -->
```

7. **Save the file that contains the newly inserted SSI with the .html or .shtml file extension as instructed by your system administrator or host provider.**

The include file itself doesn't need any particular extension. However, if you want the include file to also include another subfile, you need to save the include file as an .shtml file (or whatever extension type enables server-side includes on your server).

8. **Upload the SSI files and any documents containing SSI to your remote host server.**

If you saved the SSI files into a local folder, be sure to upload the same folder structure to the server so that the links to the SSI files match.

To change to a different SSI file after inserting one on a page, select the server-side include in the open file and click the folder icon next to the Filename field in the Properties inspector to browse for and choose a new SSI file.

The SSIs now render seamlessly in the browser window. If the SSI files are not displayed in the browser, you may need to convert your Web site linking system to use site root–relative linking, as described in the sidebar.

Document-relative versus root-relative links

When working with SSIs, their mere existence on some Web servers may require site root–relative linking rather than document-relative linking. In other words, you may need to add a forward slash before the SSI filename. For example, a document-relative link looks like this:

```
<!--#include file="ssi/serversideinclude.
    html" -->
```

A site root–relative link looks like this:

```
<!--#include file="/ssi/
    serversideinclude.html" -->
```

The forward slash at the start of the path, before the folder or filename, tells the browser viewing the site to use the root level as the starting point for locating files on the server.

Speak with your system administrator or host provider to find out if and how they support SSIs before building your pages with them. If you do ultimately choose to use server-side includes, test them on your server to ensure that they'll display properly before publishing the entire site.

For further information about relative links and site organization, see Book I, Chapter 3.

Editing Server-Side Includes

Edit a server-side include file just as you would any other HTML document by opening the file in the Dreamweaver workspace, making changes, saving it, and uploading the changed SSI file to the host server.

To open the file for editing in the Dreamweaver workspace window, double-click the SSI file in the Files panel. You can also select the SSI content in Design or Code view of the page it's inserted on and click the Edit button in the Properties inspector, or simply double-click the SSI content in Design view.

In Dreamweaver's Design view, edits to the SSI file appear immediately in the files containing them. But for site visitors to see the changes in a browser window, you must upload the updated SSI file to the host server.

Chapter 4: Creating Code Snippets and History Panel Commands

In This Chapter

✔ Understanding snippets

✔ Using Dreamweaver's snippets

✔ Making your own snippets

✔ Editing, deleting, and managing snippets

✔ Creating History panel commands

✔ Working with the History panel

*I*f you build a lot of Web sites, you know that you'll use certain elements over and over again, but each time you need them, you either have to recall a particular command or, more likely, copy and paste the code containing the content you want to reuse. Knowing that is not the most efficient way to work, Dreamweaver created a solution called code snippets that, after you create them, are available to you across all your managed sites. Snippets are valuable timesavers that every Dreamweaver user should know about and take advantage of.

Don't confuse snippets with library items or SSIs (which we cover in Book III, Chapter 3). Snippets are intended to be used as either shortcuts for inserting a single instance of content on a page or a way of quickly modifying selected content in a file.

Similar in theory to Microsoft's macros or Adobe's Actions, snippets are a fantastic way to automate some of your repetitive tasks and make your job easier. They comprise bits of code or content that you can save, edit, use, and reuse as often as you want on any Web site you happen to be working on. Dreamweaver even comes with a great set of prewritten, logically categorized, ready-to-use snippets. You can find them sitting in the Snippets panel.

Other terrific timesaving tools are the temporary and permanent custom commands you can create with the Dreamweaver History. Record to save any series of steps — such as select, bold, deselect — to play again and again at a later time.

In this chapter, you find out how to create, insert, edit, and delete snippets, as well as organize them in folders to share with your workmates. This chapter also covers how to record and play History panel commands.

Understanding What Snippets Do

The best snippets are the ones that save you time or at least limit the work you need to perform so you don't have to retype anything, such as the following:

✦ Code including HTML, JavaScript, ASP, JSP, PHP, and even CFML (ColdFusion Markup Language).

✦ Text that you use often. For instance, you may like to add a copyright notice such as © *2010 All rights reserved* at the foot of your pages.

✦ Navigation tables with bullets and text that have temporary links already applied to each navigation word so all you need to do after inserting the snippet on your page is type the real navigation names and links.

✦ JavaScript information, such as the Set Text of Status Bar JavaScript behavior, or perhaps a set of opening and closing comment tags.

There are two basic types of snippets:

✦ **Wrap snippets:** These snippets insert code before and after selected content on the page, such as adding `<span>` tags around a selected line of text, as in

```
<span>This sentence is wrapped with span tags.</span>
```

✦ **Block snippets:** These simply drop in the snippet content after the insertion point on the page, such as a line of code with JavaScript to display the current date.

Using Dreamweaver's Snippets

Dreamweaver comes with a great set of preset snippets already categorized into files for Comments, Footers, Form Elements, JavaScript, Meta, Navigation, Text, and ~Legacy. Open the Snippets panel by choosing Window⇨Snippets to review Dreamweaver's snippets folders, as shown in Figure 4-1.

Each preset folder includes a list of snippets organized alphabetically by name. To preview each snippet on the page, select it and look at the preview pane of the Snippets panel. To read a description of the snippet and review the code that it uses, click the Edit Snippet icon at the bottom of the panel to open the Snippet dialog box.

Figure 4-1:
The
Snippets
panel.

New Snippet Folder | Delete Snippet

New Snippet

Edit Snippet

To use a block snippet, place an insertion point in an open document, select
the snippet from the Snippets panel, and click the Insert icon at the bottom
of the panel. You can also drag and drop the snippet from the panel into an
open document, as you would an image or any other media file.

To use a wrap snippet, select the content in Design view that the snippet will
wrap around, select the snippet in the Snippets panel, and click the Insert
icon at the bottom of the panel.

You can find several good Web sites — including the Adobe Web site — to
exchange snippets with other Web designers and programmers. Search for
Dreamweaver snippets or *Snippets exchange.* Then, when you download new
snippets or create your own, you can file them in any existing Dreamweaver
snippets folder or create a new folder and file them there.

Creating Code Snippets

To create a code snippet, you must begin by knowing what you want to turn
into a snippet. Think about what can save you time (such as a snippet to
create a time and date stamp) or the types of content you frequently use
(such as copyright notices or meta tag information).

Snippets can be as simple or as complex as you need them to be. The following sections show you how to create four types of snippets from scratch:
text, JavaScript, wrap, and graphic.

**Book III
Chapter 4**

Creating Code
Snippets and
History Panel
Commands

To download free copies of the snippets described in this chapter, visit `www.luckychair.com/downloads.html`.

Creating a text snippet

Say you work with lots of artists and have a standard copyright notice you want to use regarding their work being displayed online. By creating a code snippet, you never have to type that copyright notice again, save for adding the correct artist name and company information after inserting the snippet on your page.

Follow these steps to insert a text snippet on your Web page:

1. **Choose Window⇨Snippets to open the Snippets panel.**

2. **Click the New Snippet icon (refer to Figure 4-1).**

The Snippet dialog box appears.

3. **Type a name for the snippet in the Name text box.**

Snippet names can't contain characters that are invalid in filenames, such as slashes (/ or \), special characters, or double quotes (").

In Figure 4-2, the snippet is named Artist Copyright Statement.

Figure 4-2:
Enter your
snippet
details.

4. **Write a brief text description for the snippet in the Description text box.**

For instance, a copyright notice description might look like this: *Inserts standard copyright statement for artists.*

5. **Select Insert Block as the Snippet Type.**

The Insert Block type is best for snippets containing only content. By contrast, the Wrap Selection type surrounds or wraps around your selected content, which is especially helpful for applying links, scripts, special formatting, and navigation.

6. Add the code for your snippet in the Insert Code text box.

Here's what to type for the copyright example:

```
All artwork featured on THIS WEBSITE is copyrighted material and may not
    be reproduced, downloaded, or used in any other format, on any other
    product, without permission from THIS COMPANY and the artist.
```

7. Select a Preview Type: Design or Code.

The Code preview type shows the code in the preview pane of the Snippets panel; the Design preview type shows a Design view-style view of the snippet in the panel's preview pane.

8. Click OK.

Your new snippet appears in the Snippets panel.

To use your new snippet, open an HTML page and, in either Design or Code view, click anywhere on the page to create an insertion point with your cursor. Then select the new snippet from the Snippets panel and click the Insert icon or double-click the Snippet name to quickly insert the snippet onto your page. The snippet appears on your page, as shown in Figure 4-3.

Book III
Chapter 4

**Creating Code
Snippets and
History Panel
Commands**

Figure 4-3:
The snippet shows up in the Document window after insertion.

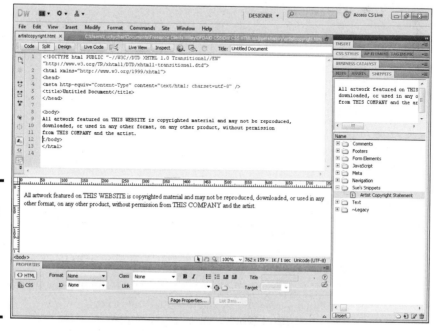

Creating a JavaScript snippet

The Internet has a lot of great free JavaScripts for use on a Web page (turn to Book IV, Chapter 2 to find out about JavaScript). You can find many useful free JavaScripts on the following sites:

+ `www.dynamicdrive.com/`

+ `www.javascript.com/`

+ `javascript.internet.com/`

+ `www.javascriptkit.com/cutpastejava.shtml`

+ `www.java-scripts.net/`

+ `www.javafile.com/`

+ `webdeveloper.earthweb.com/webjs/`

+ `www.javascriptsearch.com/`

JavaScripts that you plan to use regularly make great code snippets. Besides saving you valuable time, one of the greatest advantages to using JavaScript snippets is that you needn't understand the JavaScript code to use them. The following are some great examples of JavaScript that you can easily convert into reusable code snippets:

+ Time and date stamps and clock scripts

+ Customizable menu navigation scripts

+ Game scripts

+ Password-protection scripts

+ Text and status bar effects scripts

+ Image effects and slide show scripts

Follow these steps to make a JavaScript snippet:

1. **Open the Snippets panel by choosing Window⇨Snippets.**

2. **Click the New Snippet icon at the bottom of the Snippets panel (refer to Figure 4-1).**

   The Snippet dialog box appears.

3. **Type a name for the snippet in the Name text box.**

   Suppose that you want to create a snippet with JavaScript that displays the document's last modified date starting with the words, *This document was last modified on:*. In the Name text box, type something like **This document was last modified on: (Date).**

4. **Write a text description for the snippet in the Description text box.**

You may also want to include instructions about how to use the snippet. For example, you can add a note to insert the snippet in the <head> of the page and to remember that the snippet is supported by only particular browser versions.

5. **Choose Insert Block for the Snippet Type.**

JavaScript is code that modifies the behavior of your content, so you always choose Insert Block as the type rather than Wrap Selection.

6. **Insert the code in the Insert Code text box.**

The following JavaScript example inserts the current date into your Web page. If using CSS for styling your page, don't include the <b> and <font> tags. You can also customize the script to display something other than *This document was last modified on:* before the date by modifying the line of code that says document.write("This document was last modified on: ");. Type this data:

```
<p><font face="arial, helvetica" size="1"><b>
<SCRIPT LANGUAGE="JavaScript">
function initArray() {
this.length = initArray.arguments.length
for (var i = 0; i < this.length; i++)
this[i+1] = initArray.arguments[i] }
var DOWArray = new initArray("Sunday","Monday","Tuesday","Wednesday",
    "Thursday","Friday","Saturday");
var MOYArray = new initArray("January","February","March","April","May","
    June","July","August","September","October","November","December");
var LastModDate = new Date(document.lastModified);
document.write("This document was last modified on: ");
document.write(DOWArray[(LastModDate.getDay()+1)], ", ");
document.write(MOYArray[(LastModDate.getMonth()+1)]," ");
document.write(LastModDate.getDate(),", ",2010);
document.write(".");
</SCRIPT></b></font></p>
```

The final output looks something like this:

```
This document was last modified on: Wednesday, September 8, 2010.
```

7. **Select Code as the Preview Type.**

The Code preview type shows you the code in the preview pane of the Snippet panel.

8. **Click OK.**

To test your new snippet, click anywhere on any open page in Design view to create an insertion point with your cursor, and then double-click the snippet in the Snippets panel to insert the snippet on your page.

Book III
Chapter 4

Creating Code
Snippets and
History Panel
Commands

When you insert snippets containing JavaScript on a page, Dreamweaver's Design view may or may not indicate that you have JavaScript code on your page by displaying an invisible element icon, though you see the newly inserted code in Code view in both cases. Browsers, by contrast, display the JavaScript as it's meant to be displayed and to function. Therefore, for testing, be sure to press F12 (or Shift+F12) to launch your primary browser to see how the JavaScript snippet looks, because Live View may not always represent your JavaScript accurately.

TIP

To see the yellow invisible element icon for scripts in Design view, choose Edit⇨Preferences (Windows) or Dreamweaver⇨Preferences (Mac) to launch Dreamweaver's Preferences dialog box. Select Invisible Elements in the Category list on the left and then select the Scripts option. Click OK, and Dreamweaver indicates with the invisible element icon in Design view that you have JavaScript on your page.

Figure 4-4 shows how the icon looks as well as how this example snippet appears in a browser.

Figure 4-4:
Snippets containing JavaScript appear as invisible element icons in Design view but as fully realized script when viewed in a browser.

Invisible element   Snippets preview in browser

Creating a snippet with the Wrap Selection option

The Wrap Selection option for Snippet Type allows you to write opening and closing tags that surround whatever code or content is selected on your page. Wrap snippets are especially helpful for applying links, scripts, special formatting, and navigation. For instance, you may want to create a snippet that quickly adds link code around selected text, such as `<a href="#">link</a>`. To create a snippet with the Wrap Selection option, follow these steps:

1. **Open the Snippets panel by choosing Window⇨Snippets.**

   The Snippets panel appears.

2. **Click the New Snippets icon (refer to Figure 4-1).**

   The Snippet dialog box appears.

3. **Type a name for the snippet in the Name text box.**

   Say, for example, that you want to generate a snippet that superscripts text, such as 42nd Street. In the Name text box, type **Superscript**.

4. **Write a text description for the snippet in the Description text box.**

   For example, if you are creating a superscript snippet, your description might be something like *This snippet will Superscript any selected content using the tags.*

5. **Select Wrap Selection as the Snippet Type.**

   Use this type because the code in your snippet will surround or wrap around your selected content. When selecting the Wrap Selection type, note that the dialog box changes from displaying one box for code input to displaying two boxes for the code that goes on your page before and after your selected content, as shown in Figure 4-5.

6. **Add the appropriate code to the Insert Before box.**

   To create a superscript snippet, type the opening superscript tag:

   ```
   <sup>
   ```

Book III
Chapter 4

Creating Code
Snippets and
History Panel
Commands

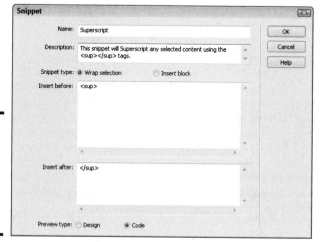

Figure 4-5:
Enter your snippet in the Insert Before and Insert After boxes.

7. Add the appropriate code to the Insert After box.

To continue creating the superscript snippet, type the closing superscript tag:

```
</sup>
```

8. Select Code as the Preview Type.

Because wrap snippets typically have no graphics, select Code as the preview type to see code in the preview pane of the Snippet panel.

9. Click OK.

To test your new snippet, click anywhere in any open page in Design view to create an insertion point with your cursor and then double-click the snippet in the Snippets panel to insert the snippet on your page (see Figure 4-6).

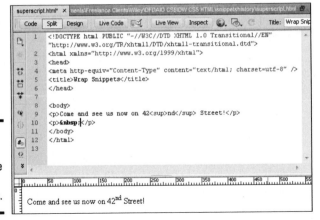

Figure 4-6: Wrap snippets are useful for superscripts.

Applying wrap snippets is a little different than applying block snippets because if you want the code to wrap around the content, you must select the content on your page that you want to apply the snippet to *before* you insert the snippet code. Using the 42nd Street example from earlier in this section, highlight the nd letters in Design view before you insert the snippet. Because this snippet contains simple HTML tags, Dreamweaver's Design view renders and displays the superscript code for you, without the need to launch a browser or click Live View to see it. Alternately, you don't have to apply wrap tags to existing text; you could insert the wrap snippet on the page first and then add content between the tags at a later time.

Creating a snippet with graphics

Snippets with graphics work the same as snippets with text and JavaScript, but with one added benefit when you select Design as the Preview Type in the Snippet dialog box. Like the Design or Code views you see when editing a page in Dreamweaver, the Snippets panel has a little preview pane above the named list of snippets. Selecting Design as the Preview Type in the Snippet dialog box makes Dreamweaver render the code in the preview pane as it would in Design view (see Figure 4-7). By contrast, if you select Code as the Preview Type, Dreamweaver shows the code of the snippet in the preview pane.

Figure 4-7:
The snippet appears in the preview pane of the Snippets panel.

If you do not see your image rendered in the preview pane in the Snippets panel, you may need to edit your snippet code to use site root–relative linking for the graphic instead of the default document-relative link.

Here's an example of a document-relative image link:

```
<p><img src="images/trademark.gif" width="87" height="87" border="1"></p>
```

To make the image link site-root relative, you must add a forward slash (/) before the graphic source location, like this:

```
<p><img src="/images/trademark.gif" width="87" height="87" border="1"></p>
```

You may also need to add the forward slash (/) to any HREF links in your graphic snippets, as in this site root–relative link example:

```
<a href="/about.html"><img src="/images/trademark.gif" width="87" height="87"
    border="1"></a>
```

For a thorough discussion about site root–relative versus document-relative linking, see Book I, Chapter 3 on root level organization.

**Book III
Chapter 4**

Creating Code
Snippets and
History Panel
Commands

Adding keyboard shortcuts for snippets

Use Dreamweaver's Keyboard Shortcut Editor to easily and quickly customize keyboard shortcuts to insert any of your snippets with key commands. You can also create, remove, and edit keyboard shortcuts at any time.

To create custom keyboard shortcuts for your snippets, follow these steps:

1. **Choose Edit⇨Keyboard Shortcuts (Windows) or Dreamweaver⇨Keyboard Shortcuts (Mac).**

   The Keyboard Shortcuts dialog box appears.

2. **Create a duplicate of the default Macromedia Standard shortcut set by clicking the Duplicate Set icon. Name your duplicate set.**

   Making a duplicate set ensures that you can always go back to Adobe's factory default settings in the future if you need to.

3. **Select Snippets from the Commands drop-down list to see a list of your custom snippets along with the standard snippets.**

4. **Navigate through the list to find the snippet to which you want to assign a keyboard shortcut.**

5. **Click the plus (+) icon to add a shortcut.**

6. **Place your cursor in the Press Key field, and then press the combination of shortcut keys you want to use as the shortcut.**

   Be careful not to use a key combination reserved for programs other than Dreamweaver, such as F11, F12, or ⌘+H on a Mac, or Alt+R on Windows.

   Be sure to press all the keys at once, such as Ctrl+Alt+Shift+9 (Windows) or ⌘+Opt+Shift+9 (Mac). Dreamweaver displays alerts for any shortcut key combos that are already assigned to another function in the program so you won't accidentally overwrite a preset. Feel free, though, to overwrite a preset if you find it useful.

7. **Click OK.**

   Your new shortcut works immediately.

To see all the existing keyboard shortcuts at a glance in a separate file, export a copy by clicking the Export Set As HTML icon inside the dialog box.

Good uses for graphic snippets include the following:

✦ **Special symbol graphics:** Create a graphic with a stylized ™ or other symbol in a particular font.

✦ **Animated GIFs:** Design an animated graphic, such as a *NEW* graphic that changes colors, to add next to special entries on your site.

✦ **Reusable page elements:** Build reusable elements with For Placement Only (FPO) text and graphics, such as a sidebar subnavigation area.

Working with Snippets

Snippets are easy to create, edit, delete, file, and manage. You can even share snippets with your coworkers.

Sharing snippets

If you want to share your custom snippets with friends or other members of your work team, you can easily copy the snippets from one computer to another. Here's how to share code snippets:

1. **Find and copy your snippets in the Configuration/Snippets folder inside the Dreamweaver application folder.**

    You can find and copy the snippet files (.CSN format) outside the Dreamweaver application using the Windows Explorer or Mac Finder.

2. **Paste the copied files into a shared folder on your computer/network or e-mail them to your friends or coworkers.**

3. **Have the recipients copy the snippet files to their Configuration/Snippets folders in their Dreamweaver application folders.**

    After the snippets are in place, they're ready to use.

You should be able to find your custom snippets in the Adobe Dreamweaver Configuration folder, but that folder can actually be in a few different places on your computer, depending on your platform:

✦ Vista/Windows 7: C:\Users\<username>\AppData\Roaming\Adobe\ Dreamweaver CS5\<language>\Configuration

✦ XP: C:\Documents and Settings\<username>\Application Data\Adobe\ Dreamweaver CS5\<language>\Configuration\

✦ MAC: MacHD : Users : <username> : Library : Application Support : Adobe : Dreamweaver CS5 : <language> : Configuration :

If you can't see your custom snippets, try adjusting the Application Data (Windows) or Application Support (Mac) folder properties to view both hidden and read-only files.

If you're interested in a faster method for sharing your custom snippets with others, visit Massimo Foti's Web site at www.massimocorner.com, where you can download his free Dreamweaver Snippets Import/Export 1.0 Extension (click the Utilities link under Dreamweaver Extensions). Install the extension with Adobe's Extension Manager (see Book IV, Chapter 2 for instructions on using the Manager). After you install the tool, you can import and export snippets straight from the Snippets panel.

Book III
Chapter 4

Creating Code
Snippets and
History Panel
Commands

Editing snippets

After you create a snippet, you'll rarely need to edit it. However, some snippets may contain specific dates or graphics that need occasional updating or editing. Additionally, you may want to create a new version of an existing snippet. In any case, editing a code snippet is simple and straightforward.

To edit a snippet, follow these steps:

1. **Select the snippet in the Snippets panel, and then click the Edit Snippet icon at the bottom of the panel (refer to Figure 4-1).**

   The Snippet dialog box appears.

2. **Make any desired changes to the snippet.**

3. **Click OK.**

Deleting snippets

To delete a code snippet quickly and permanently, select the snippet in the Snippets panel and then either click the Remove icon (refer to Figure 4-1) or press the Delete key.

Dreamweaver always displays an alert dialog box asking if you're sure you want to delete that particular snippet, giving you a chance to cancel the command if you change your mind about deleting it.

Managing snippets

One of the cool things about the Snippets panel is that you can create folders to manage your snippets into logical categories. Moving snippets around the Snippets panel, from folder to folder, is as easy as dragging and dropping.

If you want to create a new folder for your snippets, follow these steps:

1. **Click the New Snippet Folder icon at the bottom of the Snippets panel.**

2. **Type a name for the new folder and then press Enter (Windows) or Return (Mac).**

   If you don't name the folder, it is called untitled by default, but you can always change the name later.

Rename and delete snippet folders as needed. To delete a snippet folder, select it and click the Delete icon at the bottom of the Snippets panel. Organize your custom snippets into your new custom folders by dragging and dropping the snippets into the desired location.

Creating History Panel Commands

Dreamweaver users forget to take full advantage of the History panel. When a document is open in the Dreamweaver workspace, the History panel records all the actions you make in the file up to a certain number of steps (specified in the General category of the Preferences dialog box).

After you save and close the document, the history steps associated with the file go away. When you reopen the file, a fresh new history is created.

Through the History panel, you can take multiple steps backwards with the use of the panel's slider as well as copy and paste steps to use on the current document or other open documents. In addition to using the History panel to undo and redo steps, you can also record your own custom actions and save them as reusable, playable commands to automate repetitive actions in other files at any time.

Working with the History Panel

To view the History panel, choose Window⇨History or press Shift+F10. As you work, notice how the panel records each step you make. For example, when you type text, a typing layer in the panel displays the copy you just entered. When you apply bold to your text, an Apply Bold layer appears in the panel. Each action in the document creates a new action layer in the panel, as shown in Figure 4-8.

**Book III
Chapter 4**

Creating Code
Snippets and
History Panel
Commands

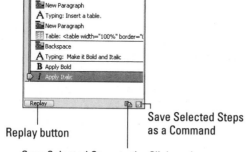

Figure 4-8:
The History
panel.

Replay button

Copy Selected Steps to the Clipboard

Save Selected Steps
as a Command

To undo a single step in your document, drag the slider in the History panel up a layer in the list (or choose Edit⇨Undo). To undo multiple steps, simply drag the slider up to the desired step in the History panel or click to the left of the path next to the slider to scroll automatically to that step. After undoing a single step or multiple steps, any subsequent new actions erase and overwrite previous actions.

Although it's not advised, you can erase the history list for a document by right-clicking (Windows) or Control+clicking (Mac) the History panel and choosing Clear History. After clearing the history in this manner, you can no longer undo any previous steps in your document.

Recording commands

To record and save a command, first be sure the History panel is open. After you perform the actions, you can record and save them.

Keep these points in mind when recording actions for your command:

✦ Use the arrow keys instead of the mouse to move the insertion point in the document. You can also use the arrow keys plus Shift to make or extend a selection. Mouse movements are unrepeatable actions that aren't saved and are identified in the History panel with a black divider line between the steps.

✦ Other actions are also unrepeatable, such as dragging an asset from one place on the page to another. These types of steps display a small red X next to the action layer in the History panel.

Follow these steps to record and save a command:

1. Open the History panel by choosing Window⇨History.

Press Shift+F10 to quickly open the panel.

2. Edit your document.

The History panel records all your actions as individual steps.

3. In the History panel, select the step(s) you want to record.

Shift+click to select multiple consecutive steps. Ctrl+click (Windows) or ⌘+click (Mac) to select or deselect nonconsecutive steps.

4. Click the Save Selected Steps as a Command icon at the bottom of the panel.

The Save As Command dialog box appears, prompting you to enter a name for the new command.

5. Name the new command.

Name your commands using simple descriptive titles, such as *Bold and Italic*.

6. Click OK.

The new command appears by name at the bottom of the Commands menu.

You can also make a temporary command by clicking the Copy Selected Steps to the Clipboard icon at the bottom of the panel after selecting a series of steps. The steps are temporarily stored on the Clipboard for easy pasting into any open document in Design view.

New commands are saved as JavaScript or HTML files in the Dreamweaver CS5/Configuration/Commands folder.

Playing commands

Playing a saved History panel command is as easy as choosing it by name on the Commands menu. For example, if you create a Bold and Italic command that bolds and italicizes a selection, select some text on your document and then choose Commands⇨Bold and Italic to play the command, as shown in Figure 4-9.

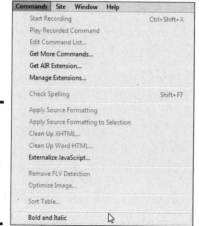

Figure 4-9:
Select the command you created on the Commands menu.

Book III
Chapter 4

Creating Code
Snippets and
History Panel
Commands

More options are available when playing commands with the History panel. You may repeat the last step, repeat a series of consecutive or touching steps, or repeat a series of nonconsecutive steps:

✦ **Repeat a single step:** Select a step in the History panel, and then click the Replay button. Or choose Edit⇨Redo (Action).

Recording temporary commands with the Commands menu

Another way to record temporary commands is to use the Commands menu instead of the History panel. Temporary commands stay on the Commands menu and you can play them on any open document as long as you have Dreamweaver open. Temporary commands disappear when you do one of the following:

✔ Close Dreamweaver (the temporary command is erased)

✔ Record a new temporary command (the new command takes the place of the old command)

To record a temporary command:

1. **Choose Commands⇨Start Recording before performing the steps you want to copy.**

   You can also begin the recording process by pressing Ctrl+Shift+X (Windows) or ⌘+Shift+X (Mac).

2. **Perform the steps.**

   Whenever possible, press the arrow keys instead of moving the mouse to reposition the cursor during the recording process.

3. **Choose Commands⇨Stop Recording.**

To play back a temporary command, choose Commands⇨Play Recorded Command.

To save a temporary command as a permanent command using the History panel:

1. **Choose Commands⇨Play Recorded Command.**

   The command plays and displays a new Run Command step at the bottom of the History panel.

2. **Select the new Run Command step in the History panel, and then click the Save Selected Steps as a Command icon.**

   The Save As Command dialog box appears.

3. **Name the command, and then click OK to save it.**

   The command now appears at the bottom of the Commands menu.

Click Get More Commands on the Command menu to launch Adobe's Dreamweaver Exchange to browse for and download additional commands.

✦ **Repeat a series of consecutive steps:** Select the steps in the History panel, place your cursor in the desired location on your open document, and click the Replay button.

To select multiple steps, either drag from one step to another or click the first step and Shift+click the last step. Whichever steps are highlighted are the ones that play.

✦ **Repeat a series of nonconsecutive steps:** Select a step in the History panel and Ctrl+click (Windows) or ⌘+click (Mac) to select other steps; then click the Replay button. Steps replay in the order in which they appear in the History panel.

✦ **Deselect a selected step:** Ctrl+click (Windows) or ⌘+click (Mac) the step.

You can also copy and paste steps from one open document to another, because each file has its own history of steps. Simply select the steps and click the Copy Selected Steps to the Clipboard icon in the History panel. Then choose Edit➪Paste in the new document to paste the steps in the desired location.

If you paste selected steps into a text editor (such as Notepad or TextEdit), Code view, or the Code inspector, you may notice that the pasted information appears as JavaScript, which can be useful for learning to write your own Dreamweaver scripts. For example, the copied command to insert and resize an image looks like this:

```
<img src="image23.gif" width="100" height="46" />
```

However, when pasted into a text editor, the line of code appears as a bit of JavaScript, like this:

```
dw.getDocumentDOM().insertHTML('<img src=\"image23.gif\">', false);
dw.getDocumentDOM().resizeSelection('100', '46');
```

Renaming and deleting commands

After saving a new command, you can easily rename or delete it.

To rename a command:

1. **Choose Commands➪Edit Command List.**
2. **Select the command in the list, and then enter a new name.**
3. **Click the Close button.**

To delete a command:

1. **Choose Commands➪Edit Command List.**
2. **Select the command in the list, and then click the Delete button.**

   Clicking the Delete button permanently removes the command from the Commands menu.

3. **Click the Close button.**

Book III
Chapter 4

Creating Code
Snippets and
History Panel
Commands

Chapter 5: Integrating Dreamweaver with Fireworks

In This Chapter

✔ **Working with Fireworks**

✔ **Setting launch-and-edit preferences**

✔ **Inserting Fireworks images**

✔ **Making changes to your Fireworks images and tables**

✔ **Image optimizing in Fireworks**

✔ **Inserting, pasting, and updating Fireworks HTML**

Dreamweaver is tightly integrated with Adobe Fireworks, a robust Web image creation, editing, and optimization program. With Fireworks, you can create animations, pop-up menus, and *rollover buttons* (buttons that change in appearance when you mouse over them); *optimize* your graphics (reduce the file size while preserving image quality to improve download times in a browser); and export graphics, HTML, and JavaScript code to an HTML editor such as Dreamweaver — all without needing to know a lick of code.

When used together, Fireworks and Dreamweaver provide you with a smooth process for editing, optimizing, and exporting graphics into Dreamweaver HTML pages. This process, called *roundtrip editing,* enables you to make seamless updates to your Fireworks graphic and HTML files while working in Dreamweaver. The code stays accurate to preserve links and other functionality such as rollover behaviors.

During the roundtrip editing process, Fireworks creates special *Design Notes* about all the graphics and HTML exported to Dreamweaver. The Notes, which are generated from Fireworks to Dreamweaver during the graphic export process, store references to the Web-ready images (GIF, JPEG, PNG), and enable Dreamweaver to quickly locate them and the Fireworks source files (PNG) they were created from. In addition, the Design Notes often include information about the export process itself, such as the location of JavaScript data in the HTML files and details about the graphics inside table cells, such as hotspots and rollover capabilities.

To be fair, the use of Fireworks is not a prerequisite for creating or designing Web sites in Dreamweaver. Please don't feel that you must run out and buy Fireworks to successfully build a Web site; you can build an entire Web site without using Fireworks or any of its features. Many designers prefer to create their Web graphics using another design, illustration, and Web graphic optimization programs, such as Photoshop, Illustrator, or an old copy of ImageReady CS2. However, Fireworks is required for the features described in this chapter.

To download a free 30-day trial version of Fireworks, go to `www.adobe.com/products/fireworks/`.

This chapter presumes that you already own and know how to use Fireworks but need help using it with Dreamweaver. Here you find out how to insert Fireworks images, edit images and tables, optimize your images in Fireworks, and add and edit Fireworks HTML in Dreamweaver.

Preparing to Work with Dreamweaver and Fireworks

Before you begin a roundtrip editing process, you must enable a few Fireworks and Dreamweaver settings to ensure the smoothest possible integration between the programs. Specifically, you must configure your launch-and-edit preferences in Fireworks, and optimize Dreamweaver for working with Fireworks by adding Fireworks as a primary image editor.

Setting Fireworks launch-and-edit preferences

If you use Fireworks to create and edit images, by default Fireworks exports those images from a source PNG (Portable Network Graphic) file. PNG is an image-compression file format that allows for the exporting of Web graphics with the highest image quality and a relatively small file size. A source PNG file is a master file that Fireworks uses to generate Web-ready graphics.

When creating graphics in Fireworks, be sure to store the PNG source files in a different place on your computer than the Web graphics generated from them for your Web site so that you don't accidentally alter the original files.

By default, when you edit a Fireworks image in Dreamweaver, Fireworks launches and automatically reopens the source PNG file. This is the Fireworks default launch-and-edit preference. You can also set the preferences in Fireworks to either have Dreamweaver open and directly edit the inserted graphics (which is not a good choice because Dreamweaver is not an image editing or optimization application) or have Fireworks open and use the inserted Web-ready image for editing instead of the image's source PNG file (which is not good either because the original source PNG always generates better quality Web graphics than an already optimized Web graphic).

You should note that Dreamweaver recognizes these launch-and-edit preferences only when certain conditions apply:

✦ You must specifically open and optimize images that include the right Design Notes path to the source PNG file. You can ensure that you're using the right Design Notes path to the source PNG by selecting the Always Use Source PNG option for the launch-and-edit preference (see the next section).

✦ The image can't be a part of a Fireworks table. Fireworks tables use a series of images with the HTML code. You must always open the source PNG file in Fireworks to edit any graphics from within Dreamweaver.

To set Fireworks' launch-and-edit preferences, follow these steps:

1. **Choose Edit➪Preferences (Windows) or Fireworks➪Preferences (Mac) to open the Fireworks Preferences dialog box.**

2. **Click the Launch and Edit option in the Category listing on the left side of the dialog box.**

The Launch and Edit options appear on the right side of the panel, as shown in Figure 5-1.

Figure 5-1:
Choose launch-and-edit preferences in Fireworks.

3. **Set the Launch and Edit preference options for editing and optimizing Fireworks images.**

These settings will be used to export images to external applications such as Dreamweaver. Select one of the following options in each of the drop-down lists:

✦ **Always Use Source PNG:** (Recommended) This setting enables Fireworks to open the PNG file defined in Design Notes as the source for the externally placed graphics. When edits are made to the source PNG, those changes are automatically updated in the exported or placed Web graphic.

✦ **Never Use Source PNG:** This option tells Fireworks to open the placed graphic for editing, even if a source PNG file is available. Changes to this graphic are permanent and appear immediately upon saving the placed graphic. The source PNG file stays the same.

✦ **Ask When Launching:** If you want to use both methods intermittently, select this option to choose the PNG file or the placed graphic on a case-by-case basis.

4. **When you finish, click OK to save your changes.**

Optimizing Dreamweaver for use with Fireworks

Make the following changes to optimize Dreamweaver for use with Fireworks.

Enable Design Notes

Verify that the managed site you're creating or using has Design Notes enabled. This is the default site setting in Dreamweaver. Follow these steps:

1. **Choose Site⇨Manage Sites.**

2. **Select your site, and then click the Edit button in the Manage Sites dialog box.**

   The Site Setup dialog box appears.

3. **Expand the Advanced Settings category and then select Design Notes from the submenu.**

   In earlier versions of Dreamweaver, the Design Notes setting was located on the Advanced Tab.

4. **Verify that the Maintain Design Notes option is selected, and then click Save to close the Site Setup dialog.**

   If you also want to share Design Notes with others on your team, select the Enable Upload Design Notes for Sharing option.

5. **Click the Done button to close the Manage Sites dialog box.**

Add Fireworks as an image editor

In the Dreamweaver Preferences dialog box, set Fireworks as the primary external image editor for selected graphics file types. This enables Fireworks to be the editor that automatically launches for editing your placed graphics files. For example, you may want to launch Fireworks as the primary editor for GIF and PNG files, and another application for editing JPEG files.

To add Fireworks as an image editor, follow these steps:

1. **Choose Edit⇨Preferences (Windows) or Dreamweaver⇨Preferences (Mac).**

   The Dreamweaver Preferences dialog box appears.

2. **In the Editors category, as shown in Figure 5-2, click the plus (+) icon to add Fireworks (and any other applications you want to include) as an editor for any selected graphic extensions.**

   Dreamweaver doesn't automatically detect that you have Fireworks installed, so you must enter the path to the Fireworks application on your machine in the Fireworks text box.

Figure 5-2:
Add Fireworks as the primary image editor in Dreamweaver's Preferences.

3. **To make Fireworks the primary editor for any selected extension in the Extensions listing, select Fireworks from the list of editors on the right and then click the Make Primary button.**

   For example, after adding Fireworks to the list in Step 2, select it and click the Make Primary button. The Fireworks application name has (Primary) appended to it.

4. **Click OK.**

Save all your Fireworks files in the same site folder

When you are working in a workgroup, save all your Fireworks PNG source and Web-ready files in the same Dreamweaver site folder. This ensures that everyone in the workgroup can easily find and edit all the source files for the site. When working alone, you may want to store your PNG source files in a separate but nearby folder to keep them better organized.

Book III
Chapter 5

Integrating Dreamweaver with Fireworks

Export Fireworks image files to the same site folder

Exporting Web graphics from Fireworks into a Dreamweaver site folder, rather than copying the files into a managed site outside Dreamweaver, ensures that the Design Notes are integrated and up-to-date. Fireworks creates a Notes folder for the Design Notes, which Dreamweaver uses to update code and graphics.

Using Fireworks Images in Dreamweaver

When you're ready to insert Fireworks images in your Dreamweaver document, you can do so in two ways. The first method is to place exported Fireworks graphics directly into a file by choosing Insert⇨Image in Dreamweaver. The other way is to design images in Fireworks to replace Dreamweaver image placeholders.

Inserting a Fireworks image in a Dreamweaver document

When you've designed, saved, and exported your graphics from Fireworks, you're ready to import those exported graphics into a Dreamweaver document. If you need help creating, saving, and exporting Fireworks graphics, refer to the Fireworks Help files or download a copy of the Fireworks manual from Adobe at `www.adobe.com/support/fireworks/`.

Follow these steps to insert an exported Fireworks image into a Dreamweaver file:

1. **In Dreamweaver, click inside the document where you want the image to go and then choose Insert⇨Image.**

Or, in the Common category of the Insert panel, click and drag the Image icon into the open document. The Select Image Source dialog box appears.

2. **Browse to and select the previously saved and exported Fireworks image.**

3. **Click OK (Windows) or Open (Mac) to complete the insertion.**

4. **If you selected an image outside the Dreamweaver local managed site folder, click Yes to the message that appears.**

The message asks whether you want Dreamweaver to copy the file into the root folder of the managed Dreamweaver site.

Now you can easily edit your images in Fireworks using the roundtrip editing feature, as described in "Editing Images in Fireworks Tables," later in the chapter.

Replacing an image placeholder with a Fireworks graphic

In Dreamweaver, you can create *image placeholders* that set aside space for graphics that you haven't created yet. (See Book II, Chapter 3 for details on creating image placeholders.) With roundtrip editing, you can select an individual image placeholder in Dreamweaver and use Fireworks to create a graphic to replace it.

Before beginning the roundtrip editing process, be sure that you specify Fireworks as the image editor for .png files (as described in "Optimizing Dreamweaver for Use with Fireworks," earlier in the chapter) and create all the image placeholders in a Dreamweaver document. Also, if you haven't managed a site in Dreamweaver yet, quickly transfer over to Dreamweaver and create a managed site before proceeding.

Follow these steps to replace a Dreamweaver image placeholder with a Fireworks image:

1. **In your Dreamweaver document, select the image placeholder that you want to replace (see Figure 5-3).**

Figure 5-3: The placeholder image in the Dreamweaver Document window.

Create button

2. **Click the Create button in the Properties inspector to launch Fireworks.**

   Fireworks opens the selected image placeholder in Editing from Dreamweaver mode.

3. **In Fireworks, design the replacement image.**

   Fireworks detects image placeholder settings from Dreamweaver, such as image width and height, alternate text, and image ID, as well as links, text alignment settings, and JavaScript behaviors, and uses these settings as the basis for the replacement graphic. As such, you will see only an empty white canvas instead of an exact replica of the placeholder image.

   Links assigned to image placeholders in Dreamweaver are maintained but are not visible in Fireworks. Therefore, if you add a new link or hotspot from within Fireworks, the original Dreamweaver link is still there. However, if you cut a slice from the image in Fireworks, the Dreamweaver link is deleted when the image is updated.

4. **In the Fireworks Optimize panel, select an image optimization setting, such as JPG, PNG, or GIF.**

   Select JPG for photographs or images with lots of gradient blends, or select GIF or PNG for images with large flat areas of color.

5. **When you finish designing the image (see Figure 5-4), click the Done button at the top of the image document window to save the original PNG file for future editing.**

   Fireworks launches the Save As dialog box, prompting you to save the PNG source file.

6. **Browse to and select the root folder of your managed Dreamweaver site as the location to save the PNG file.**

   Or save the PNG file into a different location so you can keep track of the original file separate from the optimized graphics you create from it.

7. **Enter a name in the File Name text box.**

   If you named the image in Dreamweaver when creating the image place-holder, the File Name text box is already filled in with that name.

8. **Click the Save button to save the PNG file.**

   The Export dialog box appears.

9. **In the Export dialog box, select the Dreamweaver site folder for the Save In option.**

   You'll be saving an optimized version of the file here.

Done button

Figure 5-4:
Design a
replacement
image for a
placeholder
image in
Fireworks.

10. **Enter a name in the Name text box.**

Again, the PNG filename is in the Name text box.

11. **Select a graphic type in the Save as Type drop-down list.**

Select the file type (GIF or JPEG) or choose an export option, such as HTML and Images, Images Only, or HTML Only.

12. **Click the Save or Export button to save the optimized file.**

The replacement image PNG file is saved, Fireworks is minimized, and you return to Dreamweaver, where the exported Web-ready file (or Fireworks table) has replaced the image placeholder, as shown in Figure 5-5. If you still see your placeholder image, click inside the Document window (or press F5) to refresh the page with your new graphic.

Repeat these steps for each Dreamweaver image placeholder you want to replace. If a replacement graphic file needs further editing after you insert it on the page, select the image in Dreamweaver and click the Edit icon in the Properties inspector, as described in the next section, "Editing Images in Fireworks Tables."

Figure 5-5:
The new
Fireworks
graphic
replaces
the old
placeholder
graphic in
the Dream-
weaver file.

Editing Images in Fireworks Tables

Fireworks *tables* are Fireworks-generated navigation bars, pop-up menus, and sliced images; they have nothing to do with traditional HTML tables.

Before editing any images containing Fireworks tables, be sure you've set up Fireworks launch-and-edit preferences and optimized Dreamweaver for use with Fireworks (refer to the "Preparing to Work with Dreamweaver and Fireworks" section, earlier in this chapter).

Then, if you want to edit a Fireworks image in your Dreamweaver document, you can either have Dreamweaver launch Fireworks to edit it there or use the limited image editing tools (crop, resample, brightness and contrast, and sharpen) to edit your image in Dreamweaver.

When editing images or image *slices* (graphics that are cut into smaller pieces) that are part of a Fireworks table, Dreamweaver opens Fireworks automatically, which in turn opens the source PNG file for the entire Fireworks table.

When editing images that are part of a Fireworks table, you can edit the entire table as long as the `<!--fwtable-->` comment tag is visible in the HTML code. That comment is inserted automatically when the source PNG is exported from Fireworks to a Dreamweaver site using the Dreamweaver Style HTML and Images setting.

To edit Fireworks images placed in Dreamweaver files, follow these steps:

1. **In Dreamweaver, select the image or image slice in the open document that you want to edit.**

   The Properties inspector identifies the selected graphic as a Fireworks image or Fireworks table below the Properties tab, along with the name of the source PNG file.

2. **Click the Edit icon in the Properties inspector to launch Fireworks.**

   Fireworks opens the source PNG file for editing (see Figure 5-6). If Fireworks can't find the source PNG file, it prompts you to find it. If the source file is missing, you can use the inserted image as the source for the edits.

3. **In Fireworks, edit the source PNG file.**

4. **Click the Done button.**

   Fireworks saves the changes to the PNG file, exports the updated graphic (or HTML with images), and returns to Dreamweaver, where the updated image or table appears in the open document.

Figure 5-6:
The source PNG file for the entire table is launched in Fireworks.

Optimizing Your Images in Dreamweaver

Before you add Fireworks images to your Dreamweaver document, you should optimize those images for use on the Web. By *optimizing* images in Fireworks, you can

✦ Reduce the amount of time the user's browser takes to download and display the images

✦ Reduce the image file size while maintaining image quality

✦ Change the file format of the Web-ready image

✦ Adjust color depth and other format-specific options to control the file size

After inserting your optimized images in a Dreamweaver document, however, you can still make changes to those images using an Image Preview dialog box.

To change settings for Fireworks images placed in Dreamweaver, follow these steps:

1. **In Dreamweaver, select the image you want to optimize from an open document and then choose Commands⇨Optimize Image.**

If the placed image in the document has a source PNG file, Dreamweaver uses that file. If that source file cannot be found, Dreamweaver may prompt you to locate the source PNG file. The Image Preview dialog box appears, as shown in Figure 5-7.

Figure 5-7: Change the optimization settings of Fireworks images placed in Dream- weaver files.

2. **On the Options tab, change the optimization settings to support the selected file format:**

   - **Format:** Select a file format for the optimized graphic. Choose from GIF, JPEG, PNG-8, PNG-24, or PNG-32.

   - **Palette:** (GIFs and PNGs only) Choose a color palette for the graphic. Options are Adaptive, Web Adaptive, Web 216, Exact, Windows and Macintosh, Grayscale, Black and White, Uniform, and Custom.

   - **Loss:** (GIFs only) Add a loss setting to compress GIF files for smaller file sizes. The higher the number, the smaller the file but the greater the potential loss of image quality.

   - **Dither:** (GIFs and PNGs only) Enable the dithering option to control how colors not in the selected palette are approximated using colors in the palette.

   - **Transparency:** (GIFs and PNGs only) Choose a transparency setting.

   - **Quality:** (JPEGs only) Adjust the quality setting to control the loss of image quality during compression. Higher numbers produce better quality images with larger file sizes.

   - **Smoothing:** (JPEGs only) Enable a smoothing setting to blur hard edges in the graphic and reduce the file size. Higher numbers reduce file size but can distort the quality of the image.

   - **Matte:** Select a matte color for graphic to match the color of the page the graphic or object will be on top of.

3. **On the File tab, edit the Scale and Export Area of the graphic file.**

   To modify the size of the image, adjust the Scale field in percentages or type the pixels in the Width and Height fields. To optimize and export only part of the selected graphic, enter X and Y coordinates relative to the original graphic dimensions as well as W and H sizes.

4. **Click the OK button.**

   The updated image exports with any new settings. Exporting includes updating the placed GIF or JPEG file in Dreamweaver, as well as the source PNG file.

   If the image format has changed, Dreamweaver's link checker prompts you to verify the graphic's link references. For instance, if you changed the format of a graphic from submit.jpg to submit.gif, click OK and all references to submit.jpg are converted to submit.gif.

Book III
Chapter 5

Integrating
Dreamweaver with
Fireworks

Using Fireworks HTML in Dreamweaver

You can quickly insert Fireworks-generated HTML (including all graphics, formatting, and JavaScript behaviors) into a Dreamweaver document. For example, you can create a navigation bar with a series of buttons, each of which has JavaScript rollover functionality including a hyperlink to another page. This roundtrip feature lets you design Web elements in Fireworks and add them to new or existing Dreamweaver files. Or as an alternative, you can simply copy and paste your HTML code from Fireworks to Dreamweaver. Either method allows you to design in Fireworks.

Inserting Fireworks HTML in a Dreamweaver document

After you design your Web elements in Fireworks, inserting the elements into your Web page is a two-step process: You must export the HTML from Fireworks into a managed Dreamweaver site and then insert it on your Dreamweaver page.

Follow these steps to export the Fireworks HTML into Dreamweaver:

1. **From Fireworks, choose File⇨Export.**

   The Export dialog box appears.

2. **Enter a filename for the exported HTML file, choose the Dreamweaver site folder as the Save in destination for the file, and select other options relative to the Export command.**

   Select the desired export, HTML, and slices settings, such as HTML and Images, Export HTML File, and Export Slices.

3. **Click the Save button to complete the export process.**

After you export the Fireworks HTML into a Dreamweaver site folder, follow these steps to insert the exported HTML into a Dreamweaver document:

1. **In Dreamweaver, click your cursor inside the document where you want to insert the Fireworks HTML code.**

2. **Choose Insert⇨Image Objects⇨Fireworks HTML.**

   You can also click the Insert Fireworks HTML icon from the Images menu on the Common category of the Insert panel. The Insert Fireworks HTML dialog box appears.

3. **Browse to and select the exported Fireworks HTML file.**

4. **(Optional) Check the Delete File After Insertion option if you want to delete the original files after the Fireworks HTML is inserted into the Dreamweaver file.**

   If the original Fireworks HTML is on a network drive, however, it's immediately deleted after insertion. This setting does not affect source PNG files associated with the HTML.

5. **Click OK.**

   Dreamweaver inserts the Fireworks HTML into the Dreamweaver file (see Figure 5-8). This insertion process includes HTML code, graphic images, slices, and JavaScript.

**Book III
Chapter 5**

Integrating
Dreamweaver with
Fireworks

Figure 5-8:
Insert
Fireworks
HTML in a
Dream-
weaver file.

Pasting Fireworks HTML in a Dreamweaver document

As an alternative to using the Insert Fireworks HTML command as described in the preceding section, you can copy and paste the Fireworks-generated HTML code directly in a Dreamweaver file.

To copy and paste Fireworks HTML in a Dreamweaver document, follow these steps:

1. **In Fireworks, choose Edit⇨Copy HTML Code.**

Fireworks presumes that you intend to copy the entire file, so unless you want to copy only a part of the graphic, you don't need to select anything. The Copy HTML Code dialog box appears.

2. **Use the wizard to walk through the process of exporting Fireworks HTML and images. Click the Next button to proceed through each step in the wizard.**

- **Screen 1: Select an HTML or XHTML style for the copied HTML, such as Dreamweaver XHTML.**

- **Screen 2: Enter a base filename for the copied graphic slices.**

  For example, if the graphic is for a logo for ABC company, the base filename might be abclogo. Click the Optional HTML Settings button to specify additional settings for HTML output.

- **Screen 3: Click the Browse button to select a destination for the copied HTML code.**

  Typically this is the root folder of your managed Dreamweaver site.

- **Click the Finish button.**

  Web-ready images are exported to the destination folder, and the HTML code is copied to your computer's Clipboard.

3. **In Dreamweaver, click your cursor inside the document where you want to paste the HTML code and then choose Edit⇨Paste Fireworks HTML.**

   The copied Fireworks HTML and any associated JavaScript code are pasted in the Dreamweaver file. At the same time, links to the images inside the pasted code are updated to match the freshly exported Fireworks images in the Dreamweaver site folder.

Updating Fireworks HTML in a Dreamweaver Document

To edit Fireworks HTML files inserted in Dreamweaver documents from within Fireworks and without launching Dreamweaver, use the Fireworks Update HTML command. This command lets you make changes to source PNG files in Fireworks and automatically update exported HTML and image files placed in Dreamweaver, even if Dreamweaver isn't running.

Follow these steps to update any Fireworks HTML you have in your Dreamweaver document:

1. **In Fireworks, open the source PNG file for the Fireworks HTML that you want to edit.**

   Make any edits to the source PNG file that you need.

2. **Choose File⇨Save.**

   You must save your changes before moving on to the next step.

3. **Choose File⇨Update HTML.**

4. **In the Locate HTML File dialog box that appears, browse to and select the Dreamweaver folder containing the HTML file that needs updating.**

5. **Select the file to be updated, and then click the Open button.**

   The Update HTML dialog box appears.

6. **Choose whether to replace images and associated HTML or to update images. Click OK.**

7. **In the Select Images Folder dialog box, select the folder in the Dreamweaver site where you want to place the updated image files.**

8. **Click Select (Windows) or Choose (Mac).**

   The updated Fireworks HTML and images, including any associated JavaScript code, are saved into the Dreamweaver file.

   Should Fireworks be unable to find a matching HTML file to update, you have the option of inserting new HTML into the chosen Dreamweaver file. Any JavaScript associated with the HTML is added to the document code as necessary.

Editing Fireworks Pop-Up Menus

A *pop-up menu* is a navigation menu that temporarily appears in a browser window when the user makes a specific mouse action. If you've created any pop-up menus in Fireworks 8 or later, you can now edit them either directly in Dreamweaver or use Fireworks roundtrip editing. If you created your pop-up menu in earlier versions of Fireworks, you must edit it in Dreamweaver.

If you make changes to your Fireworks pop-up menus directly in Dreamweaver and then subsequently make changes to them in Fireworks, you lose all your previous edits to the menus except for text changes. To avoid this, always create your menus in Fireworks first and then use Dreamweaver exclusively to customize the menus. However, if you prefer to do the menu editing in Fireworks, do not edit them in Dreamweaver at all and instead exclusively use the roundtrip editing feature.

**Book III
Chapter 5**

Integrating
Dreamweaver with
Fireworks

Roundtrip pop-up menu editing (Fireworks 8 and later)

If you want to edit a pop-up menu that you created with Fireworks 8 or later, you can do roundtrip editing of the pop-up menu:

1. **In Dreamweaver, select the graphic in the Fireworks table that contains the Fireworks pop-up menu and then click the Edit icon in the Properties inspector.**

   Fireworks launches and opens the source PNG file for the pop-up menu.

2. **In Fireworks, select the slice in the table that has the pop-up menu you want to edit and then choose Modify⇨Pop-up Menu⇨Edit Pop-up Menu.**

   The Fireworks Pop-up Menu Editor appears.

3. Adjust the menu content, appearance, and position as needed.

4. Click the Done button in the Pop-up Menu Editor to close the dialog box, and then click the Done button on the Fireworks toolbar at the top of the Fireworks workspace to save the changes to the menu.

The edited menu is updated in Dreamweaver.

Pop-up menu editing (Fireworks MX 2004 and earlier)

If you want to edit a pop-up menu that you built with an older version of Fireworks (MX 2004 or earlier), you can't use Fireworks' roundtrip editing. Instead, you must use Dreamweaver to edit the menu.

To edit pop-up menus created with Fireworks MX 2004 or earlier, follow these steps:

1. In Dreamweaver, select the image or hotspot that triggers the pop-up menu.

2. In the Behaviors panel (choose Window➪Behaviors), double-click the Show Pop-up Menu icon from the Actions list.

The Show Pop-up Menu dialog box appears so you can edit the menu. *Note:* The Show Pop-up Menu is a deprecated JavaScript behavior for Dreamweaver CS5, which means it is supported but no longer recommended as a method for creating pop-up menus.

3. If needed, add, change, or rearrange menu items.

4. Click OK to save the changes.

Chapter 6: Dreamweaver Cross-Application Integration

In This Chapter

✔ Working with Flash

✔ Inserting Photoshop images

✔ Accessing and using the Bridge

✔ Integrating with Device Central

✔ Getting the most out of Dreamweaver and AIR

✔ Exploring the Creative Suites Extended Services (CSXS)

✔ Collaborating Online with Share My Screen

✔ Accessing Online Help

✔ Managing Your CSXS

*I*n addition to enabling you to add Fireworks images with JavaScript and HTML to your Dreamweaver pages, Dreamweaver provides cross-application integration with several other software programs, including Flash, Photoshop, Bridge, Device Central, and AIR, as well as communication with two new online services, ConnectNow and Business Catalyst InContext Editing. Whether you currently use these applications or have never heard of some of them, this chapter provides you with a general overview of how each of them works with Dreamweaver.

In this chapter, you find out how to work with Flash to launch and edit source FLA files from any inserted SWF; insert and optimize Photoshop graphics in Dreamweaver using the Copy/Paste and Smart Object workflows; edit optimized graphics as well as the original source PSD file; access and use Adobe Bridge to browse, find, organize, preview, and insert images into Dreamweaver; preview your Web content for mobile devices in Device Central; find tips on creating mobile Web content; and discover how to set up Dreamweaver to use Adobe AIR. After that, you get an introduction to ConnectNow, Dreamweaver's screen-sharing tool, and then learn how to manage your new CSXS (Creative Suites Extended Services) through the new CS Live panel.

Working with Adobe Flash

Similar to the Fireworks workflow, Dreamweaver allows you to easily launch and edit Flash source (FLA) files for any Flash SWF files inserted on your Web pages and then return the updated files back to Dreamweaver. All you need to do is have Flash installed on your computer and configure Dreamweaver to be the primary editor of SWF files.

To make Flash the primary editor of FLA and SWF files, follow these steps:

1. **Choose Edit➪Preferences (Windows) or Dreamweaver➪Preferences (Mac).**

Dreamweaver's Preferences dialog box appears.

2. **In the File Types/Editors category, as shown in Figure 6-1, select the .swf, .swt, .spl extension group in the Extensions listing. Under the Editors heading, select Flash, and then click the Make Primary button.**

By default, FlashPlayer is set to be the primary editor associated with these files. By setting Flash as the primary editor, you can launch Flash from the Properties inspector to edit the FLA files associated with the SWF files inserted on your pages.

Figure 6-1: Set Flash as the primary editor for .swf, .swt, and .spl file extensions.

3. **Repeat Step 2 for any additional Flash file extensions for which you want Flash be the primary editor.**

For example, you may want to click the plus (+) icon above Extensions to add the .flv extension to the list and set Flash as the primary editor of that file type.

4. **Click OK.**

To launch Flash as the editor for the original source FLA files associated with the SWF files inserted in your file, make sure the SWF file is saved somewhere in your managed site, open the document containing the SWF in your Dreamweaver workspace, and then select the SWF file in the Document window in Design view. Next, input the path to the source FLA file in the Flash SRC field in the Properties inspector and click the Flash Edit icon. If Flash can't find the source file, you're prompted to find it. Additionally, if you're using the Check In/Check Out feature in the Files panel and the SWF or FLA files are locked, you may need to check out the SWF file before the file can be edited. (For instruction on using Check In/Check Out, see Book VI, Chapter 1.)

After you save the updated FLA file in Flash, the edited version of the SWF is re-exported to your document and Flash closes. You can also send the updated SWF file back to Dreamweaver without closing Flash by choosing File⇨Update for Dreamweaver.

Inserting and Optimizing Photoshop Graphics

If you don't own Fireworks but do have Photoshop, you'll be amazed at how well Photoshop integrates with Dreamweaver. You can use two different workflows, or series of steps, when working with Photoshop and Dreamweaver, depending on your specific needs.

First, you can use Dreamweaver to optimize your PSD files into Web graphics (GIF, PNG, and JPEG). When you insert the PSD file on your Web page, Dreamweaver converts it to an optimized graphic in the format of your choice. Then Dreamweaver adds to the file a Smart Object, which links directly back to the original file if you need to make any edits to the optimized graphic.

Both Fireworks and Photoshop can be installed on the same computer and each can be used for different Dreamweaver image editing tasks. To have Photoshop be the primary image editing program for particular file types, open Dreamweaver's Preferences and add Photoshop as the image editor for the desired file types in the File Types/Editors category.

Second, you can paste parts of or all of a layered or sliced Photoshop file into any Web page in Dreamweaver. Technically, the pasted graphics are not connected to the originals for roundtrip (from Photoshop to Dreamweaver, and back again) editing like you can do in Fireworks, nor are they connected to the original PSD file like Smart Objects are. But if you need to modify any graphics pasted into Dreamweaver in this way, you can easily go back to Photoshop to do your edits and then copy and paste the graphics back into Dreamweaver again.

Book III
Chapter 6

Dreamweaver
Cross-Application
Integration

The Smart Objects workflow

A *Smart Object* is a special type of image that is placed from one Adobe application into another and retains its original application's qualities. Smart Objects are linked to their original source file in case they need to be altered. With Photoshop and Dreamweaver, the Smart Object workflow is the preferred method of using Dreamweaver to add optimized graphics to your Web files.

In Dreamweaver, you can easily tell that a particular graphic is a Smart Object by the Smart Object icon that appears in the top-left corner of the Smart Object image when seen in Design view, as shown in Figure 6-2.

Smart Object icon

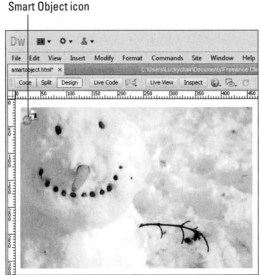

Figure 6-2:
Smart
Objects
display an
icon, making
them easy
to identify.

If at any time the original PSD file is edited after a Smart Object linked to it has been placed in your Dreamweaver file, Dreamweaver detects the change and makes one of the green arrows of the Smart Object icon turn red. You can then select the Smart Object graphic in Dreamweaver and easily update the graphic by clicking the Update from Original icon in the Properties inspector. You can update one or more Smart Objects at once through the Assets panel by selecting the image and choosing Update from Original from the Asset panel options menu.

Smart Objects can also be resized, cropped, resampled, sharpened, and have their brightness and contrast adjusted in Dreamweaver using the icons on the Properties inspector. For details about using these tools, see Book II, Chapter 3.

To keep their design files separate from their Web files, most designers save the Photoshop PSD files that are used to create the Smart Objects outside the managed Dreamweaver site. You could put a copy of the PSD file at the root level of your managed site to make the editing process go more smoothly. However, if you do, be sure to cloak the PSD file so that the source graphics are not uploaded to the server when publishing your site. (See Book V, Chapter III to learn more about cloaking.)

To place a Photoshop Smart Object into Dreamweaver, follow these steps:

1. **Insert your Smart Object by doing either of the following:**

- Choose Insert⇨Image and select the Photoshop PSD file from its location on your computer outside your managed site.

- From within your managed site, drag the desired Photoshop PSD file from the Files panel to the Design view area of your open Dreamweaver document.

  Either action launches Dreamweaver's Image Preview dialog box, as shown in Figure 6-3.

Figure 6-3: Choose image optimization settings in the Image Preview dialog box.

2. **Select the desired file format and optimization settings in the Options tab.**

Format: Select a file format for the optimized graphic. Choose from GIF, JPEG, PNG-8, PNG-24, or PNG-32.

The file format you select determines how the rest of the dialog box looks. For instance, the JPG format offers different optimization settings than the PNG and GIF formats.

GIF and PNG settings:

- **Palette:** Choose a color palette for the graphic. Options are Adaptive, Web Adaptive, Web 216, Exact, Windows and Macintosh, Grayscale, Black & White, Uniform, and Custom.

- **Loss:** Add a loss setting to compress GIF files for smaller file sizes. The higher the number, the smaller the file but the greater the potential loss of image quality.

- **Number of Colors:** Select the number of colors in your GIF or PNG-8 image from 2 to 256.

- **Dither:** Enable the dithering option to control how colors not in the selected palette are approximated using colors in the palette. Adjust the amount of dithering from 0–100% using the dithering menu.

- **Transparency:** Choose a transparency setting of No, Index (for GIF), or Alpha (for PNG-8).

- **Matte:** Select a matte color for the graphic to match the color of the page that the graphic or object will be placed on.

- **Remove Unused Colors:** Remove unused colors from the graphic, thereby making the file size smaller.

- **Interlaced Browser Display:** (GIFs and PNG-8 only) Make the image load in multiple passes in the browser window, showing a low-resolution image first and progressively improving the image until it is fully cached in the browser.

- **Optimize to Size Wizard:** Launch a wizard that allows you to optimize the graphic based on a desired file size in kilobytes (Kb). File size is reduced by making adjustments to the number of colors and dithering setting.

JPEG settings:

- **Quality:** Adjust the quality setting to control the loss of image quality during compression. Higher numbers produce better quality images with larger file sizes.

- **Smoothing:** Enable a smoothing setting to blur hard edges in the graphic and reduce file size. Higher numbers reduce file size but can distort the image quality. Select from a range of 1–8 or opt for No Smoothing.

- **Progressive Browser Display:** Make the image load in multiple passes in the browser window, showing a low-resolution image first and progressively improving the image until it is fully cached in the browser.

- **Sharpen Color Edges:** (JPEGs only) Provide a sharper image quality. Sharpen Color Edges is on by default.

- **Matte:** Select a matte color for the graphic to match the color of the page the graphic or object will be placed on.

- **Remove Unused Colors:** Remove unused colors from the graphic, thereby making the file size smaller.

- **Optimize to Size Wizard:** Launch a wizard that allows you to optimize the graphic based on a desired file size in kilobytes (Kb). File size is reduced by making adjustments to the number of colors and dithering setting.

3. **(Optional) On the File tab, edit the scale and export area of the pasted graphic.**

   To modify the size of the image, adjust the Scale field in percentages or type the pixels in the Width and Height fields. To keep size modifications proportional during scaling, select the Constrain option.

   To optimize and export only part of the selected graphic, enter X and Y coordinates relative to the original graphic dimensions as well as W and H sizes.

4. **Click the OK button to save the optimized graphic.**

   Dreamweaver displays the Save Web Image dialog box.

5. **In the Save Web Image dialog box, select a destination and filename for your optimized graphic, and then click the Save button.**

   For example, when working in a managed site in Dreamweaver, you might select the images folder at the root level of your managed site as the location to save your images into. The name of the file is up to you, although you should try to name your graphics after their purpose so they'll be easy to identify as you use them, such as nav_01.gif, onsale-now.jpg, or closeup.png.

6. **If Dreamweaver's Accessibility options are enabled for images, respond to the prompt to add Alt text for your Smart Object image in the Image Tag Accessibility Attributes dialog box.**

   Either add the information and click the OK button, or click the Cancel button to add the image without Alt text.

Editing the Smart Object's Optimization settings

To edit the optimization settings of a placed Smart Object image, select the image and click the Edit Image Settings icon in the Properties inspector. This relaunches the Image Preview dialog box, where you can nondestructively adjust the optimization settings based on the original source PSD file. When you've finished adjusting these settings, click OK to save the updated optimized graphic. Dreamweaver overwrites the original optimized graphic with the new one.

Editing the Smart Object's original PSD

To edit the original Photoshop PSD file linked to your Smart Object from within Dreamweaver, select the Smart Object in Design view of your open document and click the Edit icon in the Properties inspector. When you've finished making changes to the Photoshop file, save the file in Photoshop. Upon returning to Dreamweaver, reselect the Smart Object and click the Update from Original icon in the Properties inspector.

To watch a video tutorial about using Photoshop to create Smart Objects when inserting PSD files into Dreamweaver, go to www.adobe.com/go/vid0200. Be sure to also visit the Adobe TV Web site at http://tv.adobe.com/product/dreamweaver/.

The Copy/Paste workflow

To create an optimized graphic in Dreamweaver without inserting a Smart Object, you can use the Copy/Paste workflow. As mentioned previously, with this method, no Smart Object is created, which means there is no link to the original source Photoshop file. Therefore, to edit an image on your page that has been optimized in this fashion, you must reopen the original file in Photoshop and repeat the following steps to replace the current optimized graphic with a new one.

Any time you use the Copy/Paste workflow, Dreamweaver automatically adds Design Notes to your file that include image information such as the location of the source Photoshop file. To find out more about Design Notes, turn to Book VI, Chapter 1.

When you're ready to copy and paste your work from Photoshop into Dreamweaver, follow these steps:

1. **In Photoshop, select the slices or layers (or make a selection with any of the selection tools) and copy them by selecting Edit⇨Copy (for slices or a selection on a single layer) or Edit⇨Copy Merged (for selected layers or multi-layer selections).**

   If you're selecting slices, use the Edit Slice tool. When selecting layers, use the layers panel to Shift+Ctrl+click (Windows) or Shift+⌘+click (Mac) the thumbnails of the desired layers. For selections, use any of the marquee or magic wand selection tools. To select everything visible in the Document window, choose Edit⇨Select All.

2. **Switch over to Dreamweaver and choose Edit⇨Paste.**

   Dreamweaver's Image Preview dialog box appears (refer to Figure 6-3).

3. **Select the desired optimization, scale, and export settings in the Options and File tabs of the dialog box.**

   Refer to the previous section "The Smart Object Workflow" for details on these settings.

4. **Click the OK button to save the optimized graphic.**

   Dreamweaver displays the Save Web Image dialog box.

5. **In the Save Web Image dialog box, select a destination and filename for your optimized graphic and then click the Save button.**

   For the best results, save your optimized graphic in an images folder in your managed site.

6. **If you are prompted to do so, enter in an Image Description to add the `alt` attribute to your optimized image when Dreamweaver inserts it onto your Web page.**

   Otherwise, the image is inserted onto your page without the `alt` attribute; you can always edit the `alt` attribute or add it to the selected image in the Properties inspector.

Editing the pasted optimized graphic's original PSD

If you need to make changes to a pasted optimized graphic after you've added it to your Dreamweaver page, repeat the preceding steps, making sure to save the updated graphic with the same filename and format in the same location in your managed site so that the new version overwrites the old version.

You can launch the original source PSD file in Photoshop from the pasted image in Dreamweaver if you first set Photoshop to be the default editor for that file extension in Dreamweaver's File/Types category of the Preferences dialog box, and then select the graphic and enter the path to the original Photoshop file in the Properties inspector. After you do that, you can select the graphic in Design view and then click the Edit icon in the Properties inspector, which in turn opens the original file in Photoshop. When you've finished making changes to the Photoshop file, save the file in Photoshop, and then repeat the preceding Copy/Paste workflow steps to create a new optimized graphic for Dreamweaver. If you save the new graphic with the same name and file format as the old file, the new graphic replaces the old one.

Reoptimizing the pasted optimized graphic

To edit the optimization settings of an optimized image that you've added to your page using the Copy/Paste workflow, select the image and click the Edit Image Settings icon in the Properties inspector. This relaunches the Image Preview dialog box, where you can nondestructively adjust the optimization settings based on the original source PSD file. When you've finished, save the updated optimized graphic; Dreamweaver overwrites the original optimized graphic with the new one.

To watch a video about the Copy/Paste workflow between different Adobe programs such as Photoshop and Dreamweaver, go to www.adobe.com/ go/vid0193 or visit the Adobe TV Web site at http://tv.adobe.com/ product/dreamweaver/.

Accessing and Using Adobe Bridge

Adobe Bridge is simply one of the best cross-platform file browsing programs for finding, organizing, and previewing your files — both Adobe and non-Adobe — for all your Web, print, video, and audio projects. As an Adobe application, Bridge can be launched from within any Creative Suite program (except Acrobat) or as a standalone application from which you can select a file and launch any Adobe Creative Suite program that supports the selected file's format.

Use Bridge (see Figure 6-4) with Dreamweaver to preview, sort, and search for files, add meta data, and insert selected files into your documents. You can also do automated tasks such as batch renaming, as well as manage your digital photographs and stock art.

To watch an Adobe video on the Adobe Bridge Web workflow, go to www. adobe.com/designcenter/video_workshop/?id=vid0192 or visit the Adobe TV Web site at http://tv.adobe.com/product/bridge/.

Figure 6-4: Use Adobe Bridge to browse, find, organize, and preview your files.

Launching Bridge from Dreamweaver

Launch Bridge from within Dreamweaver in any of the following ways:

✦ Choose File⇨Browse in Bridge.

✦ Launch Bridge using the keyboard shortcut Ctrl+Alt+O (Windows) or ⌘+Option+O (Macintosh).

✦ Click the Browse in Bridge icon on the Standard toolbar. If the Standard toolbar is hidden, choose View⇨Toolbars⇨Standard to make it visible.

Launching Dreamweaver from Bridge

To launch Dreamweaver from within Bridge, choose File⇨Open With⇨Adobe Dreamweaver CS5. Or select a file and then right-click (Windows) or Control+click (Macintosh) and choose Open With⇨Adobe Dreamweaver CS5.

Inserting a file from Bridge

After you've launched Bridge, you can select and insert a file into the location of your cursor in Dreamweaver's Design view by one of two methods:

✦ Drag the selected file(s) from Bridge into your open Web document

✦ Select a single file and choose File⇨Place⇨In Dreamweaver

If the selected file is not already in your managed site's root folder or images folder, Dreamweaver prompts you to put a copy of the selected file in there. When inserting Web-ready graphics such as GIF, PNG, and JPG files, you may also be prompted to add image tag accessibility attributes for your newly inserted file.

Integrating Your Files with Device Central

With Device Central, Dreamweaver users can now preview how their files will appear in a selection of different mobile devices. By using the Opera browser's Small-Screen Rendering system, Device Central enables you to see how your mobile content looks on a small screen and test whether CSS and other Web page markup is coded correctly.

To begin previewing your Web content for mobile devices, open the file in Dreamweaver and choose File⇨Preview in Browser⇨Device Central, or click the Preview/Debug in Browser icon on the Document toolbar and select the option to Preview in Device Central.

Tips for creating mobile content

Creating and designing mobile content is a bit different than creating content for normal Web pages. For example, although individual mobile devices may support certain HTML features, the Opera Small-Screen Rendering system does not support certain elements including frames, pop-up browser windows, and font styles such as underlines, overlines, striketh-roughs, blinking, and marquees. Also, images must be made smaller than normal to render without skewing in the smaller device window. Try, too, to keep fonts, colors, and styles to a minimum, while making sure to use CSS or HTML to set `width` and `height` attributes for images as well as adding `alt` attributes for all your images. Lastly, when using Spry elements on your mobile content pages, be sure to add the following two lines of code on your pages for accurate CSS and JavaScript rendering:

```
<link href="SpryAccordion.css"
    media="screen" rel="stylesheet"
    type="text/css"/>
<link href="SpryAccordion2.css"
    media="handheld"
    rel="stylesheet"
    type="text/css"/>
```

For even more design tips and information about creating mobile content, see `www.adobe.com/go/learn_cs_mobilewiki_en`.

After Device Central launches, as shown in Figure 6-5, your Web page is displayed on the Emulate Web tab, where you can review your file as well as choose other devices listed in the Test Devices pane.

Figure 6-5: Preview your Web pages for mobile devices in Device Central.

Two popular devices, Apple's iPhone and iPod touch, are unfortunately not available in Device Central, but you can test for the iPhone online at www. iphonetester.com.

For instruction and details about using Device Central, visit http://help. adobe.com/en_US/DeviceCentral/2.0_UsingDeviceCentral/.

Setting Up Dreamweaver to Use Adobe AIR

Adobe AIR is a relatively new cross–operating system software application that lets users develop and deploy multiplatform Rich Internet Applications (RIAs) to the desktop using Flash, Flex, HTML, JavaScript, and Ajax. What makes AIR so powerful is that you can create these RIAs in a familiar environment. So in Dreamweaver, for instance, you could build an application using HTML, JavaScript, CSS, and Spry Widgets (Ajax).

To use an AIR application, you simply run it and interact with it on your desktop like your other native desktop applications. Even better, these applications work on Mac, PC, and Linux platforms, providing consistent and predictable performance to users. In essence, AIR helps you deliver desktop applications to end users without worrying about cross-platform development requirements or performance issues.

Using Adobe AIR requires two things. First, you have to download and install the Adobe AIR SDK authoring application. Second, you have to download and install the Adobe AIR extension for Dreamweaver, which lets you package and preview your AIR applications from within Dreamweaver.

You can download the latest version of both the free AIR application and the Adobe AIR SDK, which give you the tools you need to build and deploy the AIR applications.

After that, you must install the free Adobe AIR extension for Dreamweaver to begin using Dreamweaver to package and preview your Adobe AIR applications within Dreamweaver.

Follow these steps to download and install the Adobe AIR Extension for Dreamweaver:

1. **Download to your desktop the Adobe AIR extension for Dreamweaver.**

The link to download the extension can be found on Adobe's Tools for AIR and Ajax Web page at www.adobe.com/products/air/tools/ ajax/. The extension is provided in MXP format for easy installation using Adobe's Extension Manager software. Make sure you select the AIR file, not the AIR SDK file.

2. **Double-click the MXP file to launch Extension Manager.**

**Book III
Chapter 6**

**Dreamweaver
Cross-Application
Integration**

This both opens Extension Manager and begins the installation process of the MXP file. Follow the on-screen prompts to accept the terms of the extension installation disclaimer. When finished, Extension Manager notifies you that the extension has been successfully installed.

3. Exit and then restart Dreamweaver CS5.

The extension is fully functional only after you restart Dreamweaver.

After the AIR application and extension have been installed, you can begin using Dreamweaver to package and preview AIR applications by choosing Site⇨Create AIR File.

For instructions on using the Dreamweaver AIR extension, see http://help.adobe.com/en_US/AIR/1.5/devappshtml/WS5b3ccc516d4fbf351e63e3d118666ade46-7fce.html.

To find out more about developing Adobe AIR applications with HTML and Ajax, visit the following Web sites:

+ http://help.adobe.com/en_US/AIR/1.5/devappshtml/index.html

+ www.adobe.com/products/air/tools/ajax/

+ www.adobe.com/devnet/air/ajax/quickstart/

+ http://help.adobe.com/en_US/AIR/1.5/jslr/

To date, more than 800 Adobe AIR applications are available to download and use for free or for a fee. Applications in categories such as Adobe Applications, Audio & Music, Creative & Design, Entertainment, Photo & Video, and Science & Technology include such tools as the BrandGopher (a domain name research tool), Shrink O'Matic (an image batch resizer), DrawTweet (a mini-app that lets you tweet your drawings), and Timeloc (a desktop tool that tracks your time on various projects). You can find these applications and more on the Adobe AIR Marketplace Web site at www.adobe.com/cfusion/exchange/index.cfm?event=productHome&exc=24&loc=en_us.

Working with Adobe's Creative Suites Extended Services (CSXS)

Adobe's Creative Suites Extended Services (CSXS) is a group of hosted services that were developed to aid Adobe users in getting the most out of their software programs. Of the three services in the CSXS suite, two of them, Share My Screen and Search for Help, have been available since CS4, while the third, Third-Party Flash-based Services, is new in CS5.

All the services offered in CSXS run in pure Flash (AuthPlay), AIRPlay, or a combination of both, which means that they can have their own panels in Dreamweaver, providing direct access to their applications and services.

In this section, you learn more about how these online applications can help you work more effectively across the Internet.

Share My Screen (ConnectNow)

If you've ever used an online collaboration tool such as Gliffy, GoToMyPC, or Google Wave, you know how wonderful it can be to meet up and collaborate with coworkers, customers, classmates, friends, and family in a real-time, easy-to-access, secure, online environment. With Adobe's Share My Screen service (which uses a service of Adobe Acrobat.com called ConnectNow), you can not only chat and talk in real time using integrated audio but also share and make notes on your desktop and up to three other participants' desktops! What's more, ConnectNow lets you show live video, share files, and even save meeting notes from each session.

To use ConnectNow, you must have an Adobe account. To create a free Adobe account, visit `www.adobe.com/cfusion/membership/index.cfm?nf=1&loc=en_us&nl=1`.

To use Adobe ConnectNow, follow these steps:

1. **Enter ConnectNow by choosing File⇨Share My Screen.**

You can access ConnectNow also by choosing Windows⇨Connections⇨ Share My Screen. The first time you use the service, click the Set Up Access button. After that, the Sign In to Adobe CS Live dialog box appears, prompting you to enter your Adobe ID and password for access to Adobe's Acrobat.com service area.

2. **Enter your Adobe ID and Password, and click the Sign In button.**

After signing in, Dreamweaver connects you to the ConnectNow Web site, providing you with a custom URL you can use to invite up to two people to your private meeting room.

3. **Use the ConnectNow Welcome Screen to send out invitations and gain access to the different services.**

The Welcome Screen (see Figure 6-6) provides links to several areas to help you get started:

- To customize the meeting URL, click the Custom Your Meeting URL link.

- To send an invitation to up to three other participants, click the Send Email Invitation Now link.

- To learn more about using Adobe ConnectNow, click the Watch the Video button.

- To learn about upgrading your meetings for up to 20 members, click the Upgrade box Learn More button.

Book III
Chapter 6

Dreamweaver Cross-Application Integration

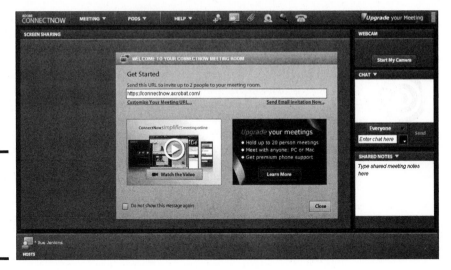

Figure 6-6:
The
Connect-
Now
Welcome
screen.

For detailed instructions on using ConnectNow, visit `http://help.adobe.com/en_US/Acrobat.com/ConnectNow/index.html`. To learn more about the program in general, visit `www.adobe.com/acom/connectnow/?promoid=ESAIW`.

Search for Help

In the past, Adobe's access to help for a particular program was limited to that program's own help files. In CS4, Adobe expanded their services to include an in-application panel that connects through the Internet to the Adobe online community, where everyone, from experts to new users, can provide additional help content to the host application.

In Dreamweaver CS5, you'll find access to this feature in the form of a Flash-based text entry box at the top of Dreamweaver's application bar, right next to the workspace selection menu.

The Help tool works in both offline and online modes:

✦ **Offline:** When an Internet connection is not detected, the Help tool displays only local help results.

✦ **Online:** When an Internet connection is detected, the Help tool displays both local help results and online community help.

To use Dreamweaver CS5 Help, simply type the term you want to learn more about in the Help tool text box and press Enter (Windows) or Return (Mac). You view the results in a pop-up window called Adobe Community Help, which by default is set to display help from the online community, as seen in Figure 6-7.

After the Adobe Community Help window displays your results, you can continue searching for other terms with the Help tool or from within the Community Help window.

To quickly clear a term from the Help search field in either location, place your cursor in the search field and press the Escape key. You may also double-click to select a term (or triple-click to select multiple words) and press Delete.

When the Adobe Community Help window appears, you can refine your searches on the left side of the window by specifying the Search as follows:

✦ **Local Help:** Filter your local help file results to the options offered in the Filter Results menu.

✦ **Community Help:** Search results here include help files found on Adobe. com along with other sources from the online community. Each entry is listed in order of relative importance and consists of a title, a brief description or a sentence pulled from the relevant results listing, and a URL to the help file online.

✦ **Adobe.com:** Search results here are from Adobe.com and are listed in order of relative importance. Each entry consists of a title, a brief description, or a sentence pulled from the relevant results listing, and a URL to the help file online.

**Book III
Chapter 6**

Dreamweaver
Cross-Application
Integration

Figure 6-7:
The Adobe
Community
Help
window.

Third-Party Flash-based Services

Dreamweaver CS5 users now have access to Flash-based services offered by other vendors and Adobe integrators. Because this feature is so new, no non-Adobe services are listed here yet. But after some services are developed, you will be able to access them through the Explore CS Live Services option on the CS Live panel, which you find out about in the following section.

Managing Your CSXS Services

Now that you know what CSXS services are, you should know a little bit more about how to manage them. To manage your CSXS services, click the new CS Live Services icon on the Dreamweaver application bar to launch the Access CS Live panel, shown in Figure 6-8. You can access the service also by choosing Windows⇨Extensions⇨CS Live.

Figure 6-8:
The Access
CS Live
panel.

Use the Access CS Live panel to perform the following tasks:

✦ Log in to Acrobat.com

✦ Sign in to the Share My Screen feature through ConnectNow

✦ Access CS News and Resources online

✦ Manage your Adobe.com account

✦ Explore other CS Live Services

✦ Access the Adobe BrowserLab

By default, the CSXS panel automatically searches for updates to any installed service when an Internet connection is detected. To turn off this feature and manually check for updates instead, deselect the Auto-Updates option on the panel's flyout menu. You may also elect to stop the CSXS panel from connecting to the Internet altogether by selecting the Keep Me Offline option. Doing this will block access to Share My Screen as well as force any Help searches to return local help files only, rather than any online help.

After you log in to Adobe.com through CS Live or Share My Screen, your login information will be remembered by the system for up to five minutes after you close your Dreamweaver CS5 application. On the other hand, if you select the Stay Signed In option when you first log in, your login information will be remembered by any CS5 product until the next time you reboot your computer.

Book IV

Energizing Your Site

Contents at a Glance

Chapter 1: Working with Layers

In This Chapter

✔ Understanding how layers work

✔ Using the AP Elements panel

✔ Creating, editing, and managing layers

✔ Setting a layer's properties

✔ Using CSS with layers

✔ Converting AP Divs to tables (and tables to AP Divs)

*L*ayers are containers for other HTML page elements. Typically coded with the `<div>` tag, *layers* can hold any kind of content you'd place elsewhere in the body of a document, such as text, graphics, JavaScript, and Flash movies.

Also referred to as *layout objects*, layers can be absolutely or relatively positioned anywhere on a page, allowing you to create interesting page layouts. In addition, you can make layers visible or hidden, styled and positioned with CSS, animated across the browser window, nested inside one another, and stacked in any order. Combined with JavaScript behaviors, you can even manipulate layers in a browser window to provide engaging opportunities for visitor interaction.

Because of their flexibility, layers have become the new solution for many complex Web layouts. Although most new browsers support layers, some very old versions do not. (This is not much of an issue because these days the ratio of browsers that don't support layers is extremely low.) Still, if you need to ensure compatibility with an isolated pool of older browsers, or if you want to cover all eventualities, you could convert your layers to a table-based layout using the Convert command (as described in the "Converting AP Divs to Tables and Tables to AP Divs" section, at the end of this chapter), so that any browser — even the oldest one — can interpret the content.

This chapter explores all the aspects of using layers in Dreamweaver. It starts with an introduction to inserting layout objects with the Layout category of the Insert panel and to layers management with the AP Elements panel, and then moves to other topics such as showing you how to set layer attributes. The chapter also covers how to use CSS to style and position layers and how to convert layers into a table-based layout and vice versa.

Understanding Layers

Layers are what the W3C refers to as a *block-level element.* Block-level elements are containers that can hold content (such as images, text, and Flash movies), be any size, and be positioned anywhere on a page when styled with CSS. Unlike tables, blocks can be aligned and positioned on a page to create fairly sophisticated layouts, including layers that overlap!

Figure 1-1 shows how you can have multiple layers on a page, each with unique content, positioning, and styles.

Figure 1-1: Position layers anywhere on a page and fill them with text, images, Flash movies, and more.

Traditionally, Web designers have used table-based page layouts to build their pages, placing graphics and content inside tables. With tables, the cells are side by side and the content can't overlap. One of the drawbacks of a table-based layout is that content and form are meshed in one document, which doesn't quite harness the full power of designing, formatting, and styling pages with CSS. The full power of CSS comes when you begin laying out pages with layers and using CSS to position and style objects on the page. Tables, by contrast, tend to be more static than layers and offer fewer opportunities for CSS formatting and styling. With layers, when you strip some of the formatting instructions from the HTML and hand them off to a Cascading Style Sheet, not only is the HTML code much cleaner, but the formatting capabilities of CSS enable you to lay out pages without the use of (or with significantly less reliance on) tables. Tables aren't necessarily a bad thing; they're just being relied on less for page layout than they used to be.

In Dreamweaver, two types of layers can be drawn or inserted into your pages. Both types are accessible in the Layout category of the Insert panel (choose Insert⇨Layout Objects). The first layer uses the regular `<div>` tag (which is a container tag that can hold any elements that appear elsewhere on the page), and the second uses the AP Div (which is controlled by the AP Elements panel, is automatically labeled with an `id`, as in `<div id="apDiv1"></div>`, and adds an ID CSS rule to your style sheet, as in `#apDiv1`).

When you insert the `<div>` tag, the Insert Div Tag dialog box is displayed, as shown in Figure 1-2, prompting you to set the insertion, class, or ID for the HTML tag:

✦ **Insert:** Choose At Insertion Point, Before Tag, After Start of Tag, Before End of Tag, or After Tag from the first menu as the location where the `<div>` tag should be placed in the code relative to the tag you select from the second menu

✦ **Class:** Apply a CSS custom Class style to the `<div>` as you're inserting the tag onto the page.

✦ **ID:** Apply a CSS ID style to the `<div>` as you're inserting the tag on the page.

✦ **New CSS Rule:** Click this button to create a new Class or ID style in your CSS on the fly and apply it to the `<div>` as you insert the tag on the page.

Figure 1-2:
Adding a
`<div>` tag
prompts you
to select
options from
the Insert
Div Tag
dialog box.

**Book IV
Chapter 1**

Working with
Layers

You can also insert `<div>` tag layers by clicking the Insert Div Tag icon in the Layout category of the Insert panel.

After the `<div>` tag layer the `<div>` tag layer is inserted on the page, you can add content to it, style it, and reposition it. However, the `<div>` tag layer is not tied into the AP Elements panel. In other words, you can't manage the `<div>` tag layer's visibility, ID, and *z-index* (stacking order) through the AP Elements panel; only AP Div layers can be managed by the AP Elements panel. The visibility, ID, and z-index of `<div>` tag layers must be managed with CSS through the CSS Styles panel.

By contrast, when you draw or insert an AP Div layer in Dreamweaver (as described in the next section), several things happen at once. The CSS style data for the layer's size and positioning are automatically inserted into an internal style sheet at the head of the open document, the `<div>` tag is inserted in the code at the insertion point with the layer id value of apDiv1, and a marker for the layer appears in the AP Elements panel. Subsequent layers added to the page in a similar manner are given id values of apDiv2, apDiv3, apDiv4, and so forth. To better identify each AP Div layer by its contents, however, you can edit the id names in either the Properties inspector or the AP Elements panel after inserting them on the page.

AP Div tags are a great way for beginners to find out about using layers and CSS without having to set technical CSS positioning and style attributes (id, positions, width, height, z-index) in the CSS panel, which can be somewhat intimidating when you first start out coding by hand. Later, as you become familiar with how the AP Div tags work, you can use the regular `<div>` tags and give them an id or class attribute with more ease.

Here's an example of the HTML code after inserting an AP Div layer on a page:

```
<!DOCTYPE HTML PUBLIC "-//W3C//DTD HTML 4.01 Transitional//EN"
"http://www.w3.org/TR/html4/loose.dtd">
<html>
<head>
<meta http-equiv="Content-Type" content="text/html; charset=iso-8859-1">
<title>Working with Layers</title>
<style type="text/css">
<!--
#apDiv1 {
position:absolute;
width:200px;
height:115px;
z-index:1;
}
-->
</style>
</head>
<body>
<div id="apDiv1"></div>
</body>
</html>
```

Don't confuse `<div>` tags and AP Div layers with the old `<layer>` and `<ilayer>` tags used for positioning, which arrived as a blip on the Netscape 4 radar but quickly went away by Netscape 6. These tags are no longer supported by any browsers nor contained in any W3C standards. Rather, the layers used in Dreamweaver refer to the `<div>` tag being paired with the id attribute and used as a block-level container for HTML content.

Creating Layers

Whether you insert a `<div>` tag or an AP Div, you can place these layers anywhere on the page, nest them, place content in them, style and position them with CSS, and size them to any rectangular shape. You can add layers to a page by three simple methods: drawing, inserting, and dropping. Use any of these methods interchangeably to suit your particular Web design needs.

Drawing an AP Div layer

The most effective way to add a layer to your page is to draw it because it can be drawn anywhere on the page. Plus, drawing a layer automatically makes it an AP Div layer, giving you more control over it through the AP Elements panel.

To draw a single AP Div layer on a page, follow these steps:

1. **In the Layout category of the Insert panel, click the Draw AP Div icon.**

2. **In Design view of your open Document window, click and drag a rectangular shape where the new AP Div layer should appear.**

The drag can flow in any direction from the insertion point. Remember that the layer size and placement is approximate at this phase (see Figure 1-3). To draw multiple layers at the same time without having to click the Draw AP Div icon each time, press and hold Ctrl (Windows) or ⌘ (Mac) as you drag and draw your layers; as long as you keep the key pressed, you can continue drawing new layers.

3. **When the size and placement of the drawn AP Div layer is acceptable to you, release the mouse button.**

4. **To add more layers to the page, repeat Steps 1–3.**

New layers added to the page are stacked directly on top of one another, each with a unique layer `id` and z-index number for identification and stacking order.

Dreamweaver provides two other ways to add AP Div layers to your page:

✦ **Insert a layer:** Place the cursor in your document where you want to insert the new layer. Choose Insert⇨Layout Objects⇨AP Div. The new layer is automatically inserted at the insertion point. New layers are added to the page stack directly on top of one another (unless you've repositioned the insertion point), each with a unique layer id and z-index number for identification and stacking order.

✦ **Drop a layer:** In the Layout category of the Insert panel, click the Draw AP Div icon, and then drag and drop the layer into the open Document window. The new blank AP Div layer is automatically inserted at the default position in the top-left corner of the Document window. Repeat the process to add more layers to the page.

Book IV Chapter 1

Working with Layers

Figure 1-3:
Draw AP Div
layers on
the page.

For more precise layout and placement of layers, some people find it helpful to enable the Grid and Snap to Grid features when drawing layers on the
page. To find out more about using and customizing the grid, see Book I,
Chapter 1.

Adding content to layers

Layers can hold most of the content you'd place in the body of a document,
such as text, graphics, JavaScript, and Flash movies. When you're ready to
add content to a layer, place the insertion point inside the layer and either
paste copied data from another source, begin typing, or insert content using
any of the options on the Insert menu, Insert panel, or Assets panel.

Creating nested layers

A *nested layer* is a layer that's controlled by, but not necessarily inside,
another layer. More simply, think of nested layers as having an interesting
parent-child relationship in which the child layer can move or function independently of the parent layer, but when the parent layer moves or changes
its visibility, the child does too. The HTML code of a nested layer is inside
the code of the parent layer, which you can see when you view the source
code, even though the nested layer may appear elsewhere on the screen due
to absolute positioning. Nested layers can be useful, for example, when creating custom navigation menus.

Figure 1-4 shows an example of how a nested layer appears in Design view, Code view, and the AP Elements panel.

Figure 1-4:
Nested
layers are
easy to
identify in
Code view
and the AP
Elements
panel, but
may be
difficult
to spot in
Design
view.

Before you can create nested layers, make sure that the Nesting preference is enabled in the Preferences dialog box (as described in the next section). Then follow these steps to create a nested AP Div layer:

1. **Choose Insert➪Layout Objects➪AP Div.**

   The new blank layer is automatically inserted at the top of the page. If you'd prefer, you can draw your AP Div instead of inserting it (see "Drawing an AP Div layer," previously in this chapter).

2. **Place the cursor in the new layer, and then choose Insert➪Layout Objects➪AP Div to create a second layer.**

   The second layer is nested inside the first layer.

3. **To reposition the nested layer (the second layer), select the nested layer in the AP Elements panel to make it active, and do one of the following:**

   • **Press the arrow keys to move the layer.**

   • **Click the AP Div layer's selection handle (on the top-left corner) and drag the layer to its new location.**

**Book IV
Chapter 1**

**Working with
Layers**

Setting layer preferences

When you insert AP Div layers onto a page, the layers are added using the default dimensions and other attributes as specified in the Layers category of the Preferences dialog box. For example, if Dreamweaver's default layer width and height is set to 200 x 115 pixels, all new AP Div layers are added to the page at that default size unless you add a layer to the page by drawing it (see the "Drawing an AP Div layer" section, earlier in this chapter). By comparison, regular Div Tag layers have no dimensions unless or until you set them with CSS.

You can edit the default AP Div layer size settings at any time by following these steps:

1. **Choose Edit⇨Preferences (Windows) or Dreamweaver⇨ Preferences (Mac).**

The Preferences dialog box appears.

2. **Select the AP Elements category to display the default AP Elements attributes, as shown in Figure 1-5.**

Figure 1-5: These settings determine the default properties of all new AP Div layers.

3. **(Optional) To set the default visibility of the layer (whether shown or hidden when the page loads in the browser), select an option in the Visibility drop-down list.**

Options are Default (visible), Visible, Hidden, and Inherit.

4. **(Optional) To set the default pixel width and height for new layers, fill in the Width and Height text boxes.**

5. **(Optional) To specify a color for the default background color for all new layers, select a color from the Background Color palette or enter a hexadecimal value.**

By default, no background color is set. If you do enter a color, be sure to enter the number symbol before the hexadecimal value, as in #FF0000.

6. **(Optional) To add a default background image for all new layers, click the Browse button to find and select the graphic.**

7. **(Optional) If you want to create nested AP Div layers, select the Nesting check box.**

   The nesting option enables you to draw a layer inside the bounds of another layer.

8. **(Optional) While still in the Preferences dialog box, select the Invisible Elements category and enable the Anchor Points for AP Elements option.**

   When you enable this option, each AP Div layer has its own yellow anchor point marker, which can assist greatly in the selection of specific layers in Design view, especially when several layers overlap or have visibility set to hidden.

9. **Click OK to close the Preferences dialog box.**

Managing AP Div Layers with the AP Elements Panel

The AP Elements panel is the place to go to select AP Div layers, name them, change their z-index, modify nesting placement, enable overlapping, and edit visibility settings. The AP Elements panel is in a panel group with the CSS Styles panel and (when opened) Tag Inspector panel. To open the AP Elements panel, choose Window⇨AP Elements or click the AP Elements panel tab within its panel group.

The AP Elements panel lists the AP Div layers on a page by visibility setting, name, and z-index number, as shown in Figure 1-6. The sorting order of the list is determined by the z-index. High z-index numbered layers appear at the top of the list, whereas lower z-index numbered layers appear at the bottom of the list.

Figure 1-6: The AP Elements panel displays information about all AP Div layers on the page.

Try not to be confused by the default layer names and the z-index numbers. The default layer names are arbitrarily assigned when you create the layers (you can rename them to reflect their purpose) and are meant to assist with identifying layers and applying CSS styles to them. The z-index, however, is used for the ordering or stacking of the layers between the browser and the site visitor. For example, on a page with 12 regular, non-nested layers, each named `apDiv1`, `apDiv2`, `apDiv3`, and so on, where you want `apDiv7` to appear on top of the other layers, assign `apDiv7` a higher stacking order than 12. When you have nested layers on the page, nested layers often appear on top of parent layers, regardless of the stacking number of the parent. In a nested group, though, normal z-index ordering applies.

If you rename your layers through the AP Elements panel, you may have an easier time arranging them into the desired stacking order. Plus, when you use the AP Elements to rearrange, the z-index numbers self-adjust as you rearrange the layers.

Preventing layer overlap

To prevent layers from overlapping as you draw, move, or resize them, enable the Prevent Overlaps option at the top of the AP Elements panel. This feature is handy if you plan on using layers for page layout or converting the layers into tables (as described in the "Converting AP Divs to Tables and Tables to AP Divs" section, later in this chapter), or if you want to add layers to your page that fit right up against one another without any gaps.

Although the Prevent Overlaps option doesn't modify existing layer over-laps until you change them manually, it does prevent you from drawing new layers on top of or inside another layer. It also prevents existing layers from being moved onto or resized over another layer, and instead helps layers snap into position next to each other.

To prevent layer overlaps, do one of the following:

✦ In the AP Elements panel, select the Prevent Overlaps option.

✦ In Design view, choose Modify➪Arrange➪Prevent AP Element Overlaps.

For most layer creation, layer movement, and layer resizing on a page, the Prevent Overlaps feature works wonderfully. However, some layer actions still allow you to add new layers that do overlap existing layers even with this option selected. For instance, layers inserted with the Insert menu and positioned with data in the Properties inspector can overlap existing layers in Design view. You can achieve the same effect when editing layer HTML source code directly in Code view.

If you like the way the new overlapping layers look in Design view and in your target browsers, the overlapping layers can be left as they are.

However, to remove layer overlaps from a page, select the Prevent Overlaps option first, and then drag the layers to a new position in Design view. The new layers snap into position next to, and not on top of, adjoining layers.

Naming AP Div layers

A layer's name refers to the layer's `id`. The `id` is used to attach CSS and positioning information to the layer. By default, Dreamweaver names AP Div layers `apDiv1`, `apDiv2`, and so on, but you can rename them with unique names through the AP Elements panel.

Layers can have a class name or an id name or both. For instance, you can reference a div class by creating a style and assigning it to a layer, as in `<div class="sidebar">`, and you could have an AP Div layer that also used the same class, as in `<div id="apDiv2" class="sidebar">`. (For a refresher on styling your Web pages with CSS, turn to Book III, Chapter 1.)

To edit the name of an AP Div layer with the AP Elements panel, follow these steps:

1. **In the ID column of the AP Elements panel, double-click the layer name you want to edit.**

   The current name of the layer is highlighted.

2. **Type the new name for the layer, and then press Enter (Windows) or Return (Mac).**

   AP Element names can't contain any spaces, may only contain letters and numbers, and can't start with a number. The new layer name is reflected in the code's `<div>` tag `id` attribute as well as in the layer's CSS style info embedded in the head of the document, in the AP Elements panel, and in the Properties inspector.

Changing the z-index (stacking order)

You can modify the *z-index*, or stacking order, of an AP Div layer with the AP Elements panel or by entering a number in the Z-Index field in the Properties inspector. The higher the z-index number, the closer to the top of the list and the closer the layer appears to the visitor in the browser window relative to the other visible layers on the page.

To edit the z-index of a layer on the AP Elements panel, select the z-index number next to the desired layer name and enter a new z-index number.

Editing layer visibility

Using the AP Elements panel with Design view, you can show or hide layers to get an idea of how the page will be displayed under different conditions in a browser window. The default visibility status for all layers is to display layers both in Design view and in a browser window.

To set or change an AP Div layer's visibility in the AP Elements panel, click in the visibility (eye) column next to the layer name for which you want to alter visibility:

✦ **Open eye:** The layer is visible when the page is initially displayed in a browser.

✦ **Closed eye:** The layer is hidden, or invisible, when the page is initially displayed in a browser.

✦ **No eye:** No visibility is set for the layer and it inherits the parent layer's visibility status or the default visibility setting, which is visible. Nested layers inherit parent visibility settings, and non-nested layers inherit the document body's visibility settings (which is visible, unless you have hidden the body with CSS).

Figure 1-7 shows the AP Elements panel with sample layers set to on (show), off (hide), and none (default).

Figure 1-7:
Use the AP Elements panel to specify each layer's visibility setting.

Show Layer

Hide Layer

No preference set

To change all the layers on the page to visible or hidden at once, click the eye header icon at the top of the visibility column. The eye header icon works as a toggle button to switch between visible and hidden for all layers. Click once to make all layers visible. Click again to make all layers hidden.

Selecting and Adjusting AP Div Layers

Before moving, aligning, resizing, or editing the contents of a layer, you must first select the layer. A selected AP Div layer is identifiable by its bold blue outline, its corner and midsection border anchor points, and the visibility of the selection handle on the layer's top-left corner, as shown in Figure 1-8.

Figure 1-8:
Selected
AP Div
layers are
displayed
with a bold
blue outline,
anchor
points, and
a selection
handle.

Anchor point

Selection handle   Outline

Selecting layers

To assist you with selecting the layer, hover your mouse cursor over the layer's edge. When you see the highlight border, click the layer's edge to select the entire layer.

You can change the color of the layer highlighting — or turn off the feature — by modifying the Mouse-Over option in the Highlighting category of the Preferences dialog box. Choose Edit⇨Preferences (Windows) or Dreamweaver⇨Edit (Mac).

You can also select a layer in any of these other ways:

✦ In the AP Elements panel, click the name of the layer you want to select.

✦ In Design view, do either of the following:

   • Click anywhere inside the layer to make the layer active; then click the layer's border or selection handle.

   • Ctrl+Shift+click (Windows) or ⌘+Shift+click (Mac) inside a layer.

If you want to select multiple AP Div layers, do either of the following:

✦ In Design view, Shift+click the border, selection handle, or inside area of any two or more layers.

✦ In the AP Elements panel, Shift+click two or more layer names.

With multiple layer selection, the corner and midsection layer border anchor points turn hollow for all but the last layer selected, which retains its solid anchor points, and the layers are highlighted in the AP Elements panel.

Resizing and moving AP Div layers

Select the layer or layers using any of the selection methods in the preceding section before making any adjustments such as resizing, moving, or aligning:

✦ **Resize a layer:** Drag the selected layer's resize handles to the new desired size. You can also adjust the layer's Width and Height sizes in the Properties inspector, or, if using CSS, adjust the size in the layer's CSS through the CSS panel.

✦ **Resize multiple layers at once:** Select two or more layers and enter Width and Height values in the Multiple CSS-P Elements W and H fields in the Properties inspector.

✦ **Move a selected layer or layers in Design view:** Drag the border. With multiple layers, drag the border of the last selected layer.

You can reposition layers on the page like you reposition graphics and other objects; however, if you've enabled the Prevent Overlaps option, you can't reposition the layer on top of another layer. (See "Preventing layer overlap," earlier in the chapter, for more on this option.)

✦ **Align two or more selected layers:** Choose Modify⇨Arrange and then select an alignment option. Align layers to the left, right, top, or bottom edge of the last selected layer. When aligning nested layers, any child layer moves along with the parent layer but isn't included in the alignment unless explicitly selected first.

Setting Layer Properties

Layers have properties that, among other things, define their size, position, name, z-index (stacking order), background color, and visibility. Although you can also set a layer's name, visibility status, and z-index in the AP Elements panel, you can easily adjust all the layer's properties in one go-around using the Properties inspector.

Properties are real-time attributes that are immediately reflected on the page in Design view when you press Tab, Enter (Windows), or Return (Mac). Therefore, any time you adjust an AP Div layer property in the Properties inspector, the AP Elements panel is updated to reflect the new layer settings. This also works in the reverse direction; when you make modifications in the AP Elements panel, the Properties inspector is also instantly updated.

The Properties inspector (shown in Figure 1-9) includes the following layer properties:

Figure 1-9:
Set
properties
for selected
layers.

Figure 1-9:
Set
properties
for selected
layers.

✦ **Layer ID:** Identify each layer using a unique name or ID. The name you enter here is used to attach CSS styles and JavaScript behaviors to the layer. Make sure each layer id is a single word using letters or numbers but without any special characters, dashes, hyphens, periods, or spaces.

✦ **L** and **T** (left and top): These are the coordinates or absolute position of the layer relative to the top-left corner of the containing box, which is usually the body of the page but can be a parent layer. For example, a setting of left:100px and top:300px places the layer exactly 100 pixels from the left and 300 pixels from the top of the browser window. Nested layers use these coordinates for absolute positioning relative to the parent layer. If you switch to Code view, you see that when the left and top are specified, the position attribute in the CSS is always set to position:absolute.

✦ **W** and **H** (width and height): These are the size of the layer. By default, layer sizes are specified in pixels, such as 100px. To enter another unit, add the appropriate abbreviation after the number without a space, such as 1in, 10pt, or 80%. Acceptable units are (px) pixels, in (inches), pc (picas), pt (points), mm (millimeters), cm (centimeters), or % (percentage of a parent layer's size).

When the contents of a layer exceed the specified size of the layer and the Overflow setting is set to Visible, the bottom of the layer grows to display all the layer's contents in both Design view and in a browser window. To use the specified width and height instead, adjust the Overflow setting.

✦ **Z-Index:** Set the stacking order of the layer. Enter positive or negative numbers. In a browser, the lower numbered layers appear behind the higher numbered layers.

Note: If you select a <layer> or <ilayer> tag in the code instead of the <div> tag, additional options appear in the Properties inspector:

• **Left, Top:** Specify the layer's position relative to the top, left coordinates of the layer's parent.

• **PageX, PageY:** Use X and Y coordinates for positioning relative to the page.

- **A/B (Above/Below):** Set the stacking order of the selected layer relative from the first A/B menu to the layer name selected in the second A/B menu.

- **Src:** Select another HTML file to display inside the layer. (This feature does not render in Design view but is displayed in Live View or in a browser.)

✦ **Vis (Visibility):** Determine whether you can see the selected layer on the Web page when the page initially loads in a browser:

- **Default:** Use a browser's default layer visibility status, which in most cases is Inherit.

- **Visible:** Display the layer and its contents in a browser.

- **Hidden:** Hide the layer and its contents from view in a browser.

- **Inherit:** Use the same visibility setting as a parent layer's visibility. Nested layers inherit the parent visibility setting, and non-nested layers inherit the document body's visibility setting, which is always visible.

You can manipulate the visibility feature with JavaScript to hide and show layers when certain events occur, such as an `onMouseOver` event. See Book IV, Chapter 2 to find out more about how to manipulate layers with JavaScript.

✦ **Bg Image:** Add a background image for the layer. The background image tiles both vertically and horizontally to fill the entire visible area of the layer.

✦ **Bg Color:** Add a background color to the layer. Be sure to enter the number symbol before the hexadecimal value, as in `#FF0000`. When you set both a background color and a background image, the background image sits on top of the background color.

✦ **Class:** Apply a custom CSS style to the layer from an internal or externally linked cascading style sheet.

✦ **Overflow:** Determine how content that exceeds the specified size of the layer is handled. This option currently has inconsistent browser support, so be sure to test this feature in all your target browsers to see if it works properly or fails acceptably (in other words, maybe it doesn't work, but it also doesn't look that terrible):

- **Default:** Display the layer and its contents in a browser.

- **Visible:** Expand the layer to fit the size of the contents and display the full layer's contents.

- **Hidden:** Hide content that exceeds the layer's size from view in a browser.

- **Scroll:** Add scroll bars to the specified size of the layer, regardless of whether the contents exceeds the specified size.

- **Auto:** Add scroll bars to the specified size of the layer only when the contents exceed that size.

✦ **Clip (L/R/T/B):** Determine the visible area of a visible layer. Set Left, Right, Top, and Bottom coordinates for the visible clipping area on the layer. Numbers are measured in pixels relative to the top-left corner of the layer. You must set the Overflow option to Hidden, Scroll, or Auto for this feature to work properly. For example, to make a clipping area of 50 x 50 pixels at the top, left edge of the layer, set L to 0, T to 0, R to 50, and B to 50. Figure 1-10 shows an example of a selected layer with a specified clipping area.

Figure 1-10:
Set a visible rectangular clip area in the AP Div layer.

Controlling Layer Style and Positioning with CSS

Dreamweaver is configured to create individual layer ID styles in an internal style sheet for all the new AP Div layers added to your page. These layer styles control all the AP Div layer style attributes — for example, the layer's background color and font preferences — as well as the layer's size and position on the page.

The benefit of using CSS with your layers — both AP Divs and `<div>` tags — is that you can

✦ Utilize all the capabilities of CSS with your layers

✦ Move the CSS information to an external style sheet and link that CSS to all the pages on your site

✦ Use these individual layer styles to control the look and placement of layers of the same name across multiple pages

For instance, you may have a layer called `navigation` that contains navigation links that go on every page of your site. You could modify the properties of the layer (not the layer's content, just its position and style) in an external style sheet file through the CSS panel, and all the pages on the site that contain a layer called `navigation` would be updated with those new properties.

Changing a CSS property should not be confused with changing a template or SSI, which is covered in Book III, Chapters 2 and 3.

When you're creating an AP Div layer in Dreamweaver CS5, two things happen in the code simultaneously:

✦ The layer is added to the code at the insertion point using the `<div>` tag, which is assigned with a temporary layer `id` value of something like `apDiv1` or `apDiv2` (rename layers at any time using the AP Elements panel or Properties inspector).

✦ The layer's size and positioning information is translated into CSS syntax and automatically inserted between `<style>` tags in the head of the open document.

Here's an example:

```
<!DOCTYPE HTML PUBLIC "-//W3C//DTD HTML 4.01 Transitional//EN"
"http://www.w3.org/TR/html4/loose.dtd">
<html>
<head>
<meta http-equiv="Content-Type" content="text/html; charset=iso-8859-1">
<title>Working with Layers</title>
<style type="text/css">
<!--
#navigation {
position:absolute;
left:0px;
top:0px;
width:760px;
height:150px;
z-index:1;
}
-->
</style>
</head>
<body>
<div id="navigation"></div>
</body>
</html>
```

Note that the layer's CSS style name inside the `<style>` tags displays a number symbol (#) before the layer's `id`, in this case, `#navigation`. Whenever the number symbol is paired with a layer's `id` as a style name in a style sheet, the style data is automatically applied (much like a tag redefine style) to the layer with the same `id`. To illustrate, a set of style definitions using the style name `#header` is automatically applied to a layer with the `id="header"`, and a set of style definitions using the style name `#closeup` is automatically applied to a layer with the `id="closeup"`.

Ideally, all style and positioning information for all content on all pages on a Web site are in one centralized location, preferably a single external style sheet. Therefore, you need to export the internal CSS style data for layers entered automatically on the page by Dreamweaver to an external style sheet. You can export internal styles two ways:

✦ Cut and paste the internal styles from the page to an external style sheet.

✦ Use the Move CSS Rules options from the CSS Styles panel options menu to move internal CSS to an external CSS file. (See Book III, Chapter 1 for information on using the export command.)

After transferring the style sheet positioning data to an external style sheet, continue adding additional styling information, such as the layer's background color, font face, font size, and font color, to the layer style through the CSS Styles panel.

To add style information to a layer style, follow these steps:

1. **In the CSS Styles panel, select the layer style name and then click the Edit Rule icon (which looks like a pencil) at the bottom of the panel.**

The CSS Rule Definition dialog box for the selected layer style appears.

2. **Edit or add new layer style definitions in any of the categories in the dialog box.**

When you select a category, the right side of the panel changes to support that category's options. For example, to add a background color, select the Background category and click the Background Color color picker icon to select a hexadecimal value for the background color. See Book III, Chapter 1 for guidance on choosing the appropriate settings in the CSS Rule Definition dialog box.

3. **To preview the adjusted style settings before committing to them, click the Apply button.**

4. **When you finish making changes, click OK.**

The updated style information is added to the style sheet and displayed in the CSS Styles panel.

In the following style example, part of the style data (from `position` to `visibility`) is used for the layer's positioning and the rest (from `background-color` to `border`) is for layer styling:

```
#sidebar {
position:absolute;
left:157px;
top:38px;
width:229px;
height:279px;
z-index:1;
```

```
visibility: visible;
background-color: #FF3366;
font-family: Arial, Helvetica, sans-serif;
font-size: 14px;
font-weight: bold;
color: #FFFFFF;
margin: 0px;
padding-top: 10px;
padding-right: 0px;
padding-bottom: 0px;
padding-left: 10px;
border: 10px solid #99CC00;
}
```

Controlling Layers with Behaviors

Dreamweaver comes with nearly 20 prewritten JavaScript behaviors that allow you to create interactive sites by controlling or manipulating objects on a Web page. Here are three behaviors that apply directly to layers:

✦ **Drag AP Element:** Provide a visitor with the ability of dragging or moving a layer in a browser window. Often used for interactive games and puzzles, the behavior offers the following features:

- **Snap-to capability:** Visitors can drag layers in any direction and they snap to a target destination within a specified number of pixels.

- **Handles:** Define a drag handle somewhere on the layer.

- **Event handlers:** Assign an event handler to the layer as the trigger for the layer's mobility, such as when a visitor moves the mouse over or clicks the layer.

✦ **Set Text of Container:** Replace the contents of an entire layer with new HTML content and formatting — including any JavaScript property, global variable, function call, or other valid expression embedded in the code — when an event is triggered by a visitor's action, such as mousing over the layer.

✦ **Show-Hide Elements:** Control a layer's visibility with user interactivity. For example, you can have a rollover button that, when clicked, reveals a hidden layer. Then, on that layer, you can include a link or graphic that, when clicked, hides the layer.

Book IV, Chapter 2 describes each of these behaviors, including how to insert, modify, and remove them.

Converting AP Divs to Tables and Tables to AP Divs

Layers, due to their flexibility, have become the new solution for many Web designers who need to create complex page layouts. A tables-based layout is still great for portions of a Web page when you have a lot of images that need to fit together tightly within a specified area, such as a navigation table or other menu-type item. By contrast, a layers-based layout can be made to look like a tables-based layout, plus you have the added control of positioning the layers and styling the layers' content using CSS. Alternatively, you may find it useful to combine the use of tables and layers for your layout.

Although now considered less contemporary and standards-compliant than a layout that relies almost exclusively on layers, tables are still a supported method for page layout (or partial page layout) because most browsers support tables, whereas layers are not supported by older browsers.

For future compatibility, accessibility, standards-compliancy, and successful validation, try to do all your layout using layers and limit table usage to holding data. If you want the flexibility of layers but need to use tables for your code, consider using layers to design page layouts and then converting the layers into tables before adding content to the page.

The conversion process is simple, and you can toggle an entire page layout from AP Div layers to tables and tables to AP Div layers. Although you can't use the conversion to convert a single layer or table, keep experimenting until you get your layout perfect.

Be forewarned that the conversion process has two major shortcomings:

✦ The conversion from layers to a table may create a table with a bunch of empty cells, which you then need to manually merge to simplify the table.

✦ You can't apply the conversion process to templates or template-based pages; you must create the table in a normal file and then convert it into a template. If the layout is simply a component of a template-based page, build the table in a new, blank document first and then paste the finished layout into the template-based page.

When creating a layout using layers, be sure to enable the Prevent Overlaps option in the AP Elements panel to constrain layers from nesting or overlapping (see "Preventing layer overlap," earlier in the chapter). Because table cells can't overlap, the layers that are converted into tables can't overlap either.

Converting AP Div layers to a table

To convert a layout using AP Div layers to a table-based layout, follow these steps:

1. **Open a page that contains a layers-based layout.**

2. **Choose Modify⇨Convert⇨AP Divs to Table.**

The Convert AP Divs to Table dialog box appears, as shown in Figure 1-11.

Figure 1-11:
Convert
a layers-
based
layout to
tables.

3. **Specify Table Layout and Layout Tools options:**

   - **Most Accurate:** Make a table cell for each layer as well as create additional cells when needed to ensure that spacing between the old layers is maintained in the new table layout.

   - **Smallest: Collapse Empty Cells:** Align the edges of layers into columns or rows of table cells when within a specified number of pixels. Although this feature creates tables with fewer empty rows and tables, the layout may not be as precise as the original.

   - **Use Transparent GIFs:** Add presized transparent GIFs to the bottom row of the table, which forces browsers to display the table using the same column widths. The drawback to this feature is that the table is not easily resized by simply dragging columns. When disabled, the columns are easily resizable, but the table itself may not display the same in all browsers.

   - **Center on Page:** Center the new table on the page using the `align="center"` attribute inside the opening `<table>` tag. By default, the table is displayed aligned to the left of the browser.

   - **Prevent Overlaps:** Prevent layers from being drawn, resized, or moved on top of one another.

   - **Show AP Elements Panel:** Open the AP Elements panel.

   - **Show Grid:** See the grid in Design view. The grid can assist you with the placement of layers on the page.

   - **Snap to Grid:** Make the layers snap to the grid when placing, sizing, and moving layers on the page.

4. **Click OK to complete the conversion.**

   If the layout contains overlapping or nested layers, an alert message may appear stating that the file isn't compatible with 3.0 browsers and the conversion is cancelled. If that happens, make adjustments to the layers and try the conversion process again.

Converting tables to AP Div layers

To convert a layout using tables to a layers-based layout, follow these steps:

1. Create the tables-based layout in a new, blank HTML document and save the file.

Only table cells with content convert into layers; table cells without content or background color disappear from the page layout during the conversion process. If you don't want this to happen, be sure to add some kind of content to the cells you want to convert into layers.

Any content on the page that wasn't in a table before is put into its own layer during the conversion.

2. Choose Modify⇨Convert⇨Tables to AP Divs.

The Convert Tables to AP Divs dialog box appears, as shown in Figure 1-12.

Figure 1-12:
Convert a tables-based layout to layers with the Convert Tables to AP Divs dialog box.

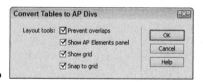

3. Enable the desired Layout Tools options:

- **Prevent Overlaps:** Prevent layers from being drawn, resized, or moved on top of one another.

- **Show AP Elements Panel:** Display the Layers panel.

- **Show Grid:** See the grid in Design view. The grid can assist you with the placement of layers on the page.

- **Snap to Grid:** Make the layers snap to the grid when placing, sizing, and moving layers on the page.

4. Click OK to complete the conversion.

Book IV
Chapter 1

Working with Layers

Chapter 2: Jazzing Up Pages with JavaScript Behaviors and Spry Widgets

In This Chapter

✔ **Understanding JavaScript behaviors**

✔ **Using Dreamweaver's default behaviors**

✔ **Changing and deleting behaviors**

✔ **Using the Extension Manager to install third-party behaviors**

✔ **Using Spry Widgets to add visitor interactivity**

*J*avaScript is a scripting language created by Netscape that enables you to create interactive sites when you embed the scripts in your HTML pages. All the newest versions of the major browsers support JavaScript because it is an open-source language, which means anyone can write and use it without having to buy a license.

JavaScript is fairly easy to learn and use, and even easier to copy-and-paste from free sources online. However, it does have a downside: Roughly ten percent of all Web visitors will have their JavaScript disabled, either by choice or by necessity. For example, people who like to surf faster sometimes keep their JavaScript disabled. Also, visitors who are visually impaired may be accessing the Web with an assistive device that requires JavaScript to be turned off, such as a screen reader.

JavaScript can enhance your Web site and provide many kinds of interactivity for the visitor. For example, with JavaScript, you can create rollover buttons and navigation menus; display dates, times, and slide shows; add cookies to a visitor's computer to remember user preferences; play games; process forms; and even control browser windows. Likewise, Dreamweaver's Spry Widgets (a combination of HTML, CSS, and JavaScript) can provide interesting ways of displaying interactive content to visitors that would otherwise not be possible.

Dreamweaver CS5 comes with the following commonly used JavaScripts, which it refers to as *behaviors,* ready to insert in your pages from the Behaviors panel:

Call JavaScript   Change Property

Check Plug-in   Drag AP Element

(Spry) Effects   Go to URL

Jump Menu   Jump Menu Go

Open Browser Window   Popup Message

Preload Images   Set Text of Container

Set Text of Frame   Set Text of Status Bar

Set Text of Text Field   Show-Hide Elements

Swap Image   Swap Image Restore

Validate Form

Dreamweaver CS5 no longer provides access to *deprecated* (old, nonstandard, and unsupported) behaviors from prior versions because those behaviors are no longer recommended for use. That said, should you inherit a Web site that uses an old behavior, Dreamweaver will support the modification of that behavior through the Behaviors panel. For further documentation about using deprecated behaviors, see the "Applying built-in Dreamweaver behaviors" Help page on Dreamweaver's LiveDocs Web site: `http://help.adobe.com/en_US/dreamweaver/cs/using/WSc78c5058ca073340dcda9110b1f693f21-7b14a.html`.

Dreamweaver also comes with the following Spry Widgets, which are easily inserted in your pages through the Layout and Spry categories of the Insert panel:

Spry Menu Bar   Spry Tabbed Panels

Spry Accordion   Spry Collapsible Panel

Spry Tooltip

This chapter shows you what JavaScript behaviors do and how you can insert, modify, and delete them. You also find information about downloading third-party behaviors from Adobe's Dreamweaver Exchange and installing them using the Adobe's Extension Manager. At the end of the chapter, you get a brief introduction to working with Spry Widgets.

Understanding JavaScript Behaviors

JavaScript is a scripting language, not a programming language. Unlike programming languages such as C or VisualBasic, JavaScript is not that difficult to learn. You also shouldn't confuse JavaScript with Java, the object-oriented programming language used for writing applets. Unlike Java and other programming languages, JavaScript doesn't require compilation to run and is much, much easier to write.

JavaScript has three main types: client-side JavaScript (CSJS), server-side JavaScript (SSJS), and core JavaScript (CJS). Because server-side and core are more complex, this chapter deals exclusively with Dreamweaver's client-side JavaScript behaviors. Client-side JavaScript builds on the core JavaScript commands by adding common functionality useful in a browser situation. For a comprehensive look at JavaScript, check out WebTeacher's entry at www.webteacher.com/javascript/. If you'd like to try your hand at some JavaScript tutorials, a fine place to begin is at the W3Schools Web site at www.w3schools.com/js/default.asp.

Client-side JavaScripts, or *behaviors* as Dreamweaver calls them, run in browsers (not on servers) and are the combination of an *event* and an *action* triggered by that event:

+ **Events:** These are either things that a visitor does to interact with a page, or things that happen to a page without visitor interaction, such as when the page loads in a browser, that trigger an action script that causes something on the page to change. Different events are associated with each page element. For instance, the onMouseOver event occurs when visitors move their mouse cursor over a particular element on the page (for example, a graphic) that contains JavaScript. That event then *triggers,* or tells, the browser to check the page's code to *call,* or put into action, any additional JavaScript based on the event.

+ **Actions:** These are the parts of a script that perform specific tasks such as opening another browser window, displaying a message in the browser's status bar, swapping an image in a rollover button, or hiding and showing layers. A great example of a script that uses the onMouseOver event to call an action is a rollover button. When you visit a site, you typically see the button graphic in its normal state. However, when you move your cursor over the button, you see a replacement image (called an *over state* image) instead of the normal state. In most cases, when you move your mouse cursor off or away from the over state graphic, the normal state graphic reappears.

Although you don't need to master JavaScript (or even understand it that well!) to use it, you would certainly benefit from any time spent learning more about it. If you're interested in reading more about this scripting language, check out *JavaScript: The Definitive Guide* by David Flanagan (O'Reilly Media) and *JavaScript: The Missing Manual* by David Sawyer McFarland (Pogue Press).

**Book IV
Chapter 2**

**JavaScript
Behaviors and
Spry Widgets**

Adding JavaScript to Your Page

Using the Dreamweaver Behaviors panel and some of the other tools that support JavaScript interactivity, you can add JavaScript to your HTML pages in four ways:

✦ As an internal script in the head of a page between a pair of `<script>` `</script>` tags, with event functions specified in the opening `<body>` tag when necessary, such as `onLoad="preloadImages();"`

✦ As an external script file using the `<script src=" . . .">` tag inside the head of an HTML page, similar to linked external Cascading Style Sheets

✦ As an *event handler* (the event that triggers the JavaScript) inside HTML elements on forms to perform certain functions, such as validating form field entries by visitors before the form gets processed, returning the results of a Celsius to Fahrenheit temperature conversion, or calling a JavaScript alert window to pop open

✦ With the `javascript:URL` protocol to add functionality to a page for actions such as link for reloading a page in the browser window, as in this example:

```
<a href="javascript:history.go(0)">Reload This Page</a>
```

Besides using the Behaviors panel, Dreamweaver supports the addition of JavaScript behaviors to your pages in a handful of other ways, although you may need to alter scripts obtained outside Dreamweaver to get them to work specifically with your Web site:

✦ Write your own JavaScripts and hand-code them in the Code editor.

✦ Copy and paste JavaScripts into your pages from another source, such as a script you used on another site or copied from a free scripts Web site.

✦ Insert JavaScript into your pages as snippets. (Book III, Chapter 4 discusses snippets.)

✦ Download, install, and use third-party behaviors (scripts for use in a Dreamweaver site that were developed by anyone other than Adobe), as described at the end of this chapter.

When hand-coding or copying JavaScript behaviors into your pages, be sure you add the code in Code view rather than Design view. You also need to pay close attention to where you place the behavior script code, because JavaScript often contains one to three parts:

✦ A script that goes into the head of the page

✦ An event handler that goes into the opening <body> tag of the page

✦ Some inline script that goes somewhere inside the body area of your page to call and display the script

For example, take a look at Listing 2-1, which is a mouse cursor effect by Marcin Wojtowicz from the JavaScriptKit Web site (www.javascriptkit.com). This example requires script between the <head> tags and between the opening and closing <body> tags. You also need to copy and upload a cursor graphic to your managed site and to the live server for this effect to function properly.

Listing 2-1:   Cut and Paste Cursor Trail

```
<!DOCTYPE html PUBLIC "-//W3C//DTD XHTML 1.0 Transitional//EN"
    "http://www.w3.org/TR/xhtml1/DTD/xhtml1-transitional.dtd">
<html xmlns="http://www.w3.org/1999/xhtml">
<head>
<meta http-equiv="Content-Type" content="text/html; charset=utf-8" />
<title>Cut and Paste Cursor Trail</title>
</head>
<body>
<script language="JavaScript1.2">
<!--
var trailLength = 8 // The length of trail (8 by default; put more for longer
    "tail")
var path = "cursor.gif" // URL of your image
var standardbody=(document.compatMode=="CSS1Compat")? document.documentElement :
    document.body //create reference to common "body" across doctypes
var i,d = 0
function initTrail() { // prepares the script
images = new Array() // prepare the image array
for (i = 0; i < parseInt(trailLength); i++) {
images[i] = new Image()
images[i].src = path
}
storage = new Array() // prepare the storage for the coordinates
for (i = 0; i < images.length*3; i++) {
storage[i] = 0
}
for (i = 0; i < images.length; i++) { // make divs for IE and layers for
    Navigator
document.write('<div id="obj' + i + '" style="position: absolute; z-Index: 100;
    height: 0; width: 0"><img src="' + images[i].src + '"></div>')
}
trail()
}
```

(continued)

Listing 2-1 *(continued)*

```
function trail() { // trailing function
for (i = 0; i < images.length; i++) { // for every div/layer
document.getElementById("obj" + i).style.top = storage[d]+'px' // the
    Y-coordinate
document.getElementById("obj" + i).style.left = + storage[d+1]+'px' // the
    X-coordinate
d = d+2
}
for (i = storage.length; i >= 2; i--) { // save the coordinate for the div/layer
    that's behind
storage[i] = storage[i-2]
}
d = 0 // reset for future use
var timer = setTimeout("trail()",10) // call recursively
}
function processEvent(e) { // catches and processes the mousemove event
if (window.event) { // for IE
storage[0] = window.event.y+standardbody.scrollTop+10
storage[1] = window.event.x+standardbody.scrollLeft+10
} else {
storage[0] = e.pageY+12
storage[1] = e.pageX+12
}
}
initTrail()
document.onmousemove = processEvent // start capturing
//-->
</script>
</body>
</html>
```

When inserted on a page, this script makes cursor trails. Although it's basic stuff, it's neat.

Another thing you may want to consider when you add JavaScript behaviors to your pages is to also add content between <noscript> tags for visitors who view sites with old versions of browsers or with browsers that have JavaScript turned off, as in the following example:

```
<noscript>
This page includes code that requires a browser that can interpret JavaScript,
    such as Internet Explorer 4.0 and above, Netscape Navigator 4.0 and above,
    Safari 1.0 and above, and Firefox 1.0 and above. If you see this message you
    may not have full access to this page's content.
</noscript>
```

Place the <noscript> tags and contents in the body of the page where you want the message to appear when conditions warrant it. You can download a free snippet of this <noscript> tag with text from the Downloads page at www.luckychair.com.

Using Dreamweaver's Default Behaviors

When you're first starting to work with JavaScript, trying to remember what goes where and when can be complicated. To ease the learning curve, try inserting a behavior with Dreamweaver's Behaviors panel.

Dreamweaver comes with nearly 20 preinstalled behaviors you can use to embed client-side JavaScript code in your documents. Many of these scripts let visitors interact with content on your pages. The behaviors are typically made up of events combined with actions that trigger those events.

Behaviors can do all kinds of things. For example, the Open Browser Window behavior can open a page and force the browser window to resize automatically to a predetermined pixel width and height. Another behavior, the Check Plug-in, can detect whether the visitor's browser has a particular plug-in installed and, if so, can redirect visitors to another page with instructions for finding and downloading the required plug-in. (Both behaviors are described in detail later in this chapter.)

Using Dreamweaver's Behaviors panel, you can quickly add these scripts to your page. All the behaviors have their own dialog boxes to guide you through the process of entering required data and inserting them on your page. You can even choose the appropriate event handler to trigger the behavior's action, as well as specify that a certain event triggers several actions at once and set the order of those actions.

All Dreamweaver behaviors have been written to work in most modern browsers. Furthermore, if they fail in an older browser, most of these should fail silently without causing display issues. Therefore, to maintain the best possible cross-browser compatibility, take care when deleting or editing a behavior's JavaScript code by hand.

Using the Behaviors panel

To open the Behaviors panel, choose Window⇨Behaviors. In Dreamweaver CS5, the Behaviors panel is nested with the Attributes panel in the Tag Inspector panel, which is part of the CSS Style and AP Elements panel grouping, as shown in Figure 2-1.

The Behaviors panel becomes active when you have a document open in the Dreamweaver workspace window. To find out more about any previously applied behaviors, select the object or tag with the behavior on the page and any behaviors associated with that object or tag appear in the Behaviors panel listing. When an event includes multiple behaviors, the behaviors are triggered in the order in which they appear in the list.

Click to open Actions menu

Figure 2-1:
The
Behaviors
panel shows
behaviors
and events.

Events column   Actions column

Behaviors are typically attached to tags for text and graphics, but you can also apply them to the <body> element, links, and form fields.

The Behavior panel's Add Behavior menu, which you open by clicking the Add Behavior (+) icon, lists all preset behaviors in Dreamweaver. Which behaviors are available or disabled on this menu depends on which object or asset on the page you select before clicking the Add Behavior (+) icon.

Attaching a behavior

Attaching behaviors to objects on your page is remarkably easy. Typically, you select an object or linked text on the page, choose a behavior from the Behaviors panel, complete the dialog box that appears associated with the behavior, and verify that the *event handler* (the event that triggers the action) matches your needs.

To attach a behavior, follow these steps:

1. **Select an object or element on the page, such as a graphic or a text link.**

When attaching a behavior to the entire page, select the opening <body> tag in the Tag selector at the bottom-left corner of the open Document window.

2. **If you'd like to attach a behavior to unlinked text, select the text and type the JavaScript null link `javascript:;` into the Link text box in the Properties inspector.**

You can't attach a behavior to plain text, but you can attach it to a link. For this reason, you must add a *null link* (a link that doesn't go anywhere) to the selected text before you can attach the behavior. Remember, the null link must contain both the colon and the semicolon.

If you want to remove the underline from linked text—and hopefully add some other property (for example, a different color) so that the behavior is available but the text that triggers the behavior to occur doesn't look like a traditional link—you could add some inline CSS to the link's `<a href>` tag to disable the default link underline and convert the text to another color, like this:

```
<a href="javascript:;" style="text-decoration:none;
    color:#000000;">Example 1</a>
```

Better yet, create and use a nonunderlining class in an external CSS, because many CSS purists frown on the use of inline styles.

3. Open the Behaviors panel by choosing Window⇨Behaviors.

4. Click the Add Behavior (+) icon in the Behaviors panel and select a behavior from the list.

The behaviors that are active in the list support the selected element; any behaviors that appear dimmed are either unusable for that selection or don't exist in the document. For example, you can't use the Drag AP Element behavior if no layers are on the page. After selecting a behavior, a dialog box appears with parameters to set and options to select that support the behavior.

5. Fill in the behavior's dialog box to specify how you want the behavior to work.

Some dialog boxes have multiple tabs with several fields for data entry.

6. When you finish, click OK.

The behavior is inserted into the page, and the default event handler for that behavior (such as `onClick`) automatically appears in the Behavior panel's Events column (the first column in the panel).

7. If you want to change the event handler to something else, such as `onLoad` or `onMouseDown`, select the current event handler in the Behaviors panel and then select a different event handler in the Events drop-down menu.

Changing and deleting behaviors

You can modify or delete a behavior at any time. For instance, you can change the event handler, add and remove behaviors, edit behavior parameters, and delete attached behaviors.

To change a behavior in Dreamweaver, follow these steps:

1. **Select the asset on the page that has the behavior attached to it.**

2. **In the Behaviors panel, select the associated behavior you want to change.**

3. **Do any of the following to change the behavior:**

   - **Change the order of the behaviors:** When two or more behaviors are listed in the Behaviors panel, you can rearrange their order by selecting a behavior and clicking the up arrow or down arrow.

   - **Edit a behavior's parameters:** Double-click the behavior name to launch the behavior's dialog box and change the behavior's parameters. You can also launch the dialog box by selecting the behavior's name and pressing Enter (Windows) or Return (Mac).

   - **Delete a behavior:** Delete a behavior by selecting it by name and clicking the Remove Event (–) icon in the Behaviors panel or pressing the Delete key on your keyboard.

In your code, some behaviors' events may appear in parentheses to indicate links, for example, when you attach some behaviors to an image. In those cases, Dreamweaver automatically wraps the `<a>` tag around images and defines a null link using the `javascript:;` syntax in the Properties inspector's Link text field, as in this example:

```
<a href="javascript:;" onClick="MM_openBrWindow('welcome.html','','width=300,
    height=300')"><img src="images/logo.gif" width="195" height="200" border=
    "0"></a>
```

In these cases, you can still edit the behavior in the Behaviors panel if you like, or edit the JavaScript behavior in Code view.

Updating old behaviors

For pages with behaviors created in Dreamweaver versions 1–4, you have to manually update the behaviors in the current version of Dreamweaver. Fortunately, this process takes a little less time because of help provided by Dreamweaver. When you manually update one instance of an old behavior on a page, Dreamweaver automatically updates all other instances of the same behavior on that page. Granted, you still need to update all the old behaviors on the rest of your site, but at least the process goes a little faster with this helpful feature.

Follow these steps to update an old behavior:

1. **Select the asset on the page that has the old behavior attached to it.**

2. **Open the Behaviors panel by choosing Window⇨Behaviors.**

3. **Double-click the behavior in the Behaviors panel. In the behavior's dialog box, verify or modify any of the settings.**

   Opening the behavior's dialog box in the newer version of Dreamweaver updates the behavior code.

4. **Click OK in the behavior's dialog box.**

   Dreamweaver automatically updates any other instances of that behavior on the same page.

Call JavaScript Behavior

With the Call JavaScript behavior, you can add your own JavaScript to your page as a custom function or a line of code that is triggered by a specified event. For example, you could add JavaScript that makes the browser window close when the user clicks a specified button. If you know JavaScript, you can write these JavaScript behaviors yourself. If you're not familiar with JavaScript syntax, you can usually find free source code on the many JavaScript tutorial and library Web sites, including these:

```
www.w3schools.com/js/default.asp
www.dynamicdrive.com/
www.javascriptkit.com/javatutors/
javascript.internet.com/
```

To add the Call JavaScript behavior to a document, follow these steps:

1. **Select an object or a text link on your page.**

2. **Click the Add Behavior (+) icon in the Behaviors panel, and then choose Call JavaScript.**

   The Call JavaScript dialog box appears, as shown in Figure 2-2.

Figure 2-2:
Enter scripts
and custom
functions.

3. **In the JavaScript box, type your JavaScript or function:**

   For example, to make a Close button, enter one of the following scripts, including the parentheses and semicolon:

```
javascript:window.close();
```

or

```
window.close();
```

4. **Click OK to close the dialog box.**

   Dreamweaver adds the JavaScript function to the `<head>` of the page for you.

5. **Verify that the event handler listed in the Events column of the Behaviors panel is the one you want to use.**

Change Property Behavior

You can use the Change Property behavior to change an object's properties, such as the background color of a layer, the text contained in a `<div>` tag, or the source file of an image. The properties that you can change depend largely on the browser type and version your visitors use when viewing the page. Most modern browsers support all the properties available for this behavior.

Because this behavior requires you to type some code in its dialog box, be sure you know HTML and understand JavaScript a little before using the dialog box, and test the behaviors in your target browsers before publishing them.

To use the Change Property behavior on a page, follow these steps:

1. **Select an object on your page.**

   You can modify these objects or tags with the Change Property behavior: `layer`, `div`, `span`, `img`, `form`, `input/checkbox`, `input/radio`, `input/text`, `textarea`, `input/password`, and `select`.

2. **Click the Add Behavior (+) icon in the Behaviors panel and select Change Property.**

   The Change Property dialog box appears, as shown in Figure 2-3.

3. **In the Type of Element menu, choose the object type that matches your selection.**

   For example, select DIV to change the background color of a layer, or select IMG to change the source of an image. The Element ID drop-down list changes to support that selection.

4. **In the Element ID list, select the object whose properties you want to change.**

   When the type of element you selected is not found on the page, you see an Element Not Found message on the Element ID menu, such as *** *no FORMs found* ***.

5. **In the Property section, select a property that you want to change in the Select drop-down list, or select the Enter Property radio button and type the property name in the Enter text field.**

   Pay close attention to spelling and letter case when typing the JavaScript property name.

6. **In the New Value text field, type the new value for the property.**

   For example, if you're changing the background color of a layer, type a hexadecimal value preceded by a number symbol (#), such as #FF3300.

7. **Click OK to close the dialog box.**

8. **Verify that the event handler listed in the Events column of the Behaviors panel is the one you want to use.**

   Because the property of the object changes when the event occurs, you need to check that the correct event is listed with the action in the Behaviors panel. If necessary, change the event handler in the Behaviors panel.

Check Plugin Behavior

The Check Plugin behavior checks to see whether the user's computer has the necessary plug-ins installed to successfully view your page. If the user has the necessary plug-ins, the Check Plugin behavior displays the current page without any noticeable delay; if the user doesn't have the required plug-in, the behavior can send the visitor to an alternate page. For example, you may have created a Shockwave movie for your site that requires the latest free Shockwave player. Use the Check Plugin behavior to detect whether the correct Flash player is installed and, if it is not, send visitors to a different page telling them how to find and install the required plug-in.

Internet Explorer can't interpret JavaScript for plug-in detection. As a work-around in Windows, when you select Flash or Director, Dreamweaver writes the VBScript to your page that autodetects those plug-ins in IE. To add the Check Plug-in behavior to your page, follow these steps:

1. **Select an object on your page.**

2. **Click the Add Behavior (+) icon in the Behaviors panel, and select Check Plugin.**

   The Check Plugin dialog box appears, as shown in Figure 2-4.

Figure 2-4:
The Check Plugin behavior can send a visitor to a page you specify.

3. **Select a plugin type in the Select drop-down list, or select the Enter option and type the plug-in name in the Enter text field.**

   Plug-in options in the drop-down list are Flash, Shockwave, LiveAudio, QuickTime, and Windows Media Player. When typing an alternate plug-in name in the Enter text field, the spelling and letter case must be accurate for this behavior to work.

   To find out more about plug-ins, including links to download the most popular browser plug-ins available today, visit `http://download.cnet.com`.

4. **Enter a URL in both the If Found, Go To URL field and the Otherwise, Go To URL field.**

   Typically, the If Found URL is the page to go to when the plug-in is detected on the visitor's computer, and the Otherwise URL is the page to go to if the plug-in is not detected. When you want visitors without the plug-in to stay on the current page, leave the Otherwise URL field blank.

   When either of the URLs are remote (not on your Web site), be sure to type the http:// prefix before the www in the Web address, as in `http://www.adobe.com`.

5. **Select the Always Go to First URL If Detection Is Not Possible option for visitors using Internet Explorer.**

   When you select this option, the visitor is sent to the URL in the If Found text field; when you leave this option deselected, the visitor is sent to the Otherwise URL. If you're not sure whether or not to select or this option, we recommend that you select this feature so that IE visitors lacking the plug-in are prompted by their browsers to download and install it before viewing the page.

6. **Click OK to close the dialog box.**

7. **Verify that the event handler listed in the Events column of the Behaviors panel is the one you want to use.**

   The default event handler for this behavior is onFocus. If desired, change the event handler in the Behaviors panel.

Drag AP Element Behavior

If you're using AP Div layers on your site and want to add some interesting viewer interactivity, consider adding the Drag AP Element behavior to allow site visitors to move and reposition these layers in the browser window. This is a great behavior for creating interactive games, puzzles, movable navigation layers, and other user interface controls.

The Drag AP Element behavior enables visitors to drag layers up, down, left, right, and diagonally in their browsers. Among other things, you can also set a target destination for the layer (think puzzles) and whether to snap the layer to the target within a specified number of pixels.

Like all behaviors, the action must be called before the behavior can be used, so you need to choose the correct event handler. For this reason, you must attach this behavior to the <body> tag and use the onLoad event handler to trigger the event. This ensures that the layer is ready for dragging the moment the page finishes loading in the browser.

Alternatively, you could attach the behavior to a link inside the layer that takes up the entire layer size (such as a linked image) paired with the onMouseOver event handler. To do this, you must first apply the behavior to the <body> tag so that Dreamweaver can add all the JavaScript to the page that defines the drag layer function. Then move by hand the onLoad script line from the <body> tag to the new link location in the code. The last thing you need to do is change the event handler in the Behaviors panel, from this:

```
<body onload="MM_dragLayer('apDiv1','',0,0,0,0,true,false,-1,-1,-1,-
    1,false,false,0,'',false,'')">
<div id="apDiv1">
<p><a href="http://www.dummies.com"><img src="images/dummies.gif" name="dummies"
    width="50" height="80" border="0" id="dummies"/></a></p>
</div>
</body>
```

to this:

```
<body>
<div id="apDiv1">
<p><a href="http://www.dummies.com"><img src="images/dummies.gif" name="dummies"
    width=""50" height="80" border="0" id="dummies" onmouseover="MM_dragLayer('
    apDiv1','',0,0,0,0,true,false,-1,-1,-1,-1,false,false,0,'',false,'') "/></
    a></p>
</div>
</body>
```

To attach the Drag AP Element behavior to an AP Div layer on your page, follow these steps:

1. **Draw an AP Div layer on the page.**

Choose Insert⇨Layout Object⇨AP Div, or click the Draw AP Div icon on the Layout category of the Insert panel and draw a layer in an open document in Design view. See Book IV, Chapter 1 for the skinny on layers.

2. **Select the opening <body> tag with the Tag selector (which is located in the bottom-left corner of the Document window).**

You must select the <body> tag to apply this behavior.

3. **Click the Add Behavior (+) icon in the Behaviors panel, and select Drag AP Element.**

The Drag AP Element dialog box appears, as shown in Figure 2-5. The dialog box has two tabs: Basic and Advanced. Each tab allows you to enter specific parameters for this behavior.

Figure 2-5:
Specify a
drop target
position and
whether to
constrain
the layer's
movement.

4. **On the Basic tab, select the layer to be dragged from the AP Element menu.**

   Layers are listed alphabetically by name (`div "apDiv1"`) to help you identify them quickly. If you forgot to rename your layers to something more meaningful, cancel out of the dialog box, select and name the layers in the AP Elements panel, and then reopen the Drag AP Element dialog box.

5. **In the Movement menu, choose Unconstrained or Constrained.**

   Select Unconstrained for free-form movement, as with puzzles and games, or choose Constrained for movements that need to be controlled, as with sliders or other movable elements.

6. **For constrained movement, type pixel values in the Up, Down, Left, and Right parameters.**

   The pixel coordinates are relative to the layer's original position, and you can enter positive, negative, and 0 values in any of the fields. For example, if you want to constrain movement of the layer to the left and right only, enter positive pixel values in the Left and Right boxes and 0s in the Up and Down boxes.

7. **In the Drop Target fields, type Left and Top pixel values for the desired finish position of the layer, relative to the top-left corner of the browser window.**

   The target is considered reached when the layer's top and left positioning values match the drop target's top and left coordinates. To get the selected layer's current top and left coordinates, click the Get Current Position button. This sometimes helps when you're trying to guesstimate pixel values for the drop target position relative to the current position.

8. **(Optional) If you want the layer to snap to the drop target coordinates when the visitor drags it within a specified range, enter a pixel value for the range in the Snap If Within text box.**

   The bigger the number, the more easily the visitor can drag the layer to the drop target.

9. **Select the Advanced tab to enter additional parameters and call JavaScript for the dragged layer:**

   - **Drag Handle:** By default, the Entire Element option is selected, which means the entire layer acts as a drag handle. If you want only a specific part of the layer to be used as a drag handle, select the Area Within Element option and enter the Top and Left coordinate values and a Width and Height in pixels for the drag handle.

- **While Dragging:** When the Bring Element to Front option is enabled, you can select Leave on Top or Restore Z-Index to alter the stacking order of the layer while dragging it.

- **Call JavaScript:** Type JavaScript code or a function name in the Call JavaScript text field. This feature requires an understanding of JavaScript and how to collect data about the layer as it's being dragged. The JavaScript code repeats while the layer is being dragged.

- **When Dropped:** Type additional JavaScript code or a function name in this Call JavaScript field to call actions when the layer is dropped or reaches its target destination.

- **Only if Snapped:** When enabled, the When Dropped Call JavaScript executes only when the dragged layer reaches the drop target.

10. **Click OK to close the dialog box.**

11. **Verify that the event handler listed in the Events column of the Behaviors panel is the one you want to use.**

    The default event handler for this behavior is `onLoad`. If desired, change the event handler in the Behaviors panel. Note: The `onClick` and `onMouseDown` event handlers don't work well with this behavior.

Spry Effects Behaviors

Spry Effects behaviors are special visual JavaScript effects that you can apply to almost any object or element on a Web page without having to add extra code or tags. To apply the effects, you must either select the object or make sure it has an assigned ID. However, for ease of use, you should give the element a unique ID before applying the effect.

Each Spry Effect has three parts:

- ✦ The JavaScript effect object (which is the script)
- ✦ The trigger element that the visitor interacts with (such as a button) to start the effect
- ✦ The target element that is being changed by the effect (such as a layer that shakes from side to side)

Spry Effects can modify any combination of an element's opacity, visibility, size, position, and CSS style properties. What makes these effects unique is that the visitor's interaction with the element causes the element to be updated only in the browser, rather than forcing the browser to refresh the entire HTML Web page.

Here's a list of all the Spry Effects you can choose from:

✦ **Appear/Fade:** Make a hidden element visible or make a visible element fade away to invisible.

✦ **Blind:** Hide or reveal an element using a simulated window blind effect that goes up or down.

✦ **Grow/Shrink:** Grow or shrink the element.

✦ **Highlight:** Change the background color style of an element. Can be applied to any element on the page except body, frame, frameset, noframes, or applet.

✦ **Shake:** Shake the element back and forth from left to right.

✦ **Slide:** Move the element up or down from its current position.

✦ **Squish:** Shrink the element until it disappears into the top-left corner of the browser window.

As you add any of these Spry Effects to your page, Dreamweaver automatically adds an extra line of code to the HTML markup between the <head> tags of your page that links to an external JavaScript called SpryEffects.js:

```
<head>
. . .
<script type="text/javascript" src="SpryEffects.js"></script>
<head>
```

This external JavaScript file, which contains the scripts for all Spry Effects in your page, is then added to the root level of your local managed site. This file can remain at the root level or be moved into a subfolder (such as js/ or includes/), as long as you ensure that the link path to the file is correct. In addition, the JavaScript file must be uploaded to the host server along with your other files for the effect(s) on your page(s) to work properly.

To add a Spry Effect to an element your page, follow these steps:

1. **Insert the element or type in the text that will become the trigger for the event.**

For example, the trigger can be a button graphic, a line, or word of text with a null link applied to it, or a layer with a unique ID attribute.

2. **Insert the element or type in the text that will become the target object of the event.**

This can also be a graphic, text with a null link, a layer, or nearly any other element in HTML. (See the effects listing before this set of steps for exceptions to each of the effect types.)

3. **Select the target element or object to which you want to apply the Spry Effect.**

Selecting the target element or object helps Dreamweaver identify where to apply the Spry Effect in the markup.

4. **From the Behaviors panel, select the desired effect in the Effects submenu.**

The dialog box of the selected effect appears. Each dialog box has its own set of options. Figure 2-6 shows an example of the Appear/Fade dialog box.

Figure 2-6: Customize your Spry Effect.

5. **Complete the dialog box with the desired settings, which may be slightly different depending on which effect you choose.**

Here's a general description of the configuration options:

- **Target Element:** Select the target element in the drop-down menu. If you don't see the name of the object you'd like to target in the listing, close the dialog box, select that object, and add an ID to it with the Properties inspector before returning to these steps.

- **Effect Duration:** The Spry Effect takes place over the number of milliseconds you set here. (One thousand milliseconds are equal to 1 second.)

- **Effect:** Select the desired effect in the drop-down menu. Most Spry Effects have two options to choose from, such as fade in or fade out.

- **Effect From/To:** Select the percentage or pixel distance of the effect, such as 100% to 0% or 1 pixel to 500 pixels, or select the desired color for start, end, and after states. Each Spry Effect has different options here.

- **Toggle Effect:** Make the trigger a toggle for the effect. For example, with the Grow/Shrink effect, clicking once makes the target object shrink and clicking again makes the target object grow.

6. **Click OK to close the dialog box and add the Spry Effect JavaScript to your page.**

   Dreamweaver automatically adds the necessary JavaScript to the `<head>` of the page, to the trigger element, and to the target object, along with adding the SpryEffects.js file to the root level of your managed site.

7. **If desired, repeat Steps 4–6 to add additional Spry Effects to your target object.**

   Many of the effects can be combined to create effect clusters in which effects run concurrently or sequentially. For fun ideas and examples of using Spry Effects, check out `http://labs.adobe.com/technologies/spry/demos/effects/index.html`.

Spry Effects are listed in the Behaviors panel along with the event handler, such as `onClick`. If desired, you can change the event handler by clicking it once to reveal the drop-down menu arrow, and then clicking the drop-down menu to select another event handler. You can also reopen the Spry Effect dialog box to modify the event settings by double-clicking the event name.

For a full description and overview of the Spry Effects available in Dreamweaver, go to `www.adobe.com/go/learn_dw_spryeffects`. You can find samples and documentation for Spry at Adobe Labs, `http://labs.adobe.com/technologies/spry/`.

Go to URL Behavior

Add the Go to URL behavior to insert JavaScript that opens a new page in the same browser window or in a specified frame. You can use this behavior with other behaviors so that the link information is placed in the JavaScript rather than in the Properties inspector (for instance, when you add a link to a graphic that has multiple rollover behaviors). When working with frames, the Go to URL behavior is particularly useful because you can set the behavior to change the contents of multiple frames with one click. (For more on frames, see Book IV, Chapter 3.)

When using the Go to URL behavior, the traditional mouse effect that changes the arrow pointer into a hand when you mouse over a link is disabled. If you want to turn the pointer for this behavior into a hand, create a CSS ID style for the trigger object that changes the cursor when visitors hover their mouse cursor over that object. To ensure that all browsers will interpret the CSS accurately, make sure your CSS style includes declarations for both hand and pointer cursors, as in the following example:

```
#triggerobject {
    cursor: hand;
    cursor: pointer;
}
```

To add the Go to URL behavior to your page, follow these steps:

1. **Select an image, object, or text link on your page.**

   The image, object, or text becomes the link that triggers the action.

2. **Click the Add Behavior (+) icon in the Behaviors panel, and then select Go to URL.**

   The Go to URL dialog box appears, displaying a list of windows or frame names, as shown in Figure 2-7.

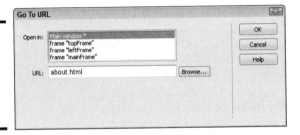

Figure 2-7: Select the main window or individual frames.

3. **In the Open In field, select a window or frame as the target destination for the URL.**

   For example, if you're using the behavior to open a page in the same browser window, the Open In field lists only Main Window as the target destination. When working with framesets, the frame names are listed, such as `topFrame`, `mainFrame`, and `leftFrame`, along with Main Window.

   Try not to name your frames `top`, `blank`, `self`, or `parent` because these filenames may conflict with the reserved frame target names (`_top`, `_blank`, `_self`, or `_parent`) and create strange results in different browsers.

4. **In the URL field, type the path and filename of the document to be opened, or click the Browse button to find and select the file.**

   If the page you want to open is outside your site, be sure to include the http:// prefix before the www in the Web address.

5. **If changing URLs in multiple frames, repeat Steps 3 and 4 to select frames and URLs.**

For example, to open two URLs with one event using frames, you can select `mainFrame` and type welcome.html in the URL field to open welcome.html in the `mainFrame`, and then select `leftFrame` and type navigation.html in the URL field to open navigation.html in the `leftFrame`.

6. **Click OK to close the dialog box.**

7. **Verify that the event handler listed in the Events column of the Behaviors panel is the one you want to use.**

    The default event handler for the Go to URL behavior is `onClick`. If desired, you can change the event handler in the Behaviors panel.

Jump Menu and Jump Menu Go Behaviors

A *jump menu* is a pop-up menu of links that automatically opens another page in the browser when an item on the menu is chosen. The Jump Menu behavior simply controls the structure and content of the menu links. The links on the menu can be to files on your Web site, pages on other Web sites, links to graphics, e-mail addresses, PDFs, Word documents, PowerPoint files, or any other kind of file that a browser can open.

Creating a jump menu

To add a jump menu to your page, follow these steps:

1. **Insert a jump menu by choosing Insert➪Form➪Jump Menu.**

    The Insert Jump Menu dialog box appears, as shown in Figure 2-8.

Figure 2-8:
Create jump menus quickly with the Insert Jump Menu dialog box.

Book IV
Chapter 2

JavaScript
Behaviors and
Spry Widgets

2. **Click the plus (+) icon above the Menu Items area to add an item to the menu, and then complete the following fields:**

   - **Text:** Type a name for the menu item.

   - **When selected, go to URL:** Type the path and filename that identifies the jump to URL destination.

   When creating a menu *header* for the first entry in the jump menu, such as *Select a State* or *Choose One,* add a null JavaScript link to the URL field, like this: `javascript:void(0)`. This null link prevents the page containing the jump menu from doing anything to the page if that option is selected. If you don't specify a destination, the script uses the menu text as the filename and tries to jump to a Web page with that name.

3. **Repeat Step 2 for each additional item on the list. Click the up and down arrows to sort and reposition list items.**

   For example, you may want to reposition the menu items so they are listed alphabetically. To sort them, select an item and click the up icon or down icon.

4. **In the lower half of the dialog box, complete the remaining fields and select or deselect the other menu options:**

   - **Open URLs In:** Select Main Window, or when working with framesets or multiple windows, select any of the other window or frame names in the list.

   - **Menu ID:** When the page has only one menu, the default menu name available for selection is called `jumpMenu`.

   - **Insert Go Button After Menu:** Add a Go button after the jump menu, which means the visitor must select an item from the menu and click the Go button to jump to the destination URL. Leave this option deselected to have the jump menu control the automatic jump to the target destination (which is the preferred method).

   - **Select First Item After URL Change:** Make the menu revert to the first item in the list after every selection. This is particularly useful if you have created a menu header at the top of the list, such as *Choose a Country* or *Quantity.*

5. **Click OK to close the dialog box.**

6. **(Optional) Verify that the event handler listed in the Events column of the Behaviors panel is the one you want to use.**

   The default event handler for the Jump Menu behavior is `onChange`, and the default event handler for the Jump Menu Go behavior is `onClick`. If desired, you can change the event handlers in the Behaviors panel.

Dreamweaver adds the jump menu form field and form tags to your page along with the proper JavaScript to control the behavior. If you add the Go button to your menu, the jump menu is included in the Behaviors panel with the Jump Menu behavior and button and Jump Menu Go behavior.

Editing the Jump Menu behavior

If you need to edit the jump menu after adding it to a page, you can reopen the Jump Menu dialog box through the Behaviors panel. Follow these steps:

1. **Select the jump menu in the open document, and make sure the Behaviors panel is open.**

2. **Double-click the Jump Menu icon in the Actions column (the second column) in the Behaviors panel.**

   If you inserted the Jump Menu with the Go button, you will be able to select and edit the Jump Menu Go behavior only if you first click the Go button on your page.

   The Jump Menu dialog box reappears, but this time you do not see options for Menu ID or Insert Go Button After Menu.

3. **Make changes to the menu as needed.**

   You can add new entries to the menu listing, rearrange entries, edit or remove entries, and specify target windows for the target URLs in any of the entries.

4. **Click OK to close the dialog box.**

Adding and removing a Go button

You can do two other things with the Jump Menu or Jump Menu Go behavior:

✦ **Add a Go button** if you originally created the jump menu without it. Adding a Go button to a jump menu is a good idea when working in framesets because it allows visitors to reselect menu options that they already have selected.

✦ **Remove the Go button** if you've added it originally and no longer want it there.

Follow these steps to add a Go button to your jump menu:

1. **Place your cursor to the right of the jump menu in the open document, and then click the Button icon in the Forms category of the Insert panel to add a button to the page.**

   You can insert a button also by choosing Insert⇨Form⇨Button.

2. **With the button still selected, select the None option in the Action area of the Properties inspector.**

   The button value and ID both change from Submit to Button.

3. **In the Value field in the Properties inspector, type Go.**

   The button's value changes from Button to Go. If desired, you can also edit the button's ID from button to Go.

4. **With the button still selected, click the Add Behavior (+) icon in the Behaviors panel, and then select Jump Menu Go.**

5. **Select the jump menu that you want the new Go button associated with.**

   If the page has only one jump menu, the drop-down menu says jumpMenu.

6. **Click OK to close the dialog box.**

   The Jump Menu Go button now has the Jump Menu Go behavior attached to it with the onClick event handler.

Follow these steps to remove the Go button from your jump menu:

1. **Select the Jump Menu Go button in the open document.**

2. **In the Behaviors panel, select the Jump Menu Go behavior, and then click the Remove Event (–) icon.**

   Dreamweaver removes any JavaScript from the code on your page associated with this behavior.

3. **With the Go button still selected, press the Delete key to delete the button from the page.**

   The jump menu now needs a behavior so it can work properly.

4. **Select the jump menu in your document, and then choose the Jump Menu behavior from the Behaviors panel.**

   The behavior picks up all the existing items in the list and reassigns the correct event handler (onChange) to the menu.

Open Browser Window Behavior

The Open Browser Window behavior lets you open any URL in a new browser window on top of the current browser window. You can also set some of the new window's properties, such as its name (id), width, and height, and specify whether certain browser chrome features appear on the new window, such as the status bar, menu bar, and scroll bars.

For instance, if you license original artwork on your Web site, you may want to have sample images open in a new browser window when a visitor clicks a particular text link. With the Open Browser Window behavior, you can have the new browser window open to a specific size with no resize handles, scroll bars, menu bar, status bar, navigation bar, or location bar, such as the example in Figure 2-9.

Figure 2-9:
The Open Browser Window behavior opens another page in a new browser window.

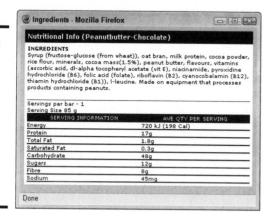

By default, none of the new window browser chrome attributes are enabled in the Open Browser Window dialog box, which means you must enter the URL to display and enable any features that you want for your new window. As long as you enter at least one attribute, the new window won't resemble the parent window's attributes and instead will have only the attributes you specify. However, if you don't enter any window attributes other than the URL, the new window opens at the same size and with the same attributes as the parent window.

Before you find out how to use this behavior, keep in mind that pop-up windows — even windows knowingly launched by the visitor — are often overused, improperly used, and abused. Some people consider new browser windows a form of Internet pollution! Also, some of the newer browsers, third-party browser plug-ins, and firewalls automatically prevent pop-ups from occurring. For these reasons, try to use this feature sparingly for specific purposes, such as showing a detailed image of a product you're selling or to display another document in a window separate from the rest of your site. In fact, you may want to add a warning message or an icon near the link that indicates that clicking the link opens a new window.

To add the Open Browser Window behavior to your page, follow these steps:

1. **Select an image or text on your page that will become the link to the pop-up window.**

   This object or text becomes the link that triggers the action to open a new browser window.

   When using text to open the new window, be sure to add a null link (a link that doesn't go anywhere) to the selected text before assigning the behavior. To create a null link, select the text and type `javascript:;` in the Link text box in the Properties inspector. Type carefully; the null link must contain both the colon and semicolon.

2. **Click the Add Behavior (+) icon in the Behaviors panel, and then select Open Browser Window.**

   The Open Browser Window dialog box appears, as shown in Figure 2-10, with a text field to add the URL of the page to display and a set of new window attribute options.

Figure 2-10:
Set target
URL and
browser
window
attributes.

3. **Next to URL to Display, click the Browse button to select a local file or type the URL that you want to open in the new browser window.**

   When entering a remote URL, you need to type the `http://` prefix before the www address, as in `http://www.adobe.com`.

4. **Specify new window attributes:**

   - **Window Width** and **Window Height:** Enter a number in pixels to set the size of the new window.

   - **Navigation Toolbar:** Display browser navigation buttons including the Back, Home, and Reload buttons.

   - **Location Toolbar:** Display browser options, including the current URL or location of the visitor.

   - **Status Bar:** Display such information as the URL, special messages, and page loading times. The status bar is located at the bottom-left edge of the browser window

- **Menu Bar:** This part of the browser window (Windows) or desktop (Mac) has menu options for your applications such as File, Edit, and View. When you deselect this option in Windows, the visitor can only close or minimize the new window. On a Mac, the menu bar stays at the top of the desktop regardless of the Menu Bar setting.

- **Scrollbars As Needed:** View scroll bars on the new browser window when the content in that window exceeds the visible size of the window. When you deselect this option, any content that extends beyond the size of the window is hidden.

- **Resize Handles:** Enable or disable resize handles from appearing in the bottom-right corner of the window. When enabled, the visitor can click and drag the handles to resize the window. If disabled, the window size is fixed and can't be changed.

- **Window Name:** Enter a name or `id` for the new window in this field. Names help target the new window with links, apply CSS styles to the window contents, and control the window using other JavaScript behaviors. Make sure the window name doesn't include any special characters, spaces, or punctuation, and is written in all lowercase letters.

5. **Click OK to close the dialog box.**

6. **Verify that the event handler listed in the Events column of the Behaviors panel is the one you want to use.**

   The default event handler for the Open Browser Window behavior is `onClick`. If desired, you can change the event handler in the Behaviors panel.

Although it's not part of the Dreamweaver dialog box for this behavior, you can hand-code additional information to specify the location of the new window when it opens. The location is relative to the top-left corner of the parent browser window. In the code directly after the width and height dimensions, add top and left pixel coordinates separated by commas and no spaces, as in this example:

```
<a href="javascript:;" onclick="MM_openBrWindow('index.html','Details','width=300
    ,height=300,top=500,left=300')">View Details</a>
```

Popup Message Behavior

The Popup Message behavior opens a JavaScript alert window with your specific text message. Because it's a text-only script, the look of the alert window is totally controlled by the site visitor's browser, which means you can't format the text message or the alert window in any way. The only thing in common as a layout feature between the different browsers, in fact, is that along with your message, they all display an OK button for the user to click to acknowledge seeing the message.

For this reason, this type of alert message is best used when you don't care how the message is formatted and simply want to communicate something to the visitor instead of needing the visitor to interact with the site in some way. If you need to control how the message looks, use the Open Browser Window behavior (described previously in the chapter) to display your message instead.

On the plus side, these JavaScript alert messages can have any JavaScript property, global variable, function call, or other valid expression embedded in the text as long as it's embedded inside braces ({ }). For example, to have visitors open an alert box that displays the current date, type the following script in the behavior dialog box: Today is {new Date()}.

After the JavaScript has been added to the page through the Behaviors panel, the behavior's code takes on the following syntax:

```
<p onclick="MM_popupMsg('Today is '+(new Date())+'') ">Click here for today's
    date.</p>
```

When a viewer clicks the link, the script returns an alert box that looks like the example in Figure 2-11.

Figure 2-11:
An example
of a
JavaScript
alert
window.

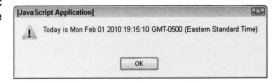

To add a pop-up message to your page, follow these steps:

1. **Select a word, a phrase, an image, or another object on your page as the trigger for the alert box behavior.**

2. **Click the Add Behavior (+) icon in the Behaviors panel, and the select Popup Message.**

The Popup Message dialog box appears, as shown in Figure 2-12.

3. **Type your text message in the Message field, including any additional JavaScript expressions.**

Using the same example, which gives the visitor the option of viewing the current date by clicking a text link, type the following:

```
Today is {new Date()}.
```

To display a brace as part of the alert, type it with a backslash before the brace, like this: \ {.

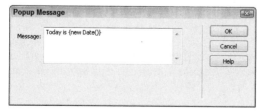

Figure 2-12:
Create JavaScript alert messages with the Popup Message behavior.

4. **Click OK to close the Popup Message dialog box.**

5. **Verify that the event handler listed in the Events column of the Behaviors panel is the one you want to use.**

   The default event handler for the Popup Message is onClick. You can change the event handler in the Behaviors panel, if desired.

Preload Images Behavior

The Preload Images behavior preloads specified images to the browser's cache so that they're ready for viewing when called by the browser. The preload process is invisible to the site visitor and helps ensure a seamless visitor experience with the Web site. Use this behavior when you want to preload images that are not on the page when the page initially loads in the browser or for images on the page that are not associated with the Swap Image behavior.

Follow these steps to add the Preload Images behavior to your page:

1. **Select an object or a text link on your page as the trigger for the event behavior.**

2. **Click the Add Behavior (+) icon in the Behaviors panel, and then select Preload Images.**

   The Preload Images dialog box appears, as shown in Figure 2-13.

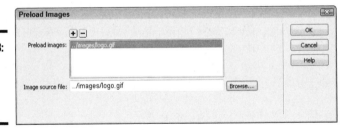

Figure 2-13:
Preload
as many
images as
you like.

3. **In the Image Source field, type the path and filename of the image you want to preload or click the Browse button to find and select an image.**

4. **Click the plus (+) icon to add the image name to the Preload Images listing.**

   The image and its path are added to the Preload Images listing, as in images/more.gif.

5. **Repeat Steps 3 and 4 to add more images to the Preload list.**

   To remove an image from the listing, select the image from the list and click the Remove Event (–) icon.

6. **Click OK to close the Preload Images dialog box.**

7. **Verify that the event handler listed in the Events column of the Behaviors panel is the one you want to use.**

   The default event handler for the Preload Images behavior is onLoad. You can change the event handler in the Behaviors panel.

Set Text of Container Behavior

The Set Text of Container behavior replaces existing text content and formatting of a layer with new text content and formatting in any container element, such as a table cell, a layer, or even a <span> tag. The new text content can have any JavaScript property, global variable, function call, or other valid expression embedded in the text as long as it's embedded in braces ({ }). You can even display a brace in the content by adding a backslash before it, like this: \ {.

By allowing you to change the content in a container, this behavior is an alternative to hiding the current layer and showing another layer with different content. For example, you could change the text in the current layer from a message that tells visitors to click for details to a message containing those details.

To begin using this behavior, you must start with at least one container with an ID on the page. For instance, you may want to apply this behavior to an AP Div layer. (See Book IV, Chapter 1 to learn more about working with layers).

To attach the Set Text of Container behavior to a page, follow these steps:

1. **Select a container on your page.**

2. **Click the Add Behavior (+) icon in the Behaviors panel, and then choose Set Text⇨Set Text of Container.**

The Set Text of Container dialog box appears, as shown in Figure 2-14.

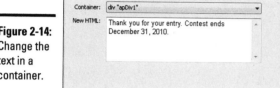

Figure 2-14:
Change the
text in a
container.

3. **In the Container menu, select the target container.**

The target container is the container where the new content is displayed. If the container you want to target isn't listed, your target doesn't yet have an ID attribute. Close the dialog box, give your container an ID with the Properties inspector, and start over at Step 1.

4. **In the New HTML text box, type or paste the replacement HTML content for the targeted container.**

Enter any HTML, including valid JavaScript and formatting code. When no formatting is entered with the New HTML text, the original text color and background color of the container is applied to the new text content.

5. **Click OK to close the dialog box.**

6. **Verify that the event handler listed in the Events column of the Behaviors panel is the one you want to use.**

The default event handler for this behavior is onFocus.

Set Text of Frame Behavior

The Set Text of Frame behavior works exclusively with framesets and allows you to replace text or HTML content in a frame with a specified action. The HTML replacement content can include any JavaScript property, global variable, function call, or other valid expression embedded in the text as long as it's embedded in braces ({ }). To display a brace, type it with a backslash, like this: \ {.

By allowing you to change the content on a page inside a frame, this behavior is an alternative to opening another page in a frame. For example, you may want to change the text inside a frame containing a graphic that, when moused over, changes to display a special message to the visitor or identifies the URL of the page inside the frame.

With this behavior, most of the frame's formatting is lost, but you can retain the background and text colors. If you need to control more than text content, you may want to open a new page in the frame instead.

To begin using this behavior, you must start with a frameset (see Book IV, Chapter 3). You can use any of Dreamweaver's preset framesets when you're creating a new document: Choose File⇨New, and then in the New Document window, select a sample Frameset from the Sample Folder in the Page from Sample category. Or choose Modify⇨Frameset⇨Split Frame and select any option to create a quick and simple frameset for an existing open document.

To add the Set Text of Frame behavior to your page, follow these steps:

1. **Select an object or a text link on your page to which you want to attach the behavior.**

    The object can be inside any of the frames in the frameset.

2. **Click the Add Behavior (+) icon in the Behaviors panel, and then choose Set Text⇨Set Text of Frame.**

    The Set Text of Frame dialog box appears, where you can enter in the new HTML content for the page, as shown in Figure 2-15.

Figure 2-15:
Enter
replacement
HTML
content for
a targeted
frame.

Set Text of Frame	
Frame:	frame "mainFrame"
New HTML:	Thank you for your submission. One of our representatives will be in contact with you shortly.

Get current HTML ☑ Preserve background color

OK
Cancel
Help

3. **In the Frame menu, select the target frame.**

   The target frame is the frame that displays the replacement content.

4. **In the New HTML text box, type or paste the replacement HTML content for the targeted frame.**

   To copy the existing page content of the selected target frame in the text box, click the Get Current HTML button. To use the same background color of the current frame's page with the new text, select the Preserve Background Color check box.

5. **Click OK to close the dialog box.**

6. **Verify that the event handler listed in the Events column of the Behaviors panel is the one you want to use.**

   If desired, you can change the event handler in the Behaviors panel.

Set Text of Status Bar Behavior

Use the Set Text of Status Bar behavior to add a text message to the browser window's status bar (at the bottom-left corner of the window) when the visitor interacts with the page in a specified way. For example, you can have the status bar display a message about a particular link or image on the page when the visitor mouses over that link or graphic (such as On Sale through July 31st, 2010!) or list the title of the given page (such as Contact Us Today for a Free Consultation!) rather than its URL, which appears by default.

Although adding a message to the browser status bar can be an interesting way to enhance a site visitor's experience of a page, many visitors don't know to look in this area for messages or may even have the status bar disabled. Also, because the status bar displays useful information from the browser, replacing it with your own text might be seen as rude to some visitors. In addition, browser support for this behavior may vary slightly, so be sure to test it in your target browsers before publishing.

For these reasons, think about using this behavior for optional information messages rather than important ones. With your important messages, consider using the Popup Message, Open Browser Window, or Show-Hide Layers behaviors, all of which are described in this chapter.

Also, just like the Popup Message behavior, any JavaScript property, global variable, function call, or other valid expression can be embedded in the status bar text as long as it's embedded in braces ({ }).

Book IV
Chapter 2

JavaScript Behaviors and Spry Widgets

To add the Set Text of Status Bar behavior to your page, follow these steps:

1. **Select an object or a text link on your page.**

   This is the object or text link that triggers the action.

2. **Click the Add Behavior (+) icon in the Behaviors panel, and then choose Set Text⇨Set Text of Status Bar.**

   The Set Text of Status Bar dialog box appears, as shown in Figure 2-16.

Figure 2-16:
Add a
custom
message to
the browser
status bar.

3. **Type your text message, including any additional JavaScript expressions.**

   For example, to display the URL for the visited page when mousing over a target object or text link using a JavaScript function, type the following code:

   ```
   The URL for this page is {window.location}.
   ```

   Try to keep your message short because many browsers that support this behavior may truncate longer messages.

4. **Click OK to close the dialog box.**

5. **Verify that the event handler listed in the Events column of the Behaviors panel is the one you want to use.**

   The default event handler for the Set Text of Status Bar behavior is onMouseOver, but you can change it, if needed, in the Behaviors panel.

   Note: This behavior is not supported by all browsers, and in the browsers that do support this behavior, its functionality often depends on user preferences.

Set Text of Text Field Behavior

The Set Text of Text Field behavior is a handy behavior that replaces the existing content of a text field on a form with specified new content. For example, you may want to enter sample text so a visitor knows the kind of content they're expected to type into the field. The new HTML content can have any JavaScript property, global variable, function call, or other valid expression embedded in the text as long as it's embedded in braces ({}). You can even display a brace by adding a backslash before it, like this: \{.

To begin using this behavior, you must start with at least one text field in a form on the page. To add a text field to your page, choose Insert➪Form➪Text Field, or click the Text Field icon in the Forms category of the Insert panel to insert a text field at the insertion point in an open document. If prompted to add the Form Tag, click Yes. When the page has multiple text fields, it's also helpful to name all the form fields to better identify them before attaching this behavior.

Follow these steps to use the Set Text of Text Field behavior:

1. **Select a text field in a form in the open document, and give it an ID in the Properties panel.**

2. **Click the Add Behavior (+) icon in the Behaviors panel, and then choose Set Text➪Set Text of Text Field.**

   The Set Text of Text Field dialog box appears, as shown in Figure 2-17.

Figure 2-17: Add example text into a form field.

3. **In the Text Field menu, select the target text field.**

   The target text field is where the new content will be displayed.

4. **In the New Text text box, type or paste the replacement text.**

5. **Click OK to close the dialog box.**

6. **Verify that the event handler listed in the Events column of the Behaviors panel is the one you want to use.**

   The default event handler is onBlur. If you'd like a different event handler, you can change it in the Behaviors panel.

Show-Hide Elements Behavior

When one or more AP Div layers are on your page, you can control a layer's *visibility* (whether it's shown or hidden) with the Show-Hide Elements behavior. You can use this behavior also to restore an AP Div layer's visibility to its default setting.

The Show-Hide Elements behavior is great for hiding and showing information as a visitor interacts with objects on your Web page. For example, you may have an online photo gallery page with a series of thumbnail images and an area to display close-up images. With the Show-Hide Elements behavior, when the visitor slides the cursor over one of the thumbnail images, an AP Div layer with a close-up image is shown, and when the visitor's cursor moves off the thumbnail, the close-up AP Div layer is hidden.

Before using this behavior, you must have at least one AP Div layer on the page. To add an AP Div layer to your page, choose Insert⇨Layout Objects⇨AP Div, or click the AP Div icon in the Layout category of the Insert panel and draw an AP Div layer anywhere in an open document. You may also want to rename all your AP Div layers with the Properties inspector or in the AP Elements panel before attaching this behavior to objects on your page to help identify them more easily. (Book IV, Chapter 1 describes layers in detail.)

Follow these steps to use the Show-Hide Elements behavior on your page:

1. **Select any object on your page (except a layer), such as a text link, an image, or any object with an `id` attribute.**

2. **Click the Add Behavior (+) icon in the Behaviors panel, and then select Show-Hide Elements.**

   The Show-Hide Elements dialog box appears, as shown in Figure 2-18. If the behavior is not available in the list of behaviors, you may need to select a different object on your page, such as the <body> tag or a link (<a>) tag.

Figure 2-18:
Alter a
layer's
visibility in
the browser.

3. **In the Elements menu, select the element for which you want to change the visibility.**

4. **Edit the element's visibility status by clicking one of the following buttons:**

   - **Show:** Show the selected element.

   - **Hide:** Hide the selected element.

   - **Default:** Restore an element's default visibility.

5. **Repeat Steps 3 and 4 for each additional element that you want to modify.**

   A single event handler controls all the elements selected here.

6. **Click OK to close the dialog box.**

7. **Verify that the event handler listed in the Events column of the Behaviors panel is the one you want to use.**

   You can always change the event handler in the Behaviors panel.

Be aware that some browsers support layers differently than others, especially older browsers. To stop browsers from altering layers, try setting layer clip parameters or adding images or text to the layer to hold the layer open to the size you want it to be. (See Book IV, Chapter 1 for more information on setting layer clip parameters.)

Another cool use for this behavior is to make a preload layer by creating a layer that covers the rest of the page as the page loads. Your visitors are engaged with other content on this preload layer, such as a Flash movie, while the main content loads. Then, when the content finishes loading, the preload layer is hidden.

Follow these steps to make a preload layer with the Show-Hide Elements behavior:

1. **Create an AP Div layer on your page in the size you need to cover the page's main content while it loads.**

   To add an AP Div layer to your page, click the AP Div icon in the Layout category of the Insert panel and draw an AP Div layer anywhere in an open document.

2. **Name the new AP Div layer "preload" or something similar in the Properties inspector or in the AP Elements panel to help easily identify the layer when attaching the behavior.**

3. **In the AP Elements panel, set the preload layer's z-index to 1.**

   The preload layer needs to be at the top of the z-index (stacking order) for the behavior to work properly.

4. **With the preload layer selected, edit the layer's background color to match the rest of the page.**

   Use the color picker in the Properties inspector to set the layer background color.

5. **To add HTML content to the preload layer, click inside the layer and type or paste the content.**

   For example, on the preload layer you may want to play a flash SWF file, display an animated GIF, or show a *Please wait . . . page loading* type of message.

   You can give visitors the option of closing the preload layer by embedding a link or button in it that closes the layer using another Show-Hide Elements behavior.

6. **In the Tag selector at the bottom of the open Document window, select the <body> tag. Then click the Add Behavior (+) icon in the Behaviors panel, and select Show-Hide Elements.**

   The Show-Hide Layers dialog box appears.

7. **Select the preload layer in the Named Elements listing, and then click the Show button.**

8. **Click OK to close the dialog box.**

9. **Verify that the event handler next to the Show-Hide Layers behavior reads onLoad.**

   If not, change the event handler to onLoad in the Properties inspector.

Swap Image Behavior

With the Swap Image behavior, you can assign a rollover button script to any graphic on the page. When the user moves the cursor over the graphic, the JavaScript tells the user's browser to display a new graphic (the *over state* graphic) in its place. You also have the option to preload images and restore the graphic to its original state with the onMouseOut event. You can even assign rollover graphics to several graphics on the page with one event handler, such as changing a button graphic and an image graphic at the same time when the visitor places the mouse cursor over the button graphic.

The script for this behavior calls an action that changes the image listed in the `src` attribute of the `<img>` tag. The two things you need to do before using this behavior are to name the normal state image in the Name field in the Properties inspector and to ensure that the over state image has the same width and height dimensions as the normal state graphic for a smooth `mouseover` effect.

To add the Swap Image behavior to your page, follow these steps:

1. **Select an image on your page.**

   If you need to insert an image, click the Image icon in the Common category of the Insert panel or choose Insert⇨Image.

2. **In the Properties inspector, type a name (ID) for the image in the Name field.**

   If you forget to name your images, you can still use the Swap Image behavior, but it may be hard to assign the behavior to the correct image when your page has multiple unnamed images.

3. **If assigning the same rollover behavior to multiple graphics on your page, repeat Steps 1 and 2 until all the graphics on your page are in place and named.**

   In other words, if you know you want images 2 and 3 to change when image 1 is moused over, insert and name images 2 and 3.

4. **Select the image on the page that you want to attach the behavior to, click the Add Behavior (+) icon in the Behaviors panel, and then select Swap Image.**

   The Swap Image dialog box appears, displaying a list of named (and unnamed) images on the page (see Figure 2-19).

Figure 2-19:
Add the
Swap Image
behavior
to named
images on
your page.

5. **In the list, select a named image that you want to assign a rollover graphic to, and then click the Browse button to select the over state graphic for that image.**

If you know the path and filename, you can type it in the Set Source To text field rather than browsing for it.

6. **Repeat Steps 4 and 5 to create multiple rollover behaviors at once.**

For example, you'd repeat Steps 4 and 5 if you want to change both a photo and a button graphic with one `mouseover` event.

7. **Select the Preload Images and Restore Image onMouseOut options.**

By default, both options are enabled, which are recommended settings:

- **Preload Images:** Add JavaScript to the head area of the page that tells the visitor's browser to preload the rollover graphics when the page loads so that the user experiences no delay in viewing the rollover effect. Leave this option selected because images that aren't preloaded could create problems for displaying the page in a browser.

- **Restore Image onMouseOut:** Add JavaScript to the page that tells the browser to restore the over state image to the normal state image when the site visitor moves the mouse cursor away from the rollover image graphic.

Figure 2-20 shows an example of how you can use the Swap Image behavior to create multiple over states for a single mouse event. When a visitor mouses over a main navigation button, such as the one for reptiles, the navigation button over state graphic appears, along with a graphic of a lizard and a graphic containing text about reptiles.

Figure 2-20:
Create
dynamic
rollover
graphic
effects.

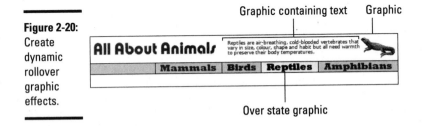

Graphic containing text   Graphic

Over state graphic

Swap Image Restore Behavior

The Swap Image Restore behavior restores a swapped image to its original state. Because the Swap Image Restore behavior is added automatically when you use the Swap Image behavior and leaves the Restore option selected, you'll probably never need to manually add the Swap Image Restore behavior.

On the blue moon occasion when you need to use it, simply choose the behavior from the Add Behavior menu in the Behavior panel and click OK in the Swap Image Restore dialog box. Dreamweaver adds the appropriate JavaScript to your page to restore the last set of swapped images to their original source graphics.

Validate Form Behavior

The Validate Form behavior verifies whether the visitor has accurately completed a form. If the form is inaccurate, the Validate Form behavior displays a JavaScript alert window with an error message. To use this behavior, turn to Book II, Chapter 7, which is devoted to creating forms.

Using Third-Party Behaviors

Dreamweaver is an *extensible* program, which means that you can enhance its functionality by installing object, command, behavior, and other extensions that perform various functions. You can find a ton of these third-party extensions at the Adobe Exchange Web site and by searching for the term *Dreamweaver Extensions* in your favorite search engine.

When you find extensions you want to try, you can download them and use the Adobe Extension Manager to install them on your computer. The Extension Manager is a standalone application that installs, manages, and uninstalls extensions in Dreamweaver and other Adobe programs. Dreamweaver installs the Extension Manager as part of the Dreamweaver software installation process.

Visiting the Adobe Exchange Web site

More than 1,500 extensions are available in the Dreamweaver Exchange section of Adobe's Exchange Web site. You'll find extensions to insert form fields, format tables, and create navigation menus and e-commerce shopping carts. Many of the extensions are offered free to registered Adobe members. Others are available as either shareware requiring small fees or as fully supported software extensions for those willing to pay full price.

Adobe has its Dreamweaver extensions grouped into several categories: Accessibility, App Servers, Browsers, Commerce, Content, DHTML/Layers, Extension Development, Fireworks, Flash Media, Learning, Navigation,

Productivity, Rich Media, Scripting, Security, Style/Format, Tables, Text, Web Analysis, and Web Widgets.

In addition to listing the platform availability (Windows, Mac, or both) for each of the extensions listed in the Exchange, you can find such helpful statistics as the number of recorded downloads, a user rating based on a five-star rating system, the Dreamweaver product version compatibility (8, MX, MX 2004, CS3, CS4, CS5), and the date the extension was released. You can also find links to a variety of discussion groups and user reviews on the site to help you make the best decision about which extensions to download.

To download and install extensions from the Adobe Dreamweaver Exchange Web site, follow these steps:

1. **Open the Dreamweaver Exchange Web site by choosing Help⇨Dreamweaver Exchange.**

   The Adobe Exchange opens in your primary Web browser, if you have a live Internet connection.

2. **Click the Dreamweaver link in the Exchanges by Product list.**

   You can also access the Exchange directly at www.adobe.com/cfusion/ exchange/index.cfm?event=productHome&exc=3&loc=en_us.

3. **Look around the various categories or search for extensions related to specific functions you're interested in.**

   To find out more about an extension before downloading or purchasing it, click the extension name.

4. **When you find a behavior you want, download or save it.**

   When accessing extensions on the Exchange, browsers often give you the option of downloading and installing the extension directly from the source or saving the extension file to your local computer.

   When you opt to save the file to your computer, Adobe recommends that you save the extensions to a Downloaded Extensions folder in the Dreamweaver application folder on your computer so you can manage all extensions in one location. Another option is to download extensions to your desktop, and then move them to another folder after installation for archiving.

Using the Extension Manager

Using the Extension Manager to install your third-party extensions is easy. To launch the application, choose Help⇨Manage Extensions. If for some reason you do not have the application installed on your computer, visit the Adobe Web site at www.adobe.com/exchange/em_download/ to download a free copy of the latest version of the application.

To install, manage, and uninstall extensions with the Extension Manager, follow these steps:

1. **From the Extension Manager's main menu, choose File⇨Install Extension to install the new extension.**

   The Select Extension to Install dialog box appears.

2. **Browse to and select an extension file with the .mxp file extension, and then click the Open or Install button.**

   Some extensions install immediately, whereas others launch the Extension Manager application panel and display the Adobe disclaimer. If the latter happens, skip to Step 4. Otherwise, continue to Step 3.

3. **If prompted, select the Adobe application under the Products listing into which you want to install the extension (for example, Dreamweaver or Fireworks).**

   This step is especially important when you have multiple Adobe products or multiple versions of the same product installed on the computer. When you upgrade your application, the extensions are installed into the newest or currently running version or you are prompted to update them.

4. **Read the Adobe Extension Manager disclaimer that appears, including any extension license information.**

5. **To complete the installation, accept the terms of the disclaimer and license.**

6. **If prompted to replace any existing extensions with the same name, click Yes (or Yes to All) to accept the newer version of the extension being installed.**

   If you click No, the current version of that file remains active. If you click Cancel, the installation stops without replacing or installing any new files. *Note:* Some extensions require you to close and restart Dreamweaver before they take effect.

Figure 2-21 shows how newly installed extensions appear in the list of Installed and Enabled Extensions in the Extension Manager. For online help with Adobe's Extension Manager, visit http://help.adobe.com/en_US/ExtensionManager/2.0/index.html.

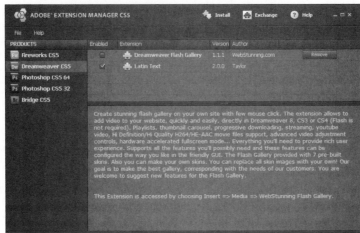

Figure 2-21: The Extension Manager lists all installed extensions along with extension details, such as version, type, and author.

Working with Spry Widgets

Spry Widgets are part of the Spry framework for Ajax that was introduced in Dreamweaver CS3. They are a special library of JavaScript *widgets* that help Web designers, coders, and programmers who have a basic understanding of HTML, CSS, and JavaScript build XLM-rich Web pages that offer unique and interesting interactive experiences for site visitors.

In addition to Spry Widgets, Dreamweaver includes Spry Validation Form Fields (which you can find out more about in Book II, Chapter 7), Spry Effects, which can be applied to elements on your pages through the Behaviors panel (see the "Spry Effects" section, earlier in this chapter), and Spry Data Sets, which let you build dynamic pages by loading and manipulating data from a specified data source. Spry Data Sets and working with Spry in general are documented in detail online in the Spry Framework for Ajax Spry Developer's Guide at `http://livedocs.adobe.com/en_US/Spry/SDG/index.html`.

What makes these Spry assets so powerful is that they're easy to use and customize after you understand how to work with them. However, to get the most use out of the Spry Widgets, you need a firm understanding of HTML, CSS, and JavaScript. Spry Widgets are a more advanced set of Dreamweaver tools intended for the experienced Dreamweaver user.

To view all currently available Spry Widgets in CS5, open the Spry category of the Insert panel, as shown in Figure 2-22. The first four widgets (Spry Data Set, Spry Region, Spry Repeat, and Spry Repeat List) are tools to use when creating dynamic pages. The Spry Validation Widgets (from Spry Validation Text Field to Spry Validation Radio Group) are for adding dynamic interactivity and validation functionality to forms. The remaining widgets are for adding general interactivity to your pages, such as creating a Spry Menu Bar, Spry Tabbed Panels, Spry Accordion, Spry Collapsible Panel, and Spry Tooltip.

Figure 2-22: Use the Spry menu in the Insert panel to insert Spry Widgets.

Here is a description of the general Spry Widgets you can add to your pages:

✦ **Spry Menu Bar:** The Spry Menu Bar is a fully customizable set of navigation buttons with unlimited submenu capabilities based on the List Item HTML tags (`<ul>`, `<li>`, and `<a>`) and CSS styling. Buttons have both normal and hover states styled with CSS, allowing for relatively easy customizable colors and fonts.

✦ **Spry Tabbed Panels:** This panel is actually a set of tabbed panels that can contain a large amount of content in a smaller defined space. Visitors can open and close panels by clicking the individual panel tabs, so that only one panel is revealed at a time.

✦ **Spry Accordion:** This panel is actually a set of collapsible panels that can contain a large amount of content in a smaller defined space. Panels can be opened and closed by clicking the individual panel tabs, and only one panel is revealed at a time.

✦ **Spry Collapsible Panel:** This panel is a single collapsible panel that can contain a large amount of content in a smaller defined space. Visitors can expand and collapse the panel by clicking on the panel's tab.

✦ **Spry Tooltip:** The Spry Tooltip provides tool tips to visitors when they hover their mouse over a particular object or bit of text on the Web page. Tips disappear when the visitors move their mouse away from the object that triggered the tool tip.

To use these general interactivity widgets, start by inserting a Spry Widget into your page, like the ones shown in Figure 2-23. After the widget is inserted, you can modify how it works by adding customized content and by editing the look and feel of how the widget appears in the browser. (All Spry Widgets are styled with an external CSS file.)

Each time you insert a Spry Widget into your page, a corresponding CSS file (such as SpryAssets/SpryTabbedPanels.css) and JavaScript file (such as SpryAssets/SpryTabbedPanels.js) is added to the root level of your managed site in a folder called SpryAssets. Sometimes, the widget may include graphics too, and those are also automatically added to the SpryAssets folder. You must upload this folder and its contents along with the page containing the Spry Widget to the host server for the widget to function properly.

All general Spry Widgets listed in the preceding section can be inserted on to your pages in the same way. After insertion, you can customize them with your own data and modify their styles through the CSS Styles panel.

To insert a Spry Menu Bar, Spry Tabbed Panel, Spry Accordion panel, Spry Collapsible Panel, or Spry Tooltip on your page, follow these steps:

1. **Place your cursor in the area on your page where you want to insert the Spry Widget.**

2. **Click the desired Spry Widget icon on the Spry category of the Insert panel.**

When inserting the Spry Menu Bar, you are prompted to select either a Horizontal or Vertical layout before Dreamweaver adds the code to the page. For all other widgets, the code is automatically inserted onto the page.

3. **With the Widget still selected (with the blue widget tab visible in Design view), use the Properties inspector to customize the widget.**

By default, the widget is generically named (such as sprytooltip1 or Accordion2); however, you can change the name, which appears as the widget's id attribute, in the Properties inspector. After you change the name, Dreamweaver updates all instances of the widget on the linked JavaScript and CSS files.

Figure 2-23:
Spry
Widgets
offer visitors
customized
interactive
content.

Customize your widget using the options in the Properties inspector:

- **Spry Menu Bar:** Add, remove, label, and reorder menu and submenu items, and add links, link title, and link targets.

- **Spry Tabbed Panels:** Add, remove, label, and reorder tabs, set the default panel that is opened when the page loads, and add content to each of the tab panels.

- **Spry Accordion:** Add, remove, label, and reorder tabs on the accordion and add content to each of the tab panels.

- **Spry Collapsible Panel:** Label and add content to the panel, set the panel display and default state to open or closed, and enable or disable panel animation.

- **Spry Tooltip:** Customize tool tip trigger and tool tip content; specify the trigger from a menu of all elements on the page with `id` attributes; set the horizontal and vertical offset; and hide and show a tool tip delay, a tool tip special effect (none, blind, fade), and whether the tool tip should follow the mouse or disappear when the cursor moves away from the trigger.

**Book IV
Chapter 2**

**JavaScript
Behaviors and
Spry Widgets**

4. **When applicable, add customized content to the widget in Design view.**

For example, the labels and content of most widgets can be adjusted in Design view.

5. **Customize the widget style through the CSS Styles panel.**

The CSS files for each of the widgets are listed in the CSS Styles panel. Finding the right one to edit, however, may be a bit difficult without Dreamweaver's Help File documentation. Here's a listing of all links for customizing each of the widgets:

```
www.adobe.com/go/learn_dw_sprymenubar_custom
www.adobe.com/go/learn_dw_sprytabbedpanels_custom
www.adobe.com/go/learn_dw_spryaccordion_custom
www.adobe.com/go/learn_dw_sprycollapsiblepanel_custom
```

To customize the style of the Spry Tooltip widget, for example, expand the SpryTooltip.css listed in the CSS Styles panel and make adjustments to the `.iframeTooltip` and `.tooltipContent` styles.

For more information about Spry Framework for Ajax, see Adobe's Online Developer's Guide at `http://livedocs.adobe.com/en_US/Spry/SDG/index.html`, where you can discover more about Spry Widgets and Spry Effects, Spry Data Sets, and building dynamic pages with Spry. You can also find helpful tutorials on the Spry Framework for Ajax Technology Center at `www.adobe.com/devnet/spry/` and informative video tutorials at `www.adobe.com/designcenter/video_workshop`.

Chapter 3: Designing Pages with Frames

In This Chapter

✔ Understanding frames

✔ Creating frames and framesets

✔ Modifying frame and frameset properties

✔ Targeting frames with links

✔ Adding noframes content

✔ Creating floating frames

*B*ack in the early days of the Internet, the most common use of frames was to ease navigation and reduce page loading wait times for site visitors using dialup modem connections. The idea behind frames is this: The browser window is divided into several panes, or *frames,* that each display different HTML pages, independent of the content in the other frames. Furthermore, by specifying the target frame in your hyperlinks, you can control which frame a new page opens in when a user clicks a link.

Suppose that a user visits a Web site comprising a three-part frameset, with company information in the top frame, some navigation buttons in the left frame, and information pertinent to the Web site's products or services, such as contact information, in the main frame. With this type of frameset, a visitor can click a link in the navigation frame, and the linked page opens in the main frame of the frameset, thereby limiting the amount of new information that needs to be loaded in the browser window. The less information to load, the faster the page can be loaded.

Today many people visiting Web sites have high-speed connections, such as DSL, cable, T-1, or broadband. With these faster types of Internet access, frames are no longer necessary as a navigation or layout tool. In addition, frames have coding, printer, browser, and SEO issues, including problems with bookmarking pages and effective search engine optimization. Today, the recommended practice is to create page layouts using layers (see Book IV, Chapter 1) and CSS (see Book III, Chapter 1).

Nevertheless, frames are still used every once in a long while, so you should know how to use them, especially in case you inherit a site that was built with them or find a compelling reason to use them on your site.

This chapter provides you with an overview of frames, including how to create and modify framesets, set attributes for frames and framesets, set the target attribute of links to display pages in specific frames, add noframes content for visitors using browsers without frame support, and insert floating frames on a page.

Understanding Frames

You can divide a browser window into multiple panes, or *frames*. Each frame contains a unique Web page that is displayed independently of the pages in the other frames in the browser window. You can control the contents of each framed area separately with regular HTML. For example, when a visitor clicks a link, you can have some frames on the page remain static while the content in another frame changes.

In the code, the page that defines the frame divisions or layout is called a *frameset*. The frameset itself doesn't display any content in the browser window (except when you use the <noframes> tag, as described at the end of this chapter). Rather, the frameset provides formatting and layout instructions to the browser on how to display the pages *inside* the frames. In other words, the frameset is merely a container in which other documents are displayed.

You can use frames to format your entire Web site or just a section or page of a site. When using frames as the layout format for your entire Web site, you typically save the frameset file as index.html so that the page loads in the browser window when people visit the URL. When the frameset page is loaded, the browser collects and displays the specified pages inside the individual frames.

You can divide frames vertically and horizontally into as many frame rows and columns as you need to achieve your layout. For example, in Figure 3-1, the browser window is divided into three frames, with static company information in the top frame, static navigation links in the left frame, and general information in the main frame. When a visitor clicks a link in the navigation area, a new page is displayed in the main frame.

In the code, <frameset> tags replace the <body> tags, and the <frame> tags further define divisions in the frameset, as in the following sample code:

```
<frameset rows="80,*" cols="*" frameborder="NO" border="0" framespacing="0">
<frame src="top.html" name="topFrame" scrolling="NO" noresize title="topFrame">
<frameset cols="80,*" frameborder="NO" border="0" framespacing="0">
<frame src="left.html" name="leftFrame" scrolling="NO" noresize
    title="leftFrame">
<frame src="main.html" name="mainFrame" title="mainFrame">
</frameset>
</frameset>
```

Top frame

Figure 3-1:
Create
framesets
with as
simple or
complex a
layout as
needed.

Left frame   Main frame

When you create new frames, rows are created top to bottom, and columns are created left to right. The smallest frameset division can contain two rows or two columns. However, you can nest a frameset within a frame of another frameset, to any level of nesting, for some highly complex page display effects.

After you divide your page into a frameset, specify the frameset and the frame parameters and attributes in the Properties inspector, just as you do with text and graphics. For instance, you can set the width and height of frames, the number of rows and columns in the frameset, the source page for a frame along with the source page margin width and height, the name or ID of a frame for targeting purposes, a border width and border color, whether the frame has scroll bars, and whether a visitor can resize each frame in the frameset.

There are both good and bad things about framesets. Frames are great because

✦ You can display multiple pages in one browser window.

✦ You can use them for displaying Web gallery images, including thumbnails and close-up images.

✦ The browser does not need to reload graphics for each page, which speeds up page display.

✦ Each page in a frame can have its own set of scroll bars, which means a visitor can scroll in one frame of the browser while referring to the unmoving area of another frame of the browser.

✦ You can use several JavaScript behaviors with frames, such as the Set Text of Frame, Go to URL, and Insert Jump Menu options. These behaviors allow you to modify the content of a page in a frame without opening a new page in the frame, create a link to another page in particular frame, and open a new page in a particular frame of the frameset using a jump menu. For details on each of these and other scripts, check out Book IV, Chapter 2.

Frames are not so good because

✦ Visitors can't bookmark individual pages in framesets. The URL of the frameset page (usually `index.html`) doesn't change as the visitor navigates through the site. Also, visitors can't save individual configurations of pages in frames.

✦ Search engines have trouble indexing pages, making search engine optimization nearly impossible.

✦ You need to define the `target` attribute of link tags so new pages open in the correct frame.

✦ Visitors with disabilities may have difficulty navigating the frames.

✦ Designing framesets can get very confusing.

✦ Precisely aligning elements between frames is more difficult than aligning elements on regular unframed pages.

✦ You're likely to create errors with links and targets.

✦ Most site visitors don't like frames, especially badly crafted framesets.

Creating Frames and Framesets

Before creating framesets in Dreamweaver, you need to do two things to customize your work environment and improve the display of the frameset document in Design view:

✦ **Open the Frames panel.** The Frames panel, shown in Figure 3-2, displays all the frames in a frameset document and can assist you with selecting the frame elements during the frameset building process. To open the Frames panel, choose Window➪Frames.

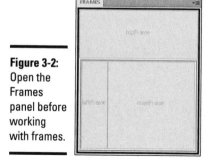

Figure 3-2:
Open the
Frames
panel before
working
with frames.

✦ **Enable the Frame Borders visual aids.** When you have this feature
enabled, the open document displays frame borders and divider bars,
as shown in Figure 3-3. To enable Frame Borders visual aids, choose
View➪Visual Aids➪Frame Borders.

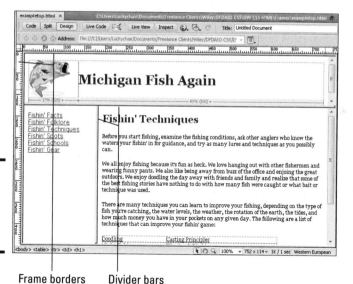

Figure 3-3:
Turn on
the Frame
Borders
visual aids.

Frame borders   Divider bars

The W3C recognized frames as of the HTML 4.0 doctype (or DTD — Document
Type Definition), and because browsers need to know what they're displaying, Dreamweaver automatically inserts the appropriate doctype when creating frames. This ensures that the browsers interpret the file accurately.
However, if you're hand-coding or inheriting a frameset from another source
(as with a Web site redesign project, for instance), be sure to add the following doctype to the master frameset file above the opening `<html>` tag:

```
<!DOCTYPE HTML PUBLIC "-//W3C//DTD HTML 4.01 Frameset//EN" "http://www.w3.org/TR/
    html4/frameset.dtd">
```

When working in XHTML, use the XHTML Frameset DTD instead:

```
<!DOCTYPE html PUBLIC "-//W3C//DTD XHTML 1.0 Frameset//EN" "http://www.w3.org/TR/
    xhtml11/DTD/xhtml11-frameset.dtd">
```

Building framesets is a complex process and you need to set them up carefully so that they are displayed correctly in browsers. For those reasons, try following these general workflow steps when building framesets:

1. **Create the frameset and select the files that you want to appear in each frame.**

   See the following sections for details.

2. **Save the frameset and all the files in each frame, and name each frame for later targeting with links.**

   See "Saving Frames and Framesets," later in the chapter.

3. **Set the properties for the frameset and the individual frames in the Properties inspector to achieve the look you want.**

   See the later section, "Setting Frame Properties with the Properties Inspector."

4. **Set the target attribute for all the links on all the pages to display in the frames of the frameset so that they'll appear where you intend them to.**

   For details, see "Targeting Frames with Links."

In the next few sections, you find out how to create a frameset and select files for the frames.

Using predefined framesets to create a new file

When you need a simple frameset with two to three frames, consider using one of Dreamweaver's predefined framesets. To create a new document with one of the predefined framesets, follow these steps:

1. **Choose File➪New to open the New Document dialog box, shown in Figure 3-4.**

2. **Select the Page from Sample category, and then select a predefined frameset in the Frameset Sample Folder.**

   If you're not sure which frameset you want, select any frameset in the Sample Page list; a preview and description of that preset appears on the right. The Fixed Top, Nested Left frameset and the Fixed Top, Nested Right frameset are the most popular Web layouts.

3. **Click the Create button.**

   The new frameset appears in the Document window. *Note:* If the Frame Tag Accessibility Attributes dialog box appears, select a frame in the frameset from the Frame menu and add a title for that frame. Repeat this process until all the frames in the frameset have titles, and then click OK. To bypass accessibility tags and just insert the frames without frame titles, click the Cancel button.

Displaying a file in a predefined frameset

Another way of using predefined framesets is to convert an existing open document into a file displayed inside a frameset. To display a file inside a predefined frameset, follow these steps:

1. **Open the file you want to display inside a frame in a frameset.**

2. **Place your insertion point somewhere in the file.**

3. **Choose a predefined frameset in the Frames icon drop-down menu in the Layout category of the Insert panel.**

   When you're trying to decide which frameset to choose, look at the thumbnail images that appear next to the predefined frameset options, as shown in Figure 3-5. The frame in blue indicates where your document appears if you select the predefined frameset. The white areas represent the frames that open in the frameset, where you can display other documents.

Figure 3-5: Use the Frames menu on the Layout category of the Insert panel to convert an existing page into a page inside of a predefined frameset.

Note: If you've enabled the Frame Accessibility features in the Preferences dialog box, the Frame Tag Accessibility Attributes dialog box appears, as shown in Figure 3-6. Select a frame in the frameset from the Frame menu, and then add a title for that frame. Repeat this process until all the frames in the frameset have titles. To bypass this feature, click the Cancel button and Dreamweaver creates the frameset without the associated accessibility tags and attributes in the code.

Figure 3-6: The Frame Tag Accessibility Attributes dialog box.

Creating custom framesets

You can create a custom frameset in Dreamweaver by splitting an existing Document window into frames. To design a custom frameset from a blank, open document, do one of the following:

✦ Choose Modify➪Frameset and choose a splitting option from the sub-menu, such as Split Frame Left or Split Frame Down.

✦ Enable the Frame Borders visual aids (choose View➪Visual Aids➪Frame Borders), and then manually drag a frame border into the open document in Design view to split the frame into a frameset. The frame borders are the thin gray bars located on the top and left edges of the Document window between the ruler (select View➪Rulers➪Show) and the content area of the page.

To further customize and refine the frameset with additional frames, continue splitting frames by these methods or the other techniques available in Dreamweaver, as described in the next section.

Adding, Removing, and Resizing Frames

Before adding, removing, or resizing frames, enable the Frame Borders visual aids (choose View➪Visual Aids➪Frame Borders), and then open the Frames panel, as described in "Creating Frames and Framesets," earlier in the chapter. Visual aids enable you to see the frame borders and frame divisions so that you can modify divisions on a frameset, and the Frames panel assists you with selecting and naming the frames.

Adding frames

To add frame divisions, do any of the following:

✦ **Divide a frame or set of frames vertically or horizontally:** In Design view, drag a frame border from the top or left edge of the window (near the ruler) to the middle of the page.

✦ **Divide a frame vertically or horizontally but do not split any existing frames:** Ctrl+drag (Windows) or ⌘+drag (Mac) when dragging a new frame border.

✦ **Split a frame into four parts:** In Design view, drag a frame border from a corner to the middle of the frame. Begin dragging when the cursor turns into a four-sided arrow.

✦ **Split a frame with a border that doesn't touch the edge of the master frameset:** In Design view, Alt+drag (Windows) or Option+drag (Mac) to drag a new frame border from an existing frame border.

✦ **Divide the frame that contains the insertion point:** Choose Modify➪Frameset and then select a split option.

Although frames are easy to split, you can't easily merge frames the way you can with table cells. Therefore, try to have a clear idea of the frameset layout you need before building it. For instance, when you need a frameset with

**Book IV
Chapter 3**

**Designing Pages
with Frames**

three frames, split the page into two frames first, and then split one of the two frames into a third frame.

Removing frames

To remove a frame division, do either of the following in Design view:

✦ Drag a frame border off the side of the page onto the ruler bar.

✦ Drag a frame border onto the border of a parent frame or frameset.

Because you can't completely remove framesets by dragging, you must delete the file and start over, or modify the code. For instance, after you remove all the frame borders from a page, the code still displays frame doctype, `<frame>`, and `<noframes>` tags, as in the following:

```
<!DOCTYPE HTML PUBLIC "-//W3C//DTD HTML 4.01 Frameset//EN" "http://www.w3.org/TR/
    html4/frameset.dtd">
<html xmlns="http://www.w3.org/1999/xhtml">
<head>
<meta http-equiv="Content-Type" content="text/html; charset=utf-8">
<title>Untitled Document</title>
</head>
<frame src="file:///C/Project Files/ProjectName/Untitled-1">
<noframes><body>
</body></noframes>
</html>
```

As you can see, the doctype still identifies the file as a page using framesets, and the `<frame>` and `<noframes>` tags identify the content as sitting inside a frame structure. If you want to use the page as a regular HTML file, you could modify the code to reflect the doctype and tags of a normal HTML or XHTML document, but creating a new document by choosing File⇨New is much faster.

Resizing a frame

To resize a frame, do either of the following:

✦ In Design view, drag the frame borders up, down, left, or right in the Document window to the size you want.

✦ Select a frameset in the Frames panel. Then, in the Properties inspector, set the exact sizes for the frames in pixels or percentages, or choose the Relative size setting.

Nested Framesets

Nested framesets occur when a frameset sits inside another frameset. Nesting is common, found in even the simplest of framesets. You can nest as many framesets as you need to achieve your layout. The three-part Web site shown in Figure 3-7 is an example of a frameset containing two nested framesets. The main window is divided into two rows, top and bottom, and the bottom row is further split into two columns, left and right. The entire bottom row is the first nested frameset inside of the master frameset. In the right column of the bottom row, another nested frameset is split into two columns.

You can create nested framesets two ways:

✦ Define the inner frameset in the same file as the outer frameset or in a separate file of its own. In other words, you can use Dreamweaver's frame-splitting tools to create the complex structure of the frameset all in the same master frameset file.

✦ Open a separate, external frameset page in one of the frames of the frameset using the Open in Frame command (as described in the next section).

Because framesets can quickly become complicated — especially when you start targeted linking — you may do better nesting with the first method.

Fortunately, when you use the frame-splitting tools Dreamweaver provides, you can virtually forget about having to oversee the complexity of nesting details because Dreamweaver handles the coding for you.

Figure 3-7: Build framesets with nested framesets for more complex page layouts.

Opening Pages in a Frame

After creating the layout for your frameset, you can add new page content to any blank, untitled documents in the frameset, or even better, open an existing HTML page in an empty frame.

To open an existing page in a frame, follow these steps:

1. **In a saved frameset, place your cursor anywhere in the frame where you want to open your page (see Figure 3-8).**

If you haven't saved and titled the master frameset yet, do so before proceeding by selecting the outer frameset in the Frames panel and then choosing File⇨Save Frameset or File⇨Save Frameset As. After you've saved the frameset, give it a title by typing one into the Title field on the document toolbar. Then start over at Step 1.

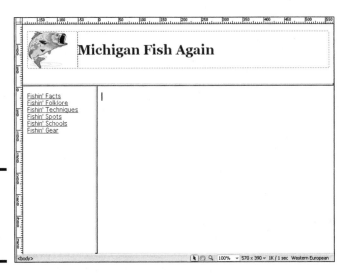

Figure 3-8:
Place your cursor in the empty frame.

2. **Choose File⇨Open in Frame.**

Do *not* select the File⇨Open option! You want the fifth option down in the list, Open in Frame, as shown in Figure 3-9.

The Select HTML File dialog box appears.

Figure 3-9:
Select the Open in Frame option.

New...	Ctrl+N
Open...	Ctrl+O
Browse in Bridge...	Ctrl+Alt+O
Open Recent	▶
Open in Frame...	Ctrl+Shift+O
Close	Ctrl+W
Close All	Ctrl+Shift+W

3. **Browse to and select the HTML file you want to open in that frame or type the path and filename of the page you want to open. Click OK (Windows) or Choose (Mac).**

The selected page appears in the frame on the frameset, as shown in Figure 3-10.

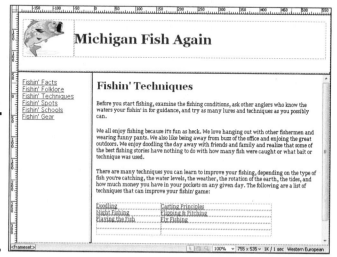

Figure 3-10: The selected page appears in the frame of the frameset.

If at any time you want to change the page that is currently open in the frameset, select the frame in the Frames panel and then edit the Src field in the Properties inspector to select another document.

Saving Frames and Framesets

After creating a frameset, you must save both the frameset document and all the individual files in each of the frames. You can save all the frames and the frameset at once by using the Save All command. Or, if you prefer, save the frameset and individual frame documents one at a time.

Saving all the files in the frameset

To save a frameset and all files opened in each of the frames at once, follow these steps:

1. **Choose File➪Save All.**

All the files associated with the frameset will be saved, including the frameset document and all the files opened in each frame. The Save As dialog box appears, as shown in Figure 3-11.

Book IV Chapter 3

Designing Pages with Frames

Figure 3-11:
In Design view, a dark border appears around the frame being saved when you're saving the frameset and its files.

The border designates which frame you are saving

2. **Name and save each file.**

   Each time the Save As dialog box appears, look at the document in Design view to identify the frame you're saving, and then enter a file-name and click Save. The frame with a dark border surrounding it is the frame you're saving. Figure 3-11 shows an example of how the border surrounds the frame.

   If you choose File➪Open in Frame to open existing files inside all your frames, you need to name and save only the frameset file.

Saving only the frameset file

To save only the frameset, follow these steps:

1. **In the Frames panel or in the Document window, select the frameset.**

   You can select the frameset with either of the following methods:

   • In the Document window, click the border between any two frames in the frameset.

   • In the Frames panel, click the master frameset border that surrounds the entire frameset. You can tell you've selected the frameset when the Frames panel displays a black border around the outermost frameset.

2. **To save the selected frameset, choose File➪Save Frameset.**

Saving an individual file in a frame

To save a file opened inside a frame:

1. Click inside the frame that contains the file you want to save.

2. To save the selected file, choose File⇨Save Frame.

Titling a Frameset

One of the most often overlooked parts of a frameset is the frameset title. The title for the frameset page appears in the title bar at the top of an open browser window. If left unaltered, the title bar reads *Untitled Document,* which is not helpful to site visitors and may be perceived as unprofessional, so be sure to title the frameset file!

It can sometimes be tricky to select the correct piece of a frameset to add the title, so be sure you're selecting the frameset and not one of the individual frames in it. Although still important, titles on these pages within the frameset don't appear in the browser window.

Follow these steps to name your frameset file:

1. Select the frameset.

You can select the frameset using one of the following methods:

- In the Document window, click the border between any two frames in the frameset.

- In the Frames panel, click the master frameset border that surrounds the entire frameset. You can tell it's selected when the Frames panel displays a black border around the outermost frameset.

2. Type a title for the file in the Title text box on the Document toolbar, as shown in Figure 3-12.

To ensure that you've entered in the title correctly, preview your frameset in a browser window to make sure the title bar of the browser matches your input.

Book IV
Chapter 3

Designing Pages with Frames

Figure 3-12:
Add a title to
the frameset
document.

Enter title here

Setting the Background Color of a File in a Frame

You can easily set the background color of a page displayed in a frame by applying internal CSS through the Page Properties dialog box. For more complex layouts and styling, however, use external Cascading Style Sheets through the CSS Styles panel to set not only the background color of a page but also other styling options (see Book III, Chapter 1).

Follow these steps to change the background color of a file in a frame:

1. **In Design view, click inside the frame where you want to change the background color of the page.**

2. **Choose Modify⇨Page Properties.**

You can also click the Page Properties button in the Properties inspector. The Page Properties dialog box appears.

3. **Click the Background Color color picker icon to choose a color for the page background.**

You can also type the hexadecimal value including the number symbol (#) in the Background color text box, such as #003300. The color is applied to your page and Dreamweaver writes the internal CSS code in the head area of the page.

4. **Click OK to close the dialog box.**

Setting Frame Properties with the Properties Inspector

The settings in the Properties inspector control different viewable parts of the frame or frameset that are displayed in a browser window, such as adding a frame border in a particular size and color or setting row and column values. Tables 3-1 and 3-2 show the attributes for framesets and frames.

Table 3-1	Frameset Attributes
Frameset Attributes	*Description*
`cols="50,25%,*"`	Set the number and size of columns (each column separated with a comma). An asterisk (*) represents a value equal to the remaining space in a browser window after frames with pixel or percentage space are allocated.
`rows="23,23,23,23"`	Set the number and size of rows.
`border="1"`	Set the frame border in pixels.
`frameborder="yes"`	Specify whether or not a frame border is present.
`framespacing="5"`	Set the frame spacing in pixels.

Table 3-2	**Frame Attributes**	
Frame Attributes	*Value*	*Description*
`frameborder="0"`	0 or 1	Enter 0 or No to hide, 1 or Yes to show a border between frames.
`framespacing="5"`	0–100	Set the frames spacing in pixels.
`marginwidth=""`	0–100	When set to 0, the frame is displayed flush with the left and right edge of the frame.
`marginheight=""`	0–100	If set to 5, a 5-pixel-wide space is between the window and the top of the frame.
`name=""`	Any name	Assign a name to your frames so you can use them as targets with the <a> tag.
`noresize`	None	Disallow the user to resize the frame.
`scrolling=""`	Auto/on/off	Decide whether to include the scroll bars on the right side of each frame. The auto setting displays scroll bars only when content in the frame exceeds the frame size.
`src=""`	filename.html	Set the filename and its location on your hard drive (or the server hard drive) to be displayed in the frame. Remember that some remote host servers use UNIX, which makes filenames case sensitive.

The next two sections show you how to specify properties for frames and framesets.

Setting frameset properties

Follow these steps to set frameset properties with the Properties inspector:

1. **Select a frameset.**

You can select a frameset using either of the following methods:

- In the Document window, click the border between any two frames in the frameset.
- In the Frames panel, click the frameset border. You can tell you've selected the frameset by the thick black border surrounding it.

2. **In the Properties inspector, check to see if the expander arrow (in the lower-right corner) is pointing up or down. If the arrow points down, click it to reveal all the properties, as shown in Figure 3-13.**

Figure 3-13:
The Properties inspector showing all frameset properties.

3. **In the Properties inspector, enter information to set the attributes for the frameset.**

Here's a rundown of the options in the Properties inspector:

✦ **Borders:** Determine if borders are displayed around the frames in a browser window. Choose Yes to display the borders, No to hide borders, or Default to use a browser's default border setting.

✦ **Border Width:** Set the width of the border to any size in pixels. If you've selected No in the Borders drop-down list, leave this field blank.

✦ **Border Color:** Use the color picker icon or type a hexadecimal value including the number symbol (#) before it, such as #999999, to set the color of the border for the selected frameset.

✦ **Row/Col Selection:** Set the frame size of any particular frame in a selected frameset by selecting a frameset in the Frames panel. Click one of the tabs (left or right for columns, top or bottom for rows) in the Row/Col Selection area of the Properties inspector, and then enter a height or width value in the adjoining Row/Col Value text box.

✦ **Units:** Determine the size of the selected Row/Col:

 • **Pixels:** Set the size of the selected row or column to a fixed pixel width or height. Choose this option for frames that you want to keep at a fixed size, as with a navigation frame. Frames with pixel values are allocated space before frames using percents and relative sizes.

 • **Percent:** Set the selected row or column to a percentage of the total width and height of the frameset. Percentages are allocated space after frames set with pixels but before frames set with relative values.

- **Relative:** Set the row or column to be as large or as small as the remaining space available in a browser window after frames sized with pixels and percentages. Any number you entered in the Value field is replaced with an asterisk (*) in the code to represent the relative value. You can also enter a number in the Value field with the Relative setting, such as 3*, which is displayed in the code as `<frameset rows="23,3*,*">`. In this example, the 3* is 200 percent bigger than *.

Setting frame properties

To set frame properties with the Properties inspector, follow these steps:

1. **Select a frame in a frameset document by clicking anywhere in the desired frame's border.**

    You can tell a frame is selected when a thin black line outlines it.

2. **In the Properties inspector, check to see if the expander arrow is pointing up or down. If the arrow is pointing down, click it to reveal all the frame properties.**

    Figure 3-14 shows all the properties of a frame.

Figure 3-14:
The Properties inspector showing all frame properties.

3. **In the Properties inspector, enter information to set the options for the frame.**

    You can change the following properties for a frame:

✦ **Frame Name:** Get in the habit of naming all your frames as you create them. The name of the frame is absolutely necessary if you want to target a frame and open a new page inside it. Name your frames with a single word that starts with a letter and does not contain any funky characters, dashes, periods, or spaces (though you can use an underscore, as in left_frame). Try not to use words that are common in HTML and JavaScript such as top or parent, but instead use descriptive terms such as left, main, or nav.

✦ **Src:** Click the Browse to File folder icon to browse for and select the document that will be displayed in the selected frame, or use the Point to File icon to select a file in the Files panel. Alternatively, if you know the path and filename, type it directly into the Src text box.

✦ **Scroll:** Decide whether scroll bars appear on the frame. The Default value does not turn the scroll bars on or off, but instead tells the page to adopt the default scroll bar settings of the browser displaying it. Most browsers use the Auto setting as the default, meaning the frame displays scroll bars when the content of a frame exceeds the display area in the browser. You can also select No for never, or Yes for always.

✦ **No Resize:** Stop users from dragging any visible frame borders and changing the size of the frame in the browser window. This option does not affect your ability to modify frame sizes in Dreamweaver.

✦ **Borders:** View or hide borders around the selected frame in a browser window. Your choices are Yes, No, or Default. The Default setting for most browsers is to show the borders unless the parent frameset has borders set to No. To truly hide all borders from displaying, choose No for the frameset and all the frames that share the border. If you have doubts about the visibility or invisibility of the border, test the page in several browsers and alter the settings until you get the effect you want.

✦ **Border Color:** Use the color picker or type a hexadecimal value in this field to set the color of the borders for the frame. The color you specify overrides the color of the parent frameset border. Be warned that the logic of frame borders is complex and may not make immediate sense. One simple solution is to use the same border color throughout the frameset. Remember to add the number symbol before the hexadecimal value, as in #FF0033.

✦ **Margin Width:** Set the width of the space in pixels between the frame borders and the content. This setting is a frame attribute, not a page attribute.

✦ **Margin Height:** Set the height of the space in pixels between the frame borders and the content. This setting is a frame attribute, not a page attribute.

Frame Accessibility Settings

To work with frame accessibility settings in Dreamweaver, you can either enable the settings in the Accessibility category of the Preferences dialog box so that you always add accessibility tags as you create the frameset, or you can disable that setting to specify accessibility values for frames and framesets individually after you create the frames. We recommend that you use frame accessibility at all times.

Setting accessibility preferences

To enable (or disable) frame accessibility settings in Dreamweaver's Preferences, follow these steps:

1. **Display the Preferences dialog box by choosing Edit⇨Preferences (Windows) or Dreamweaver⇨Preferences (Mac).**

2. **Select the Accessibility category on the left side of the dialog box.**

3. **The Frames option, as shown in Figure 3-15, should be selected by default.**

   To disable it, deselect the Frames check box.

Figure 3-15: Alter the Dreamweaver Accessibility preferences.

Adding or editing accessibility settings to a frame with the Tag Editor

To set accessibility values for an individual frame, follow these steps:

1. **In the Frames panel, click a frame to select it.**

2. **Choose Modify⇨Edit Tag to open the Tag Editor.**

3. **Select Style Sheet/Accessibility in the Category list to display a set of frame accessibility options.**

4. **Enter accessibility values, and then click OK to close the dialog box.**

   The values are added to the document code.

Book IV Chapter 3

Designing Pages with Frames

Targeting Frames with Links

How do you specify which frame should display the linked page when a visitor clicks a link? With the target attribute of the link (`<a>`) tag, of course. With framesets, you can use the default `_top` or `_parent` target attribute, or if you happen to name the frames when building the frameset, you can also use the frame names as target destinations for your linked files. Setting the target frame is exactly like setting the target on an ordinary link, only with frames you have an expanded set of options to address the different areas where a link file will open.

To illustrate, suppose you have a frameset that has the standard two rows, with the bottom row split into two columns (see Figure 3-16). Logically, you can name the top frame `topFrame`, the left frame `leftFrame`, and the right frame `mainFrame` (because that's where the bulk of your new content will appear). When you place navigation links in the left frame, you can add the target attribute equal to `mainFrame` so that the linked page opens in the main frame of the frameset, as in this line of code:

```
<a href="techniques.html" target="mainFrame">Fishin' Techniques</a>
```

So, for example, in Figure 3-16, if the user clicks any of the navigation links in the left frame (Fishin' Facts, Fishin' Folklore, and so on), a new page opens in the main frame.

Figure 3-16: Use the Properties inspector to select the target of the frame into which you want the linked page to load.

Target a specific frame when setting links with these steps:

1. **In Design view, select the text or object that you want to convert into a targeted link.**

2. **In the Link text box in the Properties inspector, select the file to link to.**

Type the path and filename, click the folder icon to browse and select the file, or drag the Point-to-File icon onto the file in the Files panel.

3. **In the Target menu in the Properties inspector, choose the frame or window where you want the linked file to display:**

- **_blank:** Open the linked file in a new browser window above, or on top of, the existing parent window.

- **_new:** Similar to _blank, this option displays the returned data in a new browser window. However because _new is not a valid target for the `<a href>` tag, we recommend that you use _blank instead.

- **_parent:** Open the linked file inside the parent frameset of the frame where the link appears, replacing the frameset with the content of the linked file.

- **_self:** Open the linked file inside the same frame the link exists in and replace the previous content. This option is the default for all links unless another setting overrides it.

- **_top:** Remove any and all framesets and open the linked file inside the main browser window.

- **(Frame_Name):** Select a frame name as the target frame. When you name all the frames, the frame names appear in this list. You must be editing the document within the frameset structure to view the frame names. Otherwise, when editing files in their own windows, type the target frame name in the Target field in the Properties inspector.

When linking to a page outside your Web site while using frames, use the `target="_blank"` or `target="_top"` option. This forces the page to open in a new window or remove the master frameset, while making it clear to visitors that the link is a separate entity from your site.

Adding Noframes Content

In HTML, elements that are not understood by a browser are ignored. This means, for example, that if the user's browser doesn't support frames, nothing is displayed on the page unless you add content inside `<noframes>` tags. Place these tags after the closing `<frameset>` tag on the master frameset and nest them with the `<body>` tags so that the content will be displayed in the body area of the page when the frames content isn't displayed.

**Book IV
Chapter 3**

**Designing Pages
with Frames**

In Listing 3-1, if the frames content isn't displayed in the user's browser window, a message appears explaining that the visitor's browser doesn't support frames.

Listing 3-1:   Using the Noframes Tag to Display a Message

```
<frameset rows="80,*" cols="*" frameborder="NO" border="0" framespacing="0">
<frame src="top.html" name="topFrame" scrolling="NO"
noresize title="topFrame">
<frameset rows="*" cols="150,*" frameborder="NO" border="0"
framespacing="0">
<frame src="left.html" name="leftFrame" scrolling="NO"
noresize title="leftFrame">
<frame src="main.html" name="mainFrame"
title="mainFrame">
</frameset>
</frameset>
<noframes><body>
Your browser does not support frames. We encourage you to upgrade your browser
    to a version that provides frame support so you can fully experience the
    content provided here:
For Windows: Internet Explorer | Firefox | Opera | Chrome | Safari
For Macintosh: Safari | Firefox | Opera | Chrome
For Unix/Linux: Firefox | Opera | Chrome
You might also find it helpful to view the <a href="noFramesIndex.
    html">frameless</a>version of our site. </body></noframes>
```

The noframes content is coded as part of the frameset syntax and is displayed only in browsers that don't support frames or have disabled frames.

To add or edit noframes content, follow these steps:

1. Choose Modify⇨Frameset⇨Edit NoFrames Content.

The Document window and the words *NoFrames Content* temporarily replace any content displayed in Design view, as shown in Figure 3-17.

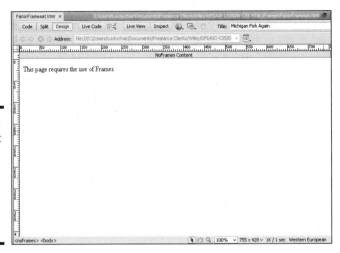

Figure 3-17: Use the Edit NoFrames Content command to edit noframes content.

2. **In the noframes area of the Document window, type or paste the noframes content, the same way you would for a regular HTML page.**

Or enter code by choosing Window➪Code Inspector. When the Code Inspector appears, add the HTML content between the <body> tags nested in the <noframes> tags.

3. **Choose Modify➪Frameset➪Edit NoFrames Content to return to the Design view of the frameset file.**

Whatever you write for your specific noframes content, try to include both a message about upgrading to a browser that supports framesets (with links to those download pages!) along with some kind of acknowledgment of the visitor's use of an old browser or a browser with disabled frames. Better yet, because nearly all browsers do support frames, consider including content and links for search engine optimization in the noframes area. Because the main point of a Web site is to provide information to all site visitors, treat the noframes content as another opportunity to communicate positively with site visitors.

Creating Floating Frames

Floating frames, or *inline frames,* are framesets or pages that you embed in the body of another page by using the <iframe> tag. Normally, frames have to stick to the sides of the browser window. However, floating frames can sit anywhere in a browser window.

When would you want to use floating frames? To display multiple pages in a bookmarkable page, such as a Web photo gallery with clickable thumbnail graphics and close-up images. Or perhaps for those times when you want to display a lot of content in a small, scrollable area within another page — for example, a long user agreement — rather than having the visitor scroll down a long page of content.

The structure of a floating frame is fairly simple. Unlike the <frameset> tags that require <frame> tags to identify the source of the content in each frame, the floating frame code uses a single pair of opening and closing <iframe> tags that include the size of the floating frame and the source file that is displayed inside it:

```
<iframe width="300" height="150" src="iframefile.html" align="left"></iframe>
```

To add a floating frame to your page you could hand-code it. If you want to use Dreamweaver's interface, however, follow these steps:

1. **Place your cursor in the file where you want the floating frame to appear.**

2. **Choose Insert➪Tag.**

The Tag Chooser dialog box appears.

**Book IV
Chapter 3**

**Designing Pages
with Frames**

3. **Click to expand the HTML Tags folder and select Page Elements on the left side of the dialog box; then select iframe from the list on the right, as Figure 3-18 shows.**

Figure 3-18: Dreamweaver's Tag Chooser lets you select and insert specific tags.

4. **Click the Insert button.**

The Tag Editor–iframe dialog box appears.

Floating frames in older browsers

Originally recognized only by IE 3.0, floating frames are now widely supported by most popular browsers, including Internet Explorer, Firefox, Safari, Opera, and Google Chrome. For older browsers, the content in the iframes isn't displayed on the page. Some tutorials on iframes may instruct you to add a `<frame>` tag with the same document source as your iframe between the `<iframe>` tags to account for older browsers, like this:

```
<iframe width="300" height="150" src="iframefile.html" align="left" frameborder="2"
        scrolling="auto" name="contactlist"><frame src="iframefile.html"></iframe>
```

Although not a perfect solution, it may improve the display of your iframe content on the page in older browsers.

Another option to consider is to add to the page containing the iframe a browser detection script in which older browsers are redirected to another page that includes the content of the iframe source file.

5. **Complete the dialog box with the attributes you want.**

Floating frames, like framesets and frames, have attributes that you need to specify if you want to override the default browser settings. Use these attribute settings to visually differentiate (or not) the floating frame content from the rest of the content on the page. Figure 3-19 shows the fields completed with sample content.

Figure 3-19:
Set
`<iframe>`
tag
attributes
easily using
Dream-
weaver's
Tag Editor.

Here's a rundown of the options in the dialog box:

- **Source:** Type the URL or path and filename of the file to display in the floating frame.

- **Name:** Give the iframe a name so you can use the name for targeting. As long as you name the iframe in the code, you can target the iframe just like a regular frame within a frameset. For example, if you name an iframe `contactlist`, you can specify that name as a target for a link:

```
<iframe src="iframefile.html" name="contactlist" width="300" height="150"
    align="left" frameborder="2" marginwidth="0" marginheight="0"
    scrolling="auto"></iframe>
<a href="contactlist.html" target="contactlist">See our Contact List</a>
```

- **Width and Height**: Set the width and height of the iframe using fixed pixels or percentages relative to the visitor's browser and monitor resolution settings.

**Book IV
Chapter 3**

**Designing Pages
with Frames**

- **Margin Width and Height:** Adjust the margin space surrounding the floating frame by setting the width and height in pixels.

- **Alignment:** Align the iframe relative to the horizontal sides of the browser with the `align` attributes of `top`, `bottom`, `middle`, `left`, or `right`.

- **Scrolling:** Add or remove scroll bars on the iframe by including the `scrolling` attribute in your iframe code. Use `scrolling="no"` to remove scroll bars, `scrolling="yes"` to always include scroll bars, and `scrolling="auto"` to add scroll bars as needed:

```
<iframe width="300" height="150" src="iframefile.html" align="left"
    frameborder="2" hspace="5" vspace="5" scrolling="auto"></iframe>
```

- **Show Borders:** Decide whether to include frame borders on the floating frame. Borders are displayed by default if you don't change this setting. When you select the Show Borders option, the `frameborder` attribute is absent and the browser displays a simple border. By contrast, when you deselect the Show Borders option, the `frameborder` attribute is set to 0 and the floating frame appears borderless.

6. **(Optional) Complete the fields in the Browser Specific, Style Sheet/Accessibility, and Alternate Content categories of the Tag Editor.**

   For example, you may want to add alternate content between the opening and closing `<iframe>` tags for older browsers:

```
<iframe width="300" height="150" src="iframefile.html" align="left"
    frameborder="2" hspace="5" vspace="5" scrolling="auto"><p>Click <a
    href="iframefile.html" title="Learn More" target="_self">here</a> to
    learn more.</p></iframe>
```

   Additionally, though it's not part of the Tag Editor, you can add (by hand-coding) the `long description` attribute with the URL of a page containing a long description of the contents inside the floating frame:

```
<iframe width="300" height="150" src="iframefile.html" align="left"
    frameborder="2" hspace="5" vspace="5" scrolling="auto"
    name="contactlist" longdesc="iframefiledescription.html"></iframe>
```

7. **Click OK to close the Tag Editor.**

   The iframe code is added to your page.

8. **Click the Close button to close the Tag Chooser.**

For even more precise placement of the floating frame on your page, you can envelop the `<iframe>` tags with floating `<div>` layer tags and use Cascading Style Sheets to create a style that absolutely positions the `<div>` by its `id`, and therefore, also the iframe. Here's an example:

```
<div id="floatingframe"><iframe width="300" height="150" src="iframefile.html"
    align="left"></iframe></div>
```

Your CSS to position the `<div>` could look something like this:

```
<style type="text/css">
<!--
#floatingframe {
position:absolute;
left:100px;
top:100px;
width:300px;
height:150px;
z-index:5;
}
-->
</style>
```

Although Dreamweaver can't display the iframe content in Design view, it does show an appropriately sized gray iframe placeholder box on the page, as shown in Figure 3-20. The placeholder box represents the width and height of the iframe embedded in the source code. To view the iframe content as you intend it to appear to visitors, click the Live View button or open the page in a browser window.

Figure 3-20: Although the actual iframe is displayed in a browser, Dreamweaver displays the iframe as a placeholder box in Design view.

Chapter 4: Making Your Pages XHTML-Compliant

XHTML *(eXtensible HyperText Markup Language)* is a form of HTML coding that extends document functionality by conforming to more strict *eXtensible Markup Language* (XML) rules. XML, a markup language for representing complex object relationships, is used by many Web applications and services.

XHTML is not just a cleaner and stricter version of HTML; you can also view, edit, and validate XHTML pages with standard XML tools. Plus, XHTML works wonderfully with Cascading Style Sheets (CSS) and is fully supported by Dreamweaver. (For an introductory tutorial about XML, visit www. w3schools.com/xml/default.asp.)

In 2000, the W3C proposed that XHTML be the new language for building Web pages, and in 2002, XHTML became an accepted standard, whereby all new browsers should contain built-in XHTML support. Using XHTML also ensures the forward and backward compatibility of your Web files. In other words, XHTML is the future of Web development. This chapter gives you the basics you need to get started.

Understanding the Benefits of Using XHTML with Dreamweaver

The biggest benefit of using XHTML with Dreamweaver is that Dreamweaver makes the transition from HTML to XHTML painless. Dreamweaver provides you with the option of selecting XHTML as the primary markup language each time you create a new page. In fact, XHTML is the default doctype setting, which means that Dreamweaver automatically inserts the appropriate doctype tag on the page and writes XHTML-compliant code. Furthermore, you can easily convert a page from HTML to XHTML (and XHTML to HTML, if needed) using Dreamweaver's Convert command, and have Dreamweaver perform code validation to ensure that the code is XHTML-compliant before publishing your pages online.

Creating XHTML-compliant documents in Dreamweaver is easy to do and provides both immediate and long-term benefits, including the following:

✦ **Simple transition to advanced technology:** Because the Web is moving toward XML, the simple transition to XHTML enables you to take advantage of this new technology for your Web sites.

✦ **Cleaner code:** With its strict guidelines, XHTML provides for cleaner and more uniform coding. Cleaner code means more accurate rendering in browsers.

✦ **Improved accessibility:** Users can view XHTML files not only in Web browsers but also on many different media types (such as Braille displays, screen readers, wireless devices, and other specialized Web environments), thereby providing wider access of information and improved accessibility for people with disabilities.

The key to XHTML is the concept of *extensibility.* XHTML combines HTML's ability to define the way content is displayed with XML's ability to describe how content functions. Because XHTML is an application of XML, any language with an XML parser can parse XHTML. For programmers, this means you can reuse any content you write in XHTML. *That's* extensibility.

Getting the Basics of XHTML Syntax

Before you can fully appreciate the benefits of XHTML, you have to know some important regulations. Check out the following sections for more information.

Discovering the strict rules you can't live without

XHTML is written with a strict set of rules. You must adhere to all the following rules:

✦ Specify a doctype tag before the opening `<html>` tag.

✦ Write all tags and attributes in lowercase.

✦ Surround all attribute values with double quotes (`"like this"`), as in `<p align="center">`.

✦ Assign a value to all attributes, as with `<input checked="checked">`.

✦ Replace attribute values containing special HTML characters such as &, <, and > with entity representations in number or in name. For example, if you need an ampersand, write the entity as `&#38;` or `&amp;`.

✦ Replace the `name` attribute with the `id` attribute when attaching attributes to elements except form input elements such as `<select>` or `<input>`.

✦ Close all tags without inner content, including non-container tags such as br, hr, and img, with />. For instance, the XHTML shorthand version of
</br> is <br />.

✦ Remove all special coding, such as inline style sheets and inline JavaScript, from the XHTML document and store it in separate external .css and .js files, with references in the head of your page(s) to those external files:

```
<link rel="stylesheet" type="text/css" ref="my_style.css" />
<script language="JavaScript" src="my_javascript.js"></script>
```

✦ Use CSS for text formatting in XHTML documents. XHTML doesn't support the <font> tag.

Taking advantage of strict and transitional rules

One key feature that sets XHTML apart from HTML is its use of markup that conforms to and takes advantage of XML rules used in Web applications and services. These rules, specified in the doctype, as shown in the following example, can be *strict* or *transitional*. Strict rules are better at automating data processing than transitional rules are, but both work great on plain static Web pages:

```
<!DOCTYPE html PUBLIC "-//W3C//DTD XHTML 1.0 Transitional//EN" "http://www.
    w3.org/TR/xhtml1/DTD/xhtml1-transitional.dtd">
```

XHTML files have three parts: the doctype, which states the *DTD* (document type definition); the <head>; and the <body>. The <doctype> tag defines the syntactic constraints allowed in the code as well as the usage and meaning of those constraints. The <head> and <body> areas are just like regular HTML files, with a few additional syntax rule changes in the code, such as properly closing and nesting tags (see the preceding section for more information).

You can set the DTD definition to *strict, transitional,* or *frameset.* Here are some sample DTD definitions for each type, along with descriptions:

✦ **Strict:** Use this DTD with Cascading Style Sheets:

```
<!DOCTYPE html PUBLIC "-//W3C//DTD XHTML 1.0 Strict//EN"
    "http://www.w3.org/TR/xhtml1/DTD/xhtml1-strict.dtd">
```

✦ **Transitional:** Choose the Transitional DTD with HTML and CSS. For example, you can add the bgcolor attribute to the <body> tag when you want to ensure that your pages render accurately in older browsers that don't support CSS:

```
<!DOCTYPE html PUBLIC "-//W3C//DTD XHTML 1.0 Transitional//EN"
    "http://www.w3.org/TR/xhtml1/DTD/xhtml1-transitional.dtd">
```

✦ **Frameset:** Use this DTD with frames:

```
<!DOCTYPE html PUBLIC "-//W3C//DTD XHTML 1.0 Frameset//EN"
    "http://www.w3.org/TR/xhtml1/DTD/xhtml1-frameset.dtd">
```

Book IV
Chapter 4

Making Your Pages
XHTML-Compliant

To learn more about XHTML 1.0, visit the World Wide Web Consortium (W3C) Web site, where you can find information about the XHTML 1.0 specification (`www.w3c.org/TR/xhtml1/`), DTD definitions (`www.w3.org/TR/xhtml1/dtds.html`), and free online tools for markup validation of published Web sites (`http://validator.w3.org/`) and unpublished local files (`http://validator.w3.org/file-upload.html`).

Handling Dreamweaver's Automatic XHTML Code Compliance Tools

In the New Document window, seen here in Figure 4-1, Dreamweaver gives you the option of selecting an XHTML Document Type Definition (DTD) for generating and cleaning up your XHTML code:

✦ XHTML 1.0 Transitional.

✦ XHTML 1.0 Strict.

✦ XHTML 1.1.

✦ XHTML Mobile 1.0.

✦ XHTML 1.0 Frameset. (This option is not specifically selectable when creating new HTML pages. Instead, the correct XHTML Frameset DTD is automatically added to your code each time you create a new frameset.)

Figure 4-1:
Select an XHTML DTD from the New Document window.

Each of these DTDs renders XHTML-compliant code. If you're unsure which DTD to use, select XHTML 1.0 Transitional.

After you select a DTD, Dreamweaver writes code that automatically meets XHTML requirements. Table 4-1 provides an overview of these requirements.

Table 4-1	Dreamweaver XHTML Compliance
XHTML Code Requirements	*Dreamweaver Automatically Writes XHTML Compliant Code*
The page must contain a doctype declaration above the opening HTML or XHTML tag and must include one of the three DTD files for XHTML (strict, transitional, or frameset).	For regular, noframe XHTML documents, adds either the traditional or the strict doctype to the file: `<!DOCTYPE html PUBLIC "-//W3C//DTD XHTML 1.0 Transitional//EN" "http://www.w3.org/TR/xhtml1/DTD/xhtml1-transitional.dtd">` `<!DOCTYPE html PUBLIC "-//W3C//DTD XHTML 1.0 Strict//EN" "http://www.w3.org/TR/xhtml1/DTD/xhtml1-strict.dtd">`For XHTML files with framesets, adds the following doctype to the file: `<!DOCTYPE html PUBLIC "-//W3C//DTD XHTML 1.0 Frameset//EN" "http://www.w3.org/TR/xhtml1/DTD/xhtml1-frameset.dtd">`
The page's root element must be HTML and it must designate the XHTML namespace. The namespace is an attribute of the HTML tag that defines the document as XML.	Adds the `html` root element and `namespace` attribute to the opening HTML tag as follows: `<html xmlns="http://www.w3.org/1999/xhtml">`
All XHTML files must have `head`, `title`, and `body` elements, and all framesets must have `head`, `title`, and `frameset` elements.	Includes the `head`, `title`, and `body` elements in all XHTML files, and includes the `head`, `title`, and `frameset` elements in all frameset XHTML files.
Any included script or style element in the code must have a `type` attribute. For example, the `type` attribute of the `stylesheet` element is `text/css`.	Adds the `type` and `language` attributes to `script` elements, and adds the `type` attribute to `style` elements for all newly generated code. Both are added, if missing, when cleaning up XHTML.

(continued)

Table 4-1 *(continued)*

XHTML Code Requirements	*Dreamweaver Automatically Writes XHTML Compliant Code*
All element and attribute names must be coded in lowercase.	Makes sure that all element and attribute names are lowercase for all newly generated XHTML code, and converts text to lowercase when cleaning up XHTML with the Clean Up XHTML command.
All area and img elements must have the alt attribute.	Adds the alt attribute to newly generated code, and inserts the alt attribute, if missing, when cleaning up XHTML. Missing alt attributes are also part of validation reports.
Elements must use proper nesting. For example: `<p><b>This is incorrect.` `</p></b>` `<p><b>This is correct.</b></p>`	Writes properly nested code and corrects bad nesting from code generated outside Dreamweaver with the Clean Up XHTML command.
All elements must have closing tags, unless specifically declared in the DTD as empty.	Adds closing tags to all newly generated code and adds missing closing tags when cleaning up XHTML.
All empty elements must have closing tags or have opening tags ending with `/>`. This includes noncontainer tags such as ` `, `<hr>`, and `<img>`. For instance, ` ` would no longer be valid, but ` </br>` and ` ` are valid and acceptable formats. This requirement applies to the following empty elements: area, base, basefont, br, col, frame, hr, img, input, isindex, link, meta, and param. The preferred method for backward-compatibility in non-XML-enabled browsers is to add a space before the `/>` when closing noncontainer tags, as in `<hr />`, not `<hr/>`.	Adds the appropriate space before the closing slash (" /") to all empty elements and noncontainer tags both when generating new code and cleaning up XHTML.

XHTML Code Requirements	Dreamweaver Automatically Writes XHTML Compliant Code
All attributes with no value must be assigned a value, as with `<input checked="checked">`. The old minimized format, `<input checked>`, is not valid. This requirement applies to the following attributes: `checked`, `compact`, `declare`, `defer`, `disabled`, `ismap`, `multiple`, `noresize`, `noshade`, `nowrap`, `readonly`, and `selected`.	Adds quotation marks around all attribute-value pairs in newly generated code, and corrects invalid coding when cleaning up XHTML. **Note:** This feature is for browsers that support HTML 4 and above. For older browsers, these Boolean attributes may not be displayed accurately.
All attribute values must be surrounded by double (`"`) quotes: `<p align="center">`.	Adds quotation marks around all attribute values for newly generated code, and adds missing quote marks as needed when cleaning up XHTML.
The `id` attribute must replace the `name` attribute or be inserted in addition to the `name` attribute, when attaching attributes to all elements except form input elements such as `<select>` or `<input>`. This requirement applies to the following: `a`, `applet`, `form`, `frame`, `iframe`, `img`, and `map`. For example, `<a name="FAQ1">FAQ Answer 1</a>` is not valid because it lacks the `id` attribute. The correct form includes both `id` and `name` attributes: `<a name="FAQ1" id="FAQ1">FAQ Answer 1</a>`.	Adds both the `name` and `id` attributes to the same value, when the `name` attribute is entered in the Properties Inspector, when generating new code, and when cleaning up XHTML.
Attributes with enumerated type values must be coded in lowercase. The enumerated type value is a value that can be chosen from a list of possible values, as with the ordered list `<ol>` `type` attribute, which allows values equal to Number, Roman Small, Roman Larger, Alphabet Small, and Alphabet Larger (1, I, i, A, and a).	Writes these enumerated type values in lowercase for new code, and adjusts the case when cleaning up XHTML.

**Book IV
Chapter 4**

**Making Your Pages
XHTML-Compliant**

Making Sure Your Documents Follow XHTML Syntax

Dreamweaver's preferences allow you to set the default DTD for your files. If you set the default DTD to XHTML 1.0 Transitional, for example, every time you create a new Dreamweaver document, it is automatically XHTML-compliant. Furthermore, if you're working with existing HTML files, you can tell Dreamweaver to convert the HTML code to XHTML-compliant markup using Dreamweaver's Convert XHTML command.

Creating a new XHTML document with Dreamweaver

Each time you create a new document, you can choose to have Dreamweaver write XHTML code instead of HTML code. Here's what you need to do:

1. **Choose File⇨New.**

   The New Document window appears.

2. **Choose a page category and type.**

   For XHTML files, select the Blank Page, Blank Template, or Page from Sample page category and then choose a Page, Template, or Sample Type from the center pane. For example, you could select the Blank Page category and the HTML Page Type.

3. **Select an XHTML document type in the Document Type (DTD) drop-down list.**

   Choose XHTML 1.0 Transitional, XHTML 1.0 Strict, XHTML 1.1, or XHTML 1.0 Mobile as the DTD. If you're creating a frameset, the appropriate XHTML Frameset DTD is automatically inserted in your frameset page when you select any XHTML DTD types.

4. **Click the Create button.**

   The new document opens in the Dreamweaver workspace window and any content you add to your page automatically conforms to XHTML rules.

Changing the default DTD

You can set up Dreamweaver to create files using a different DTD than the default XHTML 1.0 Transitional DTD by editing settings in the Preferences dialog box. Follow these steps:

1. **Choose Edit⇨Preferences (Windows) or Dreamweaver⇨Preferences (Mac).**

   The Preferences dialog box appears.

2. **Select the New Document category (shown in Figure 4-2), and then select one of the DTDs in the Default Document Type (DTD) drop-down list.**

Choose from XHTML 1.0 Transitional, XHTML 1.0 Strict, XHTML 1.1, or XHTML Mobile 1.0 for XHTML, or HTML 4.01 Transitional, HTML 4.01 Strict, or HTML 5 for HTML. If you're creating a frameset, the appropriate XHTML Frameset DTD is automatically inserted into your frameset page when you select any of the XHTML DTD types. If you're not sure about which option to select, choose XHTML 1.0 Transitional, which allows for both HTML and CSS markup and is a little less strict than XHTML 1.0 Strict.

3. **Click OK.**

Figure 4-2:
Set the default document type definition to XHTML.

Dreamweaver is now set up to write XHTML-compliant code for all new documents.

Transforming HTML document code into XHTML

Choose Commands➪Clean Up XHTML to have Dreamweaver get rid of any HTML inconsistencies and make sure your documents are XHTML-compliant. Dreamweaver does everything it needs to do — automatically — to instantly convert tag attributes to all lowercase, correct syntax errors, and add or report missing required tag attributes, such as images with missing `alt` attributes. For more detailed information on cleaning up your code with the Clean Up HTML/XHTML command, see Book V, Chapter 2.

Converting existing HTML files to XHTML

If you want to turn your existing HTML documents into XHTML documents, we could give you a set of complicated steps, but why should we? The reality is that Dreamweaver makes this task so remarkably simple that you may actually wonder if you've missed something. Simply open an HTML document in the Dreamweaver workspace window and perform one of the following tasks:

✦ If your HTML file doesn't use frames, choose File⇨Convert and select an XHTML DTD type.

✦ If your HTML file uses frames, select the frameset, choose File⇨Convert, and select XHTML 1.0 Frameset. Then place your cursor inside a document in any of the frames in the frameset, choose File⇨Convert, and select an XHTML DTD type. The HTML code in the frameset converts from HTML to XHTML. Repeat this process for each document that appears inside a frame in the frameset.

Note regarding XHTML and Framesets: Although it doesn't really matter if you mix and match DTDs, you should probably choose one type and stick with it for the entire frameset. If you're unsure which DTD to select for the pages that are displayed in the frames of your frameset, use XHTML 1.0 Transitional.

Making sure your HTML file can be converted to XHTML

Although we wish it weren't true, some HTML files can't be converted to XHTML, and not all files can be made XHTML-compliant. For example, some template-based files written in HTML can't be converted to XHTML because the converted file must be in the same language as the template file.

The best way to determine whether you can convert one of your HTML files to XHTML is to test it. After converting the file, try entering a few line breaks to the code. If the code looks like <br />, the conversion was a success. To ensure that your code is fully compliant after the conversion, however, choose Commands⇨Clean Up XHTML to perform XHTML validation on all your documents. Check out Book V, Chapter 2 for more information about this useful tool.

Validating Your XHTML

Dreamweaver has a built-in tool for validating your XHTML code. The tool looks for any tag or syntax code errors and lets you know what it thinks you should do by displaying a convenient report. In addition to validating XHTML, this tool validates HTML, XML, JavaServer Pages (JSP), ColdFusion Markup Language (CFML), and Wireless Markup Language (WML). For step-by-step instructions on validating your XHTML, as well as other tips on using reports to test your site before publishing, see Book V, Chapter 1.

Book V

Publishing Your Site

The 5th Wave   By Rich Tennant

"We're here to clean the code."

Contents at a Glance

Chapter 1: Using Reports to Test Your Site before Publishing

In This Chapter

✔ Previewing your site before you publish it

✔ Testing your pages with the Results panel

✔ Validating your code

✔ Checking and fixing broken links

*B*efore you publish your Web site on the Internet, you need to spend some time reviewing your site content to address possible accessibility issues, spelling errors, broken links, orphaned files, and code syntax problems. The benefits of following some general testing guidelines are endless. Nothing is worse than a site that doesn't work as it should. That's why this chapter gives you expert advice on performing browser compatibility checks, shows you how to test your pages with browser page previews and the use of Adobe BrowserLab, and helps you adjust page download times for site visitors.

Even when taking extreme care during the site building process in Dreamweaver, only rarely will a created Web site be perfect. No matter how hard you try, most finished sites will include one or two browser compatibility issues, spelling errors, and an occasional broken link. Making testing a priority before publication helps catch these issues so you can present a professional quality product on the Web, which will set your site apart.

Dreamweaver comes with several tools that help you tinker with your site until everything's perfect. First, you can use the powerful HTML and Workflow reports. These tools enable you to review your page content and make important improvements before publishing. In addition, the Results panel has several site evaluation tools that you can run to streamline testing and correcting problems. This chapter shows you how to use the Results panel to search code, validate tags, test pages for potential problems in specified target browsers, fix links, use the FTP log, and run a Server Debug report. You can also use the Preferences dialog box to determine page-loading times for the best viewing experience.

Testing Your Site

You've put all the work into getting your site together, and now all you want to do is publish the darn thing. Well, not so fast. You have to go through the essential testing phase before the site goes live.

In fact, you should test your site and fix problems throughout the entire Web site building process. But if you've waited until now to test your site, that's okay too.

All your site's pages should look good and function as you intend them to in all the browsers you're targeting. Browser testing should include verifying the accuracy of your links and checking download times for your larger files. Running reports can be a crucial part of this process; you can run several built-in reports from Dreamweaver's Results panel to make sure that all the code is right on the money.

Following general testing guidelines

Your main goal, ultimately, is to build a Web site that users enjoy viewing and navigating. If you follow these few simple guidelines, you'll be well on your way:

✦ **Preview your pages in as many browsers and browser versions as possible, on both Macs and PCs, to ensure browser compatibility.** You need to verify that the pages work the way you intend them to — or fail in a way that's acceptable to you — so make sure that you spend some time previewing every combination of browser version and operating system you can think of. Your Web pages should look good in browsers that both support and don't support JavaScript, layers, CSS, and plug-ins. If you don't have access to multiple browsers on a Mac and a PC, be sure you test your pages in Adobe's BrowserLab. (See the section "Previewing Pages in Adobe BrowserLab," later in the chapter, to learn more).

✦ **Check your links — both internal and external — and fix any that are broken or don't work as you intended.** The Link Check report tests internal links and identifies any that are broken, external, and orphaned. See the "Checking and Fixing Links" section, later in this chapter, for more details.

✦ **Check the file sizes of all your Web pages and pay attention to their download times.** When pages have a lot of content, especially when they include large graphic files, some or all page content may not be displayed in the browser until all the data finishes loading.

✦ **Run reports on your site.** Always test for potential errors and common coding omissions or mistakes, such as missing alt attributes on images, untitled files, and redundant or improperly nested tags. (See the "Searching Your Code for Tags and Attributes" section, later in this chapter).

✦ **Validate all your tags.** Validating tags is the best way to ensure that your code syntax meets compliance standards. If you find any broken or missing information, fix it now before you publish the site. (See the "Validating Your Code" section, later in this chapter.)

After you publish the site and begin to maintain it, continue to check the site regularly for possible errors, such as broken links, browser incompatibilities, and problematic HTML, JavaScript, and CSS. For help with specific issues, visit the Dreamweaver discussion forums on the Adobe Web site at `http://forums.adobe.com/index.jspa`. There you can find forum discussions related to common browser and platform issues as well as technical notes and helpful tips from other Dreamweaver users.

Previewing your pages in multiple browsers

Dreamweaver CS5 writes code that supports all the current industry standards and best practices, such as the use of advanced CSS, RSS, and XML feeds and accessibility requirements. The most recent versions of the main graphical browsers — Internet Explorer, Firefox, Safari, Opera, and Google Chrome — also support XHTML and Cascading Style Sheets, but not necessarily all in the same manner. The only way to know for sure whether your site will look good in all your target browsers is to check for compatibility and display issues in each browser on both Mac and PC platforms.

When fashioning a Web site, determining your target audience for the site is helpful. If you know your target, you can figure out what browsers users are likely to have. For example, if you're building an intranet site for employees who all use new PCs running the latest version of Internet Explorer, the need to test the site on other browsers isn't as critical. On the other hand, if you're building a site selling widgets on the Internet, it's essential to test a variety of operating systems and as many browsers and browser versions as possible.

You should also use the Target Browser Check report to assist you with the testing of your site in multiple browsers. This test checks the code in your files and reports tags, attributes, and CSS values and properties that are unsupported by your target browsers without altering any code. You can find out how to run the Target Browser Check report and use all the report features in the "Testing Your Pages with Browser Compatibility" section, later in this chapter.

Setting the primary and secondary browsers

Dreamweaver enables you to specify two browsers as the primary and secondary browsers that launch locally on your desktop for page previews using Dreamweaver's Preview in Browser keyboard shortcuts. To specify the primary and secondary preview browsers, follow these steps:

1. **Choose File➪Preview in Browser➪Edit Browser List.**

   You can launch the preferences also by choosing Edit➪Preferences (Windows) or Dreamweaver➪Preferences (Mac). The Preferences dialog box appears, as shown in Figure 1-1.

Figure 1-1: Add browsers and set primary and secondary browser options.

2. **Select the Preview in Browser category from the Category list on the left side of the Preferences dialog box, and then choose a browser in the browser list on the right.**

   To add or remove browsers from the list, see Step 3 and 4. Otherwise, skip to Step 5.

3. **To add a browser to the list of browsers, click the plus (+) icon, enter information about the browser in the Add Browser dialog box that appears, and then click OK.**

   In the Name field, type the browser name and version, such as IE 8.0. In the Application field, browse to and select the browser's application file. When you click OK, the new browser appears in the browser listing.

   Add as many browsers as you like to this list. Although you can select only two browsers as the primary and secondary browsers for launching with a keyboard shortcut, you can preview your page with any of the browsers installed on your computer, as described in the next section.

4. **To delete a browser from the list of browsers, select the browser you want to delete and click the minus (–) icon.**

   Deleted browser names immediately disappear from the list.

5. **To set the Primary browser, select a browser from the list and select the Defaults Primary Browser option.**

6. **To set the Secondary browser, select another browser from the list and select the Defaults Secondary Browser option.**

   Now you can press F12 (Windows) or Option+F12 (Mac) and your open document launches in the primary browser; pressing Ctrl+F12 (Windows) and ⌘+F12 (Mac) launches your open file in the secondary browser.

7. **(Optional) Select or deselect the Preview Using Temporary File option.**

   When selected, this option tells your computer to create a temporary copy of the file in the browser window for previewing and server debugging. When this option is deselected, the document may not be displayed accurately in the browser; however, you can make updates and changes directly to the file.

Previewing pages in multiple browsers locally

When you design pages in Dreamweaver, Design view provides you with only a general idea of how your page looks in a browser window. Design view can't display every part of CSS, some dynamic features such as JavaScript, or the subtle HTML display differences between browsers. Likewise, clicking the Live View button on the Document toolbar can show you roughly how your page looks in a generic browser, but it is not yet capable of rendering all features of a Web page as a real browser would. Therefore, the only way to truly see exactly how a page looks to visitors is to preview the page in individual browsers. You should test all the pages on your site on as many browsers as possible and on both the Mac and Windows platforms.

Fortunately, with Dreamweaver, you can locally preview and test your pages in more than one browser at a time. To set which browsers you want Dreamweaver to test, check out the preceding section, "Setting the primary and secondary browsers." Then follow these simple steps:

1. **To preview your page in your primary browser, press F12 (Windows) or Option+F12 (Mac).**

   The document launches in the specified primary browser.

2. **To preview your page in your secondary browser, press Ctrl+F12 (Windows) or ⌘+F12 (Mac).**

   The document launches in the specified secondary browser.

3. **To preview the file in another browser, choose File➪Preview in Browser to select any of the browsers from the Preview list.**

   Repeat this step as necessary to view the file in additional browsers.

4. **Verify the links, dynamic content, and layout of the page.**

Check all your JavaScript behaviors, links, plug-ins, ActiveX controls, and any other media files installed on the page.

If some content on your page isn't displayed accurately in one or more of your target browsers, you have work ahead of you. For example, your page may need adjustments to some JavaScript behaviors, CSS, or other features on the page.

If you're testing your page with Internet Explorer on a computer running Windows XP with Service Pack 2, the browser may display a message that some content on the page has been restricted. You can correct this problem by typing the Mark of the Web code into the `<head>` of your page:

```
<!-- saved from url=(0014)about:internet -->
```

If you want to include the code in your published projects, you should customize the URL by having it point to your domain name. You also need to modify the number, such as (0028), to match the number of characters in your domain name, starting with the h in `http` and ending with the last letter of your domain name, as with the m of `.com` in the following example:

```
<!-- saved from url=(0028)http://www.yourdomainURL.com -->
```

When you have finished testing, you can either leave the code in place or remove it by hand before you publish your site.

Previewing pages in Adobe BrowserLab

Most people building Web sites own (or use) one computer, usually a PC running Windows or a Mac running an Apple OS, and thus can test their Web sites on only that computer's platform. To be a smart designer, however, you must be willing to test on more than one platform. At minimum, you should test your Web site on PC, Mac, and Linux platforms.

In the past, to be thorough testers, designers had to take pains to get an idea of how their site looks in different browsers on the missing platform. For example, they would have to purchase another computer (or two) just for testing, use multiplatform software to run multiple operating systems on the same machine, install and use some kind of browser simulator software, or use an online site testing service such as `browsershots.org`, `crossbrowsertesting.com`, or `browsercamp.com`.

Today, thanks to the folks over in Adobe Labs, all you need to do to test your site on multiple Mac and PC browsers is to head over to the Adobe BrowserLab Web site. You can quickly access BrowserLab from Dreamweaver through a link in the Access CS Live menu. Dreamweaver displays an Adobe BrowserLab panel, as shown in Figure 1-2, where you can establish a connection with the BrowserLab Web site and choose to preview the open page locally or on a testing server. Or, if you want to access the site directly in your browser, go to http://browserlab.adobe.com.

Figure 1-2:
Log in to
Adobe
BrowserLab
to test your
pages in
different
browsers.

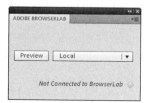

Whether you click the link or go directly to the Web site, click the Preview button to have Dreamweaver automatically launch a browser window connected to Adobe BrowserLab. When the window opens, you are prompted to log in with your Adobe ID. If you don't have an Adobe account, visit www. adobe.com/membership to create one.

After you sign in, the page you have open in your Dreamweaver workspace is displayed in Adobe BrowserLab. You may also test pages already hosted on the Web by typing the URL in the BrowserLab's address bar. In addition, the BrowserLab Web site allows you to select a 1-up, 2-up, or onion skin viewing area to compare browsers, hide and show rulers, create horizontal and vertical guides, adjust the page magnification, set a delay for taking screenshots, access a list of hot keys, select specific browsers and browser sets, and search for help.

BrowserLab currently supports the following browsers: IE (Windows XP 6.0, 7.0, and 8.0), Firefox (Windows XP 2.0, 3.0, and 3.5), Firefox (OS X 2.0, 3.0, and 3.5), Safari (OS X 3.0 and 4.0), and Google Chrome (Windows XP 3.0).

For additional help with using Adobe BrowserLab, visit http://help. adobe.com/en_US/BrowserLab/.

Setting download times and size

Dreamweaver provides you with important download times and size data to help you control the way visitors with varying connection speeds experience your pages.

Dreamweaver calculates the file size of an open document by counting the kilobytes (K) of all text and linked objects, such as images and Flash movies, and then provides a download time estimate based on the default connection speed (kilobits per second, or Kbps) you've entered in the Status Bar preferences. You can use this information to determine whether to modify the page to improve its load time.

The average time visitors connecting at 56Kbps are willing to wait for a page to be displayed without feedback is eight seconds. Thus, your goal should be to get all your pages up and working in a browser in less than eight seconds. If your page weighs in at higher than 30K, you may want to consider reducing the number of objects or linked assets on the page (for example, using CSS rollovers instead of graphic rollovers) to help lower the overall file size.

By default, the connection speed in the Status Bar preferences is set to 56K, but you can change this setting to another speed. For example, when designing a site for an intranet on a T-1 (1500Kbps speed) circuit, you can change the preference to 1500 kilobits per second. To set the download time and size preferences, follow these steps:

1. **Choose Edit⇨Preferences (Windows) or Dreamweaver⇨Preferences (Mac).**

The Preferences dialog box appears.

2. **Click the Status Bar category on the left side of the dialog box.**

Status Bar preference options appear on the right side of the dialog box, as shown in Figure 1-3.

Figure 1-3:
Choose a
connection
speed in the
Status Bar
preferences.

3. **Select a connection speed in the Connection Speed drop-down list at the bottom of the dialog box.**

Dreamweaver uses the speed you select to estimate the download time of your page. Although it's important to think about dial-up users, the majority of Web users are on some sort of higher speed connection, so changing the default connection speed from 56.0Kbps to something faster may give you a more accurate representation of Web site visitors. (See Book I, Chapter 2 for more information on building a site for a target audience.)

Examining the Results Panel

Dreamweaver offers several reports that enable you to quickly find, test, and fix the content on your Web pages from one convenient location: the Results panel. To view the Results panel, choose Window⇨Results and choose one of the options from the submenu, or press F7.

The Results panel, shown in Figure 1-4, has several tabs that provide access to the following report types:

Stop

Play

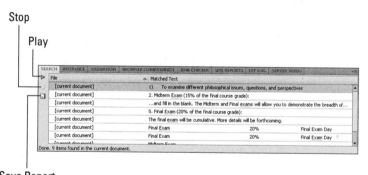

Figure 1-4:
The Results
panel.

Save Report

+ **Search:** Search your code for your tags and attributes.

+ **Reference:** Find reference information about HTML, XHTML, CSS, JavaScript, Accessibility, and programming languages.

+ **Validation:** Validate your code.

+ **Browser Compatibility:** Test your page with a targeted browser.

+ **Link Checker:** Check and fix links.

+ **Site Reports:** Run several Workflow and HTML reports.

+ **FTP Log:** View file transfer activity.

+ **Server Debug:** Debug a ColdFusion application.

A green arrow icon (a triangular icon reminiscent of a Play icon in a media player) appears at the left of the panel in every tab view except the

Reference and FTP Log tabs. Clicking the Arrow icon launches the reports related to the active tab.

The following sections discuss how you can use the Results panel to view reports and fix problems throughout your site.

Searching Your Code for Tags and Attributes

If any of the reports identify problems in your code, you may want to globally correct those problems throughout your entire Web site. Use the Search tab of the Results panel to open Dreamweaver's Find and Replace dialog box. The Find and Replace tool enables you to search for specific text, tags, and attributes in text or source code in a document, selected files, a specific folder, or all the files in a defined site. After a search string is located, you can replace that text, tag, code, or content with new information.

Turn to Book II, Chapter 2 to find out how to search for specific tags and attributes, search for text in specific tags, save and reuse search strings, and search using regular expressions.

Looking Up Reference Information

Built right into the Dreamweaver interface is instant local access to a library of reference information about HTML, XHTML, CSS, JavaScript, Accessibility, and several programming languages such as ColdFusion, ColdFusion Markup Language, ASP, ASP.NET, JSP, PHP, SQL, XML, and SXLT.

In the Reference tab of the Results panel, you can select the desired book of information from the Book menu, and then refine your search using the other menus that appear within the panel. For instance, when you select the O'Reilly HTML Reference book, you can refine your search by tag and attribute type.

You can use the Reference tab also to learn more about your current selection in Code view by choosing Reference from the Code view context menu (right-click in Windows or Control+click on the Mac) or by pressing the F1 key.

Spend a little time clicking around in the Reference tab to get a feel for the kind of information you can find here. This valuable resource is worth hundreds of dollars!

Validating Your Code

The Validation tab checks HTML or XHTML code in the current document, entire current local site, or selected files in the site for tag, syntax, and other common formatting errors. It checks in many languages such as HTML, XHTML, JavaServer Pages (JSP), ColdFusion Markup Language (CFML), XML, and Wireless Markup Language (WML). It then displays the results by File, Line, and Description (see Figure 1-5).

Figure 1-5:
The
Validation
panel.

Using the Validation tab

To validate your HTML/XHTML code, follow these steps:

1. **On the Validation tab of the Results panel, click the green Validate arrow icon and select a validation option from the menu.**

You can choose to validate the current page only, the entire local site, or selected files (from the Files panel) on the site. You can validate code for a single page also by choosing File⇨Validate⇨Markup. If your page uses XHTML or XML, however, choose File⇨Validate⇨As XML instead.

The validation results are displayed on the Validation tab of the Results panel and include messages about errors and warnings as well as a list of all the syntax and tag errors Dreamweaver detected (see Figure 1-5).

Results are displayed as errors, warnings, or messages. See the "Testing Your Pages with Browser Compatibility" section, later in this chapter, for details about each of these result types.

If the report finds no code errors, Dreamweaver displays a *No errors or warning* message. Congratulations!

2. **To fix an error, a warning, or a message in the results listing, double-click the error, warning, or message in the Validation tab list.**

The document with the error opens in the Document window and the error is highlighted, ready for you to fix it. If you want, you can correct these changes directly in the document code, and then rerun the validation report to ensure that the changes are compliant.

To find out more about any of the errors in the list, right-click (Windows) or Control+click (Mac) the error message in the list and select More Info from the context menu. The complete error message appears in its own pop-up window. This feature works for all results listed in the Validation, Browser Compatibility, and Site Reports tabs of the Results panel.

3. **(Optional) Click the Save Report icon to save the report as an XML file.**

The Save Report icon looks like a floppy disk and can be found on the left edge of the Results panel (refer to Figure 1-5). It's easy to open an XML file in Microsoft Excel and then create a spreadsheet from it for tracking, such as marking off files, errors, and status.

4. **Click the Browse Report icon to see and print the report from a browser window.**

The Browse Report icon looks like a tiny picture of the earth and can be found on the left edge of the Results panel (refer to Figure 1-5).

Setting Validation tab preferences

The Validation tab quickly finds syntax problems in your code based on the validation rules you specify in Dreamweaver's Preferences. After you set these rules, they are used to check for specific tag-based languages or problems in the code. Keep in mind, however, that the Validator preferences settings are ignored if your file contains a different doctype than the one specified.

To set Dreamweaver's Validator preferences, follow these steps:

1. **Choose Edit⇨Preferences (Windows) or Dreamweaver⇨Preferences (Mac).**

The Preferences dialog box appears.

2. **Select the Validator category to view the Validator preferences (see Figure 1-6).**

Figure 1-6:
Customize the Validator preferences.

3. **Select a doctype for Dreamweaver to validate against when no doc-type is specified in the file.**

You can select only one doctype at a time, such as XHTML 1.0 Transitional.

4. **Click the Options button to set specific Validator options.**

The Display options enable you to set the type of errors or warnings included in the Results panel. By default, all options are selected and are universal for all doctypes.

You can also have the Validator check for quotes or entries in text. Both options are selected by default in the Check For options. Leaving the Quotes in Text option selected tells Dreamweaver to include warnings about quotation marks in the document text. For XHTML compliancy, you should use the " entity rather than quotation marks. Leaving the Entities in Text option selected tells Dreamweaver to find certain characters in the text and convert them to their entity equivalents, such as & instead of &.

5. **Click OK to close the Validator Options box, and click OK again to close the Preferences dialog box.**

Changes to the Validator Preferences go into effect immediately, but you can modify them at any time.

Testing Your Pages with Browser Compatibility

The Browser Compatibility report tests your HTML files for any tags or attri-butes that are deprecated (such as <b>, <i>, <center>, or <font>) or are unsupported by the target browsers on your computer (such as the height attribute of the <table> tag in Firefox 1.0, and Safari 1.0 and 2.0). This is much different than simply previewing your page in a browser, as described earlier in this chapter, which only shows you how the page would look in a particular browser but doesn't identify the source code causing a display error.

You can run the Browser Compatibility report on the current document, the entire local site, or selected files (from the Files panel) of a site. After making corrections to the files on your site, you can run the report again to ensure that your changes haven't caused any other browser issues.

Before you run the Browser Compatibility report, set the target browsers for the report, as described in the next section, so that error results are returned for the browsers you want.

Setting the target browsers for Browser Compatibility

You can target several browsers for the Browser Compatibility report to test code against, regardless of whether you have all the browsers installed on your computer. For example, if you're working on a PC platform, you can still test for Safari on a Mac.

To set the target browsers for the Browser Compatibility report, follow these steps:

1. **Open the Results panel and then click the Browser Compatibility tab**

2. **Click the green Check Browser Compatibility arrow icon, and then select Settings.**

   The Target Browsers dialog box appears, as shown in Figure 1-7.

Figure 1-7: Select several browsers and browser version in the Target Browsers dialog box.

3. **If they're not already selected, add a check mark next to each browser against which you want to verify code in the Target Browser Check report.**

4. **Next to each selected browser, choose a minimum browser version against which you want to verify the code.**

   For example, to verify code against Safari, put a check mark next to Safari and select 1.0, 2.0, or 3.0 as the browser version.

   At a minimum, you should consider selecting Internet Explorer 6.0, Netscape 8.0, Safari 2.0, Opera 8.0, and Firefox 1.5.

   For the latest information about trends in browser usage, operating systems, and screen resolution, visit the w3schools.com Web site at www.w3schools.com/browsers/browsers_stats.asp.

5. **Click OK to close the dialog box and save your changes.**

   The browsers you selected are included in the Browser Compatibility report results.

Using the Browser Compatibility tab

To run a Browser Compatibility report, follow these steps:

1. Open the Results panel, and then click the Browser Compatibility tab.

You can run this report against the code in the current document, the entire local site, or selected files in the site. If you want to check specific files only, select them in the Files panel before proceeding to Step 2.

2. Click the green Check Target Browsers arrow icon to select the Check Browser Compatibility for this report.

The report runs and returns the results in the Results panel.

3. If the report takes a long time to generate and you want to stop it before it's complete, click the Cancel icon.

The Cancel icon appears on the left edge of the Browsers Compatibility tab.

The Browser Compatibility report defines three levels of problems: *error, warning,* and *informational message,* each easily identifiable by an icon next to the filename that contains the potential problem, as shown in Figure 1-8:

Figure 1-8:
The Browser Compatibility report.

Error

Warning

Informational message

+ **Error:** This message, displayed with a red polygon and a white exclamation mark, identifies code problems that may cause display issues in a particular browser or issues with unsupported tags that may cause an unknown problem. A typical error alert about an unsupported value looks like this: *Unsupported value: 'left' Affects: Firefox 1.5, 2.0, 3.0; Netscape 8.0; Safari 2.0, 3.0.*

+ **Warning:** Code identified with a yellow triangle and a white exclamation mark is a warning. This code won't be displayed correctly in a specified browser, but it probably won't cause additional or serious display issues. The following message about an unsupported property is a typical warning: *Unsupported property: min-height is only supported on TDs. Affects: Internet Explorer 6.0.*

✦ **Message:** Code marked with an informational white word balloon means that a particular browser doesn't support the identified bit of code. Coding found here probably doesn't have any visible effect that alters the display of the page in the browser. Rather, the message is for your information and nothing you have to worry about or respond to. For example, ignored tag attributes such as the `<html xmlns="http://www.w3.org/1999/xhtml">` HTML tag give rise to the following benign informational message: *The xmlns attribute of the HTML tag is not supported, but it has no detrimental effect. [Netscape Navigator 6.0, Netscape Navigator 7.0].*

You can perform other tasks in the Browser Compatibility tab, such as the following:

✦ **View long error messages:** Long error messages may be truncated in the Results panel. To see the complete long error messages, click the More Info icon on the left side of the panel. A Description dialog box appears showing the full error message and the browsers and browser versions that don't support the code.

✦ **Jump to code:** Double-click the error message in the Results panel. Problematic code is highlighted in the open file in Code view. This trick helps speed up the correction process!

✦ **Jump to next or previous error:** Click Next Error or Previous Error in the Browser Compatibility menu on the Document toolbar. This is just another useful way to jump directly to any code that may be problematic and speeds up the process of fixing any errors in the code by hand.

✦ **Fix errors:** Make changes directly in Code view or in the Browser Compatibility panel. You can find out how to fix errors in the next section, "Viewing and fixing errors."

✦ **Save a Report:** Click the Save Report icon on the left edge of the panel and save the report in the location of your choice with the .doc, .txt. or .html file extension.

✦ **View a report in a browser:** To see a copy of the report in a browser, click the Browse Report icon on the left edge of the panel.

✦ **Ignore specific errors:** Right-click (Windows) or Control+click (Mac) any red underlined tag or attribute in Code view and choose Ignore Error from the context menu. The errors you ignore are converted into warnings. From then on, Dreamweaver stops displaying that error type with the red wavy underline in Code view for all documents.

✦ **Edit the Ignored Issues list:** Choose Edit Ignored Issues List from the context menu in the Browser Compatibility panel. The Exceptions.xml file opens, and you can manually make changes to the exceptions listing.

Viewing and fixing errors

You can easily see the errors in the code of a document identified in the Browser Compatibility results listing. A wavy red or green underline in the code indicates that Dreamweaver has identified problematic code that may cause an error in one or more of your specified target browsers. Double-click any error in the results listing to open that document in the Dreamweaver workspace in Code or Split Code view; If Dreamweaver doesn't identify any errors, you don't see any wavy underlines in the code; instead, you see the No Errors icon on the Document toolbar to the right of the Title text box where the Browser Compatibility icon was displayed before.

You need to analyze errors in Code view to find out the best way to resolve them. Here are some tips:

+ **Warnings alert you to browser support issues:** Results that have the Warning icon next to them are highlighted in the code rather than underlined when double-clicked. Select the result in question under the Issue column on the left side of the panel to view the specific browser issue in the Browser Support Issue area on the right side of the panel.

+ **Hover the cursor over underlined code:** To find out which target browsers don't support a particular underlined tag or attribute in the code, hover the cursor over any underlined code in Code view. An error tip appears, displaying relevant error information, including browser and version types.

+ **Right-click (Windows) or Control+click (Mac) underlined code:** In Code view, you can access other target browser compatibility report commands by right-clicking (Windows) or Control+clicking (Mac) an underlined tag or attribute in the code. Choose an option from the context-sensitive menu that appears. For example, to see a report for the entire open document, choose Show All Errors from the context-sensitive menu. The Results panel displays errors, warnings, and messages.

Only target browser errors, not warnings and messages, are displayed in the Code view of an open file. Therefore, if you want to see all potential code issues, including the warnings and information messages, run a manual check on the entire document or site and review the results in the Results panel.

The Browser Compatibility report doesn't check the accuracy of any scripts in the code or validate your syntax. It evaluates any markup that specified target browsers may not support by using an editable text file called browser profiles that specifies which tags particular browsers support. For information about editing the text file, changing the existing browser profile, or adding a new profile, visit the Adobe Support Center and look for a "Customizing Dreamweaver" heading. You can find the Support Center at www.adobe.com/support/dreamweaver/.

Checking and Fixing Links

The Link Checker tab identifies broken internal links, external links, and orphaned files on your pages. *Broken links* are often associated with the wrong filename or contain typos, and *orphaned files* are files on a defined site that are not being linked to on the site and can be safely removed from the site listing. However, because Dreamweaver only verifies local files in a managed site, it displays — but can't verify — *external links*.

To view the Link Checker tab, press F7 and select the Link Checker tab in the Results panel.

By identifying and listing all the links in one location, you can quickly verify them and make manual corrections as needed. In fact, you can fix all these links right in the Link Checker tab by selecting and editing the links listed by the report or by opening the files in question and fixing the errors on the page in Code view or with the Properties inspector.

To run a report to identify broken links, orphaned files, and external links in any managed site in Dreamweaver, follow these steps:

1. **Open the Results panel, click the Link Checker tab, and press the green Check Links arrow icon to select a Check Links option for this report.**

   You can run this report against the code in the current document, the entire local site, or selected files in the site. If you want to check specific files only, select them in the Files panel before clicking the Check Links arrow icon.

   The Results panel lists the results.

2. **Select a report results type from the Show menu to view the results of each report in the Link Checker panel.**

   Your options are Broken Links, External Links, or Orphaned Files.

   To fix broken links, follow Steps 3–7.

   External links are listed for your information, but you can't test them through the panel. However, you can modify spelling errors in external links in the Link Checker panel. To test external links for accuracy, you must launch the page in a browser and click each link by hand.

You can safely delete orphaned files in the Link Checker tab or by selecting and deleting files in the Files panel. Deleting an orphaned file permanently removes the file from your computer. If you think you may need the orphaned file sometime in the future, make a backup of the site before deleting the orphans or simply move the orphaned files to a location outside the managed site.

3. **To fix a broken link, choose Broken Links in the Show menu and then select a broken link in the results list under the Broken Links column (see Figure 1-9).**

   A folder icon appears to the right of the selected link.

Figure 1-9:
Select a
broken link
to correct
in the Link
Checker
panel.

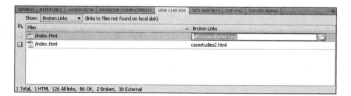

4. **Click the folder icon to browse to and select a new file to update the link, or type the correct URL or filename over the existing broken link information.**

   To correct a broken link with the Properties inspector, open the file by double-clicking the link's source page in the Files column of the Results listing. The broken link in the opened file is highlighted in Design view and Code view, and the broken link is displayed in the Link field in the Properties inspector. Correct the link in the Properties inspector, make any additional corrections, and then save the file. To verify the broken link is now correct, rerun the Link Check report.

   When fixing a broken link to an image from the document that the image is contained in, be sure to click the Refresh icon next to the image's W and H labels in the Properties inspector so that the corrected image uses its actual size, rather than the old image width and height dimensions. The W and H labels are displayed as bold characters when the new image dimensions need refreshing and as normal type when the W and H dimensions match the selected image.

5. **Press Enter (Windows) or Return (Mac) to accept the new link.**

   When multiple instances of the same broken link appear throughout the list, Dreamweaver asks whether you want to apply the same change to the other instances. Click Yes to update all instances or No to update only the current instance.

   If you've enabled the Check In/Check Out system, you need to check out the files before modifying them. If Dreamweaver can't locate a particular file associated with a broken link, a warning message indicates that the file was not found. Any broken links associated with the missing file remain broken.

6. **Repeat Steps 3–5 for each broken link.**

7. **Click the Save Report icon on the left side of the panel to save a copy of the report.**

   You can also choose Options⇨Save Results. Save your reports with the .doc, .txt, or .html file extension.

When you fix links by following these steps, the links are automatically removed from the Results list in the Link Checker panel. If you fix a link but it still appears in the list, Dreamweaver didn't recognize your corrections. Perhaps the new filename you've added is incorrect. Try fixing the link in the Reports panel, saving the open file, and rerunning the Link Check report.

After running a report, a Web site might not show any "Browser support issues" in the results panel, but this doesn't mean that the page will be displayed the same in all browsers. There is a big difference between a page being browser compatible and the page displaying the desired visual effect you are trying to achieve for a Web site. For example, a Web page might not have any issues when you run the browser compatibility check, but CSS elements on the page (height, position, fonts, margin, and so on) could have wide-ranging differences across many browsers that need to be checked. To be safe, run the browser compatibility check to fix obvious coding errors, best practices, and so on, and then view the Web site in the specified target browsers and platforms to check the consistency of the desired layout and look and feel.

Handling Workflow and HTML Reports

The Site Reports panel provides quick access to the Reports dialog box, from which you can select and run a variety of Workflow and HTML reports. Consider using these reports to begin cleaning up your site before launching it.

Launching reports

The Workflow reports are great if you're working on a major site with two or more people. The main function of the reports is to help team members work together more effectively. As long as you've defined a remote site connection in the managed site, these reports can provide important statistics on Design Notes, file modification dates, and file checkout status. For example, you can run a report to see which team members have files checked out or which files contain Design Notes. The Design Notes report can even contain specific name and value parameters, such as `Author=Sue`, for more specific search results. (Design Notes are described in detail in Book VI, Chapter 1.)

The HTML reports are a must for all Web sites, big and small. These reports identify problems in your code that could bloat file sizes, cause slower page viewing times, and even prevent your pages from being displayed properly. HTML reports include data about missing `Alt` attributes on images, removable empty tags, untitled documents, nested font tags that can be combined, and redundant nested tags.

You can run both Workflow and HTML reports simultaneously through the Reports dialog box by following these steps:

1. **Choose Site⇨Reports.**

The Reports dialog box appears, as shown in Figure 1-10, and you'll see several report options awaiting your selection.

Figure 1-10:
Select
individual
Workflow
and HTML
Reports
from the
Reports
dialog box.

2. **Select an option from the Report On drop-down list.**

Select the option that matches your specific needs. For example, if you want to check just the current page, select Current Document; to check the whole site, select Entire Current Local Site; if you want to check some, but not all, of the pages on the site, select Selected Files in Site or Folder.

3. **Select categories from the Workflow options:**

- **Checked Out By:** This option generates a report of all files checked out by a specific person.

- **Design Notes:** This report creates a list of Design Notes for either a set of selected files or the entire Web site.

- **Recently Modified:** This option makes a list of files that have been created or modified within a specific number of days or within a chosen range of dates.

4. **Click the Report Settings icon.**

   When you enable any of the Workflow reports, you should also select each report and click the Report Settings icon at the bottom of the dialog box to select customized options for each specific report. For example, to search for all the files checked out by Lee, select the Checked Out By category, click the Report Settings button, and type the name **Lee** in the Checked Out By dialog box.

   - **Checked Out By:** Enter the name of the team member this report searches for, such as Jane Smith.

   - **Design Notes:** Enter names and value pairs and choose comparison values from the corresponding menus, such as status is draft.

   - **Recently Modified:** Enter data for the report to search for files that were created or modified within a specific number of days or a range of dates, as in Files Created or Modified in the Last 7 Days.

5. **Select categories from the HTML Reports options:**

   - **Combinable Nested Font Tags:** This report option shows a list of any nested font tags that could be combined to make the code cleaner. For example, `<font size="5"><font color="#CC0000">big red text</font></font>` would be cleaned up as `<font size="5" color="#CC0000">big red text</font>`.

   - **Missing Alt Text:** Select this option to show a list of all `<img>` tags that are missing an alternate text attribute. This attribute is displayed in browsers that are set to download image files manually or in place of images in text-only browsers, and to be read by screen reader software.

   - **Redundant Nested Tags:** This setting lists any redundant tags that can be removed to create cleaner code. For example, in `<strong>Monkeys like to eat <strong>bananas</strong> and cake.</strong>`, the `<strong>` tags surrounding the word bananas are redundant.

   - **Removable Empty Tags:** Select this option to see a list of tags without content inside them, as in `<span></span>` or `<div align="center"></div>`, but not `<em>kitten</em>`.

   - **Untitled Documents:** Select this option to find any untitled documents on your site as well as files with default, missing, or duplicate title tags.

6. **Click the Run button to generate the report.**

   Some report options may require that you save any unsaved open files or select a specific folder or site before displaying report results. The results themselves are displayed in the Site Reports tab of the Results panel (see Figure 1-11).

Figure 1-11:
Site reports
results are
displayed
in the Site
Reports
area of the
Results
panel.

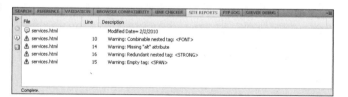

Saving reports as XML files

You can save your report results as an XML file for later importing to a database, spreadsheet, or template instance for printing or for display in a browser window. Because report data is essentially temporary information that reflects the current state of a document, folder, site, or selected files, saving report results may be useful if your company or client's company likes to archive report data.

To save and use a report, follow these steps:

1. **Run your report.**

2. **Before saving the report, you can view code, sort report data, or review report data by any of the following methods:**

   - **View Code:** To view and edit any code in a document listed in the report, double-click a line in the report to open the document in the Document window. The document opens in either Code view or Split Code view.

   - **Sort:** To sort report data, click the column heading above the category. You can sort by filename, description, or line number.

   - **Review:** To review a description of any of the problems listed in the report, select a line in the report and click the More Info icon, which appears on the left edge of the panel. The description information is displayed in the Reference panel.

3. **Click the Save Report icon.**

   The Save As dialog box appears. The default filename for your saved report is ResultsReport.xml. You can change the filename to anything you like, as long as you keep the file type as XML.

   When you finish reviewing report data, choose Commands⇨Clean Up HTML/XHTML to automatically fix HTML errors.

Viewing File Transfer Activity with the FTP Log

The FTP Log panel displays FTP file transfer activity for all the times you use the Get, Put, Check In, and Check Out commands in the Files panel. This log activity is helpful when you're troubleshooting connection errors or documenting transfer process information.

To save FTP log information, select all the content in the FTP Log panel, and then right-click (Windows) or Control+click (Mac) and choose the Select All option. Then copy and paste the data into another file, such as a Microsoft Word document, a text file, or an HTML file.

Debugging a ColdFusion Application (Windows)

The Server Debug panel displays helpful information that can assist you with debugging a ColdFusion application in Windows without having to exit Dreamweaver.

If you don't see any data in this panel, you must first assign a staging server to the site definition to specify where to process dynamic pages. The staging server can be your local machine, a testing, development, or a production server. To set the staging server, open the Site Definition dialog box for the defined site and select the Servers category. From there, you can enter the necessary information to identify the staging server. For more information on setting up a staging server, see Book VII, Chapter 1.

If you work on a Mac, press ⌘+F12 to open any ColdFusion pages in a separate browser window. From there, you can find errors at the bottom of the page.

Before beginning the debugging process, you may need to enable certain features in ColdFusion Administrator. For example, when using ColdFusion MX 7.0 and above, Dreamweaver automatically enables debugging, but if you're running ColdFusion MX 6.1 or earlier, you must enable debugging settings manually. See Dreamweaver's ColdFusion documentation for assistance with these settings by choosing Help➪ColdFusion Help.

If you're testing your pages in Internet Explorer, consider enabling Internet Explorer to refresh page data each time the page is displayed so that the browser displays the most recent data available. In Internet Explorer, choose Tools➪Internet Options and click the General tab. Click the Settings button in the Browsing History area. The Temporary Internet Files and History Settings dialog box appears. Select the Every Time I Visit the Webpage option.

To run the Server Debug report on a ColdFusion page, follow these steps:

1. **Open the ColdFusion page in the Document window.**

2. **Click the Preview/Server Debug in Browser icon on the Document toolbar.**

The page is requested from the ColdFusion server and appears on an internal Internet Explorer browser. Any errors and their possible causes appear at the bottom of the page. At the same time, the Server Debug panel also displays information to assist with the debugging process. For example, the report may list SQL queries, server variables, and an execution time summary.

3. **To expand the Exceptions category on the Server Debug panel, if one appears, click the plus (+) icon.**

The Exceptions category appears only when the server finds problems with the page. Expanding the category reveals a more detailed list of information about each problem.

4. **To fix any problems listed in the Location column of the Server Debug panel, click the page URL to open the page.**

The page opens and the code in question is highlighted in Code view so that you can edit it. You may be prompted to locate the document on your own if Dreamweaver can't automatically locate it for you.

5. **Fix errors and save the files to the server; click the Preview/Server Debug in Browser icon again.**

The browser gathers the latest information from your page and the server and renders the page again in an internal browser. The Server Debug panel is also updated to show you any remaining or new potential problems. After all the problems are addressed, the Exceptions category disappears from the panel.

6. **Exit the debugging mode by choosing View➪Design or View➪Code.**

Chapter 2: Keeping Your Code Clean

In This Chapter

✔ **Changing code preferences**

✔ **Running the Clean Up Word HTML/XHTML command**

✔ **Performing a spell check**

✔ **Cleaning code with the Clean Up HTML/XHTML command**

✔ **Applying source formatting to your pages**

✔ **Externalizing your JavaScript**

✔ **Updating links sitewide**

Whenever you build and edit Web pages in Dreamweaver — especially if you're hand-coding or pasting content — some of the markup may get crowded with redundant elements and unnecessary or unwanted code. You need to remove those extra bits of code from all the pages before you publish, whether you do that in advance (by setting preferences), during page creation (by selecting paste and import options), or as a final code cleanup (with Dreamweaver's HTML/XHTML Clean Up, spell check, and other code reporting tools) when the site is complete.

Why? Actually, you should clean up your code for a few reasons. One, that extra code adds to the overall file size, which in turn can affect page-loading times in a browser. Two, badly formatted code may confuse some browsers, causing the information on your pages to display less accurately than you intended. Even more important perhaps is the fact that some code errors can prevent browsers from displaying the HTML or XHTML entirely. If these issues aren't enough to convince you to clean up your code before publishing, you've been warned. At least think about keeping your code as clean and error-free as possible as a reflection of your professionalism. After all, anyone can look at your Web site code by simply using View Source.

So how do you go about cleaning up your Web site code without having to review the code in each file, line by line? Fortunately, the answer can be as simple as running a few quick commands in Dreamweaver. First, set up a few Dreamweaver preferences to avoid some of the issues. If you've already created your site, you should still set up Dreamweaver's preferences so any new documents you create use these settings.

After you set Dreamweaver's preferences, you should perform the following tasks, in roughly the following order, to make sure that your code is error-free and clear of miscellaneous junk: Run Dreamweaver's spell checker, use the appropriate commands to remove unnecessary code pasted from other programs, apply source formatting to your pages if it's missing, externalize your JavaScript when possible, and finally fix or change links across the site.

Eliminating Formatting Issues Before They Occur

The developers at Dreamweaver understand that previously applied formatting can be a killer to your code. Imagine this scenario: You're designing a new site. Your client, who is eager to "help" you, sends you a bunch of content for the site as text documents created with Word. (Alternatively, the file could come from some other word processor software or as Microsoft HTML files.) If the files are filled with a lot of fancy formatting (from italics to complicated styles) and structural additions (such as automatic bullet lists and tables), you need to transform them *before* you put them into Dreamweaver.

The text may start out well-formatted and well-organized in the original client-provided file. But when you copy and paste the content into Dreamweaver without first setting Dreamweaver's Copy/Paste preferences, some of the formatting data may get translated into clunky inline HTML formatting tags and be included with the text along the way. For example, a styled sentence pasted from Microsoft Word might look something like this:

```
<p class=MsoNormal><strong><span style="font-family:'Comic Sans MS'; font-
    size:20pt; color:#3366FF; ">Let's all do the Scrambled-Egg Dance</span></
    strong></p>
```

You can — and probably should — replace most of that Word-generated HTML formatting code with your own CSS formatting markup. In addition to creating and applying a style sheet, you need to remove the HTML formatting code from the page, either by hand or by using the Find and Replace tool. When you remove everything that could end up being a problem (such as the Word-generated HTML formatting), the sentence looks more like this:

```
<p><strong>Let's all do the Scrambled-Egg Dance</strong></p>
```

 Ultimately, the best defense against bad code is a good offensive strategy. The following sections list some preferences and settings that you can put into place before you even start building a site. If you use these tools now, getting your pages cleaned up before publishing will be much easier.

Setting Copy and Paste preferences

To help solve some of this transfer of undesired code, Dreamweaver CS5 allows you to set Copy/Paste preferences for pasted data from Microsoft

Word and other word processing programs. To change the Copy/Paste preferences, follow these steps:

1. **Choose Edit⇨Preferences (Windows) or Dreamweaver⇨Preferences (Mac).**

   The Preferences dialog box appears.

2. **Select the Copy/Paste category on the left.**

   On the right side of the dialog box, you see some Copy/Paste options (see Figure 2-1):

Figure 2-1:
Set your
Copy/Paste
preferences
to automatically remove
unwanted
markup
from copied
text.

- **Text only:** Not surprisingly, this option is the simplest and gives you the greatest control.

- **Text with Structure:** Dreamweaver's definition of *structure* is any formatting that affects the overall appearance of paragraphs, lists, or tables. Dreamweaver is not concerned with individual font formatting.

- **Text with Structure Plus Basic Formatting:** Dreamweaver's definition of *basic formatting* includes elements such as **boldface,** *italics,* and underlining.

- **Text with Structure Plus Full Formatting:** Dreamweaver defines *full formatting* as formatting that affects not just the basics but also individual styles.

- **Retain Line Breaks:** This option keeps any line breaks from the source when the content is pasted.

- **Clean Up Word Paragraph Spacing:** Use this option to remove extra space between paragraphs when content copied from Microsoft Word is pasted into a Dreamweaver file.

TIP

If you're unsure which options to use, select Text with Structure Plus Basic Formatting with both Retain Line Breaks and Clean Up Word Paragraph Spacing selected. Basic formatting tags such as `<strong>` and `<em>` are more effective markup for accessibility than creating styles that use bold and italic, because screen readers modify intonation for content inside these tags.

3. **Click OK to close the Preferences dialog box.**

   New preference settings take effect immediately. You can always come back and modify these preferences later if the need arises.

Using the Paste Special command

The Paste Special command enables you to control how much (and what kind of) formatting is moved from the original file to your Dreamweaver file each time you perform a paste.

When you use the regular Paste option for copied content, your paste includes all the formatting in the source content. However, when you copy information from a Word document that's been formatted with a special font, font color, font size, bold, italics, and alignment and want to paste it into your Dreamweaver file *without* the font formatting while retaining the list structure, bold, and italic settings, use the Paste Special option.

When you use Edit⇨Paste Special instead of the regular Paste command, the Paste Special dialog box appears, as shown in Figure 2-2, so that you can select a Paste preference for the copied content you're about to paste. The options in the dialog box are the same choices in the Copy/Paste category of the Preferences dialog box (refer to the preceding section, "Setting Copy and Paste preferences," for information about your options). The default setting in the Paste Special dialog box matches the setting you select in the Copy/Paste preferences, but you can override that default option on a case-by-case basis using the Paste Special command.

Figure 2-2:
Select Paste
Preferences
from the
Paste
Special
dialog box.

Cleaning up Word HTML

Microsoft Word has a feature that enables users to convert regular Word documents into Microsoft Word HTML files that are viewable in a browser window. Not a bad option, really. Unfortunately, in versions of Word 97 and later, Microsoft adds extra markup for the purpose of displaying the content in a browser window yet leaves in extra formatting data necessary only for the display of the page as a document. This extra code adds to the overall file size and may affect the speed with which the page loads in a browser.

You can easily remove the extra markup (such as redundant or unnecessary nested tags, as well as Word-specific markup) with the Clean Up Word HTML command. Using this handy tool is a good way to keep file sizes as small as possible, and cleaning up the code is essential if you plan on using style sheets.

As a precaution, always try to retain a backup copy of the original Word (.doc) and especially Word HTML (.html) files before performing the cleanup, because the Word HTML file may not reopen in Word after the cleanup.

Follow these steps to clean up an HTML file generated by Word 97 or later:

1. Open the Microsoft HTML file in the Dreamweaver workspace window.

To see the Microsoft markup in the code before it is removed, switch to Code or Split Code view by choosing View⇔Code or View⇔Code and Design.

2. Choose Commands⇔Clean Up Word HTML.

The Clean Up Word HTML dialog box appears, as shown in Figure 2-3.

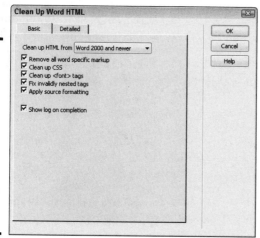

Figure 2-3:
Use the default settings in the Clean Up Word HTML dialog box for the best Word HTML cleanup results.

Dreamweaver attempts to autodetect the version of Word in which the file was generated. If the file version is undetectable, you can choose the proper version from the Clean Up HTML From drop-down list.

3. **Select any cleanup options that you want.**

   The default settings are to have Dreamweaver check for and fix everything it possibly can.

   We recommend that you keep the default settings on the Basic tab intact. These options are crucial to stripping all Microsoft markup from the document. If anything, you may want to tinker with the options even more (you can do so by clicking the Detailed tab):

   - **Remove All Word Specific Markup:** This setting removes all Microsoft Word-specific HTML, metadata, and link tags, XML markup, and other style markup.

   - **Clean Up CSS:** Use this setting to remove all Word-specific CSS, especially any inline styles that match parent styles in the markup. The options here also zap style attributes that start with Mso, styles applied to table rows and cells, and any declarations that are not CSS.

   - **Clean Up <font> Tags:** Select this setting to remove HTML font tags and convert the entire body text to size 2 HTML text.

   - **Fix Invalidly Nested Tags:** This option deletes font markup tags that Word inserted outside heading and paragraph (block-level) tags.

   - **Apply Source Formatting:** This option applies the source formatting options you selected in the SourceFormat.txt file and the Code Format category of Dreamweaver's Preferences to the page. For more on this feature, see the "Introducing your Code Category preferences" and "Applying Source Formatting" sections, later in this chapter.

   - **Show Log On Completion:** Select this option to view a log of changes performed during the cleanup. Definitely turn on this feature so you can see how much Dreamweaver has improved the file!

4. **Click OK.**

   Dreamweaver performs the cleanup with the selected settings. Depending on the size of your site, this process may take a minute or two. When the process is complete, a dialog box appears and shows that the changes have been made.

Checking Your Spelling, Grammar, and Readability

When it comes time to proofread your copy for spelling and grammatical errors, much of the responsibility sits with you. Although Dreamweaver offers a spell checking feature, it's not automatic, so you have to remember to run the spell check before publishing your Web site. And, although the spell checker may catch some of your spelling errors, it won't alert you to poorly chosen words, *homophones* (words that sound the same but have vastly different meanings, such as *sight* and *site*), words used out of context, or other common grammatical errors that can effect the meaning (such as *it's* instead of *its*).

The best way to make sure that everything makes sense is to use your eyes. No mechanical tool can substitute for taking the time to read (and reread) your site content. In fact, at least two other people should assist you in checking your site for spelling, grammar, and readability. Even better, consider setting up a temporary Web site in a folder on your Web server to share with your proofreaders to help streamline the process. Putting your site on a temporary directory on a Web server can also serve as a perfect opportunity to review the site in different browser and operating system combinations as part of your real-life, prelaunch browser compatibility testing.

Before you recruit your coworkers, friends, clients, and family members to join in on the spell checking fun, use the Dreamweaver Check Spelling command, which isolates common spelling errors in text while ignoring HTML tags and attribute values in the code.

Follow these steps to check and correct spelling:

1. **In Dreamweaver, open the document to be spell checked.**

2. **Choose Commands⇨Check Spelling or press Shift+F7.**

The Check Spelling dialog box, shown in Figure 2-4, appears if Dreamweaver finds a word or words that it does not recognize. If Dreamweaver finds no errors, you may see a recommendation that you begin a new spell check from the start of the document. Otherwise, you're presented with a Spelling Check Completed alert box.

Figure 2-4:
Use the
Check
Spelling
dialog box
to ignore
or change
unrecog-
nized words.

3. **Select an option to handle each unrecognized word:**

- **Add to Personal:** Add the unrecognized word to the personal dictionary, which appends the default or substitute language dictionary. This option is particularly helpful when working on sites that reuse particular words or often used made-up terms that fall outside the traditional vernacular, such as *knowledgeability* and *truthiness.*

- **Ignore:** Ignore the current instance of an unrecognized word.

- **Change:** Replace the unrecognized word with a selected suggestion or text typed in the Change To text box.

- **Ignore All:** Ignore all instances of an unrecognized word.

- **Change All:** Replace all instances of the unrecognized word with the selected suggestion or text typed in the Change To text box.

If you accidentally click Ignore All or Select All, errors can occur where previously there were none. Checking each found item on an individual basis is always a good idea.

The Dreamweaver spell checker uses the U.S. English spelling dictionary by default, but you can select another dictionary from the Spelling Dictionary drop-down list in the General category of Dreamweaver's Preferences. In CS5, Dreamweaver switched the spell checker engine from Wintertree software to LILO (Linguistic Library Optimized). Whereas CS4 only supported 15 languages, LILO's spell-checker supports 37 dictionaries.

Getting Your HTML and XHTML Code Consistent

Most Web designers speak a few markup dialects, such as XHTML and HTML. Like most multilingual individuals, you may lapse into a hybrid language that (unfortunately) only you understand. (We figure it's the markup equivalent of *Spanglish.*) Or maybe you're translating something from HTML to XHTML. In either case, winding up with some inconsistent tags, unneeded comments, and redundant or unnecessary tags in your code happens to the best of us. To quickly perform general HTML cleanup work on your files, such as removing empty container or redundant nested tags, run the Clean Up HTML/XHTML command on any open document.

Dreamweaver autodetects the doctype of the document open in the workspace window and displays the HTML or XHTML Clean Up command on the Commands menu to match the doctype it detects. For example, if the doctype is HTML, the Clean Up HTML command appears on the Commands menu; if the doctype is XHTML, the Clean Up XHTML command appears instead.

When your file uses XHTML markup instead of HTML, the Clean Up HTML/ XHTML command performs all the XHTML cleanup tasks, plus it instantly converts all the tag attributes to lowercase, fixes XHTML syntax errors, and adds or reports any required tag attributes that are missing, such as images with missing `<alt>` text.

To clean up HTML/XHTML code, follow these steps:

1. **Open the document.**

   For HTML documents, choose Commands➪Clean Up HTML; for XHTML documents, choose Commands➪Clean Up XHTML. The Clean Up HTML/ XHTML dialog box appears, as shown in Figure 2-5.

Figure 2-5:
Choose
options to
clean up
your text
from the
Clean Up
HTML/
XHTML
dialog box.

2. **Select any combination of clean up options:**

  • **Empty Container Tags:** Remove tags without content inside them, as
    in `<i></i>` or `<font size="2"></font>`, but not `<i>hello</i>`.

  • **Redundant Nested Tags:** Clean up any redundant tags. For example,
    in the sentence `<em>Blue frogs hop on <em>green</em>`
    `lily pads.</em>`, the `<em>` tags surrounding the word `green` are
    redundant.

  • **Non-Dreamweaver HTML Comments:** Remove any comments in the
    code that Dreamweaver didn't automatically insert. For instance, a
    comment tag to define the beginning of image slices in the code such
    as `<!-- fwtable fwsrc="fireworks.png" fwbase="index.`
    `gif" fwstyle="Dreamweaver" fwdocid="170903715"`
    `fwnested="0" -->` or a comment tag from you to another member
    of your work group such as `<!-- Phil, insert the Peanut`
    `Data table here -->` would be removed, but code to identify
    a Dreamweaver-editable area such as `<!-- #BeginEditable`
    `"doctitle" -->` would not.

  • **Dreamweaver Special Markup:** Remove the special markup tags that
    Dreamweaver uses to automatically update templates and library items.
    Removing this special markup detaches the document from its original
    source, as with a template-based file and its source template file.

  • **Specific Tag(s):** Remove specific markup from the code by typing the
    tag in the Specific Tag text box. To remove multiple tags at the same
    time, separate tags with commas, as in `span, font`.

  • **Combine Nested <font> Tags When Possible:** Combine nested font tags
    when they could be joined to do the same task. For example, `<font`
    `size="2"><font color="#006699"> little blue Thomas`
    `train</font></font>` would be cleaned up as `<font size="2"`
    `color="#006699"> little blue Thomas train</font>`.

  • **Show Log On Completion:** Display an alert box with details about
    the cleanup at the end of the cleanup process. Leave this option
    selected to see how much your file has improved.

3. **Click OK to start the cleanup process.**

   If you left the Show Log On Completion check box selected, a Clean Up Summary alert window opens when the cleanup process is finished, listing details about the cleanup. You may see messages such as *XHTML syntax fixed* or *12 comment(s) removed.*

Reviewing Source Formatting and Making Changes

Dreamweaver did a wonderful job colorizing and organizing the coding environment to assist you with reviewing and editing your code. For instance, with CSS markup, style information is color coded to differentiate between the style or selector name, style property, value, and separators between property-value pairs in the declaration, and the opening and closing style tags. And take a look at the code for any text link on a page; the `<a href>` tags are in one color (green), the link source is another color (royal blue), and any content between the opening and closing `<a>` tags is yet another color (black).

Dreamweaver provides the flexibility of allowing you to customize the coding color preferences. That means, for example, you could change the color of specific tags in the code if you're trying to isolate them. In fact, you can set Dreamweaver preferences to specify code formatting, editing, coloring, viewing, and hinting options. All coding preferences apply to both new documents and new content in existing documents created in Dreamweaver.

Setting code formatting preferences

To customize your Dreamweaver coding environment, follow these steps:

1. **Choose Edit⇨Preferences (Windows) or Dreamweaver⇨Preferences.**

   The Dreamweaver Preferences dialog box appears.

2. **Select one of the code categories on the left, and then edit the preferences for that category as needed.**

   A description of each code category and its preferences settings is listed in the following section.

3. **Click OK to save the new settings.**

Introducing your Code Category preferences

Although it may appear that you have more preferences than you know what to do with, take a quick look at the following options to see if you want to adjust anything to improve your coding environment:

✦ **Code Coloring:** Change the default code colors for different document types, which means you can use one set of colors for HTML code and another set of colors for PHP code. After you select a document type, click the Edit Coloring Scheme button. You can modify the code text and background colors, along with Bold, Italic, or Underline styles, for specific code elements such as form tags, JavaScript elements, CSS elements, and library items (see Figure 2-6). For example, if you wanted your image tags to stand out, you'd select the HTML Image Tags style and change the text color and background color, and perhaps apply bold and underline, too.

Figure 2-6:
Edit the coloring scheme for different document types.

✦ **Code Format:** Set code formatting preferences such as the default indent and tab size, the default attribute and tag case, and other options, as shown in Figure 2-7:

• **Indent:** Indent Dreamweaver-generated code (though not code you hand-code) according to the number of spaces or tabs set in the With field and drop-down list.

• **Tab Size:** Set the character width of each tab character in Code view. For instance, if set to 5, each tab is displayed as a blank space equal to five characters wide. This measure also affects the indent size when you've selected Tabs from the With drop-down list.

Figure 2-7:
Set Code
Format
preferences
for normal
coding and
use with
the Apply
Source
Formatting
command.

- **Line Break Type:** Identify the type of remote live server hosting your site. Choose Windows, Macintosh, or Unix to ensure that the line breaks in your code appear correctly when viewed on the remote server. This option applies only to binary transfer mode when connected with FTP; the ASCII transfer mode is ignored. However, when downloading files in ASCII mode, the line breaks are automatically set to match the computer's OS, and when uploading in ASCII mode, the line breaks are automatically set to CR LF (Windows).

- **Default Tag Case/Default Attribute Case:** These two settings control whether your code uses uppercase or lowercase for tags and attributes in Design view. These settings have no control over editing in Code view or over existing document attributes, unless you select one or both of the Override Case Of options.

- **Override Case Of: Tags and Attributes:** Turn on one or both of these options to have Dreamweaver enforce the case rules set for the Default Tag Case and Default Attribute Case at all times. These options automatically convert code in existing files as well as enforce case rules for content added to new files.

- **TD Tag:** Prevent Dreamweaver from adding any spaces or line breaks immediately before or after an opening or closing `<td>` tag to help with page rendering issues in older browsers.

Because the Web is moving more toward XHTML compliance and XHTML requires lowercase letters for the coding of tags and attributes, it's best to set Default Tag Case and Default Attribute Case to lowercase and select Override Case of settings for both tags and attributes.

- **Advanced Formatting:** Click the CSS button to open the CSS Source Format Options dialog box, where you can adjust CSS format settings for indents, properties, selectors, and blank line rules. Click the Tag Libraries button to open the Tag Library Editor, where, if you had some specific need, you could adjust the format for specified HTML and programming language tags.

✦ **Code Hints:** Decide how Dreamweaver's code hint preferences are displayed in Code view and in the Quick Tag Editor. Here are your options:

- **Close Tags:** Choose to have Dreamweaver automatically insert closing tags after typing "</", add closing tags after entering the opening tag's angle bracket (>), or never insert closing tags.

- **Enable Code Hints/Description Tooltips:** Choose to see code hints and description tool tips when typing in Code view. Use the delay slider to adjust the number of seconds to wait before the hints and tool tips are shown.

- **Menus:** Select from a list of menus the kinds of code hints that are displayed.

✦ **Code Rewriting:** Select how Dreamweaver rewrites or fixes invalid code. These settings can rewrite code when opening files, copying and pasting form data, and entering link URLs and attributes in Dreamweaver. However, they won't change code when you're editing HTML or scripts in Code view. When these features are deselected, Dreamweaver shows the invalid markup for HTML that it would have rewritten in the Document window.

- **Fix Invalidly Nested and Unclosed Tags:** Reorder improperly nested tags and insert missing quote marks or closing brackets. For example, `<strong><em>Monkey!</strong></em>` is rewritten as `<strong><em>Monkey!</em></strong>`, and `<div <img src="images/logo.gif></div>` is rewritten as `<div><img src="images/logo.gif"></div>`.

- **Rename Form Items When Pasting:** When pasting elements from other documents, make sure that the page has no form objects with the same name. For example, if one text field is named `textfield`, the next would be named `textfield2`, and so on.

- **Remove Extra Closing Tags:** Delete extra closing tags that don't have opening tag mates.

- **Warn When Fixing or Removing Tags:** (Available only when Remove Extra Closing Tags is selected.) See a summary of invalid HTML markup that Dreamweaver couldn't fix. The summary identifies the source of the problem by using line and column numbers so that you can easily find and fix the error.

- **Never Rewrite Code: In Files with Extensions:** (Available only when Remove Extra Closing Tags is selected.) Enable or disable Dreamweaver from rewriting code in files with particular filename extensions, such as .css or .shtml. This setting is particularly handy when adding third-party tags to your code.

The next four options do not apply to existing code or new URLs typed in Code view but do apply to all new coding added to documents in Design view and through the Properties inspector:

- **Encode <, >, &, and " in Attribute Values Using &:** Because attribute values entered or edited in Dreamweaver must have legal characters, the default setting makes sure that entered data conforms to those standards.

- **Do Not Encode Special Characters:** Stop Dreamweaver from adjusting URLs that use nonlegal characters.

- **Encode Special Characters in URL Using &#:** Make sure that URLs use only legal characters by using special encoding.

- **Encode Special Characters in URL Using %:** Like the preceding setting, make sure that URLs have only legal characters, but use a different encoding method for special characters. This option works well with older browsers, but doesn't work as well with some characters in other languages.

Applying Source Formatting

You can use the Code Format coding preferences listed in the preceding section for the creation of new Dreamweaver files and additions to existing documents. You can't, however, use them on HTML files that you created *before* these preferences were set. To do that, you'd essentially be reformatting the old code. If you want to change the original code, therefore, you must *apply source formatting*. Applying source formatting means using the Code Format settings you customized in the preceding section to reformat the code in an existing HTML file.

You can apply source formatting to an entire document or to a particular selection on a page.

Applying source formatting to a complete file

To apply source formatting to an existing file, follow these steps:

1. **Open the file in Dreamweaver.**

2. **Choose Commands⇨Apply Source Formatting.**

   Dreamweaver immediately applies all existing and any new coding preferences to the page code.

3. **Save the file by choosing File⇨Save.**

Applying source formatting to a selection

To apply source formatting to a selection in an existing file, follow these steps:

1. **Open the file in Dreamweaver and select the content in Design view that you want to modify with the new coding preferences.**

   Selected content must be *contiguous* (touching). There is no option for selecting multiple, nontouching areas of your document. If you need to apply source formatting to several sections of a page, repeat these steps for each section.

2. **Choose Commands⇨Apply Source Formatting to Selection.**

   Dreamweaver immediately applies any new coding preferences to the selected page code.

3. **Save the updated file by choosing File⇨Save.**

Using the JavaScript Extractor (JSE)

The JavaScript Extractor (JSE) is a nifty little tool that can quickly remove some or all JavaScript in your file to an external document and then link that external document to your file. You can use this tool also to remove event handlers such as `onClick` from your code and then unobtrusively attach the JavaScript associated with those handlers back to your file.

You should know about some limitations regarding the use of the JSE tool. For instance, JSE will not extract any JavaScript from editable regions in library items, a template file, or the uneditable regions of template-based files. It also can't extract any script tags from the body of a page (except for Spry). Furthermore, extraction of JavaScript associated with Dreamweaver behaviors renders those behaviors uneditable through the Behaviors panel. Lastly, extraction can sometimes produce unexpected and unwanted results, so before you commit to any extraction, test the page in multiple browsers before you close the file. You can undo your changes as long as you keep the file open; after you close the file, you can no longer undo changes.

To use the JavaScript Extractor on an open page containing JavaScript code, follow these steps:

1. **Choose Commands⇨Externalize JavaScript.**

The Externalize JavaScript dialog box appears, as shown in Figure 2-8.

Figure 2-8:
Use the JavaScript Extractor to move your scripts to an external file.

2. **Select the Only Externalize JavaScript option or the Externalize JavaScript and Attach Unobtrusively option:**

- **Only Externalize JavaScript:** Move JavaScript to an external .js file and insert a link to it. Event handlers and behaviors within the page remain intact.

- **Externalize JavaScript and Attach Unobtrusively:** Move JavaScript to an external .js file, add a link to it, and remove event handlers from the HTML and add them back at runtime using JavaScript. Behaviors on the page can no longer be edited through the Behaviors panel.

3. **Select items from the Edit column that you would like to include in the externalize JavaScript process.**

Deselect any items that you'd like to ignore. By default, the list includes script blocks from the head of the file that contain `document.write()` and `document.writeIn()` calls; function signatures related to Eolas

(Embedded Objects Linked Across Systems) handling code; and script blocks in the body of the file (unless those blocks contain only Spry widget or data set constructors).

During the extraction process, Dreamweaver automatically assigns IDs to any elements in the JavaScript that don't already have IDs. These IDs can be renamed in the ID text box, when applicable.

4. **Click OK to begin the extraction.**

   When the extraction is complete, Dreamweaver displays a summary dialog box so you can review the changes.

5. **When you have finished reading the summary, click OK to close the dialog boxes.**

After the extraction is complete, Dreamweaver saves a SpryDOMUtils.js file along with a new .js file containing the extracted JavaScript into your managed site. The SpryDOMUtils.js file is saved in a SpryAssets folder, and the .js file containing the extracted script is saved at the same level as the page from which it was extracted. You must upload the folder and both files to the live server when you publish the site for the extracted JavaScript to function properly.

Changing Links Sitewide

In a managed site, whenever you rename or move a file, Dreamweaver offers to automatically update those links for you. You can also manually change links throughout your site at any time. (To discover more about links in general, see Book II, Chapter 4. To find out how to check and fix links with Dreamweaver's Check Links report, see Book V, Chapter 1.)

The Change Link Sitewide feature enables you to change individual text, e-mail, FTP, null, and script links from one setting to another. For example, you may have a text link, such as "This Month's Menu," that needs to point to a new HTML file each month, such as /menus/september.html this month and /menus/october.html next month. Likewise, if you need to change an e-mail address across all the pages on a Web site (such as changing mailto:info@dummies.com to mailto:orders@dummies.com), you can use this command.

Follow these steps to change a link throughout your site:

1. **In the Files panel, select a file from the Local view listing.**

   If you're changing an e-mail address, FTP, a script, or a null link, you can skip this step.

2. Choose Site⇨Change Link Sitewide.

Or choose Site⇨Change Link Sitewide from the Files panel menu. The Change Link Sitewide dialog box appears, as shown in Figure 2-9.

Figure 2-9:
Change
individual
links
sitewide.

Change Link Sitewide (Site - DFDAIO)	
Change all links to:	OK
/services.html	Cancel
Into links to:	
/offerings.html	Help

3. Enter the current and new link information in the Change All Links To and Into Links To text fields, respectively.

For changing filenames, enter the old filename and new filename in the appropriate text fields. For any other type of link, enter the complete old and new text of the link you want to change. For instance, to replace one e-mail address with another, type mailto:info@example.com for the old address and mailto:contact@example.com for the new address.

4. Click OK.

Dreamweaver updates all instances of that link with the new link information. Any path associated with the former link remains intact, regardless of whether the path is site root–relative or document-relative.

After the change is made, the file with the old filename becomes an orphan with no files on the managed site pointing to it. You can safely delete it from the local site folder without fear of creating broken links. When uploading the updated pages to the remote server, don't forget to manually delete the same orphaned file from the remote server so that site visitors see the changed links.

Chapter 3: Preparing to Publish Your Files Online

In This Chapter

✔ **Setting up a remote connection**

✔ **Choosing a remote access type**

✔ **Cloaking files and folders**

*I*n Book V, Chapter 1, you discover how to run Workflow and HTML reports to check for coding errors on your pages. Then, in Book V, Chapter 2, you find out how easy cleaning up your code is when you use the Clean Up and Spell Checking commands. The next step to take before you publish your site is to set up a remote live server connection. (We cover the final step, transferring your files, in Book V, Chapter 4.)

The *remote connection* defines the folder or destination where you're publishing your files. The remote folder can be on a testing server or production server, or any other type of server for storing your published files.

In this chapter, we show you how to create a remote connection for uploading and downloading files. You also find out how to *cloak* file types and folders to make sure that specified files aren't included in sitewide operations such as uploading, report generation, and changing links.

Creating a Remote Connection

Before you set up a remote connection to a live server, you need to create a managed site. If you still need to set up a proper structure for your site, turn to Book I, Chapter 3 to find out about general Web site structure, document-relative paths, and site root–relative paths, as well as how to create a managed site in Dreamweaver.

Setting up a remote connection requires you to specify a *remote folder*. This folder is located on the host server where you store a copy of the Web site's files, separate from the local version on your own computer. You need these copies of your site in both locations so that you can test, produce, deploy, and collaborate on the site.

If you plan to run the Web server on your local computer, you don't need to specify a remote folder; as long as the local site folder points to the system running your Web server, Dreamweaver automatically uses the local site folder as the remote host server folder.

Setting up a remote folder

You can connect and access the remote folder using several methods. This section focuses on using the Server category of the Site Setup dialog box to enter all your remote folder information.

To set up a remote folder for an existing managed site, follow these steps:

1. **Choose Site⇨Manage Sites.**

Or choose Sites⇨Manage Sites from the Files panel menu. The Manage Sites dialog box appears.

2. **Select a managed site from the Dreamweaver site listing.**

If you don't see any sites listed, you must create a new *managed site* before proceeding (see Book I, Chapter 3).

3. **Click the Edit button.**

The Site Setup dialog box appears.

4. **Select the Servers category on the left side of the dialog box, and then click the Add New Server (+) icon.**

A pop-up window appears showing two tabs: Basic and Advanced.

5. **Set up a connection to the remote live server.**

In the Basic tab, the connection method you select from the Connect Using menu is simply the means you choose to transfer Web files from your local computer to the remote server location. Which option you choose depends on the size of the team of Web developers working on the site, as well as the technology you already have in place.

6. **Select an access type for uploading and downloading files to and from that location.**

After you make your connection type selection, the appropriate options for that access type appears below the Access menu. For instance, if you select FTP, you see text fields for inputting FTP access information, such as host URL, username, and password.

Here is an overview of the different connection options:

- **None:** Leave this area blank if you will not be uploading the site to a server using Dreamweaver.

- **FTP:** Select this option if you'll be using File Transfer Protocol (FTP) to connect to your remote Web server. Where prompted, enter the FTP address, Username, Password, Root Directory (if any), and Web URL in the Basic tab, along with additional options as needed in the More Options section. The FTP access method presumes you've already registered your domain name (with a company such as Network Solutions) and secured a hosting plan for your domain with a reputable host provider (check out the list of Certified Service Providers from CNET at `http://reviews.cnet.com/Basic_hosting/7026-6541_7-0.html?tag=centerColumnArea1.0`).

  To connect to and disconnect from a remote folder with FTP, all you need to do is click the Connect to Remote Host icon in the Files panel.

- **SFTP:** Select this option to create a Secure File Transfer Protocol (SFTP) connection to your remote Web server. Where prompted, enter the SFTP address, Username, Password, Root Directory (if any), and Web URL in the Basic tab, along with additional options as needed in the More Options section. The SFTP access method presumes you've already registered your domain name and secured a hosting plan.

- **Local/Network:** Select this option if you'll be running a Web server on your local computer or accessing a folder on a local area network (LAN). Click the folder icon next to the Server Folder text field to browse for and select the folder to which you want to send the remote site files. You don't need to manually connect and disconnect to a server folder with network access because you're always connected if you select this access method. You may, however, want to click the Refresh icon in the Files panel often so that you can see the latest version of your remote files.

- **WebDAV (Web-based Distributed Authoring and Versioning):** Use this access method to connect to a live server that supports the WebDAV protocol, such as a Microsoft Internet Information Server (IIS) 5.0 or an Apache Web server with the right configuration settings. Enter the URL for the WebDAV server, username, password, and Web URL before testing the connection.

- **RDS (Remote Development Services):** Use this setting to connect to your Web server using RDS. With this method, the remote folder must be on a computer running ColdFusion. Enter the Web URL in the text field provided, and then click the Settings button to enter the host name for the server, the port number, and the remote root folder's full host directory, username, and password.

To find out how to set each of the access types, see the following section, "Configuring a remote access type."

7. **(Optional) Click the Advanced tab to enter Remote Server and Testing Server options.**

   Here you can set up Synchronization options between the local and remote folders, enable the Check Out feature, and specify a testing server model:

   - **Maintain Synchronization Information:** Synchronize local and remote files automatically. Deselect this option if you don't want Dreamweaver to synchronize your files. (For details on the entire synchronization process, read Book V, Chapter 4.)

   - **Automatically Upload Files to Server on Save:** Dreamweaver uploads files to the remote site whenever files are saved locally. Most developers leave this option deselected so they can test locally before publishing the updated files to the remote server.

   - **Enable File Check In and Check Out:** When selected, three additional fields become active. These fields are the Check Out Files When Opening check box, the Check-Out Name field, and the E-mail Address field of the main person using the current workstation. Unless you work in a group setting (see Book VI, Chapter 1), leave this option deselected.

   - **Testing Server Model:** When working with a testing server, select the desired server model. Options are None, ASP JavaScript, ASP VBScript, ASP.NET C#, ASP.NET VB, ColdFusion, JSP, and PHP MySQL. When not using a testing server, leave this field blank.

8. **Click Save to save the entered information.**

   Dreamweaver saves the remote information settings and closes the Site Definition dialog box.

9. **Click the Done button in the Manage Sites dialog box to close it.**

   Dreamweaver is now set up to make a connection to the specified remote server.

Configuring a connection type

Your development environment determines which connection type you select, as well as where the remote live folder resides. If you're unsure about which option to select, we recommend the FTP method for transferring files between your local computer and your remote host server.

The following sections show you how to select and set up category options for each of the connection types.

FTP

One of the most common methods of accessing a Web server is by using File Transfer Protocol (FTP). This is a good catchall connection option and the most common protocol used for transferring files. In this section, we show you how to use Dreamweaver's built-in FTP client for transferring files, but you could also transfer your files using any of the more common standalone FTP client applications.

Access the Server category of the Site Setup dialog box, click the Add a New Server (+) icon, and follow these steps to enter FTP information (see Figure 3-1):

Figure 3-1:
The FTP
remote
access type.

1. **In the FTP Address field, enter the FTP host name where you will upload your files. Leave the Server Name field as is or edit the name to match the name of the managed site.**

   The Server Name is used to help you keep track of the remote connection locally and therefore can be anything you like. If you have already given your site a name in the Site category of the Site Setup dialog box, the Server Name field will use the same name.

   The FTP address is the full Internet name of the server, such as `ftp.mysampleURL.com` or `www.mysampleURL.com`. Don't enter any additional text such as the protocol name before the host name. You can also enter the IP address to your domain if you have it. If you do not know this information, contact your host provider or system administrator.

2. **Enter the username and password you're using to connect to the FTP server in the Username and Password fields.**

   When you order your Web hosting plan, your host provider gives you this information for your account. If you don't know your username and password, contact your host provider or system administrator.

   Keep your username and password confidential.

3. **(Optional) In the Root Directory field, enter the address of the host directory provided by your service provider.**

The host directory is the location on the remote site where the files that will be visible to the Internet public are stored. Not all servers require this information, so if you don't know it, leave this text field empty or speak with your host provider or system administrator before continuing. Some servers use a directory called `public_html` or www, or use your host account username. To see if you have a directory as part of your hosting plan, establish an FTP connection without one to see whether the Remote view lists any host directory folders, such as `public_html`. If you see a directory folder, make a note of it and complete this step later.

4. **Enter the URL of your domain in the Web URL field.**

For example, if your Web site is called Luckychair, enter http://www.luckychair.com/.

5. **Click the Test button to test your FTP connection.**

If your FTP address, username, password, and host directory are valid, Dreamweaver displays an alert message that says the connection was a success. If the connection fails, an error message appears telling you that a connection could not be established. If that happens, check the spelling and accuracy of all the information you've entered, paying special attention to character case and spelling, and try again.

By default, Dreamweaver saves your FTP login information and password. If you prefer to enter your password each time you log in to your remote folder using FTP, deselect the Save check box.

6. **(Optional) Expand the More Options area to set additional FTP options if your firewall configuration requires it.**

- **Use Passive FTP:** This setting uses the local software to set up the connection, rather than relying on the remote server to create the connection. For more information about whether you should use this option, contact your host provider or system administrator, and see the Adobe TechNote 15220 at `www.adobe.com/go/tn_15220`.

- **Use IPv6 Transfer Mode:** This is an Extended Data Connection Type that must be set when using an IPv6-enabled FTP server. For more information about this connection option, visit `www.ipv6.org`.

- **Use Proxy, as Defined in Preferences:** Select this setting when connecting to a remote server from behind a firewall. To configure Firewall Proxy settings (see Figure 3-2) click the Preferences link and refer to the sidebar "Setting FTP firewall proxy preferences" for configuration details. If you're unsure whether you need to enable this option, speak with your company's system administrator.

Setting FTP firewall proxy preferences

To edit the firewall host or port information for your FTP connection in the Basic tab of the Server category of the Site Setup dialog box, click the Preferences link next to the Use Proxy check box. The Site Category Preferences dialog box appears (refer to Figure 3-2), where you can modify the FTP connection, transfer, and hosting preferences:

✔ **Always Show:** When using Dreamweaver for FTP, adjust these settings to determine which site (local or remote) is shown by default in the Files panel. You can also choose which pane in the expanded Files panel (left or right) displays local and remote files. Dreamweaver's default is to always show local files on the right, which happens to be the opposite of most stand-alone FTP client applications.

✔ **Dependent Files:** Select one or both of these options to have Dreamweaver display a prompt when transferring dependent files (such as images, PDFs, and CSS) that the browser needs when displaying the pages being uploaded. Both options are selected by default, and we recommend that you leave these settings as they are.

✔ **FTP Connection:** Set the disconnect time after a period of idleness, such as 30 minutes.

✔ **FTP Time Out:** Set the number of seconds it takes for Dreamweaver to attempt to make a connection with the server. If there's no response after the time specified, a warning alert dialog box is displayed. The default is 30 seconds.

✔ **FTP Transfer Options:** Select this setting to have Dreamweaver use a default option after the number of seconds specified to display a dialog box during the file transfer when there's no user response.

✔ **Firewall Host:** Enter the address of the proxy servers through which you connect to remote servers when using a firewall. Leave this field blank if you don't use a firewall.

✔ **Firewall Port:** If you use a firewall host to connect to a remote server, enter the port number here. Otherwise, leave this field set to 21, the default number for FTP.

✔ **Put Options:** Select the Save Files Before Putting feature to have unsaved files automatically save before you upload them to the server.

✔ **Move Options:** Select the Prompt before Moving Files on Server option to have Dreamweaver prompt you before you move files on the server.

After making your selections, click OK or Cancel to close the Preferences dialog box and return to the FTP Setup area in the Server category of the Site Setup dialog box.

- **Use FTP Performance Optimization:** Selected by default to enhance performance of the FTP process, deselect this option only if you're having trouble connecting to the server with Dreamweaver.

- **Use Alternative FTP Move Method:** Select this setting only if you're getting errors when moving files or when rollbacks are enabled.

Figure 3-2:
Modify
the FTP
connection
settings in
Preferences.

7. **(Optional) Click the Advanced tab to set up Remote Server and Testing Server options.**

8. **Click Save to save these settings, and click Save again to close the Site Setup dialog box.**

Secure File Transfer Protocol (SFTP)

Use the SFTP connection type (see Figure 3-3) when you need to connect to the live server with SFTP for secure authentication. SFTP uses public keys and encryption to create a secure connection with the testing server running an SFTP server. SFTP is a more secure option than regular FTP, but few Web hosts support it.

Figure 3-3:
Select
the SFTP
access type
to create a
secure FTP
connection.

To set up an SFTP connection, follow these steps:

1. **In the SFTP Address field, enter the SFTP host name where you will upload your files.**

   The SFTP address is the full Internet name of the server, such as `sftp.mysampleURL.com` or `www.mysampleURL.com`. Don't enter any additional text, such as the protocol name before the host name. You can also enter the IP address to your domain if you have it.

2. **In the Username and Password fields, enter the username and password you're using to connect to the SFTP server.**

   Always keep your username and password confidential. If you don't know this information for your Web account, speak with your host provider.

3. **(Optional) In the Root Directory field, enter the address of the host directory provided by your service provider.**

   The host directory is the location on the remote site where the files that will be visible to the Internet public are stored. Not all servers require this information, so if you don't know it, leave this text field empty or speak with your host provider or system administrator before continuing.

4. **Enter the URL of your domain in the Web URL field.**

   Dreamweaver automatically configures this address for you from your SFTP address. Change it here if you think the address is incorrect.

5. **Click the Test button to test your SFTP connection.**

   When your information is valid, Dreamweaver displays an alert message that says the connection was a success. When the connection fails, an error message appears telling you that a connection could not be established. Check the spelling and accuracy of all the information you've entered, paying special attention to character case and spelling, and try again.

   By default, Dreamweaver saves your SFTP login information and password. If you prefer to enter your password each time you log in to your remote folder using SFTP, deselect the Save check box.

6. **(Optional) Click the Advanced tab to setup Remote Server and Testing Server options.**

7. **Click Save to save these settings, and click Save again to close the Site Setup dialog box.**

Local/Network

Use the Local/Network access type when you're running a Web server on your local computer or accessing a network folder.

One of the benefits of this configuration is that you're always online. From the Server category of the Site Setup dialog box, click the Add New Server (+) icon, choose Local/Network from the Connect Using menu, and follow these steps to complete the always-connected Local/Network access configuration:

1. Click the folder icon to the right of the Server Folder text field to browse and select the server folder that contains your remote site files.

On a local machine running a Web server, this folder is probably located on the Web server, as shown in Figure 3-4. If your computer is running on a network, the folder is the one on the network that stores the remote site files.

Figure 3-4: Select the Local/ Network access type to create an always-on connection.

2. (Optional) Click the Advanced tab to setup Remote Server and Testing Server options.

3. Click Save to save these settings, and click Save again to close the Site Setup dialog box.

WebDAV

Use WebDAV (Web-based Distributed Authoring and Versioning) as your connection method if you're connecting to a server that supports the WebDAV protocol. For documentation, specifications, software, and other information, visit www.webdav.org. Microsoft Internet Information Server (IIS) 5.0 and Apache Web servers with the right configuration settings are the only servers that should use this remote access setup. If you're not sure whether your server falls into this category, it probably doesn't.

To set up your configuration, choose WebDAV from the Connect Using menu and follow these steps:

1. **In the URL field, type the full URL that points to the directory on the WebDAV server you want to connect to, as shown in Figure 3-5.**

The URL includes protocol, port, and directory, like this: `http://webdav.mydomain.net/mySiteName`.

Figure 3-5:
Enter the connected server's URL including protocol, port, and directory for WebDAV access.

2. **Type your username and password in the text fields provided.**

The username and password are used only for server authentication.

3. **Click the Test button to test the connection.**

If the full URL, username, and password information are valid, Dreamweaver displays an alert message that the connection was a success. If the connection fails, an error message appears. Check the spelling, pay attention to character case, and review the accuracy of the URL before you try again.

4. **Click the Save option to store your password for future sessions.**

5. **(Optional) Click the Advanced tab to setup Remote Server and Testing Server options.**

6. **Otherwise, click Save to save these settings, and click Save again to close the Site Setup dialog box.**

RDS

Use the RDS remote access setting to connect to a Web server running ColdFusion with Rapid Development Services (RDS). To learn more about

working with ColdFusion, visit the ColdFusion Resources Support site at
`www.adobe.com/support/documentation/en/coldfusion/`. If you're
not sure whether your server is running ColdFusion with RDS, it probably
isn't. To set up your configuration for RDS, follow these steps:

1. **Choose RDS from the Connect Using menu, and then click the Settings
   button.**

   The Configure RDS Server dialog box appears, as shown in Figure 3-6.

Figure 3-6:
Select
RDS when
connecting
to a server
running
ColdFusion
with RDS.

2. **In the Configure RDS Server dialog box, complete all the fields:**

   • **Host Name:** Type the name of the host computer where the Web server
     is installed. Often, the host name appears as an IP address or a URL.

   • **Port:** Enter the port number you want to use to connect to the
     remote location. By default, Dreamweaver enters port 80. If you have
     no reason to change this setting, don't.

   • **Use HTTPS:** Provide encryption and secure identification of the
     server for transactions involving private information such as pass-
     words and online purchases. HTTPS stands for Hypertext Transfer
     Protocol Secure.

   • **Full Host Directory:** Enter the local path of the root remote folder,
     such as `C:\inetpub\wwwroot\myFullHostDirectory\`.

- **Username** and **Password:** Enter a username and password for the RDS. If you don't see these fields, you've already set the username and password in the ColdFusion Administrator.

- **Save:** By default, these settings are automatically saved. To enter these settings manually each time you connect, deselect the Save option.

3. **Click OK to close this dialog box.**

   You return to the Basic tab of the Servers setup window.

4. **(Optional) Click the Advanced tab to setup Remote Server and Testing Server options.**

5. **Otherwise, click Save to close the Basic tab, and click Save again to close the Site Setup dialog box.**

Cloaking Your Files and Folders

Cloaking is a Dreamweaver feature that enables you to exclude specified folders and file types from sitewide operations such as uploading to a server through Dreamweaver, report generation, and changing links. For example, if you transfer files to a live server using Dreamweaver's Get and Put or Check In and Check Out systems, cloaking shields some of those files from being uploaded to or checked out from the remote server.

When else does cloaking come in handy? Well, it helps if you have some files on your local site that you don't want to transfer to the server. If some files aren't being changed or updated (such as graphics or PDFs), or if some files don't need to be on the server (such as templates and library items), you have no real reason to keep transferring them, right? Say you're running a busy design services Web site that requires weekly and sometimes daily updates. If you don't want to upload the same PDF files every day, you can cloak the .pdf file type in the Cloaking category of the Site Definition dialog box. Those files on the site would then be excluded from the file transfer process until such time as you changed the cloaking information again.

You need to know a few things about cloaking:

✦ **Dreamweaver, by default, enables cloaking for each managed site.** This means you can cloak and uncloak individual files and folders through the Files panel. You can deselect the setting if you need to in the Cloaking category of the Site Definition dialog box.

✦ **When you select cloaking, you can further set Dreamweaver to automatically exclude files with specific file suffixes.** For example, you can exclude all .png and .fla files from sitewide operations.

✦ **Dreamweaver saves and uses the cloaking settings entered in the Advanced Settings⟩Cloaking category of the Site Setup dialog box for each managed site.** You don't need to reenter these settings every time you view a particular site.

You can cloak folders, files, and file types when conducting the following sitewide procedures:

✦ Transferring files with the Get and Put or Check In and Check Out system.

✦ Synchronizing a local site with a remote site.

✦ Creating sitewide reports.

✦ Updating templates and library items.

Although Dreamweaver excludes cloaked templates and library items from Get and Put operations, don't exclude them from batch operations because that might cause synchronization issues between them and their instances.

✦ Changing the contents in the Asset panel.

✦ Finding newer local and remote files.

✦ Changing or checking links.

Enabling and disabling cloaking options

To disable or enable cloaking and specify file types to exclude for any managed site, follow these steps:

1. **Choose Site⟩Manage Sites to display the Manage Sites dialog box.**

2. **Select a site from the site listing, then click the Edit button.**

The Site Setup dialog box appears.

3. **Select the Cloaking option from the Advanced Settings category.**

The Cloaking settings appear, and the Enable Cloaking option is set by default. To disable this feature, deselect this check box.

If you deselect the cloaking feature, all previously cloaked files become uncloaked. When you select the feature again, all prior cloaking settings are restored.

4. **(Optional) Select the Cloak Files Ending With check box.**

In the text box below the Cloak Files Ending With check box, enter the file types you want to exclude from site operations.

The file types can be any pattern at the end of a filename; you're not limited to merely entering file extensions. For example, you can cloak all files with the .txt extension or all files and folders that end with _bak.

As you can see in Figure 3-7, you can even specify multiple file patterns by separating each pattern with a single space. Do not use colons, commas, or semicolons to separate your parameters, as doing so causes errors.

Figure 3-7:
Enter cloaking file extensions to exclude certain files and folders during site operations.

In the Files panel, you can easily identify cloaked files because a red diagonal line appears through the icon associated with the cloaked file. When you deselect or otherwise change the cloaking setting so that the file is no longer cloaked, the red line disappears.

5. **Click Save to exit the Site Setup dialog box, and then click Done to close the Manage Sites dialog box.**

Cloaking individual folders

Although you can't cloak the root folder of a managed site (because that would mean the entire site would be excluded from sitewide operations), you can cloak any of the site's other folders, such as a folder for library items, templates, external CSS, SSIs, or JavaScript files.

To cloak individual folders on a site, follow these steps:

1. **In the Files panel, select the folder(s) you want to cloak.**

   For example, you may want to cloak the Templates and Library folders on your managed site to prevent those files from being transferred to the remote live server. The selected folders can be cloaked or uncloaked. When multiple folders are selected, you may uncloak them all at the same time.

2. **Right-click (Windows) or Control+click (Mac) one of the selected folders, choose Cloaking from the context menu, and select Cloak, Uncloak, or Uncloak All.**

   You can also access these Cloaking options from the Site category of the Files panel menu. Because the default setting for all sites is to have cloaking enabled, you can choose to uncloak individual folders, to cloak specified folders, or to uncloak all selected folders at the same time, depending on which folder(s) you have selected.

In the Files panel, folders that are cloaked have a diagonal red line through the folder icon next to the folder name.

Take caution when using the Uncloak All feature. Although selecting this option uncloaks folders, it doesn't disable the cloaking system itself. What's worse, there is no efficient way to recloak previously cloaked files and folders other than selecting the files and folders by hand to recloak them.

Uncloaking previously cloaked file types

If you change your mind after cloaking specified file types, you can easily uncloak them. Follow these steps to do so:

1. **Right-click (Windows) or Control+click (Mac) in the Files panel and choose Cloaking⇨Settings from the context menu.**

The Site Setup dialog box is displayed with the Advanced Settings expanded and the Cloaking category selected.

2. **To uncloak previously cloaked files, do one of the following:**

   - Delete the file extensions in the text box below the Cloak Files Ending With check box.

   - Deselect the Cloak Files Ending With check box. This action leaves the file extensions previously entered into the text field but temporarily disables the cloaking action.

3. **Click Save to exit the Site Setup dialog box.**

After you exit the Site Setup dialog box, any red diagonal lines appearing through the file icons of any previously cloaked files in the Files panel disappear, leaving the files uncloaked.

You can also right-click (Windows) or Control+click (Mac) any file or folder in the Files panel and choose Cloaking⇨Uncloak or Cloaking⇨Uncloak All. The first option removes cloaking from the selected file, and the second option removes all prior cloaking settings, including any file endings entered in the Cloaking category of the Site Setup dialog box. You *can't* undo this action, so be sure you really want to uncloak.

Chapter 4: Publishing Your Web Pages Online

In This Chapter

✔ Understanding the file transfer process

✔ Putting and getting files with the Files panel

✔ Synchronizing local and remote files

The final step of publishing your site is getting your files online. Luckily, with Dreamweaver's built-in FTP features, you can quickly transfer your Web site files to a remote live server.

During the transfer process, Dreamweaver can verify that both your local and remote file and folder structures match one another and even identify which files are newer on either the local or remote site to help you streamline the publishing process. You can also use the handy Synchronize Files command to copy updated files between local and remote sites, if necessary, and to decide whether or not to delete any files on the destination site that don't have corresponding files on the starting site.

You can always manually transfer individual files and folders at any time, but having Dreamweaver synchronize your files totally ensures that both locations have the most recent versions of all the files at all times.

This chapter walks you through the file transfer process as well as explains background transfers. We show you how to use the Files panel for *uploading* files (putting them online) and *downloading* files (getting them from the Internet onto your computer), and how to use the Synchronize Files command to synchronize your local and remote files and folders.

Understanding File Transfer Basics

A typical work process involves designing, building, and testing a local version of your Web site before publishing it on the Internet. After you finish all those tasks, you need to establish a connection with the remote live server (as described in Book V, Chapter 3) and send an exact copy of your local files to the live server location so that anyone on the Internet can see them.

If, after putting your files online, you need to make changes to your site, you can make your modifications to the local version of the files, and then upload the changed files to the live server to overwrite the older versions of those files.

File transfers go in one direction at a time: You either *put,* or upload, local files to the remote live server, or you *get* (download) files from the remote live server onto your local computer. For instance, while you may normally only *put* files from your local computer up onto the remote live server, you may occasionally need to *get* a copy of the remote site for your local archive or a new workstation, or to restore an old or corrupted version of a file.

When you transfer your files from local to remote, all the default read and write privileges of the original file are maintained with the transfer. However, when you get files with the Check In/Check Out feature turned on, the copies sent to your local site from the remote live server are marked with read-only privileges so you can't alter them and other team members can still access those files for check out. See Book VI, Chapter 1 for more about the Check In/Check Out feature.

Transferring dependent files

When you transfer files, you upload *copies* of the files rather than the original files themselves, much like a fax sends a copy of the original. The process may take only a matter of seconds, depending on the file size and the number of extra things that appear on the page or are linked to it (such as graphics, PDFs, style sheets, library items, server-side includes, and JavaScript files), which may or may not need to be uploaded with the file.

By default, Dreamweaver asks whether you want to include any *dependent files* — the page's graphics, movies, and style sheets, for example — during a transfer. If the prompt doesn't appear, you can force it on by holding Alt (Windows) or Option (Mac) when you click the Get, Put, Check In, and Check Out icons in the Files panel.

Also, because Dreamweaver treats library items as dependents, which could cause report errors when those files are *put* on some servers, consider cloaking the library items to prevent them from transferring automatically. To find out how to cloak library items, see Book V, Chapter 3.

Working during file transfers

During your file transfers (no matter your chosen transfer connection method), Dreamweaver enables you to continue doing any non-server-related work, such as editing text, adding images, creating style sheets, attaching JavaScript behaviors, and running reports. Dreamweaver calls these *background file transfers.*

We discuss the technology you use for file transfers in Book V, Chapter 3, so if you're curious about using your LAN versus an FTP connection to upload files, skip to that chapter to review the different transfer connection types.

You do have a few file transfer limitations, however. Dreamweaver can't perform some server-related tasks simultaneously. You can't do the following server-related work during file transfers:

✦ Additional file transfers, checking files in and out, and undoing checkouts

✦ Creating database connections and bindings

✦ Previewing live data or inserting a Web service

✦ Deleting or saving files and folders on a remote server

✦ Opening, dragging, or inserting images on files on a remote server

✦ Copying, cutting, and pasting files on a remote server

✦ Refreshing Dreamweaver's Remote view in the Files panel

✦ Previewing files in a browser on a testing server

✦ Automatically putting (uploading) files to the remote server when saving

Putting Files on and Getting Files from the Remote Server

The *Get* and *Put* commands are fantastic transfer and collaboration tools, although you can put them to good use even if you fly solo in your Dreamweaver endeavors. The Get and Put commands enable you to transfer files from your local computer to your remote host location without checking files in and out of the site. That means you can even put a version of a file you're editing on the server as you continue working on that file.

If you use Dreamweaver as part of a team, you should enable Design Notes and use the Check In/Check Out feature. Even if you work alone, you can still enable the Check In/Check Out system. For instance, though you're one person, you may work at two locations and choose to check in files to help keep track of their location and check out status. Turn to Book VI, Chapter 1 to find out more about these features.

The Get and Put commands are accessible through the Files panel, where you can upload and download files from your local machine to the remote server:

✦ **Get** copies files from the remote site to your local machine.

✦ **Put** places local files onto the remote live server.

Examining the Files panel transfer options

You can transfer files to and from your local machine and a remote server with the Files panel in the collapsed or expanded view. We recommend that you use the expanded view to see a list of all the files on both the local and remote sites at the same time.

In collapsed mode, the top of the Files panel has a simple row of icons to assist you with transferring files to and from a remote live server, as shown in Figure 4-1:

Connect/Disconnect

Site Management

Site View

Figure 4-1:
Transfer
files to
and from a
live server
through the
Files panel.

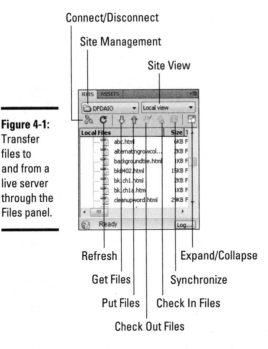

Refresh   Expand/Collapse

Get Files   Synchronize

Put Files Check In Files

Check Out Files

✦ **Site Management Menu:** Choose the site you need to transfer files for from this list. This menu appears in both the collapsed and expanded views and lists all the *managed sites* you've created in Dreamweaver. For more details on creating a managed site, see Book I, Chapter 3.

✦ **Site View Menu:** When the Files panel is collapsed, use this menu to toggle between the four site views (Local View, Live Server, Staging Server, and Repository View). In the expanded view, this menu disappears and three other icons (Remote Server, Testing Server, and Repository Files) are shown in its place:

- **Local View:** Select this view to see the file structure of the local site in the Files panel. You can also use this view to see both local and remote sites with the Files panel split into two panes.

- **Live Server:** Select this view to see the file structure of the site on the remote live server. You must set up a remote site before you can see the remote site files. For details on setting up a remote site, see Book V, Chapter 3.

- **Staging Server:** This view shows a directory listing of the testing server only in normal view, or both the testing server and local site files in the expanded view. You must set up a testing server in advance to see the testing server site. For details on setting up a testing server, see Book VII, Chapter 1.

- **Repository View:** This view shows a listing of all the files in your repository when working with Subversion (SVN), a versioning control system. For more on working with Subversion software visit `http://subversion.apache.org/`.

✦ **Connect/Disconnect:** Connect and disconnect to the remote site with FTP, SFTP, RDS, and WebDAV. With FTP connections, Dreamweaver disconnects from a remote site if there is no activity for more than 30 minutes. To increase or decrease the idle time, choose Edit⇨Preferences (Windows) or Dreamweaver⇨Preferences (Mac) and enter a new number in the Site category of the Preferences dialog box. If you're still getting disconnected after adjusting the idle time, the reason could be the Web server, because some Web hosts disconnect after only a few minutes of inactivity.

✦ **Refresh:** Manually refresh both the local and the remote file listings by clicking this icon when connected to the remote server. This icon also refreshes the local view when disconnected from a remote server.

✦ **View Site FTP Log:** This button (which bears the letters *FTP* and should not be confused with the Log button at the bottom of the Files panel) appears only in the *expanded* Files panel after the initial FTP transfer when FTP (or SFTP) is the selected live server connection method. Click this button to launch the Results panel where you can view the FTP log that contains a record of the site's FTP file transfer activity. See the "Viewing the FTP and background file activity logs" section, later in this chapter, for more information about FTP logs.

✦ **Get File(s):** Get copies of files and folders selected in the Files panel from the remote server to your local site. Any existing files and folders with the same names on the local site become overwritten during the Get process.

✦ **Put Files(s):** Put copies of files and folders selected in the Files panel from the local site to the remote or testing server. Files with the same name on the server are overwritten with the newer versions from the local site.

✦ **Check Out Files:** This option is available only when you're using the Check In/Check Out system (which is described in Book VI, Chapter 1). Click this icon to get a copy of a selected file from the remote server to your local site. If the file already exists on the local site, this process overwrites the local version of the file. After the file copies over to the local site, the file on the server is marked as checked out and a small green check mark icon appears next to the filename in the Files panel.

✦ **Check In:** This option is only available when you're using the Check In/ Check Out system. Click this icon to put a copy of a selected file from the local site to the remote server. After the file copies, the server version file is marked as Checked In and the local site file has a small lock icon next to the filename as an indication of the local file's read-only status.

✦ **Synchronize With:** This icon allows you to launch the synchronization command. For details about the synchronization process, read "Keeping Your Local and Remote Site Files Up-to-Date," later in this chapter.

✦ **Expand/Collapse:** This icon toggles the Files panel between the collapsed view and the expanded view. In the collapsed view, the Files panel displays the Local, Remote, Testing Server, and Repository views. In the expanded view, you can view a directory listing of files in both the local and remote or testing server sites. By default, the local site appears in the right pane, but you can modify this setting in the Site category of Dreamweaver's Preferences.

In expanded mode, the Files panel expands into two panes for displaying both local and remote files. You also see a complete row of icons at the top of the panel to assist you with transferring files to and from a remote server, as shown in Figure 4-2.

Putting files on a remote server

To put files on the remote server, follow these steps:

1. **In the Files panel, select the files you want to upload.**

Use either Local view or Remote view to select your files. If you're attempting to upload only local files that are more recent than their remote counterparts, see the "Keeping Your Local and Remote Site Files Up-to-Date" section, later in this chapter.

Figure 4-2:
View both
local and
remote
files in the
expanded
Files panel.

2. **Click the Put Files icon (which looks like an upward facing blue arrow) at the top of the Files panel.**

   You can also right-click (Windows) or Control+click (Mac) the file in the Files panel and choose Put from the context menu.

   If you attempt to transfer a file (or multiple files, for that matter) that you've edited but haven't saved, a dialog box may appear (depending on your settings), prompting you to save the files before copying them to the remote destination. See Book V, Chapter 3 for more information on setting these preferences.

3. **If prompted to save unsaved open files, click the Yes button to save the files or the No button to put the most recent version of the files on the remote server while leaving the unsaved files open in the Dreamweaver workspace.**

   The Dependent Files dialog box appears if the transferred files contain any dependents such as images and linked CSS files.

4. **Click the Yes button to upload dependent files, or No to bypass this upload feature.**

   For example, if the remote site already contains most or all dependent files (such as images and style sheets), you don't need to upload them again unless they have been updated.

   The file transfer begins immediately — too fast, perhaps, for you to even review the Transfer Status dialog box. If you do see the status dialog box, however, and you need to cancel the transfer, you can click the Cancel button if you're quick enough.

Getting files from a remote server

To get files from the remote or testing server onto your local site using the Files panel, follow these steps:

1. In the Files panel, select the files to download.

Although you're more likely to select files from the Remote view, you can also select the files from Local view. If you want to get only remote files that have been recently changed, use the Synchronize command instead, as described in the "Keeping Your Local and Remote Site Files Up-to-Date" section, later in this chapter.

2. Click the Get Files icon (it looks like down-facing green arrow) at the top of the Files panel.

Or right-click (Windows) or Control+click (Mac) the file in the Files panel and choose Get from the context menu. The Dependent Files dialog box appears if you've enabled this setting in the Site category of the Preferences dialog box (see Book V, Chapter 3).

3. Click the Yes button to download any dependent files. Otherwise, click No to bypass this feature or Cancel to stop the transfer.

If the local site already contains most or all dependent files, don't bother downloading them again unless the remote versions have been changed by another person in your team.

The file transfer begins immediately. When using Check In/Check Out in a collaborative situation, Dreamweaver transfers a copy of each file to the local site, and then marks it as read-only until you check it in again. When you have Check In/Check Out disabled, copies to the local site have the default read and write privileges.

When you get files from the server, you're not removing them from the server. The files are copied, and those copies are transferred to your local computer.

Viewing the FTP and background file activity logs

When you transfer files in either direction — whether you're getting or putting files — Dreamweaver keeps two logs of the file and transfer activity. The logs include operations and outcomes such as whether the transfer was a success or failure, in case you need to troubleshoot connection errors or want to keep a record of the transfer process.

Each log records and stores data in different ways and in different locations:

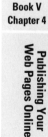

✦ **Background file activity log:** This log appears only during a background file transfer, but you can access it at any time after the first transfer. This log records details about the transfer, including start and finish times, the name of the files being transferred, and the number of files successfully updated. To view this log, click the Log button at the bottom of the Files panel. The Background File Activity dialog box appears, as shown in Figure 4-3. You can save this log as a text file by clicking the Save Log button in the dialog box.

Figure 4-3:
The
Background
File Activity
dialog box.

✦ **FTP Log:** This log keeps a running record of all file FTP transfer activity. You can access it through the expanded Files panel after the initial file transfer, or through the Results panel at any time subsequent to the first transfer. To view the FTP log, open the Results panel (choose Window➪Results➪FTP Log), as shown in the example in Figure 4-4. You can save the content on this log by selecting all the content and right-clicking (Windows) or Control+clicking (Mac) to copy it, and then pasting it into any text editor or other application before saving the file with the appropriate file extension.

Figure 4-4:
The FTP
log in the
Results
panel.

Keeping Your Local and Remote Site Files Up-to-Date

After you establish a remote connection and upload a copy of your local site to the remote server, you can use Dreamweaver's Synchronize Files command to synchronize the files between the two locations. Synchronization isn't the same as transferring files; it's mainly a cleanup or housekeeping feature, useful mostly for making sure that existing (not new) files on both your local and remote sites are up-to-date.

You can set the synchronization settings a variety of ways. Specify, if you like, the synchronization of the entire site, or override that option by selecting individual files to ignore, put, get, or delete during the synchronization. At the end of the synchronization process, Dreamweaver provides confirmation of the updated files.

Viewing the newest files without synchronization

Before you begin synching files, you may find it helpful to view all your Web site files by date. That way, you can see which files are newer in both locations *before* you synchronize.

To select the newest files that haven't been synchronized, do one of the following:

✦ In the Files panel, right-click (Windows) or Control+click (Mac) in the listing area and choose Select➪Newer Local or Select➪Newer Remote.

✦ Choose Edit➪Select Newer Local or Edit➪Select Newer Remote from the Files panel menu.

You can also search for recently modified files without synchronization by choosing Edit➪Select Recently Modified from the panel menu. The Select Recently Modified dialog box appears, as shown in Figure 4-5, and you can choose to view files created or modified within a specified number of days or view files created within a specified range of dates.

Figure 4-5:
View files
in Local
or Remote
view that
were
created or
modified
recently.

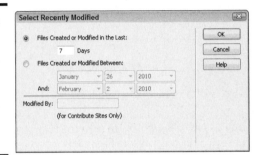

The new or recently modified files are selected and appear with gray high-lighting in the Files panel (as shown in Figure 4-6) for easy identification, making them easy to update with the synchronization command, which is explained in the following section.

Figure 4-6:
Recently modified files highlighted in the Files panel.

Synchronizing your files

When you're ready to synchronize your files, follow these steps:

1. **From the Files panel, choose a site in the Managed Site drop-down list.**

If you haven't managed a site in Dreamweaver yet, see Book I, Chapter 3. If you want to synchronize specific files or folders in the site, select them in the Files panel before proceeding.

2. **Choose Site➪Synchronize Sitewide from the main menu.**

The Synchronize Files dialog box appears, as shown in Figure 4-7.

Figure 4-7:
The Synchronize Files dialog box.

3. **Select an option in the Synchronize drop-down list:**

- **Entire "Managed" Site:** Synchronize all the files on the selected managed site.

- **Selected Local Files Only:** Synchronize selected files from a managed site (the option says Selected Remote Files Only when your most recent file selection was performed in the Remote view of the Files panel).

4. **Select an option in the Direction drop-down list:**

- **Put Newer Files to Remote:** Upload any files from the local site that have been updated since the last upload, plus any new files that don't appear on the remote server yet.

- **Get Newer Files from Remote:** Download remote files that have been updated since the last download, plus any new files that don't appear on the local site yet.

- **Get and Put Newer Files:** Put the most recent versions of all the files, including any missing files, on both local and remote sites.

5. **Select or deselect the Delete Remote Files Not on Local Drive option.**

Select this option to have Dreamweaver remove files on the destination site when originals don't exist. For example, if you delete a local file before transferring, this option also deletes the deleted file's counterpart from the remote site.

6. **Click the Preview button.**

Before committing to the synchronization process, you must review in the Synchronize dialog box shown in Figure 4-8 a list of all the files that are updating.

Figure 4-8:
The Synchronize dialog box shows the files being synchronized.

7. **(Optional) Change the action associated with each file (Get, Put, Delete, and Ignore).**

To change any of the actions associated with the files, select a file and click the appropriate icon at the bottom of the dialog box.

8. **Click OK to begin the synchronization.**

If all the files are already in sync, Dreamweaver displays a message that politely notifies you that the synchronization isn't necessary. Otherwise, the synchronization process runs. When it's finished, Dreamweaver returns to the Files panel.

Using diff tools (if you have 'em)

One of the actions in the Synchronization dialog box is to compare local and remote versions of the files with a third-party tool *before* the synchronization process. These tools, also called *diff tools,* can compare code between two versions of the same file so that you can merge changes between the files before the transfer process.

Use of a diff tool requires the installation of a third-party comparison/merging application

and the specification of that application in the File Compare category of the Preferences dialog box.

For details about Adobe recommended file comparison tools and instructions on how to use them, visit the Adobe Web site at `http://help.adobe.com/en_US/` `dreamweaver/cs/using/WSc78c5` `058ca073340dcda9110b1f693f21-` `7edda.html`.

Book VI

Working Collaboratively

Contents at a Glance

Chapter 1: Working Efficiently with a Team

Most likely, you're not working alone on your Web site project(s). The larger the Web site, the greater the odds that you're getting help from other people. Most Web sites these days require a team — someone who works on programming the dynamic aspects, a JavaScript/HTML/CSS expert, another person to design and optimize the graphics, and someone who pulls all these aspects together into one cohesive Web site. The roles in your particular situation may be different, but the overall team concept is the same.

How do you keep track of who is working on what at a certain time to avoid work nightmares such as team members overwriting each other's files or different members working simultaneously on the same file? The answers are built right in Dreamweaver.

Dreamweaver includes several features to keep you in tune with your team members, such as Design Notes and the Check In/Check Out feature. And if you customize the columns in the Files panel, you can see at a glance the status of each page in the Web site. We discuss all these features — and how you can use them to work efficiently with your team — in this chapter.

Attaching Design Notes to Your Files

Dreamweaver's Design Notes are reminder notes, like the one in Figure 1-1, that you can create and attach to individual files on a site to help you and your team with site file management. You can attach Design Notes to documents, templates, images, Flash content, ActiveX controls, and applets. The Design Notes data itself is stored in a separate linked file that allows for shared access and retrieval. This tool is a must if you're working collaboratively on site design or site management.

Figure 1-1:
Use Design Notes to remind you and your team about important site details.

Design Notes come in two flavors:

✦ **Notes you create:** The Design Notes feature is especially helpful if you're exchanging files in a design team or workgroup. For example, you may have a monthly news page that is updated to a site on the first day of each month. With Design Notes, you can add comments about file transfer data, archived file locations, and other information related to the uploading of the newest news page. You may also want to use Design Notes for storing sensitive data, such as marketing strategy guidelines or pricing arrangements.

✦ **Notes that are created for you automatically:** Adobe's Fireworks and Flash programs integrate and update Design Notes on their own (whether you want them to or not) so that you can use them later in Dreamweaver sites with the same site-root path. When you open files in either of those programs and export them to another file format, the Design Notes feature launches (behind the scenes) to store data about the original source file, such as filename, type, and location. For instance, when opening the fatcat.png file in Fireworks and exporting it as fatcat.gif, Fireworks creates a Design Note called fatcat.gif.mno that includes the name of the original .png file and the absolute location where it is stored:

```
fw_source="file:///LocalDisk/sites/assets/orig/fatcat.png"
```

In Dreamweaver, when a graphic is imported from Fireworks, the Design Notes automatically copy to the site. Then, if you need to edit the graphic in Fireworks, Fireworks can use those Design Notes to quickly locate the original .png file and open it for editing, while adding any new data to the Design Notes.

Enabling and disabling Design Notes

By default, Design Notes are enabled for each managed site, but you can edit this setting in the Design Notes category, which is in the Advanced Settings category of the Site Setup dialog box. Follow these steps:

1. **Choose Site⇨Manage Sites to display the Manage Sites dialog box.**

2. **Select a site from the site listing, and then click the Edit button.**

The Site Setup dialog box appears.

3. **Expand the Advanced Settings and select the Design Notes category.**

The Design Notes category options appear, as shown in Figure 1-2. The Maintain Design Notes option is selected by default; however, the Enable Upload Design Notes for Sharing option is deselected. Toggle these features on and off as needed.

Figure 1-2:
Select or
deselect
Design
Notes
options for
your site.

4. **Select or deselect the Enable Upload Design Notes for Sharing option.**

- **Select:** Use this setting if you want Dreamweaver to upload the Design Notes associated with files on the site along with the rest of your files when it transfers files to the remote server.

Use this setting with extreme care. Enabling Design Notes for sharing online creates security risks, especially when Design Notes are used for storing sensitive data, such as marketing strategy guidelines or pricing arrangements, as described in the previous section.

- **Deselect:** Use this setting to keep Design Notes locally and not have Dreamweaver upload them to the remote site when files are transferred.

5. **Click Save to exit the Site Setup dialog box, and then click Done to close the Manage Sites dialog box.**

Removing Design Notes

Design Notes, when selected, do increase the file transfer time slightly, so if you're working alone and do not use this feature, you may want to deselect this feature and remove all Design Notes completely.

To deselect and permanently remove Design Notes, follow these steps:

1. **Expand the Advanced Settings category in the Site Setup dialog box, and then deselect the Maintain Design Notes option in the Design Notes category.**

For details, see the preceding section.

2. **Click the Clean Up Design Notes button to delete all the Design Notes from your local computer.**

3. **To proceed, click the Yes button.**

You can't undo this step, so be sure this is something you really want to do before clicking the Yes button!

Click the No button if you have a change of heart and want to leave Design Notes as they are. If you click Yes, Dreamweaver deletes all the Design Notes on the local computer.

4. **Click Save to exit the Site Setup dialog box, and then click Done to close the Manage Sites dialog box.**

Adding Design Notes to a file

Add your own Design Notes to individual files, folders, or templates on your site every time you modify the content and want to communicate with other members of the team about it. When you add Design Notes to a template, they attach only to the template and aren't copied to any template-based documents. That way, individual template-based files can each have their own individual Design Notes! You can also attach Design Notes to graphics, Flash movies, ActiveX controls, applets, and Shockwave objects.

To add Design Notes to a file, follow these steps:

1. **Open the file you want to add the Design Notes to and choose File➪Design Notes.**

Or right-click (Windows) or Control+click (Mac) a closed file in the Files panel and choose Design Notes from the context menu.

If you want to add Design Notes to a file that's located on a remote site, you must check out the file first (see the next section, "Checking Files In and Out," to find out more about using the Check In/Check Out feature). Then you can add the Design Notes to the local version of the file.

The Design Notes dialog box appears.

2. **On the Basic Info tab, fill in the following fields to create your Design Notes:**

   - **Status:** Select a status for the file from the Status menu. The status reflects the document's current condition, relative to it being finalized and ready for publication. Dreamweaver presents you with eight status settings: Draft, Revision1, Revision2, Revision3, Alpha, Beta, Final, and Needs Attention. To create your own custom status setting (such as "Pending approval"), move on to Step 3.

   - **Date:** To insert the current date in your Design Notes, click the Insert Date icon above the right corner of the Notes field.

   - **Notes:** Type your Design Notes in the text field.

   - **Show When File Is Opened:** Select this check box to have the Design Notes appear automatically when the file is opened.

3. **(Optional) On the All Info tab, click the plus (+) icon to add to the Info list new *key/value pairs*, which you can use as custom status settings and search criteria for Design Notes reports:**

   - **Name:** Enter a word in the Name field to identify the first part (key) of the note information, such as Author or Status.

   - **Value:** Enter a word or two in the Value field to represent the attribute for the associated key, such as Sue or Draft6.

   Each *key* must have a *value* and can be composed of any words to assist you. For example, create custom status definitions, such as *Status=Draft6* or a key/value pair to refine a Design Note report, such as *Author=Sue, V=2.b,* or *Revision=4/15/10,* as shown in Figure 1-3.

   To delete an existing key/value pair, select it from the Info list and click the minus (–) icon.

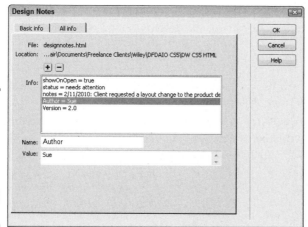

Figure 1-3: Enter key/value pairs in the All Info tab of the Design Notes dialog box.

4. **Click OK to close the Design Notes dialog box.**

   Design Notes for each file are saved in a _notes folder on your site. The individual Design Notes files are named after the document they're attached to and have the .mno file extension. For instance, if the main filename is contact.html, the corresponding Design Notes file is _notes/contact.html.mno.

Viewing and editing Design Notes

After you add Design Notes to your files, you can view, edit, and add additional information to the Notes at any time. To find files containing Design Notes quickly in the Files panel, however, you need to enable the Design Notes invisible elements icon, which by default is turned off. To turn on Design Notes icons, you must enable the visibility of the Notes column in the Advanced Settings⇨File View Columns category of the Site Setup dialog box. Turn to the "Defining File View Columns" section, later in the chapter, for details.

After you enable the Design Notes icon visibility, you can quickly identify files with Design Notes attached to them in the Files panel, in both normal and expanded mode. Look for a Design Notes icon (it looks like a little yellow cartoon speech bubble) next to the filename in the Notes column, as shown in Figure 1-4.

Design Notes icon

Figure 1-4: Files with Design Notes display a Design Notes icon next to the filename.

When you identify which files in your managed site contain Design Notes, you can easily open them through the Files panel and make changes to them as needed.

Checking Files In and Out

When you're working as a member of a collaborative team, using the Check In/Check Out Files feature is a must. The beauty of the system is that you must check in and check out files not only from the remote site but also from the shared local site — so no two people can work on the same file at the same time. This single innovation goes a long way toward maintaining the integrity of a Web site.

Dreamweaver uses a simple icon system next to filenames in the Files panel to help keep track of all the files and their check in/check out status. When a file is checked out, Dreamweaver shows the person's name and a red check mark next to the checked out file. When a file is checked back in, a green check mark appears. After checking a file back in, the local copy of the file becomes read-only and a little lock icon appears next to the filename. The remote files, however, can't be turned into read-only versions after they are checked out. That means that if anyone transfers files to the remote server with a program other than Dreamweaver, the remote files can be overwritten. To help prevent this from accidentally happening when using other programs, the .lck file usually appears next to the checked out file as a sort of visual indication of the file's checked out status.

**Book VI
Chapter 1**

Working Efficiently with a Team

To enable the Check In/Check Out system, do the following:

1. **Choose Site⇨Manage Sites to display the Manage Sites dialog box.**

2. **Select the desired site, and then click the Edit button to display the Site Setup dialog box.**

3. **In the Servers category, select the server connection you'd like to modify from the center panel, and then click the Edit Existing Server icon to reopen the server settings dialog box.**

   The Edit Existing Server icon looks like a pencil.

4. **Click the Advanced tab and select the Enable File Check-Out option (see Figure 1-5).**

   If you're using FTP, enter a check out name and an e-mail address in the fields provided. The e-mail address you enter here becomes a clickable link in the Files panel when the file is checked out.

Figure 1-5:
Enable the
Check-Out
feature.

5. **Click Save to save your settings, click Save again to close the Site Setup dialog box, and then click Done to close the Manage Sites dialog box.**

The Check In/Check Out settings work immediately and can be modified or disabled at any time. To begin checking files into and out of a remote folder in the Files panel, follow these steps:

1. **Select the files you want to check in or out.**

2. **Click the Check In or Check Out icons on the Files panel toolbar.**

   Expand the Files panel for a view of both local and remote files.

3. **Click Yes or No as appropriate when prompted to include dependent files for the check in or check out, such as graphics or CSS files.**

When a remote file is checked out, its counterpart in the local file listing in the Files panel appears with a little lock icon next to it, as shown in Figure 1-6. The lock is virtual, however, and you can remove the file's locked status if needed.

To manually unlock a file, select the file in the Files panel, right-click (Windows) or Control+click (Mac), and choose Turn Off Read Only for a regular Dreamweaver or InContext Editable site or Undo Check Out for a Contribute site. If prompted, click Yes to confirm that you want to unlock the file.

Check In

Locked file   Check Out

Figure 1-6:
A lock icon appears next to local files when checked out.

Checked in file

Using Version Control with Subversion

Subversion (SVN) is a free, open-source version control system software. You can easily integrate Subversion into Dreamweaver for even more control over file versioning, rollbacks, and editing of your files during the Check In/Check Out process.

Although it's not a full SVN client, Dreamweaver does allow users to collaboratively manage and edit files on a remote Web server, as well as get the latest versions of files, edit them, and commit the files when finished — all without having to set up a command-line interface or install any third-party utilities. Plus, in CS5, you now have the ability to Move, Copy, Delete, and Revert assets under Subversion control.

To define Subversion as your version control system, follow these steps:

1. **Choose Site⊅Manage Sites to display the Manage Sites dialog box.**

2. **Select the desired site, and then click the Edit button to display the Site Setup dialog box.**

3. **Click the Version Control Category on the left of the dialog box, and then choose the Subversion from the Access menu, as shown in Figure 1-7.**

A dialog box appears alerting you that using a version control server disables the check-in/check-out feature. Click OK to proceed.

After you choose Subversion, the rest of the Subversion settings become visible in the dialog box.

Figure 1-7:
Set version
control
settings for
Subversion.

4. Fill in the fields in the dialog box:

- **Protocol:** Select HTTP, HTTPS, SVN, or SVN+ SSH, which determines how clients authenticate themselves to the server.

- **Server Address:** Enter the server address.

- **Repository Path:** Enter the path to the repository.

- **Server Port:** Leave the server port set to the default unless you need to set it to another port number.

- **Username:** Enter your username.

- **Password:** Enter your password.

5. Click the Test button to verify the connection.

If the connection is working, Dreamweaver alerts you that the connection was successful. If the connection can't be made, you see an error alert. Check the spelling of the server address, username, and password and try again. If you continue to have difficulty establishing a connection, speak with your system Administrator for assistance.

Dreamweaver CS4 shipped with Subversion 1.4.x, which means that if you used Subversion in CS4, this version number was associated with the sites you used to with this software. Each version of the software is connected to the clients to ensure that the client and version are compatible. When you upgrade to Dreamweaver CS5, which uses the Subversion 1.6.6 client library, your older sites may not be compatible with the new version in CS5. Furthermore, if you use a third-party client application that uses a later version of Subversion, there may be additional issues with Dreamweaver communicating with Subversion. For further details, visit http://kb2.adobe. com/cps/406/kb406661.html. If you'd like more information about working with Subversion and to download your free copy of the Subversion software, visit `http://subversion.apache.org/`. Lastly, to watch a video about using SVN with Dreamweaver, go to `www.adobe.com/go/lrvid4049_dw`.

Defining File View Columns

In the expanded Files panel, Dreamweaver displays all the file and folder details in columns next to each of the filenames. Using the Advanced Settings⇨File View Columns category of the Site Setup dialog box, you can tailor which file and folder details are displayed by modifying the default column settings and adding customized columns. Here are a few of the things you can do to change the File View Columns:

+ Add up to ten new custom columns.

+ Delete custom columns.

+ Rename custom columns.

+ Show and Hide columns.

  The only column you can't hide is the filename column.

+ Realign and reorder columns.

+ Set column sharing options with users connected to a site.

+ Attach Design Notes to custom columns.

Customizing File View Columns

Member of your team can customize their computers to view the contents of the expanded Files panel to suit their specific needs. You can add, edit, remove, hide, and show Dreamweaver's built-in columns, as well as add personal customized columns associated with your Design Notes on your own computer or to be shared with the entire work team.

To add, edit, or delete File View Columns in the Files panel, follow these steps:

1. **Choose Site⇨Manage Sites to display the Manage Sites dialog box.**

2. **Select a site from the site listing, and then click the Edit button.**

   The Site Setup dialog box appears.

3. **Expand the Advanced Settings, and then select the File View Columns category.**

   The File View Columns category options are displayed, as shown in Figure 1-8.

4. **To hide any built-in categories that are set to Show:**

   a. **Select the category.**

   b. **Click the Edit Existing Column icon.**

   c. **Deselect the Options: Show check box.**

   d. **Click the Save button.**

   Categories marked with Hide in the Show column are hidden from view in the Files panel.

Figure 1-8:
Customize the Files panel by adjusting settings in the File View Columns category.

5. **To add a new custom column, do the following:**

   a. **Click the plus (+) icon.**

   b. **Enter the name of the new column in the Column Name text box.**

   c. **Choose a Design Notes value from the Associate with Design Notes drop-down menu or type your own.**

   d. **Select an alignment option from the Align menu.**

   e. **To display your new custom column, select the Show option. To keep it hidden, leave the Show option deselected.**

   Custom columns are marked as Personal (instead of Built In) in the Type column.

   f. **To share a custom column, select the Share with All Users of This Site option.**

   This option enables all users connected to the site to view and share the column. Shared columns are marked as Shared in the Type column.

   g. **Click the Save button.**

   Your new custom column will be added to the list of custom columns for Design Notes.

6. **To remove a custom column, select the column in the list and then click the minus (–) icon.**

   Deletion is immediate and not undoable, and does not come with a confirmation message, so take special care when deleting columns.

7. **To reorder any column (except for the Name column, which is always first), select the column you want to move and click the up and down arrows until the selected column is in the desired position.**

   For example, if you want the Size column to be next to the Name column, select the Size column and click the up arrow icon once to reposition the Size column next to the Name column.

8. **Click Save to exit the Site Setup dialog box, and then click Done to close the Manage Sites dialog box.**

Sorting File View Columns

After customizing columns, return to the expanded Files panel to sort column data by any of the column headings. Click a heading once to sort all the file data by that column. Click the same heading a second time to reverse the order of the sort from ascending to descending, or vice versa.

**Book VI
Chapter 1**

Working Efficiently with a Team

Chapter 2: Setting Up and Connecting to a Contribute Site

In This Chapter

✔ Building a site for Contribute users

✔ Connecting to a Contribute site

✔ Transferring files to and from a Contribute site

✔ Setting server file and folder permissions

✔ Understanding and using Contribute special files

*I*n 2003, Macromedia, before its purchase by Adobe, developed a great little software program called Contribute (the current version is Contribute CS4). For less than $200 per user, Contribute enables nontechnical people to edit some of the content on their Dreamweaver-created Web sites. Even your least technical clients or office mates can edit and update specified parts of the pages on the site without fear of breaking or ruining the site.

The Contribute program is as easy to use as Microsoft Word and comes with a fantastic built-in instructional tutorial to help you get started. Contribute has its own built-in Web browser with FTP access that enables you to navigate and download a copy of any existing page on your Web site to your local computer. From there, you can make edits to specified editable regions and publish them back to the remote server.

For example, from Contribute, users can download a local copy of a Web page from their site, modify it locally, and upload the changed page to the Web site, overwriting what was previously online. If you're working with several people in a workgroup, all members can use Contribute to edit pages on a Web site as long as copies of Contribute software are installed on their computers. One person has to act as the site Administrator. Typically that person is either the Web designer or developer who builds the site in Dreamweaver or the Contribute workgroup manager. And because you must have one Big Cheese, Contribute comes with tools that enable you to create and administer Web sites that are optimized for seamless editing and updating. We explain some of these tools in this chapter and in Book VI, Chapter 3.

To find out more about the differences between Dreamweaver and Contribute, and to find out how to manage a Dreamweaver site for Contribute users, read Book VI, Chapter 3.

Now, if you're not working with a team of contributors (which requires a bit of coordination), but are rather a single contributor who needs to make only simple updates to specific areas of a site, the browser-based Adobe InContext Editing (ICE) system might be a better, more affordable solution for you and your client. Turn to Book VI, Chapter 4 for details about using InContext Editing.

In this chapter, you discover the important differences between building a site in Dreamweaver for Contribute users and building regular Dreamweaver sites. With that understanding, you then find out how to make a Contribute-compatible site connection, use Dreamweaver to administer the site to do things such as set file and folder permissions for users, and transfer the Contribute site files to the remote live server.

Understanding Contribute Best Practices

A Contribute site isn't much different from other Web sites you build in Dreamweaver, but you do have to keep a few considerations in mind when you plan and build a site for Contribute users. For example, Contribute is intended to bring the technical elite and the technical novices together so that, as a team, they can build and maintain an excellent site. That means laying out a logical yet simple site plan that multiple users can understand and use, just as you would when designing a non-Contribute site.

The Contribute software was appropriately named. The program not only empowers users to contribute to the Web site in meaningful ways but also prevents users from making catastrophic changes that could corrupt the visual unity of the site or cripple the site's essential functions (or worse).

Setting up Dreamweaver to work with Contribute is essential before building a Contribute Web site. You need to make sure that Contribute users can get in, do what they need to do, and get out — without mucking up the site infra-structure and processes. Here are a few things you should remember to do:

+ **When you create a new managed site, don't forget to enable Contribute settings.** To access Contribute settings, expand the Advanced Settings category in the Site Setup dialog box.

+ **Build a Dreamweaver template-driven Web site with specified editable content areas.** This makes the site easier for novices to use when editing and creating new pages in Contribute. For example, you may want to specify one editable area on the template for the main text area of the page, another area for page headers, and another for graphics.

+ **Make site navigation as simple as possible.** See the section "Leaving a Trail of Bread Crumbs for Contribute Users," later in this chapter.

+ **Use Dreamweaver to create a style sheet and apply styles to the pages on the Contribute site.** Although you can apply styles (but not create them) with Contribute, it's often faster and easier to do CSS stuff in Dreamweaver.

If Contribute users are using Microsoft Word to write and format site content, consider naming styles after preexisting Word style names so Contribute can map the styles when a user copies and pastes data from a Word file into a Contribute file.

+ **Hide some styles to prevent Contribute users from changing them.** By hiding styles, you let Contribute users edit the text but not the style. To hide a particular style, edit the style name in Code view so that it starts with `mmhide_`. For instance, if you have a style called `Bold36` that makes text bold and 36 pixels, rename the style `mmhide_Bold36`.

+ **Set up read and write file and folder permissions on the server for Contribute users.** Setting up permissions designates what Contribute users can and cannot access and edit on the site after it's published.

+ **Group similar items, don't go crazy with folder nesting, and include index pages to each folder that contain links to all the other pages within the folder.** To modify or create new pages, Contribute users must be able to navigate to existing site files through Contribute's browser interface. In other words, if they can't find the page, they can't make changes to it. If your site uses folders, be sure to encourage Contribute users to save new pages they create on the site into the appropriate folders.

+ **Create a Contribute-compatible site connection and test it in preparation for uploading the files to the remote server.** That way, you know in advance that everything is functioning when you are ready to hand off the basic site maintenance tasks to Contribute users.

You must be using Contribute version 2.0 or later to administer a site with Dreamweaver CS5.

Book VI
Chapter 2

Setting Up and
Connecting to a
Contribute Site

Making a Dreamweaver Site Connection Compatible with Contribute

Before building a Contribute site, you need to create a Contribute-enabled managed site in Dreamweaver so the program knows where on your local machine you're housing all the files you create for the new Contribute site. (See Book I, Chapter 3 for details on managing a site.)

You also need to enable Contribute compatibility in Dreamweaver through the Site Setup dialog box. One of the great benefits of enabling Contribute compatibility is that Dreamweaver automatically saves a version of each file when it's opened. That way, if users ever need to revert to a previous version of that file, they can *roll back* to that version easily. Turn to Book VI, Chapter 3 for more information about the rollback process.

After you've created your managed site, follow these steps in Dreamweaver to enable site compatibility with Contribute:

1. From the main menu or from the panels menu in the Files panel, choose Site➪Manage Sites.

The Manage Sites dialog box appears.

2. Select the site you want to make compatible with Contribute, and then click the Edit button.

3. Expand the Advanced Settings category in the Site Setup dialog box, and then click Contribute.

The dialog box displays the Enable Contribute Compatibility option, as shown in Figure 2-1.

Figure 2-1: Enable your site for Contribute compatibility.

4. Select the Enable Contribute Compatibility option.

5. If Dreamweaver alerts you that you need to select a server connection method (see Book V, Chapter 3), and enable Check In/Out and Design Notes (see Book VI, Chapter 1) before enabling the Enable Contribute Compatibility option, do so.

Click OK to enable these features and type a check out name and e-mail address if prompted.

6. **Enter the Site Root URL, and then press the Test button to test the connection.**

   You must enter a URL to administer the Contribute site.

7. **Click Save to accept all the settings in the Site Setup box.**

8. **When you see a message** about the cache being recreated, click OK to proceed.

9. **Click the Done button to close the Manage Sites dialog box.**

After you enable site compatibility with Contribute, you can successfully administer the site with Dreamweaver. You can also set up and test the server connection, set server and folder permissions for Contribute users, and transfer files to the remote server—all from Dreamweaver.

You create the Contribute site just as you do any other site, including having a local and remote copy of all files. The main difference between a regular site and a Contribute site is that you set up the Contribute site in Dreamweaver so that Contribute users can log into the remote site, download pages, modify pages, and upload those pages back to the remote live server.

Using Dreamweaver to Administer a Contribute Site

Before you can administer a Contribute site from Dreamweaver, you must also have a copy of Contribute software installed on your computer. After you have both software programs installed on the same computer, you can use Dreamweaver to launch Contribute for site administration tasks such as

✦ Changing the administrative settings for the Contribute site

✦ Setting up Contribute users with individual *connection keys* (the electronic version of a password that enables them to access the remote server to download, modify, and upload edited pages on the Web site)

✦ Setting and changing permissions for Contribute roles, which determine the level of access any one Contribute user has on a Web site

One of the great benefits to being a Contribute Administrator is that you can assign user roles for each Contribute user and set file and folder permissions for each one. None of these roles and permissions settings affect the Dreamweaver Administrator, however. The Dreamweaver Administrator (that's you) is the master of all.

Follow these steps to administer a Contribute site in Dreamweaver:

1. **Expand the Advanced Settings category in the Site Setup dialog box and select the Contribute category.**

If you're not sure how to do this, follow Steps 1–4 in the preceding section.

2. **Click the Administer Site in Contribute button (shown in Figure 2-2).**

This button appears only after you enable Contribute compatibility as outlined in the preceding section.

Figure 2-2:
The
Administer
Site in
Contribute
button.

3. **In the dialog box that appears (shown in Figure 2-3), select a method for editing and then click the Yes button to become the Web site's Contribute Administrator.**

Your computer launches Contribute (if it's not already open), and the Administer Website dialog box appears, as shown in Figure 2-4.

Figure 2-3:
Assign
yourself
as the
Web site's
Contribute
Adminis-
trator.

**Book VI
Chapter 2**

Setting Up and
Connecting to a
Contribute Site

Figure 2-4:
Configure
settings
for the
Contribute
site.

4. **In the Administer Website dialog box, you can perform the following tasks:**

   • To change administrative settings, select the Administration category to enter a contact e-mail address, set the Administrator password, or remove administrative settings for this site.

   • To edit role settings, select the Users and Roles category and edit or remove existing roles and create new roles.

   • To send connection keys (Contribute site access information) to users, select the Contribute user's name from the list of connected users and click the Send Connection Key button.

   At a minimum, you should set the Administrator password. Making additional settings in the Administer Website dialog box are up to you.

   Note: This book focuses on using Dreamweaver. If you need more detailed support on Contribute, such as setting up administrative settings, connection keys, and user roles, read the Contribute Help files on Adobe's LiveDocs Web site at `http://www.adobe.com/support/contribute/`.

5. **Click OK to accept all the settings in the Administer Website dialog box.**

6. **Click Save to close the Site Setup dialog box.**

7. **Click Done to close the Manage Sites dialog box.**

Making the Most of Templates

When you conceive of a Web site for Contribute users, the design can be as elaborate as your imagination can fathom, but you need to ensure that the design has content areas that are easy to edit from the Contribute user's (read: novice's) perspective.

Although using templates is by no means required, building a Web site from a Dreamweaver template is one of the best ways to create and manage a site for Contribute users. We recommend that you use a master template in Dreamweaver to build all the pages on the site. That way, you can create editable areas in the template to define what content (including text, graphics, layers, and tables) Contribute users can edit. You (as Administrator) still maintain the look and feel of the site, which means you can easily update the layout later, should you need to. See Book III, Chapter 2 to find more about using Dreamweaver templates.

After you create the template(s) and build the site in Dreamweaver, you can upload the template(s), along with the site files, to the server to make them available to Contribute users. As long as the site root folder for each user's profile matches the site root folder you define for the site in Dreamweaver, the templates appear in Contribute's New Page dialog box when users create a new page.

If you choose not to build the Contribute site using Dreamweaver templates, you could instead designate any page on the site as a Contribute template, from which users can create new pages. For simplicity's sake, we refer to template pages designated by the Contribute administrator as *Contribute templates*.

The main difference between the two template types is that Dreamweaver templates can have editable areas and locked areas, whereas Contribute templates are completely editable, providing more opportunities for users to inadvertently "break" the look and functionality of the page. Therefore, we highly recommend that you use Dreamweaver templates because you have much more control over the integrity of any new template-based pages that are created.

To create a (fully editable) Contribute template, follow these steps:

1. **In Dreamweaver, expand the Advanced Settings category in the Site Setup dialog box and then select the Contribute category.**

If you're not sure how to do this, follow Steps 1–4 in the earlier section "Making a Dreamweaver Site Connection Compatible with Contribute."

2. **Click the Administer Site in Contribute button.**

This button appears only after you enable Contribute compatibility (as described in the earlier section, "Making a Dreamweaver Site Connection Compatible with Contribute"). If you created an administrator password when configuring Dreamweaver to administer a Contribute site, the Administrator Password dialog box appears.

3. **Enter an administrator password if prompted, and then click OK.**

Your computer launches Contribute (if it's not already open), and the Administer Website dialog box appears (refer to Figure 2-4).

4. **Select the Administrator role in the Users and Roles category, and then click the Edit Role Settings button.**

The Edit "Administrator" Settings dialog box appears.

5. **Choose the New Pages category, as shown in Figure 2-5.**

**Book VI
Chapter 2**

Setting Up and
Connecting to a
Contribute Site

Figure 2-5:
Use the
New Pages
category to
create new
pages from
existing
Contribute
pages or
templates.

6. **Select the Create a New Page by Copying a Page from This List option, click the Add button, and then select a page on the site to use as a Contribute template.**

7. **Click OK to close the Edit "Administrator" Settings dialog box.**

8. **Click Close to close the Administer Website dialog box.**

Now Contribute users can use pages in this list as a starting point for creating new pages.

Leaving a Trail of Bread Crumbs for Contribute Users

When you build a Dreamweaver site for Contribute users, try to create a site structure that is easy to navigate. Here are some basic site organization tips:

✦ **If you're building a small site, organize content in a logical manner by having all the files at the root level.** To keep things simple, don't go too crazy with nested folders. You want Contribute users to be able to easily find what they need and not feel flustered because they can't seem to open the page they need to edit. For consistency, also remember to keep your filenames short with no spaces and no funky characters.

✦ **If you're building a larger site, or if your small site necessitates a folder structure, use folders to organize similar Web pages.** When using subfolders to organize content, make sure that each folder has a main page with the filename index.html that contains links to all the other pages in that folder. Then the main page opens automatically in a browser when the URL specifies that folder name, and Contribute users can easily navigate to and open any of the pages in that folder for editing.

For example, if a company provides ten services and needs a separate Web page for each service, organizing all ten services' HTML files inside a Services folder is a logical file management solution. Then the URL, when displayed in a browser, would look something like `http://www.mysamplesite.com/services/`.

Using folders may make Contribute editing go faster than when you use a flat document structure, especially when a lot of editing is going on. With folders, the different versions of files are in separate directories, making editing a little faster.

✦ **If you have server-side includes for HTML content, such as footers or navigation tables, create a simple HTML page with links to all the include files on the site.** Contribute users can then use that HTML page to navigate to and edit the include files.

Connecting to a Contribute Site

In Dreamweaver, you can treat a Contribute site just like any other site by connecting to a remote server and editing pages as needed. However, although you can connect to a remote site in several different ways, not all of them are compatible with Contribute. Specifically, the following connections have restrictions:

✦ **Your local computer acts as the Web server:** To share your connection with Contribute users, you need to set up the site with FTP or a network connection instead of using the local folder path.

✦ **You're using WebDAV or an old copy of Microsoft Visual SourceSafe:** You're out of luck. These connection options aren't compatible with Contribute.

✦ **You're using an RDS (Rapid Development Services) connection:** You can achieve Contribute compatibility, but you need to customize your connection prior to sharing with Contribute users.

Book VI
Chapter 2

Setting Up and
Connecting to a
Contribute Site

When you enable the site for use with Contribute, Dreamweaver creates a site root URL for the Contribute site based on other information about the site. Unfortunately, this information is not always accurate, so you may need to test the connection manually. To see whether your connection is accurate, open the Dreamweaver Site Setup dialog box, expand the Advanced Settings to select the Contribute category, and then click the Test button. Dreamweaver notifies you if the connection is good or needs troubleshooting. If it's good, you're ready to transfer files. For troubleshooting help, see "Troubleshooting a Contribute Site in Dreamweaver," later in the chapter.

Transferring files to and from a Contribute site from within Dreamweaver

Just as Dreamweaver has its Check In/Out system, Contribute uses its own method of file transfer to help prevent multiple users from accessing and editing the same file at the same time. In Contribute, users download and open a *draft* of a page, edit it, and then publish it to the remote server. (Your Contribute users can learn how to do that by reading the cool Contribute tutorial that comes with Contribute.)

As Contribute administrator, you can use Dreamweaver to transfer files to the remote server instead of uploading and downloading files from Contribute. Just be sure to always use the Check In/Check Out commands as discussed in Book VI, Chapter 1 when transferring files to a Contribute site from Dreamweaver.

If you accidentally use Dreamweaver's Get/Put commands instead of Check In/Check Out when transferring files to the remote server, they may accidentally overwrite changes another Contribute user has made to a file. Dreamweaver gives you a warning if someone else checks out a file.

To aid with the Check In/Out process, Dreamweaver makes automatic back-ups of all Contribute site files upon check in and puts them in the _baks folder along with your name and a date stamp in a Design Notes file.

Turn to Book V, Chapter 4 to find out how to transfer files from a local site to the remote server.

Setting Contribute file and folder permissions

As the Contribute administrator, you can set unique file and folder permissions for every Contribute user in a group. These permissions are attached to each user's role rather than to the files and folders. Although enforced on Contribute users, these permissions don't affect the files when edited from within Dreamweaver. For example, a Contribute user with read-only permission to a folder can't write to that folder. The same goes for read access to dependent files.

If a Contribute user doesn't have permission to access an images folder, those images appear as broken image icons when viewing the file for editing in Contribute. Because templates reside in a Templates subfolder at the root level of the site, you need to be aware of read and write permissions so that Contribute users can create new files from templates as needed.

Additionally, Contribute doesn't have any way to manage read-write privileges assigned to files and folders; those must be managed directly on the remote server through Dreamweaver.

Understanding Contribute Special Files

Contribute creates a bunch of special files to assist with the administration and editing of your Contribute Web site. These special files are not viewable by site visitors, and they don't need to be edited or updated by you. They just exist in the background on the remote server to help Dreamweaver manage Contribute files for all the users making changes to pages on the site. These files are

✦ Backup files for old or rollback versions of files in the Contribute-generated _baks folder

✦ Contribute site management files with the .csi file extension that are saved in the Contribute-generated _mm folder

✦ Design Notes files with metadata about the files (see Book VI, Chapter 1 to find more about Design Notes)

✦ Temporary files with the .tmp extension created for previewing purposes in Contribute

✦ Temporary locked (read-only) files to show Contribute users when those files are opened elsewhere

When Contribute creates all these special administrative files, they are automatically updated and uploaded to the publicly accessible remote server for the Web site. If you don't want to see these Contribute files on your server (specifically the _mm and _baks folders), you can create a *staging server* (or *production server*) as a place for Contribute users to work on the site before publishing updated pages to the remote server. After users complete any changes to their pages, those site files can be copied from the staging server to the production server without the special files. To discover how to add another level of security that blocks folders beginning with an underscore from being copied to the production server, search for *Web site security* and *Staging Servers and Contribute* in Contribute Help.

Troubleshooting a Contribute Site in Dreamweaver

If you have a problem with a Contribute site in Dreamweaver, most likely it has something to do with the connection or the administration tools. Fortunately, both are easy to troubleshoot. This book gives only a large-scale view of Contribute, so if your problem falls beyond the information offered here, you should search the Contribute Help files for more information.

Fixing connection problems

You can figure out whether you have a connection problem easily because Dreamweaver enables you to test the remote connection with the root URL any time. All you need to do is click a button related to site administration for Contribute. If the URL is incorrect, Dreamweaver displays an error message.

You can manually check the server connection at any time if you are using FTP, SFTP, or WebDAV by following these steps in Dreamweaver:

1. **Expand the Advanced Settings category in the Site Setup dialog box, and then click Contribute.**

   If you're not sure how to do this, follow Steps 1–4 in the earlier section, "Making a Dreamweaver Site Connection Compatible with Contribute."

2. **Copy and paste the Site Root URL from the dialog box into a browser to see whether the URL is valid, or click the Test button.**

   If the URL is not valid, check the spelling and syntax to correct the URL. If it is valid, move ahead to Step 3.

3. **Select the Servers category in the Site Setup dialog box.**

   The right side of the dialog box displays the connection details about this site's connection to the live server.

4. **Double-click your connection in the listing to open the connection's details dialog box, and then click the Test button to test the connection.**

   When the connection is good, Dreamweaver displays an alert message that says it successfully connected with the remote server. When the connection is bad, you see an error message indicating what may be wrong with the connection, such as *Your login or password is incorrect.* If you're sure the URL is correct but you still get an error message, speak to your system administrator or host provider; the problem is probably server-related.

Checking the _mm folder

If the Contribute administration tools aren't working correctly, the problem may lie in the _mm folder, which should contain a shared settings site-management file with a long strange name and the .csi file extension.

The first thing you need to do is to verify that the read and write permissions are enabled on the server. If they aren't, enable them and try using the administration tools again. If they are enabled, you may need to reestablish a connection as administrator, which re-creates or replaces a missing or corrupted shared-settings file in the _mm folder.

If you're still having problems, follow these steps:

1. **Check the _mm folder in the Contribute site from Dreamweaver's Files panel to make sure that it contains a shared-settings file with the .csi extension.**

   The file has an odd filename such as cthubff3ce10d8490f3d1.csi. The _mm folder and this file are necessary for proper site administration.

2. **If the file is missing or possibly corrupted, you may need to create a new site connection in Dreamweaver and attempt to become the site administrator again.**

   The _mm folder and shared settings file are automatically created when you become the Contribute administrator. If they are missing or corrupted, reestablishing yourself as the site administrator creates new files.

If the problem persists, search for *Troubleshooting* in Contribute's Help files for more information.

Book VI
Chapter 2

Setting Up and Connecting to a Contribute Site

Chapter 3: Managing a Contribute Site

In This Chapter

✔ Using the rollback feature

✔ Editing remote files

✔ Making templates available to Contribute users

✔ Gaining access to checked out files

✔ Using Dreamweaver to update templates and CSS

*M*anaging a Contribute site using Dreamweaver is easy and is not much different from creating and managing a non-Contribute site. A key benefit of managing the site using Dreamweaver instead of Contribute, however, is that Dreamweaver automatically does some file management tasks for you that Contribute simply can't do.

Contribute users can, for example, browse to a page on their site; download a copy of it; edit the text, images, links, and tables on it (if the Administrator has granted them permission to do so); save the file; and then send it back to the server, which instantly displays the updated page.

Contribute users can't do some of the more complex site-management and page editing tasks, such as creating new editable regions, editing or creating new styles in a CSS, renaming and moving files, or making global changes to the site's layout by editing a Dreamweaver template. The Contribute Site Administrator in Dreamweaver must do these things.

In the preceding chapter, we show you how to create and set up a Contribute site in Dreamweaver. This chapter deals with file management. If you're ready to manage a Contribute site, we presume that you have already completed the following:

✦ Installed Contribute and Dreamweaver on the same local computer.

✦ Connected to the Contribute site with Dreamweaver. In the Dreamweaver Site Setup dialog box, you have to enter the Contribute site's Site and Server Site information. You must include a local site folder in the Site category and a Web URL for the server in the Servers category.

✦ Tested the site's connectivity by making sure that the Web URL works.

✦ Enabled Contribute compatibility in Dreamweaver. You should also turn on Design Notes and the Check In/Check Out feature (as described in Book VI, Chapter 1).

✦ Clicked the Administer Site in Contribute button, which is in the Contribute area of the Advanced Settings category of the Dreamweaver Site Setup dialog box to provide administration details for the site and for Contribute users as required.

✦ Designed, built, and uploaded a Contribute site to the remote live server.

If you haven't completed all these tasks, flip back to Book VI, Chapter 2 to find out how to do them before continuing.

Managing Contribute Files Using Dreamweaver

As the Dreamweaver Administrator, you can perform certain high-level tasks that Contribute users can't. Table 3-1 contains a list of general tasks that can be performed in one or both programs. These management tasks include *rolling back* to older versions of files; editing, deleting, moving, and renaming files; giving Contribute users access to templates even though they don't have root folder access; and unlocking locked files on the remote server.

Table 3-1	**Web Site Management Tasks**	
Contribute Site Management Tasks	*Dreamweaver Administrator*	*Contribute User*
Connect to the Web site on the remote server	Yes	Yes
Set up Contribute users and define user roles	Yes	No
Check in and check out files	Yes	Yes, as part of the Edit/Publish process
Edit files	Yes	Yes
Move and rename files	Yes	No
Delete files	Yes	Yes, if the Administrator has enabled this option for the user
Create new pages	Yes	Yes
Create new Dreamweaver template-based pages	Yes	Yes, if the Administrator has granted permission to the Templates folder on the server
Roll back files	Yes	Yes, if the Administrator has enabled this option for the user

Contribute Site Management Tasks	Dreamweaver Administrator	Contribute User
Administer a Web site	Yes	Yes, if the Administrator has enabled this option for the site
Create Contribute templates	Yes	Yes, but this is typically allowed for only one person
Create Dreamweaver templates	Yes	No
Access Dreamweaver templates	Yes	No
Modify Dreamweaver templates	Yes	No
Create, edit, delete external CSS linked to pages	Yes	No
Enable event log in	Yes	No
Unlock locked files on the remote server	Yes	No
Create Design Notes	Yes	No

Book VI
Chapter 3

Managing a
Contribute Site

Be benevolent with your power. Give your Contribute users the right access to the right tools, and you may be surprised to discover that you create less work for yourself.

Rolling back your files

You have probably enabled compatibility between Dreamweaver and Contribute by now. If you haven't, open the Site Definition dialog box in Dreamweaver, as explained in Book VI, Chapter 2.

The next step is to log in to the Contribute site through Dreamweaver as the Administrator. When the Administer Website dialog box appears, select the Rollbacks category and then select the Enable Rollbacks option, as shown in Figure 3-1. The default number of file versions to keep for rollback purposes is three, but you can increase or decrease the number if you like.

Figure 3-1:
Enable the
Rollbacks
feature.

After that, you need to enable the rollback feature in Contribute. To do so, choose Edit⇨Administer Website and select the name of the Contribute site to display the Administer Website dialog box, which looks exactly like the dialog box that opens from Dreamweaver. Select the Rollbacks category, select the Enable Rollbacks feature, and then click the Close button to close the dialog box.

With rollback turned on, Dreamweaver automatically saves every version of a file (up to the number specified in the Rollbacks category, which is typically three versions) as it is edited. If you need to revert to a previous version of a file, no problem; each version is stored with the date and editor's name for easy retrieval. You can use a previous version to roll back to and overwrite any mistakes that were made in the most recent version.

Be sure to cloak the backup folder so that it isn't copied to the live Web site when you transfer files to the Web server. (See Book V, Chapter 3 for more information on cloaking.)

You may think that the Rollbacks feature is a function you'd never need, but trust us when we tell you it will come in handy some day. The more Contribute users you have working on a site, the greater the likelihood of the need to roll back files.

To roll back a file in Dreamweaver, follow these steps:

1. **Make sure your managed Contribute site is selected and displayed in the Files panel.**

2. **Right-click (Windows) or Control+click (Mac) the filename that you want to roll back and then choose Roll Back Page.**

   The Roll Back Page dialog box appears, displaying a list of versions of the file you can select and roll back to, as shown in Figure 3-2.

Figure 3-2: Select a version of a file to roll back.

3. **Select the version of the file that you want to roll back to.**

   When there are no prior versions, the dialog box displays a message that you can't roll back to a previous version of the selected file.

4. **Click the Roll Back button to roll back to the selected version of the file.**

   The rollback version replaces the newest version of the file. To exit the dialog box instead of rolling back the file, click Cancel.

Making changes to Contribute files

Contribute users can do some tasks, such as edit and republish existing files, create new pages based on existing pages, and create new pages to add to a Contribute site. They can't delete, move, and rename files, or do certain file editing tasks on a remote Contribute site. The site Administrator must perform these tasks through Dreamweaver.

Keep in mind the following points when making changes to Contribute files:

✦ **Editing files:** Use the Check In/Check Out feature (instead of Get and Put) to check out the file to which you want to make changes, make the changes, save the file, and check it back in. We discuss editing templates and style sheets later in this chapter, in the "Using Dreamweaver to Edit a Contribute Site" section.

✦ **Moving and renaming files:** On the surface, moving a file from one location on the remote server to another, or even renaming a file, works the same in a Contribute site as it does in a Dreamweaver site. But this isn't the smartest method. Perform the same tasks in Dreamweaver, and Dreamweaver tracks and saves these changes in the _baks folder, and modifies the filename or location in all previous versions of the file. That way, if you need to roll back to a previous version, the file location or name change stays intact. Pretty smart, huh?

We strongly recommend that if you have to move or rename a file, you do so from Dreamweaver.

✦ **Deleting files:** If you're using Dreamweaver to delete a file, Dreamweaver asks whether you want to fully delete all previous versions of that file at the same time. If you say yes, they all disappear forever. If you say no, Dreamweaver saves a copy of the current version as a new version of the file in the _baks folder on the remote server for future restoration using the Roll Back Page command.

To delete a file on a remote Contribute site using Dreamweaver, follow these steps:

1. **In the Remote Server pane of the expanded Files panel, select the file you want to delete and then press the Delete key on your keyboard.**

A Confirmation dialog box appears for you to confirm the deletion.

2. **If you want to also delete any rollback versions of the selected file, select the Delete Rollback Versions option. Otherwise, deselect the option.**

If you deselect the Delete Rollback Versions option, you keep previous versions of the selected file online, including a copy of the version you're deleting.

3. **Click Yes to delete the selected file.**

You can't undo this action! Deleted files are permanently removed from the remote server and are irretrievable.

Enabling Contribute users to use templates

When you set up folder and file permissions for users on the Contribute site through Dreamweaver's Administer Website dialog box, be sure to give Contribute users read access to any files and folders on the remote server. Such folders include root-level files, images subfolders, and perhaps the Templates folder if you want Contribute users to create template-based files from Dreamweaver-generated templates. You can grant file and folder permissions by selecting a user and clicking the Edit Role Settings button. When the Edit "Administrator" Settings dialog box appears, select the Folder/File Access category from the left side of the panel, shown in Figure 3-3, and set user folder access and file deletion settings on the right.

If you're wary of granting users permission to the Templates folder, you could allow them to use Dreamweaver templates by copying the entire Template folder from the main site's root folder to the Contribute site's remote root folder through the Files panel.

Figure 3-3:
Set file
and folder
permissions
for
Contribute
users.

Thereafter, whenever the Dreamweaver templates are updated on the main site through Dreamweaver, you must remember to copy the updated templates to the Template folder on the remote Contribute site. Copying the updated templates to the Contribute site is the only way to overwrite the older files so that users can access them.

Unlocking a checked out file

When you select the Check In/Check Out feature, it may sometimes appear (by the presence of a lock next to the file on the user's computer) that a remote file is checked out when it really isn't. For any users to access the file, the lock needs to be removed. As Administrator, you have the power to do so.

Before you unlock the file through Dreamweaver, be sure the file's not really checked out by a Contribute user. If you unlock a file when it is checked out, you grant file access to multiple users with the potential of creating multiple versions of the file at once.

To manually unlock a file in a Contribute site that appears to be checked out when it really isn't, select the file in Dreamweaver's Files panel, right-click (Windows) or Control+click (Mac) it, and then choose Undo Check Out. If prompted, click Yes to confirm that you indeed want to unlock the file. To find out more about the Check In/Check Out feature, see Book VI, Chapter 1.

Using Dreamweaver to Edit a Contribute Site

As Administrator, you can perform some tasks in both Dreamweaver and Contribute. Some tasks, however, you should do only in Dreamweaver. Make any robust changes to a Contribute site, such as modifying a template or CSS, in Dreamweaver to maintain the integrity of the site's design.

Updating templates in a Contribute site

Contribute users can't change a Dreamweaver template, and that's a good thing because they're typically not Web designers. If a template needs editing, you need to do it in Dreamweaver. What part of a template might you need to edit? Perhaps you need to remove a navigation button from the layout or edit some text that appears on every page. Or maybe you need to overhaul the site design, with all new graphics, while keeping the overall content intact.

If you remove or rename an editable region from a template, Contribute users may not know what to do with the content from the old editable region. To avoid confusion, try to make changes to the templates before or after normal business hours and be sure to have Contribute users close down and relaunch their Contribute programs before making new changes to the site. Contribute users can get new remote server information to their local computers only by closing and relaunching Contribute.

To edit a Dreamweaver template used in a Contribute site, follow these steps:

1. **In Dreamweaver, open, edit, and save the Contribute site template.**

Find out more about templates in Book III, Chapter 2.

2. **Tell the Contribute users about the change so that they can close and restart their Contribute programs.**

Restarting Contribute enables Contribute users to access the site with the most recent documents and templates.

Editing style sheets in a Contribute site

Making sure that the look and feel of a site stays under tight control is important in any Web design scenario. Contribute users aren't allowed to change the contents of style sheets, which means that you don't have to worry about style sheets being messed up by anyone but you and any other Dreamweaver users on the team.

As with any site using style sheets, when you delete a style, the tag to apply that style to a particular word, sentence, or paragraph still resides in the code of the Web pages. This discrepancy may confuse your Contribute users. To quickly remove or rename style tags from an entire site, use Dreamweaver's Find and Replace tool (see Book II, Chapter 2).

Also, let the Contribute users know about any changes you make to the CSS during work hours because they can't see changes to any pages they're currently editing until they publish the page back to the site.

Follow these steps to edit a style in a Contribute site through Dreamweaver:

1. **Use Dreamweaver's style sheet editing tools.**

You have a variety of options. You can use the CSS Styles panel, use the Attributes panel (on the Tag Inspector), or edit the CSS code by hand. See Book III, Chapter 1 for information on using CSS in Dreamweaver.

2. **Tell the Contribute users about the change so that they can publish and reedit pages with the newest version of the style sheet.**

Better yet, tell users to restart Contribute so they can access all the site pages and assets with the most recent versions of everything.

Chapter 4: Collaborating Online with InContext Editing

In This Chapter

✔ Understanding editing with InContext

✔ Creating and managing editable regions

✔ Connecting to an InContext site

✔ Logging in to InContext

✔ Inviting users to an InContext site

✔ Updating pages with InContext

✔ Finding InContext Help

Recently, Adobe developed an online application called InContext Editing, or ICE, that helps Web designers and developers work more effectively among themselves and with their clients across the Internet.

Unlike Adobe Contribute, which is a software-based tool that helps Web designers and developers manage the activity of several teams of content providers for individual Web sites (see Book VI, Chapters 2 and 3), InContext Editing is a browser-based Web page editing service that puts the power of site management in the hands of content contributors. Without having to purchase and install additional software, designers and developers can now create Web sites in Dreamweaver that are easily editable by their clients through the InContext browser interface. Even better, InContext Editing requires no prior knowledge of HTML or Web editing, making it the ideal content management solution for Web site owners.

In the future (perhaps as soon as early 2011), access to the service may involve paying Adobe a nominal monthly fee of $10 to $20 for unlimited usage and access to Adobe BrowserLab. For now, however, InContext Editing is offered as a free service to registered members.

In this chapter, you find out how to create Web sites with editable InContext regions, configure pages with special text editing features, and upload the site to the live server. After that, you discover how to log in to the ICE Web site; set up Editor, Publisher, and Administrator privileges; and send invitations to content providers. The chapter ends with a list of helpful online resources about ICE for you and your customers.

Creating and Managing Editable Regions

To create InContext editable Web sites, designers and developers simply build pages in Dreamweaver as they normally would, and then customize those pages with easily definable InContext editable regions. These regions become the parts of the page that you want contributors to be able to edit.

After the pages are published online, clients and in-house contributors have the opportunity to maintain site content from any major browser without disrupting the integrity of the overall Web site design. Suppose, for example, you have a board member page with names, contact information, and photos for each member. You can easily set each component as an editable region so that when contributors log in to ICE they can easily update the data directly through their browser.

Before you begin, keep in mind that InContext Editing has some limitations and will not work properly under specific conditions. For example, Adobe AIR doesn't support ICE. For a list of known network, browser, page, and editing limitations, visit www.adobe.com/go/incontextediting_limitations.

You can create ICE editable regions in Dreamweaver in two ways:

+ **Automatic editable regions:** When creating new blank HTML pages using one of Dreamweaver's built-in CSS layouts, select the Enable InContext Editing option in the New Document dialog box. When the new page is created, the area in that file using <div id="content"> . . . </div> (in CS4, content was called mainContent) is automatically marked as an ICE editable region.

+ **Manual editable regions:** You can manually insert an ICE editable region anywhere on your page by selecting the content or region on the page that you want to become editable. For instance, you could select an image, a cell in a table, an editable region in a template, or the contents of an entire layer.

In addition to adding ICE editable regions in Dreamweaver, you may add these regions to an existing page after logging in to InContext Editing at http://incontextediting.adobe.com/.

You can insert two kinds of ICE editable regions in your pages: regular editable regions and repeating regions.

Creating editable regions

To create an ICE editable region in Dreamweaver, follow these steps:

1. **Open in the Dreamweaver workspace the page to which you want to add ICE editable regions.**

Editable regions must be created one at a time, one page at a time. When working with Dreamweaver templates, any ICE editable regions in the template will produce identical ICE editable regions in the template-based files.

If you are starting from a new blank page, you must save the page before adding the ICE editable regions.

When adding an editable region to a template or a template-based file, the ICE editable region must be in a Dreamweaver template editable region.

2. **In Design view, select the area you want to convert to an ICE editable region.**

To select the parent container of a selection, use the Tag Selector.

3. **Choose Insert⇨InContext Editing⇨Create Editable Region.**

You can also click the Create Editable Region option in the InContext Editing category of the Insert panel. Depending on what you selected in Step 2, one of the following happens:

- **If you selected a DIV, TH, or TD tag:** Dreamweaver converts the selection to an editable region by applying the `ice:editable` attribute, as in

```
<div id="header" ice:editable="*">
<h1>Welcome</h1>
</div>
```

- **If you selected a tag other than DIV, TH, or TD:** Dreamweaver opens a Create Editable Region dialog box that provides the option for you to Wrap the Current Selection with a DIV Tag and Then Transform It. Click the OK button for Dreamweaver to convert the selection to an editable region by wrapping the selection with a `<div>` tag with the `ice:editable` attribute.

- **If you selected a Dreamweaver template editable region:** Dreamweaver wraps the editable region with a `<div>` tag with the `ice:editable` attribute. *Note:* This method may produce unwanted page CSS rendering results.

- **If you selected content but not a tag:** Dreamweaver prompts you to wrap the selection with a `<div>` tag with the `ice:editable` attribute.

4. **In Design view, select the ICE editable region's blue tab. In the Properties inspector, select the formatting elements that will remain editable for content contributors.**

Formatting options (see Figure 4-1) are Bold, Italic, Underline, Alignment, Font Face, Font Size, Indent/Outdent, Numbered/Bulleted Lists, Paragraph Styles, Background Color, Font Color, and CSS Styles, as well as providing the ability to insert and edit Image/Media files and Links. To select all items, click the Check all button. To deselect all items, click the Uncheck all button.

5. Save the file.

When you create a new editable page or insert an editable region for the first time, Dreamweaver adds a folder containing a set of dependent files to the root level of your managed site. Inside this folder is another folder containing two script files and one HTML file: includes/ice/ice.conf. js. includes/ice/ice.js, and includes/ice/ide.html. You must upload this folder and all these files when you upload your page to the live server for InContext Editing to work properly.

Figure 4-1:
Choose formatting options for your ICE editable region in the Properties inspector.

Creating repeating regions

Repeating regions define a part of the page that can be both editable and repeated in the page, such as with a row of data in a table or a layer containing a heading, text, and graphics. When the page is opened in the InContext Editing browser, each repeating region can be duplicated, moved up or down, or deleted from the page. Figure 4-2 shows how a repeating region looks in the InContext Editing browser.

Figure 4-2: Repeating regions can be duplicated, repositioned, and deleted.

In the code, you can identify repeating regions by the `ice:repeating` attribute, which is added to the region's opening tag. In addition, Dreamweaver wraps the entire region inside a repeating regions group, defined by a `<div>` tag (or the parent container's tag) with the `ice:repeatinggroup` attribute. When creating repeating regions in a Dreamweaver template, the repeating region must be inside an editable region.

To create an ICE editable repeating region in Dreamweaver, follow these steps:

1. **Open the desired page and select the area to be converted to a repeating region.**

   To insert a region without making a selection, place your cursor where you want to add the new repeating region.

2. **Choose Insert⇨InContext Editing⇨Create Repeating Region.**

   You can also select the Create Repeating Region option in the InContext Editing category of the Insert panel. Depending on what you selected in Step 1, one of the following happens:

   - **If you selected a transformable tag:** Dreamweaver converts the selection to a repeating region.

   - **If you inserted a region without a selection:** You can insert the repeating region there or choose to transform the parent tag closest to your insertion point into the repeating region.

   - **If you selected a Dreamweaver template editable region:** Dreamweaver wraps the editable region with a <div> tag with the ice:repeating attribute. *Note:* This method may produce unwanted page CSS rendering results.

   - **If you selected content but not a tag:** Dreamweaver prompts you to either transform the parent tag of the content or wrap the selection with a <div> tag with the ice:repeating attribute.

3. **In Design view, select the Repeating Region's blue tab. In the Properties inspector, select the Repeating Regions Group options that will remain editable for content contributors.**

   Options are Reorder, which allows editors to reposition the region above or below other regions in the group, and Add/Remove, which lets editors add or remove regions in the group. Both options are selected by default, and you must always have at least one option selected.

4. **Save the file.**

   When you create a new editable page or insert an editable region for the first time, Dreamweaver adds a folder of supporting files to the root level of your managed site: ice.conf.js, ice.js, and ide.html. You must upload your page and this folder to the live server for InContext Editing to work properly.

Deleting editable regions

For best results, use the Properties inspector to delete regions. This way, you are assured of having Dreamweaver delete all the code associated with the region.

To remove a region, follow these steps:

1. **In Design view, select the region to be deleted by its blue tab.**

   You may select an editable region, a repeating region, or a repeating regions group.

2. **In the Properties inspector, click the Remove Region button.**

   Dreamweaver alerts you that the region will be removed but the content within it will stay on the page.

3. **Click OK to remove the region, or Cancel to cancel the action.**

Occasionally, you may encounter an error message when attempting to create ICE editable regions in your Dreamweaver files. For a complete listing of common errors, visit `http://help.adobe.com/en_US/dreamweaver/CS/using/WSDD8EB85D-905A-495d-A743-7CF9002372EA.html#WSCF97C2E7-14BA-4a1d-947C-26A00A7A59EA`.

Preparing a Site for Use with InContext Editing

After you have uploaded all your ICE editable pages along with the folder of dependent files (includes/ice/) created by Dreamweaver to the live server, the next step is for you to log in to the InContext Editing Web site to configure the site for InContext users.

To log in to InContext Editing, follow these steps:

1. **Go to `http://incontextediting.adobe.com/` to open the InContext Editing page in your browser.**

   The Sign In window appears.

2. **Sign in with your Adobe ID, and then click Enter.**

   The Add New Site? dialog box appears.

3. **In the Add New Site? dialog box, click Add Site to add your site to your account.**

4. **Follow the prompts to input the Site Name and Site Address (URL). Click Next to proceed.**

5. **Enter your FTP access information, including FTP Host, Username, and Password.**

   If you don't have the FTP access information, get it from the host provider.

6. **Click the Test Connection button.**

   If you have entered your information correctly, your connection will be successful. If you get an error message, check for spelling and letter case errors and test again. If you still can't establish a connection, speak with your host provider or systems administrator.

7. **When your connection is established, click the Next button to proceed.**

8. **(Optional) Enter information for the Host Directory, Media Directory, and Default page:**

   - **Host directory:** This directory is not a standard feature on every hosted site. If you have a host directory, click the Browse button to select the appropriate directory. Otherwise, leave this field blank.

   - **Media directory:** This directory is the location where you will store media for this site, such as an folder named images. Click the Browse button to select the desired folder.

   - **Default page:** This page is the index.html or default.html page. Enter the filename of the default page here. If you are using a programming language on your site, the file extension may be different, such as .cfm or .php.

9. **Click Save to save your site information.**

   It may take a few moments for InContext Editing to process your information. When the account has been officially created, you see a Congratulations screen. From here, you may either edit the site or invite users.

Inviting Users to the Site

To invite an editor or publisher to your site, click the Edit button and follow the prompts to add an Invitee Name and Email address. You may also specify whether this invitee will have Editor or Publisher privileges. If you would like a copy of the invitation to be sent to you, select the Send Me a Copy of the Invitation option. Click the Invite button to send out the invitation. Invitations are valid for up to 30 days; you my cancel an invitation at any time by selecting it in the Manage Users panel and clicking the Delete Invitation button.

Updating Pages with InContext Editing

When invited content contributors are ready to modify a page, all they need to do is navigate to the desired page in a browser and press Ctrl+E (Windows) or ⌘+E (Macintosh) to sign in to the InContext Editing service for that page.

After they are signed in, Editors and Publishers can create drafts of edited or duplicate pages and Publishers can publish and discard those drafts. When changes are completed, users can click the Sign Out button to return to the live version of the page.

InContext Editing is a remarkable tool. Learning to use the InContext Editing service is intuitive and straightforward, but some users may want additional training. For general help and instruction with your Adobe InContext Editing Web projects, visit, `www.adobe.com/products/incontextediting/`.

For additional training help, check out these resources:

✦ `www.adobe.com/newsletters/edge/february2009/articles/ article5/index.html`

✦ `http://tv.adobe.com/watch/learn-dreamweaver-cs4/ introducing-adobe-incontext-editing/`

✦ `www.adobe.com/devnet/dreamweaver/articles/getting_ started_with_ice_dev.html`

✦ `www.adobe.com/devnet/dreamweaver/articles/ice_product_ catalog_04.html`

Book VII

Building Web Applications

The 5th Wave   By Rich Tennant

"See? I created a little felon figure that runs around our Web site hiding behind banner ads. On the last page, our logo puts him in a non lethal choke hold and brings him back to the home page."

Contents at a Glance

Chapter 1: Preparing to Build Web Applications

In This Chapter

✔ Selecting a Web application platform

✔ Installing an application server

✔ Analyzing your choices for Web and application servers

✔ Defining Testing server settings in Dreamweaver

✔ Choosing a database

*F*rom Web site to Web app: That's the transformation that many Web developers find themselves dealing with as the needs of their Web sites expand over time. A typical scenario goes something like this: At the start, a company is content to create a static site presenting its products and services. Over time, however, the company realizes that their Web site could be far more useful to their customers if they offered more interactive and dynamic content, so they transform their static site into a full-scale Web application.

The first challenge when planning how to build applications from Web pages is choosing a set of tools to use. This chapter explores various Web application platforms and application servers and how to choose the right ones for your needs. We also touch on various languages, such as PHP, ASP, JavaServer Pages (JSP), and ColdFusion, that work hand-in-hand with the application server when generating your dynamic Web pages. Finally, this chapter gives you the lowdown on designing your database and choosing the right database application.

Understanding Web Applications

A basic Web site consists of HTML pages and related assets (images, CSS style sheets, and so on). After you place this set of files on a Web server, each file can be accessed by a browser through a unique URL. Because the content that the user sees is already contained in the HTML files, no further processing is necessary beyond sending the page to the browser to be displayed (see Figure 1-1).

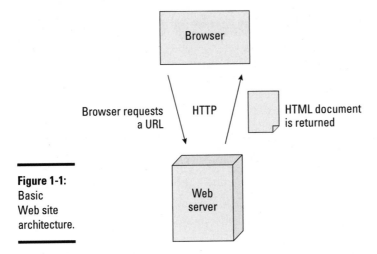

Figure 1-1:
Basic
Web site
architecture.

In contrast, Web applications don't have a set number of premade HTML files. Instead, its HTML content is generated on-the-fly by a layer on the server—often called an *application layer* or *logic layer*—based on programming code.

Consider this example. When you work with PHP, one of the most popular Web application languages, you store the programming code in text-based .php files. When the browser requests a .php file, the Web server in turn calls the PHP application server to process the .php file. When the app server has finished doing its magic, it sends a dynamically generated document to the browser to be displayed (see Figure 1-2). To the user, the dynamic document still looks like a normal Web page—but the way in which it goes to the browser is altogether different.

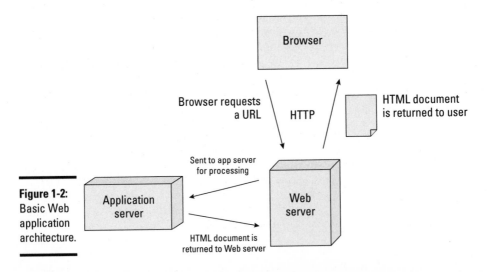

Figure 1-2:
Basic Web
application
architecture.

Choosing a Web Application Platform

Web application platforms (or application servers) run behind the scenes on the Web server. The application server supports the processing of your Web pages, acting as a helper to the Web server for processing the code that's part of the requested pages.

Dreamweaver CS5 allows you to create pages and sites that can be integrated in a variety of Web application platforms, including PHP, ASP, ASP.NET, and JSP. Each of these languages corresponds to a Dreamweaver document type (such as .php, .aspx, or .jsp).

If you're already familiar with one of these languages, choose that one. If they're all new to you, PHP and ASP are popular choices. You can find plenty of help and sample code on the Web for both of them.

Choosing a Web Server

Before you can develop Web services, you need to choose the underlying server technology. The two popular choices are Microsoft Internet Information Services (IIS) and Apache. As discussed in this section, your decision will often be based on where you plan to host the server.

Hosted sites

If your Web site is hosted by a Web hosting provider, you are already using IIS or Apache. Many ISPs even allow you to choose between Unix/Apache or Microsoft IIS server plans.

If you're still in the process of selecting a hosting company for your Web site, or if you want to test your Web application pages on your computer without uploading them to a remote server, compare the pros and cons of using the IIS Web platform versus the Apache Web platform.

For Web designers and developers, the major platform decision usually boils down to programming language and database support. Microsoft platform is the best choice for ASP and ASP.NET, whereas Apache is ideal for PHP and JSP.

When working with hosting sites, Dreamweaver enables you to generate a Web service proxy that allows the Web page to communicate with the Web service publisher. The *proxy,* also known as an *abstraction class,* contains the fields, methods, and properties of the Web service and makes them available to the locally hosted page. When you generate a proxy for your page, Dreamweaver lets you view it in the Components panel (choose Window⇨Components to open the panel).

Hosting your own site

If you're hosting the server on your own machine (either for testing or live purposes), you'll want to want to explore two options, Apache and IIS.

Apache

Apache server is the most popular Web server. It's an *open-source* product, so it's free to download and use. Apache works well with PHP and JSP, which we talk about later in the chapter.

If you're running Windows, you can download the latest Apache version at `http://httpd.apache.org`.

If you're using Mac OS X and want to run your Web application files locally, you already have Apache installed. To enable it, you simply pop over to your System Preferences tool, as described in the following steps:

1. **From the Apple menu, choose System Preferences.**

    The System Preferences application in Mac OS X controls the configuration of your system, including optional components such as Apache.

2. **Click the Sharing icon.**

    The Sharing panel tells OS X which services your computer provides, including Apache and file sharing.

3. **In the Service list, select the check box next to Web Sharing.**

    Web sharing is turned on, as shown in Figure 1-3. You're all set to start using Apache.

Figure 1-3: Turning on the Apache server.

A special host

Typically, computers have two IP addresses: the public one, such as 128.34.34.34, and the *localhost address,* which point to a special IP address, 127.0.0.1. For Web users at large to access your Web pages, they must reference the external address.

Microsoft IIS

Microsoft IIS is a good choice for hosting your Web site if you're planning to develop pages with ASP or ASP.NET programming languages because IIS has built-in support for handling those development languages.

Some editions of Windows 7 install IIS 7.0 by default. If your edition doesn't, you can select it among the list of optionally installed components. Additionally, not all editions of Windows 7 provide support for ASP and ASP.NET.

When you run IIS 7.x on Windows 7 or Vista, it restricts performance based on the number of simultaneous Web page requests but does not limit the number of connections. In contrast, for older systems, Windows XP's more restricted version of IIS 5.1 allows you to host one Web site and supports only 10 simultaneous connections.

In general, the version of Windows you're running determines which version of IIS you can run.

To install or verify that IIS is installed on your Windows 7 or Vista computer, follow these steps:

1. **Choose Start⇨Control Panel⇨Programs.**

2. **Click the Turn Windows Features On or Off link.**

   You'll need to confirm this action. The Windows Features dialog box is displayed.

3. **If Internet Information Services is already selected, you're all set and can cancel out of the you're all set. Click the Cancel button. Otherwise, select the option and then click OK to install IIS.**

To install or verify that IIS is installed on your Windows XP computer, follow these steps:

1. **Choose Start⇨Control Panel⇨Add/Remove Programs or choose Start⇨Control Panel and double-click the Add/Remove Programs icon.**

   You see the same dialog box that you've probably used to remove software.

2. **In the Add or Remove Programs window, click the Add/Remove Windows Components icon.**

   You are telling Windows that you want to change which Microsoft components (including IIS) are installed. The Windows Components Wizard appears.

3. **If the Internet Information Services option is selected, IIS is already installed and you can skip Step 4.**

4. **If the Internet Information Services option is not selected:**

   a. **Select the Internet Information Services (IIS) option.**

      Windows tells you approximately how much space you need to install IIS.

   b. **Click Next.**

      You may need your Windows Installer CD-ROM to install IIS, so make sure it's somewhere handy.

   c. **Follow the onscreen prompts to finish installing IIS and then click OK.**

When IIS is installed, it creates a default directory for storing Web pages at `c:\Inetpub\wwwroot`. This directory is often called the *Web root folder*.

Choosing an Application Server

Perhaps the most critical decision you will make as you begin developing Web applications is choosing the application server, because the actual programming you do is based on your choice. This section presents the major options to consider.

PHP

PHP is an open-source programming language and application server that is built for creating Web applications. It works well with many databases, including the popular open-source database MySQL.

It supports all major operating systems, including Windows, Mac OS X, and Linux. It integrates with either IIS or Apache to form a PHP application server. For Apache, it's loaded as an Apache module. For IIS, it's loaded as an ISAPI add-on.

Many ISPs come with preinstalled support for PHP, whereas others require you to configure it manually on your server. If you're installing it on your own computer, follow the instructions in this section for Windows and Mac OS X.

Windows setup

Installing PHP for use with IIS is fairly easy with the automatic installation available from the PHP site. Download PHP from www.php.net. Get the automatic installation package under Windows Binaries.

After you download the file, follow these steps to install PHP:

1. **Double-click the .msi file.**

2. **Click Next to install.**

3. **Agree to the license terms by clicking I Accept, and then click Next.**

4. **Click Next to accept the default installation directory of C:\Program Files\PHP.**

5. **Select a Web server setup.**

6. **Select the items to install, and then click Next.**

The standard install uses default values for many of the settings. You can use the defaults without problems.

7. **To begin the installation, click Install.**

8. **If the IIS Has Been Configured dialog box appears, click OK.**

This dialog box appears only if you didn't select IIS as your HTTP server.

9. **Click Finish in the Installation Complete dialog box.**

Mac OS X setup

Mac OS X includes the files necessary to run PHP, but those files require manual editing that's quite tedious for most users. To enable PHP support for Mac OS X without messing around with your system files, visit www.entropy.ch/software/macosx/php and then follow these steps:

1. **Download an installer file for Mac OS X based on the version of Mac OS X you're running.**

2. **The Mac installer file is a .dmg disk image. Double-click the .dmg file.**

The Mac mounts the disk image and displays a drive icon with the files.

3. **When you see the installer package, double-click it and follow the directions.**

That was pretty simple, huh? Congratulations: You've successfully installed the PHP application server for your Mac.

**Book VII
Chapter 1**

**Preparing to Build
Web Applications**

Active Server Pages (ASP)

Active Server Pages (ASP) is designed to work with the IIS Web platform. Dreamweaver CS5 supports building ASP code that can stand alone or be modified outside Dreamweaver.

ASP aims to make Web application development as easy as possible by grouping common tasks into objects. These objects are Application, ASPError, Request, Response, Server, and Session objects. The ASPError object, for example, provides functions for handling errors.

ASP pages use JavaScript or VBScript as the programming language. Dreamweaver knows what code to put in regardless of which language you choose.

ASP.NET

ASP.NET, despite its name being similar to ASP, is a complete rewrite of the ASP development platform that conforms to the Microsoft .NET platform. ASP.NET is built on Common Language Runtime (CLR), which enables developers to write ASP.NET apps using any supported .NET language.

You can download ASP.NET and related toolkits at `http://asp.net`.

Java Server Pages (JSP)

JSP uses the Java language and processor to deliver Web-based applications. JSP pages are different from other pages because they're compiled into byte code by the JSP compiler. These compiled JSP pages are called *servlets*.

Apache Jakarta Tomcat is the servlet container used for both the Java servlet and JSP technologies. Apache Jakarta Tomcat is an open-source application that helps develop large-scale, high-traffic Web applications.

Jakarta Tomcat is available from `http://tomcat.apache.org`. If you're using Windows, download the core Windows executable installer. For Mac OS X, visit `http://developer.apple.com/internet/java/tomcat1.html` to find instructions on installing the Mac OS X binaries of Tomcat.

Other commercial JSP application severs are

+ Macromedia JRun
+ Sun ONE
+ IBM WebSphere
+ BEA WebLogic

Most commercial distributions include a 30-day trial period to allow you to test-drive it before buying.

ColdFusion

Adobe ColdFusion is a Web application programming language that has markup syntax resembling HTML. ColdFusion allows people familiar with tag-based languages such as HTML to easily learn how to program Web apps.

Considering Web/Application Server Combinations

Although the Web platforms and application servers described in this chapter offer similar capabilities, they differ slightly in how they process Web application pages that contain code. The differences are in the location of the additional files and the URL to access these files.

The Web root folder for your application varies depending on the Web platform you choose and what your ISP dictates as the Web root. You want to create a directory in your Web root folder for each Web application you build.

Table 1-1 lists the default Web root folder and base URLs for each combination of Web platforms and application servers.

Table 1-1	Default Web Root and Base URLs	
Web Server	*Default Web Root*	*Default Base URL*
Apache on Windows	`c:\apache\htdocs`	`http://localhost/`
Apache on Mac OS X	`/Users/UserName/Sites`	`http://localhost/~UserName/`
IIS	`c:\inetpub\wwwroot`	`http://localhost/`
ColdFusion	`c:\cfusionMX7\wwwroot`	`http://localhost:8500/`
Jakarta Tomcat on Windows	`c:\jakarta-tomcat-4.x.x\webapps\ROOT\`	`http://localhost:8080/`

For Apache on Mac OS X, the username is the short Macintosh username (which you define when you create a user account).

**Book VII
Chapter 1**

**Preparing to Build
Web Applications**

You can verify that you have the correct Web root setup by placing a sample file in the Web root directory and then navigating your browser to the base URL. An example of a test file is a file called `index.html` that contains the following:

```
<html>
<body>
Hello!
</body>
</html>
```

If you're running IIS and place this file in `c:\inetpub\wwwroot`, for example, you can access it from your Web browser at `http://localhost/index.html`.

Setting Up the Testing Server in Dreamweaver

You can set up a testing server in Dreamweaver to indicate how to process Web application pages while you're developing them. Often, you simply use a local directory if you're using a server technology that your local Web platform can process, such as IIS/ASP on Windows or Apache/PHP on Mac OS X. Alternatively, you can connect to a remote staging server.

Follow these steps to set up a staging server:

1. **Choose Site⇨Manage Sites.**

   The Manage Sites dialog box appears.

2. **Select your site from the list, and then click the Edit icon.**

   If you need to create a site from scratch, see Book I, Chapter 3.

3. **Click the Servers item to the left of the dialog box.**

   The server list is displayed, as shown in Figure 1-4.

4. **Click the + icon to add a new server entry.**

5. **A dialog box appears for configuring the server.**

   See Book V, Chapter 3 for complete details on how to configure a server.

Figure 1-4:
Defining
a staging
server.

6. **In the Connect Using drop-down list, select how to get your files from your local computer to your remote site.**

   Your selections are FTP, SFTP, Local/Network, WebDAV, and RDS. In most testing cases, you'll want to use Local/Network.

7. **In the Web URL field, enter the URL path that your testing server uses to publish the pages.**

   If the testing server is on your local machine, it looks like `http://localhost/myapp` (where `myapp` is the specific directory for your app. If the testing server is in a remote location, the URL path includes the full domain name, such as `http://www.example.com/myapp`.

   Dreamweaver assumes, by default, that both the Web server and application server are running on the same system. Therefore, if you specify a remote location (see Book V, Chapter 3), Dreamweaver assumes that the testing server is the same URL. If you don't enter a remote category, Dreamweaver makes sure that the default testing server matches the local folder.

8. **Click the Advanced icon to display the Advanced settings.**

9. **In the Server Model drop-down list, select the server technology you want to use (see Figure 1-5).**

   Your choices are None, ASP JavaScript, ASP VBScript, ASP.NET C#, ASP.NET VB, ColdFusion, JSP, and PHP MySQL.

10. **Click Save to save your changes and begin using the new site.**

Figure 1-5:
Setting up
a staging
server.

Introducing Databases

Perhaps the most common reason that many Web designers and developers have for using a Web application server is to dynamically pull data from a database and display it in a Web document.

A *database* (or *relational database*) is a collection of data organized in such a way that you can quickly add, retrieve, or modify the information. For example, Amazon.com and Facebook use enormous databases that enable users to search and navigate the immense amounts of data on their sites. Creating your own database is nothing more than putting data into a logical system that stores and retrieves related information.

The information in a database is organized into grid-like tables. Each table has multiple *fields* (or *columns*) and individual records in *rows*. For example, take a look at Table 1-2, the Employees table.

Table 1-2	Employees		
EmployeeID	*FirstName*	*LastName*	*Department*
697882	Max	Smart	Accounting
598066	Joe	Fox	Sales
596072	Kosmo	Kramer	Sales

At the top of the Employees table are the column (field) names: EmployeeID, FirstName, LastName, and Department. The three subsequent rows contain the individual records.

To extract your data correctly, you need to set up the relationships between pieces of data properly. Data has three kinds of relationships:

✦ **One-to-one:** In a one-to-one relationship, each item is related to one and only one other item. In the Employees table, the Employee ID and the name of the employee have a one-to-one relationship. Each employee has one and only one ID number, and each ID number can belong to one and only one employee.

✦ **One-to-many:** A one-to-many relationship has *keys* (unique identifiers) from one table that appear multiple times in another table. Say you have a Department table along with an Employees table. The Employees table has a one-to-many relationship with the Department table. A department (such as Accounting) can have many employees, but each employee can work in only one department.

✦ **Many-to-many:** A many-to-many relationship means that two tables each have multiple keys from another table.

Your data should also conform to *normalization* rules (a series of progressively strict rules to help you build a well-designed database):

✦ **First normal form:** For your database to be in first normal form, every table must not have repeating columns that contain the same kind of data, and all columns must contain only one value.

✦ **Second normal form:** Stricter than the first normal form, the second normal form requires that each field be based specifically on the key.

✦ **Third normal form:** The third normal form expands on the second normal form by allowing no other column in the table except the key column to define any other column.

If you're interested in delving deeper into the subject of databases, we recommend that you check out *Database Development For Dummies* by Allen G. Taylor (Wiley).

Choosing a Database

You have many relational database choices. Any of the following databases work well with Dreamweaver:

✦ **MySQL** (`www.mysql.org`): The open-source MySQL is one of the most popular databases for Web apps. Many Web hosting providers provide support for it. You can download it for free and run it on a Windows, Mac OS X, or Linux machine.

Unless you want to go with a Microsoft-centric solution, we recommend MySQL for its quality, ease of use, and scalability.

✦ **Microsoft Office Access** (www.microsoft.com/access)**:** If you're just getting started and are accustomed to working with Microsoft Office apps, you may want to consider using Access. It's good for establishing a small, simple database when you're not overly concerned about performance. It's also bundled with Microsoft Office, so it isn't very expensive. You may even have it installed.

Some Web hosting providers provide support for Microsoft Access databases.

✦ **Microsoft SQL Server** (www.microsoft.com/sql): The popular Microsoft offering is SQL Server. Although it is more complex than other database choices, it has the power to handle a large quantity of requests from users of your Web site.

✦ **PostgreSQL** (www.postgresql.org) is an open-source object-relational database that many Web hosts support. You can download it to run on all major platforms, including Windows and Mac OS X.

After you choose the right database for your needs, consult your database system's documentation for details on how to create the database. Book VII, Chapters 2 through 6, gives you the details on setting up PHP, ASP, ASP.NET, JSP, and ColdFusion database connections in Dreamweaver.

Chapter 2: Configuring MySQL Database Connections for PHP

In This Chapter

✔ Connecting to a MySQL database

✔ Adding a database connection

✔ Editing or deleting a database connection

*I*f you've decided to go the open-source route and use PHP as your application server platform and MySQL for your database, this chapter is for you. (If you haven't set up PHP, see Book VII, Chapter 1 for details.) You'll find the discussion helpful whether you're working with a Web-hosted remote server or running PHP and MySQL on your local machine.

In this chapter, we show you how to connect to your server and create a dynamic Web page with PHP in Dreamweaver CS5. Additionally, you find out how to set up a MySQL database connection and add, edit, or delete a connection.

However, before you begin, make sure that you have a Dreamweaver site created or opened that has server settings configured and operational. Dreamweaver needs this info to connect to the database.

Adding a PHP Database Connection

To create a database connection in PHP to access a MySQL database, you need to create a new dynamic PHP page. The database connection enables Dreamweaver to interact with the database using database connections through PHP. Dreamweaver automatically adds code specific to your dynamic page type to your new dynamic page when creating a database connection.

Creating a new dynamic PHP page

To create a new dynamic PHP page in Dreamweaver, follow these steps:

1. **Choose File⇨New.**

The New Document window appears, as shown in Figure 2-1.

Figure 2-1:
Create
a new
document.

2. **Click the PHP icon in the Page Type list.**

3. **(Optional) Choose a Layout in the list.**

   For now, feel free to leave <none> selected in the Layout column.

4. **Select XHTML 1.0 Transition in the DocType drop-down list.**

5. **Click Create.**

   A new dynamic PHP page is created, as seen in Figure 2-2.

Figure 2-2:
A new PHP
document is
ready to go.

Creating the database connection for PHP

After you create a new dynamic PHP page (as described in the preceding steps), you can connect to the database. We show you how to connect to an existing MySQL database in this section. However, if you'd like info on how to get started with MySQL databases, check out www.mysql.org.

Connect to an existing MySQL database by following these steps:

1. **Choose Window⇨Databases.**

The Databases panel appears. If you have a site open and a testing server configured, the first three steps are selected, as shown in Figure 2-3.

2. **Click the plus (+) icon and select MySQL Connection from the drop-down list that appears.**

The MySQL Connection dialog box appears, as shown in Figure 2-4.

3. **Enter a name for the database connection in the Connection Name field.**

Dreamweaver uses this name to reference your database connection. The name can contain only letters, numbers, and underscores.

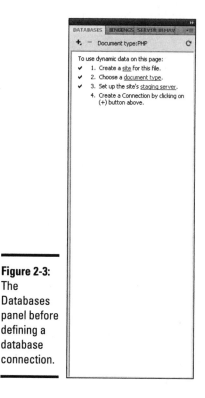

Figure 2-3:
The Databases panel before defining a database connection.

Figure 2-4:
The MySQL
Connection
dialog box.

4. **Enter the host name or IP address of the database server in the MySQL Server field.**

   This may be a host name or IP address.

   If the MySQL server resides on the same system as the Web or application server, reference it locally with the host name `localhost`. This value applies even if you're connecting to a remote server.

5. **Enter the username for the database in the User Name field.**

   MySQL enables you to create users and assign permissions in its Web-based control panel. See your MySQL control panel if you need to set up a user.

6. **Enter the corresponding password in the Password field.**

7. **Click the Select button.**

   If your settings are correct to this point, the Select Database dialog box appears with available databases, as shown in Figure 2-5.

   If you are using a Web hosting provider and receive an error, check to make sure that MySQL is configured to allow external IP connections. The exact instructions will depend on your particular Web host.

Figure 2-5:
The Select
Database
dialog box.

8. **Select your database from the list, and then click OK.**

The Select Database dialog box closes, and the name of the database you selected appears in the Database field of the MySQL Connection dialog box.

9. **Click the Test button to confirm that your connection is set up properly.**

An alert box tells you whether the connection was successful.

10. **Click OK to close the alert box.**

11. **Click OK to close the MySQL Connection dialog box.**

Dreamweaver creates the database connection (see Figure 2-6).

You can then click down on the outline structure to display Stored Procedures, Tables, and Views (see Figure 2-7).

Figure 2-6:
A MySQL connection has been established.

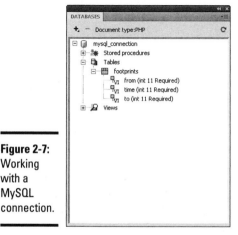

Figure 2-7:
Working with a MySQL connection.

PHP code hinting

When you have a .php file open in the Dreamweaver editor, you have full access to PHP code hinting. To access code hinting, press Ctrl+Space (Windows) or ⌘+Space (Mac OS X). A context-sensitive drop-down list of functions and operations is displayed. When you select an item, help is displayed below the item.

Editing a PHP Database Connection

In case you change the password for your database connection or the address of your database server changes, you need to know how to update your MySQL database connection settings.

To edit a MySQL database connection in PHP, follow these steps:

1. **Open the Databases panel by clicking the Databases tab of the Application panel.**

2. **Right-click the database connection you want to edit.**

3. **Select Edit Connection.**

   The MySQL Connection dialog box appears.

4. **Edit the connection properties as necessary.**

5. **Click the Test button to confirm that your connection is properly set up.**

   An alert box tells you whether the connection was successful.

6. **Click OK to close the alert box.**

7. **Click OK to close the MySQL Connection dialog box.**

   Dreamweaver saves your changes to the database connection.

Deleting a PHP Database Connection

To delete a MySQL database connection in PHP, follow these steps:

1. **Open the Databases panel by clicking the Databases tab of the Application panel.**

2. **Right-click the database connection you want to delete.**

   A list of options appears.

3. **Choose Delete Connection.**

   An alert box appears to confirm your deletion.

4. **Click Yes.**

   The database connection is deleted and removed from the list of connections on the Databases tab in the Application panel.

Deleting the database connection deletes a PHP file that Dreamweaver created in a Connections directory in your local directory. The directory itself remains. You can delete this directory if you want to keep your directory uncluttered.

Book VII
Chapter 2

Configuring
MySQL Database
Connections for PHP

Chapter 3: Configuring ASP Database Connections

In This Chapter

✓ **Gathering database connection information**

✓ **Adding a database connection**

✓ **Connecting to a remote database**

✓ **Editing or deleting a database connection**

*I*n this chapter, we show you how to set up a database connection in ASP (Active Server Pages) using Dreamweaver. You find out how to add, edit, and delete a database connection and connect to a remote database.

Before you begin, however, make sure you have the details on connecting to your database. To make a connection in ASP to a database, you need to know the following:

✦ The type of database you're connecting to (for example, SQL Server or Oracle)

✦ The host name of the database server or the IP address if no host name is available

✦ The username and password to access your database

✦ The name of the database to which you are trying to connect, or the Data Source Name (DSN)

Before starting, you need to have a site opened with a valid staging server setup, on your local computer or a remote server. See Book I, Chapter 3 for more information.

Understanding ASP Database Connections

Dreamweaver offers two ways to connect to a database when using ASP:

✦ **Data Source Name (DSN):** The DSN is a setting configured on your application server that contains the information needed to connect to your database. ASP then connects through the DSN instead of connecting directly from ASP. The advantage of using a DSN is that it's simpler than setting up the OLE DB (Object Linking and Embedding Database) driver, described next.

✦ **Custom connection string:** To set up a custom connection string, you enter information about your database server, and ASP uses that information to connect directly to your database. Connecting directly to a database requires ASP to run a small program called a *driver,* which enables ASP to speak directly with your database. Because this OLE DB driver talks directly to the database, it's faster than other drivers but requires a few extra steps (such as downloading and installing the driver).

OLE DB drivers are available for download from the provider of the database. For example, Microsoft supplies Access and SQL Server OLE DB drivers as part of its MDAC (Microsoft Data Access Components) download at `www.microsoft.com/downloads/details.aspx?FamilyID=6c050fe3-c795-4b7d-b037-185d0506396c&displaylang=en`.To download OLE DB drivers for Oracle databases, visit `www.oracle.com/technology/software/tech/windows/ole_db/index.html`. These packages come with installers that guide you through the process of installing the OLE DB driver on your computer.

If your Web hosting provider supports ASP, you can connect to a Microsoft Open Database Connectivity (ODBC) DSN provided on their server.

Before you can create an ASP database connection, you have to create a new dynamic ASP page so that Dreamweaver can interact with the database using database connections through ASP.

Creating a New ASP Page

To create a new dynamic ASP page, follow these steps:

1. **Choose File➪New.**

   The New Document window appears, as shown in Figure 3-1.

2. **Select ASP JavaScript or ASP VBScript in the Page Type list.**

   This selection is based on the type of scripting enabled on your server. For this example, we selected ASP JavaScript.

3. **(Optional) Select a layout style in the Layout list.**

   We left <none> selected in this example.

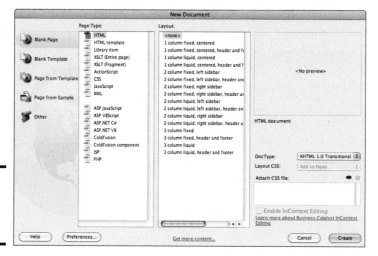

Figure 3-1:
The New
Document
dialog box.

4. **In the DocType drop-down list, select the default option, which is XHTML 1.0 Transitional.**

   This document type definition (DTD) makes your page XHTML-compliant.

5. **Click Create.**

   A new dynamic ASP page is created.

After you create a new dynamic ASP page, you can establish the database connection.

Connecting to a Database with a Data Source Name (DSN)

To create a database connection in ASP through a DSN, follow these steps:

1. **Choose Window⇨Databases to open the Databases panel, as shown in Figure 3-2.**

2. **Click the plus (+) icon. Select Data Source Name (DSN) in the drop-down list that appears.**

   The Data Source Name (DSN) dialog box appears, as shown in Figure 3-3.

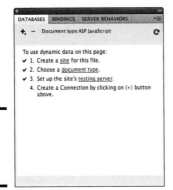

Figure 3-2:
The
Databases
panel.

Figure 3-3:
The Data
Source
Name (DSN)
dialog box.

3. **Enter a name for the new database connection in the Connection Name field.**

   Dreamweaver uses this name to reference your database connection. The name can contain only letters, numbers, and the underscore character.

4. **Enter the username for the database in the User Name field.**

   The server's administrator should provide this information.

5. **Enter the corresponding password in the Password field.**

   The password goes with the username from the preceding step.

6. **Click the DSN button.**

   The Select ODBC DSN dialog box appears.

7. **Select the Data Source Name (DSN) of your database in the Select ODBC DSN list, and then click OK.**

   The Select ODBC DSN dialog box closes, and the name of the selected DSN appears in the Data Source Name (DSN) field of the Data Source Name (DSN) dialog box.

8. **Click the Test button to confirm your settings.**

   An alert box tells you whether the connection was made successfully. The two most common causes of an error are an incorrect username and password.

   If the connection was not successful, try connecting to the database using the client that's supplied with the database. This verifies that you have the correct user, password, and database names.

9. **Click OK to close the alert box, and then click OK once more to close the Data Source Name (DSN) dialog box.**

   The database connection is created, and it's listed in the Databases panel (see Figure 3-4).

Figure 3-4: The Databases panel with the newly created database connection.

Connecting to a Database with a Custom Connection String

To create a database connection in ASP through a custom connection string, follow these steps:

1. **Open the Databases panel by choosing Window➪Databases.**

2. **Click the plus (+) icon, and then select Custom Connection String in the drop-down list that appears.**

   The Custom Connection String dialog box appears, as shown in Figure 3-5.

Custom Connection String

Figure 3-5:
Custom
Connection
String dialog
box.

Connection name: asp_sql

Connection string: Provider=SQLOLEDB;Server=WIN2K-ASP\MSSQL;Database=M

OK

Cancel

Advanced...

Test

Help

3. **Enter a name for the database connection in the Connection Name field.**

Dreamweaver uses this name to reference your database connection. The name can only contain letters, numbers, and the underscore character.

4. **Enter a connection string for your database in the Connection String field.**

For example, suppose that you want to connect to a database named Thor on an SQL server named Poseidon, with the username *dbadmin* and a password of *pass*. The connection string would look like this:

```
Provider=SQLOLEDB;Server=Poseidon;Database=Thor;UID=dbadmin;PWD=pass
```

To connect to Oracle, you use the same connection string as in the previous example, except you use the following `Provider` value:

```
Provider=OraOLEDB;
```

To connect to an Access database file, the connection string looks something like this, depending on the location of the file:

```
Driver={Microsoft Access Driver (*.mdb)};DBQ=d:\inetpub\wwwroot\data\
    myaccessdb.mdb
```

`DBQ=` specifies the path to the Access database file on the hosting server. Although this connection string lacks some of the fields, it's still a complete, valid connection string. Because we didn't specify the provider, Dreamweaver defaults to the ODBC driver.

5. **Click the Test button to confirm your settings.**

An alert box tells you whether the connection was successful.

6. **Click OK in the alert box.**

The alert box closes, and the Custom Connection String dialog box appears.

7. **Click OK to close the Custom Connection String dialog box.**

Dreamweaver creates the new database connection and lists it on the Databases panel.

Connecting to a Remote Database without a DSN

More than likely, you're planning to host your site with a commercial ISP or hosting provider. If your ISP provides a DSN, connecting to the database works the same as in the preceding steps. However, many hosting providers don't provide a DSN to connect to a remote ODBC database, so you may have to specify the ODBC connection details without a DSN.

To set up a custom connection string to access a remote database, you need to know the *physical path* to your database file.

Understanding physical paths and virtual paths

When you upload your pages to a Web server using Dreamweaver, they're placed in a folder on the Web server just like when you copy files from one place to another on your own computer. For example, if you upload your pages to a Web server running Microsoft IIS, your files may be placed in the following directory:

```
d:\inetpub\wwwroot\
```

If your home page file was named index.htm, the *physical path* to your home page would be

```
d:\inetpub\wwwroot\index.htm
```

When you use your Web browser to visit a Web site, however, you don't type the physical path. Instead, you enter the URL:

```
http://example.com/index.htm
```

This URL helps you access the index.htm page. The part of the URL that follows the Web site name is the *virtual path.* In this example, the virtual path is index.htm.

When a Web site is configured on a Web server, the server is instructed to point all requests for a particular virtual path to a corresponding physical path. In the preceding example, all requests for pages located at `http://example.com/rich` are transparently fulfilled with the files in the physical path: `d:\inetpub\wwwroot\rich`.

Finding the database's physical path when you know the virtual path

If you need to know the physical path to your database but have only the virtual path, you're in luck. The ASP `MapPath()` method allows you to feed a virtual path and get back the corresponding physical path. Follow these steps to use `MapPath()` to retrieve a physical path:

1. **Create a new ASP document based on the instructions in the "Creating a New ASP Page" section previously in this chapter.**

2. **Click the Code button or the Split button on the Document toolbar to open the code editor.**

   The Document window displays the code for your page.

3. **Enter the following ASP code inside the document body:**

   ```
   <% Response.Write(Server.MapPath("/virtualpath/fileinpath")) %>
   ```

   Replace *virtualpath* with the site's virtual path, and replace *filein path* with the name of a file in the directory. If you're just looking for the physical path of the site's root directory, simply enter a forward slash (*/*) in the quotes.

4. **Click the Design button to switch to Design view.**

   The Document window displays your page with the ASP code hidden.

5. **Click the Live Code button.**

   Dreamweaver displays the physical path, which corresponds with the virtual path you entered in the ASP code snippet.

Connecting to a remote database with a virtual path

Using a virtual path to connect to your file-based database actually calls a command on your remote server to look up the physical path. The command string used is determined by your ASP server's scripting language, JavaScript or VBScript. You need to create a custom connection string to connect to the remote database without using a DSN.

For JavaScript, your custom connection string looks like this:

```
"Driver={Microsoft Access Driver (*.mdb)};DBQ=" + Server.MapPath("/virtualpath/
    databasefile.mdb")
```

For VBScript, your custom connection string looks like this:

```
"Driver={Microsoft Access Driver (*.mdb)};DBQ=" & Server.MapPath("/virtualpath/
    databasefile.mdb")
```

In either case, replace *virtualpath* with the site's virtual path and replace *databasefile.mdb* with the name of the database file in the directory.

To prevent a user from downloading your entire database, always place your .mdb database files in a directory that isn't in your Web root.

To set up a database connection using the custom connection string, follow the steps in "Connecting to a Database with a Custom Connection String," earlier in this chapter. In Step 4, use the custom connection string you just created.

Editing an ASP Database Connection

Sometimes after you set up a database connection, several connection details may change. For example, the server that hosts the database could change, or you might select a new password for the database. To edit an ASP database connection in Dreamweaver to reflect these changes, follow these steps:

1. **In the Databases panel, right-click the database connection you want to edit and then choose Edit Connection in the drop-down list that appears.**

The Custom Connection String or Data Source Name dialog box appears, depending on which type of connection you're editing.

2. **Edit the connection properties as necessary.**

3. **Click the Test button to confirm your settings.**

An alert box tells you whether the connection was made successfully.

4. **Click OK to close the alert box, and click OK once more to close the connection dialog box.**

Dreamweaver saves your changes to the database connection.

Deleting an ASP Database Connection

To delete an ASP database connection in Dreamweaver, do the following:

1. **In the Databases panel, right-click the database connection you want to delete and then choose Delete Connection in the drop-down list that appears.**

An alert box appears to confirm the deletion.

2. **Click Yes to confirm the deletion.**

The database connection is deleted and removed from the list of connections in the Databases panel.

Chapter 4: Configuring ASP.NET Database Connections

In This Chapter

✔ Gathering database connection information

✔ Adding a database connection

✔ Editing or deleting a database connection

*L*ike PHP, ASP.NET is another application server platform that you can use inside Dreamweaver to connect to your remote or local database. In this chapter, we show you how to set up a database connection in ASP. NET using Dreamweaver CS5.

To make a connection in ASP.NET to a database, you need to gather the following necessary information about your database:

✦ Type of database you are connecting to (for example, SQL Server, Access, or Oracle)

✦ Host name of the database server, or the IP address if no host name is available

✦ Username and password to access your database

✦ Name of the database to which you are trying to connect: in the case of a file-based database such as Access, the location of the database file

Make sure you have a site open and the testing server configured before continuing. (See Book VII, Chapter 1 for details.)

Exploring ASP.NET Database Connections

Dreamweaver offers two ways to connect to a database using ASP.NET:

✦ **OLE DB connection:** With this method, you enter the information about your database server, and ASP.NET uses that information to connect directly to your database. Connecting directly to a database requires ASP.NET to run a driver program to be able to speak directly with your specific type of database. Because the OLE DB driver talks directly to the database, it's fast.

OLE DB drivers are available for download from the provider of the database. For example, Microsoft supplies Access and SQL Server OLE DB drivers as part of its MDAC (Microsoft Data Access Components) download at `www.microsoft.com/downloads/details.aspx?FamilyID=6c050fe3-c795-4b7d-b037-185d0506396c&displaylang=en`. To download OLE DB drivers for Oracle databases, visit `www.oracle.com/technology/software/tech/windows/ole_db/index.html`. These packages come with installers that guide you through the process of installing the OLE DB driver on your computer.

If your ISP supports ASP.NET, you may be able to connect to an ODBC DSN provided on their server.

✦ **SQL Server connection:** This setting is specific to connecting with MS SQL Server databases. The SQL Server connection option is nearly identical to the OLE DB connection option for MS SQL Server, except that you don't have to give Dreamweaver a Provider value in the SQL Server connection option.

Go ahead and create an SQL Server connection if using SQL Server; otherwise, create an OLE DB database connection. Before you create an ASP.NET database connection, you must first create a new dynamic ASP.NET page so that Dreamweaver can interact with the database using database connections through ASP.NET.

Creating a New ASP.NET Page

To create a new dynamic ASP.NET page, follow these steps:

1. Choose File➪New.

The New Document window appears.

2. Select ASP.NET C# or ASP.NET VBScript in the Page Type list.

This selection is based on your preference or the type of scripting available on your server.

3. Select the XHTML 1.0 Transitional option in the DocType drop-down list.

The document type definition (DTD) setting makes your page XHTML-compliant.

4. Click Create.

A new ASP.NET page is created and ready for scripting.

After you create a new dynamic ASP.NET page, you can establish the database connection. You can create an OLE DB connection using the templates or data link properties, which we cover in the next section. An alternative to connecting to an SQL Server database is to use the method provided in the Microsoft .NET Framework, which we discuss later in the chapter in "Building an SQL Server connection."

Building an OLE DB Connection

OLE DB serves as a good all-around choice for ASP.NET developers, regardless of the database you are connecting to.

If you're using SQL Server, you can use OLE DB or the dedicated connection discussed in the following section.

Using templates

To use a template to create an OLE DB connection in ASP.NET, follow these steps:

1. **Open the Databases panel by choosing Window⇨Databases.**

2. **Click the plus (+) icon, and then select OLE DB Connection from the drop-down list.**

The OLE DB Connection dialog box appears.

3. **Enter a name for the database connection in the Connection Name field.**

Dreamweaver uses this name to reference your database connection. The name can only contain letters, numbers, or an underscore.

4. **Click the Templates button.**

The Connection String Template dialog box appears.

5. **Select your database type in the Select Template list, and then click OK.**

The Connection String Template dialog box closes, and the template for the database type you selected appears in the Connection String text box in the OLE DB Connection dialog box.

You can skip Steps 6 and 7 if you selected the UDL file template.

6. **Enter the user ID for the database by replacing the [*username*] text with the username provided to access your database.**

Do not include the square brackets when entering the username. Remember to end the line with a semicolon.

Most ISPs with hosted databases provide a page for you to view your database username and password. If not, contact the person who supports the database for the username and password.

7. **Enter the password for the database by replacing the text [*password*] with the password provided to access your database.**

   Do not include the square brackets when entering the password, and be sure the line ends with a semicolon. The UDL file template doesn't require this step.

8. **Modify the remainder of the template values using the settings detailed in Table 4-1.**

   Table 4-1 provides you with details on the values to enter for each connection string template.

Table 4-1	OLE DB Connection Settings	
Template Name	**Database Type**	**Properties**
Oracle (Microsoft Provider)	Oracle	Provider=MSDAORA; Data Source=[*OracleInstanceName*]; User ID=[*username*]; Password=[*password*];
Oracle (Oracle Provider)	Oracle	Provider=OraOLEDB.Oracle; User ID=[*username*]; Password=[*password*]; Data Source=[*OracleInstanceName*];
Microsoft SQL Server	Microsoft SQL Server	Provider=SQLOLEDB.1; Persist Security Info=False; Data Source=[*serverName*]; Initial Catalog=[*databaseName*]; User ID=[*username*]; Password=[*password*];
Microsoft Jet 4.0 DB Provider	Microsoft Access	Provider=Microsoft.Jet. OLEDB.4.0; Data Source=[*databaseName*]; User ID=[*username*]; Password=[*password*];
Microsoft Access 97 (Microsoft Jet 3.5 Provider)	Microsoft Access	Provider=Microsoft.Jet. OLEDB.3.5; Data Source=[*databaseName*]; User ID=[*username*]; Password=[*password*];
UDL file	(Text file)	File Name=[*filename*]

9. **Click the Test button to confirm that your connection is properly set up.**

   An alert box informs you whether the connection was successful. The two most common causes of an error are incorrect usernames and passwords. Try connecting to the database using the client supplied with the database. This verifies that you have the correct user, password, and database names.

10. **Click OK to close the alert box, and then click OK to close the OLE DB Connection dialog box.**

    The database connection is created.

Using data link properties

To enter data link properties to create an OLE DB connection in ASP.NET, follow these steps:

1. **In the Databases panel, click the plus (+) icon, and then select OLE DB Connection in the drop-down list.**

2. **Click the Build button in the OLE DB Connection dialog box that appears.**

   The Data Link Properties dialog box appears.

3. **On the Provider tab, select the appropriate Microsoft OLE DB Provider for your database type.**

   Most applications use a provider beginning with "Microsoft OLE DB Provider for."

4. **On the Connection tab, enter the connection information for your database.**

   The database server administrator provides this information.

5. **Click the Test Connection button to confirm that your connection is properly set up.**

   An alert box tells you whether the connection was successful.

6. **Click OK to close the alert box, and then click OK to close the OLE DB Connection dialog box.**

   You are connected to the database.

Book VII
Chapter 4

Configuring
ASP.NET Database
Connections

Building an SQL Server Connection

Many ASP.NET developers use SQL Server as their database backend. As a result, the SQL Server database connection has its own connection type.

To create a .NET SQL Server database connection in ASP.NET, follow these steps:

1. **In the Databases panel, click the plus (+) icon, and then select SQL Server Connection from the drop-down list that appears.**

2. **Enter a name for the database connection in the Connection Name field.**

Dreamweaver uses this name to reference your database connection. The name can only consist of letters, numbers, or an underscore.

3. **In the Connection String field, build a connection string for your database.**

For example, to connect to a database named Thor on an SQL server named Poseidon, with the username *dbadmin* and a password of *pass*, the connection string is

```
Persist Security Info=False;Data Source=Poseidon;Initial
        Catalog=Thor;User ID=dbadmin;Password=pass;
```

The `Persist Security Info` parameter tells the ASP.NET functions to forget the password after using it to log in instead of keeping it in memory.

4. **Click the Test button to confirm that your connection is properly set up.**

An alert box tells you whether the connection was successful.

5. **Click OK to close the alert box, and then click OK to close the SQL Server Connection dialog box.**

The database connection is created.

Editing an ASP.NET Database Connection

If you need to edit an ASP.NET database connection, you'll want to do the following:

1. **In the Databases panel, right-click the database connection you want to edit and then choose Edit Connection from the drop-down list that appears.**

The OLE DB Connection or SQL Server Connection dialog box appears, depending on which database connection type you're editing.

2. **Edit the connection properties as necessary.**

3. **Click the Test button to confirm that your connection is set up properly.**

4. **Click OK to close the alert box that appears, and then click OK to close the connection dialog box.**

The connection has been edited.

Deleting an ASP.NET Database Connection

To delete an ASP.NET database connection in Dreamweaver, follow these steps:

1. **In the Databases panel, right-click the database connection you want to delete and then choose Delete Connection in the drop-down list that appears.**

An alert box appears to confirm that you want to delete the selected connection.

2. **Click Yes to close the alert box.**

The database connection is deleted and removed from the list of connections in the Databases panel.

Chapter 5: Configuring JSP Database Connections

In This Chapter

✔ **Gathering database connection information**

✔ **Adding a database connection**

✔ **Connecting to a remote database**

✔ **Editing or deleting a database connection**

*J*avaServer Pages (JSP) is a popular Java-based application server technology used to create dynamic Web pages. This chapter shows you how to create a database connection for your JSP pages and edit or delete the connection after you create it. You also find out what you need to know about the option settings that you're likely to use for this connection.

Before you begin, be sure that you have a site opened and have the testing server configured. (See Book VII, Chapter 1 for instructions.)

Gathering Database Connection Information

Dreamweaver enables you to connect to a variety of databases by modifying the database driver and *connection string* (URL) for each type of database. Before you can set up a connection to your database, make sure that you have the following information on hand:

✦ The location of the database server as a host name or an IP address. If the database resides on the same machine as the application server, this could be `localhost`.

✦ The database username.

✦ The database password.

✦ The name of the database instance. Because a database can host several distinct groups of tables, the instance provides a way to indicate which set of tables to use.

If your database resides on your own server, you must download the Java JDBC (Java Database Connectivity) driver from the database vendor site (such as Oracle or IBM). If you don't download the driver, when you try to connect to the database, you receive a Java error that the connection method is missing.

Adding a JSP Database Connection

JSP pages use a standard interface for connecting to databases called Java Database Connectivity (JDBC) drivers. The JDBC driver for your database translates the information traveling between your JSP program and your database, enabling the two to communicate with one another.

Dreamweaver offers six drivers for connecting to a database in JSP through JDBC, as well as an option for creating a custom JDBC connection. Here are Dreamweaver's built-in JSP database connection types:

- ✦ Custom JDBC Connection
- ✦ IBM DB2 App driver (DB2)
- ✦ IBM DB2 Net driver (DB2)
- ✦ MySQL driver (MySQL)
- ✦ Oracle Thin driver (Oracle)
- ✦ Inet driver (SQLServer)
- ✦ Sun JDBC-ODBC driver (ODBC database)

For the first option, Custom JDBC Connection, you enter all the necessary information to create the custom database connection. For the rest of the database types, Dreamweaver fills in the appropriate driver name and provides a URL template that you can replace with the information for your database. Table 5-1 shows the driver and URL fields for Dreamweaver's database connection types. Each of these drivers corresponds to a specific database.

Table 5-1	Database Connection Types and Their Respective Drivers and URLs	
Database	*Driver*	*Connection URL*
Custom JDBC Connection	Custom	Custom
IBM DB2 App driver (DB2)	COM.ibm.db2.jdbc.app. DB2Driver	`jdbc:db2:[database name]`

Database	Driver	Connection URL
IBM DB2 Net driver (DB2)	COM.ibm.db2.jdbc.net. DB2Driver	`jdbc:db2://[host name]:[server port]/[database name]`
MySQL driver (MySQL)	org.gjt.mm.mysql.Driver	`jdbc:mysql://[host name]/[database name]`
Oracle Thin driver (Oracle)	oracle.jdbc.driver.OracleDriver	`jdbc:oracle:thin:@ [host name]:[port]: [sid]`
Inet driver (SQLServer)	com.inet.tds.TdsDriver	`jdbc:inetdae:[host name]:[port]?data base=[database]`
Sun JDBC-ODBC driver (ODBC Database)	sun.jdbc.odbc.JdbcOdbcDriver	`jdbc:odbc:[odbc dsn]`

When you create a JSP connection to your database, replace the [*host name*] and [*database name*] shown in Table 5-1 with your database's values. For example, if you're creating a connection to a local MySQL database named `test`, use the following connection URL:

`jdbc:mysql://127.0.0.1/test`

Book VII Chapter 5

Configuring JSP Database Connections

Java Runtime Environment installation

You must have the Java SE (JRE) installed before using a JDBC driver. Visit Sun's site at `http://java.sun.com/javase` if you haven't installed the JRE.

If you're deploying your code to a remote server, be sure that the JDBC driver is installed there too. Otherwise, your application won't work when you upload it.

Installing the JDBC driver

Although Dreamweaver includes everything you need to use the Java JDBC driver classes for several databases, it doesn't include the code for the JDBC drivers.

To install the appropriate JDBC driver for your database, follow these steps:

1. **Download the Java .jar file for your database.**

   Java packages are distributed as .jar files. See Table 5-2 to find out where to download the file you need. (At some of these sites, you may need to register to download the file.)

   You can also go to Sun's JDBC Data Access API Drivers page at `http://developers.sun.com/product/jdbc/drivers` for more.

2. **Copy the Java .jar file to the configuration/JDBCDrivers subdirectory under the Dreamweaver CS5 install directory.**

3. **Restart Dreamweaver.**

Table 5-2	JDBC Database Driver Download Locations	
Database	*Driver*	*Web Site*
IBM DB2 App/Net driver	COM.ibm.db2.jdbc. app.DB2Driver	www-306.ibm.com/software/data/ db2/express/download.html
MySQL driver connector/J	org.gjt.mm.mysql. Driver	www.mysql.com/products/ connector/j/
Oracle Thin driver	oracle.jdbc.driver. OracleDriver	www.oracle.com/technology/ software/tech/java/sqlj_jdbc/ htdocs/jdbc_10201.html
Inet driver (i-net Gate)	com.inet.tds. TdsDriver	www.inetsoftware.de/Download. htm

After you install the database driver, you can create a dynamic page and the database connection in JSP, as described in the next section.

Creating a New JSP Document

Because pages that work with a database are dynamic, Dreamweaver requires you to create a dynamic page before you can add a database connection.

Follow these steps to create a new dynamic JSP page:

1. **Choose File⇨New.**

   The New Document window appears.

2. **Select JSP in the Page Type list.**

3. **In the DocType drop-down list, select the default XHTML 1.0 Transitional setting.**

   This document type definition (DTD) creates an XHTML-compliant page.

4. **Click Create.**

   Your new JSP page is ready to use.

Dreamweaver allows you to add a database connection now that the dynamic JSP page exists.

Connecting to a Database

After you create a dynamic JSP page (as described in the preceding section), follow these steps to create a database connection in JSP:

1. **Open the Databases panel by choosing Window⇨Databases.**

2. **Click the plus (+) icon and select a database connection type in the drop-down list.**

   You can choose from the database types listed in Table 5-1. After you make a selection, a connection dialog box named for the type of connection appears. The Driver and URL fields are prefilled for all standard database driver types. The fields in the custom connection dialog box are all blank.

3. **Enter a database connection name in the Connection Name field.**

   Dreamweaver CS5 uses this name to reference your database connection. The name can have letters, numbers, or an underscore.

4. **Enter the JDBC database driver in the Driver field.**

   The field is prepopulated for every database type except the Custom JDBC Database. If you're setting up a custom connection, you can usually find the Java class name in the driver's documentation. The class name tells Dreamweaver what Java code to call to access the database. For example, if you are using the MySQL driver, the class name is `org. gjt.mm.mysql.Driver`.

   If you're using a JDBC driver, you should have already downloaded it. If you click the Test button and you get a `Class not found` alert, you need to download the class. See Table 5-2 for a list of download locations.

5. **In the URL field, replace the bracketed values with the information for your database.**

   If you're creating a custom connection, refer to the documentation that came with your JDBC driver for the format of this connection string.

The URL field contains, in one long string, all the information required to log in to the database. For example, for the MySQL driver, it lists the following URL:

```
jdbc:mysql://[hostname]/[database name]
```

In this example, replace the bracketed values [*hostname*] and [*database name*] with the information for your database.

6. **Enter the database username in the User Name field.**

   The server's administrator should provide this information.

7. **Enter the database password in the Password field.**

   The password goes with the username from the preceding step.

8. **Choose the Using Driver on This Machine option.**

   This setting determines if the local machine or the remote application server's driver is used to connect to the database. If you're running Mac OS X, you can ignore this setting because Mac OS X computers always use the remote application server to connect.

9. **Click the Test button to confirm that your connection is set up correctly.**

   A dialog box confirms a successful connection or displays an error message if it couldn't connect.

   If you received a *Class was not found* error message when you clicked the Test button, you don't have the driver installed for that type of database. Download the Java package that corresponds to the type of database driver. Refer to Table 5-2, which lists where to find popular drivers on the Internet.

10. **Click OK in the Connection Test dialog box.**

   The dialog box closes.

11. **Click OK.**

   Dreamweaver creates the database, and the database connection dialog box closes.

JDBC allows you to create an ODBC database connection with the Sun JDBC-ODBC driver using a Data Source Name (DSN). See Book VII, Chapter 3 for more information on using DSNs. You need to make sure that you've set up the DSN before you use it.

Editing a JSP Database Connection

Sometimes you need to go back to your database connection and make a change. Here's how to edit the JSP database connection in Dreamweaver:

1. **Open the Databases panel by choosing Window⇨Databases.**

2. **Right-click the database connection you want to edit, and then select Edit Connection in the list that appears.**

   The database connection dialog box appears.

3. **Edit the connection properties as necessary.**

4. **Click the Test button to confirm that your connection is set up correctly.**

5. **Click OK to close the alert box.**

6. **Click OK to close the database connection dialog box.**

   Dreamweaver saves the changes to your database connection.

Deleting a JSP Database Connection

Deleting database connections in Dreamweaver CS5 is similar to editing them. To delete a JSP database connection in Dreamweaver, follow these steps:

1. **Open the Databases panel by choosing Window⇨Databases.**

2. **Right-click the database connection you want to delete, and then select Delete Connection in the list that appears.**

   An alert box appears to confirm your deletion.

3. **Click Yes to close the alert box and delete the connection.**

   The database connection is deleted and removed from the list of connections on the Databases panel.

Chapter 6: Configuring ColdFusion Database Connections

In This Chapter

✔ Pulling together database connection information

✔ Understanding how ColdFusion connects to databases

✔ Adding a database connection

✔ Editing or deleting a database connection

ColdFusion is Adobe's application server technology. What is distinct about ColdFusion compared to other app servers is that it uses a tag-based approach to programming compared to scripts or more traditional programming syntax. As a result, Web designers with no previous programming experience can often pick up ColdFusion more quickly than other languages.

Some examples of ColdFusion applications include event registration, catalog searches, directories, calendars, and even interactive training. ColdFusion applications are moderately complex; they execute on the Web server as CGI scripts. In this chapter, we explain how to set up a database connection in ColdFusion using Dreamweaver. You also find out how to add, edit, and delete a database connection.

Pulling Together Database Connection Information

ColdFusion is highly flexible in its ability to connect to different types of data sources, especially databases. Although ColdFusion supports a wide array of database types, some key pieces of information to create a connection to a database are common among all the database types. To make a connection to a database in ColdFusion, you need to know the following information:

✦ Type of database you are connecting to (SQL Server, Oracle, Access, and so on)

✦ Host name of the database server, or IP address if no host name is available

✦ Username and password to access your database

✦ Name or file location of the database to which you are trying to connect

Understanding How ColdFusion Connects to Databases

ColdFusion is designed to connect to databases at the server level, which means a database connection must be set up on the ColdFusion server itself. This task traditionally requires a ColdFusion administrator's assistance. After the connection is set up, your ColdFusion application can use it. This connection differs from other Web application platforms in that many other Web applications' database connections are created from within your Web application and don't require setup on the application server.

 ColdFusion uses Java Database Connectivity (JDBC) to connect with databases. If you're unable to find an appropriate database driver included with ColdFusion, you can enter the JDBC driver information directly.

Although the design of how ColdFusion connects to databases has stayed consistent, newer versions of ColdFusion provide greater flexibility in configuring database connections than earlier versions. Specifically, you can create ColdFusion database connections within Dreamweaver directly on the ColdFusion server.

Adding a ColdFusion Database Connection

You can connect ColdFusion to a database a couple different ways, depending on which version of ColdFusion you're running. If you're running ColdFusion 9, 8, or MX 7, you can set up the database connection within Dreamweaver. However, if you're using ColdFusion version 6.0 or earlier, you must use the ColdFusion Administration Web site on the ColdFusion server to configure your database connection.

Before you create a ColdFusion database connection, you must first create a new ColdFusion document and specify an RDS (Remote Development Services) login. (RDS is a security component of ColdFusion used to manage access to files and databases.) Creating the new ColdFusion document tells Dreamweaver the platform of the connection you're trying to set up, and ensures that you have the correct document type to use the new database connection. The RDS login tells Dreamweaver how to communicate with the ColdFusion server to publish files.

If you'd like more info on configuring the ColdFusion server, check out related articles at the ColdFusion Developer Center (www.adobe.com/devnet/coldfusion/).

Creating a new ColdFusion document

To create a new ColdFusion document, perform the following steps:

1. **Choose File⇨New.**

   The New Document dialog box appears.

2. **Select Blank Page in the Category list.**

3. **Select ColdFusion in the Page Type list.**

4. **(Optional) Specify a layout in the Layout list.**

   For this example, we kept the default <none> selected.

5. **In the DocType drop-down list, select the default XHTML 1.0 Transitional setting.**

   This document type definition (DTD) creates an XHTML-compliant page.

6. **Click Create.**

   A new, blank ColdFusion document is created.

Now that you have created a new ColdFusion document, you can establish a database connection for Dreamweaver to use.

Specifying RDS login information

Before setting up the first database connection for a Dreamweaver site, you must specify an RDS password for the ColdFusion server. This password allows Dreamweaver to interact directly with the ColdFusion server to exchange database connection information. If you haven't already entered the RDS password, a checklist appears in the Databases panel, as shown in Figure 6-1. If you installed the ColdFusion server, use the password from the installation; otherwise, contact the administrator of the ColdFusion server.

Book VII
Chapter 6

Configuring ColdFusion Database Connections

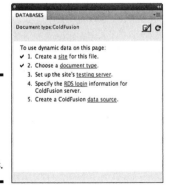

Figure 6-1:
A checklist for using ColdFusion database connections.

To set up the RDS connection, do the following:

1. **Open the Databases panel by choosing Window⇨Databases.**

A checklist appears in the panel.

2. **Click the RDS Login link in the fourth step of the checklist.**

A Login to ColdFusion Remote Development Services (RDS) dialog box appears.

3. **Enter the RDS password for your ColdFusion server.**

The ColdFusion server administrator provides the password.

4. **Click OK to close the dialog box.**

A list of existing database connections appears in the Databases panel.

Configuring a database connection with the ColdFusion Administrator

If you're using a version of ColdFusion earlier than version 7, you must use ColdFusion Administrator to create the database connection. This method works on all versions of ColdFusion, including the current one. The biggest advantage to configuring through ColdFusion Administrator is not having to open up a separate browser window to access the administration pages.

To create a database connection in ColdFusion, follow these steps:

1. **Open the Databases panel by choosing Window@–>Databases.**

2. **Click the Modify Data Sources icon (which looks like a yellow cylinder with a pencil; refer to Figure 6-1).**

Dreamweaver opens a new Web browser window with the Administrator Login page of the ColdFusion server, shown in Figure 6-2.

3. **Enter the ColdFusion Administrator username and password in the text boxes next to the Login button.**

The ColdFusion server administrator must provide this password.

4. **Click the Login button.**

After you submit the password, your Web browser is redirected to the Data & Services>Data Sources page, as shown in Figure 6-3.

5. **Enter a name for the database connection in the Data Source Name field.**

ColdFusion uses this name to reference your database connection. The name can be made up of letters, numbers, or the underscore character only. Additionally, you can't use the names *service, jms_provider, comp,* or *jms* because these are reserved by ColdFusion.

Figure 6-2:
The login
page for the
ColdFusion
Admin-
istrator
console.

Configuring
ColdFusion Database
Connections

Figure 6-3:
Adding a
database
connection
to
ColdFusion.

6. **Select the appropriate database driver type in the Driver menu.**

7. **Click the Add button.**

   You are directed to the next step of the creation process, as shown in
   Figure 6-4.

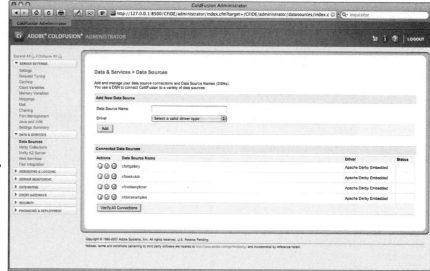

Figure 6-4:
The Add
Data Source
page for
a MySQL
connection.

8. **Enter your database connection information.**

   This information includes the CF data source name, database name, server, username, password, and a description.

9. **Click the Submit button.**

   You are directed back to the Data & Services >Data Sources page. If your connection settings contain any errors, ColdFusion displays the errors in red text at the top of the page. A green success message at the top of the page indicates a successful configuration.

   In either case, the connection is created. If an error still exists, the connection appears with a yellow background, and the error details show in the Data Source Name column in the Connected Data Sources table. The error details disappear after you correct the error.

Your new database connection appears in the Dreamweaver Databases panel. If the connection doesn't appear immediately, click the Refresh icon to update Dreamweaver's list of available connections.

Configuring a database connection in Dreamweaver

If you would prefer to create the ColdFusion (version 9, 8, or MX 7) database connection inside Dreamweaver, do the following:

1. **Open the Databases panel by choosing Window➪Databases.**

2. **Click the plus (+) icon, and then select the appropriate database connection type from the drop-down list.**

   A dialog box appears for the database connection type you selected, similar to Figure 6-5.

Figure 6-5:
Adding a
MySQL
connection
to
ColdFusion
through
Dream-
weaver.

3. **Enter the connection information for your database.**

   This information is the CF data source name, username, password, server name, and database name.

4. **Click the Test button to confirm that your connection is set up correctly.**

   A dialog box tells you whether the connection was successful.

5. **Click OK again to close the database server connection dialog box.**

   The database connection is created on the ColdFusion server.

Editing a ColdFusion Database Connection

You can edit a ColdFusion database connection in one of two ways: through the ColdFusion Administrator Web console or directly inside Dreamweaver.

Using Dreamweaver

You can edit a ColdFusion Database Connection inside Dreamweaver by following these instructions:

1. **In the Databases panel, right-click (Windows) or Control+click (Mac) the database connection you want to edit, and then select Edit Connection in the list that appears, as shown in Figure 6-6.**

   The connection dialog box appears.

Figure 6-6:
Right-
click the
database
connection
you want to
edit.

2. **Edit the connection properties as necessary.**

3. **Click the Test button to confirm that your connection is set up correctly.**

   An alert box tells you the connection was successful.

4. **Click OK to close the alert box.**

   The alert box closes, and you return to the connection dialog box.

5. **Click OK to close the connection dialog box.**

   Dreamweaver saves the changes to your database connection.

Using ColdFusion Administrator

Using ColdFusion Administrator to edit a database connection works for all versions of ColdFusion and Dreamweaver. To edit a ColdFusion database connection in Dreamweaver through the ColdFusion Administrator Web console, do the following:

1. **In the Databases panel, click the Modify Data Sources icon.**

   Dreamweaver opens a new Web browser window with the Administrator Login page of the ColdFusion server.

2. **Enter the ColdFusion Administrator password in the text box, and then click the Login button.**

   After you submit the password, your Web browser redirects to the Data & Services>Data Sources page.

3. **Select the database connection you want to edit by clicking its name in the Connected Data Sources table.**

   You're redirected to a page showing the selected database connection's settings.

4. **Edit the connection information for your database.**

   This information is the CF data source name, username, password, server name, and database name.

5. **Click the Submit button.**

   ColdFusion tests your connection. If an error occurs, an error message in red text appears at the top of the page. If the connection is set up properly, a green success message is displayed.

   In either case, the connection is created. If an error still exists, the connection appears with a yellow background, and the error details show in the Data Source Name column in the Connected Data Sources table until the error is corrected.

Deleting a ColdFusion Database Connection

To delete a ColdFusion database connection in Dreamweaver, follow these steps:

1. **In the Databases panel, click the Modify Data Sources icon.**

   Dreamweaver opens a new Web browser window with the Administrator Login page of the ColdFusion server (refer to Figure 6-2).

2. **Enter the ColdFusion Administrator password in the text box, and then click the Login button.**

   The password is submitted, and your Web browser redirects to the Data & Services >Data Sources page of the ColdFusion Administrator Web console (refer to Figure 6-3).

3. **Select the database connection you want to delete by clicking the red circle icon to the left of the connection's name in the Connected Data Sources table.**

   A dialog box appears, confirming that you want to delete the selected data source.

4. **Click OK.**

   The dialog box closes and the Data & Services>Data Sources page updates. The deleted connection no longer appears in the Connected Data Sources table.

5. **Click Logout to close your session in the ColdFusion Administrator console.**

   If no Logout button is available, simply close the window.

Chapter 7: Dealing with Database Problems and Other Gotchas

*T*alk about frustrating: You've spent a good bit of time working to create your database and configure Dreamweaver for connecting with it. But when you go to try to connect the two in a data matrimony, all you get are messages like the following:

Error. Cannot connect to database.

Connection error. Unable to locate database. See your system administrator.

Give it up, dude. You can't get there from here.

The majority of error messages that you may encounter when working with databases center on connectivity. These errors principally break down like this:

✦ Invalid host, username, or password

✦ The driver files are missing

✦ A file's permission settings prevent reading a file-based database such as Access

✦ The remote host doesn't support the database driver you're using

Within the database, errors you can encounter include

✦ Attempting to insert a duplicate record into a database with a unique constraint

✦ Creating a table that already exists

✦ Not having proper database access rights in the database, including read, modify, and create permissions

✦ Attempting to insert data that is different from the data type of a column

✦ Misspelling a table or column name

✦ Not including the same number of values as table columns

This chapter shows you how to troubleshoot database problems and resolve permissions issues.

Troubleshooting Basic Database Access

Depending on the type of database you're using, you can troubleshoot a database problem in several ways. First, ping the database to verify connectivity. If that's successful, make sure your settings for username, password, and host name are correct. The following sections give you the details on how to do these troubleshooting tasks.

Verifying contact with the database server

If your database is on a remote server, you should start your troubleshooting by verifying that your computer can reach the database server. The following steps show how to use the `ping` command to verify connectivity:

1. **Open a command prompt on the Mac or PC.**

   To reach the command prompt on a PC, choose Start⇨Run, type **cmd** in the Run dialog box that appears, and then click OK.

   To reach the command prompt on a Mac, start the Terminal application by choosing Applications⇨Utilities.

2. **On the command line, enter** ping [*host name*] **where** [*host name*] **is the name of the database server.**

   For example, if your database is on a host called `leakypipes.com`, you'd enter the following command:

   ```
   ping leakypipes.com
   ```

3. **Analyze the output from the `ping` command to determine whether it was successful.**

   If the ping attempt is successful, you see output like this:

   ```
   Pinging leakypipes.com [24.94.201.11] with 32 bytes of
      data:
   Reply from 24.94.201.11: bytes=32 time<10ms TTL=64
   Reply from 24.94.201.11: bytes=32 time<10ms TTL=64
   ```

   Unsuccessful output looks something like this:

   ```
   Pinging 12.3.2.4 with 32 bytes of data:
   Request timed out.
   Request timed out.
   ```

4. **Press Ctrl+C (Windows) or Ctrl+click (Mac) to stop executing the `ping` command.**

If the `ping` command was unsuccessful, make sure you have the right information for your host name, are connected to your network correctly, and that the database server isn't down for maintenance.

Validating your database username and password

After verifying contact with the database server (as described in the preceding section), the next step is to make sure that your username and password are correct. To eliminate any possible driver issues with Dreamweaver CS5, use your database client to test this information. Each particular database has a different protocol.

MySQL databases

For MySQL running locally on your machine, use the `mysql` command-line client to verify the username and password. Specify your database connection information like this:

```
mysql -u[username] -p[password] -h[host name]
```

For MySQL databases running on a Web host, use the Web control panel provided by your ISP to check on users and passwords. Also, make sure that you have enabled remote connectivity to your MySQL database. Many providers have a MySQL Remote Access utility in which you can grant your IP address permission.

Access and SQL Server

For Access or SQL Server databases, try connecting from Access or SQL Server through ODBC. For both Access and SQL Server, make sure that you have your DSN set up correctly. Also make sure that the remote server has DSN set up. See the "Problematic Permissions: IIS and File-Based Databases" section for more information on accessing the DSN definition through the Windows Control Panel.

Oracle

For Oracle, use the `sqlplus` command-line tool to verify the username and password. Specify your connection information as follows:

```
sqlplus [username]/[password]@[db_descriptor]
```

The syntax is `sqlplus username@database`. Oracle also provides a utility called `tnsping` that attempts to ping the database server based on its Oracle database descriptor.

Oracle names

Your Oracle database may require access through an Oracle names file called `tns-names.ora`. You can use the Oracle Network Configuration tool to set up this file, or the Oracle database administrator may supply it. To verify that your Oracle names configuration is correct, use the Oracle command `tnsping`.

The `tnsping` command takes the name of your database as an argument and pings the database server that the configuration points to. If there's a problem resolving the name or reaching the server through the network, you receive an error message. If not, you know that your naming files are configured correctly and that the database is available over the network.

IBM Universal Database

Before you test your username and password, make sure you have the DB2 Runtime Client and the ODBC to DB2 driver installed. For the IBM client, verify your login using the Command Center. To test connectivity from the Command Center, follow these steps:

1. **Start the Command Center by choosing Start⇨Programs⇨db2⇨Command Line Tools⇨Command Center.**

   The Command Center launches. If this folder isn't in your Program Files list, you don't have the client installed.

2. **Click the Scripts tab.**

3. **Enter a simple query, such as the following, in the Query field:**

   ```
   connect to sample;
   ```

4. **Click the Execute icon at the top left.**

If you're able to execute your query without an error, you know that your database details are correct.

Problematic Permissions: IIS and File-Based Databases

Although file permissions are necessary to keep your computer and servers secure, they can thwart your development process when you're working with a local Web server and a database, both of which execute with limited permissions to help keep systems secure. The unfortunate reality is that you very well may run into a permission problem or two when developing and deploying your database-driven Web sites. Permissions apply to both directories and individual files, including database files. When you don't have necessary permission to read the database file, you get error messages that don't always clearly point to the problem. Also, verifying that permissions are set correctly on more than one computer can be time-consuming.

IIS permission problems are likely to rear their ugly heads when you publish your site or attempt to use Live Data view on a dynamic page. (See Book VIII, Chapter 3 for more on Live Data view.) The same problems can happen whether you're running Windows 7, Vista, or XP; however, the Windows administrative tools you can use to correct them vary slightly.

IIS usually runs as the limited access account on Windows called `IUSR_ [computer name]`. For example, if your computer name is `server`, your limited access account name is `IUSR_server`. IIS may take on increased permissions for a Web page if the page allows a user to log in to a specific account. In that case, you still need to be sure that the login account allows access to the database file.

The default for users who don't log in is `IUSR_[computer name]`.

You receive an error message if the Web server and database driver can't read the database file as the `IUSR_server` user. Both the database file and the directory containing the database file must have read and write permissions. If the path to the database file uses a sharename, regardless of whether the share is on the local computer or a remote computer, make sure that the file share has the proper permission to access the database file as `IUSR_[computer name]`.

To check or change the database file permissions, follow these steps:

1. **Log in as a user with Administrator access.**

   Windows won't allow you to make changes if you don't have the Administrator privilege. If you don't have this privilege, you need to log out and log back in with the Administrator account.

2. **Open the folder that contains your database file.**

   You specified this directory when creating the database.

   To find out where the file is located, check the ODBC data sources from the Windows Control Panel's Data Source (ODBC) program. It's located in the Administrative tools folder.

3. **Right-click the database file and select Properties.**

   The filename usually has the .mdb extension.

4. **Click the Security tab.**

5. **Windows 7: Verify that `IIS_IUSRS [computer name]` is listed in either the Group box or the User Names box, and then skip ahead to Step 10.**

Vista or XP: Verify that `IIS_IUSRS [computer name]`, `IUSR_ [computer name]`, or the special user `Everyone` is listed in the Name column. If any of these accounts is listed, skip ahead to Step 10. Otherwise, proceed to the next step to add the `IUSR_[computer name]` account.

The user `Everyone` means that any user, including the `IUSR_[computer name]` user, receives the permission granted to it.

6. **Click the Add button to open the Users, Computer, or Groups dialog box.**

7. **Select your computer name from the list.**

    Don't worry if it appears dimmed. That just means your computer name is the only choice because you're not part of a Windows domain.

8. **Select `IUSR_[computer name]` from the list of names.**

    For example, select IUSR_GILLIGAN if your computer name is `Gilligan`.

9. **Click Add and then click OK.**

    You return to the file's Properties dialog box.

10. **While the `IIS_IUSRS [computer name]` (Windows 7) or `IUSR_ [computer name]` (Vista or XP) is highlighted, click the Edit button to display the Permissions dialog box.**

11. **Select the Allow Checkbox Beside the Full control list item.**

    Clicking this check box is a shortcut for clicking all the other permission check boxes. This ensures that the file can be used by the Web application.

12. **Click OK.**

    The file's permissions are set to allow access.

Repeat these steps for the directory that contains the database file.

If you want to restrict Web users from browsing the folder that contains your database file, you can clear the Read permission for the database folder if the database folder is a subdirectory under the Web root folder. This still allows your application to read the file (because it already knows where the file is located) but prevents users from browsing the directory. However, placing the database file outside the Web root folder means the file can't be viewed through the browser.

Troubleshooting Microsoft Error Messages

When working with IIS and a file-driven database such as Access or SQL Server, a common set of errors can sometimes crop up. These errors involve the interaction between the Web server and the database when requesting dynamic pages. In this section, I look at these common error messages:

✦ *80004005: Data source name not found.* Another variation is *80004005: Microsoft Jet database engine cannot open the file (*unknown*).*

✦ *80040e07: Data type mismatch in criteria expression.*

✦ *80040e10: Too few parameters.*

✦ *80040e14: Syntax error in INSERT INTO statement.*

✦ *80040e21: ODBC error on Insert or Update.*

✦ *800a0bcd: Either BOF or EOF is true.*

For each of these errors, the following sections summarize the root cause and the action you need to take to correct it.

80004005: Data source name not found

Another variation to the "Data source name not found" error is "80004005: Microsoft Jet database engine cannot open the file (*unknown*)." This error generally means that you can't access the database file either because of a problem with permissions or because another process is already using the file. Verify that you've set the permissions correctly and that you don't have the database open in another program such as Access. See Microsoft's page for more troubleshooting tips at `http://support.microsoft.com/kb/306345/EN-US/`.

80040e07: Data type mismatch in criteria expression

A "Data type mismatch in criteria expression" error means that you've attempted to enter a value in a database column that isn't the correct type and can't be converted automatically (for example, inserting a string like `midwest` into a number column). The solution is to supply the correct type of data or change the column's data type.

80040e10: Too few parameters

The "Too few parameters" error indicates that one of the columns you've specified to add data to doesn't exist in the database. To fix this error, check the spelling of your commands and fields. Verify that each column exists. Create a new column in the table to match the data you're trying to insert if it doesn't already exist.

80040e14: Syntax error in INSERT INTO statement

The "Syntax error in INSERT INTO statement" error may indicate that you've used an invalid character in the name of a table or column. Spaces and special characters such as punctuation symbols aren't permitted. Also, in an Oracle database, you can see this error when using the `distinct` keyword in a `select` statement. See `http://support.microsoft.com/default.aspx?scid=kb;EN-US;238164` for patch instructions.

80040e21: ODBC error on Insert or Update

The "ODBC error on Insert or Update" error indicates that the field you're inserting into isn't large enough to hold the value you're inserting. For example, if you have a string column with a length of five characters and attempt to insert `Tuesday`, you get this error. To correct the error, either increase the size of the column or reduce the size of the string you're inserting.

800a0bcd: Either BOF or EOF is true

If you get the "Either BOF or EOF is true" error, you're attempting to display an element from a recordset that doesn't exist in the database table. To resolve this error, verify that each element of your recordset has a corresponding column in the database table using the Server Behaviors tool for the deployments. The Server Behaviors panel allows you to expand your recordset; click the plus(+) icon to reveal the fields of the recordset.

Troubleshooting JSP Database Connections

The most common error you are likely to encounter when working with a Java Database Connection (JDBC) database is that the JDBC driver isn't loaded on your machine or your server. If this happens, you receive an error ending in *class not found*. Search the database vendor's Web site for the JDBC driver (see Book VII, Chapter 5 for download URLs for the most popular ones). Dreamweaver is not capable of including them all because hundreds of JDBC drivers are available. After installing the driver, restart Dreamweaver so it can detect the presence of the driver. (See Book VII, Chapter 5 for more on setting up JSP database connections.)

Identifying Problems in the Database

When working with database data, sometimes you may accidentally ask the database to do something it can't do or you don't have permission to do. For each of these scenarios, you encounter an error, regardless of which database you're using:

✦ Creating an object that already exists always causes an error unless your database supports a `replace` keyword. It's a good idea to *drop* (delete) objects such as tables before creating them to avoid creation errors.

✦ Inserting a row with a key that's already been used causes an error. To avoid this problem, either create the table without a unique requirement (if that's okay given the data you're using) or check that the value you're trying to insert doesn't already exist in the table. You can use a simple `select` statement to perform this latter operation.

✦ Misspelled table or column names cause problems. Use the database object browser to check all your column and table names before using them.

✦ Data type and size problems can also creep up in your pages. Always validate the database column type before inserting data into it. Each development model provides functions for checking the length and type of data for a variable. A little checking before your page goes live (and before your users get creative with entering data) can prevent annoying errors.

General Troubleshooting

In general, testing your queries outside Dreamweaver is a great way to make sure that you can connect to your database and that your SQL queries are correct. If your query works with the database client, you can focus on the code that is creating and executing the query. A *query* tells the database the information you're looking for. We discuss queries in detail in Book IX, Chapter 2.

Verify permissions on the database file if you're using a file-based database on both your local computer and the server or with your ISP account. You must also verify that the Web server is set to execute whichever type of code you've chosen as your dynamic site type. In general, make sure that a simple dynamic page is executable before attempting database operations. If the file is executable, you see a blank page or whatever test code you place in the file. If it isn't executable, you likely see the contents of the file with any processing.

Book VIII

Making Pages Dynamic

The 5th Wave   By Rich Tennant

"Look into my Web site, Ms. Carruthers.
Look deep into its rotating spiral,
spinning, spinning, pulling you deeper
into its vortex, deeper...deeper..."

Contents at a Glance

Chapter 1: Preparing Dynamic Content Sources

In This Chapter

✔ **Exploring your database in Dreamweaver**

✔ **Creating parameters for your form data**

✔ **Adding URL parameters to Web page requests**

✔ **Keeping track of users with session variables**

✔ **Using a database as your data source**

A dynamic Web site has content that is rendered dynamically when a user visits a site. In Book VII, we discuss how to configure Dreamweaver CS5 to work with application servers and databases. Now it's time to start working with the data itself.

When you're preparing dynamic content sources, as described in this chapter, you're actually creating code and working with variables and sessions that help you manage your Web site more efficiently. A *data source* is a source of information from which you can extract data to display in your dynamic Web pages. This data can come from several sources in Dreamweaver:

✦ A form submission from another Web page

✦ URL parameters that are part of the Web page request

✦ A session variable that you set on another Web page

✦ A database table column

✦ Other advanced sources, such as JavaBeans properties

Before you can use a data source in your dynamic Web pages, you need to define it by using the Bindings panel. This chapter shows you how to define several data sources — form parameters, URL parameters, session variables, and databases — and make them available for use in your dynamic Web pages.

This chapter also explains how to use the Databases panel to navigate your database and make sure that you're using the right column names.

Exploring Your Database in the Databases Panel

The Databases panel lists the tables and fields for an active database connection. After connecting to your database, you can view its structure and data in the Dreamweaver Databases panel, which displays your database in a tree-like structure. You can view a database table much more easily in Dreamweaver than you can by working directly through a command-line SQL client.

To explore your database visually in the Databases panel, follow these steps:

1. **Open the Databases panel by choosing Window⇨Databases.**

This panel displays all the database connections defined for your site (see Figure 1-1). Any databases with a properly configured connection are displayed with a plus sign before them. You can explore only accessible databases. If no database appears in the panel, you have to create a database connection, which you find out how to do in Book VII.

Figure 1-1:
The
Databases
panel.

2. **Click the arrow before the database to view the object types associated with that database.**

The tree view expands to show these database object types:

- **Stored Procedures:** A *stored procedure* is code stored in the database itself. Because the stored procedure runs directly on the database server, it can be faster than normal queries at complex analysis of database data. Stored procedures can also be useful for validating data.

- **Tables:** Database tables are the grid-like structures that contain the actual data. We discuss these more in Book VII, Chapter 1. As you start out with databases, you will probably work primarily with tables.

- **Views:** *Views* are tables that are based on a database query. They are read-only.

3. **Click the arrow before a database category — Stored Procedures, Tables, or Views — to see what your database contains for that category.**

4. **Click the name of the object to expand the details again.**

   You see different information, depending on which database category you select in Step 3:

   - **Stored Procedures:** List the stored procedure's parameters and return values.

   - **Tables:** List the table's columns and those columns' data types (see Figure 1-2).

   - **Views:** List the view's columns and those columns' data types.

Figure 1-2:
The Databases panel displaying the columns of a table.

For database tables, you can view the data in the table by right-clicking the table name in the Databases panel and choosing View Data from the context menu. A window appears that lists the table data.

Defining Form Parameters

The whole point of dynamic Web pages is to not return the same page each time a page is requested. One tool that's used to mix up what's returned is a form parameter. A *form parameter* allows you to pass values between Web pages. You can define a form parameter by following these steps:

1. **Open an existing or create a new Web document using the app language of choice (PHP, ASP, ASP.NET, or JSP).**

2. **Select a spot for the data-driven form and then choose Insert⇨Form⇨Form. Or insert a form using the Insert panel.**

   See Book II, Chapter 7 for the lowdown on creating forms.

Book VIII
Chapter 1

Preparing Dynamic Content Sources

3. **Choose Window⇨Bindings to display the Bindings panel.**

    Before you create any bindings, you see the Dynamic Page setup checklist in the Bindings panel.

4. **Click the plus (+) icon, and in the list that appears, select Form Variable or the appropriate form item for your dynamic page type.**

    Options appear on the list based on your dynamic page type. Table 1-1 lists the form-related option names to select for each page type. The Form Variable dialog box appears, as shown in Figure 1-3.

Figure 1-3:
The Form
Variable
dialog box.

5. **Enter the name of the form variable in the dialog box and click OK.**

    The form parameter name is usually the name of the HTML form field or object that the parameter uses to obtain its value. For example, the data field we want to display is the recipient `id` of a message (called `to`). We named the form variable `to_id` in the dialog box.

    The form parameter appears in the Bindings panel, as shown in Figure 1-4.

Figure 1-4:
The
Bindings
panel
displaying
a form field
binding.

Post or get?

When you add a form to your page (as described in Book II, Chapter 7), you need to keep track of how you submit your form data to the server. You have two methods to choose from:

✔ The POST method, which sends parameters in the body of the request

✔ The GET method, which places the data in the URL as parameters

You can use either GET or POST, but you need to be consistent about which you use between the page that submits the values and the page that processes them. Also, be sure you know the type of request when you tell Dreamweaver about your form input.

Table 1-1	Add a Binding Menu Form Item Name Based on the Dynamic Page Type
Dynamic Page Type	*Form-Related Menu Item Name*
ASP	Request Variable > Request.Form
ColdFusion	Form Variable
JSP	Request Variable
PHP	Form Variable

After you define the form parameter as a data source, you can insert the parameter in your document by selecting it in the Bindings panel. See Book VIII, Chapter 3 for details.

Defining URL Parameters

URL parameters are a simple way of passing information to the Web server as part of the Web page request. When the Web server receives the request, the URL parameter is included in that request. This allows dynamic pages to be generated based on a specific parameter from a prior page. In the URL, a question mark (?) separates the Web site location from the parameters. Here's an example:

```
http://www.example.com/?username=kramer&password=nextdoor
```

In this example, the Web site is `www.example.com`. The two parameters are `username` (which has a value of *kramer*) and password (which has a value of *nextdoor*). An equal sign (=) separates each parameter from its value. If more than one parameter exists, as in this example, an ampersand (&) separates the parameters. Passing these values to the server is important because it allows the server to determine whether the username and password are valid. Depending on how the application is written, username and password validation might determine access to subsequent pages.

When a server processes a Web page request that contains URL parameters, the server makes those parameter values available to the dynamic page before returning the page to the Web browser, where the user sees the updated page displayed.

Dreamweaver uses URL parameters automatically when you submit a form by using the HTTP `GET` method. The `GET` method specifies that the parameters are appended to the URL when the page request is sent to the Web server. URL parameters are also frequently used to pass a value to the Web server, such as an action to take, when the user clicks a link. For example, you may have a URL parameter called `action` that takes the values `insert`, `update`, and `delete` based on the action that the link indicates. Note that you can pass more than one URL parameter at a time to a Web site.

To define a data source binding for a URL parameter, follow these steps:

1. **Create a new PHP, ASP, ASP.NET, or JSP page (or open an existing one).**

2. **If the Bindings panel is not displayed, choose Window⇨Bindings.**

   Before you create any bindings, you see the Dynamic Page setup checklist in the Bindings panel.

3. **Click the plus (+) icon, and then select the URL item for your dynamic page type in the list that appears.**

   Dreamweaver uses different names for this field based on your dynamic page type. Table 1-2 lists the appropriate URL item for your page type. The URL Variable dialog box appears, as shown in Figure 1-5.

Figure 1-5:
The URL Variable dialog box for a form field called `from`.

4. Enter the name of the URL variable in the dialog box, and then click OK.

The URL parameter name is usually the name of the HTML form field or the object used to obtain its valueThe form parameter appears in the Bindings panel, as shown in Figure 1-6.

Figure 1-6:
The Bindings panel after adding the URL binding.

Table 1-2	Add a Binding Menu for URL Parameters Based on the Dynamic Page Type	
Dynamic Page Type	*URL Item Name*
ASP	Request Variable > Request.QueryString
ColdFusion	URL Variable
JSP	Request Variable
PHP	URL Variable

After you define the URL as a data source, you can insert the URL in your document from the Bindings panel. See Book VIII, Chapter 2 for details.

Defining Session Variables

Session variables store information that the user enters and make that information available to any page during the user's visit, or *session*. For example, if a user logs in to the Web site, a session variable saves that authentication information, making it available to every page on the Web site throughout the user's visit. Without a session variable, the user has to reenter the login information every time he or she visits a new page on the site.

The session variable remains in effect until the user ends the session or a timeout period expires. Because the session is tracked on the server, the information stored in session variables is also stored on the Web server. Only a small unique identifier, called a *cookie,* is stored on the Web browser's computer. (If you'd like more info on cookies, check out www.cookie central.com/c_concept.htm or http://en.wikipedia.org/wiki/HTTP_cookie.)

You have to use Code view to add a session variable to a page. Follow these steps to define the session variable on the page and add it to the Bindings panel:

1. **Create a new dynamic page or open an existing page that contains a session variable.**

2. **If the Bindings panel isn't displayed, choose Window➪Bindings.**

3. **Click the plus (+) icon, and then select Session Variable in the list that appears.**

Unlike the other binding types, Dreamweaver uses the name *Session Variable* in this list for every dynamic page type. The Session Variable dialog box appears, as shown in Figure 1-7.

Figure 1-7: The Session Variable dialog box.

4. **Enter the name of the session variable in the dialog box, and then click OK.**

Figure 1-8 shows the new binding called first_name.

Figure 1-8: The Bindings panel displays a session variable binding.

After you define the session variable as a data source, you can insert your session variable in your document from the Bindings panel. See Book VIII, Chapter 2 for details.

Using a Database as Your Data Source

If you want to use a database as a data source for your dynamic Web site, you build a *query* to gather specific data from the database to use in your page. For example, you might build a query to retrieve all the information about a user before presenting the page so the user can update the data. The data that results from that query is called a *recordset.* After you create a recordset, you can display information from your database in your page.

Understanding recordsets

The recordset lets Dreamweaver process more than one piece of data on a dynamic page. The other data sources that we cover in this chapter (form parameters, URL parameters, and session variables) work with a single piece of data. Because recordsets are the results of database queries, they can contain more than just a single piece of data. This allows the display of an entire list of results on a page.

Recordsets contain one or more results, and each result has one or more columns. Working with recordsets can be complex because of the variable number of results. To make accessing the data for a recordset as fast as possible, the database server stores the results in its memory.

You can create database queries using a graphical table linking tool or by using the standard database language called Structured Query Language (SQL). (Don't confuse SQL, the language, with Microsoft's database product, called Microsoft SQL Server.) SQL provides a standard format for specifying how information in a database is linked and then filtered. SQL is designed to describe the relationships between data and how to filter matching rows. Dreamweaver includes a simple-query building tool called SQL Builder to help build simple queries.

Microsoft's ASP.NET coding platform calls a recordset a *dataset.* Despite the different names, they're really the same thing. When working with ASP.NET document types, you can think of the terms *recordset* and *dataset* as interchangeable.

Defining a recordset

Although you build the queries for a recordset with SQL, Dreamweaver enables you to create a recordset without writing an SQL query. Instead, you can select fields graphically from a table and column listing.

Before you can define a recordset, you need to establish a database connection in Dreamweaver. See Book VII for details on setting up a database connection.

To define a simple recordset in Dreamweaver, follow these steps:

1. **Create a new dynamic page or open an existing page.**

2. **In the Bindings panel, click the plus (+) icon, and then select Recordset (Query) in the list that appears.**

The Recordset dialog box appears. Depending on your dynamic page type, the dialog box may look slightly different.

If you want to write your own SQL queries for a recordset, use the Advanced Recordset dialog box. You can display this version of the dialog box by clicking the Advanced button in the Recordset dialog box.

3. **In the Name field, enter a name for your recordset.**

Remember to use only letters, numbers, and underscores for names to be sure that the name is compatible with your dynamic page type. In the example in Figure 1-9, we accepted the default name Recordset1.

Figure 1-9:
The
Recordset
dialog box
is set to
compare the
database
column
value
against
the URL
parameter.

4. **Select a database connection in the Connection drop-down list.**

In the example, we selected the mysql_connection connection.

5. **Select the database table in the Table drop-down list.**

The database table serves as a foundation for retrieving data for a database query. The Columns field updates to display the columns in your selected table. By default, all the columns are included in the recordset. In the example shown in Figure 1-9, we chose the footprints table.

6. **If you want to specify which columns to include, select the Selected option and then select the desired columns.**

If you select the Selected option, you can select multiple columns that you want to include in the Columns listing by Ctrl+clicking (Windows) or ⌘+clicking (Mac OS X) them.

7. **(Optional) If you want to filter the records, do the following:**

- **In the first Filter drop-down list:** Select a table column to filter. You can compare the database field against one of the previously defined bindings to limit the results of the query.

- **In the second list:** Select a conditional expression (such as =, <, or >) with which to compare the data in the column that you select in the first drop-down list.

- **In the third list:** Select the data source for comparison. Your choices are any previously bound values.

- **In the fourth list:** Enter a value to compare to the database column.

For example, Figure 1-9 shows the Recordset dialog box comparing a column value (`from`) and a URL parameter.

8. **If you want to sort the records, select the table column that you want to sort by in the first Sort drop-down list. In the second drop-down list, specify whether you want the records sorted in ascending or descending order.**

9. **If your query uses a filter, enter a value to use in the filter in the Test Value dialog box that appears. Click OK.**

The value you enter should be typical of what you expect your query to encounter when it's executed as part of the Web page.

10. **Click the Test button to verify that the query works correctly.**

Dreamweaver executes your query and displays the rows in the Test SQL Statement window.

If your query uses a filter, Dreamweaver displays the Test Value dialog box and prompts you to enter a value to use in the filter before executing the Test query. Enter a filter value typical of what you expect your query to encounter when it's executed as part of the Web page, and then click OK.

11. **If the test returns the records that you expect, click OK.**

The recordset now appears in the Bindings panel, as shown in Figure 1-10.

Figure 1-10:
The
Bindings
panel
reflects
the new
recordset.

Chapter 2: Using Dynamic Content in Your Web Pages

In This Chapter

✔ Adding dynamic content to your page

✔ Formatting dynamic content

✔ Displaying multiple records from a recordset

✔ Navigating through your records

✔ Showing and hiding regions of your page

*I*f you are a code monkey, you can use PHP, ASP.NET, or some other back-end programming language and hand-code dynamic pages for your Web site. However, writing all the database integration by hand involves a steep learning curve. Fortunately, Dreamweaver comes to the rescue by allowing you to bind, or connect, your Web pages with backend data without becoming a geek in the process.

To make dynamic pages as flexible as possible and yet still organized, Dreamweaver CS5 sets all *bindings* (references) to external data before you use it in your dynamic page. After the data is bound, you can select the format to display it in. You can even hide portions of pages depending on the values of bindings. After you master these concepts, you're ready to build complex dynamic Web pages.

Displaying and Formatting Dynamic Content

When you want to insert dynamic text on your page, your key tools are the Bindings panel and the Server Behaviors panel.

To insert dynamic text, open the Bindings panel (choose Window➪Bindings), locate the item that you want to use, and drag the item to your page. Then, if you want to format the new dynamic text, you can use the Server Behaviors panel (choose Window➪Server Behaviors). The following sections describe in more detail how to add, format, and test dynamic content.

Before you can add dynamic text to your pages, you need to establish a database connection (as described in Book VII) and define a data source (as described in Book VIII, Chapter 1).

Adding dynamic text

To insert dynamic text on your page, follow these steps:

1. **In your document, place your cursor where you want to insert the dynamic text.**

2. **In the Bindings panel, locate the data source that you want to use.**

   You can choose from any existing data sources, such as recordsets, URL parameters, form parameters, and session variables. (See Book VIII, Chapter 1 for more on these data sources.)

3. **Drag the data source to your document.**

   The dynamic text appears on your page, enclosed by curly brackets { }. For example, if you add a URL parameter named from to your page, it looks like this in the Document window:

   ```
   {Recordset1.from}
   ```

   This dynamic text entry is also added to the Server Behaviors panel, as shown in Figure 2-1.

Figure 2-1:
The dynamic text placeholder in the Document window and the dynamic text listing in the Server Behaviors panel.

Formatting your dynamic content

After you get dynamic text on your page, you can modify how it appears. For example, if you're displaying a numeric field as money, you generally want it to appear in a format such as $2.43. It doesn't look very professional to list a price as $1.1 or $1.154. Fortunately, you can modify the display format of server behavior dynamic text fields.

The formatting options that Dreamweaver provides for dynamic data display depend on what dynamic page type you're using. In general, you can find functions that change the case (upper or lower) of strings, format numbers, and format dates and times.

To change the formatting of dynamic text, follow these steps:

1. **In the Server Behaviors panel, double-click the dynamic text that you want to format.**

    The Dynamic Text dialog box appears with your dynamic text already selected.

2. **Select the appropriate formatting option in the Format drop-down list.**

    For example, if you want to transform the value to uppercase, select the AlphaCase-Upper option, as shown in Figure 2-2. Or if you want to format a numeric field so that it shows dollars and cents, select Currency — 2 Decimal Places.

    You can download more formats for dynamic text by selecting Edit Format List at the bottom of the Format drop-down list.

Figure 2-2: The Dynamic Text dialog box.

3. **You can safely leave the Code field alone.**

   The Code field tells you the actual code that Dreamweaver is using to produce the dynamic text. It's populated automatically when you select a data source.

4. **Click OK to close the Dynamic Text dialog box.**

   Dreamweaver applies the formatting that you select in Step 2 to your text.

Testing your dynamic text

If you think that you have your page the way that you want it, the next step is to test it. You can test the page by using Dreamweaver's Preview in Browser command or Live Data view (both are described in Book VIII, Chapter 3).

Live Data view is a little easier to use because it gives you a dialog box for entering parameter values. For example, you can enter URL parameter values in this dialog box instead of having to manually add them to the URL like this:

```
http://127.0.0.1/url_case.php?username=jack%20bauer
```

Note that %20 is the safe way to provide a blank space in a URL.

To use Live Data view to test your dynamic text, open your document and follow these steps:

1. **Choose View➪Live View Options > HTTP Request Settings.**

   The Live View Settings dialog box appears.

   Dreamweaver menus are context-sensitive. The Live View Options menu item is available only when server-side pages, such as .php or .asp files, are open.

2. **Click the plus (+) icon to add a new entry to the URL Request list.**

3. **Enter the name of the URL parameter in the Name column.**

   The name must match the name of the parameter from the URL. For example, we entered first_name to match the name of the URL parameter in Figure 2-3.

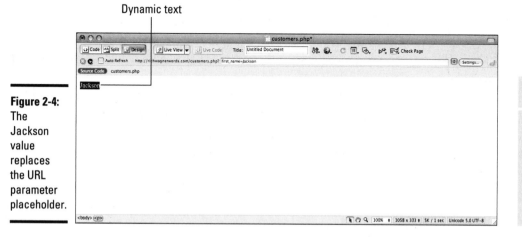

Figure 2-3:
The URL
first_name
parameter
set to a
testing
value of
Jackson.

4. **Enter a sample value in the Value field and then click OK.**

   For our example, we entered Jackson (refer to Figure 2-3.) This value
   simulates an actual value sent to your script when it runs. To find out
   how to format dynamic content, see the earlier section, "Formatting
   your dynamic content."

5. **Choose View⇨Live Data.**

   Your Document window updates to show the processing of the page's
   dynamic content. For example, in Figure 2-4, the URL parameter username is replaced with Jackson.

Dynamic text

Figure 2-4:
The
Jackson
value
replaces
the URL
parameter
placeholder.

You can update the parameter value in the URL box at the top of the Document window. Click the Refresh icon to update the document, or select the Auto Refresh option to update the value live.

Working with Database Recordsets

You can display database recordsets much as you display simple dynamic data (as described in the earlier sections of this chapter) when you're working with a recordset that has one row in its results. You can even use the Dynamic Text server behavior to display a field from a recordset. (If you have more than one row in your recordset, the behavior displays just the first row.)

Things get a bit more complex when your recordset has several rows that you want to include. The dynamic page must be able to apply formatting for each row in a recordset. Dreamweaver lets you specify the format for your results, gives you navigation tools, and uses HTML tables to display the recordsets neatly.

Repeating regions on your page

The Repeat Region server behavior lets you display multiple records from a single recordset on the same page. Select an area, or *region,* of the page that you want to repeat and specify the number of times that you want to repeat it. The Repeat Region server behavior then populates the contents of each repeated region with values from the recordset.

To add a repeat region to your page, follow these steps:

1. **Select the data fields on the page that you want to repeat.**

   For example, we're working with a recordset that's defined to return all the entries from the customers table, which has four fields: first_name, last_name, city, and state. In Figure 2-5, the four dynamic text fields appear highlighted.

2. **In the Server Behaviors panel, click the plus (+) icon and then select Repeat Region from the drop-down list that appears.**

   The Repeat Region dialog box appears, as shown in Figure 2-6.

3. **In the Recordset drop-down list, select the recordset that you want to use.**

4. **In the Show area, select the number of records that you want to display on the page.**

   The default displays ten records, but you can choose a different number. You can also display all records by clicking the All Records option. In our example, we selected two records.

Figure 2-5:
The
Document
window
displays
dynamic
text place-
holders.

customers.php	
Code	Split	Design	Live View	Live Code	Title: Untitled Document	Check Page
Source Code	customers.php	
{Recordset1.first_name} {Recordset1.last_name} lives in {Recordset1.city}, {Recordset1.state}	
<body> <p>	100%	1058 x 356	4K / 1 sec	Unicode 5.0 UTF-8

Repeating regions

Figure 2-6:
The Repeat
Region
dialog box.

Repeat Region	
Recordset: Recordset1	OK
Show: ● 10 Records at a Time	Cancel
○ All records	Help

5. Click OK to close the Repeat Region dialog box.

A gray box appears around the repeating fields with the text *Repeat* on a
tab, as shown in Figure 2-7. A repeat region (recordset) also shows up in
the Server Behaviors listing.

A repeat region is an invisible element in Design view. To view invisible
elements on your page, choose View⇨Visual Aids⇨Invisible Elements.

**6. Choose View⇨Live View to view the page with actual data from the
database.**

Figure 2-8 shows that the multiple records in this result cause the
repeated region to appear five times.

Fields that appear highlighted in Live Data view are dynamic text. In other
words, the text disappears when you turn off Live Data view. (See Book VIII,
Chapter 3 for more on Live Data view.)

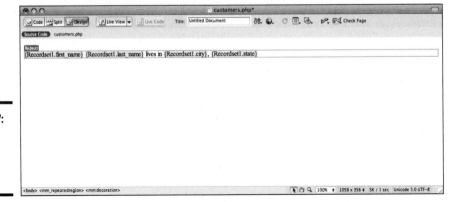

Figure 2-7:
A repeat
region in
Design
view.

Figure 2-8:
The Live
Data view
shows the
data from
the linked
database.

Repeating regions in HTML tables

To make your data easier to read, you can integrate an HTML table and a repeating region. The bulk of these steps work the same as the last example, but the dynamic text is placed into a table row:

1. **Open a new dynamic page and create a recordset, or open an existing page with a defined recordset.**

    You can use the default recordset name of Recordset1.

2. **Insert a table by choosing Insert⇨Table.**

3. **Enter the number of rows and columns you want in the Rows and Columns fields.**

    You should limit the number of rows to 2.

4. **Click OK.**

    The table appears in the Document window, as shown in Figure 2-9.

Figure 2-9:
The table that will hold the dataset.

5. **Enter the names of the fields in the column headers of the table.**

   We entered First Name, Last Name, City, and State.

6. **Select the first column of the table's second row.**

   This is where you'll place the first field of the dynamic text.

7. **Open the Server Behaviors panel by choosing Window➪Server Behaviors.**

8. **Click the plus (+) icon, and then choose Dynamic Text.**

   The Dynamic Text dialog box appears.

9. **Expand the recordset.**

   All the database table columns are displayed.

10. **Select the column from Step 6.**

    You can leave the format and code alone because you want to display these fields as they are in the database.

11. **Click OK.**

    Your dynamic field appears on your page enclosed by curly brackets { } (in our example, the field is Recordset1.first_name). The dynamic text entry is added to the Server Behaviors list.

12. **Select the second column of the second table row.**

13. **Repeat Steps 6 through 12 for each remaining field.**

14. **Select the rows in the table with both dynamic text fields.**

15. **Click the plus (+) sign in the Server Behaviors panel, and then choose Repeat Region.**

    The Repeat Region dialog box appears.

16. **Click OK.**

The default displays ten records, but you can choose a different number or display all records by selecting the All Records option.

A gray box appears around the repeating fields with the text *Repeat* on a tab. The repeat region (Recordset1) also appears in the Server Behaviors listing. Figure 2-10 shows the repeated regions defined for the table row.

17. **Choose View⇨Live View to view the actual data from the database.**

Figure 2-11 shows that the two records in this result cause the repeated region to be displayed five times.

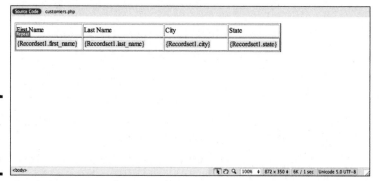

Figure 2-10: The repeat region for Recordset1.

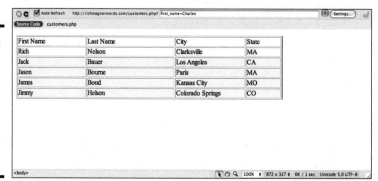

Figure 2-11: The Live Data mode shows the database data presented in an HTML table.

Adding a recordset navigation bar

Dreamweaver provides paging functions in the Server Behaviors panel for the Web user to go to the first page, last page, next page, and previous page of multipage repeating regions. You can associate these behaviors with text or with images that you select on the page itself, such as the forward and backward arrows.

When applying a Navigation server behavior to a dynamic Web page, you can display only one recordset on the page because you can't specify to which recordset the navigation applies.

To help users keep track of which record they're viewing in a multipage recordset, you can add a Record Count server behavior. You can display the total number of records, the first record on a page, and the last record on a page.

Before you can add a Recordset Navigation server behavior, you must have a Repeat Region server behavior on your page (as described in the preceding section). Although you can individually add a Navigation server behavior to your page, the easiest way to build navigation for a recordset is to use a navigation bar.

Follow these steps to add the navigation bar to your page:

1. **In the Document window, place the pointer where you want to insert the navigation bar.**

2. **Choose Insert⇨Data Objects⇨Recordset Paging⇨Recordset Navigation Bar.**

The Recordset Navigation Bar dialog box appears, as shown in Figure 2-12.

Figure 2-12:
The
Recordset
Navigation
Bar dialog
box.

Recordset Navigation Bar	
Recordset: Recordset1	OK
Display using: ○ Text	Cancel
◉ Images	Help

3. **Select the recordset that you want to control in the Recordset drop-down list.**

4. **Select Text or Images to indicate the type of navigation bar.**

We're in a graphical mode, so we chose Images.

5. **Click OK.**

The navigation bar appears on your page, as shown in Figure 2-13.

Book VIII
Chapter 2

Using Dynamic
Content in Your
Web Pages

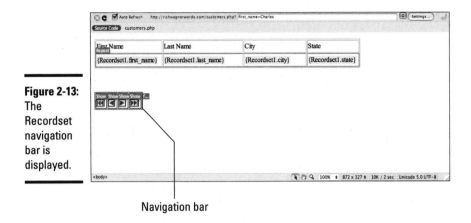

Figure 2-13:
The Recordset navigation bar is displayed.

Navigation bar

Showing and hiding regions on your page

The Show Region server behavior lets you show or hide areas of your document based on certain conditions. For example, only the site administrator should be able to see a page that displays personal information about users. Here's a rundown of the six Show Region server behaviors:

+ Show If Recordset Is Empty

+ Show If Recordset Is Not Empty

+ Show If First Page

+ Show If Not First Page

+ Show If Last Page

+ Show If Not Last Page

For example, the Show If Not First Page and Show If Not Last Page server behaviors let you display previous and next links, respectively, only when you have a next or previous page that you can jump to.

To apply one of the server behaviors to your page, open your document and follow these steps:

1. **In Design view, select the region that you want to show or hide.**

 To select the region, drag the pointer while clicking.

2. **In the Server Behaviors panel, click the plus (+) icon and then select an option in the Show Region menu that appears.**

 You can choose from the six Show Region server behaviors.

3. **In the dialog box that corresponds to the type of region you're showing, select the recordset to which you want to apply the server behavior.**

4. **Click OK.**

   The server behavior is applied to the selected region.

Adding Dynamic Form Elements to Your Page

In the same way that you use the Bindings panel to insert dynamic text on your Web page (as described at the beginning of the chapter), you can also integrate dynamic text as default values for form elements. Dreamweaver supports using dynamic data for all the major form elements, including text boxes, check boxes, radio selections, and list/menu boxes.

To insert a dynamic form element on your page, follow these steps:

1. **Choose Insert⊏>Form⊏>Form to insert a form on your page.**

   See Book II, Chapter 7 for the lowdown on creating forms.

2. **Choose Insert⊏>Form, and then select a form element that would be effective in displaying your data.**

   Be sure to give it a distinct ID that you can reference later. The form element appears on the page.

3. **In the Server Behaviors panel, click the plus (+) icon and then select a dynamic form type in the Dynamic Form Elements menu.**

   Figure 2-14 shows the Dynamic Text Field dialog box, which appears after you select a form type item

Figure 2-14: The Dynamic Text Field dialog box.

4. **In the Text field drop-down, select the form element you created back in Step 2.**

5. **Click OK.**

   The text field now gets its default value from the data source.

Chapter 3: Previewing and Testing Your Dynamic Pages

In This Chapter

✔ Testing your dynamic pages by using Live Data mode

✔ Previewing your dynamic pages in a Web browser

When you work with static HTML files in Dreamweaver CS5, previewing your Web site is easy. Just click the Preview in Browser icon and have at it. But when you are working with dynamically created pages, previewing your work is much. Fortunately, Dreamweaver comes to the rescue by providing built-in support in the form of Live Data previews. In this chapter, you find out how to preview and test your dynamic pages by using Live Data mode or a Web browser.

For your pages to work on a remote server, you must transfer your files to the remote folder. See Book V, Chapter 4 for details on publishing your site.

Viewing Live Data in Your Dynamic Web Pages

A great way to test the functionality of your dynamic Web site is to use Dreamweaver's Live View. When you use Live View while developing a page in Dreamweaver, Dreamweaver connects to your Web server, pulls the dynamic data for the page from the database, and then uses that data to replace the dynamic data placeholders on your page.

For details on adding dynamic data to your page, see Book VIII, Chapter 2.

For Live View to work correctly, you must simulate input that usually comes from the user. You also need any supporting files, such as server-side includes, so that the Web server can execute the dynamic code without errors.

Understanding how Live View works

Here are the specific tasks that are performed when you use Live View:

1. Dreamweaver transfers your dynamic page to the server temporarily.

2. Dreamweaver requests the page from the server.

3. The Web server executes the dynamic page code that may contain calls to database functions.

4. Dreamweaver integrates the page request results into the page and displays them in Design view.

5. Dreamweaver deletes the temporary file from the server.

Figure 3-1 shows how a Web page looks with placeholders. Figure 3-2 shows how the same Web page looks in Live View.

Figure 3-1:
This page, not in Live View, contains placeholders for fields in a customer database.

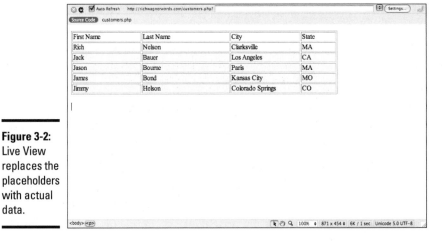

Figure 3-2:
Live View replaces the placeholders with actual data.

In Live View, Dreamweaver has to know how to get the page that you're previewing to the server and how to request that page from the server, specifically the URL path. These paths are set up as part of your testing server (see Book VII, Chapter 1).

> You can manually refresh your Live View by clicking the Refresh icon on the Live View toolbar. If you've changed any data in the database, refreshing your Live View page enables you to see how those changes affect your page.

Uploading dependent files to the testing server

Some dynamic Web pages rely on dependent files to work properly. *Dependent files* are files that your Web page references and a browser loads when it displays the page. If a dependent file is missing, your page may generate an error or images may be missing when the browser displays the page. Dependent files can include

- ✦ **Code files:** These files include JSP .jar classes, ASP .asp files, and ColdFusion .cfm files.

- ✦ **CSS files:** The files include style sheet details such as how different classes of text appear. See Book III, Chapter 1 for more information.

- ✦ **Image files:** Image files include those such as PNG, JPG, or GIF files. Depending on your image tags, you may not need to have the images on the testing server. In any case, missing images won't cause your page to fail to load.

- ✦ **Server-side includes:** These files consist of code that is included from a file as the dynamic Web page code executes. An `include` statement is replaced by the contents of the included file when the page is processed on the Web server.

Dreamweaver doesn't know which dependent files to send to the testing server, so you need to upload the appropriate files manually. Follow these steps to upload your dependent files to the testing server:

1. **Choose Window⇨Files to open the Files panel.**

The Files panel displays files for each portion of your site, including the local, remote, and testing servers.

2. **Click the Expand/Collapse icon, as shown in Figure 3-3.**

The expanded view displays two file views at the same time. By default, the local files always appear on the right half of the screen.

Book VIII
Chapter 3

Previewing and
Testing Your
Dynamic Pages

3. **Click the Testing Server icon (labeled in Figure 3-4).**

   The file view on the left displays the Testing Server files.

Expand/Collapse icon

Figure 3-3:
Displaying
local files.

Testing Server icon   Put Files icon

Figure 3-4:
The
expanded
file view.

Testing Server files   Local files

4. **Select the dependent files from the Local Files list.**

   You can select multiple files by holding down the Ctrl (Windows) or ⌘ (Mac) key while clicking the files.

5. **To upload the dependent files to the testing server, click the Put Files icon (labeled in Figure 3-4).**

   The files are displayed in the Testing Server file list, and your dynamic page code can now access them during Live View.

Providing parameters for user input

Sometimes your dynamic page code generates different output based on the user's input, such as a username or a value that indicates a database row (such as a user ID). If your dynamic page code processes user input results, such as a form submission, you may need to update the Live Data settings to supply the value (simulate the user's input). If you don't update the Live Update settings, your page may issue a warning that it can't find any data to display. Follow these steps to add parameters for user input:

1. **Choose View➪Live View Options➪HTTP Request Settings.**

   The Live View Settings dialog box appears with an empty list of parameters.

2. **To simulate the user input for each parameter, click the plus (+) icon.**

   An empty row appears in the Name and Value columns.

3. **In the Name column, enter the name of the parameter, and in the Value column, enter the value that you want to send to your dynamic Web page for that parameter.**

   For example, if you have a parameter called `user_id` and want to send the value `chucky_chase`, you enter fields like the ones in Figure 3-5.

4. **In the Method drop-down list, select a form submission method.**

   Your form submits its results by using either a GET or a POST method; select that same method from the Method drop-down list. See Book II, Chapter 7 for details on the GET and POST methods.

**Book VIII
Chapter 3**

**Previewing and
Testing Your
Dynamic Pages**

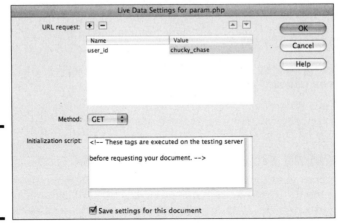

Figure 3-5:
The Live
Data
Settings
dialog box.

5. **(Optional) Set session variables in the Initialization Script text area.**

   See Book VIII, Chapter 1 for the lowdown on session variables.

6. **Click OK.**

   Your page uses the value in the parameter when updating its Live Data mode.

Troubleshooting problems in Live Data mode

Sometimes your Live Data mode may not work right the first time. The most common problem that you may encounter in Live Data mode happens when you have missing dependent files. This section provides some troubleshooting tips to try to resolve this problem.

In the Files panel, check to make sure that every file your script needs, including any database-related files, is present in the Testing Server file listing.

In the Servers category of the Site Setup dialog box, verify that your testing server folder points to a location on your testing server that can process the dynamic files — in other words, it's within the document root of the Web server. To do so, open the Site Setup dialog box by choosing Site➪Manage Sites, select your site, and click the Edit button.

Confirm that the URL prefix maps to the Web address that matches the testing server folder. Table 3-1 shows some example folders and their corresponding URLs.

Table 3-1	Typical Paths and URLs	
Web Server	*Folder*	*URL*
IIS on Windows	C:\Inetpub\wwwroot\testapp\	`http://localhost/ testapp`
Apache on Windows	C:\Program Files\Apache Group\Apache2\htdocs\testapp	`http://localhost/ testapp`
Apache on Linux	~jon/testapp	`http://example. com/~jon/testapp`

If you want to make sure that your testing server folder and URL agree outside Dreamweaver, place a simple HTML file in your testing server folder. For example, you can use index.htm with these contents:

```
<html>
<body>Smiles everyone, smiles.</body>
</html>
```

You can then check the URL by pasting the URL prefix plus `index.htm` into your browser's address bar. You should see a page with the content supplied. If you don't, double-check your paths because you have a problem somewhere.

Make sure the directory's permissions are configured appropriately so that the Web server can read the page. If you're using Windows, verify that the folder permissions allow the Web server to execute and read the directory. See Book VII, Chapter 7.

Previewing a Dynamic Web Page in Your Browser

You may find using Live Data mode great for testing your dynamic pages, but Live Data doesn't fully mimic the way that your page looks in a browser. Live Data mode won't go through multiple pages of results from the database. As a result, you should debug and test your application inside your Web browser.

To preview a Web page in your local Web browser, open the page in Dreamweaver and press F12 (⌘+F12 on a Mac). You don't need to copy any files to a temporary folder on the testing server because Dreamweaver can do the copying for you automatically, or your browser can use the files in the local folder.

Working on dynamic pages without Live Data

If you can't access your testing server or you simply like to work without Live Data, you can still develop and work with your dynamic page. Dreamweaver uses placeholders to represent where actual data would appear if you were in Live Data mode. These placeholders are surrounded by curly brackets { } to set them apart from the rest of your page.

Follow these steps to tell Dreamweaver that you want to use a temporary copy of your file when previewing with your browser:

1. **Choose Edit⇨Preferences.**

The Dreamweaver Preferences dialog box appears.

2. **Click the Preview in Browser category.**

The option for previewing appears, as shown in Figure 3-6.

Figure 3-6:
The Preview
in Browser
category
of the
Preferences
dialog box.

3. **Select the Preview Using Temporary File option.**

This option tells Dreamweaver to create a temporary copy of the file when previewing the page in a browser.

You can use this dialog box also to change the default browser that you use for previewing your pages. See Book V, Chapter 1 for details.

4. **Click OK.**

   Now the browser uses a temporary file when previewing your page.

   The requirements for dependent files that apply to Live Data also apply to the browser-based preview: Make sure that you specify in the Files panel all the files that you need to display your page. (See the section "Uploading dependent files to the testing server," earlier in this chapter, for details.)

   If you get a dialog box asking if you want to update the copy of the file on the testing server, click OK.

Chapter 4: Building Dynamic Forms

In This Chapter

- ✔ Understanding dynamic forms
- ✔ Inserting dynamic form elements
- ✔ Making form objects dynamic

*W*hen you work with application servers such as PHP and ASP, you can display dynamic pages based on data from databases. However, you may also want to build dynamic forms — providing values for the form fields and capturing the updated data to the backend database when the form is submitted.

Making forms dynamic allows users to update information because the existing values come up as the defaults when the form is displayed. You must start with a regular form and its elements before making the default values dynamic. In this chapter, we show you how to make text boxes, check boxes, radio buttons, lists, and menus dynamic.

The elements that make up a form can be supplied with dynamic data. To create a dynamic form, you must define a source for the dynamic data first by creating a binding. The *binding* tells Dreamweaver what dynamic information your program can reference. These sources can be anything from URL parameters to values for a database recordset. (See Book VIII, Chapters 1 and 2 for more on bindings.)

For more detailed information on the form objects (text fields, check boxes, radio buttons, lists, and menus) described in the following sections, refer to Book II, Chapter 7.

Inserting Text Fields

Text fields allow you to capture basic text information from the user. Dynamic text fields are useful when users are updating their information because the current values become the defaults for the update screen. To make an existing text field dynamic, follow these steps:

1. Select a text field in a form on your page.

See Book II, Chapter 7 for the lowdown on creating forms and text fields. Figure 4-1 is an example of an inserted text field.

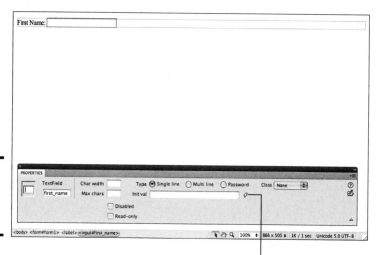

Figure 4-1: An inserted text field in a form.

The Bind to Dynamic Source button

2. In the Properties inspector, click the Bind to Dynamic Source icon (labeled in Figure 4-1).

The Dynamic Data dialog box appears, as shown in Figure 4-2, and lists the available data sources in the Field area.

Figure 4-2: The Dynamic Data dialog box.

3. **In the Field area, select the data source that will supply the default value for the text field.**

   For example, in Figure 4-2, we selected the `first_name` Recordset item. This data source provides the initial value for the text field on the page. Click the plus sign next to the category of the field (such as Recordset) to expand it before selecting a data source. Leave the Format set to None to display the text exactly as it is in the source.

   A recordset can be used as the data source for the dynamic value, but if the recordset returns more than one row, only the first value is used.

4. **Click OK.**

   Figure 4-3 displays the placeholder that's created for the dynamic text on the page (in this example, `Recordset1.first_name`).

Placeholder

Figure 4-3: Placeholder text in the text field.

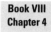

Adding Check Boxes

An HTML check box allows a user to select more than one value from a list of check box values. Dynamic check boxes have their default state of checked or not checked set by the value of a binding. Use bindings for tasks such as defaulting the check box values to their current settings for an update screen.

Check boxes are most commonly used when working with Boolean data fields with a true/false value. However, you can use a check box also based on whether a field is equal to the value you specify.

To make a check box dynamic, follow these steps:

1. **Select a check box in a form on your page.**

   See Book II, Chapter 7 for the information on creating forms and check boxes.

2. **In the Properties inspector, click the Bind to Dynamic Source icon.**

   The Dynamic CheckBox dialog box appears, as shown in Figure 4-4. The default value for the CheckBox drop-down list is the current check box.

Figure 4-4:
The
Dynamic
CheckBox
dialog box.

3. **Click a second Bind to Dynamic Source icon, which is next to the Check If field.**

   The Dynamic Data dialog box appears, displaying the available data sources (refer to Figure 4-2).

4. **Select the data source field to use for the default value comparison, and then click OK.**

   You return to the Dynamic CheckBox dialog box and Dreamweaver automatically fills in the Check If field.

5. **In the Equal To field, enter the value the field must have for the check box to be selected.**

   If the Check If value is the same as the Equal To value, the check box is selected by default.

6. **Click OK.**

Now when you use Live Data view (see Book VIII, Chapter 3) or preview the page in a browser (press F12 under Windows or ⌘+F12 on a Mac), the check box appears selected or deselected, based on the value from the data source you selected in Step 4.

You can repeat these steps for each check box in the same group.

Working with Radio Buttons

Use HTML radio buttons when you want users to select only one choice from a set of options. Radio buttons are typically used in groups (for example, AM or PM when selecting a time). Making a group of radio buttons dynamic means that the default value can come from a binding.

To make the default selection dynamic for a group of radio buttons, follow these steps:

1. **In a form on your page, click a radio button in a radio button group.**

This selects all the radio buttons in the group so you can view the group's properties. See Book II, Chapter 7 for details on creating forms and radio buttons.

2. **In the Properties inspector, click the Bind to Dynamic Source icon.**

The Dynamic Radio Group dialog box appears, as shown in Figure 4-5.

Figure 4-5:
The Dynamic Radio Group dialog box.

Dynamic Radio Group

Radio group: `"states" in form "form1"` [OK]

Select value equal to: _____ [Cancel]

[Help]

3. **Click the Bind to Dynamic Source icon, which is next to the Select Value Equal To field.**

The Dynamic Data dialog box appears, displaying the available data sources (refer to Figure 4-2).

4. **Choose a data source field to use for the default selection value.**

The Select Value Equal To field is compared to the checked value for each radio group button to determine the default selection.

You need to expand the category of the field, such as URL, before selecting a data source. In this example, we selected the language URL parameter. The radio group preselects a radio button only if its value matches the value in this field. Dreamweaver fills in the Select Value Equal To field after you select a binding.

**Book VIII
Chapter 4**

Building Dynamic Forms

5. **Click OK.**

   You return to the Dynamic Radio Group dialog box.

6. **Click OK.**

   Now when you use Live View (see Book VIII, Chapter 3) or preview the page in a browser, a radio button is selected based on the value from the data source you selected in Step 4.

You need to apply the dynamic formatting only once per radio group because a radio group can have only one value at a time selected.

Inserting Lists and Menus

An HTML form list (or menu) provides a convenient way for a user to select one or more items from the drop-down list or menu. It also dictates that only supplied values can be selected (unlike text fields, where the user can enter anything). You can insert the menu as a drop-down list or a scrollable list, which is also called a *list menu*. A list or menu could be used to select which categories you're interested in receiving. Dynamic lists and menus make updating that list simpler by using your current selection values as defaults when updating.

To set the default dynamic values for a menu or list, follow these steps:

1. **Select the menu or list in a form on your page.**

   See Book II, Chapter 7 for info on creating forms, menus, and lists.

2. **In the Properties inspector, click the Bind to Dynamic Source icon.**

   The Dynamic List/Menu dialog box appears.

3. **Select the desired recordset from the Options from Recordset list.**

4. **In the Values and Labels lists, choose the desired field from the recordset.**

5. **Click the Bind to Dynamic Source icon, which is to the right of the Select Value Equal To field.**

   The Dynamic Data dialog box appears (refer to Figure 4-2).

6. **(Optional) Specify that a particular item is selected by entering a value equal to the menu item's value in the Select Value Equal To box.**

7. Click OK.

When you use Live View (see Book VIII, Chapter 3) or preview the page in a browser, the items on the dynamic menu or menus are generated and selected based on the data source value you selected in Step 4.

Figure 4-6 displays a drop-down menu populated with values in Live Data mode.

Figure 4-6:
The menu is populated with values from the recordset.

Chapter 5: Advanced Dynamic Data Presentation

In This Chapter

✔ Working with ColdFusion Components

✔ Adding Web services to your site

✔ Putting custom server behaviors to work

You can use ColdFusion to add complex dynamic functionality to your pages without worrying about how the component does its magic. Then you can use Web services running on a remote server to process portions of your Web page. For example, you can use Web services to return a temperature based on the input of a zip code. Your site needs to know only how to access the server, not how to perform the calculation itself. Additionally, you can customize Dreamweaver CS5's tools for inserting code into your dynamic sites.

Using ColdFusion Components

ColdFusion Components (CFCs) are bits of ColdFusion code that you can use over and over again in your site. Think of CFCs as storage containers that keep your ColdFusion code organized and accessible. CFCs provide access to many more features than you'd have if you simply included ColdFusion code from a file. Here are some of those features and benefits:

✦ **Extendibility:** You can add code to CFCs.

✦ **Security:** You can limit access to portions of the code.

✦ **Speed:** CFCs are faster than other code because they're compiled.

✦ **Documentation:** CFCs automatically generate documentation.

To use CFCs, you need to use ColdFusion version 7 or higher.

By creating a CFC for code that you use throughout your site, you can reduce the amount of work you need to do to maintain the site. If you need to change your code, you only need to make the change in one spot, and the code updates throughout the site.

To use ColdFusion Components, you need to install ColdFusion on your local computer or have access to a Remote Development Services (RDS) connection. You also have to specify the testing server URL prefix in the Site Setup dialog box that Dreamweaver uses to display pages after transferring those images to the server. Finally, you should feel comfortable working directly with ColdFusion code.

Building Web pages that use ColdFusion Components

Dreamweaver comes with preinstalled ColdFusion Components, which you can find in the Components panel (choose Window⇨Components). When you select a CFC, Dreamweaver places the code to run the CFC into your page so that you have a solid starting point from which you can modify the code.

To include a ColdFusion Component call in your Web page, follow these steps:

1. **Create or open a new ColdFusion page.**

2. **Click the Code button or the Split button.**

Unlike server behaviors, ColdFusion Components don't appear in Design view. Work directly in Code view to see the added component code.

3. **In the Components panel, select CF Components in the drop-down list.**

Dreamweaver lists the component packages in the Components panel, as shown in Figure 5-1.

Figure 5-1:
The Components panel for a page that uses a connection to a ColdFusion server.

4. **Click the arrow beside a component to expand a components package.**

   The components in that package are listed, along with the components' functions in a subtree, as shown in Figure 5-2.

Figure 5-2:
The Components panel listing the component and its functions.

5. **Select the function that you want to invoke from your page and then drag that function to the point in the code where you want to place it.**

   The code from the function is inserted in the Document window. You use the `<cfinvoke>` tag to call ColdFusion Components, as shown in Figure 5-3.

   You can insert code also by right-clicking (Windows) or Control+clicking (Mac) the function name and choosing Insert Code. Or you can click the Insert Code icon on the Components toolbar.

6. **If your function needs parameters, you can add them to the `cfinvoke` tag by adding a parameter value pair.**

   For example, to add the username parameter with a value of Cosmo Crumer, use this code:

   ```
   username="Cosmo Crumer"
   ```

7. **Choose File➪Save to save your changes.**

   Your changes are saved to the local folder.

8. **To see your code in action, choose File⇨Preview in the Browser⇨*Name of Browser*.**

   Because the site contains dynamic code, you can't see the output without the ColdFusion server processing it.

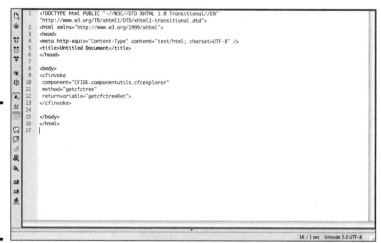

```
1   <!DOCTYPE html PUBLIC "-//W3C//DTD XHTML 1.0 Transitional//EN"
    "http://www.w3.org/TR/xhtml1/DTD/xhtml1-transitional.dtd">
2   <html xmlns="http://www.w3.org/1999/xhtml">
3   <head>
4   <meta http-equiv="Content-Type" content="text/html; charset=UTF-8" />
5   <title>Untitled Document</title>
6   </head>
7
8   <body>
9   <cfinvoke
10    component="CFIDE.componentutils.cfcexplorer"
11    method="getcfctree"
12    returnvariable="getcfctreeRet">
13  </cfinvoke>
14
15  </body>
16  </html>
17
```

Figure 5-3:
Calling the
`getcfc-`
`tree`
function
in the
Document
window.

Creating ColdFusion Components

Although you can certainly create your ColdFusion Components the old-fashioned way — by writing them in ColdFusion code — you can make the process much easier by letting Dreamweaver help you.

To create a ColdFusion Component in Dreamweaver, follow these steps:

1. **Create a new ColdFusion page or open an existing one.**

2. **In the Components panel, select CF Components from the drop-down list.**

   The available components appear in the main portion of the panel.

3. **Click the plus (+) icon next to the drop-down list.**

   The Create Component dialog box appears, as shown in Figure 5-4.

4. **Fill in the following fields in the Component section:**

   • **Display Name:** Enter a descriptive name for your component.

   • **Hint:** Enter a brief description of what your component does. This field automatically appears in the documentation for your component.

- **Extends:** Use this field to base your component on an existing component. You can leave this field blank.

- **Name:** Enter a filename for your component in the Name field. The name follows general naming rules — only letters, numbers, and underscores. Don't add the .cfc file extension to the name.

- **Component Directory:** Click the Browse button to specify where you want to save the component. Select a directory by using the Web application root folder, usually C:\Inetpub\wwwroot, or a subfolder.

Figure 5-4:
The Create Component dialog box.

5. **To define properties (variables for the component), select Properties from the Section list. Click the plus (+) icon to add properties:**

- **Name:** Enter a name for your property in the Name field. The name follows general naming rules — only letters, numbers, and underscores.

- **Display Name:** Enter a descriptive name for your property.

- **Hint:** Enter a brief description of what your property stores. This field automatically appears in the documentation for your component.

- **Type:** Select the type of data your property stores.

6. **To define a function, select Functions in the Section list on the left side of the dialog box.**

7. **Click the plus (+) icon, and then fill in the following fields, which are shown in Figure 5-5:**

- **Name:** Enter a name for your function.

- **Display Name:** This entry gives you the option to make a longer, more descriptive version of the name. Enter descriptive text.

- **Hint:** Enter a summary of what your function does. This summary appears in the automatic documentation for your component.

- **Access:** Select an access type from the drop-down list. Selecting Remote makes your function available as a Web service.

- **Return Type:** Select a return type from the drop-down list. All the ColdFusion data types appear in the list.

You can leave the Roles text box blank and the Output check box deselected.

Figure 5-5:
Defining a function in the Create Component dialog box.

8. **To define an argument for your function, select Arguments in the Section list on the left side of the dialog box.**

9. **Select the function from the Available Functions drop-down list.**

Each function can have as many arguments as you want.

10. **Click the plus (+) icon, and then fill in the following fields, which are shown in Figure 5-6:**

- **Name, Display Name, Hint, and Type:** You can enter these fields as you do in the Functions section (see Step 7).

- **Required:** Select this option if you need the argument when calling the function.

- **Default Value:** To supply a default value, enter it in the Default Value field. The function uses this value if the calling code doesn't supply a value when calling the function.

11. **Click OK to close the dialog box.**

Dreamweaver creates the component as a .cfc file and saves it in the directory that you specify in Step 4.

To ensure that Dreamweaver can use your custom component, upload the .cfc file to your remote server.

Conditional code block execution

Sometimes, you may have a chunk of code that you don't always want to execute. For example, you might want the code to display an error message only after an error. To specify that you want a code block to execute based on a condition, use this syntax:

```
<@ if (condition1) @>
codeblockif
[<@ elseif (condition2) @>
codeblockifelse]
[<@ else @>
codeblockelse]
<@ endif @>
```

Here's a closer look at this syntax:

✔ Replace `condition1` and `condition2` with any JavaScript expression that evaluates to true or false.

✔ Replace the labels that start with `code block` with the code that you want to run for that condition.

✔ You need only the `if` portion (the brackets `[ ]` represent optional portions).

✔ You can have more than one `elseif` portion of a statement.

✔ The `else` portion executes only if no other conditions are true.

Figure 5-6:
Defining an argument for the `file Exists` function.

To remove a component, delete the .cfc file from your RDS server. Dreamweaver only lists components it finds on the RDS testing server.

Creating Custom Server Behaviors

Server behaviors are blocks of code that send a request to the server and then receive data in return. Dreamweaver provides many server behaviors in the Server Behaviors panel (choose Windows➪Server Behaviors), but you can also add more.

You can use Adobe Exchange (go to www.adobe.com/cfusion/exchange and click the ColdFusion link) to add packages of server behaviors. You can also create your own server behaviors by using the Server Behavior Builder. If you're planning to create your own server behavior, first check the Exchange site to see if the server behavior that you want to create already exists.

To create a custom server behavior, you have to

✦ Write the code that performs the action of the server behavior

✦ Specify where to place the code within the HTML page

✦ Determine parameters and prompts (prompting the developer for details about how the code works when it's used in your page) for them

With the Server Behavior Builder, you enter the code block that you want the custom server behavior to insert into a page. You can use any runtime code valid for your server model. For example, if you choose ColdFusion as the document type for your custom server behavior, you have to write ColdFusion code running on a ColdFusion application server. After you build the custom server behavior, you can access it from the Server Behaviors panel.

To create your own custom server behavior with the Server Behavior Builder, follow these steps:

1. **In the Server Behaviors panel, click the plus (+) icon and then select New Server Behavior from the list that appears.**

The New Server Behavior dialog box appears, as shown in Figure 5-7.

Figure 5-7:
The New
Server
Behavior
dialog box.

New Server Behavior	
Document type: ColdFusion	OK
Name: myserverbehave	Cancel
Option: ☐ Copy existing server behavior	Help
Behavior to copy:	

2. **Select from the drop-down list the document type to which you want to add this server behavior.**

3. **Enter a name for your server behavior in the Name field.**

The name can use only letters, numbers, and underscores.

4. **Click OK.**

The Server Behavior Builder dialog box appears.

5. Click the plus (+) icon.

The Create a New Code Block dialog box appears.

6. Enter the name of your block in the Name field, and then click OK.

The name is added to the code block list. Figure 5-8 shows the updated Server Behavior dialog box.

Figure 5-8:
The Server Behavior Builder dialog box.

7. Enter the code to perform your action in the Code Block text area.

You can create the code blocks directly in the Server Behavior Builder, or you can copy and paste the code from other sources. Each code block that you create in the Server Behavior Builder must be a single tag or script block. If you need to insert multiple tag blocks, split them into separate code blocks.

8. If you want to include runtime parameters in a code block, select the point in the code block where you want to insert the parameter. Otherwise, skip ahead to Step 13.

To include parameters in your code that you supply when you include the stored procedure in a page during the page's design, you first need to mark where the parameters go in your code by using the following format:

```
@@parameter_name@@
```

9. Click the Insert Parameter in Code Block icon.

The Insert Parameter in Code Block dialog box appears, as shown in Figure 5-9.

Book VIII
Chapter 5

Advanced Dynamic
Data Presentation

Insert Parameter In Code Block

A parameter is a placeholder in the code block for information
that will be specified when the behavior is applied.

OK

Cancel

Parameter name: Param1

Help

10. **Enter the name in the Parameter Name field, and then click OK.**

    The usual naming rules apply. After you click OK, the parameter name
    placeholder appears in the code at the point you selected in Step 9.

11. **(Optional) Repeat Steps 8 through 10 to add more parameters.**

12. **In the Insert Code drop-down list, select a location where you want to
    embed the code block.**

    The Insert Code drop-down list lets you select where to place the code
    relative to the document:

    • Above the <html> Tag

    • Below the </html> Tag

    • Relative to a Specific Tag

    • Relative to the Selection (the point in the current page that's
      selected)

    The Relative to Selection position applies if you do not want to define a
    tag against which to position the code block.

13. **Select the relative position versus the selection of the code in the
    Relative Position drop-down list.**

    Depending on which selection you make for the Insert Code selection
    in Step 12, you see a different listing of relative locations in the Relative
    Position drop-down list. For example, if you select Above the <html>
    Tag, you get the following options:

    • The Beginning of the File

    • Just Before the Recordsets

    • Just After the Recordsets

    • Just Above the <html> Tag

    • Custom Position

    Because selecting the Below the </html> Tag for Insert Code rules out
    placing the code at the beginning of the file, you don't have that code
    placement as an option for that selection.

The Custom Position applies if the designer specifies a tag against which to position the code block.

14. To create additional code blocks, repeat Steps 5 through 13.

Remember that you can have only one block of code in the Code Block text area. You can create more code blocks in the server behaviors if you need them.

15. Click Next.

The Generate Behavior dialog box appears.

16. Click OK.

Your server behavior is displayed in the Server Behaviors panel.

Book IX

Developing Applications Rapidly

Contents at a Glance

Chapter 1: Building Master and Detail Pages

In This Chapter

✔ Developing master and detail pages at the same time

✔ Building your master and detail pages separately

✔ Putting together master and detail pages for ASP.NET

✔ Making sure your master and detail pages work

Simple sets of data can be expressed in a simple table, much like a traditional spreadsheet. But sometimes you don't want to display complete details on a given table. For example, suppose you want to display a master list of employees but want to view the full address and department details for an employee only when that record is selected. Dreamweaver CS5 enables you to do this by setting up what is known as a *master-detail relationship*.

A *master page* displays a list of records and corresponding links for each record. A user can click a link to see further information about a record on its associated *detail page*.

Depending on your programming language, you can either build the set of master and detail pages all in one operation, or you can separately build the master pages and then the detail pages. You find out more about both methods in this chapter.

The examples in this chapter use a simple Employee table, which you can see in Table 1-1. The first value, the empid, is a special field called a *key*. It always has a unique value. Therefore, if you query for a record in a table by using the key, you always get only the row that you're looking for because no two rows have the same key.

Table 1-1	Employee Table
Column Name	*Type of Data*
empid	Integer
first_name	20-character string
last_name	20-character string
address1	25-character string
address2	25-character string
city	20-character string
state	2-character string
zip	10-character string
deptid	Integer

Building Master and Detail Pages in One Operation (PHP, ASP, JSP, ColdFusion)

For PHP, ASP, JSP, and ColdFusion, you can build sets of master and detail pages in one operation. You can use the same method for all these languages. Creating both the master and detail pages at the same time is generally easier, but Dreamweaver gives you the flexibility of creating them separately, too.

To create a master and detail page set for PHP, ASP, JSP, or ColdFusion, follow these steps:

1. **Create a new dynamic page or open an existing one.**

   The page you created or open is displayed in Dreamweaver; this page becomes your master page in the language that you selected.

2. **Define a recordset for the page.**

   For the lowdown on creating a recordset, check out Book VIII, Chapter 1.

   The recordset provides the data that's displayed on both the master and detail pages. Make sure that you include all the table columns that you need to create your master page, including the unique key (the record ID column) for each record and all the table columns that you need to create your detail page. Typically, you display more columns on the detail page than on the master page.

   For the example in this chapter, we created an employee_records recordset and included all the columns in the employee table (see Table 1-1).

3. **Save your changes to the master page.**

   The new recordset appears in the Bindings panel, and connection code is automatically added to the dynamic page, as shown in Figure 1-1. This page allows a listing of employees to be displayed on the master page.

Figure 1-1: Dream-weaver with a recordset defined.

4. **Choose Insert⇨Data Objects⇨Master Detail Page Set to insert the master and detail pages.**

   The Insert Master-Detail Page Set dialog box appears (see Figure 1-2). You specify the properties for the master page in the top half of this dialog box and the properties for the detail page in the lower half.

5. **In the Recordset drop-down list, select the recordset that you want to use for the master page.**

   For this example, we selected employee_records. After you select a recordset, Dreamweaver fills in the rest of the fields with the columns from the recordset.

6. **In the Master Page Fields area, select which records you want to appear on the master page.**

   Click the plus (+) icon to add a field and click the minus (–) icon to remove a field. In Figure 1-2, we selected the first_name and last_name fields. These fields appear on the master page in a table format. Typically, fewer fields appear on the master page than on the detail page.

Figure 1-2:
The Insert Master-Detail Page Set dialog box.

7. **In the Link to Detail From drop-down list, select the field in the recordset that you want to serve as the link to the detail page.**

   This field is the one that a user clicks to display details for a given employee. For example, we selected the last_name field to serve as the link to the detail page for each record.

8. **In the Pass Unique Key drop-down list, select which field contains the values that you want to pass on to the detail page so it can identify the records.**

   Typically, you select the key field of the table. This key field tells the detail page which record to display for the user. For our example, we selected the empid field.

9. **Specify the number of records that you want to show at one time on the master page.**

   In the example, we chose to show 10 records at a time.

10. **In the Detail Page Name text box, enter a name for the detail page or click the Browse button to select an existing file.**

    For the example, we specified detail.php. Dreamweaver automatically uses this name when it creates the detail page.

11. **In the Detail Page Fields area, select which records you want to appear on the master page.**

Click the plus (+) icon and minus (–) icon to change the fields that appear on the detail page. Typically, more fields appear on the detail page than the master page. For the example, we selected all the fields in the table. Figure 1-2 shows the configuration of the Insert Master-Detail Page Set dialog box based on the example values.

12. **Click OK.**

Dreamweaver creates the master and detail pages and includes dynamic content and server behaviors in both. The Document window contains the automatically generated objects (a repeated region, navigation objects, record, counter, and link to the detail page), as shown in Figure 1-3.

13. **Modify the design of the master and detail pages.**

You can modify your dynamic fields just as you'd edit any other object (see Figure 1-4).

Figure 1-3:
The document shows a repeated region, navigation objects, record counter, and a link to the detail page.

Figure 1-4:
The detail page is created automatically by Dream- weaver.

When you finish designing the pages, you're ready to preview your work in a browser. See the "Testing Your Master and Detail Pages" section, later in this chapter, for details.

For ASP.NET (which is a different server technology than ASP), you need to build the master and detail pages separately (as described in the "Developing Master and Detail Pages for ASP.NET" section, later in this chapter). You can't build these pages at the same time in one operation for ASP. NET.

Developing Master and Detail Pages Block by Block

You can develop a master page block by block for PHP, ASP, JSP, and ColdFusion. Although you usually create the master and detail pages at the same time, you can also create them block by block to have complete control over the placement of the blocks.

Creating the master page

To create a dynamic master page, follow these steps:

1. **Create a page and define a recordset.**

Turn to Book VIII, Chapter 1 to find out how to define a recordset.

2. **In the Document window, place the insertion point where you want the records to appear on the page.**

3. **Choose Insert➪Data Objects➪Dynamic Data➪Dynamic Table.**

   The Dynamic Table dialog box appears, as shown in Figure 1-5.

Figure 1-5:
The
Dynamic
Table dialog
box.

4. **In the Recordset drop-down list, select the name of the recordset that you want to appear on the master page.**

5. **Specify the number of records that you want to show at one time on the master page.**

   In the example, we wanted to show 10 records at a time.

6. **(Optional) Specify border, cell padding, and cell spacing.**

7. **Click OK to close the dialog box.**

   The master table is created and added to your document.

If you don't want users to see some of the columns on the master page, delete the column from the table by following these steps:

1. **In Design view, click anywhere on the master page.**

2. **Put the pointer near the top of the column so that the column's entries are outlined in red. Then click to select the column.**

3. **Click the Delete button to delete the column from the table.**

Setting up links to open a detail page

After you create the master page (as the preceding section describes), you need to create links that open the detail page and communicate which record the user selected so that only the detail for that record displays.

To set up links to open a detail page, follow these steps:

1. **Open the master page in the Document window.**

2. **In the table, select the placeholder for the dynamic content on which you want to create a link.**

3. **In the Properties inspector, click the Browse for File button next to the Link field.**

   The Select File dialog box appears, as shown in Figure 1-6.

Figure 1-6: Configure which page to link to and which parameters to send.

4. **Browse to and select the detail page.**

5. **Click the Parameters button, which is to the right of the URL field.**

   The Parameters dialog box appears, as shown in Figure 1-7.

6. **Click the plus (+) icon to add a parameter, and then select the key value column as the parameter.**

   This parameter tells the detail page which row to display.

Figure 1-7: Configuring the URL parameter and its recordset.

7. **In the Name column, enter the column name.**

   You can also click the Dynamic lightning bolt icon and select the column from the dialog box.

8. **Click in the Value column and then click the Dynamic (lightning bolt) icon.**

   The Dynamic Data dialog box appears. This is where you select the key field from the recordset.

9. **Expand the recordset, click the key field, and then click OK.**

   In this case, we selected the empid key field. After you click OK, the Parameters dialog box displays the new parameter and the code that places it into the page dynamically, as shown in Figure 1-7.

10. **Click OK to close the Parameters dialog box.**

    The URL field in the Select File dialog box is prepopulated with the new parameter.

Each dynamic page type has different code that appears because each programming language uses a slightly different syntax to display a URL variable dynamically. Fortunately, because Dreamweaver is generating the code for you, you don't need to know the syntax differences.

11. **Click Choose to close the Select File dialog box.**

    You return to the Document window. The name of the detail page appears in the Link field in the Properties inspector. The placeholder for the dynamic content is now a link.

12. **Choose File➪Save to save your changes to the master page.**

    You now have a complete master page.

Read on to find out how to make the detail page.

Building detail pages

To create a detail page for PHP, ASP, JSP, and ColdFusion page types, follow these steps:

1. **Create a new or PHP, ASP, JSP, or ColdFusion page or open an existing one.**

2. **In the Bindings panel, click the plus (+) icon and then select Recordset (Query) from the menu that appears.**

   The simple Recordset dialog box appears.

   If you want to write your own SQL statements, click the Advanced button to display the advanced Recordset dialog box.

3. In the Name text box, enter a name for your recordset.

You can use only letters, numbers, and underscores in the name.

4. Select a database connection for obtaining the data that you want to display.

5. Select a table name for obtaining the data that you want to display.

After you select a table name, the database columns appear in the Columns list.

6. Select which columns should provide the record data to display.

Typically, your detail page uses more columns than your master page. You want the recordset for your detail page to contain at least one column (generally the id field) that matches the column that you use for the master page.

7. Complete the Filter sections as follows:

- **The first Filter field:** Select the database column name that contains values to match against the URL parameter (specified in the "Setting up links to open a detail page" section, earlier in this chapter). You use the filter to find and display the record specified by the URL parameter passed from the master page.

- **The second Filter field:** Select the equals (=) symbol, if it's not already selected. This filter requires the fields to be equal, which they must be to display only the detailed record.

- **The third Filter field:** Select URL Parameter.

- **The fourth Filter field:** Enter the name of the URL parameter that you want the master page to pass to the detail page.

The recordset (see Figure 1-8) now returns only the data for the employee who's been selected on the master page.

Figure 1-8:
Defining
a detail
recordset.

8. **Click the Test button.**

   The Test Value dialog box appears.

9. **Enter a value in the Test Value field, and then click OK.**

   This value represents which detail record is displayed. This test helps you check that the detail page brings back the data you expect.

   A table displaying data from the recordset appears.

10. **Click OK.**

    The Test SQL Statement window closes.

11. **In the Recordset dialog box, click OK.**

12. **To bind the columns in the recordset to the detail page, select the columns in the Bindings panel and drag those columns onto the detail page.**

    Your detail page can now process requests from the master page. Figure 1-9 shows the Document window after adding fields from the recordset.

Figure 1-9: The Document window after dragging several fields from the recordset onto it.

See the section "Testing Your Master and Detail Pages," later in this chapter, to find out how to preview your master and detail pages in a browser.

Developing Master and Detail Pages for ASP.NET

For ASP.NET, you can use the DataSet Web control to specify table columns and the DataGrid Web control to list the database records to display on the master page. The Web controls provide an easy way to display database data with controls for paging between multiple pages of records.

You need to define a database connection for the site before you create the master page. See Book VII for details.

Creating a master page

To create an ASP.NET master page, follow these steps:

1. **Create a new or open an existing ASP.NET page in Dreamweaver.**

2. **In the Bindings panel, click the plus (+) icon and select DataSet (Query) from the menu that appears.**

The DataSet dialog box appears.

3. **Complete the DataSet dialog box, and then click OK.**

Make sure to include all table columns that you need to create your master page, including the unique key (Record ID column) for each record. The new dataset appears in the Binding panel.

A dataset is essentially the same as a recordset; see Book VIII, Chapter 1 for more information on recordsets.

4. **In the Server Behaviors panel, click the plus (+) icon and select DataGrid from the menu that appears.**

The DataGrid dialog box appears.

5. **Select the dataset source from the DataSet drop-down list, and then click OK.**

You can leave the default column type as Simple Data Field.

Creating links that open the detail page

After you create the ASP.NET master page (as described in the preceding section), you need to create links that open the detail page and communicate which record the user selected. To open an ASP.NET detail page and display the specified record, follow these steps:

1. **Open the master page in the Document window.**

2. **In the Server Behaviors panel, double-click DataGrid.**

The DataGrid dialog box appears.

3. **In the Columns list, select the column that you want to serve as the link to the detail page.**

   You can use any field that identifies the record for expanding the detail of the record.

4. **Click the Change Column Type button.**

5. **Select Hyperlink from the pop-up menu.**

   The Hyperlink Column dialog box appears.

6. **In the Hyperlink Text section, specify the text that you want to display in the hyperlink column.**

   Here are your choices:

   - **Static Text:** Use a generic description for this column. Enter text for the link, such as Details.

   - **Data Field:** Add text for a link based on a hyperlink column. Then from the drop-down list, select a data field in your dataset. In the example, we selected the last_name column.

   - **Format String:** This field is generated automatically and displays the format of the URL text.

7. **In the Linked Page section, specify the URL for the hyperlink column text.**

   Here are your choices:

   - **Static Text:** Use a generic link for this column. Enter the URL for the link, such as Details.aspx.

   - **Data Field:** Add a link for data displayed in the hyperlink column. Then from the drop-down list, select a data field in your dataset. In the example, we selected the first_name column.

   - **Format String:** This field is generated automatically and displays the format of the URL link.

   The URL opens the detail page and uniquely identifies the record to display on the detail page.

8. **In the Linked Page section, click the Browse button next to the Format String box.**

9. **Locate and select which detail page you want to display.**

   Note the following when selecting your link page:

   - When you select a detail page, Dreamweaver adds information to the URL that specifies a parameter to use to identify the record.

   - Dreamweaver automatically names this parameter based on your database field name, but you can change the name to something else if you want to.

- Be sure to note the name of the URL parameter because you need that name when you create the detail page (which you can read about in the following section, "Creating a detail page").

- Dreamweaver uses a {0} placeholder to indicate where it places the value of the unique identifier when someone accesses the page.

10. **Click OK to close the Hyperlink Column dialog box.**

11. **Click OK.**

The DataGrid dialog box closes. The DataGrid on your page is updated.

Creating a detail page

After you create a master page for ASP.NET (as described in the two previous sections), you need to create a detail page to display the record. To do so, you need to define a dataset for the record and bind its columns to the detail page.

When creating the detail page, you need to know the database column name that you want to reference and the URL parameter that the master page uses to find and display that column's record on the detail page. If you don't remember the URL parameter name, open the master page, go to the Bindings panel, and look under the DataSet listing.

To create an ASP.NET detail page, create a new ASP.NET page in Dreamweaver and follow Steps 2 through 12 in the earlier section, "Building detail pages." Although these steps show you how to fill out the Recordset dialog box, the steps are the same for the DataSet dialog box, which you fill out when creating an ASP.NET detail page.

Testing Your Master and Detail Pages

After you create a master and detail page set, you need to test those pages. Follow these steps to preview the pages in a browser:

1. **Open the master page.**

2. **Choose File➪Preview in Browser➪*Name of Browser*.**

3. **When Dreamweaver asks if it's okay to copy the file to the testing site, click OK.**

Your browser launches with your master page, as shown in Figure 1-10.

4. **Click a hyperlink to view the associated detail page for that record.**

In the employee example, the linked field is the employee's last name. When you click a link, the browser page changes to expand the record and display the detail page.

Figure 1-10:
The browser displays the master page that uses the data from the databases.

Be sure that both your master page and detail page are transferred to the staging server. If they do not, you get a *Page not found* error message when you click a link in the master page.

Chapter 2: Creating Search and Results Pages

In This Chapter

✔ Developing search and results pages for PHP, JSP, ASP, and ColdFusion

✔ Creating search and results pages especially for ASP.NET

✔ Understanding ASP.NET requirements

You can use Dreamweaver to build *search pages,* which allow users to search your database, and *results pages,* which display the search results. Search pages are frequently used with dynamic database-driven Web pages to provide a shortcut to the information the user is looking for. For example, online stores usually give you the ability to search their products.

A basic search page contains a form with a search field and a submit button. Users enter search parameters in the form and click the submit button. The results page then receives the search parameters, searches the database for records that meet the search criteria, builds a recordset to hold the records it finds, and then displays the contents of the recordset for the users.

If you allow just one search parameter, Dreamweaver can create the recordset for you with a filter. However, if you have more than one search parameter, you need to work directly with an SQL statement and send a parameter to it. This chapter shows you how to build search and results pages for a single search parameter. We begin by looking at the techniques for PHP, JSP, ASP, and ColdFusion and then focus on the specific needs of ASP.NET.

Creating the Search Page

At a minimum, search pages consist of a form text field and a Submit button. The following steps show you how to create a basic search page:

1. **Create a new PHP, JSP, ASP, or ColdFusion document or open an existing one.**

2. **Insert a form by choosing Insert⇨Form⇨Form.**

   An empty form is displayed in the Document window. The form's boundaries appear as thin red lines.

If the form isn't visible, enable Invisible Elements by choosing View⇨Visual Aids⇨Invisible Elements.

3. **To add a text area search field, position your cursor inside your form and choose Insert⇨Form⇨Text Field.**

The Input Tag Accessibility Attributes dialog box appears, as shown in Figure 2-1.

Input Tag Accessibility Attributes

ID: search_field

Label: Search

Style: ● Wrap with label tag

○ Attach label tag using 'for' attribute

○ No label tag

Position: ● Before form item

○ After form item

Access key: [ ] Tab Index: [ ]

If you don't want to enter this information when inserting objects, change the Accessibility preferences.

OK · Cancel · Help

Figure 2-1:
The Input Tag Accessibility Attributes dialog box.

4. **Type** search_field **in the ID text box.**

You can ignore the remaining options.

5. **Click OK to close the dialog box.**

The text field is added to your page.

6. **Position your cursor just after the text field, and then choose Insert⇨Form⇨Button to add a Submit button to your form.**

You can also just click Button on the Insert panel to automatically add the new button right after the text field.

7. **In the Input Tag Accessibility Attributes dialog box, type** search_btn **as the ID value.**

8. **Click OK to close the Input Tag Accessibility Attributes dialog box.**

9. **Select the Submit button in the document.**

10. **In the Properties inspector, change the Value text to Search.**

The form should now look like Figure 2-2, which has all the basic elements that are required to request a search.

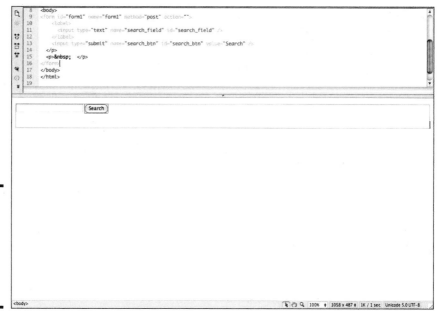

Figure 2-2:
The form
with a
Search text
field and
a Submit
button.

11. **Select the form by clicking the form tag in the Tag selector.**

    This selects the form element so that you can modify its properties.

12. **In the Action field in the Properties inspector, enter a filename for the results page (the page that will process the database search request) or click the Browse to File button to select a file.**

    You create this file when defining the results page, as described in the next section. For example, we entered results.php, as shown in Figure 2-3.

Figure 2-3:
The
Properties
inspector
for a form.

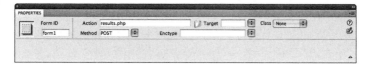

13. **Select POST from the Method drop-down list.**

    You have completed the search page. After the user fills out the form and clicks the Submit button, the information is passed to the results page as a form parameter. Read on to find out how to create the results page.

Building the Results Page

The complexity of building your results page is directly related to the number of search parameters that users can specify. If you allow only one search parameter, you don't have to modify the SQL query when building the results page. This is the type of search that we describe in this chapter.

The results page receives the search parameters from the form, plugs that data into a recordset filter, and then displays the results from the recordset on the page. The search page can optionally link to another page to expand details for a search result. For example, searching a catalog of products produces a list of matching products. If you then click one of the products, you see the full detail page for just that product.

In the following sections, you find out how to build the recordset that holds the results as well as the page that displays those results.

Building the recordset

To create the recordset that performs the search in the results page, follow these steps:

1. **Create a new PHP, JSP, ASP, or ColdFusion document or open an existing one.**

2. **In the Bindings panel, click the plus (+) icon and then select Recordset from the drop-down list that appears.**

   The Recordset dialog box appears. You need to create a recordset to query the database with the search parameters.

3. **Enter the name of the recordset in the Name field.**

   Choose a name that describes the recordset data. For example, we entered employee_search (see Figure 2-4), which indicates that the recordset relates to a search.

4. **In the Connection drop-down list, select a connection to the database you want the user to search.**

   You must have an active database connection to create the recordset. See Book VII for details on setting up a database connection.

Depending on your dynamic page type, the Recordset dialog box may appear slightly different from Figure 2-4. For example, ColdFusion calls the Connection field a data source and includes optional Username and Password fields for the database. However, these differences don't change the following steps.

Figure 2-4:
The
Recordset
dialog box
configured
to search
the last
name field
of the
employee
table.

5. **In the Table drop-down list, select the database table to be searched.**

   We selected the employee table. The Columns list is updated after you
   select a table.

6. **If you want to include only some of the table's columns in the recordset, click the Selected radio button and then select the columns to
   include.**

   Select the columns to display by Ctrl+clicking (Windows) or ⌘+clicking
   (Mac) them from the Columns list. We selected the first_name, last_
   name, city, state, and deptid columns.

7. **To create the database filter for the search, complete the fields in the
   Filter area as follows:**

   • **First Filter field:** Select the database column you want to search. For
     example, to search the last_name column of the employee table, we
     selected last_name.

   • **Second Filter field:** Select how to filter your results. Your choices
     are Contains, Begins With, Ends With, or Numeric Comparisons. Use
     the Contains item.

   • **Third Filter field:** Select Form Variable if your form uses the POST
     method, or URL Parameter if it uses the GET method. We selected
     Form Variable because the HTML form on the search page uses the
     POST method.

   • **Fourth Filter field:** Enter the name of the search field from the
     search page, which in the example is search_field.

   Dreamweaver uses the conditions you specify to filter the search
   results. If a record doesn't meet the conditions that you've specified,
   the record is excluded from the recordset. For example, if records exist
   for employees with the last names Phillips and Davis and you search the

last name field for names containing the letters *il,* the filter returns only the record for Phillips.

Figure 2-4 shows the completed Recordset dialog box for the example. This recordset returns records that contain the search parameter in the last name. For example, if you can remember only that a name contains the letters *il*, you could use this recordset to find the name.

8. **Click the Test button to execute the query and verify that it returns the data you expected.**

The Test Value dialog box appears.

9. **In the Test Value field, enter a value that represents the record to display, and then click OK.**

In the example, we entered Bo.

The Test SQL Statement window appears, as shown in Figure 2-5, displaying data from the recordset.

Record	first_name	last_name	city	state	deptid
1	Jason	Bourne	Paris	MA	0
2	James	Bond	Kansas City	MO	0

Figure 2-5: Testing the search statement.

10. **To change the order of the results, select a database column to sort by and then choose Ascending or Descending from the Sort drop-down menu in the Recordset dialog box.**

11. **Click OK to close the Test SQL Statement window.**

You return to the Recordset dialog box.

12. **If the test produced the correct results, click OK to close the Recordset dialog box.**

If your test didn't produce the results you wanted, check the filtering parameters versus the actual data in the database table.

The recordset is added to the Bindings panel list.

After you close the Recordset dialog box, Dreamweaver inserts the code that performs a search based on the search parameter passed from the search page. Only records that match the search criteria become part of the recordset. This code is hidden when you're working on the page in Design view, but you can see it by highlighting the recordset in the Bindings panel.

Displaying the results

After you create a recordset that holds the search results, you need to display the data for the user on the results page. Dreamweaver provides several tools for displaying recordsets, but the easiest is the dynamic table.

To create a dynamic table that displays results, follow these steps:

1. **In your results page, place the insertion point where you want the records displayed on the page. Then choose Insert⇨Data Objects⇨Dynamic Data⇨Dynamic Table.**

    Be sure to insert the table after the yellow code blocks because they must execute first to generate the recordset. The Dynamic Table dialog box appears.

2. **In the Recordset drop-down list, select the recordset you created in the preceding section.**

    For example, we selected the employee_search, as shown in Figure 2-6.

Figure 2-6:
The
Dynamic
Table dialog
box.

3. **Specify how many records to show at one time on the results page.**

4. **(Optional) Specify the border, cell padding, and cell spacing to use.**

5. **Click OK to close the dialog box.**

    Dreamweaver inserts a dynamic table that displays the search results, as shown in Figure 2-7.

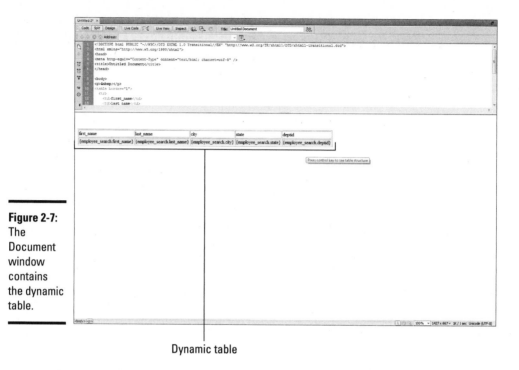

Figure 2-7:
The
Document
window
contains
the dynamic
table.

Dynamic table

Testing Your Search and Results Pages

After you create your search and results pages, it's a good idea to test them to make sure they work properly as described in the following steps for all dynamic page types:

1. **Open the search page.**

2. **Choose File⇨Preview in Browser⇨*Name of Browser*.**

3. **If Dreamweaver asks if it's okay to copy the file over, click OK to copy files to your testing site.**

    Your browser launches with your search page, as shown in Figure 2-8.

4. **Enter a search term in the Search field.**

5. **Click the Search button.**

    The browser page changes to the results page, as shown in Figure 2-9.

Figure 2-8:
The browser
displaying
the search
page to
retrieve all
names that
contain *Bo*.

ASP.NET system requirements

To get output that works with ASP.NET, keep in mind these system requirements:

✔ Make sure you have the latest version of Microsoft's database software component, which is called MDAC (Microsoft Data Acess Components). MDAC is available from Microsoft's site at `www.microsoft.com/downloads/details.aspx?FamilyID=6c050fe3-c795-4b7d-b037-185d0506396c&displaylang=en`. Download and install the most recent version available.

✔ Install the .NET Framework to allow IIS to process .NET files. Download it from Microsoft at `http://msdn.`
`microsoft.com/netframework/downloads/updates/default.aspx`.

✔ Upload the DreamweaverCtrls.dll Dreamweaver .NET component file. To publish this file on your test or remote server, click the blue up arrow in the Components panel. This places the file in the bin directory of your Web root. Without this file, Dreamweaver-generated code produces errors.

Regardless of which language you choose, if you run into an error, don't panic. Searching for the error with Google or by checking the Dreamweaver knowledge base usually turns up a solution in short order.

Figure 2-9:
Two records
are found
containing
the search
text.

Be sure that both search and details pages are transferred to the staging
server. If they don't, you get a *Page Not Found* error when you click a link in
the search page.

Chapter 3: Building Record Insert Pages and Restricting Site Access

In This Chapter

✔ **Developing a record insert page in one step**

✔ **Putting together a record insert page a piece at a time**

✔ **Making sure your record insert page works**

✔ **Building a login form**

✔ **Restricting access to pages**

So far in this minibook, we've been focusing on displaying data that is already in a database. However, in many cases, you also want to allow for the ability to add data from a Web page. In those cases, you'll want to create a record insert page.

Every *record insert page* must have

✦ A database connection

✦ A database table after which to model the insert fields

✦ A form that collects data

✦ A submit button

When designing the record insert page, you typically arrange the fields on the form in a table and include labels to identify each field. When users open the record insert page in their Web browsers, they just fill in the form fields. When they finish, they click the submit button, and — presto! — the record is added to the database.

Dreamweaver gives you two methods to add data to a database table from a dynamic Web page. You can do it in one step by using the Insert Record dialog box. Dreamweaver also supports creating a record insert page by adding the server behaviors a block at a time. We describe both methods in this chapter, as well as show you how to test your completed record insert page.

Creating the Record Insert Page in One Operation

You can add the basic building blocks of a record insert page in a single operation by using the Record Insertion Form application object. The application object adds an HTML form and an Insert Record server behavior to the page.

You must have an active database connection before you can build a record insert page. See Book VII for details on setting up a database connection.

To build the record insert page with the Record Insertion Form application object, follow these steps:

1. **Create a new or open an existing document.**

    This is where you will add the data entry form.

2. **Choose Insert⇨Data Objects⇨Insert Record⇨Record Insertion Form Wizard.**

    The Record Insertion Form dialog box appears, as shown in Figure 3-1.

Figure 3-1:
The Record
Insertion
Form dialog
box as it first
appears.

3. **Select the database connection from the Connection drop-down list.**

    For example, we selected the employee connection (see Figure 3-2). The database connection field varies slightly between the different dynamic document types. For example, ColdFusion includes a Username field and a Password field.

Figure 3-2:
The Record
Insertion
Form dialog
box after
configuring
for the
employee
data table.

4. **From the Table drop-down list, select the database table that you want to insert the record into.**

   For example, we selected the employee table in Figure 3-2. After you select a table, Dreamweaver updates the Form Fields section with the columns in the table.

5. **In the After Inserting, Go To text box, enter the page that you want to go to after the record is added. Alternatively, click the Browse button to select a file.**

   For example, we selected a page named success.php. This page simply says that the insert was successful.

   For the ASP.NET dynamic page type, you can also specify a page that you want to go to upon failure or display a debugging page. The rest of the dialog box works the same with ASP.NET as the other page types.

6. **(Optional) To remove unwanted columns from the record insert page, select the columns that you want to remove in the Form Fields section and click the minus (–) icon.**

   The Form Fields section lists the columns that appear on the record insert page. In these fields, the user can enter data before submitting the insert request.

7. **(Optional) If you want to make changes to how a field appears on the record insert page, select the field from the list and fill in the following fields:**

   - **Label:** Change the Label field to a more descriptive label for the contents of the database field. For example, you can give the first_name field a friendlier label, such as First Name.

- **Display As:** Select a form type. The default setting is Text Field. The Display As list has all the basic form types, including check boxes, menus, and radio buttons. If you select one of the types that requires additional configuration — such as radio groups — a configuration dialog box appears.

- **Submit As:** Select the data format that you want to place in the database field. The choices are Text, Numeric, Double, Date, Checkbox Y/N, Checkbox 1/0, and Checkbox –1,0. The data format that you choose here needs to match the database column's type.

- **Default Value:** Specify a default value for any field. Because many of the employees in our example are located in South Dakota, we entered SD as a default value.

  To specify a dynamic data source for the default value, click the Bind to Dynamic Source (lightning bolt) icon and select a binding. This process works the same as specifying a dynamic source for a regular form object.

Figure 3-2 shows the Record Insertion Form dialog box for the employee table example.

8. **(Optional) If you want to change the order in which the fields are displayed in the form, select a field and click the up arrow or down arrow.**

   You need to order table fields together with similar fields. For example, you'll probably want to group all the address fields.

9. **Click OK to close the dialog box.**

   Dreamweaver automatically adds the form and the submit button to your page. Figure 3-3 shows the example form in the Document window along with a submit button labeled Insert Record.

You can modify the appearance of the form by using the usual Dreamweaver functions for changing fonts, colors, and alignment. The form elements must stay in the boundaries of the form. To continue working on your form elements, see Book II, Chapter 7.

Click the Insert Record entry in the Server Behaviors panel to edit the server behavior (such as adding additional columns to the insert) in the Record Insertion Form dialog box (refer to Figure 3-1).

Figure 3-3:
The
Document
window
with a
freshly
inserted
form.

Building a Record Insert Page Block by Block

You can add the basic building blocks of an insert page separately by using
the form tools (Insert➪Form) and the Server Behaviors panel. Creating your
record insert page using the Record Insertion dialog box is faster, but building block by block allows complete control over the placement of blocks on
your page.

When creating an insert page manually, you create a form for the user to
enter the data and then add an Insert Record server behavior to process the
form submission, as the following sections describe.

Adding the form

To add the HTML form, follow these steps:

1. **Create a new page or open an existing page.**

2. **Insert a form by choosing Insert➪Form➪Form.**

    If you can't see the form, enable invisible elements by choosing
    View➪Visual Aids➪Invisible Elements.

3. **To select the form, click the form's boundaries or click the `<form>` tag in the bottom-left corner of the Document window.**

   Selecting the form lets you modify that form's properties in the Properties inspector.

4. **In the Properties inspector, enter a name for the form in the Form ID field.**

   You probably want to use something descriptive, such as insert_form. Don't set the Action or Method fields because the Insert Record server behavior sets these fields for you.

5. **Add a text field by choosing Insert⇨Form⇨Text Field.**

   You can also add other form objects, depending on the type of data that you want to insert into the database table. See Book II, Chapter 7 for more on the different form objects.

6. **In the Input Tag Accessibility Attributes dialog box, enter a descriptive ID and a text label.**

7. **(Optional) Tweak the Style and Position settings as desired.**

8. **Click OK.**

9. **For each column that you allow the user to add data to, repeat Steps 5–8.**

   For the employee table example, we added each field but arranged the fields in a slightly different order on the form.

10. **Press Enter (Windows) or Return (Mac) to insert a new line so that the element appears on a separate line.**

    You can also use a table element to align your fields (see Book II, Chapter 7 for more information).

11. **Insert a submit button on the page by choosing Insert⇨Form⇨Button.**

    If the Input Tag Accessibility Attributes dialog box appears, click Cancel.

12. **With the button selected, change the Value text in the Properties inspector to Insert.**

    The example form looks like Figure 3-4.

Adding the Insert Record server behavior

You have to add the Insert Record server behavior to your page so that it can process the data in the form submission.

You must have an active database connection before you can add the Insert Record server behavior. See Book VII for details on setting up a database connection.

| ID: | Department: |
| First Name: | Last Name: |
| Address: |
| Address 2: |
| City: | State | Zip Code: |
| Insert |

`<body>`

Figure 3-4:
The
completed
form.

To add the Insert Record server behavior, follow these steps:

1. **In the Server Behaviors panel, click the plus (+) icon and select Insert Record in the drop-down list that appears.**

The Insert Record dialog box appears.

2. **Select your form in the Submit Values From drop-down list.**

3. **In the Connection drop-down list, select a database connection that contains the table that you want to insert data into.**

4. **In the Insert Table drop-down list, select the database table that you want to insert a record into.**

The database columns appear in the Columns section, as shown in Figure 3-5.

Depending on your dynamic page type, the Insert Record dialog box may appear slightly different. For example, ColdFusion calls the Connection field a data source and includes options for Username and Password database fields. However, these differences don't change the following steps.

5. **(Optional) To modify the associated database column or data type of a field, select the column from the column list and then modify the following fields in the dialog box:**

- **Value:** Select the form field. Each form field appears in the list.

- **Submit As:** Select the data type. The data type that you select here should mirror the database column data type. The types are text, integer, date, and check box formats.

Dreamweaver automatically links the form fields that have the same name as the database field.

Figure 3-5:
Use the
Insert
Record
dialog box
to choose
which fields
supply
values
from the
form to the
database
table.

6. **For each field that you need to change, repeat Step 5.**

7. **In the After Inserting, Go To text field, enter the page that you want to go to after inserting the record. Or click the Browse button and select a file.**

For the ASP.NET dynamic page type, you have a choice also for the On Failure, Go To text box and a Display Debugging Information check box. You fill in these fields to display debugging information or redirect a user if the record insert fails. The rest of the dialog box works the same as the other document types.

8. **Click OK.**

Dreamweaver adds the server behavior to the page. You now have a complete page. Users can fill out the fields on the page and then click the submit button.

You can make any visual changes to the form by using Dreamweaver's tools for changing fonts, colors, and placement.

Testing Your Record Insert Page

After you create a record insert page (see "Building a Record Insert Page Block by Block" section, earlier in this chapter), you probably want to test your page. Follow these steps to do so:

1. **Open the Record Insert page.**

2. **Choose File⇨Preview in Browser⇨*Name of Browser*.**

3. **When Dreamweaver asks if it's okay to copy files to your testing site, click OK.**

   Your browser launches and displays the Record Insert page.

4. **Enter some sample data into the fields.**

   Figure 3-6 shows some test data for the employee table.

Figure 3-6:
Entering
data into
the Record
Insert page.

5. **Click the Insert Record button.**

   When the data is added successfully, the browser opens the success page.

Be sure that both your Record Insert page and success page transfer to the testing server. If not, when you click the button on the insert page, you get a *Page Not Found* error message.

The success page in our example simply contains the text *Inserted Successfully.*

If you want to double-check that the insert worked, follow these steps:

1. **Open the Databases panel.**
2. **Expand the database you are working with by clicking the arrow.**
3. **Expand the Tables item to display the table you are working with.**
4. **Right-click the table on the page.**
5. **Choose View Data from the pop-up menu.**

   The View Data dialog box appears, as shown in Figure 3-7.

Figure 3-7:
The View Data dialog box shows the newly inserted data.

In the dialog box, you can see that the data was inserted correctly into the table.

Building a Login Page

A login page enables registered users to log in to a Web site. Dreamweaver CS5 comes with a sample design of a login page. You can also design your own.

The following sections show you how to complete the steps to building your own login page.

Setting up a database table

If you set up the employee entry page, as described earlier in the chapter, you've already created this table.

Creating the HTML form on the login page

If you want to design your own login page, first you need to create a new page and add an HTML form with a username text box, a password text box, and a submit button. This process is similar to the process of adding a form to a data entry page.

Adding a Log In User server behavior to the page

After adding a form to your login page (as described in the preceding section), the final step is to add the Log In User server behavior, which checks to make sure that the user entered a valid username and password.

To add the Log In User server behavior to your login page, open the page and follow these steps:

1. **In the Server Behaviors panel, click the plus (+) icon and choose User Authentication⇨Log In User.**

   The Log In User dialog box appears.

2. **In the Get Input From Form field, select the form used on the login page.**

3. **In the Username Field and Password Field text boxes, select the appropriate form fields.**

4. **If you are using ColdFusion, enter your username and password.**

5. **In the Table drop-down list, select the database table that you will check the form fields against.**

   We selected the users table.

6. **In the Username Column and Password Column drop-down lists, specify the table columns for the username and password.**

   For example, the users table that we selected in Step 5 contains username and password columns, so we selected those columns.

7. **In the If Login Success, Go To text box, enter the name of the page to open if the user logs in successfully.**

   Or you can click the Browse button and select the page.

8. **In the If Login Fails, Go To text box, enter the name of the page to open if the user is unable to log in.**

   Or you can click the Browse button and select the page.

9. **Indicate whether you want to grant access to this page based on just the username and password, or based on the authorization level as well.**

   Having multiple authentication levels provides more flexibility for segregated access to information but also comes at the cost of added complexity (and time administering your user's levels and categorizing information). Most people can get by without setting up multiple access levels to their sites.

10. **Click OK.**

Your login page is now complete.

Restricting Access to Your Pages

If you have a Web page that you don't want all users to be able to view, you can restrict access to it. To do this, you add the Restrict Access to Page server behavior to the page so that only authorized users can view the page. If an unauthorized user attempts to open the restricted page, the user is redirected to another page.

Here are a few examples of when restricted access may be useful:

+ You have a page that you want to be viewed only by users with Administrator privileges.

+ You want to make sure that users log in before they can view a specific page.

+ You want to review newly registered users before allowing them to access members-only pages.

To restrict access to a page, you need to do the following tasks:

+ Add the Restrict Access to a Page server behavior to that page.

+ If you want to use authorization levels to further restrict page access, you need to add a column to your user database table to maintain information about which access privileges each user is entitled to.

Follow these steps to restrict access to a page:

1. **Open the page you want to restrict access to.**

2. **In the Server Behaviors panel, click the plus (+) icon and choose User Authentication⇨Restrict Access to Page.**

   The Restrict Access to Page dialog box appears.

3. **In the Restrict Based On area, select one of the following options:**

   ✦ **Username and Password:** Select this option if you want only users with a valid username and password to access the restricted page.

   ✦ **Username, Password, and Access Level:** Select this option if you want only users with specific access privileges to be able to view the page. Specify one or more authorization levels for the page — for example, Administrator.

4. **In the If Access Denied, Go To text box, enter the name of the page to open if an unauthorized user attempts to open the restricted page.**

5. **Click OK.**

Dreamweaver adds a server behavior to the page ensuring that only authorized users can access the page.

Chapter 4: Developing Record Update and Delete Pages

In This Chapter

✔ Creating record update pages

✔ Trying out your record update page

✔ Deleting records by using delete pages

✔ Putting your delete page to the test

*I*n previous chapters in this minibook, we've shown you how to browse, search, and insert data. But before you go away thinking that you've discovered everything you need to know about Web apps, we need to tell you — in the words of a late-night television infomercial — *but wait, there's more!*

The record update and delete operations are the last two database functions commonly used in dynamic database sites. For example, suppose that employees at your company can view their employee data online. Over time, they may want to change their employment details. Or perhaps an H.R. administrator may need the ability to delete an employee record. In any case, you need to give users the ability to update and delete database records from a Web page, which is what this chapter is all about.

Building an Update Page

Before users can update a record, they need to be able to search for the record that they want to update. Therefore, you need to create a search page and a results page. (See Book IX, Chapter 2 for full details on how to create and work with search and results pages.) Additionally, you need to create an update page so that users can enter the data for updating the record. Here's a closer look at the three pages that you need to create:

✦ **Search page:** This page allows users to search for a record that they want to update. For example, in the case of an employee record, the search page simply searches the employee that's logged in because employees can't modify other employee information.

✦ **Results page:** This page displays the record in a form. The form defaults to the values currently in the database (before the update) and has an update button.

✦ **Update page:** This page performs the update and tells the user when an update is successful.

Here's how the update process works:

1. The user enters search criteria in the form on the search page and then clicks the Submit button.

2. The browser displays the results of the search on the results page.

3. The user selects a record to update on the results page and clicks the Submit button.

4. The browser displays the update page.

The first step in the update process is to create a search and results page set. If you haven't already created these pages, check out Book IX, Chapter 2 for details. Then read the following sections for details on building the update page.

Creating link to the update page

After you create the search and results pages, you need to create a link on the results page to open the update page and display the selected record in an HTML form.

However, before you begin, quickly create a blank dynamic page of the desired type and save it as update.php (the three-letter file extension varies based on the app server you are working with). This is a blank placeholder page that will eventually be used to update a record from the results page.

After you have created a blank dynamic page, open the results page that you created based on the instructions back in Book IX, Chapter 2 and follow these steps:

1. **Select the placeholder for the dynamic content for which you want to create a link.**

   For example, we selected the last_name field to use as the link field, as shown in Figure 4-1. The field placeholder appears as {employee_search. last_name}.

2. **In the Properties inspector, click the Browse for Folder icon to the right of the Link field.**

3. **In the Select File dialog box, select the update page that you just created.**

   For example, we selected update.php as the update page. For other language types, use the appropriate file extension (such as .asp) rather than .php.

Figure 4-1:
The
Document
window for
the results
page.

4. **Click the Parameters button.**

   The Parameters dialog box appears.

5. **Enter the key field from your database record in the Name column.**

   The *key field* is a field that always has a unique value. For example, we entered empid because this field contains a unique ID for each employee.

6. **Click the Value column to the right of Name.**

   The Value edit box is highlighted.

7. **Click the Bind to Dynamic Source (lightning bolt) icon to the right of the highlighted box.**

   The Dynamic Data dialog box appears, as shown in Figure 4-2.

8. **Select the key field from the recordset, and then click OK.**

   After you click OK, the Values field in the Parameters dialog box is updated to contain the URL parameter.

9. **Click OK to close the Parameters dialog box.**

   The Select File dialog box appears with an updated value in the URL field. The value in this field varies depending on your dynamic page type. Figure 4-3 shows the results for a PHP page.

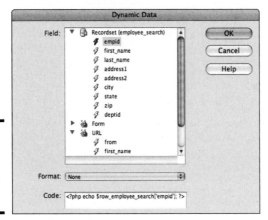

Figure 4-2:
The
Dynamic
Data dialog
box.

Figure 4-3:
The updated
URL field in
the Select
File dialog
box.

10. **Click Choose to close the Select File dialog box.**

The Document window shows the new link.

11. **Save the results page.**

The results page is now complete.

Putting the update page together

The update page must read the URL parameter from the results page and store it in a recordset. The recordset provides the default values for the form that enables users to change values. The following sections show how to create the recordset and the form.

Creating the recordset to store the URL parameter

To create the recordset, follow these steps:

Book IX
Chapter 4

Developing Record
Update and Delete
Pages

1. **Open the results page you created in the preceding section.**

You must have an active database connection to create the recordset. See Book VII for details on creating a database connection.

2. **In the Bindings panel, click the plus (+) icon and then select Recordset (Query) from the menu that appears.**

The Recordset dialog box appears.

3. **Enter the name of the recordset in the Name field.**

Use a name that describes the recordset data. For example, we entered employee_update to indicate that the recordset relates to an update.

4. **Select a database connection in the Connection drop-down list.**

Depending on your dynamic page type, the Recordset dialog box may appear slightly different. For example, ColdFusion calls the Connection field a data source and includes optional Username and Password fields for the database. However, these differences don't change the following steps.

5. **In the Table drop-down list, select the database table that you want to update.**

After you select a table, the Columns list displays the columns in that table.

6. **(Optional) If you want to include only some of the columns from the table for updating, click the Selected option.**

7. **In the Columns list, select the columns that you want to update.**

To select multiple columns, Ctrl+click (Windows) or ⌘+click (Mac).

8. **Configure the Filter area so that the database column is compared against the URL parameter from the results page:**

- In the first list, select the key column. For example, we selected empid, which is the key column for the employee table.

- In the second list, select the equals sign (=). This selection limits the result set to only the record that you want to update. You can update only one record at a time.

- In the third list, select URL Parameter.

- In the fourth list, enter the name of the URL parameter defined in the results page. For example, we entered empid, the same name as the database key column name.

If your form's field has a different name in the Properties inspector, use that name as the parameter name.

The new recordset retrieves the information needed to update the records that the user has selected to update. When the update page is requested, it uses the record ID parameter sent to the page to filter the recordset. The Recordset dialog box for the example looks like Figure 4-4.

9. **Click OK.**

The recordset is added to the Bindings panel list. Now when the user selects a record on the results page, the update page builds a recordset containing only the selected record.

Figure 4-4:
The Recordset dialog box configured to select only the record to update based on the specified URL parameter.

Adding a form to the update page

After creating the recordset for the update page (which you can read about in the preceding section), you need to create the form that enables the user to modify the record data. Dreamweaver can do the work for you with the Record Update Form Wizard. This wizard automatically creates the form in the Document window and adds the appropriate server behaviors to allow updates.

If you've used the Insert Record Form Wizard, you'll find this wizard similar.

Follow these steps to add an HTML form to your update page:

1. **Choose Insert⇨Data Objects⇨Update Record⇨Record Update Form Wizard.**

The Update Record Form dialog box appears.

Only one application object can exist on the same page. You can't have an update application object and a delete application object on the same page.

2. **Select the database connection in the Connection drop-down list.**

3. **Select the database table that you want to update in the Table to Update drop-down list.**

4. **From the Select Record From drop-down list, select the recordset that you created, as described in the preceding section.**

    This list should default to the recordset that you created in the preceding section.

5. **In the Unique Key Column drop-down list, select a key column to identify the record in the database table.**

    For example, we selected empid. Leave the Numeric check box selected if the key fields are numeric.

6. **In the After Updating, Go To text box, enter the page that you want to open after the record is updated. Alternatively, click the Browse button to select a file.**

    For example, we selected a page called success.php, which simply displays a success message. You can create the page before or after entering the filename for it.

7. **To remove unwanted columns from the update page, select the columns in the Form Fields section and click the minus (–) icon.**

    By default, Dreamweaver includes all the columns of the table in the form on the update page. The Form Fields section lists the columns in which the user can enter data before submitting the update request. For our example, we removed the empid file because it's an autogenerated key field. Removing this field eliminates the risk of the user changing the key value to a duplicate value.

8. **(Optional) If you want to make changes to how a field appears on the update page, select the field from the list and fill in the following fields in the dialog box:**

    -   **Label:** Enter a descriptive label. This label appears on the form next to the field. By default, Dreamweaver uses the column name as the label. So, for example, rather than use the default label of first_name, you could change it to First Name.

    -   **Display As:** Select a form type. The Display As list includes all the basic form types, including check boxes, radio buttons, and menus. If you select one of the types that needs additional configuration, such as radio groups, a configuration dialog box appears.

    -   **Submit As:** Select the data format. The *data format* is the type of data that the database column is expecting. The default matches the current data type in the database. Your choices are Text, Numeric, Double, Date, Checkbox Y/N, Checkbox 1/0, and Checkbox –1,0.

• **Default Value:** Specify a default value. The value that you enter in the Default Value field is the initial value that appears in the form for the particular field. If you don't enter a value here, Dreamweaver uses the current value from the database for the initial value.

You can change the dynamic data source for the default value by clicking the Bind to Dynamic Source (lightning bolt) icon and selecting a binding. The value defaults to the value from the recordset. If the data type is a menu, radio group, or check box, another dialog box appears to configure the choices available to the user. For example, a check box has a setting to determine whether it should be automatically checked when the update page appears.

9. **(Optional) Repeat Step 8 for each field that you want to modify in the Form Field list.**

The dialog box for the example looks like Figure 4-5.

Figure 4-5:
The Record Update Form dialog box after configuring an update.

10. **(Optional) If you want to change the order in which the fields appear in the form, select a field and click the up arrow or down arrow.**

Table fields should be grouped with similar fields (for example, address fields should all be placed together).

11. **Click OK to close the Record Update Form dialog box.**

The new form appears as a basic table on your update page. Figure 4-6 shows the form created for the example. You can modify the appearance of form objects as you can any other object in Dreamweaver, but remember to not move them outside the form's boundaries. (See Book II, Chapter 7 for more on form objects.)

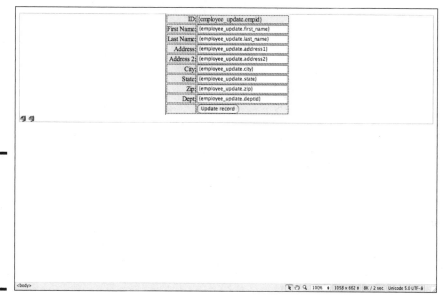

Figure 4-6:
The
Document
window
now
contains
the update
form.

Testing Your Update Page

You can test your results page by previewing it in a browser. Before doing so, make sure the latest versions of your search, results, and update pages are on your server. Then follow these steps:

1. **Open the search page in Dreamweaver.**

2. **Choose File⇨Preview in Browser⇨*Name of Browser.***

3. **Enter search criteria in the box and click the Search button.**

The results page is displayed with the matching records (see Figure 4-7).

4. **Select a record to update by clicking the link for that record.**

In our example, the last name for each employee is linked to the update page. The browser displays the update page for that record. We clicked the Jason Bourne link on the results page, and the browser displayed the update page with the record for Jason, as shown in Figure 4-8.

Be sure that both your search results page and update page transfer to the testing server. If both don't transfer, you get a *Page Not Found* error message when you click a link in the update results page.

5. **Enter a new value for one or more of the fields on the update page.**

For example, we added address info, as shown in Figure 4-9.

Figure 4-7:
The browser
displays
the rows
that can be
updated.

Figure 4-8:
The update
page is
displayed.

6. Click Update Record.

Your changes are saved to the database, and the success page appears
in the browser (see Figure 4-10).

What's more, to verify the update was saved, you can navigate back to the
update results page to verify the new value.

Figure 4-9:
More details
are provided
for Mr.
Bourne.

Figure 4-10:
Success!

Building Pages to Delete a Record

The typical process for deleting records from a database consists of a few steps. First, users select which record to delete. After they select a record, a confirmation page appears, asking them to confirm the delete request to prevent deleting a record accidentally. Finally, a page appears indicating that the record was successfully deleted from the database.

For users to be able to delete a record, they first need to be able to find that record in the database. Therefore, you need to create a search page and a results page so that users can search for the record. See Book IX, Chapter 2 for details.

The following sections detail how to build the pages that allow a user to delete a record from the database.

Creating delete links to open the confirmation page

After you create a search page and results page, you need to create a Delete link for each record in the results table that users can click to open a *confirmation page,* which is a page that asks them to confirm the deletion.

However, before you begin, quickly create a blank dynamic page of the desired type and save it as confirm.php (the extension varies based on the app server you are working with). You'll add content to this file in a moment, but for now, you just need to link to it.

To create the links to the confirmation page, open the results page and follow these steps:

1. **Select the last column in the results repeated region.**

2. **Choose Insert⇨Table Objects⇨Table⇨Insert Column to the Right.**

   An empty column appears at the end of the table. The empty column is skinny.

3. **Select the new column's lower cell, which is part of the repeated region.**

4. **Type** Delete.

5. **Select the text you just entered to apply a link to the text.**

6. **In the Properties inspector, enter the name of the confirmation page in the Link field.**

Defining the URL parameter to pass to the confirmation page

After you create a delete link that displays the confirmation page (see the preceding section), you want to modify that link so that it passes the identity of the record that the user wants to delete. To define the URL parameter that identifies which record to delete, follow these steps:

1. **Follow Steps 1–6 in the "Creating delete links to open the confirmation page" section, earlier in this chapter.**

   The deletion process follows a parallel pattern to the record update.

2. **Click the plus (+) icon to add another parameter.**

   An empty row appears in the list.

3. **Enter the name of a column that describes which record is about to be deleted on the confirmation page.**

   For the employee table example, we are using the last name field. In a real-world situation, you would probably want to add more fields to confirm the deletion. But for this purpose, the last name field works fine. Figure 4-11 shows the two parameters for the employee table.

Figure 4-11:
The
Parameters
dialog box
with the key
field and
descriptive
field.

4. **Click OK to close the Parameters dialog box.**

   The Select File dialog box appears with an updated value in the URL field. The value in this field varies depending on your dynamic page type.

5. **Click OK to close the Select File dialog box.**

   The Document window shows the new link.

6. **Save the results page.**

   The results page is complete. The delete link now appears on the page, as shown in Figure 4-12.

Figure 4-12:
The
Document
window
with the
new Delete
link.

Building the confirmation page

The Confirmation page simply displays enough information to identify the record that's about to be deleted. This page consists of a form with a confirmation button.

To create a page that confirms the record deletion, you need to send two parameters to the confirmation page:

✦ The record ID

✦ A field to display the name of that record

This page saves you from having to create another recordset with a filter to look up information that's already been retrieved from the database.

Follow these steps to create the confirmation page:

1. **Open up your confirmation page.**

We opened up confirm.php.

2. **In the Bindings panel, click the plus (+) icon and select URL Parameter from the list that appears.**

The URL Variables dialog box appears.

3. In the Name field, enter the name of the database column that is the key.

For the example, we entered empid because we need to create a binding for the URL parameter empid.

4. Click OK.

The binding is created.

5. Repeat Steps 3 and 4 for the last name parameter.

For the example, we also created a last_name parameter.

6. Choose Insert⇨Form⇨Form to add a form.

7. Choose Insert⇨Form⇨Hidden Field to add a hidden field to store the record ID.

The user doesn't need to see the empid parameter, but that ID needs to be part of the form submission.

8. With the hidden field selected, enter the name of the variable in the Hidden Field text box in the Properties inspector.

For example, we entered empid_field.

9. Click the Bind to Dynamic Source (lightning bolt) icon next to the Value field.

The Dynamic Data dialog box appears.

10. Select the type of binding (URL Parameter, for example) in the bindings list.

For the example, we selected the empid URL parameter. You can leave the other fields set to their defaults.

11. Click OK to close the Dynamic Data dialog box.

In the Properties inspector, Dreamweaver updates the Value field with dynamic code to place the URL parameter in the hidden form field.

12. Click in the hidden field in the form and type Do you wish to delete the record for ?

This text tells users they're about to delete a record.

13. Position your cursor just before the question mark, click the plus (+) icon in the Server Behaviors panel, and select Dynamic Text from the menu that appears.

The Dynamic Text dialog box appears, as shown in Figure 4-13.

Figure 4-13:
The
Dynamic
Text dialog
box.

14. **Select the empid URL Parameter in the list, and then click OK.**

If you're using a different column as the key, select that parameter instead.

15. **Choose Insert⇨Form⇨Button to add a submit button to your form.**

The Input Tag Accessibility Attributes dialog box appears.

16. **Type** delete_btn **in the ID field.**

17. **Click OK to close the dialog box.**

18. **Select the button element on your page.**

19. **In the Properties inspector, enter Delete in the Value field.**

The button's text changes to Delete, as shown in Figure 4-14.

20. **Save the page.**

Use the name that you selected when creating the Delete link (see "Creating delete links to open the confirmation page," earlier in this chapter).

But wait, there's more! The page isn't complete yet because it can't process the deletion. You need to add logic to delete the record, as described in the following section.

Figure 4-14:
The
complete
page with
Delete
button
defined.

Adding logic to delete the record

Dreamweaver adds the logic to perform the database deletion with the Delete Record server behavior. To add this behavior to the HTML form, follow these steps:

1. **In the Server Behaviors panel, click the plus (+) icon and select Delete Record from the menu that appears.**

   The Delete Record dialog box appears.

2. **Select Primary Key Value in the First Check If Variable Is Defined drop-down list.**

3. **Select the appropriate database connection in the Connection drop-down list.**

   This field may appear differently depending on your dynamic page code type.

4. **Select the table that you want to delete in the Table drop-down list.**

5. **Select the primary key column in the Primary Key Column drop-down list.**

   We left the Numeric check box selected in our example because the empid record is a numeric field.

6. **Select Form Variable in the Primary Key Value drop-down list.**

   Form Variable is the hidden field value from the form submission.

7. **In the text field next to the Primary Key Value drop-down list, enter the name of the field that contains the key value.**

   Again, we entered empid_field for the example.

8. **In the After Deleting, Go To text box, enter the page that you want to open after deleting the record.**

   We entered success.php for the example. You can make this page as simple as the statement *Deleted Successfully.* The Delete Record dialog box for the example looks like Figure 4-15.

Figure 4-15:
The Delete
Record
dialog box
set to delete
an entry.

9. **Click OK to close the dialog box.**

   Dreamweaver adds the new server behavior to the page.

   The deletion pages are complete.

Testing Your Delete Page

To test your delete page, follow these steps:

1. **Open the search page that you created in Dreamweaver.**

2. **Choose File⇨Preview in Browser⇨*Name of Browser.***

3. **If Dreamweaver asks if it's okay to copy files to your testing site, click OK.**

   Be sure that both your updated results page and the new confirmation page transfer to the testing server. If they don't both transfer, you will get a *Page Not Found* error message when you click a link in the delete results page. If they don't transfer, copy or upload them to the server before continuing.

4. **Enter search criteria in the text box, and then click the Search button to display records.**

   The modified results page is displayed, which now allows the user to select a record that she wants to delete. Your browser opens and displays a list of records that you can delete. For example, Figure 4-16 lists the employee records that we can delete.

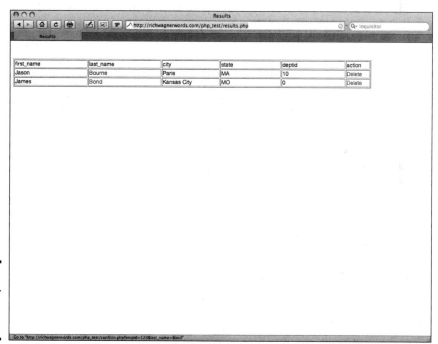

Figure 4-16: The browser displays records.

5. **Click the Delete link next to the row that you want to delete.**

   The browser page displays the delete confirmation page. Figure 4-17 shows the delete confirmation page for the example.

6. Click the Delete button.

The browser displays the success page if the operation is successful.

To verify the record deletion, you can navigate back to the delete results page to make sure the record doesn't appear on that page anymore.

Figure 4-17:
The deletion confirmation page shows the employee last name of Bond.

Index

Special Characters and Numerics

(number symbol), 122
. (period), 212
/ (forward slash), 309
: (colon), 211
{} (curly brackets), 706
"" (quotes), 469
80004005: Data source name not found error message, 667
80040e07: Data type mismatch in criteria expression error message, 667
80040e10: Too few parameters error message, 667
80040e14: Syntax error in INSERT INTO statement error message, 668
80040e21: ODBC error in Insert or Update error message, 668
800a0bcd: Either BOF or EOF is true error message, 668

A

\<a\> tag, 118, 120
absolute path, 50
absolute position, 238
Accept Anything validation setting, 195
Accept Email Address validation setting, 195
Accept Number From/To validation setting, 195
Accept Number validation setting, 195
access level, 769
accessibility of site, 39–41
actions, 385
Active Server Pages (ASP). *See also* database connections
connecting to remote database without DSN, 631–633
creating database connection with custom connection string, 629–630
creating database connection with Data Source Name, 627–629
creating new page, 626–627
custom connection string, 626
Data Source Name, 625–626
database connections, 625–626
deleting database connection, 633
editing database connection, 633
MapPath() method, 631–632
overview, 610, 625
physical path, 631–632
virtual path, 632
ActiveX controls. *See also* Java applet
aligning, 142
alternate image, 142
base, 142
class, 142
classID, 142
data, 142
defined, 140
embedding, 142
ID, 142
name, 142
overview, 138
parameters, 142
playing/stopping, 142
properties, setting, 140–142
whitespace, 142
width and height, 142
Add Object to Library, 284
Administer Website dialog box, 570–571, 573
Administrator Password dialog box, 573
Adobe After Effects, 132
Adobe AIR, 349–350
Adobe AIR extension for Dreamweaver, 349–350
Adobe AIR Marketplace, 350
Adobe Bridge
accessing, 346
inserting file from, 347
launching Dreamweaver from, 347
launching from Dreamweaver, 347
using, 346
web site, 346

G

H

Business/Accounting & Bookkeeping

Bookkeeping For Dummies
978-0-7645-9848-7

eBay Business
All-in-One For Dummies,
2nd Edition
978-0-470-38536-4

Job Interviews
For Dummies,
3rd Edition
978-0-470-17748-8

Resumes For Dummies,
5th Edition
978-0-470-08037-5

Stock Investing
For Dummies,
3rd Edition
978-0-470-40114-9

Successful Time
Management
For Dummies
978-0-470-29034-7

Computer Hardware

BlackBerry For Dummies,
3rd Edition
978-0-470-45762-7

Computers For Seniors
For Dummies
978-0-470-24055-7

iPhone For Dummies,
2nd Edition
978-0-470-42342-4

Laptops For Dummies,
3rd Edition
978-0-470-27759-1

Macs For Dummies,
10th Edition
978-0-470-27817-8

Cooking & Entertaining

Cooking Basics
For Dummies,
3rd Edition
978-0-7645-7206-7

Wine For Dummies,
4th Edition
978-0-470-04579-4

Diet & Nutrition

Dieting For Dummies,
2nd Edition
978-0-7645-4149-0

Nutrition For Dummies,
4th Edition
978-0-471-79868-2

Weight Training
For Dummies,
3rd Edition
978-0-471-76845-6

Digital Photography

Digital Photography
For Dummies,
6th Edition
978-0-470-25074-7

Photoshop Elements 7
For Dummies
978-0-470-39700-8

Gardening

Gardening Basics
For Dummies
978-0-470-03749-2

Organic Gardening
For Dummies,
2nd Edition
978-0-470-43067-5

Green/Sustainable

Green Building
& Remodeling
For Dummies
978-0-470-17559-0

Green Cleaning
For Dummies
978-0-470-39106-8

Green IT For Dummies
978-0-470-38688-0

Health

Diabetes For Dummies,
3rd Edition
978-0-470-27086-8

Food Allergies
For Dummies
978-0-470-09584-3

Living Gluten-Free
For Dummies
978-0-471-77383-2

Hobbies/General

Chess For Dummies,
2nd Edition
978-0-7645-8404-6

Drawing For Dummies
978-0-7645-5476-6

Knitting For Dummies,
2nd Edition
978-0-470-28747-7

Organizing For Dummies
978-0-7645-5300-4

SuDoku For Dummies
978-0-470-01892-7

Home Improvement

Energy Efficient Homes
For Dummies
978-0-470-37602-7

Home Theater
For Dummies,
3rd Edition
978-0-470-41189-6

Living the Country Lifestyle
All-in-One For Dummies
978-0-470-43061-3

Solar Power Your Home
For Dummies
978-0-470-17569-9

Internet

Blogging For Dummies,
2nd Edition
978-0-470-23017-6

eBay For Dummies,
6th Edition
978-0-470-49741-8

Facebook For Dummies
978-0-470-26273-3

Google Blogger
For Dummies
978-0-470-40742-4

Web Marketing
For Dummies,
2nd Edition
978-0-470-37181-7

WordPress For Dummies,
2nd Edition
978-0-470-40296-2

Language & Foreign Language

French For Dummies
978-0-7645-5193-2

Italian Phrases
For Dummies
978-0-7645-7203-6

Spanish For Dummies
978-0-7645-5194-9

Spanish For Dummies,
Audio Set
978-0-470-09585-0

Macintosh

Mac OS X Snow Leopard
For Dummies
978-0-470-43543-4

Math & Science

Algebra I For Dummies,
2nd Edition
978-0-470-55964-2

Biology For Dummies
978-0-7645-5326-4

Calculus For Dummies
978-0-7645-2498-1

Chemistry For Dummies
978-0-7645-5430-8

Microsoft Office

Excel 2007 For Dummies
978-0-470-03737-9

Office 2007 All-in-One
Desk Reference
For Dummies
978-0-471-78279-7

Music

Guitar For Dummies,
2nd Edition
978-0-7645-9904-0

iPod & iTunes
For Dummies,
6th Edition
978-0-470-39062-7

Piano Exercises
For Dummies
978-0-470-38765-8

Parenting & Education

Parenting For Dummies,
2nd Edition
978-0-7645-5418-6

Type 1 Diabetes
For Dummies
978-0-470-17811-9

Pets

Cats For Dummies,
2nd Edition
978-0-7645-5275-5

Dog Training For Dummies,
2nd Edition
978-0-7645-8418-3

Puppies For Dummies,
2nd Edition
978-0-470-03717-1

Religion & Inspiration

The Bible For Dummies
978-0-7645-5296-0

Catholicism For Dummies
978-0-7645-5391-2

Women in the Bible
For Dummies
978-0-7645-8475-6

Self-Help & Relationship

Anger Management
For Dummies
978-0-470-03715-7

Overcoming Anxiety
For Dummies
978-0-7645-5447-6

Sports

Baseball For Dummies,
3rd Edition
978-0-7645-7537-2

Basketball For Dummies,
2nd Edition
978-0-7645-5248-9

Golf For Dummies,
3rd Edition
978-0-471-76871-5

Web Development

Web Design All-in-One
For Dummies
978-0-470-41796-6

Windows Vista

Windows Vista
For Dummies
978-0-471-75421-3